TARGET
TOKYO

TARGET TOKYO

The Story of the Sorge Spy Ring

GORDON W. PRANGE

WITH DONALD M. GOLDSTEIN

AND

KATHERINE V. DILLON

McGRAW-HILL BOOK COMPANY

New York   St. Louis   San Francisco   Auckland   Bogotá
Guatemala   Hamburg   Johannesburg   Lisbon   London
Madrid   Mexico   Montreal   New Delhi   Panama   Paris
San Juan   São Paulo   Singapore   Sydney   Tokyo   Toronto

First paperback edition, 1985

1 2 3 4 5 6 7 8 9 A R G A R G 8 7 6 5

ISBN 0-07-050678-7 {PBK}
     0-07-050677-9

LIBRARY OF CONGRESS CATALOGING IN PUBLICATION DATA

Prange, Gordon William, 1910–1980
Target Tokyo.
1. Sorge, Richard, 1895–1944.   2. Spies—Soviet Union
—Biography.   3. Spies—Japan—Biography.   4. Espionage,
Russian—Japan—History—20th century.   I. Goldstein,
Donald M.   II. Dillon, Katherine V.   III. Title
UB271.R92S63 1984   940.54'8647'0924 [B] 84-3866
ISBN 0-07-050678-7 (pbk)
     0-07-050677-9

Book design by Roberta Rezk

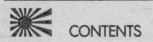 CONTENTS

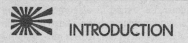 INTRODUCTION

This book represents the third of the manuscripts that the late Gordon W. Prange, professor of history at the University of Maryland, had prepared but not published at the time of his death. The first of these studies was *At Dawn We Slept: The Untold Story of Pearl Harbor;* the second was *Miracle at Midway.*

While Prange was in Japan during 1964 and 1965, *Reader's Digest* suggested the subject of the Richard Sorge spy ring. He began work on it immediately, and the *Digest* published a condensation in the January 1967 issue, under the title "Master Spy."

The Sorge story fascinated Prange. Over the next seventeen years he continued his research on the subject and his work on the manuscript with the view to publication. Because his main field of expertise at the time lay in Japan and events leading up to the Pacific war, he decided to concentrate upon the spy ring that Sorge established in Tokyo, using only so much material connected with his early life and the spy ring he headed in Shanghai as was necessary for an understanding of the man, his methods, and his associates. Sorge's Tokyo operation is much the more important historically.

Originally Prange planned that his manuscript be published without source notes. In this decision we disagree. The historical nature of this book requires source notes; so much of this story is the stuff of which legends are made that credibility demands documentation. By far the most time-consuming contribution we have made to this book has been tracking down and recording the sources. This book is the most thoroughly documented study of the subject available in English.

Prange's voluminous files failed to disgorge the origin of a number of quotations and incidents, but we have been able to pinpoint the sources. In this connection we are most grateful to William Lewis of the Military Records Department, National Archives Records Center, Suitland, Maryland.

In the course of our work on this project we discovered material in the Prange files that he intended to work into his manuscript, and we have made use of it where appropriate.

The Preface, Introduction, and Conclusion are our work. Prange ended his manuscript with what is now the Epilogue, and dramatically he was right to do so. However, we believe that some conclusions remained to be drawn, and we have taken the liberty of doing so. For the rest, we have pruned and edited; we have not improvised.

We should mention certain aspects of the text. In Japan the family name precedes the given name. However, for the sake of clarity and uniformity we have adopted the Western usage of given name first—for example, Hotzumi Ozaki rather than Ozaki Hotzumi.

Transliteration of Japanese names is no simple matter. One ideograph can represent more than one pronunciation. For example, the ideographs of Ozaki's given name are frequently rendered as "Shujitsu," but Ozaki preferred "Hotzumi." In all cases we have used the transliteration accepted by Japanese scholars.

Since the days of Richard Sorge many places in the Far East, especially in China, have been subject to a major change in Western spelling and even to change of name. We have retained the names current in his time, for as such they appear in the testimony and in most cases the traditional name is more familiar to Westerners.

In a few instances, for clarity and dramatic effect, Prange changed indirect quotations to direct quotations. But neither Prange nor we have put words into anyone's mouth. When a thought is expressed as a direct quotation, evidence of that thought in exactly those words appears in the source document or interview.

Many direct quotations are not in perfect English. Except

for a few occasions when clarification is necessary for understanding, we have followed Prange's practice of leaving the quotation as it came from the hands of his translator. In many cases a triple translation was involved—from the original English or German into Japanese, then into English for this study. Further adjustment might only confuse the sense further. Then, too, the slightly Japanese flavor and rough-cut texture carry their own authenticity, and indeed, men who are testifying with their lives in the balance seldom have the time or inclination to worry about their grammatical structures.

The major primary source for the Sorge case is *Gendaishi Shiryo, Zoruge Jiken* (*Materials on Modern History, the Sorge Incident*), published in Tokyo in 1962. This is made up of surviving records of the interrogations and procedures of the investigation that followed the arrest of Sorge and his key associates in the fall of 1941. Important related sources are two documents prepared in the office of Major General Charles A. Willoughby, G-2 (Intelligence), Far East Command, Tokyo, for presentation to the United States House of Representatives Committee on Un-American Activities. These are entitled "A Partial Documentation of the Sorge Espionage Case" and "Extracts from an Authentic Translation of Foreign Affairs Yearbook, 1943, Criminal Affairs Bureau, Ministry of Justice, Tokyo, Japan." Another valuable G-2 study, "The Sorge Spy Ring—A Case Study in International Espionage in the Far East," has been reproduced in the *Congressional Record*. Much authentic and hitherto unpublished primary material came from personal interviews that Prange or persons acting for him conducted in Japan.

We have divided this narrative into four parts. The first, "Forging the Ring," covers biographical backgrounds of Sorge and the major members of his *apparat,* their selection for the Tokyo assignment, their contacts, and their *modus operandi*. This section closes with the arrest and torture of Teikichi Kawai. The second part, "Turning the Ring," opens with the February 26, 1936, Incident, when for the first time the *apparat* functioned as a true unit, and closes with the Tripartite Pact. During this period the spy ring was exceedingly active, and both Sorge and his principal assistant, Hotzumi Ozaki, rose to positions of considerable prestige and influence in their respective spheres.

The third portion, "Spinning the Ring," covers events in 1940 and 1941, with particular emphasis upon the German attack on the Soviet Union, Moscow's failure to heed Sorge's warnings thereof, and Sorge's subsequent frantic efforts to determine whether Japan would follow Germany's example. The fourth part, "Breaking the Ring," deals with the capture of the *apparat* members, their imprisonment, trials, and fate.

Grateful thanks are due to those interviewed for this study; their names appear in the list of interviews. Many of these people not only contributed such information as they knew firsthand but also recommended others who they believed might be able to help with the project. As always, Prange's Japanese representative, Masataka Chihaya, was a tower of strength; so was Seiichi Fukuoka, at that time head of *Reader's Digest*'s Tokyo Bureau. Special acknowledgment is made of the contribution of Ms. Chi Harada, who conducted a series of exceedingly important interviews on Prange's behalf after he had left Japan early in 1965 and who translated much of Ms. Hanako Ishii's memoirs.

On this side of the Pacific we should like to single out Kiyoshi Kawahito, who translated much of the Japanese source material that is absolutely basic for any work on Sorge and, in addition, offered illuminating comments upon it. We should also like to cite a number of Prange's students at the University of Maryland who prepared papers on various aspects of the case and otherwise helped in research. All provided interesting viewpoints and suggestions. They are: Mark Arisumi, James H. Carter, Larry Hall, H. W. Henzel, Hideo Kaneko, Sarah Marie Mumford, William Renzi, T. George Sakai, Jeff Singman, James M. Sweeney, Milton J. Uzelac, Thomas E. Volz. There may be others of whose names we are not aware. If so, we ask their pardon.

Dillon's friend and neighbor Irene Belvoir plunged in with her typing skill to help us.

Two of Goldstein's associates, Larry Lehmann and Paul Herman, have performed yeoman service as translators of respectively German and Russian material, and Ms. Claudia Rivi, who has done everything from brewing coffee to typing correspondence, keeping records, and setting up interviews and television appearances, rates a most special vote of thanks.

If Prange were here to express his wishes, we believe he would want this book dedicated in gratitude and friendship to Maurice Ragsdale and his colleagues at *Reader's Digest*, who suggested the subject of this book and who never failed in their encouragement and assistance.

DONALD M. GOLDSTEIN, PH.D.
*Associate Professor of
  Public and International Affairs
University of Pittsburgh
Pittsburgh, Pennsylvania*

KATHERINE V. DILLON
*CWO, USAF (Ret.)
Arlington, Virginia*

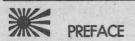

PREFACE

Richard Sorge headed a spy ring for the Soviet Union in Tokyo from his arrival in September 1933 until his arrest in October 1941. Thus he and his colleagues, a mixed bag of Occidentals and Japanese, operated successfully for eight years during a period when Japan was so suspicious of foreigners as to be almost neurotic and was spy-conscious to the point of mania.

Sorge's Tokyo base was the German Embassy, outpost of a nation as distrustful and tightly organized as Japan, which he penetrated so thoroughly that he became virtually a member of the staff of the two ambassadors resident during his time in Tokyo.

One reason for the ring's long immunity was that the Japanese police were so preoccupied in those years with mass arrests of known and suspected Communists that they lost their sense of proportion and wasted their energies on trivia. The police had Sorge under observation long before the events of 1941 that led to his arrest. However, they watched him not as a suspected spy but as a foreign newsman, a class that aroused their darkest suspicions. His arrest came as the result of an unexpected tip, which led to him through a chain reaction.

Another contributing factor to the ring's longevity was that its two most important members, Sorge and Hotzumi Ozaki, operated at a level that made them well-nigh above suspicion. In addition to his position in the German Embassy, where ultimately he became the best friend as well as the unofficial consultant to the ambassador, Sorge was a stringer for the

Frankfurter Zeitung, one of the most prestigious newspapers in Europe. Ozaki wrote for the highly respected newspaper *Asahi Shimbun,* was a noted author, and had connections at high levels in the Japanese government.

Yet members of the ring were not supermen; they were human beings of varying degrees of intelligence, dedication, and moral values, of such diverse backgrounds that in the normal course of events their paths never would have crossed. With only its work in common, held together by the centrifugal force of duty, the ring carried within it the seeds of its destruction. The breakup at the hands of the police may have come just in time to prevent the *apparat* from flying apart from its inherent stresses.

Sorge himself is a fascinating historical figure of many contradictions, and it is not surprising that different sources present diametrically opposed views of the man. For example, in 1951 the West German magazine *Der Spiegel* introduced the reader to a drunken braggart and compulsive womanizer, pitiably eager for acceptance as a serious journalist, although intellectually shallow. In contrast, in the Soviet press of 1964 one meets a paragon of purity and selflessness, a brilliant writer and deep thinker. Both versions contain a germ of truth.

Sorge was clever enough to keep his masquerade confined to the political area. He operated on the excellent principle that the fewer lies one tells or lives, the fewer chances of being caught. Even though he had a police record for underground Communist activity in Germany, he used his real name, Richard Sorge. Despite the inherent risks, he made no attempt to curb his heavy drinking and among his German friends did not pretend to be a convinced Nazi, although he joined the Nazi Party, a necessity for his cover. He indulged his taste for women freely, and at least two of his affairs were with prominent members of the German community whose husbands could have had him recalled to Germany had they been so inclined.

History does not readily let such a personality disappear; inevitably legends have grown up around his name: that he single-handedly saved the Soviet Union in 1941; that he was the power behind the Tripartite Pact; that the Japanese never executed him but traded him to the Soviet Union. Only extraordinary personalities evoke such different responses and such postmortem mythology.

The question of whether or not Sorge was a double agent, working for Germany as well as for the Soviet Union, has been raised persistently, and it was a very real cause for worry to the Japanese authorities at the time of his arrest. It would have been in keeping with his iron nerve to have made some such arrangement as part of his cover. This would explain much— the ease with which he penetrated the embassy and the reluctance of the German official and social community in Tokyo to deal with him as one might have expected on the basis of his personal life. However, no evidence has come to light that Sorge was other than what he claimed to be: a convinced, almost devout Communist, working wholeheartedly for the Soviet Union.

An unavoidable occupational hazard of historians is the problem of assessing sources, all of whom have their own interests to protect, their own axes to grind, their own personal, national, social, and political biases, and all of whom are subject to lapses of memory. Most of the existing documentary evidence on the Sorge case comes from the records of officials' interrogation of the members of the ring after their arrests, and these are not complete. Much testimony went up in flames during the fire bombing of Tokyo during World War II. A particular example is Branko de Voukelitch. His vivid narrative of how he came to join the ring has survived; after that the writer must rely upon the recollections of acquaintances and the testimony of his associates in the ring, sources not above suspicion.

For many historical problems of this kind, supporting evidence is available—letters, diaries, official documents, and the like. In the case of the Sorge ring no such checks exist. The historical events of the day—the stage against which Sorge enacted his drama—are well known, but his exact part in them remains in question. For obvious reasons he kept no personal diary and wrote no frank, detailed letters mentioning current problems and how he was dealing with them. Even the surviving radio messages Sorge sent to Moscow are fragmentary. Some of them the Japanese communications agencies picked out of the air and could not decode until after the case had been broken. The Soviet Union released a few in later years; these may or may not be accurate. Some were reconstructed from the memory of members of the ring and from the notes made by the ring's radio operator; again, these may or may not be trustworthy.

The testimony in the interrogation records shows no signs of coercion; the responses are not the terse, reluctant replies of men unwilling or unable to speak freely. They are detailed, almost voluble, and reveal distinct personalities in keeping with the individuals in question. Sorge told a number of provable lies concerning his early life, none of which is important in relation to his Tokyo period but which unavoidably cast doubt upon his veracity.

There is no valid reason to doubt the honesty of the police and prosecutors whom Dr. Prange interviewed for this book. Far from being prejudiced against Sorge, they liked and admired him, for they considered him a Russian patriot working for his country in his own way, just as they were serving Japan in theirs. Much personal information about Sorge came from Ms. Hanako Ishii, his mistress, who loved him and remained devoted to his memory. Having played no part in his espionage, she had no cause to be other than honest. She was candid in two areas where many would have been tempted to embroider: she did not pretend that he truly loved her, and she did not claim before-the-fact intuitions.

Cases such as Richard Sorge's are never really closed, and the future may bring forth further information. The authors have attempted to tell as complete and comprehensive a story of the Sorge Tokyo spy ring as history allows at this time.

MAJOR CHARACTERS

Name	Position
Akiyama, Koji	Translator for ring
Aoyama, Shigeru	Police officer, Toriizaka Station
Araki, Ms. Mitsutaro	Tokyo society figure
Asanuma, Sumitsugu	Sorge's defense lawyer
Berzin, General Ian Antonovitch	Chief, Fourth Department, Red Army
Clausen, Anna Wallenius	Wife of Max Clausen
Clausen, Max	Radioman, Tokyo ring
Dirksen, Herbert von	German ambassador to Japan, December 1933–February 1938
Fukuda, Tori ("*Ama-san*")	Sorge's housekeeper
Fuse, Ken	Voukelitch's prosecutor
Hashimoto, Takashi	Member, outer ring
Hirota, Koki	Prime minister of Japan, March 19, 1936–February 1, 1937
Ichijima, Seiichi	Governor of Sugamo Prison
Inukai, Ken	Associate of Ozaki
Ishii, Hanako	Mistress of Sorge
Ito, Ritsu	Associate of Ozaki
Kawai, Teikichi	Member of outer Tokyo and Shanghai rings
Kazami, Akira	Secretary, first Konoye cabinet
Kitabayashi, Tomo	Friend of Miyagi
Konoye, Prince Fumimaro	Prime minister of Japan, June 4, 1937–January 3, 1939; July 22, 1940–October 17, 1941
Koshiro, Yoshinobu	Military expert, outer ring
Kretschmer, Colonel Alfred	Military attaché, German Embassy
Kuzumi, Ms. Fusako	Member, outer ring

Leitzmann, Captain Joachim	Naval attaché, German Embassy, 1938–1940
Matsumoto, Shigeharu	Chief, editorial bureau, Domei; member of Breakfast Group
Matsumoto, Shin'ichi	Friend of Ozaki
Matsuoka, Yosuke	Foreign minister of Japan
Matzky, Colonel Gerhard	Military attaché, vice Air attaché
Meisinger, Colonel Joseph A.	Police attaché, German Embassy
Mirbach-Geldern, Count Ladislaus von	Chief, Press section, German Embassy
Miyagi, Yotoku	Member, Tokyo ring
Mizuno, Shigeru	Member, outer Tokyo and Shanghai rings
Nakamura, Toneo	Chief, Prosecution Bureau, Tokyo District Criminal Court
Ogata, Shinichi	Chief, Foreign Section, Tokko
Ohashi, Hideo	Tokko official
Oshima, Major General Hiroshi	Military attaché, later ambassador to Germany
Ott, Major General Eugen	Military attaché, German Embassy; later ambassador to Japan (April 1938–January 1943)
Ott, Helma	Wife of Eugen Ott
Ozaki, Eiko	Wife of Hotzumi Ozaki
Ozaki, Hotzumi	Member, Tokyo and Shanghai rings
Ribbentrop, Joachim von	Foreign minister of Germany
Ritgen, Wilhelm von	Chief, German Press Department
Saionji, Prince Kinkazu	Friend of Ozaki
Saito, Harutsugu	Tokko agent
Schellenberg, Walter	Chief, German Foreign Intelligence
Schol, Lieutenant Colonel Friedrich von	Assistant military attaché, German Embassy
Shinotsuka, Torao	Member, outer ring
Smedley, Agnes	Member, Shanghai ring; friend of Ozaki
Sorge, Christiane Gerlach	First wife of Richard Sorge
Sorge, Richard	Chief, Soviet espionage rings in Shanghai and Tokyo
Sorge, Yekaterina ("Katcha") Alexandrovna Maximova	Second wife of Richard Sorge
Stein, Günther	Associate of Tokyo ring
Suzuki, Tomiki	Tokko official
Taguchi, Ugenda	Member, outer ring

Takahashi, Yosuke	Tokko official
Tamazawa, Mitsusaburo	Procurator, Ministry of Justice
Urach, Prince Albrecht von	Friend of Sorge
Uritskii, General Semion Petrovitch	Assistant, then successor to Berzin
Ushiba, Tomohiko	Friend of Ozaki
Voukelitch, Branko de	Member, Tokyo ring
Voukelitch, Edith Olsen de	First wife of Branko de Voukelitch
Voukelitch, Yoshiko Yamasaki de	Second wife of Branko de Voukelitch
Wendt, Bruno	Radioman, Tokyo ring
Wenneker, Captain Paul	Twice naval attaché, German Embassy
Yabe, Shu	Member, outer ring
Yamana, Masazano	Member, outer ring
Yasuda, Tokutaro	Member, outer ring
Yoshikawa, Mitsusada	Chief prosecutor, Sorge trials
Zaitsev, Viktor Sergevitch ("Serge")	Second secretary and consul, Soviet Embassy, Tokyo; contact for ring

The German Embassy in Tokyo as Sorge Knew It in 1941

Service Attachés*

Military: COL. ALFRED KRETSCHMER
Naval: RADM. PAUL WENNEKER
Air: COL. WOLFGANG VON GRONAU

Not responsible to ambassador but conferred regularly with him.

*These officials were not responsible to the ambassador; they reported directly to their respective headquarters in Berlin.

Ambassador

M/G EUGEN OTT

Command and supervision of the embassy departments and all German consulates in Japan; liaison with Gestapo Department and service attachés; control of Nazi branch HQ as Hitler's representative.

Gestapo Department*

COL. JOSEPH A. MEISINGER

Coordinated with ambassador and supervised liaison with Japanese police; branch HQ of Nazi party, and moves of German nationals in Japan.

Propaganda and Information Department

COUNT LADISLAUS VON MIRBACH-GELDERN, secretary of legation

Controlled receipt of propaganda and information; issued press dispatches and propaganda for Japanese consumption.

Cultural Department

REINHOLD SCHULZE

Supervised cultural relations with Japan, schools, and schoolteachers.

Economics Department

DR. ALOIS TICHY, counselor of legation

Supervised economic relations between Japan and Germany; received reports from German businessmen in Japan, and furnished funds when remittances from Germany were overdue.

Code Department

Under direct supervision of ambassador. Full text of a message known only to him. Decoders saw only segments. The service attachés had their own code setup.

Political Department

DR. ERICH KORDT
DR. HANS ULRICH VON MARCH-THALER (counselor)
A secretary

Controlled political and diplomatic affairs.

General Organization Department

CONSUL KARL WENNE, chancellor

Supervised typists, translators, couriers, mail, finance, security within the embassy, maintenance of automobiles and buildings, gasoline, general repairs, etc.

This chart is based upon "Extracts," Part XV, Sorge's Notes, Record Group 319, File 923289 Part 37, Box 7482

Soviet Union, Japan, and China

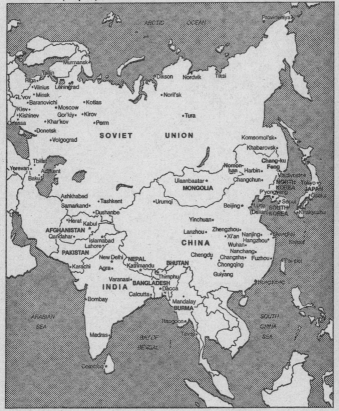

PART 1

FORGING THE RING

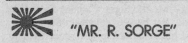

CHAPTER 1

"MR. R. SORGE"

The schedule for the Canadian Pacific Line's *Empress of Russia* announced that she would dock at Yokohama at 5:00 A.M. on Wednesday, September 6, 1933, but whatever gods control Japanese weather seemed reluctant to let her touch Japan's shores. A storm at sea delayed her for several hours. However, by noontime the protecting spirits apparently had resigned themselves to the inevitable, for when she finally nosed into her berth at 1:00 P.M., no one could have asked for a more beautiful day.[1]

From the newspaper accounts, the week in Japan had been fairly quiet. On September 1 the entire nation commemorated the tenth anniversary of the Great Earthquake with solemn ceremonies and prayer.[2] The next day twenty lepers of Communist persuasion fled from the National Leper Sanatorium in Osaka "because of the denunciation of their beliefs by other patients."[3] A story datelined Hsinking in west-central Manchuria reported that the Soviet Union would pursue an active policy in the Far East "to destroy further advance of Japan's imperialism and to prevent possibility of Soviet-Japan clash. . . ."[4] In Dairen authorities were hunting for "five tall and beautiful female agents of the O.G.P.U.,"* whose reported arrival had caused "the latest spy scare in the Manchurian capital."[5]

All this would be exceedingly interesting to one of the

* Later GPU (Gosudarstvennoe Politicheskos Upravlenie), the Soviet Union's secret police from 1922 to 1935.

passengers aboard the *Empress of Russia*. Both the *Japan Advertiser* and the *Japan Times and Mail* noted this man's arrival modestly enough, listing "Mr. R. Sorge" among those disembarking at Yokohama.[6] Yet he was obviously Somebody, born to be noticed. And he would stamp his name, Richard Sorge, upon the annals of his time.

Sorge had lived hard all his thirty-eight years, and the record of his days was etched in the deep ridges of his forehead and the heavy grooves in his cheeks. Behind the surface creases, his brow had the height and breadth of Shakespeare's. Lines running from blunted nose to rounded chin enclosed, as if parenthetically, full, sensual lips. Richly waving brown hair beginning to recede at each temple lent a Mephistophelian touch. From beneath dark, winging brows clear blue eyes, slightly tilted, looked forth with the chill wariness of a jungle animal.

His was a face both beautiful and ugly, as some who knew him said. He was German by birth, and many considered him typically so. Yet his features reflected the Germany far to the east, where Slavic blood helped form the Prussian. With his high, prominent cheekbones and slanted eyes, his face would have appeared more at home beneath a Mongol fur hat than beneath a German steel helmet. For Sorge was half Russian, and the Slavic strain injected into his personality a sizable dose of the Muscovite temperament.

His arresting features displayed none of the hopeful, expectant diffidence of a stranger in a strange land. He was far too self-assured to be able to imagine himself as being out of place anywhere. Instead, he surveyed the Japanese scene with the interested benevolence of one who just might buy the place if it satisfied his needs.

He was descending upon Dai Nippon (Japan) with an improbable mission: to establish and operate a Soviet spy ring in the heart of the most spy-conscious nation on earth. His mission called for him to gather every available scrap of pertinent information and to relay it to Moscow. To accomplish this feat, he and his colleagues would have to infiltrate the rigid, sensitive Japanese society and government at the highest levels—a task that seemed almost impossible at the outset.

From the beginning he must suppress his Slavic side. He must speak no word of Russian, make no Russian friends, allow no Russian book in the extensive library he would amass. Above all, he must stay away from the Soviet Embassy. He must appear German to the core. A Nazi Party card, then being processed in Berlin, would certify him as a member of the "superrace." In the meantime, he would establish himself as a respected member of the German community. What is more, he hoped and fully expected to infiltrate the German Embassy itself, to make himself such an expert upon Japan, its people and its politics, that he would be indispensable to the ambassador and his staff.

By a natural process of reciprocity, his standing with the German diplomatic set would enhance his prestige with the Japanese and open still more doors to him. From one side or the other, preferably both, he should be able to determine the answers to the questions that his superiors in the Fourth Department (Intelligence) of the Red Army had posed when they sent him to Tokyo: Did Japan intend to attack the Soviet Union, and if so, when, where, and in what strength?

Sorge brought formidable assets to his mission. He was intelligent, shrewd, and thorough. He had the ability to seize opportunity and to charm people into doing his bidding. He could sense danger like an animal and fend it off with cool courage.

He carried with him bona fide credentials from several German periodicals. Karl Haushofer, the leading exponent of geopolitics—the study of the influence of geography upon world history and statecraft—had given Sorge valuable letters of introduction to influential Germans in Tokyo. In addition, Sorge brought similar missives from other highly placed dignitaries. So he had reached Japan with an excellent, ready-made cover.

Yet he would have to work under formidable handicaps. The balance of suspicion would be against him as a foreigner. In this year of 1933 not even Nazi Germany was more racist than Japan, so he could expect to be a prime target of official and unofficial snooping. While Sorge, the citizen and faithful servant of the Soviet Union, could not reasonably bring to this prospect any sense of moral outrage, it would constitute a nuisance and a danger. For he must play the cloak-and-dagger game on Japan's home field against a tightly organized, well-trained, and dedicated team of professionals.

Then, too, his personal experience of Japan was almost nil. He had dabbled a bit in Japanese, but he did not speak the language well, and never would. He could count his Japanese acquaintances on his fingers, and those he did know might be forbidden him, for his superiors had ordered him to avoid Japanese Communists and Communist sympathizers. Yet what other Japanese could he trust?

So far he had set eyes on only one of his prospective colleagues: Bruno Wendt, a Red Army radio technician, who would handle communications between the Sorge *apparat** and the Soviet mainland when in the fullness of time he had anything to broadcast. The radioman Sorge really wanted and eventually would receive was Max Clausen, a chunky, likable expert in radio techniques whom Sorge had met and worked with in Shanghai. At the moment Clausen was in the Soviet Union.

Already in Japan was another man, thus far unknown to Sorge, whom he was to contact when he believed the time was ripe. Moscow had furnished Branko de Voukelitch via the Paris cell in response to Sorge's request for someone to work the opposite side of the ideological fence while Sorge took care of the totalitarians. Presumably the comrades knew their business, but Sorge had an ingrained suspicion of anyone for whom he could not vouch personally. So he would withhold judgment.

He awaited with similar reservations the appearance of Yotoku Miyagi, who was being recruited in the United States. Sorge badly needed a trustworthy Japanese assistant, yet it would have been asking for trouble to bring into the inner circle of his ring a Japanese citizen with known Communist tendencies, perhaps even a police record. So the American Communist Party had come to the rescue with a young painter who had established himself as a good party worker but who lacked any experience in espionage.

Living in Japan, however, was the one man Sorge hoped and planned to recruit personally at the earliest opportunity:

---

* Russian term for a highly disciplined Communist organization, usually applied to an espionage group.

Hotzumi Ozaki. Ozaki had collaborated with Sorge before, demonstrating the quality of his mind, his work, and his dedication to communism. Yet so cleverly did this intelligent, amiable journalist conceal his beliefs that to Japanese officialdom and society he presented the perfect picture of a promising writer and scholar of no more than mildly liberal tendencies.

For the rest, Sorge's excellent newspaper and diplomatic introductions would provide a good start, but only a start. Everything else would be up to him. After presenting his letters, he must make himself so charming, so useful that his new contacts would be eager to have the acquaintance ripen into friendship, trust, and mutual cooperation.

But he knew he could never relax—not for a minute. Twenty-four hours out of every day he would be living amid and working with Japanese and Germans, who at that period in their history were neurotically suspicious. In some ways that might be the most difficult part of his task, for Sorge had a complex nature. The scholar and foreign correspondent; the pacifist who hated war as only a former soldier can hate it; the single-minded worker for international communism; the student of world affairs; the urbane gentleman—these all were valid facets of Sorge's personality. But he possessed a monumental ego and at times could be unbelievably careless. He was a hard drinker, a compulsive womanizer, a man who loved to hold the conversational spotlight. Much would depend upon how tight a rein Sorge the responsible could keep upon Sorge the swashbuckler.

All these considerations bounced off Sorge's self-confidence without even denting it. Neither he nor the Fourth Department expected concrete results overnight. He was to move slowly, operate cautiously, and avoid unnecessary risks. Thus he would spend his first years in remedying his deficiencies of experience, establishing himself in his chosen circles, and building his *apparat*. Espionage is not a career for the impatient. His whole life had been preparation for this supremely important mission. He would establish the most valuable, the most successful, the most highly placed of Soviet espionage rings or perish in the attempt. In the end he did both.

CHAPTER 2

"SLIGHTLY DIFFERENT FROM THE AVERAGE"

Far from the flood tides of history a small hook of land juts into the Caspian Sea. There lies the Russian oil city of Baku. Not far away stands the small Azerbaijani village of Adjikent, where on October 4, 1895, a German petroleum engineer and his Russian wife became the parents of a son they named Richard. The occasion was not a novelty for Adolf Sorge and Nina Semionova Kobieleva Sorge, for Richard was the youngest of nine.[1] The household spoke German, which accounts for the nickname his intimates always used. A baby trying to lisp the name Richard would make a sound like *Ika*, the name that stuck to Richard.

A picture of the father, taken when the son was eight years old, shows a handsome, imposing figure who looks the image of the stern and rockbound late-Victorian father almost mathematically certain to produce rebel children. Adolf Sorge was "a nationalist and imperialist. . . . He was strongly conscious of the property he had amassed and the social position he had achieved abroad."[2]

Richard Sorge claimed as his grandfather Friedrich Adolf Sorge, an associate of Karl Marx and Friedrich Engels. He was one of the founders of the Socialist Workers Party in the United States and served as secretary-general of the First International in New York City.[3] In later years, when building up Sorge as a hero, the Soviet press was delighted to accept Richard Sorge's version.[4] However, the relationship was in fact less close, the revolutionary Sorge being a great-uncle rather than a grandfather of the spy.[5]

When Richard was eleven, Adolf Sorge's contract with the Caucasian Oil Company expired, and the family moved back to Germany. They settled in Lichterfelde, a pleasant residential section of Berlin, to the life of comfortable upper-middle-class citizens. Ika went to school in Berlin, carrying in his satchel that sense of being, in his own words, "slightly different from the average" that can be such an embarrassment to a child. But Richard Sorge was well satisfied with himself. By his own account he was a difficult pupil—defiant, obstinate, and sullen. Yet in any subject that interested him enough to make him willing to study it, he stood far above his classmates. For his proficiency in history, literature, philosophy, and political science his classmates nicknamed him the Prime Minister. If the title carried a hint of derision, it passed over Richard's head. He accepted it at face value as a compliment. By the age of fifteen he had gulped down Goethe, Schiller, Lessing, and the other German immortals and was soaking himself in the lore of the French Revolution, the Napoleonic Wars, and the era of Bismarck, as well as in current events and problems.[6]

The loss of his father in 1911 made no material adjustments necessary. In the Sorge home "economic worries had no place." A vacation in Sweden in 1914 climaxed his late teens. Then the cyclone of World War I swept him from his placid millpond. Sorge returned to Germany immediately and joined the army. This burst of patriotism was made up of the atmosphere of excitement generated by the war, and a desire to leave school, to have new experiences, and to shed what he considered "the whole meaningless and purposeless pattern of living of an 18-year-old."[7]

After six weeks of inadequate training Sorge became one of thousands of youths on the Belgian front, where he experienced the full ugliness of the battlefield. Soon he had had his fill of excitement and novelty. Crouching miserably in the mud, Sorge wondered what the war was all about. "Who cared about this region, or that new mine or industry? Whose desire was it to capture this objective at the sacrifice of life?"[8]

Then one day he met his first pacifist. This man, a "real Leftist, an old stonemason from Hamburg," told his impressionable comrade about "his life in Hamburg and of the persecution and unemployment he had gone through." The association was short-lived, for the stonemason died in action early in 1915, but it left its mark on Sorge.

Soon thereafter, on the bloody field of Ypres, Sorge stopped enemy steel for the first time. Back in Germany to nurse his wound, he learned more about the jungle of German wartime life. "Money could buy anything on the black market. . . . The initial excitement and spirit of sacrifice apparently no longer existed. . . ." Not only that: "The material objectives of the struggle were gaining increasing prominence, and a thoroughly imperialistic goal, the elimination of war in Europe through the establishment of German hegemony, was being publicized." [9]

Sorge used his convalescence to prepare for his graduation examinations and to enter the medical department of Berlin University, but he attended only two or three lectures. Nothing in Berlin had real significance for him any longer. He decided he would rather be back in the trenches with his "naïve brothers-in-arms." Before his convalescent leave expired, he volunteered for frontline duty and returned to combat in 1915, the year the Germans hammered the Russian armies into a jelly that oozed homeward over everything in its path to escape this relentlessly efficient enemy. Thus Sorge returned to Russia for the first time since childhood as an invader. He observed that "all men dreamed of peace in their spare moments." Yet as the German offensive plunged ever deeper into Russian territory, only to face more endless miles, he began to experience a nightmarish panic that the war would never cease, that he and his comrades were doomed to march eternally into an ever-melting horizon. In this unspeakable horror of the eastern front he fell wounded a second time. In early 1916 he went back to Germany by a long trip across occupied Russia. [10]

The German government's policies were becoming brutal with the first stirrings of unease about final victory. Sorge's own middle class, feeling itself slipping downward into the "proletariat," was clinging to the lifeline of "German spiritual superiority." This concept and this class, which Adolf Hitler would make his own, filled Sorge with contempt. Discontented in this atmosphere, he volunteered to return to the front as soon as he was physically able.

He had not long been back with his unit when at Baranovichi, a town southwest of Minsk, numerous shell fragments slashed into his body; two of them smashed bones in his thigh and left him with a slight limp and a lifetime of nagging pain. The fates placed him in a field hospital in Königsberg under the care of a doctor and his nurse-daughter, both radical Socialists. They recognized a potentially valuable convert, plied him with literature, and encouraged him to go back to his neglected studies.[11]

So Sorge dug into a heavy course of economics, history, the fine arts, and the philosophies of Immanuel Kant and Arthur Schopenhauer. Despite the seriousness of his injuries and "the excruciating pain involved in their treatment," he "was happy for the first time in many years." He left the field hospital "an apostle of the revolutionary labor movement."[12]

He returned to the university but abandoned medicine for political science. He had lost two brothers in combat,[13] and by the end of 1917 he had decided that the Great War had been meaningless: ". . . millions had perished on either side. . . . The highly vaunted German economic machine had crumbled in ruins. . . . Capitalism had disintegrated into its component parts, anarchism and unscrupulous merchants."

Before his eyes he had seen "the downfall of the German Empire, whose political machinery had been termed indestructible." Nor were the victors in better shape.

But all was not dark. Sorge found a "fresh and effective ideology . . . supported and fought for by the revolutionary movement," which "strove to eliminate the causes, economic and political, of this war and any future ones by means of internal revolution." He spent his time at Berlin University digging into this "most difficult, daring and noble ideology."[14]

Then came the news of the Bolshevik Revolution. Sorge promptly "decided not only to support the movement theoretically but to become an actual part of it." Upon his discharge from the army in January 1918, he headed for Kiel University. There he joined the revolutionary Independent Social Democratic Party, working as agitator, party recruiter, and instructor in Marxist dogma. He conducted many "secret lectures on socialism before groups of sailors and harbor and dock workers."[15]

Early in 1919 Sorge moved to Hamburg to study for his Ph.D. in political science, which he obtained in August of that year. He worked for his party to such good purpose that by the end of the year he had become training chief of its local guidance department. About that time the newly established German Communist Party absorbed, among other revolutionary groups, the Independent Social Democratic Party. So Sorge became a Communist Party member.[16] He served the Hamburg unit as training chief and as adviser to the Hamburg Communist paper.

Then he moved to Aachen as assistant to Dr. Kurt Gerlach at the College of Technology. Sorge had swung into the orbit of Dr. Gerlach, a professor of political science, while in Kiel. A Communist and a very wealthy man, Gerlach had carried his pupil still further into the revolutionary movement.[17] From Aachen Sorge wrote a revealing letter to his cousin and friend Erich Correns:

> . . . I have almost totally cut myself off from everyone in Germany, which is not something I would call sad in the usual sense. For a vagabond such as I, who cannot keep anything in his hands, this seems the only possible state. In no way, not even internally, do I need another person to be able to live; that is, to really live and not just to vegetate. I am so completely up in the air, so completely homeless that the road is my preferred place and path. . . .[18]

After consulting with the party, Sorge decided to enter the mines to earn his living and to intensify his already active propaganda work among the miners. Soon he had made the Rhineland too hot to hold him, and he departed with a prod from the authorities. An attempt to follow the same pattern in Holland fell flat. He departed at that country's urgent request almost before he had unpacked his bags.[19]

Sorge's own account of his postwar career in Germany is confusing, no doubt deliberately so, for as a conspirator and agitator he knew how to cover his tracks. But independent evidence where available gives him the lie. For example, he claimed to have remained in Aachen until late in 1922, and his only mention of Solingen, a small town in the Ruhr, is his claim that during a school vacation he edited a Communist newspaper "for two months while its editor was in prison."[20]

However, German police records reveal him as a resident of Solingen as early as February 28, 1921. What is more, he did not edit the paper; he was the political editorial writer, and contributions with his "R.S." by-line appeared between August 21, 1921, and June 1922.[21]

From early 1920 well into 1922, Sorge wrote to Correns from Solingen. He did not live alone there. A letter to Correns dated April 29, 1921, sheds light on Sorge's difficulties in Solingen. He apologized for being unable to put up his cousin for a long visit. He might have to leave Solingen in short order.

> Because of the police, I must unfortunately make a burdensome compromise. We won't be able to stay here without the registrar's office [i.e., a civil marriage]. Because they naturally want to throw me out of Solingen, but have no grounds to do so, they will try to do it on grounds of creating a public scandal. To the bourgeois, living together constitutes creating a public scandal. It annoys both of us, but we will have to bite the sour apple.[22]

The "we" of the letter were Sorge and Christiane Gerlach, who had been the wife of Kurt Gerlach. Over the preceding two years she and Sorge had fallen in love; they were married in May 1921. According to Christiane, her husband agreed to an amicable divorce, and she lived with her stepmother in Bavaria until the legal formalities were settled.[23] But according to Sorge's letter to Correns, he and Christiane had jumped the gun.

Next Sorge went to Berlin, whence the Central Committee dispatched him to Frankfurt am Main. According to him, he was to become an assistant in the social science department of the city's university, in the meantime engaging in "positive activities" for the party.[24] German police records show that he reached that city on October 20, 1922;[25] however, no record of employment at the university exists. Instead, he went to work with Gerlach—with whom he remained on cordial terms—in his Society for Social Research, which had no official connection with Frankfurt University.[26]

While Sorge was in Frankfurt, the Communist Party was outlawed in Germany, so Sorge and his comrades had to go underground. He became the liaison between Berlin head-quarters and Frankfurt. He handled all secret documents, propaganda material, even the party's funds and membership register.[27]

During the Frankfurt period Sorge and Christiane made the acquaintance of Hede Massing, the former wife of Gerhard Eisler, a prominent Communist. An attractive, slender brunette of Austrian Jewish background, inclined to schoolgirl crushes on people and causes, she admired Sorge extravagantly. She sketched this picture of his life with Christiane:

> Their home was the center of social life within this group. I remember how quaint it looked, with its antique furnishings carried over from Christiane's past as a rich bourgeois professor's wife. There was a fine collection of modern paintings and rare old lithographs. I was impressed by the easy at-mosphere and grace with which the household was run. I liked the combination of serious talk and lust for living that was shown.[28]

But this gracious life-style received its death blow in 1924. The party Central Committee required a bodyguard for four Soviet delegates to a convention being held at Frankfurt in April and called upon Sorge for this duty. His charges turned out to be key figures in the Comintern: Dmitri Manuilsky, Ossip Pyatnitsky, Otto Kuusinen, and Solomon Lozovsky.[29]

Sorge defined the Communist International (Comintern) as "a world organization made up of the representatives of the Communist party of each country which belongs to it. And the mission of the Comintern lies in mobilization of activities of the Communist Party in each country in order to develop a socialistic and communistic social order."[30] This was not a bad definition, except that Sorge neglected to mention that its ends included violent revolution.

His guard duties, which were not arduous, threw him into close contact with these VIPs. By the end of the convention he had so impressed them that they invited him to join them at Comintern headquarters, there to set up an intelligence bureau. Of course, the German Communist Party approved Sorge's transfer.[31]

Sorge and Christiane reached Moscow toward the end of 1924, and by January 1925 Sorge was deep in his new work. In March Sorge switched his party membership to the Soviet Communist Party, receiving card number 0049927, and the same year he became a Soviet citizen: "Profession: intellectual. Vocation: Party worker."[32] Obviously he kept his change of allegiance a secret from his former homeland, for he was soon traveling on a German passport made out in his own name, evidently issued without difficulty and in good faith.

During 1925 and well into 1929, considerable mystery surrounds Sorge's activities. The available evidence is fragmentary and often contradictory.

He spent his first two years in Moscow assisting in the expansion of the Comintern Intelligence Division and establishing himself as a party stalwart. He polished up his English and Russian, for despite his mother's nationality, he had not grown up speaking Russian. He wrote two books, *The Economic Provisions of the Versailles Peace Treaty and the International Labor Class,* and *German Imperialism,* which he considered "competent pieces of work."[33]

His personal life was less successful. Christiane found work at the Marx-Lenin Institute, but if Ms. Massing is correct, she did not care for the Russians, at least at first.[34] Sometime in 1925 she noticed a growing atmosphere of intolerance and oppression as Stalin's star commenced to rise. Even those who had been friendly started to shun this bourgeois German woman. By October 1926 Christiane had had enough of Sorge's drinking, other women, and general neglect of her. She sought and received permission to return to Germany, and Sorge saw her off at the station.[35]

Christiane did not give chapter and verse, but Sorge was proud of his sexual prowess and had no respect for the marriage bond. Any woman who for whatever legal, moral, or social reasons did not follow her physical urges he stigmatized as a "bourgeois goose."[36]

Nevertheless, Christiane kept a soft spot for Sorge. Eventually she emigrated to the United States, but she did not marry again and maintained a warm correspondence with him. Although no evidence of a divorce has turned up,[37] Sorge considered himself a bachelor and wrote off home life as not for him.

He suffered no sexual frustrations, for he exerted an almost mesmerizing attraction on women. When amused and somewhat envious comrades protested it was time he settled down, he merely grinned and countered that he was not made for conjugal happiness.[38]

Free of domestic ties, Sorge became involved in espionage:

> . . . it grew increasingly necessary to supplement previously acquired basic data with first-hand information obtained by special Intelligence Division espionage agents operating in all countries and at all times. It had long been a practice to send special emissaries from the Organization Division of Comintern headquarters to assist local parties with organizational problems, and it was decided that such functions would have to be expanded to include intelligence work.[39]

Accordingly, for the next few years his bosses sent Sorge up and down Europe "to engage in intelligence activities concerning their communist parties, their economic and political problems, and any important military issues which might arise. . . ."[40]

Sorge's dating of visits he claimed to have made to Denmark, Sweden, Norway, and elsewhere is so at variance with other evidence, such as that turned up by the German investigation which followed his arrest, as to lend considerable credibility to two theories: that Sorge invented the Scandinavian story to cover an entirely different mission in Germany, perhaps for Soviet military intelligence, or that the German police might have confused him with another Richard Sorge.[41] There is no doubt that he spent some time in Germany. On one such occasion he recruited Hede Massing as an active agent.[42]

He became more and more interested in espionage and grew severely irritated when the political side of his work impinged upon intelligence. Following a trip to England in 1929, he suggested to the Intelligence Division that the political and espionage aspects were not homogeneous; for the espionage agent secrecy was imperative. His superiors accepted this con-

cept and severed his connection with the Comintern, charging
him to cease all nonprofessional contact with his Comintern
comrades. The only exceptions were Pyatnitsky, Manuilsky,
and Kuusinen, who were and remained Sorge's unofficial
advisers.[43]

Accordingly, he broke off all relations with party cells,
became a member of the Secret Department of the Soviet Communist Party Central Executive Committee, and was put in
touch with General Ian Antonovitch Berzin, chief and virtual
founder of the Fourth Department (Intelligence) of the Red
Army. From Pyatnitsky, Berzin had heard of Sorge's wish to
engage in political espionage. All concerned were so pleased
with Sorge that they offered him a choice of returning to Europe
or going to the Far East. He requested China, much to the
satisfaction of his superiors.[44]

Tremendous upheavals in the Orient seemed to offer unlimited potential for Communist activity, and China was the
heart of Asia. The next few months found Sorge occupied with
preparations for an immensely important task: the organization
and operation of a Red Army spy network in Shanghai.

CHAPTER 3

"WE COULD WORK WELL TOGETHER"

Built on yellow mud, shored up by treaties, Shanghai was three cities in one: the Chinese city, the International Settlement, and the French Concession.* Ships poured into its spacious harbor from the seven seas. In bank and business along the majestic Bund, the city's modern European quay and shopping area, at the end of each day counting machines chattered of black figures and ever-increasing bank accounts. Yet for all its wealth, Shanghai was wretchedly poor, and the margin between life and death was razor-thin. By 1930 Shanghai had a large industrial proletariat and a host of radicals, agitators, and agents from and acting for the Soviet Union. For Moscow took aim on China through this great gateway. This city was Sorge's target.

He started on his journey in November 1929. First he stopped at Berlin, where he established his cover as a writer for the *Soziologische Magazin*. He obtained his passport legally and traveled under his own name. From Berlin he moved on to Marseilles, where he boarded a Japanese passenger ship. It reached Shanghai in January 1930.

With him sailed two other key members of the ring, who boarded the ship at different ports. These were Seppel Weingarten, a radio expert, and "Alex," otherwise unidentified, who actually outranked Sorge in both age and length of party service.[1]

* For many years certain Occidental nations had enjoyed virtual sovereignty over assigned parts of several Chinese cities. These were usually called concessions.

Sorge's mission was to report on all possible facets of the Chinese government in Nanking—its social and political character, military strength, foreign and domestic policies—as well as on Chinese agriculture and industry. He was also to cover the social and political character of factions opposed to Nanking, British and American policies in China, the military strength of all foreign powers in that country, and extraterritoriality. And he had orders to report on anything else of interest he considered worth noting—a comprehensive and formidable task.[2]

Shortly after his arrival Weingarten introduced him to an old friend, Max Clausen. Weingarten and Clausen had been comrades in the same cell in Hamburg, and Clausen was now Weingarten's opposite number in one of the two other Red Army espionage units in Shanghai. For Sorge's was by no means the only Soviet espionage group in Shanghai. At least three other such organizations worked in the city. Clausen's *apparat*, known as the Jim or Lehman group, was strictly a technical one, establishing radio contacts between Russia and Shanghai and other parts of China.

Both the Jim organization and Sorge's "were allowed to use Max Clausen according to the necessity,"[3] so across their drinks Sorge took careful note of him. He knew that good radio technicians were worth their weight in diamonds. He saw a man of about his own height (five feet ten inches), but heavier, with a square, good-humored face topped by brown hair parted on the side, waving back loosely from a low, wide forehead. Deep-set dark eyes looked out with direct simplicity from beneath level brows almost meeting over a high-bridged nose. Lips with a humorous quirk at the corners offset a deeply cleft chin.

After Sorge had put Clausen through an oral examination, he remarked, "I believe we could work well together."[4] Thus Sorge met the man who was to be one of the most important members of his future Tokyo spy ring.

Sorge and Clausen both were under orders of the Fourth Department of the Red Army, and both were graduates of the Hamburg branch of the German Communist Party. Otherwise they were about as different as two men could be. Born in 1899 on Nordstrand, an island off the coast of Schleswig-Holstein,

Clausen was the son of poor parents who could give him no
education beyond the public schooling available in a German
country district. He was the only principal member of Sorge's
Tokyo ring with direct experience of manual labor. In his teens
he helped in his father's bicycle repair shop and was apprenticed
to a blacksmith who happened to be an enthusiastic Communist
and instructed Clausen in the lore of the hammer and sickle as
well as that of the bellows and anvil. The boy entered the radio
field when he was drafted into the German Signal Corps in
1917.[5]

Following his discharge in 1919, Clausen wandered through
a number of jobs on both land and sea. Troubled by the unemployment and unhappiness around him, he sought a solution
in Communist literature and found an answer to his satisfaction.
Through associations formed in the Seamen's Union, he joined
the Communist Party in 1927. On a voyage to Russia he "was
impressed by the various industrial facilities of Soviet Russia,"
he explained naïvely. "And thus I became convinced that the
achievement of communism would establish the happiest society." Within a year of his becoming a party member, the
Soviets enlisted him in an espionage group as a radioman and
sent him to Russia for indoctrination and training. On his graduation the Fourth Department dispatched him to China as a
member of the Jim group.[6]

Sometime after their encounter Sorge instructed Clausen
to move into an apartment, so he found quarters in the Hong-
Ku district, renting two loft rooms as a work area. He would
have preferred to live on the third floor directly under his
workshop but had to settle for a second-floor bedroom because
a woman named Anna Wallenius, whom he had encountered
in the dining room without really noticing her, occupied the
bedroom he wanted. He trudged purposefully up the stairs and
tapped on her door with the view to negotiating an exchange
of territory.[7]

The door opened to reveal a woman of about his own
age, pretty in a china doll fashion. Although blue shadows
smudged the big, deep-set eyes, a hint of a dimple lurked in
the full cheeks. A wide, sweet mouth topped an exceedingly
determined chin.

Courteously Clausen presented his proposition. Would

she trade quarters with him? Anna was suspicious. Why should a man prefer a small third-floor room to a large second-floor one? Besides, his quarters rented for $40 a month; hers, for $25. Gallantly Clausen offered to pay the difference. This well-meant suggestion triggered an explosion that sent him clattering downstairs.[8]

What had brought Anna to a Shanghai boardinghouse? She was born of Finnish parents in 1899 in Siberia. At the age of sixteen she had married Edward Wallenius, of a good Finnish family. He bought a flour processing factory in Siberia and converted it to leather production. After the Revolution the Reds took it over, and the young couple went to China. Eventually they settled in Shanghai in the lumber business, but in 1927 Edward died. The Finnish Consulate sold his factory to pay his debts, and Anna found herself with no assets but a small house, which she sold. Shanghai in the 1920s was not the ideal spot for a widow with no protection, money, or specialized training. Anna supported herself by sewing and practical nursing, always on the knife-edge of security.[9]

Clausen was no glamour boy or towering intellect, but he was kind, steady, and affectionate, exactly the qualities most calculated to appeal to a woman in Anna's circumstances. "Being impressed that he was a healthy, hard-working, and nice man," said Anna later, "I came to feel like marrying him." This was not exactly a passionate declaration, but Clausen had no complaints. Within a month of meeting, the couple decided to marry eventually, and in the meantime, why wait?[10]

Soon Sorge discovered that Clausen had a live-in lady friend. He cautioned Clausen to tell her nothing about their activities and asked to meet her. So Sorge, Weingarten, Clausen, and Anna gathered for dinner at a café. Anna did not appear to be a promising convert, either to Sorge's Shanghai group or to communism.[11] Still, Sorge considered her harmless and told Clausen a little later, "It's all right for you to marry the girl, but be careful of our secret work. If your marriage threatens our work, you will be recalled by Moscow, so be careful." Clausen did not know whether or not Sorge had contacted the Moscow authorities before granting this permission, but Clausen knew that they did not like their agents to marry "immigrants."[12]

Little by little Anna ferreted out clues to Clausen's activities. At first she put down his absorption in radio to his being a ham radio operator, a hobby popular in Shanghai at the time. She suspected his sallies forth by night indicated he might have another girl friend stashed away somewhere. But eventually she pried out of him an admission that he had a connection with the German Communist Party. From this she deduced that he was a member of an anti-Nazi group. Then a meeting in Canton with a White Russian named Konstantin Mishin added a touch of vodka to the pot. Clausen assured her that in his organization nationalities did not matter.

Anna did not swallow this whole. "I am stupid, but when I hear that he is from Moscow and that the headquarters exists in Moscow, I can tell that the secret group belongs to the Communist International, and thus at that time I clearly realized that my husband was working for the Communist International of Soviet Russia," said Anna.[13]

Afraid that she might leave him out of her dislike of his work on behalf of Moscow, Clausen, in his words, "tried to educate her on communism." He put his beliefs simply. "Communism is trying to create a happy world without exploitation of the workers and farmers," he said to the skeptical Anna. "It will nationalize all the industries, and all the people will receive equal and fair distributions . . . it will make the world a paradise."[14] Anna could have pointed tartly to her own experiences with communism: her husband robbed of his livelihood and herself paddling frantically to keep her chin above financial water.

Doggedly Clausen told her about his troubles as an unemployed laborer in Germany. "In the Communist world there will not be such unemployment, and in the future all the world will be like Russia." This was just what Anna was afraid of. At this point, Clausen noted unhappily, "My wife said that communism is not good and yelled at me!"[15]

Much later, in East Germany, Clausen declared that when Anna discovered his real work, she "didn't hesitate for a minute."[16] This may be true, for by that time Anna loved him too much to leave him. One thing speaks more clearly than any number of eloquent speeches. Three times during their life together Anna became pregnant. Each time she had an abortion, although she and Clausen liked children and Anna craved a normal family life. She would not bring into the world the child of a Communist spy.[17]

After working with Sorge capably since their first meeting, Clausen moved offstage. In September 1931 Sorge informed him that Moscow had ordered him to Manchuria and sped him to the Harbin unit, which functioned as "a mailbox for Sorge" and belonged to the Fourth Department. Clausen resented this action, especially because Sorge gave him no reason for his transfer. ". . . I suppose it was because I was regarded as a 'bastard son' under the Sorge regime," he wrote long afterward, "my status being that of a sort of honorary member as long as Weingart* was around to handle the radio work."[18]

While Clausen and Anna were establishing their life together, Sorge worked hard to fulfill his obligations to Moscow. The sort of intelligence he wanted he could only obtain at high level. He presented to the German Consulate General a letter of introduction from the German *Grain* magazine, stating that he wanted to write a series of articles on Chinese agriculture and nutrition. Thus sedately vouched for, Sorge cultivated Lieutenant Colonel Hermann von Kriebel, the senior military adviser to Nanking, who stood high amid Chiang Kai-shek's advisers. Soon Sorge was a general favorite, much in social demand. He traveled widely in China, studied long and hard, and gathered about him an efficient ring of willing workers.[19]

To them Sorge, who spoke English well, posed as an American reporter named Johnson. He made an exception of Agnes Smedley, who was much too intelligent to accept him as a fellow American and who as a journalist would encounter him in the course of business.

When Sorge landed in Shanghai, he had only two assets: his credentials as a newspaperman and the name of this woman, who had been in Shanghai since May 1929 as a correspondent for the *Frankfurter Zeitung*.[20]

"The only person in China upon whom I knew I could depend was Agnes Smedley, of whom I had first heard in

---

* That is, Weingarten. The name sometimes appears as "Weingart."

Europe," said Sorge. "I solicited her aid in establishing my group in Shanghai and particularly in selecting Chinese co-workers. . . . She was used in Shanghai by me as a direct member of my group."[21]

Sorge was so pleased with Smedley that he personally recommended her registration with Comintern headquarters, offering himself as one of the two sponsors required for each new recruit.[22] So, while Smedley never joined the Communist Party, she was registered in Moscow as a reliable worker, and the Soviet Union received the benefit of her activities without having to assume technical responsibility for them.

With her hair cut as though with a lawn mower, a wide mouth that seemed to sneer even when smiling, and a chin like the prow of a battleship, she was not Sorge's cup of tea. He respected her for her "good educational background and . . . brilliant mind" and for her abilities as a reporter, but the very qualities that made her valuable as a colleague made her sexually repulsive to Sorge. "In short," he wrote in later years, "she was like a man."[23] Clausen delivered an even more acute summation. Intellectually Smedley might bat out of his league, but she impressed him as "a hysterical, conceited woman."[24] Nonetheless, she had the entrée into all leftist circles and a flair for picking the right man for the right job.

Sorge had been rapidly reaching the conclusion that the key to evaluating the Asian scene was Japan. At this time he had no more understanding of Japan than any other well-read European, so he asked Smedley to put him in touch with a suitable Japanese to fill the gap.[25] Thus it came about that one crisp day in the autumn of 1930 the big hand of "Johnson" swallowed the delicate fingers of Hotzumi Ozaki.[26]

Sorge saw a dapper young man already growing chubby. Heavy black hair cut in Western style set off a wide, smooth forehead. His mouth was oddly like Sorge's: full-lipped and sensual between deep grooves. Only his eyes hinted that he might be anything more than an amiable extrovert. An acquaintance once observed, "Ozaki was always in smile; however, his eyes were not. Although his eyes were narrow and meek as those of an elephant, there was something strikingly cold at the bottom of the eyes." [27]

Sorge liked Ozaki at once. Socially the two men shared

a number of traits. Both were hearty drinkers, and Ozaki, like Sorge, loved to boast of his sexual adventures. Between them loomed no language barrier, for they had German and English in common, and Ozaki spoke a smattering of Russian. His grasp of written Chinese was flawless; but spoken Chinese was another matter, and he labored with no fewer than three tutors to master the Shanghai dialect.[28]

Ozaki was born in Tokyo on May Day 1901. His parents, though poor, came of rural samurai stock. When he was six months old, the family moved to Taiwan, where his father became editor in chief of a newspaper and something of a local celebrity.[29] But he was not too busy to teach his son Chinese and to instruct him in Confucianism and the classics. Later he sent the boy to Japan to the Tokyo First Higher School, the Imperial University, and the political science department of the Teidai Law School.[30]

Two events in 1923 left an imprint on Ozaki. Immediately following the Great Earthquake, rumors flamed that Koreans planned to join forces with Japanese Communists to take advantage of the disaster and establish a revolutionary government. As a result, many innocent Koreans suffered from mob violence, and the police arrested Communists wholesale. Kind-hearted and sentimental, Ozaki began to identify with underdogs in general and with Communists in particular, although not to the extent of committing himself openly and thereby jeopardizing his chance of a solid position in life.[31] Then and for some years thereafter Ozaki tried to reconcile a comfortable conscience with a comfortable body.

He dawdled pleasantly over his education, financed by his father. His one bout with reality concerned the higher civil service entrance examinations, which anyone hoping for a top government position had to pass. Ozaki's failure to do so and the circumstances of that failure changed the direction of his life, personal as well as professional. Instead of devoting his full attention to the civil service tests upon which his whole future depended, he spent much time mooning over a young divorcée with whom he was in love. But she preferred another man, and Ozaki ended up with neither a government job nor the woman of his dreams.[32]

Throughout his college days Ozaki used to say, "All or

nothing! I detest half measures. I will be the best official and pile up the best records if I enter government service. If I can't do that, I'd rather not begin my career in government." He put off a decision about his future by doing a little graduate work, with the financial aid of a family friend. Emerging from the university and having not yet settled upon the course he wished to pursue in life, he "chose the newspaper field as a kind of neutral observation point."[33] Needless to say, with this self-centered attitude he fell flat on his face at *Asahi Shimbun*, where he had found employment as a city desk reporter. The city editor recalled that "both his news sense and writing style were completely hopeless."[34]

Instead of firing Ozaki, *Asahi* transferred him to its magazine section, where he found his niche in evaluating and interpreting the stories that other men rustled up and brought in. From his modest ivory tower he looked down upon these laborers in the vineyard, whose aggressiveness he found distasteful.[35] Ozaki was a born commentator and interpreter, for his brain, though first-class, was retrospective rather than creative.

Now settled into journalism, with his civil service career and his great love lost, in 1927 Ozaki married a woman he had known from childhood—his first cousin and former sister-in-law, Eiko, a sensitive, intelligent woman who went more than halfway to make the marriage a success. Ozaki was an unfaithful and somewhat offhanded husband, but he was good-natured, generous, and in time an affectionate father to their daughter Yoko.[36]

Although Ozaki had done much reading and studying of Marxism, at the time of his marriage he was not yet a convinced Communist. He "tagged along half-heartedly" to some leftist cultural gatherings and joined the Kanto Publishing Workers' Union under an alias. These activities were enough to compromise him seriously when, on March 15, 1928, the police rounded up more than 1,000 Communists and fellow travelers. With amazing luck, Ozaki escaped the dragnet. But many of his friends did not. Beatings and torture accompanied these arrests. Bitterly ashamed that Japanese would behave in such a manner, Ozaki asked for a transfer to *Asahi*'s Shanghai office. In November 1928 he and Eiko arrived in China.[37]

The March 15 Incident was a symptom of the repression

gradually spreading over Japanese life. In the 1920s Japan showed the world the face of democratic institutions: a Diet of two houses; an independent judicial system; an efficient civil service. But Japanese democracy had serious flaws. Not until 1925 did the Diet enact full suffrage for all Japanese males over twenty-five; before that date restrictions limited the actual voters to about 1 percent of the male population (female suffrage was unthinkable). Another problem area was the military. The framers of the Meiji constitution, in an effort to keep the army and navy from under the thumb of potentially selfish, unpatriotic politicians, had placed the army and navy directly under the Emperor. Inevitably this arrangement allowed the military to dominate the cabinet.

The Japan of Ozaki's student days was relatively liberal, at least on the surface. The post-World War I period was one of somewhat hectic prosperity and a general loosening of traditional bonds. Japan had its equivalent of the flapper and Joe College, its "parlor pinks," even a few who turned to radical ideas. But communism had a strike against it, being associated with Japan's old enemy, Russia. And 1925 saw the enactment of the Peace Preservation Law, which made criminal offenses the advocating of both a basic change in the political system and the abolition of private property. This statute was to become a dependable workhorse for the arrest of Communists.

In 1927 Japan had a depression, and conservatives of all classes and types began to see past Westernization as an enormous mistake. The stringent measures to spur economic recovery were directed toward strengthening the state rather than raising the citizens' standard of living. Harsh social restrictions went into effect: strict censorship of communications media; banning of certain student associations; the death penalty for serious violations of the Peace Preservation Law; thousands of Communists thrown into jail, as Ozaki could testify.[38]

Although Ozaki had been studying Chinese affairs for some time, when he first set foot in Shanghai his ideas about China were contemporary with the hobble skirt. Convinced that the British were the chief exploiters of the Chinese, he received a severe jolt when he discovered that Japan was the leading imperialist in China and the nation against which Chinese leftists demonstrated and boycotted. Ozaki remembered his boyhood amid the privileged Japanese of Taiwan, then an integral part of the Japanese Empire, and in retrospect worked up an outsized guilt complex.[39]

Yet such considerations did not complete Ozaki's shift to the left. He came to communism not from an abstract quest for social justice but from a detached observation and analysis of events being played out before him. He wrote that "it was not the study of Marxism which led me to the study of the 'China problem' but rather it was, for me, the observation of factual developments of the 'China problem' that matured my interests in the Marxist theory. . . . [the] stages of the world revolution were unfolding themselves, right in front of my very eyes, precisely according to the formula."[40] Thus convinced of the validity of communism, he fell an easy prey to Sorge and Smedley.

Sorge described Ozaki's information as "the most accurate and the best" that he received from any Japanese source. He served as one of Sorge's most important sources of information about "Japan's new Manchurian policy, the effect of said policy on the Soviet Union, . . . Sino-Japanese clashes and the general problem of Japanese expansion. . . . Ozaki acted as my teacher in connection with these problems."[41]

In addition, he was a valuable recruiter and produced two new agents for Sorge, both of whom would join him later in Tokyo. The first of these was a bright, personable Japanese youngster of twenty-two. Shigeru Mizuno impressed Sorge as "more of a scholar than a political spy,"[42] but Sorge accepted him in his group, for Mizuno had Ozaki's enthusiastic backing.

The two had met in late 1929, when Mizuno visited Ozaki in his office to solicit his help in editing a student newspaper. Basking in the obvious admiration of the eager-eyed young man, Ozaki became host to Mizuno and a small group of students who gathered in his home for an extracurricular seminar on Marxism.

By October 1930 Mizuno had set up a party cell in the school and was busy fomenting student strikes, only to fall afoul of the Japanese consular police, who in December arrested him for distributing Communist propaganda to Japanese naval cadets. This exploit earned him ten days in jail and expulsion from school. His police record should have removed him immediately from any consideration for espionage, but in the following May he began to collect military and political items for Sorge's ring. In August, however, the city police picked him up on a charge of student agitation and turned him over to the Japanese Consulate, which deported him to Japan.[43] His Shanghai espionage career had been brief; he would last somewhat longer in Tokyo.

Ozaki's second recruit was Teikichi Kawai, like Ozaki a Japanese newspaperman. He had already proved his ability to collect and evaluate military and political data for one of the many amateur and professional intelligence groups in Shanghai when Ozaki recruited him in October 1931. Kawai having agreed to sever all ties with other groups, Ozaki arranged a meeting with him, specifying a certain street corner.[44]

At the designated site Kawai had scarcely time to exchange greetings with Ozaki when a car pulled up to the curb and Smedley's vividly ugly face peered at them from behind the wheel. Ozaki and Kawai piled into the car, and Smedley drove them to a Chinese restaurant on Nanking Road. Sorge was waiting for them and lost no time in getting down to business. Having no language in common with Kawai, he addressed him in English with Ozaki as interpreter.

Instructing him in his first assignment—observation of the Japanese Army in North China and Manchuria—Sorge cautioned, "Take your work step by step. Do not rush things."

Later Kawai recalled, "Sorge's words lived with me. I think I am alive today because I followed Sorge's advice." Sorge's dynamic personality; his no-nonsense way of coming to the point; an electric quality in his handshake—all impressed Kawai: "One meets one like him only once in a lifetime."[45]

Kawai struck Sorge as "very active and very eager to work."[46] His new recruit was a small man of about Ozaki's age with the wiry strength of a fox terrier. Kawai's eyes twinkled with a peasant's cunning. His cheekbones were high; his lips, full; his teeth, slightly protruding. Sorge could sense a shrewd intelligence that, if properly channeled, could be productive but that might lose itself in the marshes of impatience. Kawai was a queer fish to have swum into the Communist net.

He was an individualist, not the type one would expect to accept unquestioningly a personal or doctrinaire pattern.[47]

He recoiled from steady work as a small boy shrinks from a bathtub, but his material wants were few, so he had drifted from one temporary job to another less from laziness than from restlessness. Upon graduation from Meiji University in 1925, he took a newspaper job in Tokyo, but soon the vast magnet of China drew him. At Shanghai in 1928 he became a Communist, principally for pacifist reasons. A gregarious soul, he joined a whole sheaf of left-wing and Communist-front organizations. Now, obedient to Ozaki, for whom he had conceived an inordinate admiration, Kawai swore off his other leftist groups and took service with the Sorge ring of spies.[48]

The Sorge-Ozaki partnership came to a halt when, shortly after the Shanghai Incident of January 30–31, 1932—fierce fighting in which a landing force of Japanese marines engaged the Chinese Nineteenth Route Army and a body of Chinese students—*Asahi* recalled Ozaki to Osaka. Sorge wanted him to resign from the newspaper and remain in Shanghai. However, Ozaki did not wish to give up his job, preferring "to go back to Japan for a while and watch the situation." [49]

Sorge asked Ozaki to pick out his successor, so he introduced his friend Masayoshi Yamakami, who terminated the association after only two meetings. Kawai, who for a short while operated as a liaison between Sorge and the Japanese leftists in and out of the ring, selected as substitute Hisao Funakoshi, whom he knew through various left-wing groups, and presented him to Yamakami, who in turn introduced him to Sorge. The latter accepted Funakoshi, who worked loyally with Sorge and later with his successor in Shanghai.[50] Sorge was very cagey about his relationship with Funakoshi. "I can no longer remember what kind of information I received from Funakoshi," he wrote.[51]

The full story of Sorge's gaudy Shanghai period is beyond the scope of this study, for our target is Tokyo. Yet the Tokyo adventure had many roots in Shanghai, and the ring Sorge established in China was in many ways the pattern for his Japanese *apparat*. There two major and several minor dramatis personae first appeared in connection with Sorge; there he demonstrated techniques and established a system that matured in Japan; there he established the reputation with the Fourth Department of the Red Army that made him the logical choice for the Tokyo assignment.

CHAPTER 4

"YOU MIGHT TRY TOKYO"

The Fourth Department had planned to keep Sorge in Shanghai for only two years, but his assignment proved more difficult than expected, so he remained for an extra year. He left Shanghai in December 1932 and reached Moscow in January 1933.[1]

The ice of a Russian January melted before the warmth of his reception at Red Army headquarters. He reported to General Ian Antonovitch Berzin, who had been chief of the Fourth Department since 1926. Starik, as Berzin was known, and his new assistant, General Semion Petrovitch Uritskii, were charged with the job of building a worldwide apparatus that would infiltrate espionage agents into the very heart of the government of any country. The two generals considered Sorge's work in China "most satisfactory," but they met his request for an indefinite assignment in Moscow with a flat refusal. To both of them, his activities abroad were more valuable. Berzin agreed that Sorge could remain in the capital long enough to expand into a book some articles about Chinese agriculture that he had written for a German agricultural journal.[2]

Sorge had another reason for wanting a permanent Moscow job. He was getting married or at least going through the motions of marriage. While in Japan, Sorge is said to have remarked of his second wife, "Naturally, I never legally married, but she is still known throughout Russia as Mrs. Sorge."[3]

The lady in question, Yekaterina ("Katcha") Alexandrovna Maximova, was nine years younger than he. A picture shows a darkly lovely girl with straight hair drawn over her ears in a style that reveals the regular oval of her good-humored face. Until 1928 Katcha had studied at the Institute of Dramatic Art in Leningrad but had left the institute to work in a factory near Moscow, where she had many friends among the foreign comrades. Sorge's Russian was never perfect, and Katcha helped him through its mazes.[4]

Married or not, the couple spent very little time together—a few months in early 1933; a few weeks in mid-1935; then separation forever. But tragedy was far from Sorge's mind at this time. When Berzin telephoned him one day around the end of April, he was full of self-confidence and eager to prove his mettle.

"I promised to let you finish your writing," the general said, briskly apologetic. "I am sorry, but we cannot keep the promise. We have to ask you to go abroad again. Where do you want to go?"

Sorge swallowed any disappointment he may have felt. "Anyway, it will be some place in Asia," he said thoughtfully. "There are three places possible: China, Manchuria . . ." He broke off. He had spent a most pleasant three-day vacation from Shanghai at the Imperial Hotel in Tokyo. So half-jokingly he added, "Tokyo is not bad, either!"

Berzin neither accepted nor rejected the idea at the time, but after a few meetings at Sorge's hotel and his own home the general brought up the matter "with sudden enthusiasm."

"We are very interested in your saying that you might try Tokyo," Berzin told him. Sorge had the impression that "we" were very high up and perhaps included War Commissar Kliment Y. Voroshilov and even Stalin. Sorge suggested that they go into details at their next meeting.

Berzin gave him permission to meet with Pyatnitsky, Manuilsky, and Kuusinen. Their talks, "although they touched on political problems of a general nature, were purely personal and friendly." They were, in Sorge's words, "quite proud of their protégé." He claimed that Pyatnitsky in particular "was extremely worried about the hardships I would face but delighted with my enterprising spirit."[5]

The general also approved of Sorge's calling on Karl Radek of the Central Committee to help with his arrangements. In one of his visits to the committee Sorge ran into an old friend named Borovitch, whose code name was Alex.* Sorge, Radek, and Alex engaged in long talks about political and economic problems involving Japan and East Asia. Though not in a position to give Sorge orders, Radek and Alex offered many suggestions. For information about living conditions and the general situation in Tokyo, Sorge got in touch with the Foreign Commissariat.[6]

Moscow had cause to question Tokyo's intentions at this stage of world history. Japan had been pursuing an expansionist policy since the Sino-Japanese War of 1894–95, when the Treaty of Shimonoseki gave Japan Formosa (Taiwan), the Pescadores Islands, and the Liaotung peninsula. Already alarmed, Russia joined France and Germany in pressuring Japan to return the latter.

The Russo-Japanese War of 1904–05, fought primarily over control of Korea, gave the Russians something to worry about. In a preview of Pearl Harbor, the Japanese Navy bottled up the Russian fleet units at Port Arthur, then demolished the main Russian fleet at Tsushima. The Japanese Army proved no less effective. By the Treaty of Portsmouth, mediated by President Theodore Roosevelt, among other items Russia conceded Japan's special interest in Korea and ceded to Japan the southern half of Sakhalin Island. Nevertheless, the Japanese always believed that Roosevelt had shortchanged them and nursed a national grudge against the United States.

Japan annexed Korea in 1910, then, as a result of very limited participation on the Allied side, emerged from World War I with a thriving economy and mandates over former German possessions in the Pacific north of the equator. More disquieting to Moscow, Japan participated with the United States in the postwar Siberian campaign. Each agreed to limit its troops to 7,000, but Japan hurled in massive forces and occupied strategic spots in the Maritime Provinces, in northern Sakhalin, and as far as the Lake Baikal area. It quickly pulled out of Lake Baikal and took troops out of northern Sakhalin but received substantial oil and other concessions there.

Both Russia and Japan cast acquisitive eyes on Manchuria, a region of 413,000 square miles in northern China which

---

* This was not the Alex of Shanghai days.

the Chinese called the Three Northern Provinces. Under a secret protocol of 1907, Russia and Japan divided Manchuria into spheres of influence. But Japan had no intention of being permanently satisfied with crumbs or even with half a loaf. It coveted Manchuria, particularly its rich deposits of coal and iron, both seriously deficient in the home islands and absolutely necessary to sustain the national economy, which boomed after World War I.

Yet it was not the government or even the War Ministry that precipitated the issue but the Kwantung Army, a Japanese force stationed along the South Manchurian Railway. Engineering a blowup on the railroad and claiming the Chinese were responsible, the Kwantung Army occupied the city of Mukden in what became known as the Mukden Incident, which rapidly expanded into the much broader Manchurian Incident. Soon the Kwantung Army spread beyond the railroad to occupy all the major cities of South Manchuria. By January 1932 Japan was in complete command of virtually all China north of the Great Wall. This gave Japan control of a long border adjacent to the Soviet Union, and Moscow had no reason to suppose that Japan had slaked its appetite. For their part, the Japanese had always dreaded Russia's vast material and military potential and now almost equally feared the Soviet Union's ideological imperialism.[7]

After several meetings among Berzin, his Fourth Department staff, and Sorge, they decided that first he should simply attempt to establish a Soviet spy ring on Japanese soil. In this early, tentative mission he was to try to determine the answers to four questions: Could he and his fellow members enter Japan legally? Was real communication possible between Japanese and foreigners? Were radio and other communications with the Soviet mainland technically feasible? Could his ring collect information concerning Japan's future policy toward the Soviet Union?

After two years in Japan, Sorge was to return to Moscow to report progress in person—that is, if he was alive to do so.[8]

Then Berzin turned him over to a Fourth Department code expert, who drilled him for a full day in the agreed-upon cipher, which was based upon the 1933 edition of the *German Statistical Yearbook*.[9]

As Sorge and his superiors laid down the broad outlines of his new spy ring, he asked to be supplied with a foreign national for work among the non-German Europeans in Tokyo and with a Japanese national with a solid knowledge of English because English was to be used in the code for radio communication with the Soviet Union.[10]

Sorge planned to go to Tokyo as a reporter, the only cover that would serve his purpose. Journalism offered the perfect operating base for espionage, particularly for a man of Sorge's stamp. With his inimitable loose stride, his striking features, his eyes as blue and hard as aquamarines, he was a commanding, unforgettable figure. So he would make a virtue of necessity, cultivating the image of an unconventional but distinguished German newsman. "Johnson," the American persona he had used in Shanghai, had outlived his usefulness. Sorge could not hope to get away with pretending to be American in Tokyo, where he planned to deal with Japan's top crust, many of whom spoke better English than he did and knew the United States well. Moreover, he had high hopes of penetrating the German Embassy in Tokyo, and this he could do only as a fellow countryman, representing some reputable German newspaper or periodical and entering Japan with a folderful of German credentials. So he would have to go to Germany to arrange his cover.

It would be difficult to imagine a worse time for a Soviet agent to attempt to infiltrate the Reich. On January 30, 1933, Hitler became chancellor, and within a few days the Nazis had declared war on Communists. They outlawed the party, destroyed its newspapers and magazines, beat its members senseless, clapped them into jail, and shipped them off to concentration camps by the hundreds. In this atmosphere there could be no friendly gatherings in cozy apartments for Sorge and his old comrades. Every German Communist who could do so had disappeared with the silent speed of an eel into a mud bank.

This was the state of affairs when Sorge approached the German border in May 1933. His papers were in order. Still, he might be—and should have been—on the "watch" lists at the German frontier posts. Not so long ago he had been well known for his activities in behalf of communism in Germany.

With typical luck he reached Berlin in good shape. But

could this really be the Berlin of his school days and early manhood? Where was the bustling, comfortable city that, in spite of being the capital of a great nation, had never lost its provincial flavor, never quite attained the knowing grace of Paris and Vienna?

On every surface that could hold a banner hung long, thin red, white, and black bunting stamped with the swastika. Berlin swarmed with uniforms, flags, banners, and men who marched confidently to the stolid blat of a German brass band. In his speeches Hitler was still preaching peace, goodwill, and international understanding, but the atmosphere was one of war. Definitely it was not a pretty scene into which Sorge walked in the late spring of 1933. It behooved him to move delicately. But he had much in his favor, not the least being self-assurance and dauntless physical courage.

Equally to the point, in Shanghai he had established himself as a bona fide reporter, hence did not have to start from scratch in the newspaper world. As always, he aimed high, as high as the *Frankfurter Zeitung*. Sorge claimed that he became the Japanese correspondent of the prestigious newspaper around July 1933.[11] Hede Massing[12] and two former officials of the newspaper have endorsed this claim.[13] The *Frankfurter Zeitung*, however, later averred that the first time the paper heard from Sorge was in a letter dated February 4, 1936, when he offered to send it articles.[14]

Sorge mentioned "a Comintern contact man" in Berlin. He did not name him, but it probably was Yakov Gregorievitch Goriev. They met at a café, exchanged passwords, and posed as old wartime friends, speaking in German. Goriev wrote that this meeting was "truly a race against the watch," for they had only one hour to exchange information. Sorge knew that he would experience problems in Tokyo because of Japanese counterespionage. "The idea of difficulty is relative," he pronounced. "It is possible to attain your objective, in all circumstances if you can see clearly and use the chances, the possibilities, which offer themselves to you. Of course," he added with a rueful smile, "you also need a little luck."[15]

Nevertheless, Sorge was not the man to stand around with his mouth open, waiting for the fruit to fall in. So he called at the office of the *Zeitschrift für Geopolitik* ("Journal of Geopolitics''), which wielded considerable influence in Nazi circles, and made the acquaintance of its editor, Kurt Vowinckel, a well-known Rhenish publisher and ardent supporter of Hitler's. Vowinckel had read Sorge's essays on China in the agricultural magazine, was pleased to meet the author, and asked him to contribute to the *Zeitschrift für Geopolitik*. Naturally Sorge was delighted to accept. Vowinckel also furnished him with an open letter of introduction to the German Embassy in Tokyo and personal introductions to secretaries Josef Knoll and Hasso von Etzdorff. After selling himself to Vowinckel, Sorge traveled to Munich to pay his respects to Dr. Karl Haushofer.[16]

Haushofer, who had founded the *Zeitschrift für Geopolitik* with Vowinckel, believed deeply in the influence of geography upon world history. A professor at the University of Munich, he had an enormous reputation as the director of the Institute for Geopolitics and as an author. He had served in Japan prior to World War I as an officer in the German Army and had written extensively about Japan; he greatly admired the country and its people, whom he believed destined to rule all Asia. Haushofer had connections with the highest levels of the National Socialist Party, and his friendship with Deputy Führer Rudolf Hess dated back to 1918, when Hess was his student at the University of Munich.[17]

By ironical chance, Hess and Haushofer had written a book together entitled *Japan and Espionage*. In imitation of the Japanese, the Nazis took a particular interest in Germans living abroad in the hope of obtaining from them the sort of information that Japanese living and traveling overseas sent home as a matter of course—namely, virtually everything they saw or heard. Nazi cells were established among such "outlanders" as early as 1930, and in 1931 a Foreign Department of the Nazi Party was organized, with Hess at its head, which kept a special card on every Nazi Party member. Through Hess, Haushofer came to know Hitler.[18] Therefore, any credentials from this well-connected and distinguished geopolitician carried a special stamp of authority. Haushofer obligingly provided Sorge with a letter of introduction to the German ambassador to Japan and another to the Japanese ambassador to the United States.[19]

Having stormed Haushofer's citadel, Sorge made his way

back to Berlin to the *Täglische Rundschau*, a mildly anti-Nazi paper that was not to last much longer. The editor in chief, Dr. Zeller, was glad to meet Sorge, whose work he knew. When Sorge proposed that he write some articles for him in Tokyo, he made out a contract on the spot and gave him a valuable letter of introduction to the embassy of the "To Whom It May Concern" type, indicating that the *Tüglische Rundschau* would appreciate any support the embassy could give its correspondent.[20]

Zeller also gave Sorge what was to prove his most important introduction, a letter commending him to Lieutenant Colonel Eugen Ott, an exchange officer with a Japanese artillery regiment at Nagoya. In this missive Zeller went much farther out on the limb than he had in his letter of introduction to the embassy. He requested Ott to trust Sorge "in everything; that is, politically, personally and otherwise." Unhappily for Ott, he did so.

Sorge prized this letter, for with Hitler in power, Germans living overseas were suspicious of strangers from home trying to strike up acquaintance. Zeller's letter provided Sorge with his "first opportunity . . . to get closely acquainted with Colonel Ott and to win his confidence."[21]

Sorge did not realize how very valuable Zeller's introduction to Ott would become, for he had his sights on bigger game than exchange officers. Nevertheless, anyone connected however remotely with the German Embassy was worth cultivating. As Sorge explained, "Moscow rightly thought I would be able to establish sound connections in high German circles in Japan. Of course, it was assumed that I would get a firm foothold in the German Embassy, which was the sole place where I could study such developments in detail."[22] That last sentence provides a clue to Sorge's fantastic success: The possibility of failure never entered his mind.

During these months in Berlin the most ticklish and perhaps for him the most satisfying of Sorge's exploits was acceptance into the Nazi ranks. He read reams of Nazi propaganda, memorized all the catchwords, copied the standard gestures, and devoted particular attention to the ubiquitous bible of the Nazis, *Mein Kampf,* by Adolf Hitler.

Soon he was shouting and arguing with the best of them,

bolstering his arguments by spouting verbatim whole pages of
Mein Kampf. His new friends took him to so many beer parties
that, lest his tongue betray him, he made the supreme sacrifice
and went on the wagon. "That was the bravest thing I ever
did," he told Hede Massing sometime later, grinning. "Never
will I be able to drink enough to make up for this time." [23] For
Sorge to give up the bottle voluntarily shows that for all his
bravado and self-confidence he knew that he walked a tightrope
in Berlin in 1933.

Now for the critical moves. He submitted an application
for membership in the Nazi Party, such membership being
required of newspaper correspondents. He applied through the
editor in chief of the Berlin newspaper *Pozendai Zeitung* and
the monthly magazine *Heidelberg Geopolitik*, who knew Sorge
because he had contributed some articles to the magazine when
in China. Acceptance customarily depended upon a Gestapo
check of the applicant's background. Sorge's luck held. He
was accepted, although his membership card, which certified
him as a full-fledged Nazi, did not catch up with him until
sometime in 1934, when he had been in Japan for months. [24]

How could the Gestapo possibly have overlooked Sorge's
long Communist record in Germany? As the Military Intelligence Section (G-2) of General Douglas MacArthur's Far East
Command later observed:

> Having just seized power the Nazi Party and the
> Gestapo had not yet acquired the efficiency and
> thorough national coverage they were to develop
> later. Nevertheless, there must have been a Soviet
> agent in a responsible post at Gestapo files. When
> a check was made in 1941, highly derogatory in-
> formation was turned up at once, yet in 1933 Sorge's
> application for party membership and for travel
> abroad as a correspondent were unchallenged. [25]

Hede Massing confirmed G-2's guess. She wrote that
Sorge had a guardian angel, "another Soviet agent who had
been planted in the Gestapo. Sorge never knew his name,
although he knew of his existence. At the crucial moment, this
agent had been able, temporarily, to remove all the incriminating evidence from the file on Sorge." [26]

By July 1933 Sorge was ready to leave Germany. He obtained his passport without difficulty and set out for New York via France and England, where he embarked at Southampton.

In the United States he broke his trip for fifteen days, eight of which he spent in New York City, where he stayed at the Lincoln Hotel. No one knows exactly what he did during that time. However, according to him, he got in touch with a man whose name he did not know, who instructed him "to meet a certain employee of the *Washington Post* at the Chicago World's Fair."[27]

From New York Sorge proceeded to Washington, where he presented his letter from Haushofer to Ambassador Katsuji Debuchi. His Excellency unwittingly did his bit by giving Sorge a valuable letter of introduction to Amaha Temba, head of the Information Department of the Japanese Foreign Ministry.

Sorge spent three days in Washington,[28] then headed west. He stopped in Chicago for four days to take in the world's fair and meet the representative of the *Washington Post,* from whom he received instructions for contacting the Japanese assistant being furnished him. To get in touch with this person, Sorge was to place an advertisement in the *Japan Advertiser,* a Tokyo English-language newspaper, indicating a desire to purchase Ukiyoe, a particular type of Japanese print.[29] The Japanese assistant would reply to the advertisement.

Having finished his business in the United States, Sorge swung aboard a train and rocked westward to Vancouver, where he boarded his ship, the *Empress of Russia,* well armed for his foray into Japan.[30] The preliminaries over, he could look forward to the main bout with formidable foes in Tokyo.

CHAPTER 5

 "NO EQUIVALENT IN HISTORY"

A few days before Christmas 1933 the new German ambassador, Herbert von Dirksen, walked down the gangplank of the *Hakusan Maru* at Kobe and proceeded to his little kingdom. "Little" is correct, for the staff he inherited was a distinct comedown from what he had been accustomed to as ambassador to the Soviet Union, where he had presided over the largest staff of any German Embassy in the world. With the exception of Counselor Otto Bernard von Erdmannsdorff, who soon returned to Germany, the Tokyo staff consisted only of the counselor, Dr. W. Noebel; four secretaries; the two service attachés; and two typists.[1]

By the time Dirksen reached Tokyo Sorge was practically an embassy fixture. After landing in Japan in September, he had registered at the Sanno Hotel and allowed himself only a brief breathing spell before approaching the German Embassy armed with his letter of introduction from Haushofer. Finding that the current ambassador was out of town and that a replacement would arrive later in the year, Sorge presented his letter to Erdmannsdorff, the acting ambassador.[2]

He and his staff received Sorge courteously and heartily, the more so because asked whether he knew anyone in the Japanese Foreign Ministry and whether he wanted an introduction, Sorge "somewhat proudly" answered, "You do not need to worry about it. I already have a letter of introduction from the Japanese Ambassador to the United States, Debuchi." They were surprised and impressed to find that Sorge had such high and wide connections, and this little incident broke down any latent resistance to immediate acceptance of the newcomer.

The next day Sorge submitted his letter from Debuchi to Amaha Temba, head of the Information Department of the Foreign Ministry, who greeted him cordially, introduced him "to many Japanese and foreign journalists," and gave him a number of valuable tips concerning travel in Japan.

Within the embassy Sorge had set out to become intimate first with Erdmannsdorff, then with Hasso von Etzdorff, and succeeded.[3] The importance of this infiltration cannot be overestimated. "The fact that I successfully approached the German Embassy in Japan and won absolute trust by people there was the foundation of my spy activity in Japan," Sorge observed. ". . . I could carry out my spy activity only standing on this foundation. Even in Moscow the fact that I infiltrated into the center of the embassy and made use of it for my spying activity is evaluated as extremely amazing, having no equivalent in history."[4]

By the end of 1933, between his new friends and his first intensive studies of Japanese politics, Sorge considered himself ready to publish. He sent to the *Täglische Rundschau* a political essay on Japan that "received a very good evaluation in Germany. Hearing this," Sorge continued complacently, "Knoll came to trust me not a little." Josef Knoll, commercial secretary at the embassy, was, in Sorge's words, "the number one as far as political knowledge was concerned and I was greatly stimulated politically by him."[5]

Herbert von Dirksen, Hitler's envoy to the Japanese empire, was a Prussian aristocrat who looked something like a Teutonized version of Sibelius. Above a strong chin and big nose loomed a bald, rather flat skull and a craggy forehead jutting over intelligent but weary eyes that gave the impression that he had seen everything at least twice and was tired of it.

Dirksen's appointment disquieted Sorge, for the ambassador was a lifelong "Easterner" by both birth and preference. Long service on the Eastern desk at the German Foreign Ministry had preceded his five-year stay in Moscow. In Sorge's eyes, the advent of Dirksen in Tokyo seemed to signal an abrupt turn in German foreign policy. Whereas the mission of Dirksen's predecessor had stressed "cultural ties between Japan and

Germany," Dirksen's was to plan and promote close military and economic relationships between the two countries, and to work toward "a common policy against Soviet Russia."[6]

Possibly he spoke from hindsight, for Dirksen wrote long after, "I have never succeeded in discovering the real reasons for this transfer. . . . The assumption that a change of policy was intended was without foundation. . . . After surveying the whole problem I came to the conclusion that the transfer was purely a matter of routine, and had no connection with political considerations."[7] All that Dirksen brought with him in the nature of instructions was "a hint dropped by General [Werner] von Blomberg, the War Minister," that Hitler intended "to establish closer relations with Japan." This was fine with Dirksen, who "realized the necessity of applying some kind of brake to the Russian machine, after the relations with Germany and the Soviet Union became more strained. I never believed in the possibility of a Russo-Japanese war on Japanese initiative. . . ."[8]

Dirksen accepted Sorge without question as a reputable German journalist. Nevertheless, Sorge did not achieve the hoped-for degree of chumminess with him.[9] Their relationship was friendly, and Dirksen admitted Sorge to his confidence to a certain extent; but a barrier remained. Dirksen was a typical topflight diplomat of the old school, who knew exactly how to keep lesser mortals in their place without antagonizing them, and he had reached the pinnacle of his profession. Sorge had nothing to offer that Dirksen needed. He could expect only such cooperation as the ambassador would give any well-connected newsman who also happened to be a pleasant, witty gentleman with a useful gift for getting along with the Japanese. Sorge could not hope to plant the hammer and sickle banner on the enemy heights by a direct charge on the opposing commander in chief; he knew he had to make a flanking attack. And this he set out to do.

In the fall of 1933 he traveled to Nagoya to seek out Lieutenant Colonel Eugen Ott, liaison officer with Japan's Third Artillery Regiment. When Sorge presented himself, letter of introduction in hand, Ott was living a far from luxurious existence in military quarters. He was employed in observing and reporting on Japanese Army training, "which took place as though behind an iron curtain." This left him little time to study the Japanese language. One reason why Ott was pleased to have Sorge's friendship was Sorge's grasp of Japanese, which, while weak, was better than Ott's. "Because of his language skills, it was easier for him to make contact with Japanese and gain information from them."[10]

The colonel was about Sorge's height, five feet ten inches, rather slender, with the flat back and stomach, broad chest and shoulders of a man at least ten years younger than his forty-four years. He carried himself bolt upright, thanks in part to the rigid German military tradition and in part to nagging rheumatism.[11] A high brow merging with a receding hairline plus a long, square jaw gave his face an oblong look. Mouth and nose were straight and thin, forming a T square in the middle of his face. His eyes were large, deep-set, and blue, holding the observer with a direct gaze. The disciplined features could break into an unexpectedly charming smile, which printed a deep fan of wrinkles at the outer corner of each eye.

Ott was born in southern Germany. During World War I he served on the western front as a young officer of artillery. He also worked with and was a favorite disciple of Colonel Walther Nicolai. That inoffensive-looking officer, the type born to be referred to vaguely as "You know, what's his name," was at the time chief of the German High Command's Intelligence Service (Bureau IIB). During the secret buildup of the German Army in the early 1920s, Nicolai acted as a channel between the Defense Ministry and General Kurt von Schleicher. A man of large ideas and petty intrigue, Schleicher perfected a widespread system of espionage. So in view of the Nicolai connection, it is not surprising to find Ott serving for about a decade as chief of Schleicher's Political Department.

In 1932, when Schleicher was chancellor, he sent then Major Ott to Munich to meet Hitler and ask the future *Führer* to join Schleicher's cabinet, an offer Hitler rejected with disdain. Ott being thus identified in Hitler's sight as an adherent of Schleicher, his superiors in the High Command arranged to have him stashed away in Japan after Hitler had come to power. As a result, Ott was safely across the world when his chief and friend Schleicher met an abrupt end on June 30, 1934, on the Night of the Long Knives, Hitler's purge from the Nazi Party of those he considered undesirable.[12]

However, there was more to Ott's appointment in Japan than appeared on the surface. Nicolai was once more actively working to establish the espionage service of which he had long dreamed. The Germans and Japanese had much to offer each other in the way of a mutual espionage assistance pact. In the Far East the Japanese could be of enormous help to the Germans, and the Germans could spy for the Japanese in areas where Orientals would be conspicuous. Therefore, Ott had to pay particular attention to Japanese intelligence and act as something of a liaison between the Germans and Japanese.[13]

Eugen Ott is not the least mysterious personage in the Sorge drama. The general view is that he was an officer doing his duty for Germany, though having no love for Hitler. Yet some have believed he had been Hitler's agent in Schleicher's headquarters in his pre-Japan days.[14] Inevitably the question has arisen of whether or not he might have been more deeply involved in the Sorge case than anyone has ever admitted. No student of Sorge and his ring has been able as yet to find proof of either of these last two allegations.

Like all men of personality who have achieved a degree of success in their chosen field, Ott had his detractors. "Ott is a little Swabian who wanted to play Grand Prussian," said General Walter von Reisenau, Ott's onetime immediate superior, "but after all he was only a pale copy of a Prussian noncom, not an officer."[15] Dirksen's tribute stood in direct contrast: "I was fortunate in having as my military attaché one of the most prominent officers in the German Army—both as regards his character and his ability—in the person of General Ott. . . . By his character and ability he won the esteem of the Japanese General Staff as well as that of the Diplomatic Corps."[16] Dirksen had the ambassadorial gift for masterly understatement honed to a fine edge, so this is high praise indeed.

"Ott was a man of fine character," Sorge concurred. "One of the reasons why we became so close is that I once participated in the First European War as a German soldier and was wounded and that Ott participated in this war at the same time as a young officer."[17] This tie between a good officer and a good soldier who have served in similar circumstances is one of the subtlest yet strongest of human bonds, and Sorge could have had no better entrée. Another common interest, more cerebral, was chess; both loved the game and frequently sat across the board for hours in motionless concentration.[18]

Sorge termed Ott "shrewd, able, politically realistic."[19] He had the knowledge, background, and intelligence to become a successful diplomat, especially in that day, when the military and statecraft were so interwoven in the totalitarian states. What he lacked was Sorge's flair and charisma, while his military duties allowed him no time or opportunity to amass the fund of information about Japan that Sorge was beginning to collect.

But for all of Sorge's usefulness and charm, he had one failing that, from Ott's point of view, could have negated all the rest. He drank heavily, a fact that worried Ott considerably. "I had him watched for months," said Ott, "because I feared that while drunk he might talk about things from our conversations."[20]

Sorge did not establish a full intimacy with Ott until March 1934 when Ott, recently promoted to colonel, became military attaché at the embassy and moved to Tokyo with his wife and their eldest son. Sorge was a frequent guest at their home and became a friend of the family.[21]

Ott came to rely heavily upon Sorge's judgment and advice, and Sorge was glad to oblige. Yet the benefits of the friendship were far from one-sided. Onto Ott's desk at the embassy was funneled all the information about the Japanese Army to be evaluated and sent to Berlin, and from Berlin came data to keep Ott current on the home scene. This word included any advance notice of German plans for the Far East. So if Sorge boosted Ott to the top, Ott pulled Sorge up after him.

Yet Sorge's dependence upon Ott professionally, and the genuine liking and respect he felt for the man, did not prevent Sorge from entering into an affair with Ott's wife.

If a group gathered in the drawing rooms of Japan's German colony was small enough or intimate enough, mention of Helma Ott brought a slight hesitation with the teapot, a lowering of the voice just half a tone, and some such comment as "Frau Ott? Charming! But my dear, slightly *pink*, you know!"[22]

The whispers had some foundation in fact. Her first husband, Ernst May, had been a Communist, and during the Red uprising in Munich in 1919 she had been a member of the party.[23]

The colonel's lady was a rather remarkable woman. Standing six feet tall, with prematurely gray hair, she was a glowing Valkyrie, though no longer in her first youth. Her attraction lay less in her features than in her striking height and the atmosphere of warmhearted intelligence that she generated.[24] Her surface amiability concealed a certain arrogance; she could be amazingly rude to wives of Ott's subordinates, and she looked down, figuratively as well as literally, upon Japanese women.

Sorge saw no reason why seducing Ott's wife should shadow his conscience toward his friend; he did not take any woman that seriously. Nor was the affair the unforgivable risk to his mission that it might have been. Although Ott always treated his wife tenderly, a consideration which she did not reciprocate, and suffered keenly during her liaison with Sorge, he was no longer in love with her, so he chose not to interfere or to take any of the steps that could have ruined Sorge's espionage career in Tokyo.[25]

Some years later, after Max Clausen had married and joined Sorge in Tokyo, Anna teasingly asked Sorge what he thought of Ms. Ott. "She is a beautiful woman," Anna offered.

"Oh, don't talk to me of that woman," answered Sorge. "But what do you want me to do—we need her. . . ."[26]

Another incident of a later time offers a less ugly picture. One day, while looking over some of Sorge's snapshots, his Japanese girl friend noticed one of a gray-haired Western woman whose eyes were "full of happiness and shone beautifully." The Japanese girl was positive that the woman in the photo loved whoever had taken it. When she quizzed Sorge on this subject, he identified the woman as Ms. Ott and admitted that he had had an affair with her. "But there is nothing between us now. She is just a friend. Ms. Ott is kind and good," he said gently.[27]

Nothing in Sorge's attitude toward Ms. Ott was uncharacteristic. Sorge the man could appreciate and salute kindness and goodness wherever he found them; Sorge the spy could and did exploit those qualities ruthlessly for his own purposes.

He made another friend and unwitting colleague when Captain Paul Wenneker reported for duty as naval attaché, a post he held from 1934 to 1938. Dirksen affectionately characterized him as "a frank and outspoken sailor, a cheerful and reliable comrade."[28] Ms. Mitsutaro Araki, a Japanese society woman often at the embassy, remembered Wenneker with smiling warmth as a "very sociable, charming, and friendly" man, popular with his Japanese associates—"a great fillip, because Ott was so rigid and stiff."[29]

"Wenneker . . . had a noble character," wrote Sorge. However, he had little political experience, and Sorge gladly helped indoctrinate him. Socially the two men became "very chummy,"[30] but never enough for Sorge to secure information from Wenneker on naval affairs comparable to his knowledge of the Japanese Army and Japanese politics.

Sorge's conquest of the German Embassy was not difficult. At the time of his adventures in Tokyo that city's German population comprised fewer than 1,000 families. In effect, he had entered a small town where everyone knew everyone else. Any newcomer was an event, and Sorge made quite a splash in this little pool. Everyone who met him always remembered him with total recall. Mention his name, and with the glint of an eye, the quirk of a brow, he emerges from the mists of memory with a casual stride, cocktail glass in hand, a pretty woman on his arm.

He impressed different people in opposite ways. Ms. Araki, who knew Sorge well, spoke of the curious duality of his features: "first the beauty, then after study the ugliness of his face, but always it was an interesting face."[31] To some who knew him, he appeared typically German, and they were astounded later to learn that he had Russian blood;[32] others claimed to have sensed something un-German in him from the beginning.[33]

However, in spite of the wariness the political atmosphere engendered, no one suspected him for what he was. The embassy staff thought of him as "an eccentric, first-class journalist" who was "completely isolated from political parties and factions, being neither a follower of nazism or communism.'' Sorge remarked a bit quizzically, ''Also, I think I gave not a little humanistic charm to Ott and other members of the embassy because I was not ambitious. I did not seek for position; I did not seek benefits. . . .''[34] This statement is only half-true. Sorge was not bucking for anybody's job at the embassy, but certainly he was seeking benefits.

Now that he had secured a beachhead in the embassy, his most important object was to establish himself as a topflight newspaperman at whose knock all doors would fly open. Soon he was on terms of personal friendship with the other German newsmen in Japan, particularly with Rudolf Weise, head of the official German news bureau, Deutsches Nachrichtenbüro (DNB). Weise was useful to Sorge not only because of his position but also because he sometimes passed on bits of political gossip. He was cynical and fond of backstage scuttlebutt, so Sorge found him amusing and held down the DNB desk for him when he went on vacation.[35] On at least one such occasion, when Weise was in Berlin, he discovered to his horror that Sorge's reports made almost no sense. Later he learned that his substitute had been drunk most of the time he was in charge.[36]

Sorge cultivated Western journalists for their goodwill and to establish his image as ''a slightly lazy, high-living reporter,'' always willing to do a favor for fellow members of the Fourth Estate.[37] The news value of Japanese reporters proved nil, and he could not rely on the anemic fare the government-controlled press handed out. Such stories had only one value: They indicated the current propaganda line and what the government wanted the public to believe. However, gradually he jockeyed himself into a position where Japanese officials would accept him. He soon realized that his access to the many and varied data in the embassy, plus the embassy's backing, would increase Japanese trust in him.[38] To probe beneath the surface, he ''plunged into an exhaustive study of Japanese affairs'' which was basic to his establishing a reputation as an authority on Japan and indispensable to his espionage activities:

> . . . I did not believe that I should concern myself
> exclusively with the technical and organizational

work of receiving orders and conveying them to my co-workers and forwarding reports to the Moscow authorities. I could not reconcile myself to such a simple concept of my responsibilities as the leader of an intelligence group operating in a foreign land. I had always felt that a man in such a position should cultivate a thorough understanding of all problems related to his activities. The collection of information had an importance of its own, but I was convinced that the ability to appraise it and to evaluate the over-all political picture was of vital importance.[39]

So Sorge set about making himself the best-informed Occidental in Tokyo on Japan and the Japanese. By the time of his arrest he had accumulated almost 1,000 books, most of them on Japanese history, economics, politics, and thought. If a suitable translation was not available, he commissioned one. He was proud that his library contained collector's items and by no means neglected such Japanese classics as *The Tale of Genji*. With the view to eventually writing a book on the subject he paid special attention to those times in Japan's long history when it had embarked on expansionist adventures.[40]

However, despite the formidable knowledge of Japan he was acquiring, he had to rely upon translations, hence perforce absorbed his facts at second hand. For he never learned Japanese beyond the smattering necessary to move about on his own and carry on a simple conversation.

In addition to his books, Sorge collected many manuscripts, translations of Japanese magazines, and government pamphlets. He had access to the German Embassy's official library and eventually had the run of the ambassador's personal library. He haunted the Tokyo East Asia German Society, the fine collection of which was particularly rich in the scientific field, and he kept in touch with Germans of interests and tastes similar to his own, thereby picking any number of brains.[41]

He never mentioned his informal ties to *NS Partei-Korrespondenz*, the paper of the Nazi Party—he was on cordial, if long-distance, terms with its editor, Wilhelm von Ritgen.

His information for this journal, however, went in the form of personal letters to Ritgen, who came to value as practically indispensable the facts and estimates they contained.[42]

Along with his professional aims, Sorge had a personal motive for all this effort. ". . . had I lacked the ability to evaluate a given problem and erroneously analyzed a situation, I would have become a target for ridicule of my Japanese co-workers," he confided.[43]

At the German Club, the German Chamber of Commerce, and embassy receptions Sorge encountered many of the German businessmen and engineers in Tokyo. During his first years he cultivated them because the interweaving of the German and Japanese economies was of considerable professional interest to him. But he soon discovered that he obtained nothing from these sources that was not readily available in the files of the German Embassy. In time he pruned down his relations with the business colony to a few personal friendships and was not sorry to do so, for he disliked and distrusted businessmen. Of the two, he preferred the engineers, who, he said, "were not as timid as the businessmen, and who at least knew their own fields." In fact, the businessmen clammed up on him, behavior that Sorge put down to fear "that their competitors might learn something from me. . . ."[44] He was always indignant when anyone sidestepped his probing, attributing such cageyness to either timidity or stupidity.

In those early days Sorge also had friendly relations with the Dutch colony in Tokyo, mainly in order to weigh the extent of possible Dutch resistance to the Japanese economic infiltration of the Netherlands East Indies, secondarily to learn something of Japanese-Dutch commerce as well as Japan's foreign trade and financial condition.[45]

He picked up another source in 1934, when his Nazi Party card, No. 2,751,466, caught up with him. On October 1, 1934, he became a member of the local Nazi organization and began to attend its meetings. When its leader left Japan that year, some of Sorge's German friends urged him to take the position. Privately Sorge thought the idea absurd, but he took it up with Dirksen and Ott, who told him ambiguously, "You should become head of the branch; then the Nazis will have another intellectual leader."[46]

He never accepted leadership, but he found the Nazi gatherings useful as a sounding board of party opinion. One segment openly deplored close cooperation between Germany and Japan. This dissenting opinion held that Germany had nothing to gain economically from such a partnership and suggested that it should seek instead a firm bond with China.[47]

Thus in a remarkably short time Sorge had constructed for himself a triune base of operations in Tokyo: the German Embassy, the German community, and the newspaper world. Each supported and intermingled with the other, but the embassy was the true foundation of his espionage edifice.

CHAPTER 6

"YOU ARE GOING TO TOKYO"

Paris and Los Angeles are a long way from Moscow, Shanghai, or Tokyo, but not too far for the Soviet Union to finger a likely prospect. Thus it came about that in March 1932, somewhere in Paris, a woman with a Finnish or Baltic accent carried on an earnest conversation with a certain man. She called herself Olga.[1]

Although the man was only twenty-eight, his brown hair was retreating rapidly before the advance of his bald skull. Round glasses with thin dark rims perched on a high-bridged nose, and behind them large, dark, myopic eyes regarded the world with measuring watchfulness. His lips were compressed. Slim and well built, this Croatian held himself with the responsive tension of a violin string. But with his friends he could relax, chattering on and on—gentle, happy, and mischievous.[2] Branko de Voukelitch did not know it, but he was about to become a charter member of an exclusive organization, the Soviet Union's Tokyo spy ring under Richard Sorge.

Voukelitch was born in 1904 in Geijek on the Drava River, not far from the Hungarian border in what is now Yugoslavia. His father, Milivoje Voukelitch, was an army officer, and the family traveled about between garrison towns. At the end of World War I they settled in Zagreb, where the boy attended high school.[3] Following graduation, he dabbled briefly in art, then entered the University of Zagreb as a major in architecture. In 1926 his mother, Vilma, carried him off to Paris to work toward a law degree. He was graduated from the

University of Paris in 1929 and took a job with the Compagnie Générale d'Electricité.[4]

At roughly the same time he came up against life's realities with a tooth-jarring bump. His mistress, a Danish woman named Edith Olsen, a maid in the household of a Danish family living in Paris, announced that she was pregnant. She had assisted Voukelitch with occasional gifts of money in his days as a struggling young student. Voukelitch packed her off to Denmark to have her baby, and when she returned with a fine little boy, he legalized the union, although his parents firmly opposed it.[5]

In the early fall of 1931 he resigned from the General Electric Company and went to Yugoslavia to serve his hitch in the army, where he made something of a study of the class and nationalist conflicts among his fellow soldiers.[6] Returning to Paris in January 1932, he found that his firm had abolished his job. Wandering through the Latin Quarter searching for work, he ran into two old friends from Zagreb, where they all had belonged to a Marxist student group. Voukelitch soon realized that his friends Klein and Budacq were still actively involved in the Communist movement. They promised to help him find work and suggested that he write a personal history that included his Communist period and his recent experiences in Yugoslavia.[7]

The idea charmed Voukelitch. He enjoyed nothing more than rambling on and on about himself and his thoughts. So he wrote a brief autobiography of some sixty pages, coupled with some of his observations about the Yugoslav Army. This he took to his friends' apartment, for they did not wish to visit him lest Edith become suspicious. Klein and Budacq kept the document for two or three weeks. During that time, they heard of a conspiracy in the Yugoslav Army which bore out some of Voukelitch's observations. So the two Communists were impressed, or at least said they were when he visited them to hear the verdict.[8]

"This report shows really excellent observation and analysis, considering that you were in the army only four months," declared Klein. "A man who can write such a report is always in demand, so you needn't worry about getting a job.

"This report is useful to the movement," he continued.

At this, Voukelitch pricked up his ears; in the old days they had used the word *movement* when they meant *communism*.

"Won't you rejoin the movement?" Klein invited. "I can arrange it so that your five years without activity will be considered a vacation and not held against you." [9]

Voukelitch did not agree immediately, for his revolutionary ardor had cooled considerably in the past few years. "I'm not a convinced Communist any longer," he replied. A little more conversation, however, revealed that he had not abandoned the Marxist creed; he merely doubted that the revolution could come about in present world conditions. Its only chance would be if peace could be maintained long enough for a socialist force, such as that represented by Stalin's Five-year Plan, to be developed in Russia.

Klein rushed into this opening. "Let us give a chance to Soviet Russia to establish socialism by maintaining peace for another several years," he urged, "until the Comintern in convention has definitely thrown out the Trotsky theory of permanent revolution and Stalin has adopted the one-country socialism theory. This is the main duty of the Comintern." [10]

Voukelitch posed another objection: the Comintern's lack of any realistic knowledge of what was going on in the world. This gave Klein the opportunity he wanted. "That is why this new organization has requested you to do a certain activity," he declared smoothly. The legal Communist parties were busy with elections; their members were well known. In some countries the legal parties had been destroyed. Therefore, the information the Comintern received from these countries was often unreliable. This explanation surprised Voukelitch because he had always supposed "that the Comintern probably collected more information than any other organization except the Pope." [11] As a result of this conversation, Voukelitch returned to the party.

A meeting was arranged between him and a comrade who was to instruct him in his duties. Thus it happened that the mysterious Olga briefed him that March evening. Voukelitch tried to pump her about the nature of the organization he would be joining and what part he was to play, but for the time being she refused to be drawn into specifics. "Our task is to protect Soviet Russia," she explained. "This is the duty of all good communists, but our special duty is to collect information."

"I haven't any military knowledge except for my four months in camp," Voukelitch protested. "I'm not qualified as a spy because I haven't had any experience in conspiracy work."[12]

"Our work isn't that of a military detective as it appears in [E. Phillips] Oppenheim's detective stories," Olga replied, half-smiling, half-contemptuous. ". . . We won't expect you to crack safes, but we will expect you to use your experience as a journalist.* . . . You will have to utilize your observational and analytical ability as a Marxist. No matter what country you go to, there will be experienced comrades who will guide you and sympathizers who will cooperate with us in our work." Fixing Voukelitch with a keen look, she asked, "Do you have sharp sensitivities or not? This is the most important condition for this kind of work."

"No," answered Voukelitch frankly, and once more Olga seemed amused.

Nor did his long break in service upset her. "This is convenient because that means you haven't had many relations with the police."[13]

Although virtually committed, Voukelitch still questioned his qualifications for espionage, so he hesitated for a few months.[14] Well into the summer, Klein, Budacq, and Olga pressed him to accept the proffered assignment. Despite his inexperience and self-doubt, he was a skilled amateur photographer, a talent very useful to an espionage ring, and his ability to speak eight languages was another potentially valuable asset.[15]

To Olga he betrayed an abysmal ignorance of the nature of the work he was contemplating. "Why couldn't the Comintern use the Russian Embassy as the headquarters for collecting intelligence?" he asked.

With patient indulgence she explained that other countries could use their embassies for such purposes, but that "our

---

* Olga's words as reported by Voukelitch are confusing because no evidence exists that he had much experience as a journalist. In view of developments, no doubt she meant that he would have to use his linguistic and photographic skills in the capacity of a journalist.

activity relies on young communists like you and sympathizers in each country." Having served this appetizer, she got down to the main course. "The Soviet Embassy is watched particularly, so we can't use it. If we used the Embassy, in an emergency Soviet Russia itself would be exposed to danger as a chain of the Comintern." Olga hastened to qualify this revealing remark. "Russian diplomatic agencies and the Comintern do not necessarily have the same opinion," she said with a smile.

Eventually Voukelitch agreed to take up the work and made an appointment for another meeting. Olga came prepared for his capitulation. She gave him some papers to translate and about 3,000 francs as living expenses, along with instructions that he was to adopt a cover career. Having promised to determine just what his duties would be, Olga disappeared amid the gray buildings of the Latin Quarter.[16]

At a subsequent rendezvous she introduced him to "an elderly comrade of the business type with white hair," who Voukelitch thought "was from some Baltic coast area." During their brief meeting the white-haired man did not have much to say and seemed to be sizing up the candidate. Evidently he was satisfied, for by early summer Voukelitch's assignment had begun to take shape. He received instructions to make general preparations to go to Japan, but because his area of activity was not yet definite, he did little along those lines.[17]

Voukelitch suggested to Olga that he had a ready-made cover in that Edith was a qualified instructor in Danish gymnastics, which were very popular in Japan at the time. So Olga arranged that Edith be inspected. Ms. Voukelitch duly met with "a senior comrade," an elderly woman who looked like a Russian immigrant. Edith passed the test and went to Denmark to spend the summer brushing up on her gymnastics and obtaining letters of recommendation from Danish schools that had good relations with Japanese gymnastic societies. However, Edith's primary role was to play herself—Ms. Branko de Voukelitch, housewife.[18]

Shortly thereafter Olga dragged herself from a sickbed, where she was recuperating from appendicitis, to keep a rendezvous with Voukelitch. "It has been finally decided that you are going to Japan," she told him. "I envy you for going to such a beautiful country."

"How long will I stay there?" he asked.

"About two years," replied Olga. She looked squarely at the happy-go-lucky spy-to-be and issued a grim warning: "If you can't make up your mind to go to Japan, you can turn down the order now. But once you go to Japan you must perform your appointed work honestly. You will not be allowed to retire at any time for your own convenience."

Voukelitch accepted these conditions and put forth a suggestion: "I would like to go to Moscow as soon as possible to study Marxism." Olga was rather evasive but hinted it might be arranged. He fervently hoped so, for this was his dream: ". . . that someday I would be allowed to go to Soviet Russia as a compensation for my effort and enjoy the peaceful and cultured life in the paradise of socialism."[19]

Voukelitch's last contact with the Paris cell was with a black-haired man of some thirty-five years, whom he took to be "a southern European Jew, probably Hungarian." This comrade instructed him, "You will leave for Japan by the end of this year. Take a ship to avoid traveling by way of Siberia and select one which does not stop over at either the United States or Shanghai."[20]

Autumn was well along before Voukelitch had to face the necessity for action. In a last-minute burst of speed he had to find a legitimate job that would give him a legal reason for going to Japan, obtain visas from Yugoslavia and Japan, and secure several letters of recommendation, which his former employer, the president of the electric company, was kind enough to arrange.

Luckily the French pictorial weekly *Vue* was planning a special issue on the Far East and agreed to employ Voukelitch to take a series of pictures; having proved his worth, he subsequently continued on *Vue*'s payroll in Tokyo. For the present a business card proclaiming him as a member of *Vue*'s staff helped him secure his visa. He also managed to be appointed a special correspondent for the Yugoslavian daily *Politika*, for which he had written a few essays in the past.[21] On December 30, 1932, Voukelitch, Edith, and little Paul boarded an Italian ship at Marseilles, to begin their long voyage to Japan by way of the Suez Canal and Singapore.[22] He had received absolutely no instruction in the art of spying or any indoctrination in what sort of information he was expected to produce.

While Voukelitch was preparing to leave Paris, half a world away a Japanese named Tsutomu Yano and an unidentified Caucasian Comintern agent threaded their way through the crowded streets of Los Angeles's Little Tokyo.[23] California's antipathy toward Orientals, who would work for ridiculously low wages, was never more virulent than during the Great Depression. Discrimination bred resentment, which in turn fertilized the field of Communist endeavor among the disenchanted of Little Tokyo. Among these was an artist named Yotoku Miyagi, the target of the two Communist agents. At the time Yano tapped on Miyagi's door, little in his background indicated any special gifts for espionage. Nevertheless, Miyagi was to develop into a first-class agent.

He was born in 1903, the second son of a peasant family in a village on the island of Okinawa. Two years later his parents set out for greener pastures, eventually settling in California. They left their children with Ms. Miyagi's father, who exercised an early and decisive influence over Miyagi. "When I was a little boy, my grandfather's discipline was: 'Do not maltreat the weak and be conscientious,' " Miyagi remembered.[24] To the end of his days he was considerate and dutiful.

While his unfortunate father wandered from one failure to another in California, finally winding up on a farm near Los Angeles, Miyagi attended the village grade school and the Okinawa Prefecture Normal School, but he was not graduated, for the first symptoms of tuberculosis appeared when he was sixteen. In the hope of improving his health and studying art, he joined his father in June 1919.

In the United States he secured a diploma from the San Diego Public Art School, and after a year in the Imperial Valley, letting the clean, dry air fill his tormented lungs, Miyagi moved to Los Angeles. He set up shop as an artist and joined three Japanese friends in establishing the Owl Restaurant. Both ventures were moderately successful. Miyagi earned enough by his brush for his simple needs, and when he left California for Japan, the Owl was still operating.[25]

Miyagi's tragedy was this: He had exactly the wrong amount of talent. A little more, and the painter's compulsion would have chained him to his easel. If he had developed a social consciousness at all, it would have come out through his brush, perhaps to make him the Goya of his people. A little less, and economic necessity would have kept his nose to the grindstone of the restaurant or sent him back to the land, retaining his painting as a relaxing hobby in youth and a joy in his old age. Unfortunately he had just sufficient gifts to bring in a small income and leave him free to get into mischief.

The year 1926 marked the true beginning of Miyagi's Communist career. It was then that he and his fellow restaurateurs established a Marxist study group. It had not held more than two or three meetings before the party took over, and the membership grew by leaps and bounds. However, the next year, when the group, now a club with the name Romei Kai ("Society of the Dawn"), split into Communist and non-Communist factions, Miyagi stayed with the latter.[26]

At this point his social and political beliefs were in turmoil. He hated Americans for what he called "the wild conduct of the capitalist and ruling class" and especially its treatment of Japanese; on the other hand, he detested the Japanese for their inability to cope with this situation, for Japan's contempt toward emigrants, and for the way Japanese diplomats in the United States seemed to knuckle under to "U.S. capitalists."[27]

For this last reason, and because of the way doctors, bankers, and retired government officials from Kagoshima prefecture had come to Okinawa and exploited the Okinawans, Miyagi could not bring himself to join any of the pro-Japanese groups springing up on the West Coast. He believed wholeheartedly in the Marxist revolution yet hoped to work as a nationalist within the Communist frame. He continued to read Russian literature and to drift leftward, but when he was first approached in 1929 to join the Communist Party, he declined. He pleaded poor health, the uselessness of joining an American party when he did not have the franchise, and his suspicion that his Communist friends depended too much upon mere book learning; not one of them understood the situation in either Japan or China.[28]

By 1931 he was in a more receptive mood. Along with his wife, Chiyo, whom he had married in 1927, he joined not only the Communist-front Proletarian Arts Society but also the Communist Party itself. He had come to believe that only through communism could humanity be saved, and he could not have helped being flattered when Tsutomu Yano himself urged him to join, for Yano was quite an important man in the party, sent to California all the way from New York to shore up the sagging West Coast organization. Yano even filled out Miyagi's card, gave him the code name Joe, and filed his membership.

In the spring of 1932 Miyagi and Chiyo went their separate ways, so Miyagi moved into a room in the home of a family named Kitabayashi.[29] The husband, Yoshisaburo, was neither a Communist nor a fellow traveler. However, his wife, a tiny, anxious-faced woman named Tomo, was a member of the party and the Proletarian Arts Society. In light of subsequent developments, it is important to remember that Miyagi was living with the Kitabayashis when Yano and his colleague came to recruit him in the winter of 1932.[30]

At first glance Miyagi had little to recommend him as a spy. He had neither experience nor training along that line; he had no influential contacts in the homeland. Yet he had formidable potential. Once in Japan, he would have a ready-made cover as a painter and as such need account to no one for his comings and goings. He spoke both Japanese and English fluently and had no inconvenient police record. He had a good mind and a retentive memory.

From Yano's sales pitch, Miyagi gained the impression that the party wanted him to go to Tokyo for a month or so to establish a Comintern group there; in fact, he would be working as a spy for Richard Sorge and the Red Army. After Miyagi had accepted, the unidentified white man told him to keep in touch with Roy, an American Communist living in Los Angeles, who was an old acquaintance of Miyagi's.[31]

Miyagi felt no sense of urgency about leaving for Japan. Tuberculosis was rampant there, and even a short stay might undo the work of years in the California sun. So he continued to wander about Los Angeles with his painter's kit and to dabble in local agitation.[32] But not for long. In September 1933, the month Sorge made his debut on Japanese soil, Yano and Roy paid Miyagi a visit, demanding that he leave for Japan immediately. By way of softening the blow, Roy assured him that he would be gone for not more than three months. So in the expectation of returning to the United States soon, Miyagi collected only the barest necessities for travel.

Shortly before his ship sailed, Roy gave Miyagi $200 for expenses, and an extra dollar bill for identification when he reached Japan. His contact would be carrying a dollar bill with the consecutive serial number. Thus armed, Miyagi boarded the *Buenos Aires Maru* at San Pedro and arrived in Japan late in October.[33]

Roy must have believed his promise to Miyagi that his stay in Japan would be short, for from time to time after Miyagi's departure he stopped by the Kitabayashi residence to inquire whether or not he had returned. Roy and his like could not have been welcome callers. Either on orders of the party or because some inner hunger was not satisfied by the austere fare served up by the Communist Party and the Proletarian Arts Society, Ms. Kitabayashi had abruptly severed her connections with them and become a Christian, joining the Seventh-Day Adventist Church; she also joined the Women's Christian Temperance Union.[34]

At this point, Ms. Kitabayashi could have easily qualified for the title of the least important resident of Los Angeles. Gifted indeed would be the seer who could have predicted how important she would be to her former boarder, Miyagi, let alone to Richard Sorge, pursuing his self-confident path in far-off Tokyo.

CHAPTER 7

"HE WILL BE YOUR BOSS"

Meanwhile, Voukelitch had landed at Yoko-hama on February 11, 1933, with only the vaguest notion of what was expected of him. He had received only one instruction: He was to take lodgings in the Sanno Hotel in Tokyo, then watch the newspapers for an advertisement announcing a vacancy in the Bunka Apartments,* which would probably appear around the beginning of summer. "When you see this ad, move into the apartment and wait. Eventually a German person will come to look for you. He will be your boss. This person will have a code. He will ask you, 'How is Mr. Johnson in Paris?' "[1]

Voukelitch installed himself and his family in Tokyo, not at the Sanno, as instructed, but at the Imperial Hotel. Not surprisingly, he found himself strapped on his unrealistic allowance of 300 yen per month. His budget did not permit even a short sight-seeing trip. So in this early period he had no opportunity to see the country and meet the people—basic requirements both for his espionage and cover activities.[2]

Not until late in September did Voukelitch see a vacancy in the Bunka Apartments advertised. He promptly moved in and patiently waited for his unknown chief to get in touch with him.[3] But Sorge was in no hurry. He was waiting for the arrival of Bruno Wendt. He believed in sending out a scout to survey

* At the time the Bunka Apartments were among the best in Tokyo, and during the occupation of Japan they became a U.S. Army billet.

the terrain and never made a direct initial contact. Wendt, whose code name was Bernhardt, was a former member of the German Communist Party and a graduate of the Moscow Radio School, and the Fourth Department had assigned him to Sorge as his radioman.[4]

Sorge greeted Mr. and Ms. Wendt in the lobby of the Imperial Hotel in October. Immediately he instructed Wendt to build a radio. This posed an immediate problem, for Wendt had set up his cover business, a small company supplying samples of Japanese products to foreign firms, in Yokohama instead of Tokyo. Since Wendt had to install the radio in his home, this was extremely inconvenient for Sorge.

November came before Wendt telephoned the Bunka Apartments on Sorge's behalf and confirmed Voukelitch's presence. Sorge sent him to sound out Voukelitch and announce his impending approach.[5] Voukelitch would have been made of iron had his pulse not stepped up at his visitor's question "Do you know Johnson?" For this signified that his waiting period had ended and business was about to begin. "Yes, I do," he replied, and Wendt answered, "I am not Schmidt, but I have come from Schmidt."[6]

The next day Sorge visited Voukelitch and gave him detailed instructions about their future spy activity and the precautions he must observe. Voukelitch would have plenty to do, for Sorge planned to use him to collect data from and about the British, French, and Americans; to act as the ring's photographer; and to use his quarters as a radio site. Sorge found him in "a pitiful state . . . ill, homesick and broke." He took care of him financially and advised him "to rent a house, move there with his wife and child, and begin to work in earnest as a reporter." Nevertheless, Voukelitch's first impression of Sorge "was not very good." He suspected that Sorge considered him "not the serious kind," and he later discovered that Sorge thought of him "as an outsider and could not get out of this feeling until the last day of our cooperative work."[7]

Sorge soon dropped the Schmidt pseudonym, for the two men met frequently thereafter, a convenient rendezvous being a European-style restaurant, the Florida Kitchen in the Ginza. As fellow reporters they were certain to meet under their real names at the Japanese press agency Domei and at official press conferences. However, Sorge took care that his friends at the German Embassy should not know how often he met Voukelitch,[8] who was on the other side of the ideological fence from them.

Soon Voukelitch made his first move toward active participation in the ring. His apartment provided insufficient space for a photographic darkroom and did not offer the necessary privacy for use as one of the ring's radio sending or receiving sites. So he took Sorge's advice and soon moved to a house at 22 Sanai Cho, Ushigome-ku.[9] He was still in financial difficulties, so he augmented his income by giving language lessons at home in his free time, while Edith taught gymnastics at the Tamagawa Gakuen School.[10]

At Sorge's direction Voukelitch placed a certain advertisement in the *Japan Advertiser* in early December. Scanning the classified section of this paper, Miyagi finally spotted his signal. Under the heading "Wanted to Buy" appeared: UKI-YOE—prints by old masters. Also English books on the same subject. Urgently needed. Give details, titles, authors, prices to Artist, c/o The Japan Advertiser, Tokyo."[11] A telephone number for replies was that of an advertising agency in Tokyo's Kanda section. Through this firm, Miyagi arranged to meet the person who had inserted the advertisement and found himself face-to-face with Voukelitch in front of the agency.

The two men checked their dollar bills. Miyagi carefully returned his to his wallet in case he needed it again, for he recognized that Voukelitch was a go-between, not his ultimate contact and real boss. Not until much later did he realize that Voukelitch belonged to Sorge's spy ring.[12]

Very shortly after this encounter Miyagi met Sorge in person in front of the Ueno Art Gallery, but that time they did not use the dollar bill as a means of recognition. Instead, Sorge wore a black tie; Miyagi, a blue tie.[13] Sorge did not need the prearranged signal because no one could readily mistake Miyagi for anyone else. Physically he was not prepossessing. The heavy, prominent jaw was wider than the low forehead, and dense black brows lent a menacing air to his long, folded eyes. His muddy complexion mutely testified to poor health, and a thick thatch of unkempt black hair spoke the nonconformist. But such first impressions dissolved upon acquaintance. When

Miyagi spoke, his large mouth showed itself firm and well shaped; his lids opened to reveal bright, intelligent eyes.

Miyagi was a curious mixture of brisk practicality and political innocence. His vocabulary was rich, for his literary taste ran to Tolstoy and Gorky. His paintings showed technical skill and sensitivity. The colors he used were more muted than the popular taste of the day dictated, his palette leaning to the blue end of the spectrum. Miyagi was well acquainted with the works of the Chinese and Japanese masters, and since Sorge took a keen interest in Oriental art, at times the two men pushed espionage aside until they had refreshed themselves at the limpid pool of Far Eastern painting.[14]

In those early days Sorge gave Miyagi no hint that their association involved anyone else. On the contrary, he told him, "Since we have no help, we will have to find people to work with us." He amplified this remark with specific instructions: "Look for left-wing elements who have considerable position socially and are not yet watched by the police." Miyagi had been laboring under the delusion that he had come to Japan to work with a Comintern unit, perhaps to help reconstitute the Japanese Communist Party by organizing a cell. But soon he realized that his superior expected him to be a spy, coming to this conclusion because "what Sorge asked me was things about Japanese political and military issues and . . . he was not trying to organize a Comintern ring even though he was working for the Comintern."[15]

In January 1934, after five meetings had convinced Sorge that the American comrades had made no mistake in their choice, he confirmed Miyagi's suspicions and put the issue to him squarely. The party wished him to stay in Japan and engage in espionage.[16]

This unmasking plunged Miyagi into a brief but sharp tussle with his conscience. If they had been in the United States, he would not have hesitated, but to conspire on Japanese soil with a white man—how could he reconcile this with his convictions? For Miyagi's most earnest desire was to help free the Oriental peoples, particularly the Japanese, from the white man's exploitation as revealed to him in California at the height of the Yellow Peril psychosis. But in the final analysis he was a soldier of the revolution, and a soldier obeyed all orders, not just the ones he liked. So Miyagi agreed to do Sorge's bidding in the belief that his would be "an important mission from the viewpoint of world history and . . . the main task was to prevent a Japanese-Russian war."[17]

However, he had qualms about his suitability and extracted from Sorge a promise that if anyone better qualified could be found, that person would take over his duties. No replacement ever appeared, and Miyagi continued to serve. "So I participated in the ring, understanding completely that this activity was against the laws of Japan and that I would be executed in wartime for my espionage."[18]

Now Sorge had the makings of an *apparat,* but as the spring came, he had little cause for satisfaction with it: Wendt, dickering over his radio apparatus and breaking into a cold sweat at every real or fancied danger; Voukelitch, a fuzzy-minded chatterbox with no experience in espionage! Miyagi was the pick of the bunch: sharp-eyed, long-memoried, and ready to learn. He had a valuable knack for making friends and a flair for military matters. Yet the *apparat* still lacked what might be its most important component: a Japanese with entrée into the highest social and political circles.

A picture emerged from Sorge's memories of Shanghai: a sleek pigeon of a man, neat, plump, fluttering about ingratiatingly to peck crumbs from a friendly hand. Just the man, if he were willing, and Sorge had little cause to doubt Ozaki's willingness. Once the Soviet underground got its claws into anyone, it did not let go easily. And Ozaki had never shown any disposition to struggle.

One could scarcely have recognized the fleshed-out, self-confident Ozaki who had returned to *Asahi Shimbun*'s Osaka office early in 1932 as the likable but ineffectual young reporter who had left for China four years before. Although he was still unknown to the general public, his own newspaper world now acknowledged him as a man who wrote of the China scene from firsthand experience. So *Asahi* welcomed him home and gave him a desk in the foreign section.[19]

Ozaki settled down in Inanomura, a suburb of Osaka, and spent more time than usual with his family. During this domestic idyll his Shanghai experience seemed like a dream. His wife and daughter, too, were happiest in this period.[20] Yet the spring of 1932 was not a tranquil one in Japan. The rightist lunatic fringe engineered a number of assassinations, which reached a peak on May 15, when the prime minister, Tsuyoshi ("Ki") Inukai, fell beneath the bullets of a group of young army and navy officers who claimed to be Naval Academy cadets.

They had three objectives: to destroy the political party system by murdering the prime minister, to bring about martial law by bombing the House of Representatives of the Diet, and to increase the power of the military by provoking war with the United States, which they proposed to bring about by murdering Charlie Chaplin, who was then visiting Japan.[21]

The social and political malaise represented by this last proposal was deadly. Officers of Japan's armed forces seriously believed that the United States would plunge two great nations into war over the murder of one man—granted a much beloved man. Small wonder the whole world eyed Japan with the nervous apprehension of men fixing a leaky gas main and seeing nearby a child playing with matches. Fortunately for Mr. Chaplin, the plot fizzled out.[22]

Ozaki had met the prime minister, and he had a slight acquaintance with his son, Ken Inukai, that was to ripen into friendship when the two became fellow members of Prince Fumimaro Konoye's famous Breakfast Group,* but the officers' plot did not touch him personally. Much more dangerous to him was the nationwide roundup of known and suspected Communists in February 1933, which broke the back of the Japanese party as then constituted.

Similar police strikes continued throughout the year, along with much chivying of intellectuals whose involvement with communism was either nonexistent or academic. The net caught some of Ozaki's acquaintances, yet not Ozaki, in spite of his many questionable associations. Ozaki flirted with Communist ideology but never backed up his convictions by joining the party, although he said he would have done so had it not been for the wholesale arrests of Communists in 1928. So the police

---

* The Breakfast Group consisted of young intellectuals who gave Konoye the benefit of their expertise as a sort of kitchen cabinet. See Chapter 23.

did not have him listed as a known party member, a fact that undoubtedly saved his skin during this and other anti-Communist drives. Nor did Ozaki's name appear among the few who dared to protest these arrests, for he walked delicately through these perils.[23]

Yet where his own friends were concerned, Ozaki acted with no judgment whatever. Late in 1933 he introduced Mizuno to his friend Karoku Hosokawa at the Ohara Social Problems Research Institute, a well-known private organization of many years' standing, where Hosokawa set him to work researching Chinese matters. Considering Mizuno's record and the narrow squeak the institute had just had during the police crackdown,[24] Ozaki was indiscreet, to say the least, in foisting this agitator on his friends. But he was earnestly bent on helping out regardless of the consequences.

So by ideology, temperament, and circumstances, Ozaki was ripe for the plucking when Sorge decided to spread his net.

CHAPTER 8

"SPY ACTIVITY WITH SORGE"

Few cities in Hirohito's empire wore the green, blossom-brocaded kimono of spring with more aristocratic charm than Nara, ancient capital of Japan. On any fine Sunday crowds of eagerly respectful sightseers thronged there to enjoy the beautiful natural setting and to pay tribute to their history. No spot rewarded the faithful more handsomely than the famous deer park with its fairytale landscape and friendly animals.

There on one of those enticing Sunday afternoons in the spring of 1934 Sorge sat on the bank of Sarusawa Pond. He was on one of the most important missions of his career in Japan thus far: the personal recruitment of Hotzumi Ozaki.[1] But would Ozaki work with him in Japan as he had done in Shanghai? A foreigner would be asking him to spy for the Soviet Union against his own country, his own people, on his native soil. Just how heavily these considerations would burden Ozaki would depend upon how much, if at all, he had changed since Shanghai days. For all Sorge knew, Ozaki might have been caught up in the rhythm of Japanese life, sipping the heady sake of nationalism, his flirtation with clandestine left-wing activity just a youthful wild oat to be plowed under.

Yet Ozaki had served Sorge well in Shanghai with no noticeable qualms, patriotic or otherwise. Furthermore, as was his custom in Japan, Sorge had sent a member of his ring to make the initial contact and to appraise the situation for him. Earlier that week Miyagi had visited Ozaki at the *Asahi* office in Osaka. He handed Ozaki a name card which read "Ryuichi Minami" and asked to speak with him, adding in a nervous

71

voice that a foreigner with whom Ozaki had been closely associated in Shanghai was in Japan and eager to see him. Ozaki was cautious at first but after a number of questions "became almost certain that the foreigner was Johnson. "After two more meetings, during which Ozaki learned Miyagi's identity, he agreed to see the foreigner.[2] So Ozaki was more than halfway committed to the venture before Sorge opened his mouth that day in the deer park.

At their meeting Ozaki called Sorge Johnson, and Sorge did not correct him. Until Ozaki proved himself, let him know only Johnson, who could fade into nothingness if Ozaki turned out to be untrustworthy. Two years passed before Ozaki learned, and then only by accident, his associate's real name.[3]

During their conversation amid the murmuring pines of ancient Nara, Sorge filled in Ozaki on a few points of background, then asked him to gather information for the Comintern, just as he had in China. Ozaki did not hesitate. "I made up my mind to do spy activity with Sorge again," he stated some years later, "accepted his request readily, and since then up to the time of my arrest I have been engaged in espionage activity."[4]

Those words *accepted his request readily* distress Japanese left-wing aficionados of the Sorge case. For that phrase jerks the rug from under their image of Ozaki as a Hamlet-like figure torn between ideology and patriotism.[5] Yet his ready agreement was the logical result of what he believed and what he was. He was a dedicated Communist in everything but name, and after his arrest he made no secret of his allegiance to the Soviet Union:

> I have thought that . . . the role of protecting Russia was one of the most important activities, and that informing accurately the Comintern or Russia of the various situations inside Japan, which is the most probable attacker of Russia among the world powers, and let her take measures against it as a means of protecting Russia, was the most important mission for us. . . .
>
> I sometimes thought secretly that, as a Communist in Japan, it is even something to be proud

of that I engaged in such a difficult and disadvantageous work.[6]

Sorge sponsored Ozaki as a reliable agent, as he had Agnes Smedley, "and had him registered in Comintern Headquarters." He offered himself "as one of the two sponsors required for each new member." A member in Moscow consented to be the other sponsor, on the strength of Sorge's recommendations and reports.[7] So Sorge laid his own reputation with Moscow on the line as surety that Ozaki was an efficient, trustworthy worker.

Opinions on the type and scope of Ozaki's activities for the Sorge ring differ. Was he truly a spy in the conventional sense of the word, actively seeking forbidden data, or was he a source—a willing but basically passive accomplice, submitting to Sorge such information as legitimately came to his notice? Yet Ozaki's actions were not ambiguous; he was a spy, albeit an unusual and sophisticated one. When anything needed was not at Ozaki's hand, he went out and dug for it. Among the data he gave Sorge were highly classified matters of Japanese national policy and national defense.[8]

He delivered an interesting lecture on the art of spying that leaves no doubt about the depth of his plunge into those murky waters:

> (1) One should not give an impression that one is eager to obtain news. Especially these days people engaged in important matters are cautious and never tell the truth to those people whose motive seems to be collection of information.

> (2) If one succeeds in giving others an impression that one already knows more than they do, they will display the information they have.

> (3) At drinking parties or banquets which relatively have not yet reached the wild stage one can often receive fairly important news by general hints.

> (4) It is very convenient on many occasions to have some special talent. As in my case I was an expert on Chinese problems, various inquiries

came to me from many areas and my opinion was asked. At such times I was able to obtain much important information from the inquirers.

(5) For getting information directly and indirectly, it was convenient that I was active in newspapers and journals as critic.

(6) I frequently attended table-talk meetings and lecture meetings in rural areas. I was able to use these opportunities available to me to learn the local opinions fairly accurately.

(7) By trying to establish direct relations with important information sources . . . one can achieve excellent contacts naturally.

(8) The greatest secret, in short, is to win personal confidence from others and to generate conditions wherein one can exchange data without seeming unnatural.[9]

This complacent dissertation should remove any lingering doubt that Ozaki was a spy, knew it, and took pride in his competence.

Much in Ozaki's personality was likable, for as surely as his intelligence won admiration, so his sociability and sense of fun brought him popularity. He sympathized with anyone in difficulties. Yet he took this fateful step without a thought for what discovery and disgrace would mean to his father, to his wife, and to his little daughter, who adored him.

For all of Ozaki's humanity and warmth, there was something calculating about him. Prosecutor Mitsusada Yoshikawa, who came to know Ozaki well, believed that he "wanted to be associated with Sorge because the latter was an important source of information and analytical interpretation."[10] Sorge was perfectly willing to give Ozaki's career a boost in exchange for his help; the higher Ozaki rose, the better for the ring. The relationship paralleled Sorge's with Ott, with one significant difference: Ott did not know that Sorge was using him for the benefit of Moscow.

Ozaki's acquiescence to Sorge's proposal had scarcely left his mouth when he added a warning. Disciplined, monolithic Japan was a far cry from casual, polyglot Shanghai, and the efficient Japanese police were very different from their Shanghai equivalents. Sorge needed no reminder of that fact. So far as he knew, the Soviet Union had never successfully established an effective *apparat* in Japan.

Under the circumstances Sorge could not have his flock scattered all over the country, so he asked Ozaki to resign from *Asahi* and come to Tokyo, suggesting that he find employment as a private tutor, a position which would leave him plenty of time to work with Sorge. This was not one of Sorge's brightest ideas, for immured in such a sterile occupation, Ozaki soon would have lost touch with the very contacts that made him so valuable a recruit. Ozaki demurred at quitting the newspaper, but he agreed to request a transfer to *Asahi*'s Tokyo office.[11]

He could not pull up stakes overnight. He was a family man—a fact of which Sorge was not aware—and as such had many loose ends to tie before he could uproot himself from Osaka. Equally important, he had to wait until *Asahi* approved his transfer, for he needed a steady, remunerative job. He would have no salary from the *apparat*, only an occasional gift and reimbursement for expenses incurred on ring business, usually in the neighborhood of $100. He was not too happy to take even these token sums, but when he tried to refuse, "Sorge looked unpleasant" and forced payment on him.

Sorge worked under a $12,000 annual limit, with a monthly maximum allowance of $1,000,[12] yet he pressed money upon Ozaki, presumably to place him in an employee relationship with Moscow. Ozaki's accepting a slim expense account placed him as much legally and morally in the pay of the Soviet Union as Sorge himself was.

Also, before Ozaki moved, he wanted to finish a task he had undertaken, the translation into Japanese of Agnes Smedley's autobiography, *Daughter of Earth*. He had been dabbling with it ever since returning to China; by speeding up his tempo, he hoped to submit the manuscript to his publisher by early autumn. With the help of his *Asahi* friends, Ozaki completed the job in time for it to roll off the press in August 1934, although the censors liberally peppered it with black spots.[13]

Through a remarkable stroke of luck Ozaki was able to come to Tokyo in the full light of day, haloed in the respectable aura of *Asahi*. The newspaper decided to sponsor in Tokyo an affiliated research office, known as the East Asia Problems Investigation Association (Toa Mondai Chosa Kai), and asked Ozaki to join the staff. Naturally he agreed with alacrity and by the middle of September was busily getting acquainted with his colleagues, while Ms. Ozaki established their new home.

The association was organized "to investigate broadly subjects related to East Asia, make them available for the basic activity of the newspaper, and at the same time cooperate with the national policy." *Asahi*'s editor, Taketora Ogata, served as president of the board. Members included specialists on mainland economics, political analysts, representatives of the information offices of the Foreign Ministry, army and navy, delegates from the General Staff, and various other representatives of the government, industry, and intellectual life—even an expert on Soviet affairs.[14]

Sorge could have done no better if he himself had planned the whole setup. Ozaki's selection considerably enhanced his prestige. Through the group he would meet some of the best minds in Japan, acknowledged experts in their areas, and through this association his own knowledge would increase proportionately. Given such heavy representation from the Fourth Estate, Sorge could expect little highly classified information to emanate from the East Asia Problems Investigation Association, but that was its only flaw.

The situation gave Sorge access at one stroke to half a dozen important sources through one agent—a highly desirable economy. To plant a reliable leak or find one in each of these government and industrial organizations would have cost Sorge months, perhaps years, plus a young fortune in money. And with each new agent he would have increased his chances of discovery and betrayal.

Throughout late 1934 and 1935 Ozaki entrenched himself in the East Asia Problems Investigation Association. There his firsthand knowledge of China, mastery of the Chinese language, and wide readings in the historical, economic, and political fields rapidly brought him to the forefront. Whatever he learned he passed to Sorge, who used as much of this authoritative information as he safely could in briefing Ott. In his turn, the grateful military attaché discussed his problems freely with this friend of his who had such an amazing grasp of Far Eastern affairs. To complete the circle, Sorge relayed back to Ozaki the fruits of this contact with the Germans, along with the gleanings from the French, British, and Americans that Voukelitch picked up.[15]

Sorge was the shuttle weaving these complicated threads in and out, picking everybody's brains, extending his influence, building up his position as a political thinker and journalist, and strengthening his ring.

However, the cozy arrangement benefited all concerned. From Sorge's European sources Ozaki came to know the trend of Western political thinking in relation to the Orient as perhaps no other Japanese layman of his time. From Sorge's Japanese contacts Ott had a window on Japan that he never could have opened through normal diplomatic and military channels. With this information and Sorge's shrewd analyses added to his own considerable gifts and official connections in Japan, Ott was rapidly becoming Dirksen's most valuable adviser, putting him in an exceptionally influential position, for Dirksen had to depend upon his staff more than an ambassador normally would. He had developed bronchitis, which by the autumn of 1935 had afflicted him with severe asthma. For the rest of his years in Japan he suffered agonies of suffocation from October to early spring, during which months he was a semi-invalid.[16]

Success drove Sorge to even greater efforts to add feathers to his nest at the embassy. When Dirksen sent Ott on an official visit to Manchuria in the late summer or early autumn of 1934, Sorge went with him, ostensibly as an official courier, but undoubtedly in order to give Ott the benefit of his knowledge and political judgment on the spot.[17]

Dirksen had a number of reasons for desiring a report from someone he could trust. Problems concerning Manchuria were rapidly turning what remained of his hair even grayer than it had been. Almost the first item of diplomatic business Foreign Affairs Minister Koki Hirota had brought to Dirksen's attention had been a request for German official recognition of Manchukuo.[18] Early in 1932 the Japanese had established Manchuria plus portions of Inner Mongolia as a puppet state named Manchukuo. Colonel Kenji Doihara, who later became one of Ott's connections in Japan, provided Manchukuo with a regent, the deposed Emperor of China, Henry Pu Yi, by the simple expedient of kidnapping him. The bayonets of the Kwantung Army propped up the whole edifice. Japan formally recognized Manchukuo in September of that year[19] and hoped that other major nations would follow suit.

Dirksen considered that German recognition of Manchukuo would be a practical, effective means of demonstrating the Reich's friendliness toward Japan; but at first the German Foreign Office reacted coolly, and a "somewhat lively exchange of letters" passed between Dirksen and State Secretary Bernhard von Bülow.[20]

When Sorge returned to Tokyo, he wrote an essay on Manchuria, based on what he had seen and heard on his visit. It included nothing secret, and for good reason, because he handed it not to Moscow but to Ott, who was so impressed that he sent it to the army General Staff headquarters in Berlin for the attention of General Georg Thomas, chief of the Economic Department. Ott generously gave credit where it was due, and a long-distance association between Thomas and Sorge resulted. In the future Thomas often asked Ott to have Sorge prepare reports for him.[21]

Of more direct interest to Sorge were the transactions going on between the Soviet Union and Japan for the purchase of the Eastern Chinese Railway. Ozaki briefed Sorge on this subject early in 1935, and they concluded that Japan would not attack Russia, at least during the negotiations for purchase of the railroad.[22]

The Eastern Chinese Railway was a long-standing burr under the saddle of Russo-Japanese relations until Hirota took advantage of the resignation of the war minister, bellicose Lieutenant General Sadao Araki, shortly after Dirksen had arrived in Tokyo, to start the ball rolling toward settling the matter once and for all. After long-drawn-out haggling Japan purchased the railroad at a bargain price.[23] At this time the Soviet Union was not strong enough in the Far East for a direct confrontation with Japan. Better to sell it the railroad and keep its goodwill than hang on to it and have Japan take it anyway.

During this period Ozaki was full of zeal. Early in the spring of 1935 he decided to try recruiting once more. He wrote to Teikichi Kawai, suggesting that he return to Japan. Always ready to come at Ozaki's call, Kawai arrived in his homeland in March, whereupon Ozaki asked him "to stay in Tokyo and study the situation in Japan." Kawai took a room with Isamu Fujita, a friend of his since Shanghai days and a virulent rightist. At Ozaki's behest Kawai had collected specimens of the far right as cover and as sources of information since his Shanghai days. During their residence together Fujita practically supported Kawai, who had no compunction about taking his money.

Kawai collected so little information for the Tokyo ring that he poses something of a puzzle. He was not just a mercenary willing to serve any cause, left or right, that would guarantee him a free meal.[24] Moreover, he was devoted to Ozaki, deeply respectful of Sorge, and honored to be of service to them. He may have tackled men too disciplined to pour confidences into every ear bent in their direction. However, Kawai had other uses; soon he would help guide Miyagi through the mazes of the Japanese Army's power structure and its factions, whose policies, rises, and falls depended primarily upon the personalities of their leaders.

Miyagi had been doing a little recruiting on his own. One of the tasks originally assigned to him was translating documents from Japanese into English for Sorge's consumption and for radioing to the Soviet Union. Soon, however, such translating threatened to become a full-time occupation, so he had an eye open for a substitute when he ran into Koji Akiyama, whom he had met in California in 1931 through Ms. Kitabayashi.[25]

That Akiyama was either a full-fledged Communist or a fellow traveler during his American period is clear from Sorge's brief comment: "Lately it seemed that Miyagi was often meeting with a former friend from America. . . . He talked about him several times, and whenever I expressed my anxiety about his association with this former friend from America he declared emphatically that the man was trustworthy."[26] Miyagi would consider no one trustworthy who was not a Communist or a deeply committed sympathizer.

Forty-five years old and unemployed, Akiyama jumped at Miyagi's offer of the important, if pedestrian, job of translating. He was well qualified to do so, being a graduate of the California Business College. He must have known that the military and technical documents given him to translate were curious items to be in an artist's possession, but he did as he was told and asked no embarrassing questions. His small but regular fee, never more than 100 yen a month, kept the wolf from the door, and that was all that concerned him.[27]

Akiyama had been working as a translator for the ring for at least a year, freeing Miyagi for valuable fieldwork, when, in May 1935, Ozaki introduced Kawai to Miyagi. Ozaki hoped to add Kawai to Miyagi's bag of assistants in accordance with Sorge's arrangement that the ring's Japanese lower echelon should report to Miyagi.

Ozaki, Kawai, and Miyagi met for dinner at the Annex of the Sakai Restaurant near the Ueno Pond.[28] Playing his cards carefully, Ozaki told Kawai that Miyagi was an artist from France. Right on cue, Miyagi obliged with imaginary reminiscences of that country, while the three took on board a heavy cargo of drinks.

At midnight Ozaki left the party. His two friends moved on to a *machiai*,[29] an appropriate choice of setting, because *machiai* were traditional locations for shady sub rosa political dealings.[30] Kawai and Miyagi called for some geishas, Miyagi expressing a preference for the round, chubby type. Between the geishas and the drinks that they continued to absorb, the new acquaintances made a night of it. The next day they dragged their remains to another restaurant to try to quell the insurrection in their outraged stomachs with some solid food.

There Miyagi admitted that he had come to Japan not from France but from America. They agreed that this formed a bond of sorts, both having reached Japan from big areas, Kawai from China, Miyagi from the United States. With owl-like solemnity born of the bottle they discussed the influence of geography upon the individual, pointing out to each other that in narrow, restricted Japan people minced along with small steps, whereas in broad, open China and America, men stepped out with big strides.[31]

After lunch they adjourned to Miyagi's room and got down to business. They talked over their espionage methodology, agreeing that because both were Japanese, there was no reason why they should not visit each other openly. When Kawai had any information for Miyagi, he would report orally, and Miyagi would take it down in tiny letters on small pieces of paper to be rolled into tight balls and squirreled away among his painting equipment.[32] Shortly after this meeting Miyagi changed residence again. In those early days he was a bird of passage, never staying for more than a few months in any one location.[33]

With Miyagi beginning to assemble an efficient subring, Ozaki burrowing into the influential East Asia Problems Investigation Association, and Sorge a trusted, if unofficial, aide to the German military attaché, the Fourth Department had good reason to be well pleased with its Tokyo spy ring.

Yet unknown to Sorge, the Soviet Union had been attempting to set up another *apparat* in Tokyo. Head of the embryonic ring was John Sherman, an American, whose party designation was Don. In his attempt to secure a Japanese agent he contacted Whittaker Chambers with "somewhat staggering" specifications. He wanted a Communist Party member, Japanese by race and American by citizenship, highly connected in Japan. By some sleight of hand Chambers pulled this exotic rabbit out of the hat, coming up with Hideo Noda, a Communist Nisei,* a promising artist—a pupil of Diego Rivera's—and related to "one of the Japanese premiers." Noda's code name was Ned.

This second ring began to coalesce around the end of 1934, but it collapsed with Don's arrest in 1935. His ring had only one triumph to show for its efforts: Don won the Japanese handball championship at a contest held in the Tokyo YMCA.[34] Either Sorge never knew he had a rival in Tokyo, or else he never admitted the fact. It is unlikely that his path would have crossed Don's, for the imagination staggers at visualizing Richard Sorge playing handball at the YMCA.

---

* Second-generation Japanese-American.

CHAPTER 9

"COLLECTING INFORMATION
AND INTELLIGENCE"

Sorge marked the first anniversary of his arrival in Japan with satisfaction, for he now had adequate coverage of every major type of intelligence. As he observed:

> The membership of my espionage group automatically determined to some extent the manner in which the work of collecting information and intelligence was divided. . . . Ozaki obtained information chiefly about political and economic affairs, Miyagi gathered economic and military data and took charge of the translation of all documents written in Japanese and Voukelitch collected news primarily from foreign correspondents and French acquaintances and handled such technical work as photography. I myself gathered and collected information from foreigners, principally Germans.[1]

In 1934 one of Sorge's tasks was to ensure that his Three Musketeers did not fall into a rigid pattern of specialization, so he stipulated that in his individual conferences with them each agent would bring anything he considered of particular interest, whether or not it fell within his primary field. He went over with each agent the information the latter had brought in, pointing out what was significant and what was not and calling attention to any contradictions. He urged them not to be satisfied with reporting surface facts but to dig for the causes.[2]

No one but Sorge knew exactly what information he passed to Moscow, for Wendt did not have the code. Sorge examined and correlated the reports, reworded and boiled them down to the essence, and coded them for Wendt to send to the Soviet Union. He also editorialized when he considered this desirable, and his superiors wisely encouraged him to do so. Never known for his modesty, Sorge observed, "Moscow frequently hinted that it placed a high value on my power to judge and appraise the general situation."[3]

The process of evaluation, screening, and interpreting was laborious and time-consuming. In this area Sorge's painstaking researches into Japanese history and current events paid off handsomely. "This ability to select material and present a general appraisal or picture of a given development is a prerequisite for intelligence activity of genuine value, and it can be acquired only through much serious and careful research," Sorge said of himself. He added, "I took it upon myself to see that our information was screened most carefully, and only what I considered essential and absolutely safe from criticism was sent. . . ."[4]

In those first years his *apparat* never met as a group. Sorge decreed that only he would have direct communication with the key members. Whenever he could, he set up meetings that would appear accidental, and the agents and he never met in the same place twice. Eventually this policy broke down because legitimate reasons for mutual acquaintance among the members of the ring developed naturally or were arranged deliberately.[5] At this early time, however, the ring resembled a wheel, the agents radiating from Sorge like spokes from the hub.

Between his own agents and the rumor mill, Sorge had an astonishingly effective communications system. He was too shrewd to discount Japanese gossip. Like robins chirping the advent of spring, a flock of rumors preceded every important event in Japan.[6] Take an alert, intelligent, and literate population, clamp on a lid of strict official censorship, and the resultant steam will escape in an unending mist of scuttlebutt. Thus Japanese censorship defeated its own purpose. Endlessly inquisitive and with extensive family ramifications, the Japanese always knew someone who knew something, and they made their own news, which in general was quite accurate.

Meanwhile, Voukelitch had established himself as a favorite in the newspaper world, remembered with pleasure for his friendly, mischievous personality and for his willingness to share tips with his fellow newsmen. Just where and how he got those tips were something of a puzzle. "No one knew why Voukelitch was so well informed," said a colleague. "One only knew that he entertained very good relations with the German journalists. . . ." [7] Voukelitch kept to himself just how good those relations were.

Relman Morin, chief of the Associated Press's Tokyo bureau, recalled Voukelitch as "a pleasant little man with a Cheshire-cat grin and a high-pitched voice." Voukelitch often asked for some clarification of an American policy, but it never occurred to Morin that he might be a spy. [8]

By bits and pieces, a picture emerges of a rather carelessly clothed man, "very talkative, very intelligent and somewhat blundering," with "an extraordinary fertility of wit . . . a certain instability and a great curiosity."

Another colleague remembered Voukelitch as "a 'ferret' who loved to sniff out the terrain. He had a prodigious memory. . . . " This gift allowed him to absorb foreign vocabularies easily, but his mastery of tongues went only so far; he was a scatterbrain. "He knew foreign languages but he never was able to speak only one of them at once and had a tendency to employ several vocabularies, indeed several syntaxes," in one conversation. [9] This made life interesting for those of his acquaintances who did not share his tendency to shift linguistic gears in the middle of a sentence.

Incurably frivolous, Voukelitch could not resist occasionally pulling a leg, especially the leg of the ubiquitous police. This habit worried his friends. A fellow reporter warned him, "In Japan where police suspicions become troublesome, it could be dangerous to joke." [10] But Voukelitch went his merry, garrulous, convivial way and became quite a character in Tokyo's news world.

The story was different on the Voukelitch home front. A friend recorded one fleeting glimpse of a human family life: Branko and Edith had a little boy "who was very nice," and "Voukelitch bought his son an electric train and played with it himself," in the habit of fathers everywhere. [11] But relations between the boy's parents were disintegrating. In this year of

1934 the Voukelitch marriage had not yet broken, but it had cracked badly.

So Sorge's photographer was ripe for trouble when, one fine evening in 1934, he attended the celebrated *No Gaku Do* to see one of the No plays peculiar to Japan. His Japanese not yet being equal to the task this imposed upon it, he arranged for a translator. The assignment fell to Yoshiko Yamasaki, a Japanese girl of good family. She brought along her father, as befitted a respectable unmarried woman.[12]

Voukelitch's nearsighted eyes almost popped out of his head, and he paid more attention to the slim figure beside him than to the stage. The true masterpiece of Japanese art is the well-bred woman, and of this class Miss Yamasaki was a conspicuous ornament. Beautiful and cultivated, she was a graduate of the Tsuda English College in Tokyo and spoke the language perfectly. Voukelitch may already have been window-shopping, for, according to one of his interrogators, Moscow had ordered him to divorce Edith, marry a Japanese woman, and thus become closer to the Japanese community.[13] Whether helped along by a sense of duty or not, Voukelitch fell deeply in love. Soon he was meeting Miss Yamasaki without the benefit of chaperon.

The situation held explosive possibilities, but Sorge gave no indication of noticing it, much less of being uneasy. Indeed, on the professional front Voukelitch gave him cause for considerable satisfaction. By the following spring Voukelitch had taken hold as a reporter with such intelligence and energy that he was asked to affiliate himself with Havas, the French news agency.[14] This was a break for the ring. His Havas credentials gave him prestige and authority that he had lacked, new friends among influential Western reporters, and access to news conferences with top Japanese public figures.

On that first anniversary of Sorge's he had only one genuine problem area in his inner ring: Wendt. The radioman had been in Japan almost as long as Sorge, yet in all those months he had set up nothing better than a makeshift station in his home in Yokohama. Under these circumstances Sorge could send only very short messages at long intervals. He had nagged Wendt to set up a station in Voukelitch's home, but Wendt would not be rushed. Not until April 1934 had he started assembling a second set under Voukelitch's roof, and he had not finished until late May. Before, during, and after this operation Wendt had been in a state of constant panic lest the Japanese intercept his messages, spot their origin, and swoop down for the kill.[15]

Sorge had no patience with Wendt's fears. Having deluded the Japanese police for a few months, he had exuded the brash confidence of the successful beginner when he radioed the Fourth Department on January 7, 1934: "I am no longer afraid of the constant and varied surveillance of which I am the object. It seems to me that I know the cops and their methods well enough. I have the impression of leading them along by the tip of the nose."[16] With such an attitude, no wonder Sorge held his radioman in contempt. Wendt's nervousness and technical incompetence kept Sorge in a ferment of anger and frustration.

Wendt's cover activity, a small trading firm, required considerable correspondence with his customers. Fearing that too much radio activity would draw police attention to his business, Wendt sent off as few messages as he could. Sorge bore down on him relentlessly to dispatch more and more information to the mainland, and under this strain Wendt began to drink heavily. He resented the pressure, for he believed Sorge was attempting to build a big name for himself with Moscow at the expense of possible discovery of them all.[17]

At about this time during the autumn of 1934 Sorge ordered Wendt to Shanghai to meet a courier. The meeting went off without incident, Wendt meeting his contact in a coffee shop. One man carried a package wrapped in red paper, the other a bundle wrapped in yellow, by which means they recognized each other.[18] But in Sorge's eyes a successful courier exchange by no means balanced Wendt's shortcomings as a radioman. He would need a first-class, reliable radio expert if his entire mission were not to become an exercise in futility. For the best intelligence is useless unless there exists the means to furnish it promptly and accurately to the office of primary interest.

In the months before Wendt assembled his first radio, Sorge's only contact with Moscow had been by courier. His first such meeting occurred on a crisp winter day, when he loped into the German Embassy, where a telephone message awaited him, confirming an appointment. Sorge thanked his informant and hastened away. This was the signal previously conveyed to him in a letter that he had committed to memory and destroyed—to approach the doorman in the lobby of the Imperial Hotel. The doorman escorted him to a European, whom Sorge immediately pigeonholed as a Scandinavian. For the benefit of whatever curious ears might be listening, Sorge and the courier chatted for a few minutes and during their conversation exchanged the passwords. The two men agreed to meet the next day for a sight-seeing visit to Nikko, a national shrine about ninety miles northeast of Tokyo. There they traded packages. The courier told Sorge the number of a post office box in Shanghai for use in case of emergency, and they decided to meet again in Shanghai sometime in May.[19]

When Sorge opened his package after the initial contact, he found its principal contents to be a stack of money to cover the ring's expenses for several months. Other financial arrangements for the Tokyo ring would be made in the future, but for the time being the courier exchanges were the most efficient method of payment. Cash told no tales, so Sorge received and paid out Japanese yen and American dollars.[20]

The procedure established during Sorge's briefings in Moscow was for the couriers themselves to arrange the next rendezvous, advising Moscow if anything developed to make the meeting impossible. But over the course of time this method was used only when two parties met fairly frequently. For the most part Moscow arranged the courier contacts by radio.[21]

These messengers formed Sorge's only personal contact with Russia. Most of them were youngish men, professional couriers of the Soviet government, who combined the carrying of official documents with that of clandestine material. If when face-to-face the courier and his contact discovered that they had never met before, they exchanged special signals and passwords. Conversation between courier and contact was brief and generalized. Only rarely, and then when Moscow specifically sanctioned it in advance, would there be any mention of secret matters regarding the work. They had a certain amount of leeway in purely personal subjects, especially if the courier and the agent had met several times and thus become acquainted. But for the most part the meetings remained impersonal: The men exchanged signs and passwords, transferred packets; then each went his own way.[22]

If courier contacts were highly suitable for exchanging money they were proportionately unsuitable for passing on timely information, for months elapsed between meetings. Bulky material and such items as pictures, photostats, and maps had to be hand-carried, but radio transmission was vital for urgent messages and to arrange courier rendezvous. Hence Sorge's concern over Wendt's failure to establish an efficient sending and receiving station.

With Ott's appointment as military attaché in the spring of 1934, Sorge's already formidable program of research and writing intensified, for Sorge was determined to become indispensable to Ott. Between Sorge's rapidly expanding paper work and his social life, he outgrew his hotel room, so he rented a two-story house in Azabu-ku, 30 Nagasaki Machi, which was one of three Japanese-style houses in a fenced-in compound.[23]

One of the three approaches to his new home passed the Toriizaka Police Station. Any interested policeman could look out of the station directly across to Sorge's bedroom window. This proximity was excellent embroidery on Sorge's cover. What spy would deliberately set up housekeeping in the shadow of a police station? However, its agents frequently questioned Sorge's maid and laundryman and often tailed Sorge to restaurants and even into the Imperial Hotel. The authorities had no definite idea that he was a spy; they entertained a general suspicion of all foreigners. Nor was this watch careful and constant, for the police did not have the necessary manpower. The checkup was intermittent, in the nature of a sample survey,[24] nothing to cause Sorge alarm or to interfere with his way of life.

The neighborhood was a pleasant collection of neat middle-class dwellings, each with its well-manicured patch of garden. Among these spruce dolls' houses, Number 30 cried for the services of a painter and a carpenter, and weeds had established mastery in the garden.[25]

On the inside this tiny dwelling, "hardly more than a summerhouse," was even more disreputable. One of Sorge's fellow journalists, Friedrich Sieburg, remembered the two or three rooms he saw as scarcely larger than tables, "stuffed full of books, papers and all possible kinds of articles of everyday use. . . ." Weise, Sorge's crony from the German news bureau, said that the shortcomings of the two upstairs rooms, "in furnishings, comfort, and even cleanliness, cannot easily be described." One or two good bronzes and porcelain pieces were the only evidence that here lived a man with some pretensions to good taste.[26] This bohemian lair accorded ill with the reputation Sorge was attempting to build of a man of the world and a lover of Japanese art. Almost the only pictures on the walls were a few of Miyagi's oils.[27] Sorge accumulated nothing he could not walk away from without a pang.

But while not acquisitive, he was no ascetic. His clothes, although soon shabby, were well cut and of excellent material. He frequented Tokyo's bars and restaurants, while considerable funds went up in smoke in the form of expensive American cigars and cigarettes.[28]

He acquired a housekeeper, Tori Fukuda, a small woman about sixty years of age. Sorge called her Ama-san,* treating her with courtesy and consideration, which she repaid with steadfast devotion. She was an excellent cook, and Sorge did full justice to her efforts, while she beamed with approval. Bottles of the best brands of whiskey, brandy, gin, and sake stood by for action in his liquor cabinet.

As if to compensate for his heavy eating and drinking, he established a rigid daily routine. Ama-san arrived at five each morning and prepared his bath. The master of the house awoke at six so uniformly that the neighbors could have set their clocks by him. Then he bathed.[29] Despite the clutter of his surroundings, Sorge was fanatically clean about his person and reveled in Japanese-style baths, scrubbing himself outside the tub, then soaking in it.[30] After his bath he wrapped a towel around his loins and went through a brisk round with a chest expander. His exercise completed, Sorge dressed, breakfasted, then attacked his typewriter.

After lunch, no matter what the pressures on him, he

---

* *Ama,* or *amah,* was a term used among Europeans in the Orient to denote a maidservant or wet nurse. In this case, "Honorable Housekeeper" is probably the most suitable translation.

threw himself down on the sofa-bed in his study and napped for a full hour, to wake refreshed and ready for another twelve hours' work. At about 3:00 P.M. Ama-san departed, leaving Sorge's late afternoons and evenings free for social activities or clandestine visitors without her knowledge. During each afternoon Sorge had a quick workout with barbells, then took off on his rounds: newspaper offices, embassy, German Club, and parties to see what intelligence he could pick up.[31]

CHAPTER 10

"THE BRIGHT PROSPECTS
I FORESAW"

The Fourth Department had given Sorge two years to determine whether or not he could establish an effective spy ring in Japan. The anticipated order to return to Moscow immediately for a conference reached him in May 1935, at exactly the right moment. He was eager to announce in person his triumph in setting up an *apparat*, and to shift the operation into high gear, he needed specific instructions from his superiors on the nature of the intelligence they wanted him to collect and submit. This was a particularly auspicious time for Sorge to leave Tokyo temporarily because Ozaki was scheduled for an inspection trip to China with a team from the East Asia Problems Investigation Association. The two collaborators would return to Japan in the fall and could exchange information then. Moreover, the Comintern would hold its Seventh International Convention in Moscow from July 25 to August 20, and Sorge hoped to attend.[1]

He traveled from Japan to Moscow via the United States. In New York a Communist Party contact gave him a genuine passport bearing an Austrian visa and the "long and outlandish" name of its original owner, together with Sorge's picture and description. Thus on his return trip his own passport would not show that he had been in the Soviet Union.[2]

While in New York Sorge ordered a suit at a tailor's, using his real name and indicating that he would pick it up on his way back through the city, then went to a steamship company to buy his ticket. There, much to his annoyance and

embarrassment, he had to consult his false passport to refresh
his memory of his assumed name.

In boarding his ship, he neglected to pay his exit tax,
hence had no receipt. A customs official was about to whisk
him off the vessel; but Sorge slipped him $50, and the man
suffered an immediate lapse of memory. "Things are very
flexible in the United States," Sorge remarked.[3]

By the time he reached Moscow he was his usual confident self. Acting as his own courier, he had brought a large
volume of material, ignoring his instructions which expressly
forbade him to "make a long journey carrying articles to be
delivered through many countries."[4]

Uritskii had succeeded Berzin as chief of the Fourth
Department. A Bolshevik since 1917, he had studied mathe-
matics, physics, and astronomy, spoke quite good Polish and
French, and could get around in German. On the lighter side
he had written short stories and a novel in his spare time.[5]

Sorge had the impression that Uritskii had discussed him
with the party leaders and had gone very thoroughly into his
background and the material he had submitted. Uritskii extended Sorge every kindness, fully appreciating the difficulties
he had met and would still meet in Japan.

First of all, Sorge told Uritskii what the general must
have gathered indirectly: that "spy activity was possible" in
Japan. He reported in detail his experience in establishing
the ring and, as he put it, "the bright prospects I foresaw
there."

In return Uritskii gave Sorge a general indication of areas
of primary Soviet interest. Sorge would have "freedom of
activity to select problems to work on as the situation would
develop and change."[6] This was the only practicable arrangement. In short, Uritskii outlined the strategy; he left the tactics
to Sorge, the field commander. The areas of interest broke
down into seven, all of which were closely interrelated:

1. Japan's policy toward the Soviet Union, with particular attention to whether or not Japan planned to attack.

This was by far Sorge's most important duty. At that
time the Soviet Union darkly suspected all its neighbors but
most of all Japan. So deeply ingrained was this obsession about

a Japanese strike that Sorge's repeated reassurances "were not always fully appreciated in Moscow. . . ." Uritskii made plain the direction of Russian fears by saying that he especially wanted information relating to the Manchurian-Siberian and Mongolian-Manchurian borders.

2. Any reorganization and strengthening of such Japanese army and air units as might be directed against Russia.

In effect, this meant the entire Japanese Army, for the military used the Soviet Union as an ever-ready excuse for constant budget increases.

3. German-Japanese relations.

Moscow believed that a rapprochement between Germany and Japan was inevitable, with the consequence of a two-pronged attack on the Soviet Union, and was so certain of this that "when Japan took the last great turning in her career* Moscow was taken completely by surprise.[7]

4. Japan's attitude toward China.

At the time Moscow did not foresee the China Incident which broke out in July 1937 but "merely supposed that a knowledge of Japan's China policy would, to a certain degree, reveal Japanese intentions toward the U.S.S.R., and that the course of Japan's future relations with other countries easily could be deduced from her China policy."

5. Japan's posture toward Britain and America.

This was in line with the Soviet Union's national persecution mania, which visualized all the great powers pouncing upon it in concert, with Japan, Great Britain, and the United States allied to handle the Pacific front.

6. All possible information concerning the Japanese Army, not only such professional information as number and quality of troops and equipment but also the extent to which the military influenced national policies.

7. The development of Japan's heavy industries.

The reason for Moscow's interest in this area was twofold: The effectiveness of the Japanese Army would depend upon how well industry could support the economy, and Russia

---

* When Japan attacked Pearl Harbor.

could profit from Japan's techniques for converting from agriculture and light industry to heavy industry.[8]

All this boiled down to finding the answers to two questions: Does Japan, either alone or as one of an entente, intend to attack the Soviet Union, and how well equipped is it to do so?

In later years Sorge turned the full power of his personality and wit to smoothing over the military aspects of his espionage in Japan. ". . . General Uritskii told me that he was not interested in purely military problems, but interested in the military problems only to clarify the Japanese foreign policy," he averred.[9] Nevertheless, of the seven points outlined, three deal specifically with the Japanese Army, so military information ranked high on his agenda.

He made three requests of Uritskii. He asked that "the central authorities recognize Ozaki as a direct member of our group." Sorge had already vouched for Ozaki, with another comrade as cosponsor on the strength of Sorge's word, but now he personally submitted Ozaki's name, which was registered officially.[10] Just exactly what Sorge meant by "a direct member of our group" is somewhat obscure. Possibly this agreement between Uritskii and Sorge acknowledged that Ozaki was strictly Sorge's pigeon, not subject to transfer to another spy ring in Asia without Sorge's approval.

He asked for "absolute freedom to contract any relations I deemed necessary with the German Embassy."[11] This request hints at tales left untold since his instructions from Berzin of two years before presupposed that he would worm his way into the German Embassy. Possibly he needed Uritskii's confirmation of Berzin's orders, but possibly he might have gotten wind of some suggestion that he was too friendly within German circles. In any case, he made the stipulation, and Uritskii agreed.

He asked for either Clausen or Weingarten to replace Wendt. Permission was necessary, for graduates of the wireless school could not "be taken out of Russia without the approval of the Red Army." This was all right with Uritskii, too, and he left the choice to Sorge.[12] Both were in Moscow. So was Wendt, who was on the spot to brief his replacement, whichever of the two Sorge should select.

Sorge had not told Wendt frankly that he was not satisfied with his work and his attitude and wished to replace him. Instead, he had cleverly played on his fears. With the delicate insistence of a dentist's drill, he had stressed the dangers of the situation until the hapless Wendt wanted only to get out of Japan while the getting was good. Sorge had gladly packed him and his wife off to the Soviet Union in May.[13]

Sorge chose to interview both candidates in a bar near the radio school where Clausen was studying the structure and capacity of American transmitters and Japanese shortwave receivers—the same bar where a week previously Wendt had told him that he had left his Tokyo post because it was becoming too dangerous. Sorge was already entrenched in the bar when his two colleagues of Shanghai days came in.[14]

Clausen had had an adventurous career since Shanghai. After his spell there he had been ordered to Mukden in Manchuria, his cover to be a motorcycle shop. Curiously enough, he made a hash of his professional duties. The cover shop failed, and Clausen sent out only fifteen messages in a year. He admitted that this Manchurian adventure was a failure.[15]

Ordered to return to Moscow, and for cover to travel with a woman the party would provide from among its trusted agents, Clausen laid back his ears and balked. With obstinate courage he defied the Kremlin.[16] Technicians of his caliber being in short supply, Moscow agreed to let him travel with Anna. A representative of the Fourth Department met them at the station and escorted them to the Hotel Moscow, where on their first night all their personal belongings, including their precious passports, vanished. For this and other reasons Anna found Moscow less than the paradise Clausen's enthusiastic word picture had painted.[17]

After this wrist slap the Fourth Department left Clausen alone for a while. Since he often strolled around Moscow in his uniform, Anna was able to fit into place the last pieces of the jigsaw puzzle: Clausen was an officer of the Red Army, and his clandestine work was connected with the Red Army.[18]

After six weeks' medical leave at a Black Sea resort and advanced training at a Moscow radio school,[19] in January 1934 the Fourth Department called him on the carpet, informed him that his work in China had been unsatisfactory, and consigned him to a period of "reform through labor" at the motor tractor station (MTS) at Krasny Kut, which is slightly southeast of Engels, capital of the German Volga Autonomous Soviet Socialist Republic. Motor tractor stations operated over much of Russia, renting heavy farm equipment to the collective farms in return for a share of the wheat crop.[20]

In the first months of Clausen's exile, life was difficult, for he had no expertise with farm machinery and his salary was low. But his mechanical aptitude rose to the challenge. Anna found a part-time job, and between them they managed to eke out a living. Soon Clausen's superiors assigned him to set up a system of radiotelephones to establish communications between the factory and the individual tractors as they chugged about the vast wheat fields and to place radiotelephones at "mobile clubs," one to each collective, so that broadcasts from Moscow could edify the farmers.[21]

With a job at hand Clausen did it thoroughly. Slowly but steadily his salary rose. He and Anna shared two pleasant rooms, and although still resentful of the Fourth Department for sending him into exile, he was contented enough. Anna was somewhat less reconciled. "Our living standard there was very low," she said.[22]

But Clausen did not suffer under his banishment. He had work he liked, and he had his Anni, always affectionate and faithful, if sometimes acid-tongued. Traveling through the collectives, installing telephones and repairing tractors, Clausen was a popular figure in his rural world. By the end of a year his communications network was famous. Officials from the MTS headquarters in Engels came to inspect it and were so impressed that they asked him to set up a radiotelephone system there.[23] Not bad for a simple mechanic supposedly in disgrace!

Then, in February 1935, a sour note crashed into Clausen's domestic symphony. A telegram from the Fourth Department ordered him to return to Moscow. Not at all ready to abandon his pleasant lot and still sulking over his official slap, he ignored it. The Fourth Department did not follow through for approximately a month. Then it sent a second, sharper message, which received the same treatment. The Fourth Department could not let that go by, so in April the branch chief of the Communist Party emerged from Engels bearing a telegram signed with the awe-inspiring name of General Voroshilov. Moscow had called in the first team. Handing Clausen the message, the chief said almost whimsically but definitely, "So Max must go back to Moscow."

Later Clausen said that this meeting was "the crossroad of whether I would lead my life as an honest worker or whether I would be sent abroad as an international spy." At the time, however, he accepted his orders with as good grace as possible.[24] Being in the Red Army under military discipline, he had little alternative. Temporarily leaving Anna behind, he returned to Moscow, where the Fourth Department claimed its wandering boy.

Clausen found Berzin, who still headed the department, in no pleasant frame of mind. "Why did you twice reject the telegram requesting you to come back to Moscow?" he demanded.

Clausen faced the general serenely and replied simply, "I rejected them because my position was stable and life was getting better in the Volga Republic. As a result I did not want to return to Moscow."[25]

Unfortunately no witness has told what Berzin did or said in the few minutes after he dismissed Clausen. Perhaps he laughed; perhaps he cursed; perhaps he held his head in his hands; perhaps all three. What could he do with a man like that? The Clausens of this world are indestructible. And Clausen was a good radioman who had taken his medicine.

After leaving Berzin, Clausen paid his respects to the head of the European Department, who told him that he was being transferred to that department for assignment in Germany. This was all right with Clausen. He set out for the Volga Republic, picked up Anna, and returned with her to Moscow.

A few weeks later Clausen was sitting in the bar near the radio school with Weingarten, hearing Sorge explain that he wanted one or the other for the Tokyo job that Wendt had found too dangerous. Both were willing to go, but Clausen added, "I am supposed to go to Germany as I belong to the European Department."

If Sorge had not yet made up his mind which man he wanted, this remark would have settled the question, posing as it did a challenge to his influence. "That doesn't matter at all," he assured Clausen loftily. "I will arrange things so that you will go to Tokyo." Weingarten being already scheduled to leave for China or Mongolia, taking Clausen to Japan was the best arrangement. This important decision made, Sorge took his two friends home to meet his wife.[26]

Between conferences with Uritskii and Clausen, writing reports, and briefing the party Central Committee, even though Manuilsky vetoed his request to attend the Comintern convention, Sorge had very little time to look up his Russian friends and not much time to spend with his wife.[27]

Some special arrangements had to be made about his membership in the Soviet Union's Communist Party, though usually, when a party member left a country for another for any length of time, he transferred his membership to the Communist Party of the new location. For obvious reasons Sorge could not join the Japanese party. So he relinquished membership in the Communist Party of the Soviet Union. When and if he returned permanently to Russia, he would requalify himself. To avoid too great an accumulation of fees, he would continue to send his dues to Moscow.

In the meantime, he was solely responsible to the Fourth Department "and did not have any duty to receive any instructions from any other place . . . even if Stalin ordered me."[28]

After a few more conferences with Clausen and a last interview with Uritskii, Sorge left Moscow by plane. The whirling propellers of the aircraft chopped his lifeline. Unknown to him, he had done many familiar things, seen many familiar sights for the last time and had spoken a last farewell to many friends. For Katcha, this parting was particularly poignant. In Sorge's line of work every good-bye might well be forever; this time her husband left her pregnant.[29]

Not much is known about Sorge's return trip to Tokyo. Presumably he stopped off in Berlin for a few days to establish his bona fides. He had been absent from Tokyo for several weeks and could not permit the ever-suspicious Nazis to discover that he had been in Europe without touching home base; by the same token he needed some anecdotes of current vintage about Germany to tell his friends in Tokyo or he risked blowing his cover. He had the time for a brief visit with his mother and sister. He stopped over in the Netherlands, where he destroyed his fake passport and once more became Richard Sorge.[30]

On the way back to Japan he touched American soil one last time. In New York he phoned a longtime comrade. "But how did you find me?" Hede Massing exclaimed with pleasure at hearing the familiar voice. Sorge laughed. This was an old ritual. He liked to mystify Hede with his unexplained comings and goings.

They dined together in the Café Brevoort, and Sorge brought Hede up to date on his adventures. She listened enthralled but noted that Sorge had changed and not for the better: "Little of the charm of the romantic, idealistic scholar was left. He had been transformed into a boisterous, hard-drinking man. . . . His cold blue eyes, slightly slanted and heavy-browed, had retained their quality of looking amused for no reason at all; his hair was still thick and brown, but his cheeks and the heavy, sensuous mouth were sagging, his nose was thinner."[31] They agreed to meet a second time, but Sorge did not keep the rendezvous. Their paths never crossed again.[32]

In New York Sorge had one small embarrassment. He went to pick up the suit he had ordered on his way to Russia and on this occasion used the name on his false passport. The surprised tailor noted the difference, but fortunately for his customer he was interested only in the business transaction. "People in the United States do not think it strange if the same man uses two different names," Sorge pronounced.[33]

Then once more Sorge was airborne—over the long sweep of the United States, over the Pacific, and back to Japan, scene of his ultimate triumphs and tragedies—to touch down in Tokyo on September 26, 1935, never to see Europe or America again.

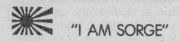 "I AM SORGE"

On his fortieth birthday, October 4, 1935, in the soft dusk of a warm evening, Sorge sauntered down a narrow street in the Ginza to one of his favorite haunts, the Rheingold Bar. Business was brisk that night. Japanese waitresses in bright kimonos flitted among the customers like butterflies, noiseless and graceful. With the ease of long practice Sorge wove his way down the long room to a booth near the bar.[1]

The decor of the Rheingold left no doubt that its proprietor, Helmut Ketel, had Nazi sympathies. On the wall behind the semicircular polished wooden bar surmounted by a large sign advertising a brand of German beer the Nazi swastika touched a Japanese flag. Elsewhere about the place swastikas and photographs of Hitler explained why the Nazi element of Tokyo's German colony patronized this particular establishment.[2] Almost half the customers were Japanese; the other half, foreigners. The Japanese came in search of the exotic; the Germans, among them embassy personnel, for a touch of home; the other foreigners for a change from Japanese fare.

The Rheingold opened at 10:00 A.M. and spiced the life of its customers with German beer, whiskey, wine, sake, and any cocktail the imagination might dream up. Sometimes quiet, sometimes noisy, its tone varied with the day, the hour, and the mood of the customers. One way or another made little difference to Ketel. He let his patrons set the pace so long as they did not actually smash the furniture or bring the police down on his neck.

In his restaurant Ketel was affectionately known as Papa.

This stocky, medium-sized German had a broad, beaming face and a personality oozing *Gemütlichkeit*. A good crop of gray hair topped a high, sloping forehead and a sharp nose; his tufted eyebrows hung over rather small, twinkling eyes. His first taste of Japan had been as a prisoner of war after the Japanese had captured him in China early in World War I. After his release he had remained in Japan and married a Japanese woman.

But Ketel was too sensible to make any embarrassing attempts to go native. No stuffing of his rotund body and large feet into robe and tabi, no shaky squatting on his heels for him. He had remained superbly German, and the Japanese loved him for it. Wisely capitalizing on his biggest asset, himself, he had opened his bar shortly after the Great Earthquake of 1923. Twelve years later he presided over one of the most popular bars in the Ginza.[3]

Soon Ketel joined Sorge in his booth. As they chatted, one of the waitresses glided up to take Sorge's order. In keeping with the Rhineland atmosphere, Papa had given each of his waitresses a German name, which he selected alphabetically. As fate would have it, on this evening a girl called Agnes was on duty at Sorge's booth. His back was toward her, so until she stood before him, she saw only broad shoulders and rather unkempt hair. The first full sight of Sorge made a distinct impression on her. When she returned to the bar, she edged up to the waitress called Berta and asked, "Who is that foreigner talking to Papa? Is this his first visit here?"

Berta shot a quick glance at Sorge. "No, he used to come here quite frequently, but he has not come recently. He is a very nice person." She amplified the phrase by adding with a laugh, "He does not speak Japanese, but he is very generous."

With that, Agnes carried Sorge's drink to his booth and placed it in front of him. Then she took a small folding chair from one of the nearby tables and joined the two men.[4] At the Rheingold an easy friendliness prevailed among host, waitress, and customer, for this was Papa Ketel's way. The customer who did not like this informality could take his trade elsewhere.

As the men continued their conversation, Agnes eyed this foreigner with curiosity no less keen for being covert. His face impressed her as being very German, and she began to take inventory of his features. After a short while Sorge looked at her as if really seeing her for the first time and broke into a smile.[5] Saying something in German, he ordered champagne. Ketel beamed as he relayed the order and turned to the girl. "Agnes," he announced, "today this man turned forty. It is his birthday." Sorge nodded, smiling broadly, and said, *"So des, so des ["It is so, it is so"]."*

When the champagne arrived, they popped the cork and drank to Sorge's health. By this time he had tired of waiting for a formal introduction to the lovely girl seated beside him. "Are you Agnes?" he asked.

"Yes, I am," she answered.

"I am Sorge," he replied. As he spoke, he stretched out his big hand, and she slipped her slender fingers into his. His kind tone surprised her, for it seemed at odds with his rather harsh features and his voice, which sounded to her Japanese ears somewhat hoarse and unmusical. But his whole demeanor proclaimed a man of good breeding.[6]

At this moment a customer at a nearby table insisted that Ketel sit with him. Papa cocked an experienced eye at him, excused himself, and joined the man, who obviously had looked too long upon the beer when it was brown. He plied Papa with a long, involved, drunkenly humorous story that made Agnes and Sorge chuckle and helped bridge the first awkward moment of their being alone. They fell into conversation.[7]

From their first meeting this foreigner with the face of a fallen angel attracted Agnes. She was favorably disposed toward him because he was friendly and kind. Then, too, at five feet five inches she was taller than many Japanese men and felt ill at ease with a man shorter than she. Germans stood high in her good graces, for Papa Ketel was an indulgent employer and his many German patrons were pleasant and generous. Her new acquaintance seemed to her German "to his last bone."[8]

"How old are you, Agnes?" Sorge asked casually in English.

"I am twenty-three years old," she replied in German, for she had picked up a few words of Ketel's native tongue. Sorge's face crinkled in amusement at Agnes's quaintly accented German, and he nodded.[9] Still smiling, he appraised her with a connoisseur's scrutiny.

Her wide lips were full over even white teeth that protruded slightly, pushing the upper lip a trifle forward. Jet black hair cut in a thick bang contrasted with light, clear skin. Two pinpoint moles interrupted the smooth surface, but by good fortune one rested on the tip of her pert nose, the other near her left eye, as if to draw attention to her best features. For all else was mere background for a pair of beautiful eyes, framed by delicate brows and long, brush-like lashes. Sorge knew at a glance that this young woman was no ordinary member of the serving class or demimonde, for those eyes were neither archly inviting nor demurely lowered; their direct regard held honesty and intelligence leavened by a quick sense of humor.[10]

As Sorge and Agnes surveyed each other covertly, someone turned on the phonograph. Here and there customers laughed and thumped the tables with their beer mugs. Soon the Rheingold was jumping as Papa's patrons sang German songs in rolling waves of exuberance. Amid the cheerful commotion Sorge sat almost immobile, sipping his champagne, with Agnes beside him in quiet contentment. She had the Oriental quality of stillness and saw no need to fill the silence between them with small talk. Occasionally Sorge's eyes burned into hers, so that Agnes felt a little embarrassed and wished that Berta or someone else would join them.

Sorge made no move to take part in the hilarity. Experienced lady-killer that he was, he bestowed on Agnes the tribute of undivided attention. He talked to her in his throaty voice, now in English, now in German.[11] About the only words she understood were "I am very happy today" and "Agnes, what would you like to have? I want to buy you a present."

She made no coy protest, accepting the idea placidly. She hesitated briefly. What should it be? Not too much—she was not a gold digger. Not too little—that would mock his generosity. The answer came almost at once. She loved music passionately. "If you are going to give me a present, please give me a record," she said softly.[12]

If she had known Sorge for years, she could not have made a better selection. For he, too, loved music, in particular the German classics, Russian folk songs, and the rousing chants of the Red Army.[13] Beaming with satisfaction, he nodded agreement. "Let us go buy you one tomorrow," he suggested. Out came his notebook, down went the time and place where Agnes would meet him the next day.

Presently Berta joined them, and soon thereafter Sorge left the Rheingold. The size of his tip delighted Agnes.[14] Although Sorge could be downright stingy in paying salaries or giving money for other purposes to members of his spy ring, he was a lavish spender on the luxuries he permitted himself: women, good liquor, fine food, the best tobacco.[15]

Agnes generously shared her tip with Berta. But her mind was elsewhere. "Berta," she asked hopefully, "does that foreigner have anyone he likes especially in this bar? Does he have a favorite?"

The question pleasantly amused Berta, who thought for a moment, then replied, "Dora used to serve him occasionally when he came here, but since he does not call for anyone specifically, I don't think he has a favorite."[16]

When Agnes slipped into the music store the next day, Sorge was already there, listening to records. He told her to pick out anything she wanted, so she chose three records of arias sung by one of her favorite tenors, Beniamino Gigli. Sorge selected several of his favorite piano and violin sonatas and added them to the gift. "I am very fond of Mozart," he explained. "Please accept these." The gesture was typical. By all means let Agnes have what she wanted, but he would try to guide her taste.

Sorge suggested dinner. Agnes readily accepted. He took her to Lohmeyer's, a small restaurant in the Ginza that specialized in German food and service to foreigners, where he often dined. Agnes felt a trifle reserved, but Sorge soon put her at ease and lost no time in suggesting another date. Once more down in his notebook went the time and place of their next meeting. After dinner he told Agnes that he had to go to Domei, so could not see her home. "Is your office in Domei?" she asked. "Yes, I am a foreign correspondent of the German newspaper *Frankfurter Zeitung,*" Sorge replied.[17] Later she found out about his close affiliation with the German Embassy, but that was virtually all she ever discovered from Sorge about his work.

He made no effort to conceal his identity from Agnes or

from anyone else he met legitimately in his character of German newspaperman. The more people outside his spy ring who knew Richard Sorge the journalist, the better for his cover and his prestige.

Sometime later Sorge learned that Agnes called herself Miyake Hanako. Miyake was her mother's maiden name, which she found more melodious than her father's family name, Ishii. Thinking Miyake to be Agnes's given name, Sorge called her "Miyako" and continued to do so even after she had corrected him. She did not object, for she did not like Hanako, "a child's name."[18] Yet it suited her best, for she was a true flower of Japan.*

Although she was not yet in love with Sorge,[19] she was to look back on this encounter as the watershed of her life, an irrevocable break with the past. For Sorge the meeting was a significant but not vital event. He had made the first tentative moves toward initiating another amour, no novelty to him. Yet this one would last.

---

* *Hana* means "flower"; *ko* is an affectionate feminine ending. There is no equivalent name in English; however, the French Fleurette and the Italian Fiorella are almost exact translations.

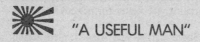

CHAPTER 12

"A USEFUL MAN"

Before he left Moscow, Sorge gave Clausen a blow-by-blow account of the rather cold-blooded way he had got rid of Wendt, and he made his reasons very clear: He "drank all the time and often neglected to send out the information. Spying work must be done bravely. He was too cowardly and did not send out as much as half of my information." In his turn Wendt bitterly accused Sorge of risking radio detection to build up his image in Moscow. Weighing the two viewpoints, Clausen decided that the trouble was really a personality clash, not anyone's fault.[1]

Various officials plied Clausen with advice and instructions. Wendt briefed him on the Tokyo operation and what Sorge would expect of him there. The Far Eastern Division executive warned that he must be extremely careful to attract no more attention than necessary. He would be conspicuous because fewer Westerners lived in Tokyo than in Shanghai. The division chief himself urged Clausen to learn Japanese. Clausen took this counsel to heart. In addition to his native German, he spoke fairly good Russian as well as English, which he had picked up in China.[2] Sorge, who had been in Tokyo for two years already, was by far Clausen's superior in formal education, and prided himself upon his expertise on Japan; but he never spoke its language well, and Clausen came to surpass him in Japanese.

Along with good advice, Clausen received one suggestion he did not appreciate. "Why don't you divorce your present wife and take a German woman?" asked the Far Eastern chief.

"If you are willing, I can introduce you to one." Clausen refused, explaining that though he and Anna were not yet man and wife, they had lived together since Shanghai.[3]

He was eager to set out for Japan and do his bit to better the world. He had an ingrained anti-Japanese prejudice dating from his school days and had indiscriminately lapped up the Communist Party's propaganda, which taught him "that capitalist countries . . . are all the same, that they exploit their own people, and that taking advantage of opportunity, they subdue weaker nations and exploit them for their capitalism."

As a workingman he objected to the Japanese low standard of living and cheap production, but he had no hostile feelings toward the Japanese people. He directed his anger at their rulers. He "thought that Emperors and kings in capitalist countries were something like advertising boards for their people and that by attracting attention of the people to themselves they tried to keep the people unaware of the true substance of things." Therefore, he thought that "the Japanese Emperor system and political system tried to keep their aggressive activities from people's eyes."[4]

Clausen did not understand that no such camouflage was necessary. Suzuki-san, the Japanese man in the street, fully supported his government and was proud of it. Nothing in its methods or policies was alien to his traditions and way of life; rampant nationalism was a logical, if extreme, extension of the bone-deep respect for the warrior. The totalitarian, militaristic clique that controlled Japan in the thirties and early forties took nothing from Suzuki-san that he had ever had and gave him pride on an international scale. No longer was he a quaint little figure in a kimono; he was a force to be reckoned with. When Tokyo spoke, the world might not like what it heard, but it listened.

Clausen's third grievance against Japan was the fact that the Soviet Union considered that nation one of its prime enemies, and in spite of the treatment Clausen had received at Russian hands, he was still "a 100% Communist" and a faithful servant of the Marxist homeland. All things considered, he saw himself as "an enemy of the Japanese Government but at the same time as a friend of the Japanese people"; hence, when "appointed by Moscow as a wireless operator in the spy ring

in Tokyo, I felt a big pride."[5] This pride fortified him for
another long separation from the unhappy and fearful Anna,
whom he left behind in September. The authorities refused to
let her go with him, holding her in Moscow virtually as a
hostage for his good behavior.

Clausen left Moscow armed with $1,800 in American
currency and two false passports—one Austrian; one Canadian.
Headquarters had selected these from the hundreds on file as
conforming generally with Clausen's description. The documents in this large stockpile were valid, the Soviet government
having purchased them from their rightful owners. Substitution
of a false name and a photograph produced, with very little
doctoring, a convincing set of false credentials.[6] In Clausen's
case, however, this efficient machine slipped a cog.

His journey from Moscow to Tokyo is worth following
as a case study in the Communist espionage methodology and
operations of that time. The original plan called for Clausen to
depart from Odessa, go to New York via Constantinople and
Geneva, then cross the United States and the Pacific to Shanghai, where he would pick up Anna and take her to Tokyo. But
when he showed up in Odessa, a sharp-eyed OGPU man sent
him packing back to Moscow because the workmanship on the
Austrian passport was so sloppy.

The Moscow experts whipped up another Austrian passport and sent Clausen on his way again, but the delay necessitated a change of route. This time he traveled by rail via
Leningrad to Helsinki. To avoid any appearance of undue haste,
he spent a day in Helsinki, then took the train to Turku, where
he boarded a ship for Stockholm. There he changed to rail
again and chugged along to Malmö, where he transferred to a
Dutch aircraft for Amsterdam. There he secured a transit visa
at the Belgian consulate, entrained for Paris, and checked in
at the Hôtel du Nord.

His Austrian passport having served its purpose, he tore
it up and flushed the pieces down the toilet.[7] Then he slipped
the Canadian passport from its hiding place in the false bottom
of his valise to become a Canadian tourist named Titleman. As
the Canadian document already carried the necessary visas, the
newly hatched Mr. Titleman journeyed to Vienna, an innocuous

tourist on his way to sample Viennese culture after a brief stay in England.

Clausen had business in Vienna, a rendezvous in a theater where a comrade returned to him his own genuine passport, which had expired in 1933. This Clausen stashed away in the false bottom of his case and hastened back to Paris. From the Gare St.-Lazare his train rattled across Normandy to Le Havre, where he embarked for New York.

On shipboard he had the disconcerting experience of watching one page of his Canadian passport slowly fade, and he presented it to the New York customs official with his heart nudging his tonsils. But luck was with him. To most Americans, a Canadian is not really a foreigner, so the official gave him a pleasant greeting and sent him on his way.

Now came the problem of updating his own passport. With a prefabricated story and a sailor's identification book, which he had bought from an American seaman during his first stopover in Paris, he presented himself at the German Consulate General, claiming to be a sailor who had left his ship and worked for some time as a garage mechanic in Camden, New Jersey. The consulate renewed his passport, and after acquiring a visa from the Chinese consulate, he was ready for his trip to Shanghai via San Francisco.[8]

During Clausen's stop in New York an agent who rather unimaginatively gave his name as Jones contacted him and asked if he needed money. Clausen declined, for his original $1,800 was holding up well. But when he embarked on the *Tatsuta Maru* in San Francisco on November 14, he had cause to wish that he had accepted. He ran into some sort of difficulty; later he claimed that $300 "was taken unreasonably at the American customs." Clausen never explained this peculiar incident, which drastically changed his plans. Now he lacked funds to marry Anna in Shanghai and take her to Japan.[9] This proved to be just as well, for Anna was not in Shanghai as anticipated. Not until the spring of 1936 did the Russian authorities permit her to leave Moscow.

Clausen passed through Japanese customs with no difficulty. He climbed into a small car the Hotel Sanno had waiting on the dock and was whisked off to Tokyo. Learning at the hotel that the German Club was giving a masked ball that night, he decided to treat himself to an evening of fun.

Before Sorge left Moscow, he had arranged the time and place of contacts with Clausen. "Let's go to the Blue Ribbon Bar near Sukiyabashi in Tokyo in the evening every Tuesday," Sorge had said.[10] If one or the other missed a rendezvous, he would try again the next week at the same time and place.

Having no worries about getting in touch with his chief, Clausen took off for the masked ball with a light heart. He paused in the hall of the club to look at some pictures a painter was exhibiting and, glancing up, saw Sorge disguised as a German sausage vendor. They ignored each other. Clausen introduced himself to the club director, who with expansive German hospitality made him known to several members, among them Sorge.

This happy change gave Sorge and Clausen an open acquaintance and the opportunity to meet freely. They agreed that for the time being they would rendezvous at the Fledermaus, which Clausen described as "a little shop which had a better reputation than the others, chiefly frequented by foreigners who had money."[11] Other visitors to Tokyo during the thirties recalled the Fledermaus as a dismal, smoky spot with only a few tables and two giggling waitresses. It would seem an unlikely haunt for Richard Sorge, that cultured gentleman at home in the German Embassy and Imperial Hotel, but something in the Fledermaus appealed to the dark side of his nature, for he went there often and got thoroughly drunk.[12]

One of Sorge's friends who witnessed his behavior at the Fledermaus was Prince Albrecht Eberhard Karl Gero von Urach, a correspondent for the Nazi paper *Völkische Beobachter* and a first cousin to the King of Belgium. He brought a letter of introduction to Sorge from Etzdorff, and the two hit it off immediately. Urach was an engaging young man, welcome at the embassy for his own sake as well as for that of his father, under whom Ott had served in World War I.[13]

Urach painted a devastating picture of Sorge at the Fledermaus: "Sorge went through all the stages of an alcoholic's intoxication: euphoria, tearful misery, aggressiveness, delusions of persecution, megalomania, delirium, passing out in a stupor, and finally the gray desert of a hangover that could be driven away only by more alcohol.''

One of the bar girls at the Fledermaus, Keiko, was hopelessly in love with Sorge. Once, when he turned up with a beautiful European in tow, the despairing Keiko left a farewell note and a gift of flowers on Sorge's doorstep and took a steamer for Oshima, where she planned to throw herself into a volcano. The bartender, by no means willing to part with such a drawing card, enlisted the aid of the police and brought her back. Apparently reconciled to living, she hovered over Sorge as before, spitting into his dice cup for luck.[14]

With Clausen's arrival, the major actors in Moscow's espionage drama were onstage in Tokyo. Even though separated from his beloved Anni, he was in good spirits and determined to do his job well. In Sorge's words, Clausen's "technical ability and enthusiasm for his work knew no bounds.''[15] He spent his early days in Japan conferring with Sorge, getting his bearings, keeping a sharp eye open for the police, and sizing up the radio situation from every possible angle.[16]

Throughout the winter he labored mightily to construct his own radio set to replace Wendt's relic. He had brought no parts with him from Europe, but thanks to Wendt's tips and his own shopping, he found what he needed in Tokyo stores that sold radio parts. Except for the transmitter vacuum tubes, which were American, all the parts were of Japanese manufacture. For tuning coils in the transmitter he used copper gasoline tubing intended for automobiles, which he purchased at a hardware store in Kyobashi-ku. The transmitter itself was a Bakelite panel attached to a wooden box, the tubes and coils readily detachable. He used a receiver from an ordinary radio with three tubes modified for shortwave reception, and he discarded the cabinet and loudspeaker in favor of headphones. The entire contraption fitted into a suitcase. The transformer for the transmitter was too large and heavy to carry about easily, so he built one at each sending station as the need developed.[17]

Having no instruments for measuring wavelengths, Clausen had to improvise in establishing contact, using, as Sorge ordered, thirty-seven to thirty-nine meters for transmitting and forty-five to forty-eight meters for receiving. Otherwise Sorge gave him no instructions except to put together something that would meet the technical requirements he had established in Shanghai and Mukden. Clausen's inventive construction was so good that he established contact with the Soviet mainland station, "Wiesbaden," within a week of finishing the set. At that time he received directions to modify his sending wavelengths to thirty-eight meters, the only correction needed.[18]

A Japanese official called Clausen's finished product "one of the strangest conglomerations of various stray parts I have ever seen—a terrific assortment of materials that included one or two beer bottles and other miscellaneous items."[19] It might not have been beautiful, but it worked. Clausen needed an average of ten minutes to install it and start sending, and fewer than five minutes to dismantle it. To avoid outdoor antennas, he suspended two tin-plated copper-stranded wires about seven meters long in the room. He used one wire about a meter long for reception.[20]

When the set was ready for use, the question of a suitable sending site arose. Clausen specified three requirements: First, the location must be in a densely inhabited section; the more residences in the area, the more difficult it would be for the police to trace any emanations they might pick up. Secondly, the building must be wooden because a steel skeleton interfered with transmission. Thirdly, the building must be at least two stories high, for a second-floor location would avoid both "the earth's magnetic qualities" and the prying eyes of visitors.[21] He did not add, for it went without saying, that the occupant must be a willing, reliable associate.

Clausen was in no position to send from his own quarters. A month after his arrival he had taken a room in the Bunka Apartments with a German who, Clausen said, "had nothing to do with the spy ring." Furthermore, he was having difficulties in establishing his cover. He had planned to engage in exporting and importing, but "this did not turn out well," so after two ineffectual months he abandoned this project and started planning a firm for manufacturing and selling blueprint copying machines. This company, M. Clausen Shokai, did not go into production until the summer of 1937.[22]

In the meantime, Clausen had neither private home nor office, so he and Sorge faced a dilemma: What to do? Voukelitch's home was still cluttered up with the machine Wendt had left behind, and Miyagi was flitting from one small furnished room to another. Though Sorge's home fitted Clausen's conditions perfectly, when Clausen tried to set up a station there, "the results were not good, and we resolved to use it only when we had no alternative."[23] Circumstances aside from technical ones dictated this prudence, for Sorge's embassy and press cronies dropped in at odd hours, and the Toriizaka Police Station was much too near for safety.

Sorge approached Günther Stein, a fellow journalist, and asked permission to use his apartment. This encounter took place at Sorge's house, with Clausen present. Sorge's request to Stein "visibly disturbed him." But he was not too disturbed to agree immediately. Clausen recalled, "Stein and I discussed radio and he drew a map to show me where he lived. I visited him several days later at his home in Azabu Ku, Motomachi Cho, examined the house to see whether it was suitable for the installation of radio equipment, and decided, with his consent, to use two of his upstairs rooms." Clausen installed the equipment and began testing around the middle of February.[24]

Born in 1900 in Germany, Stein had served as correspondent for the *Berliner Tageblatt,* but when Hitler came to power, that newspaper no longer had a place for a leftist half Jew, and Stein moved his base of operations to London. He had come to Japan as a correspondent for the *London News-Chronicle.*[25]

Sorge's first meeting with Stein took place in the spring of 1935 at a Foreign Ministry press conference. This encounter "was an extremely happy event" for both men. Apparently the pair had known of each other for a long time, for Sorge said, "Stein tried to see me in China around 1932, when he traveled from Moscow to London via China, Hongkong and Switzerland, but failed, inasmuch as I had already left." At first the two men confined their conversation to "political topics," but soon Sorge hinted that he "was engaged in something more than news reporting" and still later indicated that he "was working for the Moscow authorities." Sorge explained, "I maneuvered him gradually toward participation in our work," and Stein agreed to help.[26]

Stein had a likable personality and endeared himself to

Clausen because "being opposite to Sorge he is a very quiet and kind person." An expert on politics and economics, he was something of an introvert who spoke little and preferred to stay at home, writing his books and articles.[27]

On the question of Stein's involvement with the Sorge ring, some have taken the attitude that Stein was a misunderstood bystander. In later years he protested his innocence: "I never had anything but a common receiver in my house. I performed no courier service. I was never a spy for anyone. My links to Sorge were of a purely journalistic and social nature, just as were my relationships with other colleagues as well."[28]

Stein had not been assigned to the Tokyo ring through Red Army or Communist Party channels, as were Sorge, Clausen, Miyagi, and Voukelitch. Sorge, however, attempted to place him on the same footing as Ozaki. He informed Moscow that Stein, "a useful man," was helping him and petitioned the Fourth Department for permission to bring Stein into the ring as a full member. Very possibly Sorge, never satisfied with Voukelitch, entertained hopes of trading him in for Stein, whose expertise and prestige more closely approximated his own and Ozaki's. His superiors rejected his request, but Sorge believed that Stein "would have been accepted as a member if he had stayed longer in Japan." In 1938 the Japanese authorities spotted him as "a leftist writer" and suggested that Japan could get along without him.[29]

Before that event removed Stein from Sorge's sphere, his "assistance was extremely valuable" to him. He supplied "information, obtained at the British and American embassies, concerning the diplomatic and political policies of foreign powers with respect to Japan and China."[30] He was particularly useful for his connection with the British ambassador and with Sir George Sansom, commercial counselor at the British Embassy. On the other side, he was close to Dirksen, whom he had known since his stint in Moscow for the *Berliner Tageblatt* and who considered Stein "an intelligent and important person." Then, too, Stein was "on very intimate terms with all foreign newspapermen, especially the British and American reporters." Not the least of his uses was his very considerable knowledge of the Japanese economic situation.[31]

In addition, Stein acted as a courier for Sorge, carrying microfilm and photographs to Shanghai and bringing back other packages.[32]

Students of the Sorge case have debated whether to categorize Stein as a "member" or a "sympathizer" of the ring. In his testimony Sorge wavered between the two but leaned toward the latter.[33] Clausen, too, hesitated between "sympathizer" and "member" but inclined toward "member."[34]

By whatever term one might prefer, both Moscow and the Sorge ring knew him by a code name, Gustaf,[35] and Sorge had him down in his notebook as one of the ring.[36] Occasionally, when Sorge was out of town or ill, he entrusted Stein with the task of contacting Ozaki or Miyagi.[37]

This was a marked demonstration of trust, for Sorge took care that his co-workers not learn too much about each other. He introduced Clausen to Voukelitch at the Fledermaus shortly after the radioman's arrival, and they soon developed a close relationship,[38] yet Clausen knew none of the Japanese associates—only that Sorge was pleased with his agents. Clausen had known of Miyagi by his code name, Joe, for four or five years before he met him in the summer of 1939 at Voukelitch's home, upon which occasion Miyagi deduced that Clausen belonged to the group.[39]

As for Ozaki, Clausen met him only twice in all the years the ring existed, and that was in 1941 at Sorge's house; he did not learn Ozaki's true identity until just before the end of the line. Not until late 1936 or early 1937 did Miyagi realize that Voukelitch was a member of the ring, and Ozaki never set eyes on him.[40]

Thus Sorge's net was not particularly close-knit. Each member did his part to sustain the whole but did not come into intimate contact with every other operative. Sorge worked with all members of the inner ring and knew a number of those in the outer circle, but he left personal association with them to Ozaki and Miyagi.

Toward his own choices, Ozaki and Clausen, Sorge showed a degree of trust that he did not bestow upon any of the others. Ozaki was far and away his favorite both as friend and as colleague. Yet although Sorge treated Clausen as a social inferior, it was to him that he came to entrust part of the ring's financial accounting, to him that he would instruct Miyagi to report when he was not available, and to him Sorge would turn in an unexpected crisis.

Clausen was not a party member. After 1929 he had paid no dues to the German Communist Party, and he never bothered to transfer his membership to the Soviet party. Unlike Sorge and Ozaki, he never tried to mitigate his work for the ring by playing up his lack of party status, which with innate realism he knew to be irrelevant. "Since I came to engage in spying activities by the order of the Fourth Headquarters, I thought it would not matter much whether I was a Party member or not," he remarked straightforwardly.[41]

To be literal, Clausen never was a spy like Sorge, Ozaki, Voukelitch, Miyagi, and the members of the subring. He never brought to Sorge a single item of intelligence, and there is no evidence that he ever tried to do so. He was a technician and part-time courier. Yet the ring never moved into productive operation until he was in place, his blunt, skillful fingers holding the line between Tokyo and Moscow.

CHAPTER 13

"HE HIMSELF RESPECTED
OZAKI VERY MUCH"

Miyagi, ringmaster of the network's outer circle, had to contend with one performer who refused to jump through the hoop docilely. Kawai was a tiger of a very different stripe from Miyagi's own recruits. He made a number of efforts to put Kawai to genuine use, but privately he held little hope of success. Ill in body, stern of mind, Miyagi was not the man to approve of his tough, offhand colleague.

". . . Kawai was taken care of by Ozaki, and he himself respected Ozaki very much," Miyagi acknowledged. Then he continued primly, "But Kawai's Communist conviction was low and his private life was not good either. Therefore, from the viewpoint of spying activities, he could not be trusted."[1]

Miyagi was extremely busy in Tokyo, where he had been collecting and interpreting military intelligence since "about the summer of 1935." At that time Sorge told Miyagi that the "Comintern" had ordered the ring to furnish "information on the Japanese Army based on documents and pamphlets." Accordingly, at a store in Kanda, Miyagi bought monthly magazines and military and technical pamphlets from which he extracted "opinions by Japanese military officers on the introduction of Soviet weapons, anatomy of Red forces and the new weapons of France, Germany and England." He gave to Akiyama for translation into English "those opinions of Japanese military officers on Japanese military problems."[2]

Kawai procured a copy of a pamphlet entitled *Opinions*

on the Reform of the Army, which Miyagi approved, copied in black ink (the better to be photographed), and gave to Sorge.[3]

Miyagi was also in touch with a new recruit, Torao Shinotsuka, owner of a small factory in Kansai producing military equipment, of which he had made a special study since boyhood.[4] In Sorge's words, Shinotsuka was "an old friend of Ozaki's who was brought into our work soon after I arrived in Japan, but who turned out to be far from what we expected. Instead of a military expert . . . he gradually turned into a money 'expert.' "[5]

Ozaki first asked Shinotsuka for military information in the autumn of 1935, on the pretense of needing a briefing before he attended "a meeting to study military affairs," but he was unable to understand Shinotsuka's technical language. He introduced Shinotsuka to Miyagi several days later, with the explanation that "Miyagi was studying military affairs and was helping Ozaki with his work."[6]

So, as early as October 1935, Miyagi met with Shinotsuka at a Japanese restaurant behind the Ginza. On that occasion the new recruit discoursed on army aircraft, particularly the Kawasaki 88 and the Mitsubishi 92, describing their features and capabilities. The two men met again later that month, and Shinotsuka rattled off exact figures of army bombers and their capabilities, naval "reconnaissance planes, fleet scout planes, fleet attack planes, fleet fighters, fleet torpedo planes." He supplied details about the machine guns and bombs attached to both army and navy planes. He outlined the setups and locations of the army's flying units and the navy's bases at Yokosuka, Kasumigaura, Sasebo, and Omura. He also spoke briefly about naval weaponry in general and about the aircraft carriers *Akagi* and *Kaga,* names that six years later at Pearl Harbor would be written in blood on American memories. He finished by recommending a list of books for Miyagi to study.[7]

If Sorge begrudged Shinotsuka payment for the type of information he gave Miyagi, the master spy had a poor sense of relative values. Shinotsuka's information was detailed, factual, and straight from the source. Ozaki had such faith in Shinotsuka that he had him prepare notes concerning the formation and equipment of the armed forces of every country on the globe.[8] Yet Sorge neglected the opportunity to profit from Shinotsuka's specialized knowledge. His own military experience had been exceedingly unpleasant and limited to the lower enlisted ranks, so he had little concept of, and less interest in, strategy and tactics. Nor was Miyagi as yet the sensitized recorder of military affairs he later became.

Grappling with these manifold activities, Miyagi could not make field trips through Japan to gather on-the-spot information, so he conceived the idea of sending out Kawai in the guise of a traveling salesman dealing in books. Kawai did not relish the thought of becoming an itinerant purveyor of literature, so Miyagi had to abandon the plan.[9] He need not have pondered so conscientiously over what to do with his colleague, for fate was brewing a kettle of hot soup into which to plunge Kawai shortly.

Even as Miyagi was considering the Kawai proposition, in far-off Manchuria the Japanese police, in its constant pursuit of leftists, arrested one Tatsuoki Soejima. Three years previously Smedley and Ozaki had set Kawai to work on a two-year stint gathering intelligence in northern China and Manchuria. Soejima had been a member of Kawai's network. In the course of his interrogation Soejima mentioned Kawai, charging him with giving military information to the Comintern. The Japanese Consulate in Hsinking therefore requested that the Tokyo police pick up Kawai and bring him to Hsinking for questioning.[10]

So at 5:00 A.M. on January 21, 1936, eight policemen pounced on Kawai as he lay asleep in his apartment in Suginami-ku. They dragged him out of bed, flourished a warrant, tied him up, and hustled him to the Suginami Police Station. After two days there the police spirited him to Manchuria, passing him from one station to another for about two weeks, stopping over at some, continuing through others. It was no secret that the Japanese police had unpleasant ways of extracting information from suspects. Later Kawai admitted freely that he was a badly frightened man when his captors flung him into a prison at Hsinking to answer to thirty-seven separate charges of violation of national security.[11]

Reading the charges against him, Kawai was relieved to find that the police had no inkling of the Sorge ring's existence.

Furthermore, he felt sure that Soejima had never heard of it either. Certainly he had not done so from Kawai, who had a strong sense of loyalty. For Sorge he entertained an almost superstitious reverence, for Miyagi a sincere respect for the artist's dedication, and as for Ozaki, Kawai would have died rather than betray him. And he almost did.

Soejima had had no direct connection with the Tokyo *apparat*, and Kawai had told Soejima no more than was absolutely necessary. So Kawai believed that by answering all questions as briefly as possible, volunteering nothing, and confessing only what the police already knew, he could spare his friends in Tokyo and save the ring. He categorically denied having given thirty-seven military secrets to the Comintern, as charged.[12]

Naturally, his unsupported denial did not satisfy the Shinkyo police. On February 11, around midafternoon, they pulled him from his cell and propelled him into the basement with the intention of jogging his memory. Kawai found himself in a bare, windowless room, cold as the Scandinavian hell and lit feebly by a single electric light bulb hanging from the ceiling. The only furnishings were a single round stool in the center of the room and various instruments of torture hanging on the walls.

A burly policeman stripped Kawai of his quilted kimono (tenzen) and the shirt of his long woolen underwear, leaving him naked above the waist, then pushed him down on the stool. The kimono and shirt had offered little protection, but their removal left Kawai with a despairing sense of vulnerability and loss of dignity. Through the walls he could hear the screams of other unfortunates in adjoining cells, the sound making a hideous accompaniment to his own inquisition. In his vivid imagination Kawai suffered tortures before anyone laid a finger on him.

Only two men entered the basement with Kawai: the chief of the Shinkyo police, a medium-sized, slender-faced man of some twenty-two years, and a powerfully built man, who might have been a former soldier. The latter took down from the wall an iron bar, not heavy enough to break bones or inflict permanent damage but strong enough to bruise and sting wickedly. The two men fell upon Kawai at once, the chief screaming a staccato of questions which the torturer punctuated with smashing blows with the iron bar.[13]

Fortunately for Kawai, his anticipatory fears, the whole grisly setup, the clammy cold of the basement, and his suffering on behalf of his unseen but acutely heard neighbors all combined into an anesthetic effect. The impact of the rod felt like the flick of a red-hot wire crisscrossing his shrinking flesh, but not until later, when his blood began circulating freely, did he feel the full impact of his punishment. During the experience his mental anguish pushed physical pain into the background.

From Kawai's huddled position, as he cringed from the iron bar whistling through the air, the man wielding it seemed a veritable ogre. His massive torso towered up to an impassive, blank-eyed face, while the shrill bat's squeal of the chief's questions pierced Kawai's eardrums with exquisite torment. Trying to parry the questions while wondering how much more he could take was the real core of Kawai's torture. The inquiries centered on the alleged thirty-seven military secrets. "When did you steal them?" "Where?" "Why?" "Why were you in Manchuria?" "Who are your associates?"

As best he could Kawai answered honestly, insisting that he was in Manchuria on a research project for his friend Yang Liu-ch'ing in Shanghai. All his information, said Kawai, went to Yang, not to the Comintern. Of course, Kawai did not know exactly what Yang did with the information, and under the circumstances he was not about to hazard a guess.[14] Nor did he mention that the same Yang had introduced him to Ozaki in Shanghai.[15]

Strangely enough, Kawai believed that the physical beating actually helped him keep his secrets. He could only gasp out a brief "yes" or "no" between blows, and through the blur of pain he could not think clearly enough to give detailed information, even had he been inclined to do so. Later he deprecated his physical suffering, but the human mind is mercifully equipped with a shutter that clamps down over unbearable memories. The police gave him a pitiless beating that left his wiry body a quivering mass of black and blue. More than a coldly logical determination to keep quiet is required to sustain a man through that sort of ordeal. From some reservoir of

stubborn heroism deep in the human soul, beyond logic, beyond
ideology, even beyond friendship, Kawai drew strength to en-
dure. When he passed out after about an hour's inquisition, he
had kept the secret of the Sorge ring locked within him.[16]

He came to in a pleasant room and was served tea and
cakes in one of the abrupt swings from bestiality to suavity
that can make the Japanese such an enigma to the Westerner.
After soothing Kawai down, the police questioned him again,
this time in a civilized manner. Since he had not confessed
under torture to supplying the Comintern with information, they
were ready to hear his side of the story.

But Kawai had nothing more to say, and in due course
the police abandoned the effort. They did not torture him again
but kept him on ice for some months of a three-year suspended
sentence—almost literally on ice a good part of the time, for
a prison cell in Manchuria in late winter was bitterly cold. He
received no medication and with the help of his sympathetic
cellmates treated his wounds as best he could with cool water.
Almost immediately his once-thick hair began to fall out. By
the time of his release in June he was almost bald, a condition
that he attributed to his mental sufferings rather than to the
actual beating.

After about a month in jail Kawai noted a vast change
in the attitude of his captors, who began to treat him more like
a guest than a prisoner. This politeness was a backwash from
the February 26 Incident, which was an outbreak of mutiny
and assassinations by certain army officers known as the Young
Officer group. This incident was a clear demonstration of the
power of an extreme right-wing element of the army. For cover
purposes Kawai usually posed as a rightist, and a number of
his overt contacts were hand in glove with the Young Officer
group.[17]

What is more, Kawai was often characterized as a *Shina
ronin*. The customary polite rendering of the term as "China
adventurer" does not convey the flavor and implications. At
the time the *Shina ronin* were agents in China and Manchuria
of the huge assortment of Japanese "patriotic" secret societies
that proliferated like rabbits and in most cases were just about
as dangerous. Some of them, however, were both sinister and

powerful, enjoying an unacknowledged but semiofficial status. To Westerners the most famous was the Black Dragon Society.*

A number of army officers belonged to one or more secret societies. These particularly attracted the Young Officer group, which thrived on assassination. It was whispered that army intelligence funds helped finance the activities of the *ronin* in China and Manchuria, where they spied for the secret societies and stirred up ugly incidents to order.[18]

As well as being the lowest dregs of the Japanese underworld, the *ronin* had high connections. So when the February 26 Incident occurred and it appeared that the Young Officers would take over, the Manchurian police began to treat Kawai as if he were a particularly fragile piece of porcelain. They thought they had a genuine specimen of *Shina ronin* in their hospitable jail, and it behooved them to handle it with care.

Of the February 26 Incident and its ramifications Kawai knew nothing at the time. He knew only that when his cell door creaked open on June 25, he was now branded as an object of police attention and that for a long time he would have to be extremely careful about contacts with Ozaki and Miyagi. So he remained in Manchuria, lay low, and did not return to Japan permanently until 1940.[19]

The other members of the Sorge ring preserved a complete silence concerning this incident, but they knew that something was amiss when Kawai abruptly disappeared from his usual haunts with no word of explanation. In the climate of the time it was easy to guess what had happened when an underground revolutionary suddenly was lost to view. While a rightwinger could murder almost at will and, like Hitler at Munich, turn the dock into a soap box from which to denounce the government, the left-winger hardly dare swat a mosquito lest he be jailed for inciting to violence.

* The name might more accurately be translated "Amur River Society," for "Black Dragon" is the literal meaning of the Chinese name for the Amur River, which forms most of the boundary between northern Manchuria and the Soviet Union. So the group's title gave a fair indication of the society's aims to take over all Manchuria up to the Siberian border.

The individual droplets of the endless stream flowing from the left into prison were under constant pressure to turn informer. A nagging doubt about what, if anything, Kawai was confiding to the police must have given Sorge, Ozaki, and Miyagi many a pang during the spring of 1936. None of them held a very high opinion of Kawai and never would have credited him with the courage and loyalty he demonstrated on their behalf. Neither Sorge nor Miyagi displayed any gratitude or appreciation. Sorge remained supercilious; Miyagi remained disapproving. In the future Ozaki would continue to assist Kawai financially and find jobs for him. Still, he was willing to slough him off on Miyagi to avoid having such an unconventional figure visit his office, where he might raise eyebrows among Ozaki's upper-crust colleagues.

The danger to the Sorge ring from Kawai's arrest had been very real. Unknowingly the police had held the key in their hands. Kawai knew personally most of the major members of both the old Shanghai and the new Tokyo organizations. Like Ozaki, at this time he knew Sorge as Johnson, an American reporter, but if the police had checked the small American community, they would soon have found that no such person existed. Kawai had been a friend of Ozaki's since Shanghai days and knew the extent of Ozaki's implication in both the Shanghai and the Tokyo rings; except for Sorge himself, Kawai was one of the very few who could spill all the beans on Ozaki. Even Miyagi, who worked closely with Ozaki in Tokyo, knew nothing of the Shanghai operations. What is more, Kawai knew all about Miyagi's covert activities. With all this to tell, Kawai could have spared himself the torture of which he bore the marks for the rest of his life, and had he been merely a mercenary, he had plenty of opportunity in prison to earn a nice little nest egg and a steady income by turning informer.

All the other members of the ring talked when they were finally arrested, from Sorge right on down the line, and none of them experienced the sort of punishment Kawai endured. Yes, they all talked—Sorge the magnificent, Ozaki the sociable, Miyagi the purist, Voukelitch the flippant, Clausen the stubborn. In the moment of truth only one stood firm—Kawai, on whom the others looked down. Some inherent strength, some resource within himself enabled Kawai to lock the secrets of the Sorge spy ring behind his lips. And by so doing, he saved the *apparat* at the very time it was moving from its trial period into actual operation.

PART 2

TURNING THE RING

CHAPTER 14

 "RISEN IN REVOLT"

The rumbling that shook the building was not the familiar tremor of an earthquake, but it propelled Hanako and her young friend Masuda to the window of his apartment in a flash of movement. Peering out into the darkness, they saw one large black object after another roar past. "Tanks! tanks! tanks!" shouted the onlookers in high excitement.

With the sunrise Tokyo wore a strange, indefinable air. Troops swarmed around the Imperial Palace and occupied government buildings. The Imperial Guards stood almost nose to nose with rebel forces entrenched in the nearby structures. Papa Ketel did a roaring business that day and night. Rumors were begetting rumors, each one more fantastic than the other. Foreign and Japanese patrons alike were thoroughly upset, fearful of the army and disappointed in the failure of the police to cope with events.[1]

Wild as were the rumors on February 26, 1936, they scarcely could have been stranger than the truth. Some 1,400 soldiers, led by company-grade officers of the First Division, which was on orders for Manchuria, marched out of their barracks to occupy the government buildings. Military trucks conveying select murder teams armed with submachine guns roared through the snow to the homes of their predestined victims. The "hit list" read like a *Who's Who in Japan:* Prime Minister Admiral Keisuke Okada; Minister of Finance Korekiyo Takahashi; Grand Chamberlain Admiral Bunjiro Suzuki; Lord Keeper of the Imperial Seals Admiral Viscount Makoto Saito; Inspector General of Military Training General Jotaro Watanabe; and

Count Nobuaki Makino, who held no office but was close to the Emperor.

Saito had just returned from dinner and a movie at the American Embassy when the killers burst in on him. His wife tried to shield him, but the bullets wounded her in the arm and sped past her into his body. Watanabe was shot out of hand, while Suzuki escaped with a wound. Rumor later held that the officer selected to assassinate the grand chamberlain owed him a favor and aimed at his arm instead of a vital spot. Eighty-year-old Takahashi died by a shot from an automatic and hacks from a sword.

The prime minister escaped by hiding in a toilet, and the murderers shot his brother-in-law by mistake. Two days later the dead man's funeral procession wended its mournful way out of the house. Behind it walked Okada, disguised as a mourner over his supposed corpse. With great presence of mind the family pretended that the killers had succeeded in their mission, and Okada stayed under cover until the danger blew over.[2]

A squad of reservists led by a captain converged on the country inn where Count Makino was staying with his wife and granddaughter. The policeman detailed to guard Makino shot the leader of the thugs and himself fell under rebel fire. Makino and his granddaughter slipped out the back door to face an almost perpendicular hillside. Supported by the young lady and an unidentified man, Makino had struggled several yards up the bank when the assassins poured out of the inn and wounded the man with rifle fire. As he fell, Makino fell with him. They both feigned death, and the soldiers hastened off.

That ended the bloodshed.[3] The rebels issued a fascinating manifesto. One cannot envy Sorge the task of rendering it into comprehensible German. However, it is worth quoting as an example of the sort of thing that confronted him in his endeavors to understand enough about the Japanese to predict national policy toward the Soviet Union:

> . . . Now is the time to bring about an expansion
> of the power and prestige of Japan.
>   In recent years many persons have made their

chief purpose in life the amassing of wealth regardless of the general welfare and prosperity of the people, with the result that the majesty of the Empire has been impaired. The people of Japan have suffered in consequence. Many troublesome issues now confronting our country are due to this situation.

The Elder Statesmen, the financial magnates, the government officials, and the political parties are responsible. . . .

The recent strained relations between Japan and the other powers are due to our statesmen's failure to take appropriate measures. Japan now confronts a crisis. Therefore it is our duty to take the proper steps to safeguard our fatherland by killing those responsible. On the eve of our departure to Manchuria we have risen in revolt to attain our aims by direct action. We think it is our duty as subjects of His Majesty the Emperor.

May Heaven bless and help us in our endeavor to save our fatherland from the worst.[4]

All very impressive, but what did it mean? For Sorge the key question was just where and when did Japan intend to expand its "power and prestige."

The opening of the second paragraph was the old cry that selfish materialism was sending the country to the dogs. The people of Japan had indeed suffered, especially economically, yet one officer, when asked just what the army wanted in 1936, replied, "We desire a community in which all people are able to work to the fullest degree, accepting twenty per cent of the results of their labor as their private income and turning the rest over to the government as national income."[5] An 80 percent income tax was a curious method of relieving Suzuki-san's troubles, especially since the money would be slated for the insatiable maw of the armaments program.

For what were the elder statesmen et al. responsible? What were the "appropriate measures" they had failed to take? What was this latest in Japan's perennial series of crises? In

what way would the "proper steps"—i.e., wholesale murder
—"safeguard" the fatherland from "the worst," whatever that
ominous phrase might mean?

Small wonder that Sorge immediately mustered his entire
espionage army to try to find what this was all about and what,
if any, indication it contained of Japanese intentions toward
the Soviet Union, so that he could boil it down to something
that would make sense to Moscow.[6]

". . . the Incident had a very typical Japanese character
and hence its motivations required particular study," Sorge
explained. "A discerning study of it, and, in particular, a study
of the social strains and internal crisis it revealed, was of much
greater value to an understanding of Japan's internal structure
than mere records of troop strength or secret documents. . . ."[7]

He found his friends at the German Embassy thoroughly
bewildered by the revolt and, with their strong sense of discipline, unable to understand the failure of the government and
the army's top brass to control it.[8]

Dirksen was in Nagasaki to welcome the German cruiser
Karlsruhe when the police advised him that "some political
murders had been committed in Tokyo during the night." He
hastened back to Tokyo, where the embassy, which stood near
the War Ministry, was virtually under siege. With the aid of
some gendarmes Ott smuggled Dirksen through a maze of narrow alleys to his office. Food and furniture had been carried
to the cellar to form a sort of underground command post, with
the confidential files near the boiler in case of emergency.[9]

Sorge pointed out the importance of the social implications of the incident to Dirksen, Ott, and Wenneker, the naval
attaché, and said that he was studying them. As a result, the
embassy devoted considerable attention to these aspects of the
affair.

Ott set to work on the army, Wenneker on the navy.[10]
Of the two, Wenneker had the easier job. The navy had its
Young Officer element, but in general its members confined
themselves to meetings, delegations, and expostulations. The
February 26 Incident was strictly an army matter.

Ott had many contacts in the army and any number of
elbow-bending cronies among the Young Officers, but since
becoming military attaché, he had directed much of his energy

to fathoming the Japanese system of espionage and sabotage and how the secret societies fitted into the pattern,[11] so in this situation he was somewhat out of his element. Indeed, the affair was especially puzzling to a Teutonic officer such as Ott. Was not the Japanese Army supposed to be styled after that of Germany? How then could this absurd revolt have arisen in the first place, and once it had arisen, why was it not crushed within the hour?

The Japanese were confirmed transplanters, but no plant can be removed from one environment to another without some transmutation. The German military system took a native quirk in Japanese soil. Control of the German Army ran in a direct line upward; control of the Japanese Army followed a bell curve. As the German officer rose in rank, his duties and responsibilities rose with him; his superiors encouraged and expected him to be an original thinker in his field. But after the Japanese officer had passed a certain point, he shucked his duties and responsibilities, leaving him with a resounding title but extremely vulnerable to his juniors. The Japanese preferred conformity to originality, so the man who attained the rank of general officer was not necessarily the most brilliant. Often he was the one who fitted himself most closely to the mold until he had acquired enough seniority and moss for promotion.

In this scheme the junior officers assumed that they who did the spadework should call the tune. And the generals had abdicated their responsibility for so long that they did not know how to recover it. This situation existed in the civil branches of the government as well as in the military.[12]

The February 26 Incident did not, as has been suggested in recent years, place the military in control of the nation.[13] Japan's government had long been under the thumb of the armed forces. Typically the War Ministry's announcement of the revolt and the resulting deaths contained no word of censure, no promise of investigation, no assurance against any repetition.[14] And when certain ringleaders were brought to trial and sentenced, there was no mention of assassination or murder; the charge was that of using the imperial army without imperial sanction.[15]

To all intents and purposes, the Japanese Empire had a

collective dictator—the army. The army controlled the government; ergo, whoever controlled the army controlled Japan. If Sorge could isolate and identify the power behind the throne, by watching it he could predict national policy. That is why he had more than an academic interest in interpreting the February 26 Incident and in anticipating its results.

Several rebels made speeches in public places to explain their actions to the people. Thus Sorge had no trouble in following the rebellion's events, which were open for all to see. Both Miyagi and Voukelitch saw and heard one of these orators near the Sanno Hotel.[16]

After the first big push obviously something went wrong. The rebels came to the end of their prepared script when they hoisted over the prime minister's residence the banner of revolt—a tablecloth from the Peer's Club purchased with a 100-yen note. They made no move to extend their lines or consolidate their position. For four days they just sat around, waiting for someone to tell them what to do next.[17]

During these four days the Sorge ring worked ceaselessly. Sorge himself took a special interest in the documents that Ott obtained from the Japanese military. These and other papers the embassy collected were so important that he photographed the lot on the spot for dispatch to Moscow—the first time he used this technique in the embassy, but far from the last.[18]

His prime Japanese source, Ozaki, submitted a long dissertation which boiled down to four conclusions:

1. Many of the rebels came from agrarian backgrounds, and the Young Officers who came in contact with them had developed an anticapitalist slant.

2. While Kazuki Kita, author of a book that influenced the Young Officers considerably, did not advocate communism, he did have "a revolutionary ideology."

3. The Japanese right wing would gain in strength.

4. Japanese foreign policy might become "anti-Russian."[19]

While expert evaluations poured in, Sorge combined business with pleasure by pumping Hanako over dinner at Lohmeyer's. She hesitated to pass on the gossip she had heard.

Sorge was a foreigner, and in her opinion the incident reflected "great shame for the Japanese that precious lives were taken by military force, right or wrong." Marshaling her scanty English and German, she did her best.

"People are saying that Japan did good things for Manchuria. Soldiers want repayment or bonus for taking Manchuria. There is none. The soldiers are angry. They did bad things. No good!"

Sorge nodded and laughed, as much at Hanako's fractured German-English mixture as at this naïve interpretation. "Yes, but what do *you* think?" he persisted. "I want to know."

"I really don't know," she admitted. "My friend says that Japan took Manchuria. The army likes power. The government is weak. The army gets mad and had a riot. My friend said, 'They are savages.' "[20]

Sorge cocked a quizzical eye at her. The German construction made clear the gender of the friend. "Is your boyfriend smart?" he asked.

"Yes," answered Hanako with some pride. "He is very smart. He reads books," she added triumphantly. "He is gentle. He does not make riots. He told me about the French Revolution, but I am not in favor of a guillotine," she concluded severely.

Amused and refreshed, Sorge set aside politics for the moment. "Yes, you are a girl who does not like violence," he told her. He added teasingly, "I am not violent. Let us become good friends."[21]

But such entr'actes were few in this turbulent period. By the end of February, shortly before the incident fizzled out, Miyagi was ready with his oral report, a detailed one to follow. After some general comments he got down to cases. The serious-minded artist was surprised that the average Japanese seemed remarkably little concerned and that such public opinion as existed supported the Young Officers.[22]

Sorge could have predicted this reaction. He was familiar with Japan's favorite play, the *Forty-seven Ronin*, a tale of clan revenge, and he expressed his admiration of the *ronin*, who pretended to be footloose drunkards until their mission was accomplished.[23] The play's key theme is loyalty; the Japanese have overwhelming respect for this virtue and can carry it to gruesome lengths. At every production of this classic handkerchiefs dampen with admiring tears when one of the *ronin* sells his daughter into prostitution to obtain money to keep the gang together. The Young Officers took full advantage of this thin spot in the national morality to proclaim their actions as evidence of their loyalty to Emperor and nation.[24] Suzuki-san could not be expected to probe more deeply.

Nevertheless, Miyagi believed the revolt doomed from its inception. The Young Officers had only small arms to oppose the establishment's tanks and airplanes, and the revolt had erupted earlier than planned because of a breakdown in communications. Moreover, the army authorities had quickly arrested rebel leaders in the provinces before they could reach their planned destinations. Miyagi predicted an early end to the rebellion.[25]

He proved a true prophet. At the end of the four days the city came out of its paralysis. Warships lay at anchor in Tokyo Bay, awaiting orders. Troops under trustworthy officers surrounded the occupied area with tanks and heavy guns. Appealed to in the name of the Emperor to return to their barracks with the promise of a full pardon if they obeyed, the rebel soldiers gradually complied. The tablecloth came down from the prime minister's roof, its brief day of glory over. Then followed a two-hour pause while the rebels were tacitly invited to commit suicide. Only one obliged. The others knew they stood a good chance of escaping with token punishment after a wonderful opportunity to publicize their cause.

The real motive for the rising has never been revealed. If the rebels ever divulged it, it remains buried in the records of the closed court-martial that tried the ringleaders, fifteen of whom were shot on an undisclosed date.[26] Later in the year Miyagi told Sorge that the public could not understand why certain generals had been cleared or given light sentences when obviously they had been connected with the rebellion.[27] That may have been true of individual cases, but in the Japan of that day the fact that any court-martial convicted any officer of any crime was astounding.

The immediate result of the incident was the fall of the cabinet. The Supreme Military Council, having squelched the rebellion, exacted its pound of flesh by blocking the new prime minister, Koki Hirota, from appointing Shigeru Yoshida foreign minister. Yoshida was the son-in-law of Count Makino and firmly opposed to trouble with Great Britain or the United States.[28]

An able man and a diplomat by training, in theory Hirota advocated settlement of international disputes through diplomacy. But to a Japanese official of that time, diplomacy meant give-and-take—you give and I take. In practice under Hirota's premiership the most pernicious of Japanese governmental customs attained the force of law. On May 18, 1936, at the army's demand, his government issued an ordinance that the war and navy ministers must be active-duty officers of the rank of lieutenant general or above. The new war minister was appointed by a triumvirate of the current minister of war, the chief of the General Staff, and the inspector general of military training. The last was almost equal to his two colleagues in power and, like them, had access to the Emperor.

By law these three chose their own successors, so in effect they constituted a self-perpetuating monopoly from which there was no appeal. If the prime minister did not approve their nominee, they refused to appoint another, so no cabinet could be formed. If the prime minister found a general with the courage to accept the portfolio over the heads of this brass-plated trio, they could cancel his eligibility by removing him from the active list.[29] A military takeover on the Occidental pattern—a coup d'état placing officers in civil positions—was unnecessary in Japan. The army was in control; the only changeable factor in the situation was which faction of the army was in the saddle.

Miyagi understood this very well. A month before Hirota's legislation went into effect he told Sorge that whether or not Japan struck the Soviet Union would depend on which of the three principal factions in the military came out on top when the smoke of the incident blew away. If the Action group, composed of such young, radical officers as General Shunroku Hata, were in the saddle, Japan would attack the Soviet Union fairly soon. But if either the Control Faction or that of General Issei Ugaki came to power, a strike on the Russians would not be in the cards for some time. At the moment the Control Faction still held the reins, therefore, Russia was probably safe for the immediate future.

Miyagi pointed out, however, that no matter who held the balance of power in the military, the domestic situation must be considered carefully. If Japan's economy broke down, the government might stir up a war with Russia to build up the economy and to direct public dissatisfaction into foreign channels. If this came about, Miyagi believed that April or August would be Japan's best time for an attack.[30] However, by the time summer rolled around the Control Faction was still in command so Miyagi predicted, "Japan will seek a weaker area of expansion. This means she will not attack Russia but will expand in China."[31] Within a year his prophecy came true.

Sorge incorporated Ozaki's and Miyagi's early information and evaluations into a long report, which he submitted to his friends in the German Embassy. This document made Sorge's stock skyrocket with Dirksen, Ott, and Wenneker. "In this way," said Sorge smugly, "I accomplished the same effect of killing two birds with one stone, in that I gained trust from the Germans by studying and writing. . . . And at the same time I spied valuable materials."[32]

In reality, Sorge slew a whole flock with scattered buckshot. The admiring Ott sent a copy of Sorge's report to General Thomas in Berlin. Delighted with it, Thomas requested more of such fine work. This gave Sorge an airtight excuse for research in the embassy files and improved his ties with this valuable friend at court. His newspaper articles lifted his prestige with his fellow reporters and in the German colony.[33] Also, he had reason to hope that his coup might induce the *Frankfurter Zeitung* to look favorably upon his suggestion that he submit articles concerning political, economic, or general-interest areas in Japan or Manchukuo.[34]

In May 1936 a long article entitled "The Army's Revolt in Tokyo" appeared in Karl Haushofer's magazine *Zeitschrift für Geopolitik*. It bore the by-line "R. S." Sorge had arranged with Haushofer not to publish his material under his full name, since he wanted to avoid having the name Richard Sorge become too well known in Germany, where he had an unfavorable record.[35] But he could bask in the knowledge that he had established himself with Haushofer. So much for Sorge the German journalist.

For the Soviet spy Sorge, this was the first real test of strength, and he came through magnificently. He knew the mettle of Ozaki and Miyagi, and Moscow knew his. For the reports most important to Sorge went to the Fourth Department. (Because Clausen's radio was not yet ready for such a heavy load, he sent this bulky material by courier.[36])

The February 26 Incident launched the Sorge spy ring as did no other single event. From this date forward the *apparat* gathered operational momentum. Sorge's coverage of the rebellion and its aftermath reflected his ability to absorb and refine the information his assistants brought him, his gift for turning events to his advantage, and his talent for playing both ends against the middle. And by increasing his knowledge, he grew in power and prestige.

CHAPTER 15

"HOT AFTER SOME SORT OF QUEER ENTERPRISE"

The February 26 Incident did not occupy the whole of Miyagi's attention. He strove mightily to secure accurate information on a number of important subjects. His first task was to serve as a channel between Sorge and Ozaki. In that capacity he met with Ozaki once a month in such places as restaurants and teahouses.[1]

Miyagi's second and more significant duty was to gather intelligence on his own. To help him cover as wide a field as possible, he built up a formidable subring of individuals who worked with and for him.

One of his first and most valuable recruits was Ms. Fusako Kuzumi, "a dedicated, brave underground worker for the Communist party in Japan."[2] Ms. Kuzumi was born in Okayama Prefecture in 1888. Her marriage to a Christian minister had ended in divorce in 1920. At the time she was at least skirting the edges of the Communist movement, being well known among the party members at Waseda University in Tokyo. By August of the next year she had moved in with a leading Communist, Shiro Mitamura, and she lived with him long enough to attain the status of a common-law wife. Long active in labor movements, she joined the Communist Party in November 1927 and was appointed to the Hokkaido District Committee.

A wholesale arrest of Communist leaders in April 1929 put Ms. Kuzumi in jail for five years. A large number of her fellow prisoners renounced their Communist faith, and upon reading of their recantations, she joined them.[3] Kawai, who knew her quite well, considered her more a humanist than a theorist.[4] Nevertheless, she drifted back into the movement and met Miyagi in March 1936 through a number of mutual friends. He lost no time in recruiting this promising contact to help him with the February 26 Incident and to secure the benefit of her many leftist associations.[5] Ms. Kuzumi was a valuable addition to Miyagi's forces, and he grew to prize her friendship and assistance.

Among other things she immediately set about rounding up new agents and sounding out prospects. She promptly tipped off Tokutaro Yasuda, Miyagi's physician, that his patient was a Communist agent. This was no news to the doctor. Miyagi had first visited Yasuda in January 1935. "Friends have told me that one may consult you on other matters besides ill-nesses," Miyagi murmured. Yasuda was quite a large fish for Miyagi to have hooked. He had a good practice in a fashionable location and was to become a well-known anthropologist and historian, the author of a five-volume history of humankind. In possibly romanticized reminiscences, Yasuda claimed that on that very first visit he agreed to cooperate after Miyagi had handed him the standard party line: "It is necessary to try to disrupt the plans to destroy the U.S.S.R., to prevent a Japanese-Soviet war. We need your help." Thenceforth Yasuda proceeded to feed Miyagi items picked up from his patients.[6]

In March 1936 Ms. Kuzumi introduced Miyagi to another contact, Masazano Yamana. Thirty-four years old at their meeting, Yamana was one of the few members of the ring without a sound formal education, having failed to progress beyond primary school. He belonged to several agrarian societies and had worked for a time in Manchuria. He became a Communist in November 1927. He was one of a large group arrested on March 15, 1928, and soon after his release from jail joined forces with Ms. Kuzumi.

Miyagi gave Yamana 60 yen a month for the next two years, his explanation being, "I did not intend to use him in connection with our group except to learn something about Japan's agrarian problems, but after he became connected with the Current Politics Society and began to bring me news about political and economic affairs, I started to make use of him. . . ."[7]

Miyagi sent Yamana to Hokkaido to report on the army's

buildup there, the location and equipment of airports, and conditions in the agricultural villages. Yamana monitored rumors that army camps were being built or had been built near the Russian border in Karafuto.*[8]

As the next step in the chain reaction, Yamana introduced Miyagi to Ugenda Taguchi, who evidently had some source of military information. Born in 1902 in Hokkaido, Taguchi spent some time at the Oriental University, transferring to Meiji Gakuin. Apparently academic life did not suit him, for he quit before graduating and joined a labor union in Sapporo, a hotbed of Communist activity. He became a party member in 1927, was sentenced to three years' imprisonment for subversion in March 1928, but was freed on good behavior in November 1929, when he moved to Tokyo.[9]

Miyagi had his doubts about Taguchi, and Ms. Kuzumi warned him that Taguchi was "unsuitable for espionage"; but he took him on in the hope that he would be useful in reporting on economic matters concerning Hokkaido. Miyagi's remarks about Taguchi are revealing, perhaps more so of Miyagi than of his Hokkaido agent: "He has already arranged to set up a peat factory in Manchuria. According to my standards he was not a genuine communist because he was going to Manchuria to make money. He was always hot after some sort of queer enterprise. . . ."[10] To Miyagi no one who joined the movement from other than ideological motives was a genuine Communist. Sorge had this to say about Taguchi:

> Miyagi had a connection of long standing with a man from Hokkaido who provided much detailed information on Hokkaido and, sometimes, Sakhalin. The information was chiefly on military matters. Occasionally this source supplied economic information. . . .
>
> According to Miyagi's story about this source, he was a friend of many years' standing who had had Leftist tendencies for a long time. However,

* Karafuto, the southern portion of Sakhalin Island, was then part of Japan.

I understood from what I heard that he had abandoned a positive political stand long before and
was now engaged strictly in business. . . . The
man was obviously engaged in the fishing business
in Hokkaido.[11]

Another assistant Miyagi recruited in 1936 was Takashi
Hashimoto, who had just returned from Manchuria. Because
Miyagi had been working on the question of how many troops
Japan would require in Manchuria if it planned to attack Russia,
he was glad to secure Hashimoto, who had firsthand infor-
mation.[12]

That summer Hashimoto brought in a scoop, not from
Manchuria but from Karafuto. Miyagi took a double interest
in that location, for he had heard of a movement to increase
the labor force in northern Karafuto, which might be significant
in light of Japanese petroleum sales to the Russians. Hashimoto
explained, however, that when the government wanted to expand its military establishment in Karafuto without broadcasting the fact, it usually sent soldiers disguised as construction
workers. As a result, the Soviet Union did not know how many
troops were parked on its doorstep. Hashimoto reported a camp
under construction in Karafuto that would be big enough to
hold additional units should the need arise.[13] This tied in with
Yamana's report and demonstrated the reliability of the rumor
mill.

In Sorge's words, "Miyagi's oldest connection, whom
he apparently met frequently," was Shu Yabe, confidential
secretary to General Ugaki, one of Japan's most influential
generals. Miyagi told nothing about when and how he brought
Yabe into the ring, but they must have met very early in the
game. In view of his position, Yabe was a potentially valuable
source of information about Japan's military and political life.
He brought in advice on development of internal policies, Russo-
Japanese relations, and Japan's intentions toward China.[14]

Some of Miyagi's sources were not collaborators but
dupes. Into this class fall two newspaper reporters, Masahiko
Sano and Hachiro Kikuchi. Sorge had the impression that Kikuchi was connected with the military and believed both men

leaned to the far right.[15] Miyagi cultivated them for cover as well as for information. He could not afford a strictly Marxist group of acquaintances.

It is highly unlikely that either he or Ms. Kuzumi, a seasoned underground worker, would have tipped their hand to recent acquaintances. Japan swarmed with informers, and one whisper of leftist activity guaranteed swift seizure. Although technically Miyagi's membership in the American Communist Party had lapsed, and Sorge explicitly forbade him to join the Japanese one,[16] his circle of friends indicates that the artist stood high in the confidence of Japan's underground Communists.

Geographically, Miyagi's operations ranged from his hometown in Okinawa, where he pumped his unwitting neighbors, to the northernmost Japanese islands and from Tokyo to Manchuria. Socially they covered the ground between the confidential secretary to a general to a nobody in the fishing business in Hokkaido. Miyagi combed newspapers and magazines for information that might be of interest to Sorge. He lounged on street corners and wandered through restaurants and bars. Indeed, he complained to Sorge about the amount of time he had to spend in bars drinking with chance acquaintances who might provide him with information.[17]

His personal appearance was an asset. If he neglected to shave for a morning, dressed carelessly, and let his shock of coarse black hair hang wildly, he could walk into any dockside bar and be accepted as one of the boys. A clean shave, spruce clothes, a comb through his stubborn locks, and Miyagi became a suitable companion for any respectable government functionary or reporter. Miyagi could hold his own in any company. His extensive vocabulary and orderly mind enabled him to present his thoughts admirably. He had almost total recall and knew the background and personality of virtually every important figure in the government or army.[18] What is more, with all his espionage activity Miyagi still earned his living with his brush.[19] That in itself gave him entrée to Tokyo's social life, for an artist enjoyed great respect in Japan. Withal he was "a very simple, good-natured man" who looked "very naïve and kind."[20]

By a curious interweaving of fate, at the very time Miyagi's subring was widening, so was the police net. On July 4,

1936, the Tokubetsu Koto Kaisatsu Bu (Special High Police Bureau) was established in the Metropolitan Police Department in Tokyo. The Tokko, as it came to be called, had been instituted originally in 1911 as a counterirritant to the left wing. The creation of July 4 was a reorganization and expansion of the original bureau and comprised in effect a thought police to ferret out and crush subversive ideas.

Tokko agents were career policemen, in many cases handpicked, proud of their outfit as an important section of the police and of themselves as guardians of the Japanese spirit. A similar organization in each prefecture's police force maintained liaison with the Tokyo bureau, but since the provincial bureaus were not in a direct chain of command, they operated through the normal police channel of the Home Affairs Ministry when unified action was required.

The Tokko set up shop in the Metropolitan Police Department building, an ugly structure topped by a tower facing the imperial moat. The bureau was divided roughly into four sections. The First Section, staffed by from fifty to eighty men at peak strength, was charged with watching the activities of the left wing, while the Second Section, of approximately the same strength, took care of the far right. The Third Section, with no more than thirty men, kept its eye on residents of hostile nations, and the Foreign Section, a group of some fifty agents, looked after friendly or neutral nations. This was a very thin spreading of manpower. The Tokko never had enough bodies to do a really first-class job of shadowing.[21]

Whether the police, civil or military, made the best possible use of their manpower and resources is questionable. They spent a great deal of time and effort collecting informants, many of whom were ignorant or unreliable or both. By persuading or forcing so many to turn stool pigeon, the Japanese police defeated their own purpose. Their informers so inundated headquarters with every imaginable type of datum that the police had no time to pan for gold. They drowned in trivia, while Sorge and his men operated under their noses.[22]

Evidence of whether or not Sorge received a report on the Tokko's reorganization is lacking. Certainly it merited his consideration, for it represented an unmistakable indication of increasing official repression. It behooved Sorge and his inner quartet to be more and more cautious about associating with known Communists and fellow travelers, who henceforth would be under even closer scrutiny than before. Yet the very opposite happened. Any reasonably prudent person, let alone an experienced *apparatchik* like Sorge, knows that the more people know a secret, the slimmer are its chances of survival as a secret. With each new member or fringe assistant, the possibility of a mistake and possible detection grew proportionately. Yet there is no hint that Sorge ever tried to check Miyagi's well-meaning but dangerous increase in his helpers. Thus from its hard core Sorge's ring steadily widened. And from its headquarters in downtown Tokyo so did the scope of the Tokko. Someday, inevitably, the two were destined to meet.

CHAPTER 16

"BUSY WITH THE
SECRET WORK"

At the time of these events in Tokyo, across the world in Moscow a brisk rat-tat-tat broke the silence of a little room. The sound was no novelty to Anna, and she was not a coward, but no one under totalitarian skies can hear an unexpected knock at the door without a sudden lurch of the heart. She eased the door open, peered out cautiously, then resignedly flung it wide. A woman strode in, bringing with her the bone-biting chill of an early March morning.

By this time this woman, a German who never revealed her name to Anna, was a familiar figure. Within a few days of Clausen's departure for Japan she had appeared, identified herself as being from the Fourth Department, and instructed Anna "not to associate with other people." From that time on she had dropped by almost daily.

Anna was not ill-treated during her stay alone in the Soviet Union. When she complained that her room in the suburbs was too far from Moscow for convenience, the Fourth Department moved her into a room in the city. By nature Anna was a city mouse and had had her fill of roughing it in the Volga Republic. Various men came at intervals and gave her money for living expenses, so she did not lack necessities.[1] Nevertheless, she was lonely and bored and maintained her opinion that under communism "there is no life, no freedom, and no peace.[2]

Now, on this cold March day, the German woman ordered, "Be ready to leave immediately. A car will pick you up at ten o'clock this morning." To Anna's nervous query the messenger replied, "I have no idea where you are to go—just be ready to leave." With that she stalked out as abruptly as she had arrived.

A short time before, one of the men who came periodically bearing expense funds had instructed Anna to pack and be prepared to travel to a destination that would be disclosed later. So when a car pulled up in front of her apartment building on the dot of 10:00 A.M., she was ready to go with her grim German acquaintance, who rode with her to the station.[3]

Ten minutes to departure time a man approached the two women. "Your destination is Vladivostok," he informed Anna, and he handed her some American money, which he said she would need later. "The train conductor will give you a passport in the name of Emma Koenig," he added. Perhaps the appeal in her eyes touched him, for he told her kindly, "In Vladivostok a big, tall nice man will meet you and tell you where to go from there."

Something in this elaborate plan went wrong. Anna arrived in Vladivostok with no passport but with "a very uneasy feeling." To add to her fright, the promised contact did not show up, so she went to a hotel, where an OGPU representative questioned her sharply because she did not have a passport. On her third day in Vladivostok the "big, tall nice man" at last gave her money and the missing passport. He instructed her to travel to Shanghai, where she must destroy the passport and check with the central post office and the Cook travel agency. At one or the other she would find a letter from Clausen, who would take care of her from that point.[4]

Because of the mixup about the passport and the delayed rendezvous, Anna missed her ship for Shanghai and had to wait in Vladivostok for almost a month before the next one departed. Once in Shanghai, she destroyed the false passport and rented a room.

But her troubles had not ended. The travel agency had lost Clausen's letter. A sympathetic travel agent offered to try to locate him. So Anna was temporarily stranded again.[5]

The Soviets had released Anna at this point because Clausen had established his new radio station to their satisfaction.

When Clausen first went into operation, the volume of radio messages was relatively small. Because atmospheric conditions were best at sunrise and sunset and because Clausen preferred the latter time, the hours from 4:00 to 7:00 P.M. usually found him on the air approximately once a week.[6]

The end of each message from the Soviet Union consisted of three letters and a number, which designated the day and time for the next contact. To arrange this aerial rendezvous, the Soviets employed an old German proverb, *Morgenstunde hat Gold im Munde,* the meaning of which is something like "The early bird gets the worm." The German sentence minus the last word contains twenty-one letters. These were divided into three columns of seven letters each, corresponding to the days of the week, thus:

Monday:	M	T	T
Tuesday:	O	U	G
Wednesday:	R	N	O
Thursday:	G	D	L
Friday:	E	E	D
Saturday:	N	H	I
Sunday:	S	A	M

The next contact was indicated by the three letters representing the day of the week plus the hour in Greenwich mean time, and the date. For instance, EED 36 at the end of a transmission meant that the next contact would be on Friday (EED), the nineteenth, at 5:00 P.M. GMT. The number 36 broke down to 19 plus 17, or 1700—that is, 5:00 P.M. At the designated hour Clausen would click out his call sign XUAC, the *XU* being the signal, *AC* designating that the Ramsey (for Sorge) group was ready for action.[7]

The message code substituted numbers, arranged in groups of five figures, for letters. Because the letters *A, E, R, S, T, N, O,* and *I* constitute about 70 percent of every English sentence, they were expressed in single digits, making the code relatively easy to memorize. Double digits for the rest of the alphabet helped complicate the arrangement for the bafflement of would-be interceptors. The number 94 alerted the recipient that a number would follow, and another 94 closed the number. For emphasis the figures in the number were repeated twice— i.e., 150 would appear as 115500. Of course, a simple substitution cipher would have been child's play for an experienced decoder to break, so the system called for the use of random numbers selected from the tables in the *German Statistical Yearbook*. Thus, the coder could easily memorize the substitution alphabet, while the *German Statistical Yearbook* was readily available and its possession entailed no suspicion. There was considerably more to this system, but these were the basics.[8]

In this period Sorge still encoded and decoded, using the 1935 edition of the *German Statistical Yearbook*. Clausen did not know the contents of the messages he sent, for Sorge seldom discussed the text with him.[9]

Coding of the text was not the only protection the Fourth Department specified to frustrate the curious. Each member of the ring had a code name. Sorge was Ramsey or Fix, Clausen was Fritz, Ozaki answered to Otto, and Miyagi to Joe, while Voukelitch was Gigolo and Günther Stein was Gustaf.[10]

Individuals and positions frequently referred to also had code names, which probably originated with Sorge, for an intelligence officer in Moscow would have scarcely dreamed up Anna for Ott, Richard for Joachim von Ribbentrop, Max for Yosuke Matsuoka, and Max's Successor for Admiral Teijiro Toyoda (who succeeded Matsuoka as foreign minister).[11] This use of the first names of three members of the ring was dangerous.

Such bravado extended to locations. Sorge had set up housekeeping opposite a police station. Stein had chosen a home with "police boxes on both sides of the street"; when Clausen used Stein's premises, he had to sneak around to the back of the house.[12] Now, shortly after having put his station in order, Clausen established himself right under the eye of Japanese officialdom. Located at 12 Shintatsuda Cho, Azabuku, his apartment consisted of two floors of a somewhat isolated house. That only some fifty meters separated it from a barracks of guards impressed him as being excellent cover.[13]

He furnished his apartment with some secondhand furniture and set to work on another transmitter. The walls of his new home being paneled, he hid the new transmitter behind the wainscoting. He also took the precaution of carrying a small piece of the set with him at all times, so anyone who happened to find his transmitter could not use it.[14]

By May he was ready to establish a third station in Voukelitch's house, but to do so, he had to get rid of the clumsy relic of Wendt's days, which was no longer needed and was so big that it attracted attention. He talked over the problem with Voukelitch, and they decided to throw it into Yamanaka Lake.[15]

They removed the apparatus from the phonograph cabinet that housed it and stuffed the parts into a knapsack. Dressed as hikers, complete with walking sticks, the two men set out from Shinjuku Station very early one fine spring day. The whole time they were on the train they worried themselves into a gentle sweat lest their baggage be checked. Disembarking at Yoshida Station, they took a taxi to a hotel near the lake.[16]

A hotel attendant picked up the knapsack as Voukelitch and Clausen climbed out of the taxi. Sagging under the unexpected weight, he asked in amazement, "What do you have here?"

Clausen stammered the first thing that came into his head, "We brought a half dozen bottles of beer."

Bringing beer to a Japanese hotel was carrying coals to Newcastle with a vengeance. No doubt concluding that all foreigners were mad, the attendant remarked, "If you want beer, we have lots of beer." With that he lugged the bag into the lobby.[17]

Alone in their room Clausen and Voukelitch decided to ditch the set immediately. The hotel management was almost sure to report to the police anything unusual about a foreign visitor, such as a suspiciously heavy bag. Renting a rowboat, they rowed to the middle of the lake and tossed in the radio, knapsack and all. Then, considerably lighter in back and mind, they returned to Tokyo. There Clausen recounted his adventures to Sorge, who merely observed dampeningly, "Instead of going that far away you could have discarded the radio in Tokyo."[18]

Not long after having thus cleared the communications deck for action, Clausen had the opportunity to visit Shanghai to arrange for his marriage to Anna. Sorge took the occasion to deputize him as a courier, giving him a packet containing twenty to thirty rolls of microfilm to be turned over to the Soviet contact.

Aboard the train for his embarkation point, Nagasaki, Clausen was acutely conscious of the lump in his left-hand trousers pocket. The little package seemed like a live thing poised to nip him as he parried the questions of the sharp-eyed Japanese seated beside him in the second-class coach. The train was stuffy with the sun-baked July air, but more than heat beaded Clausen's brow with perspiration.

The man had got on at Fukuoka Station, dropped down beside Clausen, and immediately begun to question him closely. From the tenor of their conversation and the man's attitude Clausen assumed he was a policeman.[19] In response to a request for his name and occupation, he gave him the business card of his still inoperative company. The inquisition continued for about half an hour, and Clausen replied to all the probings with assumed lightness. Satisfied that this genial German was harmless, the policeman left the train at one of the scheduled stops without checking Clausen's luggage or clothing. Nevertheless, the incident so rattled Clausen that even aboard ship and well on the way to China he worried in case the man on the train had set someone else on his trail. He kept the film in his pocket the whole trip, ready to fling it into the sea at the first sign of trouble.[20]

In Shanghai he and Anna embraced happily after a separation of almost a year. Clausen told her that he would take her back to Japan with him but they had to get married first.[21] In the Soviet Union their unconventional status had presented no problem, but to enter Japan and take their place as prominent members of the small German community, they had to legalize their union.

The couple gave the German consul general official notice of intent to wed. Then Clausen set about his courier duties. The day after his reunion with Anna he took the film to a left-wing bookstore on Bubbling Spring Road, where he exchanged the password with the proprietor and thankfully handed over the packet. Because it took several weeks for the official red tape to unwind between notice of intent and the marriage ceremony, he returned to Japan after a few days, promising to come back to Shanghai in August.[22]

Accordingly, in late summer Clausen returned to Shanghai, there formally to seal his bond with Anna in the city where they had first met and linked their lot. The German consul general officiated at the ceremony. In the evening the newlyweds entertained a few friends for a little celebration. As the wife of a German citizen Anna was eligible for a new passport, and arranging for this was the Clausens' first order of business. That important document procured, they took ship for Japan, where they made their home in Clausen's house in Azabu-ku.[23]

"Are you busy with the secret work as usual?" Anna asked her husband shortly after they had settled in.

And he replied, "Of course, but just a little bit." He had not yet told Anna that Sorge headed the Tokyo ring, so she was vague in her mind about the *apparat*, although except for Sorge and Clausen, she was the only one who knew, or admitted to knowing, of its affiliation with the Red Army.[24]

In time Anna became more and more involved in the secret work, at first with outspoken resistance, later with resignation, but always with reluctance. For the moment, however, she was called upon only to fill a position in life very much to her liking: Ms. Max Gottfried Friedrich Clausen, wife of a respected businessman of the German colony in Tokyo.

CHAPTER 17

"LOVE AND TENDERNESS"

While Anna and Clausen, awaited their long-deferred wedding and Miyagi recruited espionage assistants, Sorge began to reel in Hanako. He genuinely liked her, so his moral sense had given him pause thus far. Also, the thought of Katcha carrying his child in Moscow made him think twice about initiating what a later generation called a meaningful relationship in Tokyo. A letter he wrote Katcha in April projects a sense of genuine affection and rather mournful tenderness:

> If I am melancholy, it is only because you must do everything alone and I cannot help you with anything, cannot prove my feelings of love for you. This is sad and, perhaps, cruel, as is our separation on the whole. . . . But I know that you exist, that there is a person whom I love very much and about whom I can think, whether my affairs go well or badly. And soon there will be something that will belong to both of us. . . .
>
> Of course, I am very worried about every-thing you are enduring, and if everything will be all right. Please take care to see that I receive the tidings at once, without delay.

He hoped her parents were not angry because he had left her alone. "Later," he promised, "I will try to rectify all this with my love and tenderness for you."[1]

He never had the chance. An almost incoherent letter from Sorge, undated but written in late spring, makes clear that

Katcha had lost the baby.[2] His subsequent published letters to her are of a subtly different quality in that he rather than she takes the center stage.

In a letter to her dated August 1936 he complained of the "unbearable" heat; he was working hard and was very tired.

> Sometimes I am very worried about you. Not because something might happen to you, but because you are alone and far away. . . . Would you not be happier without me? Don't consider that I am reproaching you. It has already been a year since we have seen each other. . . . Even if everything goes well there is still a year remaining. All this brings on reflection and, therefore, I write to you about it, although personally I am more and more attached to you and more than ever want to return to you.

"Personal desires," Sorge wrote in this letter, "must withdraw to the background,"[3] but his personal desires were very much to the fore when he treated Hanako to dinner and some phonograph records, then suggested, "Agnes, let us go to my house. I have something to show you." Feeling no fear, she accepted the invitation. They bought a box of chocolates at a German bakeshop and caught a taxi to his house. Having exchanged shoes for slippers at the entrance, in accordance with Japanese custom, they went up to his study.

Hanako looked about her curiously. Using the Japanese standard, she judged the room to be of approximately ten-mat size,* with a rug of noncommittal color on the tatami. A big desk with a swivel chair stood against one wall. On the opposite side, near the window, was a smaller desk and chair. Against the other wall rested a low couch and tea table.

While Sorge brewed coffee over an alcohol lamp, Hanako perched on the couch, nibbling candy and picking up the details: a typewriter on the big desk, with a nearby lamp rising like a

---

* She referred to the standard thick, woven straw mats, about three by six feet. Their size was often used to estimate the dimensions of a room.

lighthouse from a sea of books, papers, and documents, and built-in bookshelves crowded with books, clock, and camera. The tokonoma (a niche usually used to display one or two decorative objects) held a flower arrangement and painted scroll, but instead of forming the usual oasis of uncluttered refreshment, it also housed Sorge's portable phonograph and various odds and ends. Covering every inch of the walls and sliding doors were maps and more maps, with one little French scene hung among them by a pin, as if it had wandered in by mistake. Floor-length curtains of garnet velvet hung at the windows. It was a truly weird mixture of East and West.[4]

Magpielike, Hanako fixed her dark eyes upon the glitter of an antique gold buckle set with a red jewel. When she took it up, Sorge immediately gave it to her. Then he seized a big Japanese sword from the tokonoma and swung it about, burlesquing a sword dancer. His clowning eased the little awkwardness. While they both laughed, he set a stack of records near the phonograph and began feeding them to the machine. As the music filled the room, he sat down beside Hanako and there, in an atmosphere of German classics, rich chocolates, and hot coffee, pushed her abruptly back on the couch.

His pounce came so suddenly, with no preliminary caress or kiss, that it took Hanako by surprise, and his hand groping at her skirt alarmed her. She pushed violently at his circling arm and cried out, "*Dame o, dame o!* [It is wrong, it is wrong!]"

Sorge's lips brushed Hanako's ivory ear, and he whispered, "Why?"[5]

But he was too experienced to mistake real agitation for coquetry. Seeing tears flood Hanako's frightened eyes, he immediately released her and helped her up courteously. She adjusted her skirt, burning with embarrassment, and muttered like a sulky child, "I want to go home."

Sorge said, "I will see you as far as the top of the hill."

They walked in silence through the dark, quiet streets until he halted abruptly and asked, "Will you have dinner with me again sometime?" Hanako nodded and agreed. Sorge hailed a cruising taxi and handed her into it, giving her the cab fare. Peering through the window, Hanako thought that his face looked very sad.[6]

Not an introspective woman, Hanako might have had some difficulty in explaining even to herself why she had repelled Sorge's advances instinctively. She was not an innocent girl, and although not in love with him, she liked him very much. She was not angry with him; having accepted his gifts and shown a preference for his company, she could not in good conscience charge him with presumption.

By no means had Sorge given up. Once again, shortly after his rejection, he asked Hanako to go home with him. Once again she got in a taxi with him without any fear.

She had no cause for alarm. Sorge was too much of a man to take a woman against her will. However, he would exercise every iota of his charm and sex appeal to make sure her will marched with his. On this occasion he decided something stronger than coffee might not be amiss. He poured her a cordial and mixed himself a stiff highball. Once more they climbed to the study. Accepting a Turkish cigarette, Hanako noted several books on a special subject. "Do you read Japanese ancient history?" she asked.

"I have studied it," Sorge replied. "You may read them if you wish."

Hanako smiled doubtfully. "Ancient Japanese is very difficult," she said.

Well mounted on his hobby, Sorge launched into an enthusiastic lecture on the Japanese classics. He had particular praise for *The Tale of Genji,* which he urged her to read in modern translation. Gravely she promised to do so, thinking, "What an extraordinary conversation!"[7] It was indeed. Picture James Bond alone with a Folies Bergère beauty, earnestly discussing the *Chanson de Roland.*

Although both protagonists had lively senses of humor, neither saw anything amusing in this situation. Sorge was simply being Sorge, and whatever else he might mock, he always took himself seriously. Hanako was acutely embarrassed that a foreigner should know so much more than she about her country's classics. If only she had not wasted her time reading so many Russian and French novels!

As if sensing her discomfiture, Sorge brought out the record player, and while the music spun its magic, Hanako taught him a few words of Japanese. She had just about concluded that he had no designs on her when suddenly he pulled her into his arms.[8]

Hanako's principal characteristic was an unadorned honesty, and in this moment of decision she was honest with herself. Sorge was over forty; she, in her mid-twenties. "I wonder if I came here expecting this to happen?" she asked herself silently, gazing questioningly into the compelling blue eyes near hers. Sorge had already declared his intentions. By accepting his second invitation, in effect she had accepted the man. So she made no protest as Sorge lifted her in his arms and carried her to the bed, but she closed her eyes tightly.

When she opened them, Sorge was smiling at her tenderly. She touched his hand, and he snuggled her close, kissing her gently. All the love she had not felt for him before welled up in her heart.[9] From this point her lot would be linked to Sorge's. What was to him a pleasant but not profound embellishment to his existence was to Hanako the love of her life.

Late one evening shortly after this, Sorge came to the Rheingold and waited until Hanako was through for the day, passing the time by sampling Papa Ketel's stock. When Hanako joined him, he was distinctly blurry around the edges, although still able to navigate and escort her through the door with elaborate courtesy. She was disconcerted to find Sorge's big motorcycle awaiting its master and viewed the machine with the liveliest alarm. The combination of a well-oiled motorcycle and Sorge in the same condition held explosive possibilities.

But at his urging she climbed aboard gamely, commended her soul to her ancestral gods, and clung to his waist with the strength of desperation as he pushed his steed into action. With a bang and a roar they disappeared into the night, Hanako quaking with fear as the motorcycle settled into a steady purr at high speed.[10]

This was the first night that Hanako spent with Sorge. She awoke with a start at the sound of a female voice calling out that it was six o'clock. Sorge was already awake and smoking. He went through his customary routine of bath and chest expander.[11] His skin was much fairer than his sunburned face and hands suggested, and his body was almost as hairless as an Oriental's. Old scars crisscrossed his chest, back, arms, and legs, where shrapnel had plowed through in World War I. Sorge could never forget his experiences in uniform; the sight of his body reminded him every time he bathed, and the gnawing pain in his right leg constantly muttered "war, war, war" in cold or damp weather.[12]

At Sorge's suggestion Hanako went to the downstairs bathroom to bathe, feeling somewhat awkward at meeting the housekeeper. But if Ama-san was surprised to find herself expected to prepare two baths and two breakfasts, she gave no sign and smiled at the guest in motherly fashion. They chatted while Hanako soaked, feeling herself drawn to the elderly woman with intelligent face and kind spectacled eyes, subdued gestures and soft voice.

Sorge spent the morning pounding his typewriter. He tossed an occasional smile to Hanako, who had propped herself on the couch with a book. During one of his breaks Sorge took the book from her, riffled through it curiously, and asked her what it was about.[13]

"It is *The Absent Landlord* by Kitazo Kobayashi," she told him. "As it is Proletarian Literature it is not interesting," she added, destroying a whole school of writing in one sentence. He questioned her about the author. The lack of common language made conversation difficult, but he concentrated intently on what she said and caught the gist, especially as her expressive eyes and vivid gestures spoke the universal language of pantomime. Thus she conveyed to Sorge that the author had died by torture. It seemed an unlikely volume for an extrovert like Hanako to have selected.

"Did you buy this yourself?" Sorge asked.

"No, my boyfriend gave it to me," she replied.

While Sorge digested this information, Hanako tried to explain Masuda to him. "My friend is a student," she said falteringly. "He has many books. I read and talk with him. It is very interesting."

Sorge nodded thoughtfully. "Your boyfriend is a Red," he announced. "What does he tell you?"

Hanako was much troubled in case her limited political understanding and vocabulary were not equal to the task. She dredged up the necessary words and pulled them loose with some difficulty. "My friend says that the Emperor is the richest man in Japan. Wherever you go there are forests of the imperial household. We should build more schools and hospitals instead of so many shrines and temples. Farmers and workers are always poor, and we do not need rich people."

Sorge nodded his approval of this sound, orthodox doctrine.[14] It is a measure of his self-confidence and his disinclination to take any woman seriously that he made his approval of Masuda's views so obvious. Then he veered to another tack. "Is this boyfriend your lover?" he asked coolly.

Slightly flustered, Hanako stammered, "No, just friends." But something in Sorge's sardonic eye compelled the truth. "A little more, perhaps . . ."

She trailed off, fearful of Sorge's reaction, but he tossed off one of his shouts of laughter. "From now on, if you want books, I am the one who will buy them."[15]

After lunch Sorge settled down for his usual sleep, urging Hanako to acquire the habit. "If you take a nap in the middle of the day, you can get up early in the morning and work until late at night," he explained. Hanako was not eager to rise with the larks and go to bed with the owls, so she let this go by. After his rest Sorge returned to work and paid no more attention to her until Ama-san brought them coffee at three.[16]

In those early days Hanako's association with Sorge made no major change in her mode of living. She continued to dwell in a small apartment, spending a few days each week with Sorge and going with him on occasional weekend trips.[17] For personal and professional reasons he could not bring her to live with him. Full-time company would have cramped his style. However, he had no wish to hurt her and he kept his transient amours from crossing her path. In this period Clausen was the only member of the ring to enter Sorge's home, and if the light at the front door was on when Clausen turned up Sorge was with Hanako or another visitor and not at home to other callers,[18] so Clausen made himself scarce. But Sorge needed privacy for his espionage activities and for his incessant study, evaluation, and writing.

Shortly after having linked her lot with Sorge's, Hanako traveled to Osaka to break with her boyfriend Masuda, who was now living there. She did not relish her task, but the boy deserved a face-to-face explanation.[19] Sorge was somewhat upset at her departure and required her earnest assurance that she would be back the next day.

She had outgrown the relationship with Masuda, yet her life would not have been the same without him. He had introduced her to the world of books and the life of the mind. Without this early experience she would not have been able to meet Sorge on anything like common ground. Furthermore, Masuda was a Communist, and his views colored her thinking more than she realized. This early conditioning allowed her to listen with approval when Sorge expressed, as he often did, ideas that would have sent another woman scurrying to the nearest police station. As usual, luck beamed upon Sorge. He had chosen a woman who could share his thoughts and whose only feelings for him were love and loyalty.

CHAPTER 18

"ON THE EDGE OF A
PRECIPICE"

Surging rollers of learned verbosity broke against
the majestic scenery of California's Yosemite National Park as
the Institute of Pacific Relations (IPR) met for its sixth annual
conference. In this August of 1936 interest inevitably centered
on Japan. Many eyes lingered on the correct, smiling delegation
from the Land of the Rising Sun. Anyone with the gift for
spotting up-and-coming young men would have noted three
brisk, intelligent Japanese much in one another's company.

First of the trio by virtue of a distinguished name was
Prince Kinkazu Saionji. Both name and title were by his adop-
tion. A Japanese family does not accept extinction just because
the ancestral gods do not see fit to bestow a son to carry on
the line; it ensures continuity by adopting a likely candidate.
So it happened that this man found himself about as high on
the Japanese ladder as one could climb, outside the imperial
family itself, as adopted grandson of a unique, revered figure:
Prince Kimmochi Saionji, the last of the elder statesmen.[1] The
princely house might have looked farther and fared better, for
this scion grafted on the family tree was not the stuff of which
the old gentleman was made.

A liberal, Saionji senior believed in representative government and the genius of his people. During the twenties and
early thirties he assumed that Japan would follow the lead of
Great Britain and enjoy a constitutional monarchy, with the
prime minister's portfolio automatically tucked under the arm
of the majority party leader.[2] Yet the Japanese constitution was

a monstrosity that practically begged for a military dictatorship. By 1936 many Japanese were fervently convinced that only the imperial system would work for them, some were sure that the whole structure was rotten and should be scrapped, and many more were uneasily aware that something was amiss but had no idea how to fix it.

Prince Kinkazu Saionji belonged to the second group. From an overbred rodentlike face his large, protruding eyes peered at his world and did not find it good. The first-class, Oxford-educated brain behind the high, smooth forehead was combined with a shrewd eye to the main chance and a sharp list to port. In 1936 he resigned from the Foreign Ministry to become a secretary to the Japanese council of the IPR. Once China officially turned Communist, Saionji abandoned his native soil for the yellow clay and red flag of the People's Republic. In mid-1936, however, he presented to a respectful public the picture of an intellectual, ambitious young nobleman ensured of a solid political future under the sponsorship of such family friends as Prince Fumimaro Konoye and Yosuke Matsuoka.[3]

Second of the three friends at Yosemite was Tomohiko Ushiba, like Saionji, a secretary of the Japanese Council of the IPR. Ushiba was a well-bred, exceedingly bright young man with alert, cautious eyes. His thin mouth knew how to keep a secret, and he generally selected his friends and associates with care. He had the slender bones and sleek grace of a greyhound, and like the greyhound, he would speed after the mechanical rabbit of fortune wherever it might lead him. Governments might totter, but with a skill and wit worthy of Talleyrand, Ushiba always landed on his feet well up the path to the top. It was Ushiba who introduced the third young hopeful into the IPR. That third man was none other than Ozaki.[4]

On the way to California Ozaki shared a stateroom aboard the SS *Taiyo Maru* with Saionji. He turned on his roommate the full voltage of his undoubted charm to such good effect that at the close of the two-week conference he had twisted him around his little finger.[5]

As the *Taiyo Maru* plunged on her stately way, Ozaki had the opportunity to renew and consolidate his friendship with Ushiba. They had been classmates throughout high school and college, and Ushiba entertained much respect for Ozaki's brainpower, so when he was in a position to bring Ozaki into the institute, he did so.[6]

This circumstance accorded Ozaki international recognition as an expert on the "China Problem." From this time until his arrest the name of Hotzumi Ozaki, if not exactly a household word in Japan, was mentioned with respect in political and intellectual circles.

The IPR was made up of national councils of countries the shores of which touched Pacific waters. By 1936 the institute had accumulated a vast reputation as a forum for exchange of information and discussion of the political, socioeconomic, and technological matters concerning its member countries. It also became a platform for presentation of and apologia for national policies and aspirations. While the organization was unofficial, funded by grants from various foundations and individuals, it numbered among its members and supporters many holding government positions.[7]

It was a target of Communist infiltration. For many years Frederick Vanderbilt Field was executive secretary of the American council. He could always be counted upon to use the millions inherited from his great-grandfather to make up the operating deficit. Field's by-line frequently appeared in the *New Masses* and *Daily Worker*. Corliss Lamont, whose books on the Soviet Union read embarrassingly like fan letters, was active in the IPR, as was Brigadier General Evans Carlson, close friend of Agnes Smedley and admirer of the Chinese Communists. Günther Stein, collaborator with the Sorge ring, in 1942 became the IPR's Chungking correspondent and contributed more than twenty articles to its magazine.[8]

These are but a sample of the many available names. Nevertheless, the IPR had so many powerful figureheads, such high backing, and such prestige in international circles that it was virtually unassailable. Needless to say, it also benefited from the activities, financial backing, and moral support of many non-Communist representatives of the governments and the social and the economic lives of the member nations. Ozaki may have been selected for the Japanese council strictly on his merits as a China expert, though it is possible that someone pulled strings to secure him this position so helpful to the Sorge ring.

The appointment gave Ozaki the chance to shine before an international audience, make many useful contacts, obtain firsthand, inside information on Pacific affairs, and pick brains right and left. Yet his experience at Yosemite was not unalloyed bliss. "The atmosphere of this conference was very aristocratic and also pedantic, and did not fit a heretic like me," he remarked sarcastically. "It was observed conspicuously how exclusive the Japanese were when they were fastened to nationalistic consciousness and what a narrow-minded attitude they possessed; how the British and Americans did not try to cover their arrogance as the rulers of the world; that many of the Chinese intelligentsia seemed to follow and depend upon Britain and the United States. . . ."⁹

But he did not let his displeasure dim his sharp eyes and ears. He concluded "that a basis for joint operation of [Chinese] Nationalists and Communists did actually exist; and that in Chinese relations with Japan, Britain and the United States would probably side completely with China." He could not put his finger on it but felt that this represented "the real mood of the conference." Later he found this observation helpful "in understanding the course of development of subsequent historical incidents in east Asia."¹⁰

Ozaki observed with satisfaction, "The fact that I was able to promote my personal friendship with Japanese delegates through this conference was another crop worth special note."¹¹ Indeed, it would be difficult to overestimate the importance of his new friendship with Saionji and his renewal of old acquaintance with Ushiba.

The delegates to the conference had the opportunity to consider a report contributed by Ozaki. Written in English and entitled "Recent Developments in Sino-Japanese Relations," it was a carefully worked-out, persuasive rationalization of Japan's "special position" on the continent.

He began by admitting that since the Manchurian Incident the relationship between Japan and China had been tense. "One might say that the two nations are standing face to face on the edge of a precipice."¹²

Ozaki urged that his listeners eschew idealism in studying

Sino-Japanese relations and adopt an economic and social approach.[13] It must have pained him considerably to have to assert that:

> Japan's diplomatic policy in dealing with the present stage of Sino-Japanese relations has gradually come to be shaped in the so-called Three Principles of Hirota, now Prime Minister.* The Three Principles may be summarized as follows: First, that China should abandon the policy of balancing one foreign power against another by relying upon the United States, and European powers, second, that China should respect the *de facto* existence of Manchukuo, and last that Japan and China should collaborate in adopting an expedient and effective policy against the invasion of the Reds in China.[14]

What is more, Ozaki, the Sinophile par excellence, in his capacity as Japan's apologist, had to pooh-pooh China's demand for Sino-Japanese equality. Nearly all of China's economic vitality was in the hands of the Great Powers. In contrast:

> Japan has become a World power; yet, a still more important fact is that she is in a special position as an important Asiatic power. . . . It is true that the Chinese markets have important significance both for Great Britain and the United States, but the importance of the Chinese market for these countries is not so urgent as it is in the case of Japan. Hence, it is natural that Japan's activities should be more expressive than those of the other two countries.[15]

Ozaki must have searched through his extensive English vocabulary for some time to come up with the tiptoeing delicacy of that word *expressive* to characterize Japan's actions in Manchuria and China.

He considered China's social and economic organization

---

* Ozaki referred to a speech which then Foreign Minister Hirota delivered before the lower house of the Diet on January 21, 1936.

at least in part the cause of the "multifarious phases and difficulties" of Sino-Japanese relations. He ended with a hope for "more amicable and closer relations between Japan and China."[16]

It was a clever performance and a tribute to Ozaki's neat footwork that he managed to sound like an intelligent man with an understanding of China's socioeconomic structure and at the same time a supporter of Japan's expansionist policy. At Yosemite Ozaki walked a very slippery path. On one side loomed the necessity for demonstrating some originality to certify his expertise; on the other, the chasm of dangers that would yawn for him if he deviated too far from the national line. He could not risk being sent home in disgrace, with the subsequent loss of the contacts that made him so valuable to Sorge.

Then, too, at the time anything that weakened China worked greatly to the Soviet Union's advantage. The last thing Russia wanted was a resurgent, nationalist China across the border. The Russians might publicly deplore Japanese aggression in China, but it was in their interest to aid and abet it because it weakened China and distracted Japan from designs on the USSR. Moscow's friends in the IPR would do their best along these lines, so Ozaki's overt position as apologist for Japan's China policy was not as incongruous as it appeared.

Ozaki returned to Japan established as a promising intellectual. He had more than justified Ushiba's faith in him and had the sleek black scalp of Saionji hanging at his belt. Had Ozaki's appointment to the IPR and his voyage to the United States brought about no other result, the Saionji connection would have been worth the time, money, and effort. The friendship was a definite leg up the social ladder for Ozaki and helped push him into the gravitational pull of Prince Konoye's star.

Ozaki was complacent about his intimacy with Saionji. "In my *Asahi* newspaper era he visited me almost every day," Ozaki explained. "I myself visited the prince's residence, and he visited my home frequently. Also, when Saionji came to publish the magazine *Graphic*, I cooperated with this project and contributed my writings frequently.

"Such being the case, Saionji trusted me well, treated me as a bosom friend, and disclosed secret matters to me without any caution. Thus, as his political position rose, I was able to obtain important information from him."[17]

Saionji became Ozaki's firm friend and supporter. Throughout Ozaki's imprisonment and even after his conviction he made strenuous efforts to save his neck from the noose. Then and thereafter he proclaimed that his friend's motives in spying for a foreign power were strictly patriotic.[18]

The Yosemite conference had a curious aftermath. In September 1936 Ozaki attended a reception held in the Imperial Hotel to honor the Netherlands East Indies delegates to the IPR. During the affair a member of the Dutch colony introduced Ozaki to a German newspaperman, Dr. Sorge. Ozaki looked up into the quizzical blue eyes of the man he knew as Johnson.

Ozaki was not genuinely astonished. Sorge had already let drop that he was not an American but of mixed German-Russian parentage and he was a spectacular figure in the journalists' world that Ozaki also inhabited. The new knowledge made no change in their contacts.[19] Between *apparatchiki* nothing was of less importance than each other's real names.

All in all, this period was a time of triumph for Ozaki. He had moved into the big leagues, proved he could represent Japan with intelligence and dignity, and made two valuable contacts in positions that would place the spy ring in the very residence of the prime minister.

CHAPTER 19

"WORK ONLY WITH SORGE"

"**S**o you are Meissner." The German Embassy's latest acquisition, Third Secretary Dr. Hans-Otto Meissner, grasped the extended hand and felt the warmth of the smile that softened the harsh features. "I heard you had just arrived," continued the friendly voice. "Welcome to our Oriental paradise!" The man tipped his glass to the young diplomat in half-mocking, half-gracious salute, tossed off the drink, and immediately disappeared in a swirl of dancers. Meissner gazed after him in bewilderment, for he had no clue to the identity of the stranger. The man obviously took it for granted that everyone knew him.[1]

Sorge, greeting Meissner with such royal aplomb that July evening in 1936, was relaxing at an embassy ball among his ever-widening circle of German acquaintances. The staff of Hitler's outpost in Tokyo was gradually expanding as Japan increased in importance to Germany. Young Meissner, son of a prominent career diplomat, was only one of several promising Foreign Service men to arrive in Tokyo in 1936.

Closest of them to Sorge was Lieutenant Colonel Friedrich von Schol, the assistant military attaché. Shortly after Ott had introduced them, they found they both had belonged to the 201st Reserve Infantry Regiment and fought at Ypres. Any reservations Schol might have entertained toward Sorge the journalist fell victim to Sorge the *Kamerad* of the western trenches, and he welcomed him into full friendship.[2]

Sorge also considered a friend, if not an intimate, Count Ladislaus von Mirbach-Geldern, who came to Japan in 1936

169

to head the embassy's Press Section. Mirbach brought with
him a letter of introduction to Sorge from Etzdorff in Berlin.[3]
Differences in personality kept Sorge from becoming a particular crony of Mirbach's. The count is said to have characterized
Sorge disdainfully as "the most uncultured fellow in the world."[4]
Mirbach was not the type to paint the town red with a newspaperman, although their positions inevitably drew them together professionally. Heir to an old, aristocratic Bavarian name,
he was a courtly and somewhat exclusive bachelor, faithful to
the traditions of his family and his class.[5]

Sorge had nothing to say of Meissner, but he fascinated
the third secretary, whom he both repelled and attracted. He
did not fit into any category with which Meissner was familiar.
Eventually he put Sorge down as "a gay, dissolute adventurer
with a brilliant mind and an unassailable conceit" and an incorrigible lady-killer. On the other hand, "Sorge was accepted
by everyone, everywhere," and Meissner soon acted on the
hints of his colleagues that Ott's pet could not be snubbed with
impunity. Meissner gained the impression that Ott believed
Sorge was a German special agent. In any case, the young
diplomat found it "hard to resist his obvious high zest for living
and careless disregard for pomp and ceremony."[6]

Sorge was never more in evidence at the German Embassy than during 1936, for a knotty problem was coming to
a head there. It had begun in March, when Ott burst into the
little embassy room Dirksen had allotted Sorge. In great excitement Ott asked Sorge to come with him to his own office.

The door had scarcely shut behind them when Ott ex-
ploded in agitated speech. "According to what I just heard
from the General Staff headquarters of the Japanese Army,
some talk is going on in Germany between Oshima and Ribbentrop through Admiral Canaris. Neither I nor Dirksen know
anything about it. This talk must be something important and
may be a negotiation for an alliance between the two countries." Having sketched the background, he explained where
Sorge came in. Ott wanted his friend to help prepare a coded
telegram to the German General Staff headquarters, asking it
to tell him what was going on. "But," he continued, "I want
you to swear that you will not tell this to anyone else."

Sorge was more than happy to oblige. In the seclusion

of Ott's home he worked out a message to be coded, for the attaché considered the matter so secret that he would not ask help from anyone else in the embassy.[7] Thus as early as March 1936 Sorge had so thoroughly cast his spell over Ott that the colonel trusted him more than he did the accredited embassy staff.

Ott shot off his telegram to Berlin but received no answer. "As a result Ott suffered very much," said Sorge, "and finally told Ambassador Dirksen about it."

"You had better check with them once again, using the army's code," Dirksen instructed Ott, "but I want you to work only with Sorge without showing it to anybody else absolutely." With Sorge's help Ott wrote a second coded telegram, and this time he received an answer of sorts. The German General Staff advised that it could not put details in a telegram and suggested that Ott go personally to the Japanese General Staff for information.

He did so immediately and hastened back to Sorge with his discoveries. The gist was that talks were under way between Japan and Germany toward a political and military alliance, but nothing about them was being revealed in case politicians impeded the negotiations, so neither the Japanese nor the German Foreign Ministry knew about these talks.[8]

This was a juicy morsel for Sorge and his Russian employers to chew on. From the day he concocted the first telegram with Ott until the last moment, Sorge "reported the development of these negotiations constantly to Moscow through wireless. Since at that time nobody in the world knew about such negotiations except a limited number of related persons, the report to Moscow must have been highly sensational to them."[9]

The news of a possible German-Japanese alliance so disturbed Sorge that he decided upon a bold step. "The early form of the pact was clearly a military-political alliance of Japan and Germany against Russia . . . ," he believed, and being naturally "absolutely against such an alliance," he determined to do his bit to stop it. Entirely on his own, without Moscow's knowledge or permission, he moved outside his roles of journalist and helpful friend. To both Ott and Dirksen he argued against the proposed entente with all the eloquence at his command.[10]

He invoked the shade of Bismarck, reminding his German friends of the Iron Chancellor's immutable policy—Germany must never risk a two-front war with Russia to the east and France to the west—a policy that World War I proved wise indeed. Germany would be smart to tie in with Russia and so be able to cope with Britain and France.

He also pointed out that with Japan just coming out of the February 26 Incident, "internal problems were heating up and the inside of the military itself could not be trusted. Therefore, it would be dangerous for Germany to conclude a military alliance with Japan under such conditions."

Moreover, Sorge classified as entirely wrong the popular view long prevailing in Japan and Germany "that the Russian Government was about to collapse and that the Red Army was absolutely powerless. . . ." These early negotiations, he thought, constituted "an adventurous attempt by . . . Oshima and Ribbentrop to obtain their own advancement . . . ," so the whole business was a question of private ambition rather than national policy.[11]

In all this Sorge was dead right, from the German as well as the Russian point of view. But the decision did not rest with either Dirksen or Ott, although the latter was visibly uneasy over the prospect of a military alliance with Japan in its current state of mind and preparedness.[12]

The news of the proposed rapport was not altogether a shock to Dirksen. Since the previous December he had been receiving confidential tip-offs from the Japanese General Staff that Ribbentrop and Oshima had started talks. Dirksen wrote somewhat dryly, "As I still clung to the old-fashioned belief that in such cases the advice of the Ambassador on the spot might be of some value, I resolved to go a little more closely into the matter." Accordingly, on April 9, 1936, he sailed for Vancouver on the *Empress of Canada* to return to Germany with the view to checking on these rumors and also to clearing up his asthma.[13]

The three moving spirits of the German-Japanese discussion were an odd trio to be negotiating a foreign alliance. Admiral Wilhelm Canaris was chief of the German High Command Intelligence Service (Abwehr); Major General Hiroshi

Oshima was the Japanese military attaché in Berlin; Joachim von Ribbentrop had no official connection with the Foreign Office, being directly responsible to Hitler.*

From the heartiness of the thanks with which the Foreign Office received Dirksen's information he realized how completely the diplomats had been left in the dark. "It need hardly be mentioned that the Foreign Office was dead against the pact with Japan," Dirksen wrote. Furthermore, at the time the War Ministry disagreed with Hitler's pro-Japanese policy, being keenly interested in entrenching the German military mission with Chiang Kai-shek.[14]

The negotiations in Berlin proceeded slowly. Canaris, Ribbentrop, and Oshima sent a representative to Tokyo "to scout to what extent the Japanese Government would go along with the military concerning this alliance problem and to what extent Japan could be a strong ally to Germany in the military field." This advance guard was Dr. Friedrich Wilhelm Hack, officially an employee of the Heinkel Aircraft Company, who had been Ribbentrop's agent for his original proposal of an alliance to Oshima. At first Hack was not at all inclined to talk to Ott concerning his mission, but when the attaché told him that he already knew the story from the Japanese General Staff, Hack relaxed. He "disclosed many things to Ott, asking him at the outset to keep them absolutely secret because there would be trouble if the Russians should learn about the negotiations."

One of the "many things" of which Ott and Hack spoke was the reluctance of the German Foreign Ministry to be quite so closely committed to Japan as the Oshima-Ribbentrop discussions implied.[15] Hack's presence in Japan was undoubtedly another reason why Berlin was marking time. Neither Ribbentrop nor Canaris could afford to climb too far out on the limb until he heard from Hack's own lips everything he had discovered in Japan.

A touch of high comedy is added to the story by Hack's confiding to Sorge that Soviet agents had been posted outside the homes of Oshima, Ribbentrop, and Canaris, "that they had even taken pictures during the secret negotiations for the Anti-

* Soon he was appointed ambassador to Great Britain.

Comintern Pact, and that he [Hack] had served as a go-between
among the three officials so that the negotiations could continue
without further Russian detection.''

Sorge immediately reported this chat with Hack to the
Kremlin and believed that Hack, too, was watched thereafter.
(Sorge later claimed that the Russian agents had watched Oshima,
Ribbentrop, and Canaris as a result of his previous information
to Moscow.)[16]

Through the late spring and summer of 1936 Ott showed
Sorge ''very detailed reports on to what extent Japan had military force for an anti-Russian war.'' The meat of Ott's final
analysis was this: Japan's eight or nine divisions in Manchuria
were insufficient to fight Russia, nor could the Japanese Army
as a whole, then about sixteen divisions, withstand a full-scale
conflict. Japan would require considerably more training, better
weapons, border fortifications and the like before it would be
in a position to wage war on the Soviet Union. Therefore, he
decided that ''it is a little too early for Japan and Germany to
conclude a military alliance and enter a war against Russia.''[17]

Between Ott's dampening report from Tokyo and Dirksen's bringing the German Foreign Office into the act, by the
end of summer the more wild-eyed aspects of the discussions
had been squelched. The Soviet Union might have been reassured had not Hitler chosen the Nuremberg Party Congress
of the Workers' Front, held in September, for one of his tirades.
Before an assembly full of German diplomats he lifted his shrill
voice in a ''terrific diatribe against Bolshevism.''

Since occupying the Rhineland, Hitler had given a respite
to his number one whipping boy, the Versailles Treaty, and
turned to his second infallible rabble-rouser—the iniquities of
the Bolsheviks. The Foreign Office had the unhappy task of
explaining away Hitler's ravings in acceptable language without
visibly weakening his pet self-image as the hero with his finger
in the dike holding back the floods of communism.

This time he had thrown a real curve. The diplomats
present at Nuremberg gathered around the dismayed Count
Friedrich Werner von der Schulenburg, the newly appointed
ambassador to Moscow, in much the same spirit that Daniel's
cellmates must have clustered about him just before he was
tossed into the lions' den. They commiserated with Schulenburg

on his "terrible task and the unpleasantness awaiting him in the Russian capital." But Dirksen, delicately cynical, "congratulated him that he would now no longer be bothered by requests from Berlin, that nobody would expect him to press our demands and that he would be able, at long last, to live perfectly at his ease." That is how it worked out. Personally Schulenburg got along well with the Russians and traveled freely around the western reaches of the Soviet Union, happily collecting carpets and icons.[18]

All things considered, Dirksen was glad to return to Tokyo. He disembarked from the liner *Gneisenau* at Kobe on November 9. The very next day his asthma came back worse than ever.[19] Perhaps Dirksen's disease was psychosomatic; perhaps he was allergic to Japan.

Sorge was well pleased with himself over his activities in this diplomatic exercise and hinted as much in a letter to Katcha that October: "I hope that soon you will have the opportunity to rejoice for me and even to be proud and convinced that 'yours' is quite a useful fellow."[20]

He had proved his usefulness to the Soviet Union. The lengthy negotiations between Japan and Germany took form in the Anti-Comintern Pact, which was officially announced on November 25, 1936. It was remarkably innocuous on the surface. It contained three public articles: Germany and Japan agreed to exchange information on Comintern activities and to collaborate in preventive measures; the signatories invited "third states" to adopt anti-Comintern defensive measures, either in the spirit of the pact or actually participating in it; and the pact was to remain in force for five years. In the accessory protocol Germany and Japan agreed among other administrative details that they would "take drastic steps within the bounds of existing law, in dealing with persons who, at home or abroad, directly or indirectly, are serving with the Communist International or foster its destructive activity."[21]

Both parties denied that the pact contained any secret clauses. This was false. In a secret agreement, effective on the same date and for the same period as the pact, the signatories agreed that should either become the object of an unprovoked attack or unprovoked threat of attack by the Soviet Union, the other party would carry out no measures that would "be apt to relieve the position" of the Soviet Union; both would "immediately consult which maneuvers they will use to preserve their common interests." Both parties contracted for the duration of the agreement to conclude no political treaties with the Soviets that did not conform to the spirit of the pact, unless by mutual assent.[22]

The Russians did not believe for a minute that anything so banal as the published portion of this agreement was the full result of approximately a year's secret negotiations. On December 3 Soviet Ambassador to Japan Konstantin Yurenev told U.S. Ambassador Joseph C. Grew that "his Government possessed definite evidence that a secret military pact existed." Sorge's earliest information gave the Russians good cause for this assumption, as did the entire supersecret atmosphere surrounding the discussions. Yurenev complained to Grew that "Soviet-Japanese relations had suffered a severe setback as a result of the German-Japanese agreement"[23]

The pact represented Hitler's first big step toward fulfilling his dream of a worldwide anti-Comintern bloc and set the cornerstone of his policy of collective security for the Fascist states. For Japan the pact relieved the pressure of isolation it had suffered since quitting the League of Nations in 1933 and gave reassurance that it would not have to fight single-handedly against the Soviet Union.

Yet Dirksen's report to Berlin of Japanese reaction, which Sorge photographed and sent to Moscow, was to the effect that Japan could not take decisive action because of internal splits. Because of these, the negotiation to formulate a Japan-Germany military alliance dwindled into a somewhat weak set of commitments, and since the public version was meaningless, it elicited hostility rather than support from inside the Japanese government and various political organizations. However, Dirksen thought that these unfavorable reactions would die down gradually.[24]

Fear of what might hide behind the façade of the Anti-Comintern Pact conditioned Soviet foreign policy for years. The effort to avoid a two-front war was the key to virtually every Russian diplomatic action from the last months of 1936 almost until the end of World War II. Undoubtedly Sorge's initial reports of the ominous trend of the discussions played their part in exacerbating the Soviet Union's preoccupation with a possible secret treaty for which the agreement as published was a front.

Sorge's intelligence work on the Anti-Comintern Pact was a unique experience for him. This was the only one of his projects in Japan that was virtually his alone from start to finish. Neither Ozaki nor Miyagi gave him any assistance of appreciable value.

Just how much, if at all, Sorge's arguments against the pact affected the outcome is questionable. They failed with Dirksen because, in Sorge's words, "he himself was in charge of these negotiations and was anxious for their settlement."[25]

This is not quite true. Ribbentrop and Oshima had been discussing a possible German-Japanese rapprochement for some months before Dirksen got wind of it. Had his Japanese friends not tipped him off, he might have known nothing until matters had gone too far for him to do more than sign the completed papers. Dirksen's principal contribution was to bring the negotiations into proper channels.

Unquestionably Ott's opinion carried some weight in Berlin. His lack of enthusiasm may well have tipped the scales toward an ideological rather than a military alliance. The question is just how far Sorge influenced Ott. Sorge's account of the proceedings gives the impression that he led Ott around by the nose. Yet there is independent evidence that Ott was truly, in Sorge's own words, a "shrewd, able, politically realistic"[26] individual with a mind of his own. Nor was Sorge Ott's only fount of information and advice. The resources of the entire German colony were at his disposal. More important, he had many Japanese friends, including Oshima and Major General Kenji Doihara, the so-called Lawrence of Manchuria.[27] Ott probably knew as much about the relative strength of the German and Japanese armed forces as any man.

Sorge gave Ott information from Ozaki, Miyagi, and the subring about Japan, but when it came to German actions, policies, and intentions, Sorge depended upon Ott, not vice versa. Sorge placed at Ott's disposal his exceptional gifts of analysis, interpretation, and expression, and Ott took full advantage of them. But where German national interests were concerned, no evidence exists that Sorge influenced Ott in anything but phraseology.

An international pact is a complex work of many hands. Full responsibility for even one of its provisions cannot be credited definitely to any one person. Sorge may or may not have added his touch to the final product. In any case, he had good cause to congratulate himself, for he had served the Soviet Union well.

CHAPTER 20

"DANGEROUS POLITICAL EXPERIMENTS"

Throughout the remainder of 1936 and well into 1937 Ozaki spared no pains on Sorge's behalf. Aside from his labors in connection with the February 26 Incident, in the spring of 1936 he did for the ring a few chores related to military matters. He secured from Shinotsuka a general description of all the major arms firms in Tokyo, which he passed directly to Sorge. At Miyagi's request he procured a copy of the *Principles of National Defense*, a pamphlet that offered helpful information about trends in the army. Miyagi translated an outline of it into English and gave it to Sorge with the original, which he later recovered and returned to Ozaki.[1] In appreciation of these and other favors Sorge presented Ozaki with a silver cigarette case on his birthday, May 1, 1936, saying, "This is a present from our group," which Ozaki took to mean the Comintern group in which he believed his name was enrolled.[2]

In those days and for about a year thereafter Sorge and Ozaki met approximately once a month, usually in restaurants, occasionally in houses of assignation. Ozaki made the reservations, using at first the alias Otake but because he soon "thought that might rather show the cloven hoof," thenceforth he used his real name.[3]

A subject of major and continuing interest to him was the progress of talks going on between Japan and China. Tokyo's demands on Nanking boiled down to Chinese membership in the Anti-Comintern Pact, with certain secret provisions, among them "establishment of an Anti-Comintern defense zone in northern China; establishment of Japanese special service agencies, and exchange of information.''[4]

Ozaki's information about the talks came mainly from the European and American department of *Asahi* and consisted of confidential reports from the paper's correspondents abroad and various other foreign sources. These items could not be published in Japan but were available for Ozaki's inspection. Naturally the matter also came under discussion in the East Asia Problems Investigation Association.[5]

Ozaki considered the talks doomed long before they started. As early as January 1936 he reported to Sorge that matters were not going as smoothly as the Japanese would have liked and that the masses in northern China were becoming more and more anti-Japanese. He was not at all surprised when the negotiations broke down late in the year.[6]

Around that time, November 1936, Ozaki joined an organization after his own heart. Hisao Funakoshi, Ozaki's successor-once-removed at Shanghai, had left that city for Tientsin, where he represented the newspaper *Yomiuri Shimbun*. In November he and Kawai formed Shina Mondai Kenkyo Sho (China Problems Research Institute), "for the purpose of carrying on scientific research on the political and economic situation in North China." A number of well-known leftists graced its rolls.[7]

Ozaki became a member of the institute and received its monthly and weekly reports. He "was impressed that especially the monthly report was so left-leaning that even the translated articles in it would be banned in Japan."[8] It was typical of Ozaki to join this organization, exactly the type he should have avoided like the Black Death. Kawai frankly designated it "a link in the espionage ring," which "brought the movement one step closer to its goal."[9] However, Ozaki could derive no possible benefit from membership in the China Problems Research Institute that outweighed the danger of a provable connection with such a frankly subversive group.

Late in December 1936 the arrest-prone Mizuno once more fell afoul of the police, who picked him up on a charge of participating in the attempted reconstitution of the Japanese Communist Party. They turned him loose after a few days either for lack of evidence or in the hope that he would lead to bigger game.[10] However, Ozaki did not heed the warning and drop Mizuno for the good of the team, as he should have done. And the fates not only let him get away with it but also wove a modest laurel wreath for him.

It so happened that the newspaper-reading public had its choice of two fantastic stories to absorb over the breakfast table in December. Any publisher of serious fiction would have tossed out of his office an author brash enough to submit either of them in novel form. But here they were, preempting the front pages, blatantly or somewhat apologetically, according to the nature of the sheet: Edward VIII spoke the words that cost him the crown of England; and in Sian, capital of China's Shensi Province, Chang Hsueh-liang, warlord of Manchuria, kidnapped Chiang Kai-shek, leader of the Kuomintang. The first of these events meant nothing in Ozaki's life, but thanks to the second, intellectual and political circles would soon ring with his name.

Ozaki wrote an article entitled "The Significance of Chang Hsueh-liang's Coup d'État." Drawing on his studies of Sinology and observations made at the IPR conference, he made a prediction that was in some quarters in Japan an unpleasant dose to swallow: The Kuomintang and the Chinese Communists would bury the hatchet long enough to form a united front against Japanese aggression.[11] That was exactly what Chang Hsueh-liang's Manchurian soldiers demanded as ransom for Chiang Kai-shek.

A Communist-Kuomintang alliance of expedience had existed in the twenties, when each party needed something the other had to give, but it had lasted only until one—in that case the Kuomintang—gained the upper hand. Ozaki's conclusions, therefore, had historical basis. They also had roots in wishful thinking, for his great dream was a coalition among the Soviet Union, a Communist Japan, and a Red China.[12] The Chinese Communists would fly to power hanging to the tail of Chiang's Nationalist kite. Ozaki never foresaw that they would not immediately hand over their country to the Soviet Union.

However, Ozaki had made quite a coup. To predict and publish in rabidly aggressive Japan that the Kuomintang and the Communists would close ranks in the face of Japanese threats required insight and courage and greatly enhanced his reputation as an expert on China, both inside and outside the *apparat*.

Ozaki's article so boosted his stock that within approximately a month of its publication an *Asahi* editor arranged for Ozaki's membership in the Showa Kenkyu Kai (Showa Research Association). Because of the increasing emphasis on Chinese matters, this organization was adding a China Problems Research Department under the leadership of Akira Kazami. The parent Showa Research Association was formed originally in 1936. Ryunosuke Goto founded this organization, a curious group, being a sort of shadow cabinet for a would-be premier, Prince Fumimaro Konoye.[13]

Despite impeccable social position, powerful associates, and an excellent education, Konoye had a singularly fluid personality. A combination of ancient tradition and modern education had produced in him political and social schizophrenia. He was considered a moderate and as such acceptable to the proponents of civilian rule, yet the military respected him. No one knew exactly where Konoye stood; perhaps he did not know himself. Sir Robert Craigie, British Ambassador to Japan, referred to him as ". . . the *dilettante* Konoye, who, surrounded by the young men of his 'brains trust,' delighted to toy with dangerous political experiments. . . ."[14] Konoye badly wanted to be premier but prudently had refused the honor in the chaotic period immediately after the February 26 Incident. Knowing that he was not omniscient, he was willing to take advice, the reason the Showa Research Association came into being.

Goto, a close friend of Konoye's, hoped thus to draw together a group of reputable, public-spirited men, experts in their fields, who would give Konoye the benefit of their counsel. In addition to Kazami, among the members were political scientist Masamichi Royama; labor lawyer Juso Miwa; sociologist Kazuo Okochi; Shigeharu Matsumoto, the able chief editor of the Domei News Agency; and Kiyoshi Miki, the eminent philosopher. A batch of political economists, agricultural experts, educators, and writers radiated from the central core of luminaries.[15]

The members represented every imaginable political opinion except the militarist; opposition to the military was their only common ground. Yet they had no dynamic, unified program to offer the nation as an alternative; indeed, no overt loyal opposition could function within the framework of Japanese law in the 1930s. And Konoye's subsequent career did not indicate that he was genuinely antimilitary.

Ozaki worked hard for the Showa Research Association. He had known Konoye slightly through his friend Ushiba at the IPR since "about the end of 1936."[16] But the two never became personal friends; the relationship was not analogous to Sorge's with Ott.

Ozaki's direct superior in the Chinese department was Kazami, who had "a fine genius-like intuition concerning politics." At the time Kazami's principal field was domestic affairs; however, he took a keen interest in the Chinese Revolution.[17] Kazami's record was no straight and narrow path. A nationalist in his boyhood, he later fell somewhat under the spell of the Chinese revolutionists. He was to serve Konoye as chief cabinet secretary and later as minister of justice, again maintaining a relatively nationalist position. During and after World War II he made himself scarce on the political scene, and he reemerged in 1952, carrying the torch for Communist China. In 1955 he formally became a Socialist and served a number of terms in the Diet's lower house. From Ozaki's fall in 1941 until Kazami's death in 1961, he stoutly upheld Ozaki's reputation as a patriot. How much of this was real conviction and how much a rationalization, Kazami himself might have difficulty in assessing. Ozaki worked Kazami for all he was worth in the Showa Research Association and later in the Konoye cabinets.[18]

Sorge had no complaints on the score of Ozaki's diligence, indicating his appreciation by a birthday present of $40 in American currency in 1937 and saying, as usual, that it was a gift from "our group."[19]

Meanwhile, Japanese politics marched on. General Ugaki failed to form a cabinet. He never had the chance, for his opposition to the pro-Nazi officers' faction and his ability to get along with the politicians and other civilians damned him in the eyes of the army triumvirate. He tried for a week to buck the system, and many of his fellow generals implored the trio to reconsider, to no avail. They refused to appoint a war minister, so Ugaki could not form a cabinet.[20]

Instead, Konoye became premier. The formation of the Konoye cabinet caught Sorge somewhat by surprise, and he asked Ozaki to brief him. Basing his report on information available within the Tokyo *Asahi*, Ozaki informed Sorge that Konoye's rise was due to the following factors:

1. The Konoye cabinet was "the last trump card of the upper class in Japan, which arranged for its appearance to let it cope with the internal and external tense situation of recent years."

2. This action of the upper class implied that Konoye's appointment would check the "political pressure of the army."

3. ". . . the congressional strength, the financial world, and the civilians welcomed" the Konoye cabinet, hoping the prince could control the armed forces and thus harness Japan's military and civilian strength in a tandem effort.

4. "On the other hand, the military welcomed it because, taking advantage of Konoye's reputation, position, and liberal character," they saw in him the means of bringing about the aggressive national policy they had always wanted.[21]

That each of several different elements adopted Konoye as its own champion underlined his gift for being all things to all people, a talent valuable to a politician but fatal to a statesman. Sorge heard that Konoye "accepted the request to form the cabinet with the premise that he himself would possess the real power and the military would follow him."[22] If this is true, one can only marvel at Konoye's optimism, in view of the fact that the army had just checkmated a distinguished, popular general because he tried to take the lead.

Ozaki cherished his own private hope "that there would be some possibility that Prince Konoye would perform some new role for a new era—that is, a Kerensky-like role."*[23] Ozaki never doubted that the Japanese revolution, like prosperity, was just around the corner.

---

* Aleksandr Feodorovitch Kerensky was premier of Russia between the last czarist regime and the final Communist takeover of the government.

CHAPTER 21

"VERY STRENUOUS WORK"

One evening during those exciting times when Ozaki was enjoying his newly augmented prestige, the Japanese government was host at a full-dress reception at the Kaikan Restaurant. Gold braid glittered and orders blazed as generals rubbed shoulders with ministers and as one official toast after another was proposed, downed, and duly acknowledged with another toast.[1]

At a table slightly apart, newsmen enthusiastically seconded all the toasts. Inhibitions sank proportionately as the alcoholic content rose, and the atmosphere teetered on a knife-edge between truculence and hilarity as the correspondents discussed the Spanish Civil War, now some six months old.

"It's a good thing that the Soviet Union is supplying the Spanish Republicans with tanks and planes, or else we in Germany would not have enough scrap iron." Sorge's voice rose provocatively above the clink of glasses and rumble of male voices. His tone swung every head at the table in his direction. His blue eyes flicked insolently over Vladimir Leontievitch Koudriatsev, representative of the Soviet Union's news agency Tass, who sat opposite him. Stung beyond the limits of discretion, the Russian replied in kind. His words were swallowed in a roar as the rest of the reporters, delighted with the prospect of livening the occasion, jumped into the discussion with gusto.

At the exact point of no return a listless drawl drifted across the tumult. "How fed up I am with all these political tiffs!" murmured Prince von Urach. "Let's talk about women." The tension poised, hesitated, then broke in a crash of laughter.[2]

Sorge's sneering remark was that of an arrogant Teuton contemptuous of Soviet technology, consistent with his public pose as a Nazi sufficiently in the good graces of the party to be offered the leadership of its Tokyo branch. Koudriatsev, who knew Sorge well through the give-and-take of Tokyo's foreign correspondents, stated that he "always emphasized his devotion to Nazism, sometimes overemphasizing it," and Koudriatsev heard other German newsmen in Tokyo praise Sorge's commitment to Nazi Germany.[3] Yet with those closer to him Sorge adopted an attitude of a man somewhat detached from politics. "Ambassador Ott knew that I was a member of the Nazi Party as a formality but he could not have thought that my own view of life and ideological stand reflected a genuine Nazism."[4]

In this little incident, Sorge appeared at his tiresome worst following immediately upon Sorge at his brilliant best—Sorge of the narrowly averted drunken brawl following upon Sorge of the Anti-Comintern Pact.

Besides combining in one person the dedicated Soviet spy and the trusted, if unofficial, adviser to Hitler's embassy in Tokyo, Sorge was a mass of many contradictions.

One aspect of his complex personality was the journalist who not only kept a number of official and unofficial clients happy but also strove to improve the extent and quality of his background knowledge. At this point in his career Sorge traveled extensively. On Sundays he hiked into the country west of Atami "to inspect the rice crop in all seasons and under varying conditions." He also visited Nara and Kyoto frequently, covering Kobe, Osaka, Shikoku, and the Inland Sea, following the Kyushu coast to Kagoshima. No member of his ring ever accompanied him on these occasions, and he did no spying on such trips, which he undertook "to obtain a better knowledge of the country and its people; to provide a substantial intuitive basis for my study of history and economics."[5]

Two projects dating from the summer of 1937 were typical of Sorge's literary output in this middle period of his life in Japan. One was a study of Japanese agricultural products, which he undertook at the request of General Thomas. For source material he used English and German translations of various Japanese books and statistics, together with items from magazines devoted to economics.[6] This article was one reason why in the summer of 1937 Sorge asked Miyagi to gather agricultural material along with the usual military information. Among Miyagi's findings were a detailed map of Japan showing rice-raising areas and the conclusion that the peasantry was solidly behind government policy.[7]

Sorge's article covered tenant-landlord relations, living conditions on the farms, demands of agrarian organizations, the function of the middleman, and farmers' debts. It was a straightforward, intelligent bit of research and presentation. General Thomas was delighted with it and urged Sorge to produce more of the same.[8]

The other article typical of Sorge's resources appeared in June in *Die Wehrmacht*, the official organ of the German Army. Entitled "The Japanese Army Today: Samurai of the Armored Divisions," it was a knowledgeable exposition of the army's traditions, strategy, organization, and equipment.[9] Sorge had a number of acquaintances in the Japanese Army.[10] Whatever his sources, he could never have written that article without thorough study, inside information, and both knowledge of and interest in the material.

Sorge claimed that most of the Western journalists in Tokyo were cool to him as a purported Nazi.[11] But he maintained friendly, if not intimate, relations with Relman Morin of the Associated Press. Once a week, usually in the middle of the night, Sorge, bubbling with good nature and alcohol, would phone Morin and ask him to come to the Silver Slipper, a tiny bar in the Nishi Ginza that foreign correspondents patronized. Sorge usually had a girl friend with him, seldom the same one twice, most of them Japanese but some European. When Morin appeared in the doorway, Sorge would bang on his table and roar, "Bring my friend your cheapest bottle of beer!"

Morin liked Sorge very much. He was "wonderful company—cultured, amusing, and a sparkling conversationalist on any subject, but especially politics and women." He seemed to take no precautions against the ubiquitous police, who watched all foreign correspondents. "He rode his motorcycle everywhere," wrote Morin, "and how he kept from being killed on it after drinking so much is a mystery." Sorge never attempted to pump Morin, who had no idea that his German friend was other than he seemed.

Once Morin needed some economic statistics, and Sorge obligingly translated one of his articles for him. He found it hard sledding. "This is heavy going for the customers, Sorge. You ought to try to get more sex into your stuff," he complained.

"Sex is too important to waste on newspapers," Sorge said with a grin.[12]

Sex did indeed loom large in Sorge's life. There is no evidence that he ever tried to gain any woman's favors by promising more than he would or could deliver. He never pretended that he wanted or would give more than an affair undertaken simply for pleasure at the physical level.

Even Hanako, who remained the center of his personal life and who adored him, had no illusions that he really loved her. Yet to her he was unfailingly considerate and as generous as his means allowed. When, toward the end of 1936, she expressed her lifelong wish to study music, he arranged for her to take lessons with Professor August Junker of the Musashino Music School. "Your voice is alto," Sorge told her. "The professor says Japan does not have many altos; there are many more sopranos. . . . Please study hard!"

Hanako plunged into singing lessons, and Junker urged her to take piano. Her tiny apartment being too small to hold the instrument Sorge bought for her, she rented a house and asked her mother to join her in Tokyo.[13]

It was typical of Sorge that on January 1, 1937—the very day on which Hanako rearranged her life and her mother's along lines Sorge mapped out—he penned a solicitous letter to his wife:

> . . . I wish you the very best in this year and hope that it will be the last year of our separation. . . .
>
> Recently I had a period of very strenuous work, but in the immediate future it will apparently be somewhat lighter. . . . It was very pleasant to receive two letters from you in recent months. . . . In one of them you wrote that you were ill. Why don't you now inform me how your health is and

what you were ill with? I was very worried about you. . . .

You will undoubtedly be surprised that now we have twenty degrees of heat here. . . .

Nevertheless, I would rather be with you in the cold than in this damp heat. Well, everything will be better, dear, when my time is up.[14]

Sorge was not exactly suffering. Hanako was always ready and eager to keep him company, and on the side he combined business with pleasure. Koudriatsev spotted him one evening at the Fledermaus, squiring a striking-looking woman clad in a low-cut black velvet gown. As the couple swept past, Sorge dropped Koudriatsev a conspiratorial wink.[15]

A photograph exists of a friend of Sorge's in just such a décolleté black velvet gown as Koudriatsev described. Her head is turned to reveal an exquisite profile like Greta Garbo's. Her blond hair, swept up in front and swinging free to her shapely shoulders in back, catches a thousand highlights. Her name was Birgit Lundquist, and she was a reporter for a Swedish newspaper. Clausen listed her as a member of the spy ring.[16] Sorge told Clausen that "she was extracting information from well-known Japanese leaders." Her code name, Ingrid, appeared several times in messages.[17]

Sorge later claimed that "Ingrid" or "Olga" was "an old acquaintance" from Scandinavia who "came to Tokyo unannounced on a special mission."

He professed ignorance of her assignment but guessed it to be some kind of military mission. He added, surprisingly, "She had been strictly forbidden to have anything to do with me or my group. . . ." But she sent radio messages and letters through the Sorge ring and borrowed money from him about once a month. Sorge added, "She was recalled to Europe after about five months through a telegram addressed to me."[18]

In late May 1937 "Berta" resigned from the Rheingold, and Hanako decided to follow her example. She enjoyed her work at Papa Ketel's, but because of the late hours and because she wanted to devote all her time to music, she discussed with Sorge the possibility of her leaving. Sorge agreed and offered to pay the living expenses of her little home. She tried to convince him that she would not need pocket money, but he knew better. "I am not a very rich man," he told her with a troubled sigh. "You are a girl who likes to spend a lot of money. You can't help it! But I'll do something. You need not worry."[19]

In view of Sorge's commitment to support Hanako, it is ironic to find him writing to Katcha on May 15, 1937, ". . . here, in spite of everything, it is very hard, above all this solitude. . . ."[20]

Solitude could not have ranked high on Sorge's list of problems. Hanako asked for a key to his house so that she could come to him whenever she became lonely. He agreed immediately, although this made a dangerous breach in his privacy, but told her to ask Ama-san to secure a duplicate key. "I am a drunkard, and I broke the other one already."

Ama-san confirmed that Sorge had indeed ruined the extra key. "Probably he was too drunk to fit the key in the keyhole." But she expressed no disapproval, only awe. "Master has a big power! He bent down such a strong key!"[21]

Hanako effaced herself when Sorge's men friends visited him. Although Sieburg described her as "radiantly lovable and polite," she appeared to him "very ordinary," even "a sort of slave." And he felt sorry for Sorge because he did not have "a closer companion."[22] His sympathy was wasted. Hanako was by no means devoid of intelligence, and if she had not suited Sorge, he would have sent her packing long before. His one venture into matrimony with a woman of his own social and intellectual level had ended in divorce. Had he wanted to try the experiment again, he would have met with little difficulty, for in addition to his prominent position and sex appeal, he could be polite when the occasion demanded. Ms. Araki recalled that in a group, and especially around ladies, he was "always quiet, with perfect manners, a true gentleman."[23]

Possibly the strangest of Sorge's affairs was his long-running liaison with the wife of a German businessman. Sorge made only one mention of this man:

> In my notes with regard to my personal friendships, the names "Mohr" and "Kaumann" appear very frequently. In both their houses . . . I was made

to feel most welcome by their families. . . . These friendships were entirely apart from my espionage activity. They were rather the exact opposite, since they were social contacts I maintained to strengthen my legitimate cover in Tokyo or because I was favorably disposed toward the persons as individuals.[24]

Sorge felt no need to spell out just how close was his relationship with Anita Mohr, for everyone in Tokyo—with the possible exception of Helma Ott—seemed to know all about it. Anita Mohr was not the reticent type.

In her late thirties and her third marriage, Anita seemingly had no thought in her blond head but to be known as "the most beautiful, best dressed and most successful woman with men in Tokyo."

The German colony wives might have been expected to freeze her out, but she had so sunny and good-humored a disposition that she was welcome everywhere.

That she and Sorge should have been mutually attracted was almost inevitable. Yet the reason given for Sorge's becoming Anita's lover is one of the most bizarre aspects of a life outré enough in all its facets. In brief, Ott was enamored of Anita, and the theory is that Sorge planned to be a sort of channel to give Ott access to her. In less convoluted terms, Sorge not only stole the wife Ott did not particularly want but preempted the woman his friend did want. No wonder that Franz Huber, the embassy's police attaché, advised Ott "to take a closer look at those people in whom he placed his trust." For this good counsel, Huber received the only snub of his Tokyo career.[25]

Sorge, too, could have profited by "a closer look" at himself. His conversations with Hanako demonstrate that he could be dangerously revealing with an admiring woman. And his drinking threatened his control of his tongue as well as his health. Indeed, soon it would almost cost him his life.

CHAPTER 22

"AN INCIDENT IN
NORTHERN CHINA"

A staff car from *Asahi* pulled up in front of the official residence of the prime minister, and Ozaki sprang out. He scurried into the building and anxiously sought out Kazami, now the chief secretary of Konoye's cabinet. Ozaki had learned at *Asahi* that the cabinet was to meet in extraordinary session in three days. He did not doubt that the subject of the meeting would be what action to take about the Marco Polo Bridge Incident which had occurred the day before, July 7, 1937. In Ozaki's opinion, whether or not this crisis developed into a second world war depended entirely upon how Japan handled the situation. He believed that when Konoye and his cabinet met, they would hold the peace of the world in their hands, so he was duty-bound to make the cabinet understand its awesome responsibility.[1]

In his agitation he was somewhat incoherent, and Kazami could not make head or tail of his protégé's viewpoint. "Everything is all set," he said soothingly. "There is no worry about it." But to Ozaki there was plenty of worry about it. In despair he hurried to Ushiba's office in search of a more responsive audience. Ushiba, too, had found a home in Konoye's administration as one of the junior secretaries.

Having shared his mental burden, Ozaki hastened off as if pursued by demons.[2] Perhaps he was, for he, along with many another intellectual, had been playing the role of Sorcerer's Apprentice. By such actions as his report to the IPR conference he had helped set the Japanese military broom to hauling water. Now it was painfully evident that neither he nor his fellow dilettantes knew the magic incantation to stop it. The monster might keep on bringing water until Japan drowned and much of Asia with it.

Had the Japanese possessed the will to peace, the Lu-kouchiao, or Marco Polo Bridge, Incident could have passed off with minor damage on both sides. Briefly the background is this: Under the Boxer Protocol of September 7, 1901, the powers with legations at Peiping had the right to station guards at certain points along the railroad between Peiping and Tient-sin. The other powers maintained a sketchy guard and conducted infrequent maneuvers, but by July 1937 the Japanese had thousands of soldiers in North China and conducted maneuvers nightly. The Japanese had agreed to notify the Chinese of these exercises, but on July 7 they held maneuvers without notice. They claimed that the Chinese garrison in the city of Wanping opened fire. A Japanese soldier was reported missing. The Japanese demanded and received permission to search Wanping for him. After considerable fighting in the area they proclaimed their man had been found and asked for a truce under reasonable terms. There the whole unpleasant mess might have ended, but the Japanese chose not to abide by the truce.[3]

The Japanese Army did not want to permit the Chinese situation to lapse into the status quo ante, and as a result, Marco Polo Bridge, like Sarajevo and Pearl Harbor, came to signify the place where a major war started. Thus began what the Japanese called the China Incident, destined to become a long, bloody war that raged for years over a vast territory. Lieutenant General Hideki Tojo, chief of staff of the Kwantung Army, the Japanese force in Manchuria, had suggested to the General Staff about a month previously that the time might be ripe for a major offensive against the Chinese, to precede war with the Soviet Union. Within twenty-four hours Kwantung Army troops were on the way to the scene.

On July 11 the cabinet decided to postpone mobilization within the homeland but did nothing to halt the Kwantung Army. On July 27, in an address to the Diet, Konoye made the usual smooth protests that Japan coveted no Chinese territory, that it wanted only "cooperation and mutual assistance—a contribution from China to Far Eastern culture and prosperity." Then he slipped the brass knuckles into his velvet glove: Local solutions to Chinese problems would not suffice; Japan must "obtain a fundamental solution of Sino-Japanese relations."[4]

The Marco Polo Bridge Incident was so important that Sorge put all the members of his ring to work to determine the reasons for it and its potential consequences. In this case his position was the opposite of what it had been in the Anti-Comintern Pact emergency. He could expect no information of any importance through the German Embassy: ". . . there was not a single expert on Chinese affairs in the Embassy; neither Dirksen nor Ott were [sic] versed in these problems and there were almost none in the Embassy who were familiar with China." Sorge continued, "Such being the case, when the China Incident broke out in July 1937, the Incident was something unexpected and unknown to all the people in the Embassy. And not a single person could tell about its causes and its prospects for the future." So his highly placed German friends looked to Sorge for explanations and interpretations. Thanks to his Japanese associates, he did not fail.[5]

"The Japanese Army states that it wants to solve the problem on the local level," Miyagi reported skeptically. "But the military plans to occupy three provinces in North China. . . ." He thought the entire affair a deliberate plot to shift public attention from Japan's domestic problems to a spectacular action abroad. "And Japan can't face Soviet Russia," continued Miyagi, "so she turned her attention to China."[6]

In search of specific data Miyagi dispatched Yamana and Hashimoto to seek intelligence on such items as troop strength and aviation equipment in place at various airfields. Although each man carried out Miyagi's instructions, neither brought back news of particular interest.[7]

It was a bit early for anything definite of a military nature. Taking the Marxist economic viewpoint, Miyagi believed that the head of steam built up through years of inflation had broken out in "the form of military action and was directed to China which was weakest." But he admitted that the "emotional anti-Japanese movement of the Chinese since the Manchurian Incident" had not helped matters.[8]

To a certain extent, Ozaki also believed that the Marco Polo Bridge affair was an extension of the Manchurian Incident and that the army had deliberately created this latest crisis.[9] In the four days between the initial flare-up and the cabinet meeting, opinion in the government on what course to pursue was divided. Foreign Minister Koki Hirota wanted to isolate the clash and deal with it as an individual case. Others had what Ozaki called "a positive opinion." Konoye kept his thoughts to himself. Ozaki had no hope that Hirota would prevail. The Japanese Army had been waiting for years for just such a chance. Ozaki explained:

> . . . I thought that the problem of northern China
> had been hanging since 1934 and Japan intended
> to provoke such an incident in northern China. . . .
> the Marco Polo Incident was provoked by military
> plan when there already was the possibility of war,
> and even if the Japanese government should try its
> best to solve the incident as an isolated problem,
> the military would probably carry out its prede-
> termined policy aggressively, that . . . the incident
> would become a long war. . . .[10]

Ozaki had become so accustomed to using the official Japanese euphemisms that he had lost the ability to call a spade a spade. *The problem of northern China* referred to Japanese plans for brazen aggression in that area; *solving the problem* meant crushing nationalist China into abject agreement with any Japanese demand; and the *China Incident* was diplomatese for the Sino-Japanese segment of World War II. Still phrasing in this diplomatic tradition, Ozaki continued:

> . . . whether she wants to or not, Japan must face
> and struggle with Anglo-American imperialism
> which, just like Japan, looks for Chinese markets
> as necessary for carrying out world policy. There-
> fore, disputes between Japan and China have an
> inevitable destiny not to end simply as problems
> between Japan and China. Moreover, in China there
> is another cause of complication in that a unique
> force, i.e., Russia, has come into it, and this point
> cannot be overlooked.[11]

Ozaki would never admit that the Soviet Union was on the spot with any idea of pulling Muscovite chestnuts out of the fire. To his blind faith, the Soviet Union was "a unique force," above the self-interests that impelled other nations.

He did not underestimate China's will to fight. "China has achieved a national awakening. . . ." he pointed out. He noted that this "national consciousness has been centered absolutely on Japan only, and consequently, along with economic strengthening after the monetary system reform, China would be able to show a substantial capacity for resistance. . . ."[12]

Ozaki had the courage of his convictions, for this was not a popular view. Most Japanese believed that unwieldy China would be a pushover for disciplined, aggressive Japan. As the war dragged on and on, it became increasingly evident that Ozaki had been right, and his prestige grew accordingly.

Not only would the war be long, in Ozaki's opinion, but it was bound to spread. "Now world capitalism has reached a deadlock, and imperialistic countries are compelled to find their way in reallocation of the world market by their strong military power to open their way out of the deadlock. This means that a world war is inevitable and unavoidable. The outbreak of the China Incident is nothing but the beginning of such a world war. . . ."

Having obtained Sorge's agreement with his analysis,[13] Ozaki toned it down somewhat and incorporated it in an article, "The New Phase in the North China Problem," which was published in August.[14]

Ozaki was correct in predicting a long war, but in one important respect he erred. The Marco Polo Bridge Incident did not make World War II inevitable. Nothing that happened to China that day in July made the slightest difference to Adolf Hitler, then contemplating an early draft of Operation Otto, his scheme to take over Austria. And Japan's economic problems were largely of its own making. Many nations less blessed by nature than Japan thrived by fitting their pattern of life to the size of their resources. Both Germany and Japan, while crying for living space, exerted heavy pressure on their people to have children and more children. Of more interest to Sorge than such theorizing was Ozaki's observation that as a result of "the outbreak of this China Incident the danger of Japanese attack on Russia . . . became dim for the time being. . . ."[15]

Sorge's German friends brought him such information as they could. Dirksen received an analysis of the situation from Hirota, with whom he was on very cordial terms. Ott obtained a similar report from the Japanese Army General Staff headquarters. Both "had an optimistic opinion that the incident would be solved in a very short time because of the weakness of the Kuomintang in China. . . ." However, Sorge insisted that "the Kuomintang was not such a weak organization, but considerably strong and therefore the Incident would suddenly become a long-term war. . . ." For the time being Dirksen and Ott remained skeptical, but the situations in China developed as Sorge had predicted, so in the end they had to accept his opinion. As a result, his already high stock rose another point.[16] Dirksen assembled his entire staff so that Sorge might instruct them in this latest turn of events. "It was a fascinating lecture delivered with incisive clarity," Meissner recalled.[17]

Dirksen was not at all happy over the way matters were shaping. He believed the events that occurred at the Marco Polo Bridge were accidental, not because he put it past the Japanese to manufacture incidents to order but because this particular incident was so clumsy. Unless someone had blundered, "it would be inexplicable that the Japanese Army, generally averse to taking any risks and noted for the careful preparation of its *coups* . . . should so obviously have bungled this big undertaking. . . ." He believed Hirota sincere in his personal efforts toward peace but admitted "that Japan must be held responsible for the outbreak of the war with China for the reason that she pursued a continuous policy of aggression."

A Sino-Japanese conflict at this time was highly detrimental to German interests. The object of the Anti-Comintern Pact was to exert pressure on the Soviet Union, and Japan's entanglement in China distracted its attention from the Russians. To add to Dirksen's headaches, Germany's current relations with China were friendly and profitable. The ambassador had many long, earnest conversations with Ott about the military implications. Finally, both agreed that Germany should maintain its military mission to Chiang, thus remaining in a position to mediate the war. In view of this latest world crisis in his own backyard, Dirksen agreed to stay at his post until mediation had either succeeded or failed and canceled his scheduled departure on the *Gneisenau* in September.[18]

In the meantime, Sorge sent Moscow his conclusions on the Marco Polo Bridge affair. These were largely similar to Ozaki's opinions. Sorge further noted that "there had been instances when the Japanese military carried out an expansion policy without consulting the government. This incident was an instance of the kind."[19]

As a result of the Marco Polo Bridge Incident, Sorge became deeply involved in military matters in the German Embassy, which immediately started an exclusive study group, composed of Ott, Schol, and Sorge, to investigate the general subject "The Japanese Army in relation to the Chinese Incident." The purpose of these studies was "to understand the prevailing conditions of the Japanese Army as accurately as possible."

Ott and Schol collected material on a variety of themes, including mobilization plans and their execution, equipment and facilities, allocation of troops in Manchuria and China, battle techniques in China, logistics, aircraft, mechanization, training of officers, the army's casualties, and the wartime economy of the nation. "In addition, when a particularly important battle was fought in China, a detailed investigation and study were made of it and a report was sent to Germany." Sorge had access to all these reports, which he photographed and dispatched to Moscow.[20]

In addition, Lieutenant Colonel Nehmiz, who joined the staff that year as a junior air force attaché, reported monthly on Japanese Army aircraft and the aircraft industry in general. Wenneker did much the same investigation of the Japanese Navy, but naval affairs did not hold as much interest for Sorge as the army to the Fourth Department, so he passed on only some of Wenneker's information. These sessions continued until the summer of 1940, gradually fizzling out after Schol, the most enthusiastic of the three, had returned to Germany. In the meantime, however, Sorge not only was a member of this triumvirate but also saw all the reports of the various field trips to the combat areas which Ott, Schol, Nehmiz, and their successors made.[21]

Sorge's career in the German Embassy offers the perfect object lesson in the importance of a principle of security called "need to know," whereby only those who genuinely need to know the contents of a document or discussion of a problem in order to perform their duties are allowed access to them. The highest security clearance is not enough. Sorge's membership in this exclusive embassy military study group was in flagrant contradiction of "need to know."

Violation of this principle was the one unforgivable aspect of Ott's relationship with Sorge. Regardless of the number of Sorge's Berlin connections and their influential character, regardless of whether Ott did or did not believe him connected with the German government, regardless of how much he liked the man, the bald fact remains that journalist Richard Sorge had no legitimate need to know German Embassy business. Whether the material was classified or not, Ott was far out of line in giving Sorge information above and beyond that which he gave every other reputable German foreign correspondent, and later he paid for it dearly.

In many respects Eugen Ott was a tragic figure. He was cold-bloodedly exploited by a man he liked and trusted, and the career to which he had given his life was broken. Yet he wove his own rope when he made himself an exception to the rule drilled into his head since his earliest manhood. Nor did he stand alone. Dirksen, Wenneker, Schol, and Nehmiz were at fault. But it is doubtful if they would have been so indiscreet with Sorge had not Ott sponsored him so enthusiastically.

CHAPTER 23

"THE CHINA INCIDENT WILL SPREAD"

If one had to reduce the mission of the Sorge ring for late 1937 and early 1938 to a single word, that word would be *China*. Just as Ozaki had predicted, what began as an apparently isolated incident at the Marco Polo Bridge escalated into a major, if undeclared, war.

As the Japanese approached ever closer to the capital, Nanking, a stream of pathetic refugees poured into the foreign concessions in Shanghai, and it looked as though those who boasted that Japan could conquer China in six months might be correct. Shanghai, however, offered no haven to these unhappy people, for fierce fighting raged in the area.

Long before the Shanghai battle reached its inevitable conclusion, Miyagi understood its significance. "Now if the war spreads into Shanghai, then the China Incident will spread into all of China," he told Sorge. "In that case, it will be very difficult to reach a solution on the China problem."[1]

Even the Japanese Navy had a share in the conflict in the Shanghai area. Early in December nine naval planes sank the American gunboat *Panay* off Shanghai and machine-gunned its survivors. Miyagi reported to Sorge that Kingoro Hashimoto* deliberately attacked the *Panay* to see how the United

---

* Hashimoto was an outspoken admirer of military dictatorship and an enemy of party politics. He had been involved in the conspiracy of May 1932 to assassinate Premier Inukai. An ardent advocate of arms buildup and of alliance with Germany and Italy, he was sentenced to life imprisonment at the Tokyo postwar tribunal.

States would react. But this action caught Tokyo by surprise, and Japan acceded to the United States' demand for compensation.

Capture of Nanking attracted much more attention from the Japanese than the *Panay* Incident. "With the report of the fall of Nanking, the general public judged that the end of the war was at hand, and they were intoxicated with the feeling of victory," Miyagi reported to Sorge. "But some of the intelligent people thought that it was too early to view the fall of Nanking in that way." A difference of opinion on the next move arose. Some thought that Japan should talk with Chiang Kai-shek and keep the war isolated in northern China. "But," Miyagi continued gloomily, "headquarters stated that if we do not hit all China now, we may in a hundred years regard it as a very serious mistake."[2]

At Nanking the world had an object lesson in just how bestial the human race can be if it really tries. Ozaki did not protest. He had displayed courage and judgment in warning his countrymen that in attacking China they might have engaged in a much more difficult undertaking than anticipated, but farther than that he did not go. He had developed to a fine art the knack of standing out just enough to be noticeable and not enough to arouse suspicious resentment in a nation of conformists.

Thanks to his expertise in Chinese matters, he scrambled one more rung up the professional ladder, succeeding Kazami as chief of the China Department of the Showa Research Association, a post he held until the association folded in 1940. The China Department met once a month and was a fertile source of ideas for Ozaki to pass along to Sorge. Another useful contact was a gathering of journalists knowledgeable about Chinese affairs, sponsored by the Planning Department of the Foreign Ministry, which wanted informed opinion on the "China Incident." He obtained fairly good information from this group's monthly meetings to hand on to Sorge.[3]

Meanwhile, German efforts to mediate between Japan and China absorbed Sorge and his friends at the embassy. In late autumn of 1937 a representative of the Japanese Army's General Staff visited Ott to inquire whether or not Germany would be willing to mediate. If so, the only mediator satisfac-

tory to Japan was Hitler. Ott "reported this proposal to Dirksen
and at the same time to the German Government." Berlin
replied: "It is impossible that Hitler himself will actively participate in the arbitration between Japan and China. However,
he can play the role of a postbox . . . and arbitrate by letting
both sides know each other's intention." The Foreign Ministry
also wanted to know Japan's peace terms.[4] In other words, *der
Führer,* playing it cool, was not at all averse to appearing before
an admiring world as the dove of peace. But he did not care
to be associated directly with a failure.

Berlin informed Chiang Kai-shek through the German
ambassador to China that the Japanese were ready to enter into
peace negotiations. Naturally suspicious, Chiang replied that
he was willing to talk peace but wanted to know Japan's demands. The ambassador forwarded Chiang's answer to Tokyo,
and Ott carried it to the General Staff. Fairly beaming with
geniality, Ott's Japanese Army buddies assured him "that Japan
would not present any particularly excessive demands and . . .
would only demand political reformulation in northern China
and Shanghai. . . ."[5]

In everyday language, that meant ceding those areas to
Japan. This would seat Japan firmly in the Soviet Union's
backyard, with a never-failing stream of stalwart Chinese manpower at its disposal, a prospect not in the least pleasing to the
Russians. Therefore, when Ott talked over this proposal with
Sorge, the latter tried to dampen his enthusiasm. He emphasized
that the Japanese would not stop at that point "but would
increase their demands more and more later on"—a reasonable
assumption under the circumstances. Ott disagreed.[6]

Back through channels went the General Staff's reply to
Chiang, and in due course back came his answer. The proposal
was good in itself, but it was only the General Staff's opinion,
therefore not reliable. He would appreciate "more official and
responsible guarantees." Upon receipt of this snub the Japanese
had to put the problem into the hands of the Foreign Ministry,
where it belonged. So Dirksen took Chiang's reply to his friend
Hirota, who advised him that peace conditions had not yet been
determined. They were just about to hold a meeting to make
the decision. Hirota told Dirksen off the record that he did not

believe Japanese demands would be excessive. Dirksen replied cautiously he would like to be shown "more concrete terms."[7]

The cabinet meeting of which Hirota spoke took place in mid-January. In the meantime, the Japanese victory at Shanghai and the fall of Nanking put an entirely different complexion on the matter, and the negotiations died on the vine.

Dirksen showed Sorge the reports he sent to the German government. In each case Sorge radioed a summary to the Fourth Department, then photographed the entire report and sent it to Moscow by courier. The major points he made, "as those in which Russia might be most interested," were three: In the early stages of the negotiations "Japan intended to go to the north, that is, toward Russia, after concluding a peace treaty with Chiang Kai-shek"; by comparing the demands each side would present, Moscow could estimate the respective national power of Japan and China; when the discussions fell through, the China Incident would be prolonged for a long time.[8]

Early in 1938 Sorge made a courier run to Hong Kong and met Ozaki, who was there on an *Asahi* assignment and also picking up information for the ring.[9]

Sorge was kept exceedingly busy on this trip, for he had legitimate business to transact as a courier for Ott, met with his Moscow contact, and also collected enough information and impressions for a two-part article, part of which was "somewhat secret," entitled "Hong Kong and Southwest China in the Japanese-Chinese Conflict." This he sent to General Thomas through Ott. The article appeared in Haushofer's *Zeitschrift für Geopolitik.*[10]

But this was small change compared to the prize that came Ozaki's way as a result of his expertise on China.

In November 1937 Ozaki had become a charter member of the famous Breakfast Group (*Asameshi Kai*), an assortment of writers and scholars "versed in politics and economy." Originally the group consisted only of Ushiba and Kishi, Konoye's two secretaries and its leading spirits, plus Ozaki and Prince Kinkazu Saionji, whom Ozaki had charmed at the Institute of Pacific Relations conference.[11]

These men and others who joined later constituted a sort

of kitchen cabinet to give Konoye the benefit of their experience and ideas. It was not, as it is sometimes called, a society, which implies a formal organization, but was simply a group of men with a common goal.[12] From mid-1938 they got together around twice a month. In 1939 they met weekly. They had breakfast together and exchanged opinions on politics, diplomacy, economics and current problems. During the first Konoye cabinet they met at the secretariat office. Sometimes Kazami sat in on these sessions, but Konoye never attended. Naturally this organization was a valuable source of information for Ozaki, and he remarked complacently, "It can be said that this meeting made me achieve a substantial result for my spy activity."[13]

Nevertheless, he had no voice in policymaking; he was just one of a number of bright young men selected for their expertise in some area who placed their counsel at the premier's disposal. It would be a mistake to picture Ozaki at this point as a potent force behind the scenes of the Japanese government.

CHAPTER 24

"SECRET AND IMPORTANT"

As 1937 began, a certain amount of emotional shaking down took place on the Clausen home front. Years of living with Clausen as his mistress had denied Anna the happy self-confidence that would have helped her adjust to a new life in a new country. Periodically she brought up the idea that he had married her only for camouflage. All very well for a reporter like Sorge to be a bachelor, but a prosperous businessman would be conspicuous if unmarried.

"I will go away," Anna threatened when her devils plagued her.

Clausen, who did not understand and was too inarticulate to reassure her if he had, could only reply miserably, "You must not."

"There is no need for my being here, is there?" prodded Anna. "What should I do? I don't have anything to do, do I?"

To which Clausen replied exactly the wrong thing: "You have to be at home as a lookout."

"Lookout for what?" demanded Anna suspiciously.

"Lookout for me!" answered her husband, reasonably, if inadequately.[1]

But the couple's mutual devotion was sound enough to survive Anna's insecurity and Clausen's clumsiness, and Anna took up the role of lookout efficiently. Most of the daytime hours Clausen spent at his office, but two or three times a week found him at his radio set, commencing with the late-afternoon hours, which he preferred. "You keep watching the street outside from the window of the bedroom on the second floor,"

205

he instructed his wife. "If someone should come, let me know. If the person is related to the business you won't need to. But if any strange person should come, let me know."[2]

So Anna took up her post on the second floor, which commanded a clear view of the street. Lest the maid become suspicious, she sent the girl home or told her that the master was sleeping so she must not work upstairs. Occasionally, when Clausen did not feel the need of a lookout, he sent the two women out "for a couple of hours to do shopping or to see a show."[3]

By this time Anna realized that Sorge headed the spy ring. He kept the telephone jangling constantly, and if Clausen was not at home, he would order Anna "in a commanding tone and very arrogantly, 'When your husband comes back tell him to come over here immediately!' "[4]

Meissner had pigeonholed Clausen as "an oaf out of his class."[5] But this particular "oaf" had a gift which even a well-born man of the diplomat class should not despise: the ability to buckle down to a job diligently and well. By this time M. Clausen Shokai, Clausen's blueprint machinery company, had opened for business. He had set it up entirely as a camouflage but grew genuinely interested in it.[6] He carried a good product for which there was a real need. This circumstance, coupled with Clausen's good sense and dutiful nature, almost guaranteed success.

Soon the Clausens had prospered sufficiently to rent a cottage at the seashore resort of Chigasaki, which they used in the summers of 1937 and 1938. Clausen dug a hole under the cottage, which was built on pilings above the sand, put his transmitter in a box, and buried the box in the hole. Contrary to legend, he never sent messages from aboard a boat. He transmitted from the house and in the open air at other places within sixty to eighty kilometers of Tokyo. For all these wanderings Clausen needed a car, so he took the calculated risk of procuring a driver's license, which necessitated a visit to the police station to have his fingerprints taken.[7]

He had good cause to be self-satisfied, but the fates love to jolt the smug. So it happened that one afternoon in the autumn of 1937 Clausen arrived at Voukelitch's home ready to transmit to "Wiesbaden." Just as he entered the door, he stopped abruptly and slapped frantically at every pocket. His wallet had disappeared. In the clammy certainty that this could mean utter disaster, he forced himself to retrace his movements mentally: a taxi from his home to the German Club; his nonchalant entrance; his unobtrusive exit; a second taxi to Voukelitch's house. Yes, he had had the billfold in the second taxi, for he had opened it to pay the fare. With a convulsive jerk Clausen leaped past the dumbfounded Voukelitch and flung himself out of the house. He was too late. The cab had vanished.

Replacing his wallet after paying the driver, he had missed his pocket. At this very moment his billfold lay in the cab, begging to be discovered. In addition to about 230 yen and his driver's license, it contained a financial report of the ring's operations, written in English in Sorge's handwriting, which was one of the items he had intended to transmit from Voukelitch's home that afternoon.

At a loss what to do next, Clausen resolved to ask Voukelitch's advice, though without mentioning the nature of the report, in case Voukelitch, the blabbermouth, ran to Sorge with the whole story. So he told his comrade only that he had lost his billfold containing a large sum in Japanese currency, his driver's license, and some notes in English on scratch paper.

The two men decided upon a bold course. They would go to the nearest police station and report the loss. If the driver had turned in the wallet and if they hurried, they might be able to retrieve it before the police could have the English manuscript translated. Speed was the essence of this scheme, and Clausen should have sped off like a startled hare. Unfortunately he had other duties. His black bag held coded material ready for transmission, and the receiving station awaited his call signal. Since it was almost 3:00 P.M. when he discovered his loss, he had no time to go to the police station after he had finished sending.

The next day he and Voukelitch seized their courage in both hands and advised the police of the missing wallet. To their dismay no such item had been turned in. This circumstance left Clausen in suspense, until, as the days sped by and no axe fell, he concluded that the danger had passed. This was only one of a number of narrow squeaks which kept him from taking his safety for granted.[8]

Clausen and Voukelitch had become fairly close asso-

ciates. In fact, Sorge's quartet of major assistants had broken
into natural halves: Clausen and Voukelitch, Ozaki and Miyagi.
This was due not to race but to the nature of their duties. The
second pair worked the Japanese side of the street, although at
different levels. As radioman Clausen had no reason for direct
contact with either of them. No question of using Ozaki's home
as a sending site ever arose, and Miyagi's quarters were obviously unsuitable, for he lived in a rented room. Voukelitch,
however, made his home available. Then, too, he, the ring's
photographer, and Clausen, its radioman, had technology in
common, if nothing else.

During this period, when Clausen and Anna had settled
into a happy, if at times stormy, marriage, Voukelitch was
thoroughly embroiled in personal woes. For three years he had
been meeting Yoshiko Yamasaki and was fathoms deep in love
with her. Hanako told Sorge that it was common knowledge
Voukelitch made love to Miss Yamasaki downstairs while his
wife cried her eyes out upstairs. Hanako took a dim view of
Voukelitch, who came to Sorge's home often in his capacity
as a foreign correspondent: "Voukelitch was very talkative,
but he had no manners to speak of." His habit of slouching
down in a chair or stretching out on the couch offended her
sense of propriety.

The Voukelitch situation disturbed Sorge very much, and
he agreed with Hanako that something had to be done about
it.[9] He saw nothing incongruous in joining with his Japanese
mistress in deploring the goings-on of Voukelitch and his Japanese mistress. Either Sorge did not know, or did not tell
Hanako, that this story had its second side. Edith Voukelitch
was dating other men.[10]

From the standpoint of the ring the problems Voukelitch's
love life raised were professional, not moral. Japanese public
opinion frowned upon associations, marital or otherwise, between foreigners and Japanese women of the upper social brack-
ets. If Voukelitch did not watch his step, he would incur the
enmity of the local community, thus closing many valuable
doors and decreasing his value as a reporter and as a spy. Havas
might receive a delicate hint that it could find a more acceptable
representative in Japan than Branko de Voukelitch.

Suppose Edith stopped crying and acted? What if she

marched to the nearest police station to announce, in effect, "My two-timing husband is a Soviet spy?" The Tokko would be lenient with an informant having such a fabulous yarn to spin. Edith could have told much about the Sorge ring. She had been briefed in Paris; she assisted Clausen with his sending problems; she knew Sorge.[11] All things considered, in those critical days the Voukelitch triangle put many a gray hair in Sorge's head.

At approximately the same time as the billfold scare, being extremely busy, Clausen suggested to Sorge that Anna, rather than he, should be the next courier to Shanghai. Sorge agreed and received permission from Moscow. Early in October Anna gave Clausen the perfect opening by remarking that she was thinking of visiting Shanghai, partly on business of her own and partly to run a few errands for the firm. He immediately approved, adding that she could take along a small package for the ring.[12]

"What is in it?" asked Anna warily.

"Secret films," replied Clausen. "When you hand it to the contact man he will give you some funds for the group. You can shop for various things at the same time."

Anna temporarily ignored this tempting red herring. She "did not want to participate directly in the spy work" and feared she would get into trouble, for she had never been a courier before. "It is dangerous to take secret films, so I don't want to do it," she answered firmly, adding for good measure, "I don't like communism!"

"Don't say that!" pleaded her husband, alarmed to hear such blasphemy uttered under his own roof. "Please go! If you don't go, I'll have to tell that to Sorge and we will have to change the contact procedure. In that case I shall lose face. So please go. When you get the money you may buy anything you want."[13]

Anna still demurred, so Clausen pressed her with a mixture of arguments, pleas, and reproaches. "Everything is already decided and there is no one but you who can go. Don't you feel ashamed of rejecting just one assistance to our ring?" He admitted that the films were "secret and important." But he added, "Since you are a woman, if you hide the films under your breast, no one will search there. So don't worry. In case of emergency, you can throw it into the sea." Summoning his most winning smile, he coaxed, "Just once, please!"

Anna capitulated.[14] She harked back to a really interesting subject: shopping in Shanghai. "Then may I buy . . . ?" And Anna reeled off a staggering list of expensive clothes. Thinking, "My wife would fight the devil if she could get something good out of it," Clausen agreed. So he queried Moscow concerning contact procedures and signal words.

Instructions called for Anna to wear a large black brooch and a shawl with broad brown and yellow stripes that Günther Stein had brought back from a courier run to Shanghai early in the year. Clausen collected them from Stein and gave them to his wife, along with some thirty rolls of microfilm folded into a handkerchief.[15]

Anna set forth for Shanghai, reluctant and somewhat worried but trusting her husband's promise that this would be her one and only courier trip. She kept the film in her handbag but twice—just before embarking at Nagasaki and disembarking at Shanghai—tied the bundle between her breasts. As Clausen had predicted, the police respected this sanctuary.[16]

After one missed rendezvous Anna made contact and exchanged the microfilm for $6,000 in Chinese money. Free of the less agreeable aspects of her trip to Shanghai, she started on a shopping spree.[17] Then she relaxed in Shanghai for twenty days before returning to Tokyo in November.[18]

Not long after her return fate gave her husband another scare. One late December evening, when the clock hands stood near nine, Clausen entered a taxi outside Voukelitch's house and stowed the black bag containing his radio set on the back seat beside him. Just as the taxi came to Roppongi, a traffic policeman signaled it to a halt. "Where are you going and what is your name?" the policeman demanded.

All cooperation, Clausen produced his business card. "I am just going home from the German Club and this is who I am," he answered with a reasonable facsimile of a smile. The Japanese fixed his eyes on the bag, and Clausen's pulse accelerated. But the policeman stepped back and waved the taxi to proceed.[19] Lady Luck was still minding the store.

CHAPTER 25

 "FREE RUN OF THE EMBASSY"

"The German Ambassador and Mrs. von Dirksen are leaving Japan in a few days in order that Dr. von Dirksen may recover his health during a prolonged home-leave," the "Social and General" column of the *Japan Advertiser* informed its readers on February 3, 1938. "The Ambassador has been the victim of renewed and severe asthma attacks, from which he suffered last winter and the winter before. He and Mrs. von Dirksen, in compliance with the request of attending doctors, are asking all their friends who might wish to see them off at the station to abstain, for Dr. von Dirksen's condition makes it detrimental for him to talk."

Dirksen was indeed a sick man, if not exactly as near death's door as the crepe-hanging reporter would have led the readers to believe. When the news of his illness spread over the country, dozens of medicines and suggestions for cure or comfort deluged the embassy from sympathetic Japanese. The spontaneous demonstrations of goodwill touched and pleased Dirksen.[1]

His impending departure came as no surprise, for in the previous spring he had asked to be relieved on the ground of his chronic asthma.[2] Before he departed, he officiated at Meissner's wedding, a gala occasion held in the embassy grounds. Meissner wrote a few interesting notes on the subject.

> Sorge and his associates were present, and after the ceremony they came to offer congratulations. Sorge bowed from the waist and kissed my wife's

211

hand. Then came the bluff Klausen [*sic*] surprisingly charming in his good wishes for our future.
I almost liked him. He was followed by Voukelitch
whose polished, punctilious and utterly impersonal
attitude turned a lighthearted scene into a stiffly
correct occasion. Toward the end of the hand-
shakes, Ozaki and Miyagi appeared to offer congratulations. I liked Ozaki, but did not know Miyagi
well. Both were exquisitely polite to my bride.[3]

This event marks the only known occasion when all five
major members of the Sorge spy ring were at the same place
at the same time and free. Of Sorge's presence there is no
doubt, for he appears in the wedding picture, "for once reasonably well-dressed," as Meissner put it tartly.[4]

On February 6 the Dirksens left Japan by the *Empress
of Canada*. Despite the attending doctors' suggestion, a group
of Tokyo college students sped them on their way. Dirksen
spoke a few graceful words, "urging Japanese youths to fight
for permanent peace."[5]

During February Sorge wrote his first missive to Katcha
in quite some time:

> . . . I asked myself if you had not ended up by
> losing patience, by dint of waiting for me. But it
> was truly not possible to act otherwise. . . .
>
> Life without you is very hard for me, it passes
> so slowly. . . .
>
> If you can, I would like you to hold off your
> summer vacation until my arrival: we will take it
> together, because I probably will return about that
> time. . . .[6]

Sorge had reason to suggest that he was about to leave
Japan. His future in the German Embassy would depend upon
Dirksen's successor. To all intents and purposes Sorge had
been a member of Dirksen's staff. He functioned openly as
Ott's political adviser and had his own room in the embassy.[7]
Sorge had no need to bribe a clerk or a guard to bring him the
contents of a wastebasket or a carbon copy here and there. He

sat right down at the conference table, and what he wanted was handed to him. Later he was to emphasize this point, claiming that he had not actually spied in the embassy because everything was freely available.[8]

Since the spring of 1936 he had been photographing documents within the embassy for dispatch to Moscow by courier. This he was able to do because he had Dirksen's permission to use the embassy library freely. This was a central file of all unclassified or relatively low-classified documents sent to and from the embassy. All that was denied him was the ambassador's secret file, which only Dirksen could use. But he had ready access to the service attachés' files through his friendship with Ott and Wenneker. In general, he photographed these papers within his own office, but whenever he feared someone might break in on him, he used any available vacant room.

Such documents as Sorge could not take from the embassy or to which he had only brief access he snapped on the spot with his small Robot camera, which "did not require legs and was easy to handle." When he took documents and other material home with him, he used either the Robot or a Leica; sometimes, when time permitted, he had Voukelitch photograph them.[9]

How long would this ideal arrangement last if the new ambassador took a dislike to him or even cracked down on him for security reasons? No matter how firmly Sorge had fastened himself to Ott's coattails, Ott would not dare continue the official intimacy that was the foundation stone of Sorge's espionage structure in the face of ambassadorial disapproval.

What is more, Ott had been military attaché for four years and in the normal course of events was due for reassignment. In fact, he had been besieging Berlin with requests to return to Germany for duty with troops. So far his superiors had ignored his pleas.[10] But all such situations were subject to rapid change.

Then, in April 1938, came the event that secured Sorge's position and ultimately sealed his fate. Ott received a telegram from Berlin, signed by Colonel General Ludwig Beck: "The Führer has ordered your release from active service in the army. At the same time he intends to appoint you ambassador to

Tokyo. You are to report immediately whether you are prepared to accept the post. If not, you are to verbally explain your reasons and report upon arriving in Berlin.''

As had become his habit, Ott asked Sorge for advice. Sorge replied, ''Don't do it, because by so doing you will lose all of your human qualities.''[11]

At first glance this reaction appears astounding, almost unbelievable. At second look it becomes more credible. As military attaché Ott could maintain a somewhat aloof attitude toward Hitler's regime. As ambassador he would have to follow the Berlin line regardless of his private convictions. Then, too, this promotion in protocol-conscious Japan might mean that Ott no longer could keep up his almost familial association with a mere reporter. Yet the very fact that Ott asked his opinion on such an important personal and professional matter signified that Sorge had no cause for worry on that front.

Ott did not take Sorge's advice. Actually he had little choice in the matter. He remarked later that Beck, a close personal friend, virtually blackmailed him into accepting.[12] Indeed, a threat was implicit in the last line of Beck's message.

On April 27 the Japanese invested Ott with the Order of the Sacred Treasure, second class, ''in appreciation of his services in German-Japanese friendship while military attaché here.'' That evening the military attachés of the Tokyo embassies honored Ott at a banquet in the Imperial Hotel. The United States, France, Britain, Rumania, Turkey, and Poland sent representatives; even the Peruvians and the Siamese were there. Conspicuous by its absence from the list was the name of the Soviet Union's attaché, although a few months earlier Ott had lent his presence to a similar affair in honor of the Soviet naval attaché.

The next morning an imperial carriage bore Ott to the palace to present his credentials to the Emperor. Eugen Ott, who bowed to the Emperor of Japan that sunny spring day with Foreign Minister Koki Hirota at his side, had come a long way from the obscure lieutenant colonel packed off to Japan two jumps ahead of Hitler's long knives.[13]

Whatever Sorge the man felt about Ott's promotion, Sorge the spy could not regret it. His place in Ott's friendship and councils was secure. And there can be little doubt that Ott's close association with Sorge was one of the background factors responsible for his elevation. Not that Sorge had consciously groomed Ott for the ambassadorship. He had given his time and knowledge unstintingly to ingratiate himself with a valuable source of information and power. If his assistance had helped fill his friend's personnel file with favorable effectiveness reports, that was all to the good. The more valuable Ott became to the German government, the better for Sorge.

Events had given Moscow a direct line into the office and home of Hitler's ambassador to Japan. There could be no further question of Sorge's spending a summer vacation with Katcha. With this turn of the wheel, Sorge had enlisted for the duration. As long as Eugen Ott represented Nazi Germany in Tokyo, Richard Sorge must be his gray eminence.

To fill the post vacated by Ott's promotion, and which Schol had been occupying temporarily, Colonel Gerhard Matzky reported for duty as military attaché early in the summer. The "army executives of Germany" had assured Matzky that "he could trust Sorge." Furthermore, he brought a message from Thomas requesting an article from Sorge on Japanese wartime industries. As the local German merchants and engineers had become even less communicative than usual, which he attributed to intensified police surveillance, Sorge asked Matzky to obtain the necessary information from these reluctant sources. Of course, Matzky was glad to oblige such an esteemed colleague of the top brass.[14]

On a similar occasion Sorge asked to read one of Matzky's reports. Matzky told Ott who immediately approved the request. Matzky later claimed that unlike several other reporters, Sorge never tried to pump him. On the contrary, he was always ready to supply Matzky with information and surprised him by his knowledge of troop strength, location, and movements. Moreover, Sorge was helpful on the personal level, assisting the newcomer to find a house, servants, and summer quarters.

But the two men never became really close. This may be because on one of his few visits to the Matzkys' home, Ms. Matzky asked him half jokingly, "Aren't you really Russian? You have a certain look about you."

After a split second Sorge replied with an air of innocence, "Oh, no . . . I come from Thuringia." Some years later, after Matzky had left Japan and the balloon had gone up, he could congratulate himself that he had kept his relationship with Sorge "within limits."[15]

Meissner claimed that the relationship between Ott and Sorge "was now so close that all normal reports from attachés to Berlin became mere appendages to the overall report written by Sorge and signed by the Ambassador. Ott depended on Sorge for Japanese news, gossip in high military and political circles and for interpretations of events."[16]

All of Sorge's newspaper brethren knew him as a man from whom the German ambassador had few, if any, secrets. Steadily Sorge's position grew in strength. Officials coming and going between Berlin and Tokyo formed a shuttle weaving Sorge and the German government ever closer together. Dirksen spoke of him warmly at the Foreign Office and elsewhere and gave letters of introduction to him to many Germans going to Japan. Also, Sorge's friend Prince von Urach had returned to Germany and was hand in glove with the Foreign Ministry.[17]

From 1938 until the outbreak of the Russo-German war on June 22, 1941, couriers came to Tokyo once every two weeks from the German's Foreign Ministry, carrying important military and political documents as well as propaganda material. Each of these official trips included one German officer to protect the courier and to carry out special duties for the War Ministry and for the General Staff of his service. Most were from the air force, but some came from the navy and from the army—infantry, artillery, and tank corps. Nearly all of them brought letters of introduction to Sorge from Dirksen, Etzdorff, or the *Frankfurter Zeitung*. Some had orders from Thomas to see Sorge. These officers freely discussed Germany's problems with him and shared with him their thoughts about the Japanese Army, Air Force, and industry matters. He considered them among his most important sources of information.[18]

Sorge did not just rely heavily upon the German couriers; he became one. As the time for his contact with Ozaki in Hong Kong early in 1938 drew close, Sorge told Ott that he would like to go there on newspaper business. Ott asked Sorge if in that case he would act as an embassy courier. "That's good!"

thought Sorge, and accepted with alacrity. He then secured from the embassy a letter identifying him as its courier. Wrapping a bundle of reports, letters, and films over his stomach, Sorge set out on a six-week trip that took him first to Manila, then to Canton and Hong Kong. Thanks to his diplomatic status, he had to undergo no customs or police examinations. His business in Manila being strictly for the German Embassy, he transacted it quickly and went on to his real mission.[19]

In Hong Kong he made prompt contact with the Russian courier, using as a recognition signal a conspicuous pipe that Stein had brought to Japan on one of his courier runs for the ring. "Greetings from Katcha," said the Hong Kong courier. Sorge courteously replied, "Greetings from Gustaf." Having thus exchanged passwords, they traded packets.[20]

Of course, Sorge did not have everything his way. Late in 1938 he had to adjust to the loss of several valuable contacts and become acquainted with their replacements. The navy ordered Wenneker home late in 1938 to command the pocket battleship *Deutschland*. Ms. Mitsutaro Araki was one of the group who saw him off. He stood on the dock like a "grand seigneur" with his protocol-conscious German friends on hand to bid him *auf Wiedersehen*. And there to watch their favorite sail away twittered, bowed, and smiled a group of *geishas* from Tokyo in their best kimonos. "It didn't worry Wenneker, he merely laughed good-naturedly and waved good-bye to them," Ms. Araki said. "What a contrast! And what a scene! It just fitted Wenneker!"[21] When his replacement, Captain Joachim Leitzmann, reported for duty, he brought with him Wenneker's introduction to Sorge.[22]

From Sorge's viewpoint, the most regrettable loss was Schol, who transferred out early in 1938.[23] Schol was one of Sorge's best friends and unwitting sources of information, as well as the sparkplug of the military evaluation meetings.

Early in 1939 Colonel Hans Wolfgang von Gronau arrived to take over as senior air force attaché from Lieutenant Colonel Nehmiz, who moved down to become Gronau's assistant. Although Sorge and Gronau naturally became acquainted, he was never as close to him as to Nehmiz.[24]

Gronau remembered Sorge as "an iridescent and fascinating personality." He recalled one enlightening experience.

One day his assistant gave him some pictures he had received from Sorge. These were most secret by Japanese standards of the day, being of the Air Force Research Center. Gronau understood that traitors were very rare in Japan, so he wondered how the prints had come into Sorge's hands.[25]

Pondering on the problem, he reflected that eventually the Japanese authorities would catch up with the source of the photos, in which case his own office would be compromised if he kept them. He had the pictures returned to Sorge. He preferred to obtain information about Japanese air power from official sources, and he did not want to be under that sort of obligation to Sorge.[26]

Shortly after this incident Gronau found his desk, which he had locked the previous evening, opened and the lock ruined. Because the desk contained only insignificant statistical documents, he made no issue of the matter, assuming it to be the work of the Japanese surveillance authorities. Least of all did he suspect "Dr. Sorge, who had free run of the embassy, day and night."[27] Quite likely Gronau's first suspicion was correct. Sorge had no need to pick locks, and if he had done so, certainly he would not have been clumsy about it.

CHAPTER 26

"THE ACCIDENT COULD HAVE KILLED ME"

Papa Ketel cut off his hospitality at 2:00 A.M., turning the Rheingold's remaining patrons genially but firmly into the night. Among those for whom the bell tolled in the small hours of Saturday, May 14, 1938, were Sorge and Urach, who had returned to Tokyo. Sorge heaved his motorcycle off its rest and vaulted into the seat; Urach climbed aboard the pillion. The big black motorcycle with its incongruous crew of Soviet spy and German prince hummed through the night.[1]

Even cold sober, Sorge drove his machine as if racing time itself, for slowness, whether of understanding or of transportation, maddened him.[2] And on this Saturday he was already well in his cups.

Sorge and Urach reached the Imperial Hotel safely and went to Urach's room, where Sorge tried to persuade his friend to a joint descent upon another resident of the hotel, a wealthy Austrian businessman whose friends were welcome to help themselves from his private bar, whether their host was home or not. Sorge was one of those thus favored, although the Austrian once warned Urach, "Watch out for Sorge. He is a marked man." Marked by whom and for what, he did not elucidate. But on this particular occasion Sorge obviously had programmed himself to self-destruct, so Urach declined. Sorge conducted the raid by himself and downed an entire bottle of whiskey. Then he returned and asked Urach to ride home with him. By this time the prince's instinct for self-preservation had come to the fore, and he wisely turned down the invitation.

Alone once more, Sorge kicked his motorcycle into action and headed for his home a few miles distant. With the alcohol sloshing amidships, he thundered toward Toranomon, where he left the broad street and turned onto a narrow dirt road running by the wall of the United States Embassy. He had already passed the embassy grounds when suddenly in front of him loomed an obstacle with which his whiskey-soaked reflexes could not cope. He smashed full tilt into the wall.[3]

Luckily a policeman on duty at the embassy gate heard the crash and hurried to investigate. The injured man cried out, "Here, here!" The policeman ran to his side, and Sorge managed to gasp Urach's name. The obliging man phoned the Imperial Hotel, and Urach hastened to the scene.[4]

As Sorge lay there waiting for his friend and for medical attention, he knew that he was on the spot. Instinctively he had called for Urach, but in this emergency he needed someone fully in his confidence. So when Urach reached the site of the accident, Sorge mumbled through his blood and pain, "Tell Clausen to come at once!"[5]

By some miracle his body had escaped major injury, although it was a mass of cuts, bruises, and strained muscles. His left arm had been seriously sprained. One of the handlebars had smashed into his mouth, shattering his teeth and virtually knocking apart the inside of his jaws. Urach arranged that his friend be taken to the American hospital, St. Luke's. Within minutes an ambulance sped the patient on his way.[6]

The telephone splintered the silence in Clausen's home in the predawn. He piled out of bed to listen to a voice telling him that Sorge had been in an accident. He must come to St. Luke's immediately. Knowing that this could mean big trouble and having a tendency to lean on his wife, Clausen asked her to come with him. They managed to arrive at the hospital while Sorge was still conscious. He lay fully clothed on a stretcher, his powerful body limp. Bruises showed livid on features marked with exhaustion.

He could not talk to Clausen with doctors and nurses hovering around, so he ordered them all out. With the room cleared, he crooked a finger at him. "Empty my pockets!" he panted through swollen lips. Clausen obeyed instantly. Thus Sorge rid himself of some highly compromising documents—reports written in English ready to be radioed to the Soviet

Union—and a quantity of American currency. With this incriminating evidence and the keys to his house safe in Clausen's hands, Sorge fainted.

As soon as his chief lost consciousness, Clausen scuttled out of the hospital and drove to Sorge's house. There he scooped up every document even remotely relating to the ring's activities, including Sorge's diary. His departing footsteps had scarcely cooled on the threshold when Weise of the DNB arrived to seal Sorge's effects.

For days afterward Clausen shuddered as he reflected upon the inevitable disaster had Weise been a few minutes more prompt, because Sorge's papers had been scattered all around his office. From the information they contained, Weise would have seen immediately that he had stumbled upon something outside the bounds of journalism. Furthermore, Clausen expected the police to appear, wanting to know why instead of a close friend or a representative of the German Embassy, he, a businessman and a mere acquaintance of Sorge, had been summoned to his bedside.[7]

Thanks to Urach and Clausen, Sorge had narrowly escaped not only serious bodily injury but also equally serious professional injury at the hands of the Kremlin. For Sorge had not committed a mild error of security, an excusable slip that anyone might make. This was a flagrant violation of the basic rules of espionage. The security of the Soviet Union in the Far East might depend upon his discretion. But in the full knowledge of what was at stake, he had been ramming around Tokyo at all hours on his motorcycle, drunk and with secret documents on his person. Had eyes other than Clausen's read those papers, it could have meant at the least the end of his usefulness as an *apparatchik*, if not of his life. His bosses in Moscow were not gentle with failures.

To Sorge had been granted a unique opportunity. If he were unmasked, the Soviet Union would have no possibility of repeating his coup. Never again would the German ambassador accept anyone without an exhaustive investigation, and Sorge estimated that a good 60 percent of the entire output of his ring originated in the embassy.[8] At least another generation would have had to pass to allay Japanese and German suspicions sufficiently to establish a capable espionage net in Japan.

Should this spy ring be exposed, the Tokko would stage a last roundup of party members and fellow travelers. Every Japanese or foreigner who had ever spoken to Richard Sorge would be caught and persuaded to talk as only the Japanese police knew how to persuade. Considering the level at which he and Ozaki operated, the reverberations would rock the very government of Japan and unleash the militarists, already straining to get at the Russians. In that event, and with no devoted Soviet agent inside the German Embassy to play one Fascist state against the other, the Anti-Comintern powers would be sure to band together against the common enemy.

But the fates had not yet become bored with Sorge. Instead of the unpleasant consequences he had richly earned, he received the best of care in a good hospital, where many solicitous friends visited him.

Early in the morning of May 14 Hanako received an urgent telegram from Ms. Fukuda: "Sorge hurt. Come at once." Hanako rushed to his home and found Ama-san packing a suitcase for Sorge. Blinking back tears, she told Hanako that Sorge was seriously injured. Her heart in her throat, Hanako burst outside, flagged a cab, and hastened to St. Luke's, leaving Ama-san to follow with the suitcase.

Hospital attendants ushered her to Sorge's room. He lay in a high hospital bed, his upper body raised to help him breathe. Bandages swathed his head, and his left arm hung in a sling. The room was darkened because his eyes had been so severely jarred that they were sensitive to light; for a time the doctors feared for his sight. Hanako asked, "Sorge, can you recognize me?" He nodded faintly, and this relieved her slightly. At least his brain was normal! She promised to visit him again on the morrow, and once more Sorge nodded feebly.

At home Hanako's mother promptly went to the household shrine to pray for Sorge. As Hanako pitched herself onto her bed, she made up her mind that no matter how disfigured Sorge might be under those bandages, he was the only man for her. Silently uttering disjointed prayers, she finally fell asleep.[9]

Each day that Sorge remained in the hospital, Hanako visited him. She knew nothing of the espionage aspects of his accident, but from Ama-san she heard about the physical details: the drunken crash, the hospitalization; Clausen's coming at his call. Hanako asked if all that was so, and he admitted with an embarrassed grin, "That's true, that's true."

Later he told her that she had saved his life, that he wanted her so much it filled him with the will to live. During this period he underwent painful facial surgery. A number of his teeth had been knocked out completely; others were so shattered that they had to be pulled immediately. Then his gums became infected, and most of the remaining teeth also had to come out. The ordeal left him with barely enough of his own teeth to anchor a set of gold bridges, upper and lower. These never fitted him properly, and for the rest of his life he had to eat his meat ground or finely chopped. Often he groaned from the pain.[10]

Opinions on how the accident affected Sorge's appearance differ. Dr. Friedrich Sieburg, one of Sorge's press colleagues and friends, stated that the scars gave his features an "almost demoniacal expression."[11] Hanako did not see so much of a difference. A bad gash on his forehead required stitching, and while a scar remained, it was small. Because his forehead had always been furrowed, the scar was unnoticeable unless one knew where to look for it. And his heretofore heavy lips appeared thinner. But Hanako's adoring eyes would have found Sorge's looks in no way repulsive had he suddenly turned into a gargoyle. To her, of prime importance was the fact that his eyesight returned to normal as the shock wore off.[12]

The "Social and General" column of the *Japan Times and Advertiser* of May 14 drew the attention of Sorge's friends to his plight. "Dr. R. Sorge, a correspondent here at the Hamburger *Fremdenblatt*, was in St. Luke's International Medical Center yesterday after a motorcycle accident early in the morning. His injuries were reported serious."

Ott was in Hong Kong en route to Berlin and telegraphed his good wishes.[13]

Sorge learned from Ozaki a bit about the background of the switch in foreign ministers which took place in May, but he did not remember the details.[14]

However, he digested the meat of the situation: Konoye decided that Hirota was dragging his feet on the China war. He dismissed him in favor of Ugaki, with the idea that the latter might discuss compromise with the United States. The whole cabinet was not sold on Ugaki, and "public opinion in Japan was against the compromise with the United States and Britain."[15]

Schol visited Sorge nearly every day. From him the spy heard of the appointment of General Seishiro Itagaki to succeed General Gen Sugiyama as war minister. This switch came about because the army faction that favored pushing the China war vigorously overcame a group that preferred to stop the war at its present point and consolidate Japanese gains. Such an occurrence held much interest for Moscow, and Sorge reported it to the Fourth Department.[16]

Sorge had reason to feel sorry for himself. As his wounds started to heal, each day the doctors would peel off a bit more of the bandages, revealing another inch or two of alarmingly purplish, swollen flesh.[17] But as soon as he began to heal, he exuded all his usual charm. Meissner was visiting him one day when a fairly severe earthquake shook the hospital. To Meissner's mingled exasperation and amusement, three nurses, ignoring the rest of the patients, burst into the room and flung themselves on top of Sorge's prostrate body to save him from the chunks of plaster falling from the ceiling.[18]

Ms. Araki heard that five nurses were involved. "The director of the hospital wondered what kind of man Sorge was to merit such treatment," she recalled. "Sorge was there for only a few weeks, but he earned the favors of the nurses in so short a time."[19]

As soon as he could walk, Sorge began to itch to be back on the job. While still heavily bandaged, he talked the doctors into releasing him. "Sorge put his whole life into his work," said Hanako. "He was so engrossed in his work that even after his serious accident he plunged right back into it as though he had absolutely to make up for all the time he had missed."[20]

•Sorge's hospitalization ended too soon to suit a certain Japanese secret policeman. This man, who had been shadowing Sorge, dropped into the office of Harold O. Thompson, correspondent for the United Press. The policeman rejoiced to Thompson's Japanese assistant that Sorge was in St. Luke's, so he could look forward to some time to himself. Thompson, who liked Sorge as "a friendly, accessible guy," checked and found that he had already been released from the hospital, whereupon the policeman scurried off to return to duty,[21] the routine shadowing of a foreign reporter.

Before Sorge dived back into work, he spent a brief period of convalescence in the German Embassy, where Ms. Ott took care of him. This was truly kind of her. She and her son had scarcely moved into the embassy when Sorge's accident occurred, and being scheduled to sail on June 2 to join Ott in Berlin, she had a great many arrangements to make in addition to her normal social routine. "Ms. Ott took the accident very much to heart," recalled Sieburg, "and since then had been permanently uneasy." According to Sieburg, she was responsible for ensuring that Sorge never rode a motorcycle again.[22]

Hanako played her part, too. She protested vigorously against his continuing to use the motorcycle. "It is dangerous! It is dangerous!" she cried forcefully, over and over.

And Sorge admitted, "The accident could have killed me." Reluctantly he gave up the idea of purchasing a new motorcycle. Instead, he bought from Clausen a small Datsun, to which he gave none of the tender loving care he had bestowed on the motorcycle. He seldom bothered to wash it and parked it in front of his home or in any handy spot in all kinds of weather. Once it was stolen, and Sorge merely shrugged, saying that he would buy another from Clausen. A friend found it and returned it, and after a couple of years he rented a garage from a neighbor to provide shelter for his sturdy mechanical beast.[23]

The accident marked a watershed of sorts in Sorge's life. Much later Ott reported to Berlin that thereafter Sorge "was subject to nervous disorders."[24] One wonders to just what extent that terrible blow to the head affected Sorge's brain, for Hanako's memoirs reveal him as increasingly out of control of himself.

Yet the mishap with its appalling possibilities for himself and his mission did not sober Sorge. He sacrificed the motorcycle, but the machine had not been intrinsically at fault. Typically he did not admit to himself that the problem lay within. So the spy continued to be a boon to Tokyo's liquor dealers, sacrificing security upon the altar of his appetite.

CHAPTER 27

"IF IT IS SHANGHAI,
I WILL GO"

"Do you have a cigarette?" Voukelitch obligingly extended a pack. Clausen extracted one and moved to
hand back the rest, but Voukelitch stopped him. "I have another
pack with me, so you may have that one." With a word of
thanks Clausen stuffed the pack into his pocket. He knew that
along with two or three cigarettes it contained several rolls of
microfilm, this being one of their favorite devices for exchanging film. After finishing their drinks, the two men parted.[1]
Although Voukelitch had recently plunged Clausen into hot
water with Sorge, both were too good-natured to nurse a grudge
over a triviality.

The occasion came about when Voukelitch, having decided upon formal separation from Edith, tried to persuade her
to leave Japan and take their son to Moscow. He made the
suggestion in all good faith, for Moscow was the city of his
dreams. Nevertheless, although he wished Edith and the boy
well, he also wanted them out of his sight. He looked forward
to marriage with his adored Yoshiko as soon as his divorce
was final and wanted no reminder of the past to shadow his
new life.

Edith consulted with Anna Clausen about this recommendation, and Anna gave her a firsthand account of life in
the Socialist paradise. "Communism is not good," she said,
as she often did, and added, "Russian conditions are terrible."
Edith mentioned this conversation to Voukelitch, who passed
it on to Sorge. Furious at this example of Anna's heresy, Sorge
read Clausen a severe lecture on controlling his wife's tongue.

Clausen absolved Voukelitch of malicious intent. "He is a man who cannot keep his mouth shut," he told himself resignedly.[2]

The Voukelitches separated amicably. Having severed the marital relationship in which they were incompatible, they relaxed into the comfortable status of old comrades. Far from betraying her husband's spy ring in reprisal for his casting her aside, Edith was willing to continue working for it. This circumstance had nothing to do with ideological commitment. "She was not interested in politics, nor was there any hope of her conversion to Communism," Sorge wrote. He could always use another transmission station, so he helped Edith find a new home at 2113 Kami Meguro, 4 Chome, Meguro-ku—a two-story wooden building, of course.[3] However, the ring sent no messages from Edith's home until the following year.

This development meant a financial loss for Voukelitch. He had been receiving from the ring a monthly stipend of 400 yen, but after his separation from Edith and in view of his newspaper earnings, Sorge cut off his salary, permitting him only an occasional 100 or 200 yen.[4]

The Clausens, too, were househunting. During the spring Clausen had begun to notice a car parked near his home every day at about 7:00 or 8:00 A.M. The two men in the car were looking around as if they were investigating something. What Clausen called his sixth sense told him that these were plainclothesmen probably keeping an eye on the neighboring Soviet trade agency, but they might be watching him, too. Feeling uneasy, he reported it to Sorge, who did not like the look of matters. "That is dangerous," he said. "I suppose this is because there is a regiment nearby and some Russians are also near there. Anyway, if they find out what we are doing, *that is it!* So you had better move quickly."[5]

Clausen had another reason for changing addresses. A typhoon had damaged his home, the roof began to leak, and the damp affected his electrical wiring. But between Sorge's accident and a rush of business during the summer, he did not move until early September, when he rented a house a 2 Hirobi Cho, Azabu-ku.[6]

He also took on a heavy new load of responsibility. At last Sorge received Moscow's permission to allow Clausen to encode messages.[7] Thankfully Sorge dumped this task on his radioman, whose salary rose by 100 yen a month, bringing his monthly pay to 700 yen. Each month he also received 175 yen as a rental allowance, 80 yen for transportation, and a special expense account to defray costs in connection with the radio set.[8] Anna had no regular salary, but when she served as a courier, the ring paid her expenses.[9]

Through no fault of his own Clausen got into a minor scrape. Before leaving for China on a courier run, Sorge left a manuscript with him for transmission, and hesitating to use his chief's name when he was not around, Clausen sent the message over his own name. The recipients thought Clausen had gathered the information himself and sent him "a big compliment." When Sorge returned and heard about this, he was angry with Clausen.[10] In such matters his sense of humor remained in abeyance. If Moscow tossed any bouquets, he liked to catch them himself.

If he wanted revenge on Clausen, he soon got it. After the China Incident had engulfed Shanghai, Sorge had recommended that Hong Kong would be a more suitable rendezvous point. For some time a trip there had been tentatively scheduled, with Sorge to carry the mail. However, he could not break away from his duties in Tokyo, so the Fourth Department sent a message suggesting Anna as a substitute and asking for details by radio on the time of her departure, the name of her ship, and the place of contact.[11] Clausen broke the news to Anna and braced himself for the anticipated barrage of opposition.

As he expected, she roundly refused to go, bitterly reminding her husband of his promise that her first trip would be her only one.[12] Along with a general dislike for taking an active part in the espionage work, she felt a particular aversion to meeting a courier in Hong Kong, which was unfamiliar territory to her. Nor was Clausen happy with the idea of sending his wife to a British colony. Her English was poor, and while she might get around by using Russian, it would make her conspicuous. He suggested that Moscow might agree to hold the rendezvous in Shanghai. Still Anna demurred.

"You must go so that I will not lose face," Clausen pleaded, and his wife softened.

"I don't like Hong Kong because I have no friends and

there is nothing to buy there," she said, "but if it is Shanghai, I will go, because it is like my home."

Sorge made no objection to the change. As a former resident of Shanghai Anna had a ready-made reason to go there—to visit old friends. He authorized a message to the Fourth Department asking that Shanghai be selected and received a favorable reply, inquiring whether "Fritz's wife" could be in Shanghai by October 20. Clausen wired an affirmative.[13]

The selection of Shanghai pleased him. He had promised a business partner that he would help him send money via Shanghai and Switzerland to his wife and children in Germany since it was difficult to send money direct from Japan to Germany. One of Anna's errands would be to send $3,000 to his partner's wife.[14]

A third message advised that the Moscow courier would be waiting in Shanghai from October 18 on and gave instructions about the recognition signals.[15] Clausen coached Anna. The place of contact would be either the café of the Palace Hotel or the lobby of the Cathay Hotel. She would carry a yellow handbag and white gloves and would place the handbag on the table with the gloves crosswise over the bag. "It's funny to wear white gloves when it isn't summer," observed Anna.[16] Clausen waved aside this feminine objection as irrelevant, incompetent, and immaterial, though the point was valid: in normal times a woman carrying a summer purse and gloves in a fashionable Shanghai hotel in winter could have drawn undesirable attention.

Sorge did not dispatch Anna to Shanghai for approximately two months. On the very eve of her departure she balked again.

This second insurrection came when Clausen asked her to take along twenty to thirty rolls of film. She had been under the impression that she was expected only to obtain $6,000 of expense money from the courier and give him a small parcel to take to Sorge's wife. Clausen was on the verge of tearing his hair. Without the film the Soviet agent would not give up the money or anything else he might have for the ring.

"If you don't go, I'll go," he said despairingly. "But

it is already decided that you are to go to Shanghai and the place of the contact is arranged already. If you don't go, we will have to negotiate again by wireless and I cannot leave within two weeks. If you don't go, I don't know what will happen to me, and to you, too."[17]

Anna hesitated. She did not want to cause trouble for her husband. She told herself that her refusal would not seriously interfere with the spy operation. The mission would still go forward with Clausen as the courier. If she refused to go, he would be disgraced in Sorge's eyes. Weighing the pros and cons, she thought, "I would be sorry for him if some time in the future, when he goes back to Moscow, he receives some punishment, just as he was sent to the MTS before."[18]

So Anna capitulated and accepted the microfilms. She carefully rolled them into a cloth, which she tied around her body beneath her breasts, and set out on her journey. She arrived in Shanghai around December 10. After one missed rendezvous she made the contact and exchanged the film and the package for Katcha for a packet containing $6,000 in mixed Chinese and American money.[19]

The next day Anna sent the $3,000 to Switzerland for Clausen's partner, $500 to Hamburg for Clausen's business, and deposited about $1,000 in the Hong Kong-Shanghai bank to the Clausen account. After a number of business purchases for her husband she was free to smother her conscience in the soft fur of a coat costing 700 Chinese dollars. Following the contact, Anna visited with a friend for two weeks before returning to Tokyo.[20]

This was the current arrangement. Clausen explained that "the fund was mostly not brought back but was used for shopping or was deposited at the Hong Kong-Shanghai bank. . . ."[21] Thus the money received from the Moscow courier was in the nature of a reimbursement for funds already expended to support the ring in Tokyo.

This trip was a milestone in Anna's journey through life. Having once succumbed to the most insidious of all arguments—"If I don't do this, someone else will, so I might as well"—Anna never again seriously protested against playing her part in the ring's activities. Sorge had caught her in a net woven of love and fear.

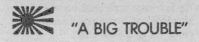

CHAPTER 28

"A BIG TROUBLE"

Circumstances in the summer of 1938 presented Sorge with a concrete problem with which to test his spy ring. Not far from where the borders of the Soviet Union, Korea, and Manchuria form a triangle, the Tumen River flows a short distance west of Lake Khasan. Between the river and lake and overlooking both lies a range of hills that for some years had attracted the covetous attention of both Russia and Japan. The former claimed that the border ran along the crest of Chang-kufeng [Broad Drum Peak], while the latter held that it followed the western shore of Lake Khasan.

The area was of considerable strategic importance, commanding a view of the railway and also of the roads leading to Vladivostok and other points in the Maritime Provinces. Early in July 1938 the Japanese moved in field troops to strengthen the border guards. Then, around July 15, the Japanese claimed—but the Russians denied—that Soviet troops had entrenched themselves on the Manchurian side of Chang-kufeng.

Foreign Minister Ugaki kept his head and dispatched Mamoru Shigemitsu, the Japanese ambassador to the Soviet Union, to Moscow to negotiate a settlement, suggesting a return to the status quo ante July 11.

Then matters took an ugly turn. War Minister General Seishiro Itagaki, along with the chief of the General Staff, sought an audience with the Emperor to obtain imperial sanction for securing Japan's demands by force of arms. To do so, Itagaki lied to his sacred Tenno, falsely claiming that his policy had the backing of Ugaki as well as the navy minister, Admiral

231

Mitsumasa Yonai. On July 29 Japanese forces attacked the Soviet border guards.[1]

Because this was the first large-scale clash between Japan and Russia during the China Incident, Sorge took a deep interest in it. He called on his group for an all-out effort.

Relying upon his resources in the prime minister's official residence, the Information Department of the cabinet, dispatches from the governor-general of Korea, and similar sources, Ozaki soon decided that this was simply a border clash, not a deliberate Japanese provocation of the Soviet Union. What particularly struck him about the occurrence was that "as soon as it took place, contact between the cabinet and military was cut completely, and this is characteristic of Japanese politics."[2]

Miyagi reported that he heard through Yamana that no large troop movements were under way. These assurances led Sorge to decide early that the matter would blow over with little harm done. He confirmed this belief through the German Embassy. The Tokyo government had told the embassy that the incident probably would not expand.[3]

In slightly amplified form this is what Ott told Grew: Japan's top brass informed Ott "that they want no trouble with Russia at present because they are far too occupied in China and that they would therefore not allow the incident to develop." This satisfied the American ambassador, who was confident that Ott would not mislead him, for their personal relations were "of the friendliest." The incident did not overly disturb Grew, who believed that the Japanese neither wanted nor could afford war with the Soviet Union under the current circumstances.[4]

Nevertheless, the Japanese government could not speak for the USSR. Japan's armed forces pushed several kilometers into Siberia and inflicted quite heavy casualties, whereupon the Russians brought in their airpower. This worried Tokyo, for it might mean the Russians would seize the initiative,[5] so the Japanese Army took care not to call in its own aircraft in answer to this move.[6]

Sorge quickly advised his Soviet chiefs that the "Japanese government and military would take a nonexpansion policy."[7] The Soviet Foreign Office demanded as the price of peace that Japan return to the borderline of July 29, 1938. Japan was glad to pay it. The incident closed on August 1.[8]

It was a Russian victory well worth pondering in Tokyo. The Soviets had displayed the will and the ability to defend a spot of land which in that vast country was almost invisible to the naked eye. They could be expected to do so again, if need be. Later Miyagi reported to Sorge that after 1938 the Japanese defense budget allocated 60 percent for the inactive northern sector against 40 percent for the China Incident.[9]

Very few of Sorge's projects can be docketed as neatly as the Chang-kufeng Incident, with exact starting and completion dates. As a general rule the subjects he investigated ran longer and were less well defined, with several cases running concurrently. Such was one that began in the early summer of 1938, on which Sorge did not make his final report until early 1939.

This cause célèbre commenced on June 13, when General Third Grade G. S. Lyushkov defected from the Soviet Union and fled over the Manchukuo border, where the Kwantung Army picked him up.[10] As Sorge understated, it was found "that he had abundant knowledge about political and military affairs in Russia, and that he was rather volunteering to tell about these." A division commander in the Far East, Lyushkov was in an excellent position to know the state of Soviet strength and preparations in that area, and as a general officer of the GPU undoubtedly he knew where many a political body was buried. The Japanese Army was delighted with the unexpected and distinguished catch and hustled him off to Tokyo for a thorough interrogation at the General Staff headquarters.[11]

Sorge learned of the case either before Lyushkov reached Tokyo, probably from Schol, or on July 1, when the Japanese officially announced Lyushkov's border crossing.[12] At first he considered this a simple case of a man "dissatisfied with Russian attitudes and treatment," who might have been mixed up in some shady business in Siberia, had fled the Stalinist purges, and represented himself as belonging to an opposition group to lend his defection an aura of political respectability. Therefore, "since the betrayer's behavior is always stereotyped like this case," Sorge "did not have any particular interest in him."

Once in the General Staff headquarters, Lyushkov became very communicative, and the staff extracted enough from him to alarm Sorge seriously. The Japanese kept Schol informed of their progress, and he in turn briefed Sorge.[13] By this time recovered sufficiently to be at work in the embassy, where Ott was also back on the job, Sorge knew everything the Germans knew as soon as they did. He put Ozaki and Miyagi on the scent, but in this matter they were of little help. As Miyagi remarked, Sorge was in a better position to investigate. Both Ozaki and Yamana told Miyagi that Lyushkov was "only a colonel of an ordinary division, and therefore, he could not give any more detailed information than Japan already had."[14] Although far from the truth, this was probably what Miyagi's colleagues believed.

However, Miyagi reported that "the general had been spying for some time for Japan." He added, "Many of his men who were mostly Jewish were arrested. He therefore felt himself in danger and came over to the Japanese side."[15] Evidently Sorge did not credit Miyagi's interpretation for shortly after Lyushkov's arrival in Tokyo he sent a radio message indicating that the ring could not find out much about Lyushkov because the Japanese were too vigilant.[16]

Sorge sent Moscow three or four messages during the summer, relaying the most important items from Lyushkov's testimony. These included his anti-Communist attitude; his accusations against Stalin and the Central Committee; his opinion of the Red Army in Siberia—including his evaluation that a very strong and dissatisfied opposition group existed within it "and that therefore if the Japanese Army stands up and attacks the Red Army, it may collapse in a day"—and, last but far from least, the disposition of the Red Army in Siberia and its military wireless code. Sorge added that in his opinion "there was danger of the Japanese and German military action picking up the weakness in the Red Army pointed out in Lyushkov's report."[17]

The Japanese propagandized in the German Embassy that Russia was on the verge of a breakdown. Using the customary party technique of downgrading the source, Sorge worked hard to correct this impression.

"Lyushkov is not a big figure but an unreliable person,"

he stressed to Ott, Schol, and Matzky. "It is very dangerous to judge the internal condition of Russia by trusting such a person's words. When the Nazis took over the government of Germany," he added slyly, "many Germans escaped abroad and by reading their books many people got the impression that the Nazis would be collapsing any day. But it wasn't so, and Lyushkov's case is exactly the same."[18]

During this early period Moscow showed no interest in Sorge's reports; however, he believed that the Fourth Department's failure to instruct him resulted from the fact that he was constantly reporting on his own initiative, and therefore no comment was necessary.[19] The exceedingly dangerous situation in Europe following Hitler's takeover of Austria that spring and his bellicose gestures toward the Czechs had given the Soviet Union more urgent matters to think about than the Lyushkov affair, although the Fourth Department by no means underrated its seriousness.

Toward the end of the summer a new element entered the picture. When the Japanese General Staff informed the German Embassy that Lyushkov "knew many things about the internal situation in Russia," the embassy wired Berlin asking for a special mission to Tokyo to interrogate Lyushkov on matters relating to German interests. When Sorge heard this, he pricked up his ears and asked Moscow if it wanted this mission's report.[20] The reply left Sorge in no doubt that Moscow was very interested indeed in what this defector might spill: "Devote all of your effort and capacity to obtaining a copy of the document which Canaris will obtain from the Japanese Army and a copy of the document which the special mission will receive at the personal interview with Lyushkov. Send immediately what you obtain."[21]

The wire from Dal* somewhat mystified Clausen. He deduced, however, "Probably there must have been a big trouble at the time in relation to the Lyushkov incident. And they wanted to know what kind of things Lyushkov was going to say in Japan."

---

* The word means "far" in Russian, hence stood for "Far East," and probably stood for the head of the Far Eastern Section of the Fourth Department (*Gendai-shi Shiryo*, Vol. III, p. 171).

Sorge remarked to Clausen, "It is very difficult to obtain such materials," and Clausen dispatched a message to that effect.[22] Sorge's remark is odd, for he had no reason to suspect that Ott might exclude him from his councils at this late date. On the contrary, he was more deeply than ever in the confidence of Ott and the service attachés, so much so that he "could obtain information without trying at all." These worthies had formed the habit of bringing their problems to Sorge. They even consulted him concerning "very important telegrams and report documents," bringing him their drafts for his opinion.

At other times, as he had arranged with the Fourth Department, Sorge would bait his line with a minnow to catch a tuna. By volunteering some tidbit obtained from Ozaki or Miyagi, he would open the floodgates of ambassadorial confidence, and information of real importance poured out.[23] This technique was clever psychology and a large factor in Sorge's long-lasting success. A direct question is remembered, often resented, but a simple statement usually calls forth an answering statement, the whole exchange more often than not forgotten in the mass of the day's conversations.

In the instance of Lyushkov, however, Sorge would not be able to count on his embassy friends for help. The special mission was coming from the German Intelligence Department; its members did not have to show anyone in the embassy its findings unless they chose to do so.

Admiral Canaris dispatched to Tokyo from his Intelligence Department (Abwehr) a select group headed by an Abwehr colonel who spoke excellent Russian. Sorge claimed that he "met the man in the Embassy several times, but did not know his name."[24] This is somewhat peculiar in view of German punctilio. Possibly Sorge deliberately dodged the Russian-speaking colonel to avoid any slips of ear or tongue.

By the end of the year the special mission had come up with a report of several hundred pages. The embassy received a copy, which Schol showed to Sorge. Sorge read it through, photographed all that seemed to him of particular interest—about half the report—and sent the films to Moscow early in 1939.[25]

Throughout the Lyushkov case Sorge had an excellent opportunity to continue his own propaganda war in the German

Embassy. He stressed that the Soviet Union "was much stronger than many people believed" and urged peaceful relations between Russia and Japan and Germany, for the economic benefit of the two last. Playing on a sentimental string also, he reminded Ott that during post-Versailles days, when Germany was forbidden to rearm, the Soviet Union had permitted Germany to send its army officers to Russia to engage in secret tests of cannon and aircraft. Because his hearers thought Sorge was arguing for the benefit of the Reich, he grew in favor and prestige.[26]

Sorge's role in the Lyushkov case, albeit a key one, was simply to furnish Moscow information about the revelations of a defector. Nevertheless, he performed a signal service for the Soviet Union by being in a position to reveal exactly what Japan and Germany—its potential enemies—discovered as fast as they found it out. Sorge's reports may well have contributed to Marshal Georgi K. Zhukov's later victory at Nomonhan because through them Moscow knew whatever Lyushkov had told the Japanese about Russian strength and military dispositions.[27]

One cannot know what, if any, influence the Lyushkov case had on Japanese affairs. It may be only coincidental that the reorganization of the Japanese Army to conform to the structure of the Red Army began around this time and was still going on at the time of Sorge's arrest. The fact of the reorganization, however, "was extremely important to Russia"; it seemed to indicate that "the Japanese were planning an anti-Russian war."[28]

If nothing else, through Sorge the Fourth Department learned that Lyushkov had compromised the military code. This information in itself was priceless. It gave the Fourth Department the opportunity to change the code and thus plug a dangerous leak in its Far Eastern intelligence dike. Once more the Sorge ring had proved its worth.

CHAPTER 29

"THE TIME IS NOT RIPE ENOUGH"

Shortly before the Chang-kufeng Incident broke out, Ozaki's thriving career moved up another notch. Kazami, who valued Ozaki's judgment, was agitated to learn that Ozaki, his expert on China, considered accepting the invitation of the Foreign Ministry to join its economic research agency. He summoned Ozaki to the premier's official residence, asked him to reconsider and to work for the Konoye cabinet as a *shokutaku* ("unofficial assistant"). Ozaki agreed and began duties on July 8, 1938.[1]

The term *shokutaku* covered a wide range of appointments with government and other corporate bodies. The position might or might not be salaried, and the appointment was usually for less than three years. Selection was made outside regular administrative rules and procedures, in order that the appointee need not be covered by the rights and privileges— or bound by the obligations—applicable to a regular staff member. This system enabled the agencies concerned to take on badly needed personnel outside their budgets.[2]

Ozaki's orders read, "You are requested to do survey work,"[3] a statement which is nothing if not specious. In practice he became an assistant to Kazami. So Hotzumi Ozaki, dedicated agent of world communism, set forth sedately each morning for his office in the basement of the official residence of the premier of Japan.

At first Ozaki had no definite tasks as a cabinet consultant; he merely offered opinions on the conflict in China and other matters when so requested. In time, however, his area fell into five main categories: disposition of the China Incident, the possibility of working with Great Britain to handle the China problem, evaluation and forecast of the course of the China Incident, the puppet Chinese regime under Wang Ching-wei, and the National Reorganization.

Wisely he made no attempt to bring about his own ambitions for China because "the government's intention was already clear. . . ." Ozaki was too smart to bat his head against a brick wall. He furthered the Soviet cause by more subtle means: ". . . it was most appropriate and convenient for me to make use of this position, grasp accurately the actual trend of Japanese politics, and obtain reliable information instead of trying to realize my political intentions. Accordingly, it goes without saying that I passed on to Sorge the information that I obtained in the cabinet."

To do this, he was well placed. In addition to his own office under Konoye's roof, he was free to enter the offices of the secretary and chief secretary, where these men showed him all the papers necessary to his work, with or without his asking for them. They talked before him without restraint. Both the information received and his interpretation of it he promptly submitted to Sorge.[4]

However, as a member of the Breakfast Group and as a special consultant Ozaki was not in a position to give Sorge direct assistance from the military angle. This was not for want of trying;[5] but he had no access to war plans, and he had nothing whatever to do with the military aspects of Japan's national strategy. His province was political and economic, with particular emphasis on interpreting and forecasting Chinese reactions to Japanese moves.

Nevertheless, during this period Ozaki had much to tell Sorge, for two exceedingly important projects were in the Konoye mill. The first was the attempt to work out a peace settlement with China through Wang Ching-wei. Wang was vice-chairman of the Kuomintang and vice-chairman of Chiang Kai-shek's National Defense Council. For some time he had been secretly negotiating with the Japanese.

On December 18, 1938, Wang fled from Chungking to Hanoi, as prearranged. Four days later Konoye issued a statement of terms for the settlement essentially as follows: Japan,

Manchukuo, and China must unite to establish a new order; Japan and China must conclude an anti-Comintern agreement; Konoye disclaimed any intention of securing an economic monopoly in China but demanded that China must recognize freedom of residence and trade for Japanese and must extend to Japan facilities for developing China's natural resources.

On December 29, safe in Hanoi, Wang declared these terms acceptable and urged that China make peace with Japan.[6]

Ozaki reported to Sorge that public opinion was divided. Most were unsatisfied with Konoye's statement, "and part of the military was very skeptical about it." Sorge believed that "the Japanese people as a whole were thinking that in order to solve the Chinese Incident quickly Japan had to negotiate with Chiang Kai-shek instead of Wang Ching-wei."[7]

Over the next few years this project occupied much of Sorge's and Ozaki's attention. But in its early stages Ozaki took little direct part in it. He served primarily as an assistant to Kazami, who specialized in domestic policies and therefore was relatively indifferent to the Wang Ching-wei maneuver. Saionji, Inukai, and Shigeharu Matsumoto of Domei kept Ozaki posted on progress, and several times during the year he reported to Sorge about the matter.[8]

Ozaki's principal target was the National Reorganization Plan. He frequently discussed the project with Sorge, who also heard about it from Miyagi and other Japanese friends. Sorge claimed that he did not recall having reported to the Soviet Union on this movement. This is incredible, for such a vast concept, which occupied the best minds in the Konoye cabinet, must have attracted Sorge's liveliest attention. In later days he gave a clue to this pretended indifference, admitting that he "could not comprehend the core of the problem." Sorge usually claimed disinterest in any subject he could not conquer. As far as he could fathom, the movement "was a trial to lead the many sorts of parties which had been struggling against each other into a unique national movement." He doubted that the plan could succeed.[9]

Sorge did not stand alone in not knowing exactly what National Reorganization was all about. There was remarkably little effort at coordination among Konoye's bright young men. No one ever worked out a blueprint for the future or even formulated a statement of aims and policies to serve as a platform. According to historian Chalmers Johnson, the New Structure Movement—i.e., the National Reorganization—was an "attempt to create a strong political instrument on the Japanese domestic scene which could force the military to heel." To bring this about, a resort to Nazi models was permissible to create "a totalitarian party of the masses which could impose its will on the Army and on the Army-dominated bureaucracy."[10]

Some such ideas might have found a home in the heads of Ozaki, Saionji, and Kazami, but it is unlikely that Konoye could have entertained them for a minute. The notion that Konoye was a moderate who wanted to curb the military has enjoyed a long life, although it has no visible means of support. He never could have become prime minister without the consent of the military, which flourished in each of his three premierships. Whatever was going on in Konoye's brain, the armed forces were very much a part of it.

Moreover, Konoye, a Japanese to his meticulously manicured fingertips, could not have deceived himself that the "masses" were panting to be delivered from the military. In the 1930s the Japanese people were immensely proud of their army and navy and identified with them, for the military of Japan was not a class in the sense of the German *Junker*. No social barrier stood between any Japanese boy, however humbly born, and a brilliant career in his country's armed forces, provided he could pass the stiff physical and mental examinations to either service academy. Even more important, the warrior was the national ideal of manly perfection. Not until the military led the Japanese people to utter disaster was the image shattered, broken by the only power that could smash it—the military itself. Certainly in 1938 Suzuki-san saw no reason for trading a military dictatorship for a civilian one.

For Ozaki, a "totalitarian party of the masses" could take only one form: a reincarnation of the defunct Japanese Communist Party. To add a final touch of irony to the situation, for years the military had been trying to get rid of the existing parties. If Konoye succeeded in replacing them with his National Reorganization, the armed forces would be the first to stand up and cheer.

"National Reorganization was the problem to which Mr. Kazami put in his effort most enthusiastically," said Ozaki, "and he was trying to establish Prince Konoye's political foundation through this movement." If this circumstance came about Kazami's own future would be secure.[11]

A plan along the lines of National Reorganization was first submitted in the summer of 1938. Ozaki observed, "In political parties there rose a movement to consolidate and make Konoye head of the combined party." Ozaki spoke about this to the premier in the autumn of that year.

"People's understanding still is lacking, and the time is not ripe enough," the premier replied. "If I just wanted to unify the existing parties, I would be able to do it even tomorrow." From this remark, Ozaki gathered that Prince Konoye wanted to avoid merger of the prevailing political parties and was expecting a new political system to be born. . . ." This Ozaki passed on to Sorge.[12]

At Kazami's order Ozaki worked on this concept, and in November 1938 he submitted a plan. He kept Sorge posted "once in a while," telling him that Konoye was "very enthusiastic about this problem" and that Kazami was also "very anxious to see the plan achieved." Ozaki recalled that "Sorge paid attention to it from the viewpoint that a new political system to give a fundamental change to the Japanese political system might be made with the leadership of Konoye"—a much more believable statement of the master spy's attitude than Sorge's pose of disinterest.

The plan of Count Yoriyasu Arima, presented to the cabinet in December, was based on Ozaki's outline but did not succeed "because of opposition in the cabinet." Then Admiral Nobumasa Suetsugu, minister of internal affairs, submitted his scheme, which was adopted. If Konoye was indeed attempting to curb the military, he chose some odd associates, for Suetsugu was the navy's number one fire breather. The premier proclaimed his new order on December 22, but before it could go into effect, his cabinet resigned.[13]

Konoye out of office, Ozaki out of a job—those days when the autumn of 1938 blended into early 1939 were not the most propitious of Sorge's Tokyo years. On October 7 he wrote a brief but typical letter to the chief of intelligence in Moscow:

"Dear Comrade: Do not worry about us. Although we are exhausted and tense we remain disciplined, obedient and resolute, prepared to carry out the tasks of our great cause. Our warmest greetings to you and your friends. Be so good as to pass on the enclosed letter to my wife and add my regards. Please look after her from time to time."[14]

"Do not forget me," he wrote gloomily to Katcha. "I am sad enough without that." He gave his wife an account of his accident, described his wounds, complained about the weather—"so difficult to support above all when the work demands a perpetual tension"—feared that she might become tired of "this eternal waiting," but hoped mournfully that there still remained "a little chance of realizing our old dream of five years of living together."[15]

Ozaki might be out, but he was not down. Far too canny not to keep a reserve bowstring at his belt, shortly before Konoye's resignation he got together with Inukai and Saionji. The glib trio talked Kazami into financing a China Research Office, the avowed purpose of which was to work for a basis upon which to end the China Incident and restore cordial relations through Wang Ching-wei.

Ozaki used this organization as a refuge for his needy Communist friends, bringing in Mizuno as administrator and writer. Mizuno also collected material for Ozaki's articles and helped translate into Japanese Sun Yat-sen's *Three Principles of the People*. Ozaki selected as manager Karoku Hosokawa, an old friend who in the future became a Communist member of the Diet. Later Ozaki also recruited Yuichi Horie and Shin'ichi Matsumoto.

Through the China Research Bureau Ozaki solidified his friendship with Saionji and Inukai. He also secured valuable sources of information and remained in the political eye.[16] Thus he was ready to swing aboard when the wheels of power rolled his way again.

CHAPTER 30

"MUCH VALUABLE
INFORMATION ON
JAPANESE POLITICS"

Miyagi could consider the year just commencing as peculiarly his own, for 1939, like his birth year of 1903, was a Year of the Rabbit:* "Rabbit people are temperamentally melancholy. . . . They are somewhat pedantic . . . what they know they know well. . . . They are a bit conservative and do not plunge into anything without first thinking it over carefully. Rabbit people will have a placid existence . . . provided they do not become involved with unmanageable elements."[1]

This could be a description of Miyagi, who sacrificed the "placid existence" he might have enjoyed as an artist by becoming "involved with unmanageable elements." From January to April 1939 he briefed Sorge on no fewer than twenty-seven items, ranging from the establishment of the Hiranuma cabinet to the explosion of a weapons warehouse.[2]

Miyagi and Sorge had a difference of opinion on Japan's occupation of Hainan Island, located off the south coast of China. For some time the artist had predicted that the Japanese would take it over. Sorge disagreed, claiming that they would not for fear that the war in China would spread into the south, where "Japan would inevitably collide with the United States

---

* The Oriental Zodiac has a cycle of twelve years instead of twelve months. Each year bears the name of one of the twelve animals that came at the Buddha's call to honor him. Every individual is said to partake of the qualities of the animal belonging to his natal year.

and Britain.'' With his growing knowledge of military affairs and his contacts in the army, Miyagi believed that Japan would run this risk, both to cut off Chiang's supply lines and to raise morale at home with news of a victory.

Miyagi compared notes with Ozaki, who agreed with him because he had heard through his friends at *Asahi* that for months troops had been waiting in southern Formosa for this operation and because journalists were leaving Hainan. His views reinforced, Miyagi wrote a report to Sorge to this effect and was pleased in his dour way when, a few days later—on February 10, his thirty-sixth birthday—his prediction came true.[3]

But as always, in this period of transition between two governments, Sorge relied most heavily upon Ozaki to guide him through the bewildering mazes of Japanese politics. At the end of the Konoye regime Ozaki explained that the prince had resigned voluntarily because relations between the administration and the military still were not going any too well; the China Incident was being prolonged beyond all expectations; the cabinet was unable to decide whether to adopt a pro-German foreign policy or one favorable to the United States and Britain, and the National Reorganization Plan was proving difficult to realize.[4]

The Breakfast Group continued to gather each Wednesday and for the first three months of 1939 met in various places. Ozaki's membership in that select body still offered him his best source of ''much valuable information on Japanese politics and foreign policy from pieces of talk of these people, their attitude, atmosphere of the meeting, and their conversation.''[5]

The Showa Research Association continued in full swing. Ozaki participated in its deliberations and lectured at the Showa Academy, which the organization sponsored. The association was pushing the Greater East Asia Co-Prosperity Sphere,* and in January 1939 a well-known essay by Ozaki on this subject

---

* Although certain Japanese preferred the name *Toa Kyodo Tai* (''East Asian Cooperative Body''), the author uses the phrase *Greater East Asia Co-Prosperity Sphere* (*Dai Toa Kyoei Ken*), for this is the title under which the concept became generally known in the United States.

appeared in *Chuo Koron* (*Central Review*). Ozaki was considered one of the top philosophers of this movement, along with Masamichi Royama and Kiyoshi Miki.

Royama was Ozaki's colleague in the Breakfast Group and Showa Research Association. He had been known for some time as one of Konoye's advisers. Miki was a leading intellectual of the day. He did not belong in the Breakfast Group but did belong to the Showa Research Association. He had studied philosophy at Kyoto, in Germany, and in Paris. Returning to Tokyo, he became a columnist for *Yomiuri Shimbun*. Although he did not become a formal Communist, he dabbled in Marxism during his Tokyo years. He also donated money to the party and in consequence had been arrested in 1931.[6] So an academic politician, a pink-tinged intellectual, and an undercover Soviet agent were among the leading lights of the Greater East Asia Co-Prosperity Sphere! In those days some strange ingredients went into the upper crust of a nation supposed to be a monolith of rightism.

Ozaki's testimony left no doubt what he hoped to gain from a Greater East Asia Co-Prosperity Sphere. He believed that a world war that would rapidly bring about the collapse of capitalism and the triumph of communism was in the making. He envisioned Russia, Japan, and China forming a nucleus to which all other Asians would gravitate. "This," said Ozaki, "is a summary of the so-called 'East Asia New Order Society' which I intended to realize. . . ." This and similarly phrased remarks reveal clearly that Ozaki planned to play an active part in this vast Communist coalition.[7]

Of course, he did not air these views in public. His articles and books followed rather closely the Miki line, which one author summarized as the advocation of "a 'new order' . . . on the basis of an anti-capitalist, anti-imperialist liberation of the colonized peoples in Asia and the creation of a pan-Asiatic culture. . . ."[8]

Both Miki and Ozaki pointed out that one price Japan would have to pay for such a "new order" would be a lessening of Japanese nationalism. Japan and China must cooperate to resist European imperialism.[9]

No one in the Showa Research Association understood the meaning of cooperation. No one suggested that Japan prove good faith by offering to return to China a portion of occupied territory, to restore any of the property destroyed as its army spread over the land like a plague of locusts, or to pay token reparation—for full reparation was impossible—for the flood of Chinese blood and tears the invaders spilled. China was to do all the cooperating. It must forget the past, accept the status quo, and grasp Japan's hand without reservation or resentment.

For all practical purposes the attitude of the Showa Research Association amounted to complete support of the army's aggression on the mainland. It offered a perfect example of the Konoye team's ability to give the army what it wanted while throwing up a smoke-screen of verbosity for the benefit of moderates and intellectuals.

So it is not surprising that the militarists adopted the Greater East Asia Co-Prosperity Sphere as a slogan for their aggressive policies and actions. Not that the military establishment needed Ozaki or anyone else to convince it of its right, indeed its duty, to dominate East Asia. Even those in the armed forces who opposed a full military agreement with Germany and Italy enthusiastically supported the China war as a logical, heaven-sponsored step toward destiny.

His article out of his system, Ozaki plunged into writing what became his best-known book, *On Modern China,* a straightforward work about post-Manchu Chinese society and politics, destined for publication in May 1939.

Ozaki was sure enough of himself in those days to become personally involved in two police cases, although discretion and common sense should have kept him from any action that might turn the Tokko's searchlight in his direction.

The previous November the police had picked up Shin'ichi Matsumoto, a leader of the Tokyo-Yokohama Communist Group, and kept him without trial in Tokyo's Sugamo Prison for almost a year. Always a loyal friend and a soft touch for any Communist in trouble, Ozaki helped support Matsumoto's family throughout his ordeal. When he was finally released with a suspended sentence in late 1939, Ozaki put him to work with the China Research Office.

In February 1939 Ozaki testified in court on behalf of Tatsuzo Ishikawa, whose novel, *Living Soldiers,* was banned for having portrayed the face of war in all its ugliness. Ozaki had read the controversial book, and when its publisher asked him to be a witness, he agreed, testifying that in his opinion the novel did not contain antiwar sentiments.[10]

Not only did Ozaki's fantastic luck steer him away from such shoals, but it guided him to a safe harbor in one of Japan's most influential organizations. On June 1, 1939, he became to all intents and purposes an employee of the Kwantung Army: He went to work for the Investigation Department of the South Manchurian Railroad (*Mantetsu*).[11] This was a genuine coup on Ozaki's part, in some ways even more significant for the *apparat* than his appointment as Kazami's assistant. In that spot Ozaki had been subject to the shifting winds of political fortune and indeed survived there only six months. In the South Manchurian Railroad he had all the advantages of a government position and none of the disadvantages; he would be secure as long as he produced. Having done so, he was still firmly entrenched in his office on the fourth floor of the Mantetsu Building in Tokyo's Toranomon section at the time of his arrest.

The South Manchurian Railroad was a vast network of subsidiaries, including mining and manufacturing companies. The Japanese government had established the company in 1906, with shareholders limited to the government and Japanese nationals. It was really an agency of Tokyo created to administer official Japanese interests in Manchuria. The charter provided that in military affairs the army commander in the then leased territory could issue orders to the company. What is more, if the military situation so justified, this authority extended to the company's business affairs.[12]

Thus the *Mantetsu* maintained the closest possible relations with the Kwantung Army, which under the Treaty of Portsmouth had been stationed in Manchuria to protect Japanese interests, including the railroad. From this modest beginning the Kwantung Army had gradually taken over to the point at which by 1936 its commander indirectly controlled Manchukuo's internal administration.[13]

The Investigation Department, which Ozaki joined, worked in concert with the Kwantung Army. As Ozaki explained, ". . . not only the survey plans and results of the Investigation Department are reported to the Kwantung Army, but also it is requested by the Kwantung Army to do various researches and receives orders related to the operation of the army." It was a snug arrangement. The railroad operated what amounted to a second G-2 for the Kwantung Army, appearing on no organization chart and making no drain on the military budget.

Formally Ozaki "was supposed to participate in the operational planning of the Investigation Department of the main office of the Manchurian Railroad broadly and take charge of part of it." In practice he was "in the Consultant Office of the Investigation Department of the Tokyo Branch and was related to the Chinese Resistance Capacity Measurement Council and International Situation Research Council, which were projects of the Investigation Department of the main office."[14] The titles tell their own story. The situation could have been tailored to Sorge's requirements.

Ozaki also belonged to the department's Current Materials Section, which gathered "information and materials through which large movements of politics and economy could be grasped." These data were "arranged, organized, and sent to the main office" by Ozaki's co-worker Hisatake Kaieda, and Ozaki wrote the political information column of the *Current Materials Monthly Report (Jiji Shiryo Geppo)*. "Among these materials there were very many which were treated as extreme secrets, and frequently codes were used in the case of telegrams," he explained. Some of these monthly reports he gave in their entirety to Sorge through Miyagi; in other cases he sent only his political column.

Ozaki fairly beamed with satisfaction over his new position. "Since the Investigation Department, which has a long history and a huge organization, is full of rich materials and new information, it goes without saying that this information and materials were very valuable to us," he observed smugly. ". . . I was able to obtain a large amount of information and materials on politics, economy, foreign policy, etc.; moreover, I was able to find out some part of the movement of the Kwantung Army and, furthermore, the movement of the Japanese military."[15] In fact, Ozaki had a front-row seat for a preview of any major moves the Kwantung Army might contemplate, hence could not have been in a better position to know when and if Japan planned to wage war against the Soviet Union.

Ozaki did not reveal just who secured him this choice

assignment, but one thing is certain: As an undeclared Communist he had plenty of company. The South Manchurian Railroad was a prime target for infiltration. Out of approximately 1,000 Investigation Department employees, about 30 were Communists, overt or covert. They had organized an efficient little investigation department of their own within the official department. Among them were two former associates of Ozaki's from Shanghai days, Ko Nakanishi and Kuraji Anzai.[16]

For many years, the aim of the department had been to collect source data for the Kwantung Army and the General Staff in the furtherance of Japan's expansionism. Yet the means whereby the information was gathered and evaluated came close to academic freedom. Hence the company was able to employ a number of intellectuals either blind to the dichotomy or else able to rationalize that the means justified the end. When one Suehiro Okami joined the department, he espoused the Marxist economic theory, a decision that played an important part in forming the organization's policies[17]—and presumably its recruitment of personnel.

In the spring of 1939 Miyagi engaged in some recruitment of his own, at the instigation of the Fourth Department, which had instructed Sorge to acquire a few Japanese Army officers for his ring.

"That is a very difficult problem," remarked Sorge when Clausen handed him this message.[18] This was a masterpiece of understatement. If Moscow had directed him to recruit a few little green men from outer space, the task could scarcely have been more formidable. The Japanese Army, that stronghold of rampant nationalism, was the last place on earth to look for potential Soviet agents. Sounding out possible contacts might trigger the army's security apparatus and put the dreaded military police, the Kempeitai, on his trail. Yet hopeless as the assignment looked, Sorge attempted to accomplish it through his reliable director of the outer ring. Miyagi could not unearth a suitable officer, but he produced a man destined to be one of his ablest assistants, a reserve corporal named Yoshinobu Koshiro, recently returned from active duty in Manchuria.

Koshiro was born in 1909 and became interested in communism and introduced to Miyagi by a friend of his while attending Meiji University, from which he was graduated in

1935. After being drafted in March 1936, he spent most of the
next six years in the army, first in Manchuria, then in North
China. In November 1938 he was promoted to corporal and
almost immediately placed on the reserve list. He was called
back to active duty almost immediately, first in Manchuria,
then in Korea. But by March 1939 he was home, employed in
a paper shop.[19]

"If a war should break out between Russia and Japan,"
said Miyagi to Koshiro at what is alleged to be their first
meeting, "it would mean a great sacrifice not only on the part
of the farmers and laborers of both countries but also on the
part of the whole Japanese people. To avoid such a tragedy,
that is to say a Russo-Japanese war, I am sending various data
on the situation in Japan to the Comintern." Inasmuch as Koshiro made no comment, Miyagi continued his pitch. "Will
you help me by telling me what you know about the army and
by obtaining military information from your friends? You will
be paid."[20]

A slight smile twitched Koshiro's lips. "I don't know
many secret matters," he replied lightly. But he added, "You
don't have to worry about money, for I have some savings."

Well satisfied with this oblique agreement, Miyagi mentally put Koshiro down for about 50 yen a month plus traveling
expenses. He had high hopes for Koshiro. "I intended to train
him for a couple of years and then make him an independent
member of our group," he explained. "Meanwhile, I thought
it would be convenient to have him employed in some office
where he would have access to military information. I thought
the War Ministry; if possible, the Mobilization Bureau would
be a good place, but before I could arrange it, he found a
job . . . through a friend of his father's."[21]

Obviously Miyagi had no doubt that the ring would continue to operate for a long time. And he spoke with casual
assurance of placing Koshiro in either the War Ministry or the
Mobilization Bureau, as if spotting a Communist agent in those
top places was all in the day's work. Sorge and his men were
very sure of their ability to infiltrate the highest agencies of the
government.

Miyagi discussed his plans with Sorge,[22] who was interested enough to meet Koshiro once or twice. Although no

longer on active duty, Koshiro was the only prospect so far
who had firsthand experience of army matters. So Sorge "sent
Koshiro's curriculum vitae to Moscow," and Koshiro received
the code name Miki.[23]

It is possible that Koshiro had been working on the fringes
of the *apparat* before these events took place. Clausen believed
that he "had been already cooperating with us as a friend of
Joe's [Miyagi] . . ." before Moscow's instruction reached
Sorge.[24] Certainly Miyagi would never have compromised himself by saying that he was supplying information to the Soviet
Union unless he had good reason to believe Koshiro would
keep his secret.

Sorge made a curious statement on this subject: "The
main information source for Miyagi was Koshiro."[25] Yet Miyagi had been feeding Sorge with excellent information for five
years before Koshiro officially appeared on the scene. Cautious,
as always, when discussing his associates, Sorge had this to
say about the data Koshiro brought in:

> I got the impression that most of our information
> on the mobilization of the Tokyo and Utsunomiya
> divisions came from Koshiro, and that he was also
> responsible for two or three reports on the organ-
> ization of new combined units . . . from the old
> Tokyo and Utsunomiya divisions. Koshiro gave
> Miyagi a variety of data on the living and working
> conditions of troops on the Siberian border, and I
> believe he also furnished several individual pieces
> of information about the army's new artillery and
> tanks.[26]

Koshiro supplied considerably more than Sorge's words
indicate. While he was not an officer, as Moscow had specified,
Koshiro was to bring in information of a sort not normally
available to a corporal. And very soon Sorge would stand in
acute need of just such data.

CHAPTER 31

"A VERY CRUCIAL MEANING"

Sorge was thoroughly aware of the tentative discussions under way since the latter part of 1938, sparked by General Oshima in Berlin, toward a Japanese-German rapprochement. As the new year 1939 began, the Japanese position seemed ambivalent, to say the least. Oshima had moved up from military attaché to ambassador. He was a general officer, whose first loyalty was to his military superiors. And the army, like Oshima, ached to join Hitler in a full-scale agreement to replace or amplify the ambiguous Anti-Comintern Pact. By giving Oshima the dignity and authority of ambassadorship, the Konoye government seemingly signified its approval of Oshima's policy. Yet by some deft footwork Konoye avoided committing himself and left office with his reputation as a moderate uncompromised.

Neither Oshima and Ribbentrop nor Toshio Shiratori, now ambassador to Italy and second only to Oshima in enthusiasm for a Rome-Tokyo-Berlin axis, let matters drop just because the Konoye government fell. They continued to exert every possible pressure through the new war minister, Seishiro Itagaki. But Navy Minister Mitsumasa Yonai and his vigorous assistant, Isoroku Yamamoto, were dead set against lashing Japan to Hitler's mast by such an all-inclusive alliance as Hitler, Oshima, and the army hotheads desired. Foreign Minister Hachiro Arita was no more than lukewarm. Yet the question was not a clear-cut one of pro- or antinazism. Both Arita and Yonai would have agreed to a military alliance with Germany if it had specified Japanese involvement only in the event of war

253

with the Soviet Union. The new prime minister, Kiichiro Hiranuma, was considerably under the army's thumb and his inability to bring Arita and Yonai into line made him the target of much flak. He pointed out unhappily that while he could dismiss the foreign minister, Yonai had him treed for as long as the navy cared to back up its minister. The navy would refuse to name a successor, and the cabinet would fall.[1] Thus, temporarily at least, the army was cornered by the very beast it had unleashed: the law that the war and navy ministers must be flag officers on active duty.

There was no telling how long this stalemate would last. Yonai and Yamamoto had a formidable pair of opposites. War Minister Itagaki had been the founder of the Cherry Society, a group of officers that had been a prime force behind the Manchurian Incident, and he himself bore a large share of responsibility for Japanese military aggression in that area. Later he had served as chief of staff of the all-powerful Kwantung Army. And now his deputy minister was none other than Lieutenant General Hideki Tojo, who had succeeded him as the Kwantung Army's chief of staff.[2]

It looked like a fight, and Sorge stripped for action. He cut himself off from many of his former contacts, to allow himself to concentrate entirely on the German Embassy.[3]

To Clausen he delegated certain new duties. Sorge had kept the *apparat*'s purse strings in his own fingers, receiving funds from Moscow through American and Dutch banks. He began to entrust Clausen with some financial responsibility. This happened through a process of evolution rather than by specific order. Now the radioman paid himself his own salary and expenses and dispensed those of Voukelitch and Edith. The other wages and expenses Sorge continued to administer, and he required a monthly accounting from Clausen.[4]

Thus free of extraneous details, Sorge could devote his full attention to the diplomatic front, where the tug-of-war between the pro-Nazi, militarist elements of Japan led by the army and the relatively moderate faction bolstered by the navy raged with all the bitterness of a minor civil war. The army was ready and eager to ally itself with the strong man of Berlin, who had torn up the Versailles Treaty, made a monkey out of a British prime minister, mesmerized France, and stamped on

Communists right and left. If Italy wanted to come along for the ride, that was all right, too.

On the other hand, the navy hierarchy understood that if Japan entangled itself unreservedly with Germany, it would be covering Hitler's eastern flank at no possible advantage to itself. Indeed, if he continued on his present course, Japan could find itself at war with the United States and Britain, perhaps with the Soviet Union as well, with the China war still going full blast. The more responsible civilian elements of the country, such as the business community and certain court circles, realized that Japan's dependence upon American and British raw materials necessitated keeping up formal, if not friendly, relations with those nations.[5]

Sorge had cause to regret that his ring did not boast a true expert on economics who could tell him exactly how matters stood, but Ozaki did his best. Reporting the flow of gold, that sensitive barometer of economic weather, he informed Sorge that Japan had purchased 80 to 90 million yen in gold from Taiwan toward the end of 1938, and noted at that time a conspicuous expansion of currency. Nevertheless, the market appeared strained. Now, in the spring of 1939, coal and electric power had begun to run short. Ozaki's source, the economic staff of the South Manchurian Railroad, told him that the financial world feared these conditions might come to a head around April or May and generate a crisis.[6]

In these early German-Japanese negotiations Sorge's position was extremely delicate. No one knew exactly what they were arguing for or against. As Sorge said, ". . . the difficulty of this particular negotiation lay in the very obscure nature of the content of the German proposal. The content may be summarized as (1) Japan and Germany will conclude a political and military alliance, and (2) the foreign country to which this alliance will be applied is the country which becomes an enemy of either Japan or Germany—it was as vague as that."[7]

Naturally Sorge opposed the agreement. Equally naturally Ott worked vigorously to crown his ambassadorship with such a triumph. Sorge dared not antagonize Ott or raise his suspicions, but he threw cold water on the ambassador's enthusiasm. "Of course Prime Minister Hiranuma is anti-Bolshevik," he argued, "but even the former Konoye cabinet could not bring about such an alliance. Therefore, the Hiranuma cabinet won't be able to conclude it. Since there is danger that the alliance might be directed against Britain, proposing such an alliance to the cabinet is ridiculous, judging from the character of the Hiranuma cabinet. Japan may conclude a treaty if she can get the benefit of it directly, but she will never agree to a treaty only to be made the cat's-paw of Germany.''

With this argument Ott had to concur.[8] But the matter was out of his hands. Exactly what, if anything, Germany had to offer Japan in exchange for a blank check against the future depended on the direction in which Hitler jumped. He showed his hand in March, annexing what was left of Czechoslovakia on the fifteenth. This was Europe's turning point. Hitler stood revealed as an aggressor and a liar. It came as a nasty jar to all the well-meaning souls who had thought they could do business with him. On March 31 Britain pledged all support in its power to Poland if asked to provide it.[9] Thereafter the march of events in Europe should have left no doubt in Tokyo that the proposed alliance was not aimed solely at the Soviet Union.

From this point on Sorge played what for him was a very inconspicuous game at the German Embassy. He continued to point out to Ott and occasionally to Matzky that Germany could not expect Japan to sign a treaty of no direct advantage to itself.[10] German policy was being dictated from Berlin, where Ribbentrop controlled the Foreign Office, so Ott had little or nothing to say about the nature of the alliance. As ambassador he had the duty of doing his best to implement whatever arrangement Berlin made and to report progress on the Japanese side. Under these circumstances Sorge's voice could not be truly influential. Moreover, political activity was not part of his mission. He had taken it upon himself in the past, and would again in the future, when he considered that he could thereby best serve his country. At this stage exceeding his authority would have no real purpose.

It was becoming increasingly clear that the real target of the proposed German-Japanese treaty was Great Britain, despite the smoke-screen of words concerning the containment of communism. From Sorge's standpoint a treaty of this kind would be no bad thing. If the Fascist states and the Western democracies went to war, and if the Soviet Union could stay out of it, this would be exactly what the founding fathers had forecast: the breakup and mutual exhaustion of the capitalist powers. Such a conflict would result in nothing but good for the Russians.

So Sorge kept his ear to the ground at the embassy, where Ott and Heinrich Stahmer, Ribbentrop's aide for the discussions, informed him regularly about the progress of the negotiations, intelligence that Sorge immediately radioed to Moscow.[11] He asked Ozaki and Miyagi for information about Japanese intentions, but despite Ozaki's position, neither could give him anything concrete about the nature and progress of the proposed alliance.[12]

A strange scene in the spring of 1939 hints that the pressure was pushing Sorge beyond the bounds of normality. Wistfully Hanako expressed a wish to bear his child. At first he tried to joke her out of the notion: Did she want a baby with one blue eye and one black eye? At her indignant reaction he swung to the other extreme. If she had his child, she would be in a "pitiful" position. "I am an old man. I am going to die soon," he said, stretching himself on his bed. "I can do without a baby! Oh, poor Sorge!" he moaned. "You should study so that you can get along without Sorge. . . . An old man always dies sooner. . . ."[13]

Distraught, Hanako cried out, "I don't think you are an old man—I don't!" He looked at her for a moment, then murmured slowly, "I feel sleepy. Good night, good night! I don't need to live any longer." With that he closed his eyes and dropped his arms limply to his sides, as if feigning death. Thoroughly frightened and fathoms over her head psychologically, Hanako could only stare down at him in dismay.[14]

Sorge had some reason to feel a draft from the Grim Reaper's scythe as it swung toward Europe. Upon the timeliness and accuracy of his information might well depend the foreign policy of the Soviet Union. If he made a mistake or tipped his hand, he could expect no mercy from the Fourth Department.

On May 4 Hiranuma went over Oshima's head to Hitler through the German and Italian embassies in Tokyo. He indicated that Japan would support Germany and Italy with political and economic aid and as far as possible by military means

if one of them were attacked by one or more powers without
the participation of the Soviet Union. However, in view of
Japan's current circumstances, they could not count on Japan
at that time or in the near future for any practical military
assistance.

This so-called Hiranuma Declaration was a fairly safe
statement. The chances of either Germany's, or Italy's being
attacked by a power other than the Soviet Union were exceedingly slim. Naturally enough, Ribbentrop asked for clarification, whereupon the Japanese ambassador, the ever-eager Oshima,
assured him that if Germany went to war, Japan would consider
itself at war also, whether or not it gave Germany any actual
help. When this word hit Tokyo, it brought on a cabinet crisis,
although not yet its fall.[15]

On May 22 Germany and Italy signed the Pact of Steel,
a genuine military alliance obligating them to join in any war
in which either party became involved.[16] "The attitude of the
Japanese people as a whole is that they should naturally join
this alliance," Miyagi told Sorge. "However, the leaders of
the Japanese government manipulated by the *Zaibatsu** think
it is dangerous to join the alliance and they cannot make up
their minds."[17]

Miyagi overestimated the influence of the business community upon foreign policy, but he was correct about the government's ambivalence.

The event that sent the Hiranuma cabinet tumbling down
caught the whole world by surprise, although one piece of
news had given a strong hint of what was in the wind. On
May 3 Stalin dismissed Maksim Litvinov as foreign commissar
and brought in Vyacheslav Molotov. How could any diplomat
have doubted Russian intentions thenceforth? With his Jewish
blood and English wife, Litvinov was anathema to Hitler and
symbolized Soviet attempts at friendly relations with the
Western democracies. In contrast, the new commissar had
always favored diplomacy by power and therefore respected
Germany.[18]

Shortly before that, on April 16, Stalin had begun fishing

---

* Literally "wealth-family," *Zaibatsu* was Japan's industrial-
financial complex.

in the international waters, casting the first fly to the West by offering a mutual assistance pact with Britain and France, a pact that might include Poland. The very next day, long before he could expect a reply from London or Paris, he tossed a second line, this one to Berlin. Which fish he hooked was a matter of indifference to Stalin; he would haul in whichever struck his bait first, provided the catch was big enough to make it worth his while. Unfortunately Britain kept the Russians dangling and at last rejected the offer in terms so chilly as to amount to insult. In the meantime, Hitler eagerly seized this chance to protect his eastern flank and continued negotiations with the Soviet Union very much under the rose.[19]

Sorge caught wind of these secret moves almost immediately from both Ott and Stahmer. This word that his fatherland and his motherland were considering a rapprochement put an entirely new complexion on the German-Japanese negotiations, especially after Ott had hinted that the discussions might blossom into a military alliance rather than a mere neutrality pact. Sorge knew that from this point his reports to Moscow would be of increasing significance. He summed up the new situation clearly:

> For the Soviet Union this negotiation for a Japanese-German alliance had a very crucial meaning, for Russia at that time was already having secret negotiations with Germany, and it was by all means necessary to know what Germany . . . was negotiating with Japan at this time. If this Japanese-German negotiation had been about a military alliance against Russia, Russia would have discontinued the secret negotiations with Germany, since she did not entirely trust Germany.[20]

In other words, the Russians would spin out the discussions with Hitler until they heard from Sorge whether or not the Germans were double-crossing them by negotiating an anti-Soviet military alliance with the Japanese—even as Stalin was double-crossing the Germans by offering an anti-Nazi alliance to the British and French at the same time that he extended a friendly hand to Hitler.

On May 30 Ribbentrop flashed the green light to Schulenburg in Moscow: Germany had decided to begin negotiating with the Soviet Union in earnest.[21]

British-Japanese discussions had been in progress but had ended unsuccessfully for a number of reasons, and Sorge so advised Moscow. "It seems," he said, "that Russia came to conclude the treaty with Germany after she realized through my report that the Japanese-German negotiations were being directed against Britain."[22]

The Russo-German Nonaggression Pact, announced on August 24, 1939, set the world back on its heels. In addition to the usual public portions, the pact contained a secret protocol in which Hitler and Stalin divided the Baltic states into spheres of influence and established a demarcation line in Poland for their forthcoming invasion.[23]

It would be difficult to say who was the most astounded and baffled by this turn of events: the Western democrats, the Japanese, or the Germans and Russians themselves. For years the Soviet leaders had portrayed Hitler and his Nazis to the Russian people as the lowest form of insect life, while Hitler never ceased to proclaim himself the lone defender of mankind against the bestial Communists. Now they had arranged a marriage of convenience, and neither the German man in the street nor his Russian counterpart knew what to make of it.

Since World War II theorists have held that Stalin agreed to this pact to gain time for the Soviet Union to build up its strength. In view of the raw materials that he poured not into Russian storehouses but into Hitler's Reich, it is more likely that he fell victim of his own psychology and propaganda. Some believe that Stalin had always leaned toward cooperation with Germany.[24]

For his part, Hitler was certain that his pact with the Soviet Union ensured his planned invasion of Poland against British and French intervention.[25] He had no qualms about double-crossing the Japanese. Of that he left no doubt when he broke the news to his generals on August 22:

> . . . I have decided to go with Stalin. On the whole,
> there are only three great statesmen in the world:
> Stalin, myself, and Mussolini . . .

I have left to Japan a whole year's time to decide. The Emperor is the companion piece of the latter Czars. Weak, cowardly, irresolute, he may fall before a revolution. My association with Japan was never popular. . . . Let us think of ourselves as masters and consider these people at best as lacquered half-monkeys, who need to feel the knout.[26]

In an amazing feat of security, Berlin and Moscow had kept any hint of their negotiations from reaching Tokyo. Up to the last minute the Japanese press was clamoring for a full alliance with Germany. So Hitler's brazen violation of the Anti-Comintern Pact enraged the Japanese government. In almost any other nation a political and diplomatic about-face might well have resulted. A rapprochement with Great Britain, France, and the United States had much to offer Japan: ready access to the raw materials so vital to its economy; relief in large measure from the crushing load of an overbalanced armaments program; powerful allies sharing an interest in keeping the Pacific free of both Germany and the Soviet Union.

But a fundamental condition of any agreement with the Allies of the future would be honorable peace in China, and Japan was not ready to drop the handful of silver to pick up the handful of gold. Instead of seeking new friends, Japan withdrew within itself, sullenly suspicious of all foreigners.

The Hiranuma cabinet fell. Shinosuke Abe, who understood the military but had no vigorous views of his own, became prime minister, with the Emperor's former chief aide-de-camp, General Shunroku Hata, as war minister. Yonai remained in the navy spot. For a brief period, General Nobuyaki Abe became foreign minister, but on September 25 he was succeeded by Admiral Kichisaburo Nomura, well known as an advocate of Japanese-American friendship. While he held the helm of foreign policy, he could be counted upon to stamp a large foot on any suggestion of further alliance with Nazi Germany.

"This cabinet will be much weaker than the previous one," said Ozaki to Sorge, "and will be cooperative with the United States and Britain."[27]

Sorge believed that "a do-nothing government appeared" because "Konoye at that time had not made up his mind to return to the government again, and Japan itself was unable to determine its attitude. Konoye wanted to wait until the appropriate time came. . . ."[28] However, this transitional period did not mean a rest for Sorge and his *apparat*.

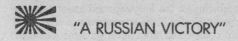

CHAPTER 32

"A RUSSIAN VICTORY"

No piece of real estate appeared a less likely object of aggression than Nomonhan,* a spot where the eastern boundary of Outer Mongolia touches Heilungkiang Province. This was a desolate region of deep ravines, quicksands, and voracious mosquitoes, without so much as a bush to be seen for miles around. Even the wood for Russian campfires had to be hauled 600 kilometers to the site.[1]

But the strategic implications were enormous. Mongolia bordered the Soviet Union from Manchuria almost to Lake Baikal and if controlled politically or militarily by an unfriendly power would be a very real threat to a vast expanse of Soviet territory. Of immediate importance was the Trans-Siberian Railway, which for a considerable distance ran parallel and close to Outer Mongolia's northern border. If the Japanese were to sever this stretch of track, in effect they would cut off eastern Russia from its West.

Recognizing these uncomfortable facts of life, on March 12, 1936, the Soviet Union and the Mongolian People's Republic signed a mutual assistance pact that enabled the Russians to station troops at key locations in return for a commitment to defend Mongolia from aggression.

Since its failure at Chang-kufeng, the Kwantung Army had made a number of annoying but insignificant stabs at Outer Mongolia. On May 11, 1939, with world attention centered on Europe, the army struck at Nomonhan.[2]

* Khalkin Gol to the Russians. See map on page xxi.

This incident disturbed Sorge more than he ever cared to admit.[3] There was one sure way to find out whether or not this was the beginning of the long-expected major Japanese assault on the Soviet Union: If the Japanese troops engaged at Nomonhan were confined to those already on the mainland, Japan meant to keep the incident isolated; if large numbers of replacement troops were sent to Nomonhan from the home islands, Japan intended a major war. Once again Sorge rallied his shadow army for a special campaign. Each was "to concern himself exclusively with discovering what reinforcements Japan will send to the Mongolian border."[4]

Ozaki soon brought him encouraging news: "The Japanese government is adopting a policy of solving the problem locally and not expanding it. It does not have any intention of daring an overall war with Russia. Also the general public does not want to have a war with Russia."[5]

Miyagi immediately set to work with Koshiro, concentrating on the organization and equipment of the Hasegawa mechanized division stationed at Koshuryo, Manchuria, the number of divisions stationed along the eastern border, and the plan for implementation of the Ko and Otsu divisions. The Ko Division, consisting of four regiments, heavy artillery, cavalry, and special corps, was the Japanese Army's "anti-Russian system," whereas the Otsu Division, with four regiments, was the "anti-Chinese system." Of course, Miyagi and Koshiro took a particular interest in the current condition of the Ko Division.[6]

Sorge checked the publicity releases at Domei. Japan was pouring out propaganda; Russian releases were somewhat scarce. His German Embassy friends indicated that the Japanese military was being evasive with them, but he had the impression that the Japanese would go as far as they dared without bringing the whole weight of the Soviet Union down on them.[7]

Tanks, heavy artillery, and aircraft were moving from Japan to Nomonhan, but since no major troop movements developed from the homeland, Sorge concluded that his inside information was correct. He radioed that he did not believe "the incident would lead into a war, because no extensive troops were sent to the spot from Japan, but that there was a possibility that reinforcements might come from northern China and Manchuria."

He might have saved himself the trouble, for the Red Army did not believe him.[8] It was positive it had to deal with no mere border probe but with genuine, major aggression against the Soviet Far East.[9]

The first accounts Sorge received of the actual fighting were not encouraging for the Soviet Union.[10] The Russians and Mongolians were ill-prepared to wage modern warfare in this area, where they had strung neither telephone nor telegraph wires, had constructed no landing strips, no command post. Zhukov admitted to Stalin that in these early stages Japanese pilots flying superior planes bested their Russian counterparts until better-quality Soviet aircraft reached the front.[11]

As the clerks in Tokyo's German Embassy ripped the page headed May 1939 from their calendars, Sorge was somewhat surprised to find that the Nomonhan Incident, which he had anticipated would be over quickly, was nowhere near a settlement.[12] On this point he had miscalculated. Could he be equally mistaken about Japanese intentions?

Sorge tried to give the impression that he never seriously considered the possibility of Nomonhan's being the start of a full-scale attack on the Soviet Union. But Hanako knew better. "This incident greatly affected Sorge," she said. "Even when it was clear to him that Nomonhan was a Russian victory, Sorge still was very much concerned. This was because he wondered whether the Japanese might not try to hit the Russians again, whether they might after all organize a serious invasion of Siberia from Manchuria."[13]

Busiest of all of Sorge's group was Miyagi, who labored ceaselessly with Koshiro to uncover every possible scrap of information about the progress of the Nomonhan Incident. He also talked with Shinotsuka, who declared that Japan was winning a victory in the air. But Miyagi was not convinced. Despite exaggerated Japanese claims, he believed the two air forces were about evenly matched. The public was equally skeptical of official tall stories crediting each Japanese fighter with three to thirty Russian planes.[14] The arrival in mid-June of replacement Soviet aircraft and twenty-one crack pilots, every one a

Hero of the Soviet Union, soon gave the Russians a distinct edge in the air, but the Japanese command was still so sure of a victory that it invited foreign correspondents and military attachés to view the triumph.[15]

Voukelitch was among the newsmen selected. "Since you are going there at the invitation of the Japanese government, you will be shown only those places that Japan wants to show," Sorge told him disagreeably. "You had better not go." This remark conveyed an aroma of sour grapes. Sorge would have been glad to go to Nomonhan, even as a guest of the Japanese Army. Voukelitch could not have refused to be one of this party, even had he so wished, as Sorge knew very well. "But anyway," he warned, "don't make a move which might bring you under suspicion."[16] He "ordered Voukelitch to watch tanks and heavy guns carefully. . . ."

Voukelitch spent from July 3 to 15 in the neighborhood of Nomonhan. While he could hear the pounding of guns, he was not permitted near the front, and he saw no air action. He talked with some Russian prisoners "and found that they were not politically trained," to use Sorge's expression. Sorge was somewhat unhappy over the caliber of Russian propaganda concerning the Nomonhan Incident and discussed this matter several times with Voukelitch.[17]

The latter returned with information about heavy artillery, trucks, and airfields, adding that in his opinion "this incident would not lead to a war." He further advised that "the Russian Army was much better than was being reported in the Japanese newspapers, that the Russian artillery had more heavy guns than the Japanese artillery, and that he saw very many trucks moving behind."[18]

He had had a glimpse of some of the behind-the-lines activities relating to the hard-fought engagement of July 3–5, when the Japanese launched a powerful surprise attack at Bain-Tsagan Mountain. Initially the Russians were outmanned and outgunned, but they hurried aircraft, tanks, armored vehicles, and artillery to the scene. They forced the Japanese to retreat with such heavy losses that the Japanese never again tried crossing the Khalkin Gol.[19]

Voukelitch talked with an unnamed army officer who told him that "the incident was a means for Japan to have friendly relations with Germany." Sorge discounted this because at that very time the Germans were trying to convince the Hiranuma cabinet that Japan's real enemy was Britain, not Russia.[20]

Voukelitch's account contained the same conclusions Sorge sent to the Soviet Union as his own, yet he claimed that his report to Moscow "was not based on the on-the-spot inspection report by Voukelitch."[21] No wonder the Croatian later remarked that to the very end of their association Sorge could never rid himself of the feeling that he, Voukelitch, was an outsider.[22]

As for Miyagi's intelligence about Nomonhan, Sorge declared contemptuously, "It was found that his information was wrong and that he brought just rumors." Sorge also asserted that Miyagi's information was meaningless to him. Yet to the objective eye Miyagi's detailed data about Japanese forces, plus his evaluation of popular opinion, would seem to have been well worth Sorge's approbation.[23]

Miyagi traveled to the Osaka area in search of intelligence not available in Tokyo. He dropped in on Mizuno, who was in Kyoto recuperating from an illness. From the convalescent he learned that the Sixteenth Division from Kyoto had left for Central China instead of for the Mongolian-Manchurian border.[24] This confirmed the report that Japanese home troops were not being rushed to Nomonhan and proved that the Japanese planned to keep the incident localized as far as possible.

Miyagi poured data on his chief. In July he briefed Sorge on the type and number of units at various points around Nomonhan, as well as training conditions in Manchuria, in northern Korea, and along the Russian border; and passed along the rumor that "about August . . . Russian tank corps would counterattack and the general offensive of the Japanese Army would not be successful."[25]

On the twentieth of that month, exactly as Miyagi had reported, the Soviets launched a counterattack in force at Nomonhan. Led by Lieutenant General Georgi Zhukov and supported by aircraft, artillery, and infantry, Russian tanks "retaliated like clouds and fog." They rolled over the Japanese.[26] It may or may not be significant that the Soviet Union waited until Sorge had furnished the Red Army with data on the strength

and equipment of the Japanese. Zhukov had some harsh words
to say about the quality of the on-the-spot information in preparation for this critical August engagement: Intelligence men
were wasted in difficult but meaningless assignments, and frequently intelligence officers misled the command by assump-
tions based on nothing more than speculation.[27]

By August 30 the Japanese invaders had been virtually
destroyed. Miyagi noted the timid sprouting of a few antimilitary ideas. When the official announcement of the result came
in September, it confirmed public fears. By September 15 the
Japanese were glad to agree to a cease-fire.[28] The adventure
had cost Japan an estimated 50,000 casualties. Stated Procurator Mitsusada Yoshikawa, "It was like putting Japan's
hand in a charcoal brazier."[29]

On the basis of information from Koshiro and other informants, as well as of interviews with returning Japanese soldiers, Miyagi summed up the results of Nomonhan. In neither
morale nor equipment were the Japanese particularly inferior
to the Russians, but in quantity the Soviet Union had more than
thrice that of the Japanese. One exception was a new Russian
two-engine bomber which had both armament and speed, so
"the Japanese troops could not do anything against it." In
tanks Japan was inferior in both quantity and quality.[30]

Zhukov's memoirs tend to confirm Miyagi's estimate.
He paid tribute to the training, discipline, and persistence of
the enemy soldiers and junior officers. He had less use for their
seniors, who seemed to lack initiative. And he considered Japan's armament obsolete.[31]

The chief of staff of the Kwantung Army was recalled
because of his responsibility for the Nomonhan Incident, but
instead of being properly chastened, he demanded of the General Staff why it had not carried the battle through to a conclusion. Headquarters planned strategy and tactics, so the
Kwantung Army on the spot "could not take proper measures."

"The general public feels safe and secure by the announcement of the cease-fire," Miyagi said to Sorge. "There
are two intermingling feelings: One is that we do not want to
fight Russia at the same time as the China Incident and [the
other is] that the army does things that are not necessary."
Oddly enough, he found the populace favorably disposed to-

ward the Soviet Union. "The Japanese people have a low standard of political sense," he observed. "So when they win, they feel strong, but when they lose, they easily become pessimistic—even if the battle is limited to an extremely small one." Because of the Russian victory, "the general public as a whole has come to embrace the idea that Russia is powerful."

Miyagi gave Sorge a sensible word of caution: "Japan discontinued the Incident because she had the China Incident to contend with at the same time. Therefore, Soviet Russia should not overvalue its success in this victory."[32]

By way of follow-up, Miyagi combined his information with notes from a scratch paper from Ozaki, containing the names of divisions, their locations and division chiefs, of Japanese units in Central and North China. These, plus other data from Koshiro and Yamana, he worked up in the form of a map and gave to Voukelitch to photograph for Sorge.[33]

The latter turned up his nose at this effort. ". . . the list was made by Ozaki and Miyagi based on what was written in the *China Weekly Review*, so I thought it was of no value," he observed. ". . . Materials in China could have been collected more reliably by the Russians in China than I, and if I had given a report to Moscow based on such materials obtained in China, I might have been scolded."[34] That was absurd. Independent confirmation of data is always welcome, in espionage as in any other field.

Sorge made good use of the Nomonhan Incident to return to his political activity in the German Embassy. "The achievements announced by the Japanese side are completely false," he told Ott. "Judging from my experience as a soldier, it is absolutely untrustworthy that Japan destroyed a thousand Russian airplanes. Such reports are completely false no matter what Japanese Staff Headquarters may propagandize.

"The military weakness of the Red Army," he continued, "which was exaggeratedly reported by Lyushkov and others, is entirely groundless. For the Japanese Army to expel the Red Army from this area, Japan will need four to five hundred tanks, but such a thing is impossible judging from Japan's current industrial power.

"Germany should study the Nomonhan Incident thoroughly," he stressed, "and let it be a lesson to the German

Army to discard the long-dominant view that there is no resisting power in the Red Army.''

Sorge saw nothing at all quaint about an ex-buck private lecturing a major general about airpower on the basis of his experience in the infantry more than twenty years before. He was somewhat aggrieved to find that as matters worked out, ''it seems the German side probably did not trust such words of mine, but the word of Lyushkov and others.''[35]

It was all very frustrating. The Fourth Department did not believe his assessment of Japanese intentions, and the Germans did not credit his warnings about the Red Army's capabilities. He could only wait for events to justify him. And over the next few years they would amply do so.

As the days passed, Sorge continued to be jittery about the Russo-Japanese border situation. Shortly before the Nomonhan armistice, Ozaki reported on a large troop concentration of the Kwantung Army on the Manchuria-Mongolia border.[36] What was Japan up to now? ''The Japanese government is always grabbing,'' Sorge snapped to Hanako. ''What will they grab next?'' In his talks with her he became increasingly critical of Japanese aggression. ''They are always stealing from others,'' he would repeat. And from time to time he demanded of her abruptly, ''Do you know what I am in Japan?''[37]

She neither knew nor cared. He was there, and they were together. For Hanako that was enough. But not for the Red Army, which knew precisely why he was there and exactly what it wanted from him.

CHAPTER 33

"SOMETHING FISHY WAS
GOING ON"

Thus far, in view of the climate of the times, the Sorge ring had operated with an almost eerie invulnerability. Always suspicious of foreigners, by the late 1930s the Japanese were entering a period when this nebulous antipathy crystallized into a spy mania amounting to national psychosis. Any Japanese in the company of a Caucasian had better be able to give the Tokko or the Kempeitai* a rock-solid reason why.[1]

On the day the *Japan Advertiser* announced Dirksen's imminent departure it broke out the headline GOVERNMENT PLANS TO STATION "THOUGHT HAWKS" ABROAD TO KEEP RADICAL IDEAS OUT OF JAPAN. San Francisco, Rome, and Berlin were the sites selected for Japanese agents on the lookout for radicals who might send "literature from the Comintern to Japan."[2]

Antiespionage propaganda flooded the country: exhibitions, posters, slogans, shopwindow displays, antispy days and antispy weeks, even antispy matchboxes. Always the spy was represented as a white man.[3] This preoccupation with race was one reason why Ozaki and Miyagi avoided arrest so long. Concurrent with the anti-Western-spy drive went the usual roundups of native leftists. That February Mizuno, who had managed to stay out of jail for an entire year, found himself in again for violation of the Peace Preservation Law. Once more he escaped with a suspended sentence.[4] How often the

---

* The military police charged with counterespionage.

finger of fate hovered over Sorge, only to lift at the psychological moment!

In April 1938, with blithe disregard of the obvious dangers involved, the indefatigable Miyagi ventured afield to sign
up another recruit. He visited his old friend Tomo Kitabayashi
and persuaded her to collect information for him.[5]

How did she happen to find herself once more within
Miyagi's orbit? The sequence of events had begun almost two
years before. In 1936 a thin stream of reverse immigration was
trickling to Japan from American ports as Japanese living in
the United States faced a choice. Those not born on American
soil were not eligible for citizenship at the time. So they had
to do some serious thinking. Should they remain in the United
States, their longtime home and source of livelihood, where
they must be forever aliens? Or should they return to start life
anew in the almost forgotten homeland, where they must accept
a lower standard of living but where they would be citizens of
the country and members of the dominant race?

Among those who cast their lot with the Rising Sun were
the Kitabayashis, with whom Miyagi had roomed in Los Angeles. They decided that Ms. Kitabayashi would return to Japan, find a place to live, and get a job. Then her husband would
join her. Accordingly she packed her meager possessions and
returned to her native Wakayama, southernmost prefecture on
the island of Honshu. There she settled in the little town of
Kokawa and found work as a sewing teacher. Both her home
and her work were conveniently near the local Seventh-Day
Adventist church, of which she was still a member.[6]

Miyagi shepherded back into the fold his former landlady, a woman of known Communist background, who moreover had a personal association with him dating back to their
residence in the United States. Later he paid a bitter price for
this action.

As yet the police had taken no special interest in Sorge
or Clausen. By 1938, however, both from its own resources
and from tip-offs from the Korean government, the Japanese
Ministry of Telecommunications knew that unauthorized coded
radio messages were crackling between Tokyo and the Asian
mainland. This information was duly passed to the police,

including the Toriizaka Station—Sorge's local police station—and efforts were under way at all levels to decode the messages and pinpoint their source. These early attempts were fruitless. The code defied all efforts to break it, and Clausen's mobile apparatus baffled the Japanese tracking instruments of the day. But the Tokyo police continued to work on the problem, and careful hands added another and another as yet undecoded item to their ever-thickening file.[7] For this was a major weakness of Sorge's operation. Any message entrusted to the airwaves could be picked up not only by its intended recipient but also by eavesdroppers.

The motorcycle accident rather than the ring's activities brought Sorge to the attention of Shigeru Aoyama, a bright young officer of the Toriizaka Station, who was assigned to handle the red tape in the case, such as caring for Sorge's property in his absence. For this reason, and because Aoyama's duties brought him into frequent contact with embassy employees, he and Sorge became quite friendly. Aoyama liked and admired his interesting neighbor, but from the very beginning of their association he "had the impression that something fishy was going on."

Aoyama did not suspect that Sorge might be a spy; he was simply suspicious on general principles. Sorge did not fit into the conventional mold. In a nation and at a time when *different* was a dirty word, this was enough to attract official attention. For one thing, although Sorge was associated with the embassy, where he met many people socially, he rarely entertained at home and seemed to have very few outside contacts. In the second place, he always worked upstairs and after typing his documents would burn them, as Aoyama discovered through routine questioning of Ama-san. But his shadowy doubts were not sufficiently substantial for him or anyone else to act upon or to interfere with his friendship with Sorge.[8]

The military police attempted a flanking attack upon Sorge. A "gentle-looking" young man visited Hanako to ask about Sorge. Making the best of it, she ushered the agent into her home and served him tea. "How long have you known him? And how close is your relationship with him?" he asked, adding apologetically, "This is a very impolite question, but please answer." Hanako replied briefly that she lived on the money Sorge gave her. After ascertaining Sorge's occupation, he asked, "Can you steal Mr. Sorge's papers?"

"I could not steal without telling him!" protested Hanako.

Smiling slightly at this incongruous reply, the man went on, "If you were my sister, I would ask you to do some work." That was a delicate touch, the hint that he intended no disrespect, that he would ask nothing of Hanako that he would not ask of his own sister.

He requested that she not tell Sorge of this encounter, but of course she did. Sorge seemed interested but unconcerned. "The policeman said that he wants to get your papers," she told him. "Why? Funny, isn't it?"

Sorge burst out laughing. "Would you like to have my papers?" Hanako disclaimed any such wish but admitted to a little worry. Sorge reassured her, instructing her that if the agent came back, she was to send him to Sorge in person.[9]

Clausen continued to have frightening experiences with the Tokyo police. Early in 1939, as his taxi bowled toward Shimbashi, he clutched the black bag containing his transmission apparatus. As always, with that incriminating object in his possession, he felt nervous. The driver mistakenly raised his turning signal. Instantly an alert policeman waved him to a halt and summoned him to the nearby police box. Peering out the window of the taxi, Clausen saw the officer's curious gaze come to rest on him and his bag. Then the man turned to the driver and began to question him. The next thirty minutes were "very painful" to Clausen. But the officer made no effort to interrogate him. Eventually the driver emerged from the box and climbed behind the wheel. As the taxi sped off, Clausen relaxed at last, feeling "as though I had just emerged from a tiger's lair."[10]

Retrospectively Clausen's near misses with policemen seem more humorous than dangerous, but many a criminal case has been broken through just such incidents, so Clausen had good reason to worry.

After the opening of the European war, security measures tightened in all areas, and in October 1939 the Tokko quietly began checking up on Sorge.[11]

In the monolithic, racist Japanese structure of the day, any foreign element was as intolerable as a cinder in the eye. In 1939 Japan was a police state, requiring neither actual wrongdoing nor evidence of evil intent to attract the attention of the authorities.

The watch on Sorge was in no sense the thorough, constant tailing merited by any concrete evidence of lawbreaking or definite suspicion of espionage. But from the Tokko's point of view the Japanese had three excellent reasons for watching him: He was a foreigner, he was a journalist, and he frequented the German Embassy. Foreigners were intellectual Typhoid Marys, carriers of un-Japanese ideas and possible corrupters of Japanese youth. Journalists poked and pried into matters that were none of their business. And the German Embassy was suspected of being a clearinghouse.

Army and civil police agents haunted the seventh floor of the Domei building, where most foreign correspondents had their offices. In the words of American journalist Joseph Newman, ". . . with Japanese nationalism mounting to the point of fanaticism, almost anything in the possession of a foreign correspondent could be construed as evidence of his guilt as a spy." These agents informed Newman frankly "that they suspected German and Italian newsmen much more than Americans. They understood that the Axis correspondents had been sent to Japan not only to report to their newspapers and agencies but to gather whatever secret information they could for the German Embassy."[12] So it is likely that the Tokko suspected Sorge of spying not for the Russians but for the Germans.

If the Tokko had wished to subject Sorge to a day-by-day, hour-by-hour tailing, it would have been hard put to do so. In 1939 the German subdivision of the Tokko's Foreign Section boasted only 5 employees to cover some 700 Germans in Tokyo.[13] Each agent had 140 Germans under his wing. This impossible proportion of workload to manpower reveals just how sketchy was the Tokko's surveillance.

Nor were all Tokko detectives brutalized fugitives from a propaganda film. They could be exceedingly tough when in their opinion the occasion called for it, they did not believe in coddling their prisoners, and as in any police force, a few psychopathic cases may have slipped in. But many were sin-

cere, dedicated policemen, proud of their role as protectors of
the domestic front.

Such a one was Harutsugu Saito, the sharp young agent
of the Foreign Section detailed to watch Sorge. At twenty-eight
years of age Saito was taller than the average Japanese, handsome and intelligent, with the wide shoulders, narrow midsec-
tion, and grace of a welterweight. Brisk, ambitious, cool-headed,
he would have been a credit to any police department. He took
immense pride in his Japanese heritage and in his status as a
Tokko agent.[14]

At first Saito was not pleased with the job of following
an embassy habitué. These types usually sported high-powered
cars that left the modest Tokko vehicles behind and caused
agents to lose valuable time in flagging down taxis. However,
Sorge's little Datsun proved well within the Tokko capabilities,
and Sorge, a flamboyant figure, one of the best known in the
foreign community, was an easy subject to follow. Saito knew
that if he bungled this job, someone might demand his badge,
for Sorge was a favorite of the German ambassador, who in
turn had numerous powerful connections in the Japanese Army.

But Saito was not clumsy; he eased into his assignment
with the delicacy of an expert safecracker adjusting a dial.
Slowly, carefully he tabulated his man's habits and routines.
At times he picked up the trail from Sorge's house; on other
occasions, so well did he come to know Sorge's tastes he waited
in one of his drinking haunts until Sorge turned up. Always he
took care to keep out of sight, for Saito's strong, mobile face
was memorable. He did not want to give his quarry an opportunity to notice the same set of features frequently bobbing up
in the background.

Thus cautiously, never for more than an hour or two at
any time, Saito kept watch on Sorge and managed to glean a
large bagful of information. He took a special interest in his
acquaintances. Clausen caught Saito's eye, for he seemed an
unlikely friend for one of Sorge's stamp. Yet so skillful was
Sorge in dealing with his Japanese contacts and so necessarily
sporadic was Saito's surveillance that the agent never saw Sorge
meet either Ozaki or Miyagi, nor did those two names as yet
appear on the Tokko's records in connection with Sorge's.[15]

In the course of his surveillance Saito became acquainted

with Tori Fukuda, Sorge's faithful Ama-san. She was loyal to Sorge and loved him as a son, so when Saito first tried to question her, she sent that personable young man about his business. "I won't answer your questions or those of the Kempeitai," she snapped. "My master is a fine man. Leave him alone!"

Far from resenting his oral spanking, Saito admired her spirit and became fond of the spunky little woman. Soon Ama-san melted so far as to permit him to accompany her to the temple to pray to her favorite deity, Oinari-san, the fox god, who had many devotees among Japanese peasants. They would walk together to the nearby temple, Saito matching his buoyant stride to her slower pace. Having made her devotions, Ama-san would be in a softened mood, more open than usual to Saito's gentle questioning. Gradually he won her confidence. In a mental duel she was no match for the clever agent and let slip small items, none important in itself, but all helping round out the picture.[16]

Whenever a person talks, however innocently, however innocuously, what he or she says contains bits and pieces with meaning for the trained interrogator. It is unlikely that Ama-san intended to provide Saito with information that might be used against her master. Sorge had the knack of inspiring devotion. Perhaps as she knelt in the tiny temple she asked the protection of the fox god upon her adored employer, and what could be more appropriate? Surely Oinari-san would look benignly upon Sorge, the foxiest of spies.

CHAPTER 34

"A CONSIDERABLY HIGH POSITION"

Ms. Mitsutaro Araki acknowledged her partner's heel-clicking bow of thanks with a dainty tilt of her glossy head. The German Embassy was in gala array, with a tide of German gutturals and Japanese sibilants ebbing and flowing. The most attractive features of the evening were the Japanese women, as gracefully elegant as Siamese kittens.

The first notes of the next dance would have brought more than one eager suppliant to Ms. Araki's side, but by Oriental standards the room was stuffy, and she felt a sudden need to escape momentarily from the heat, lights, and noise. Unobtrusively she slipped from the ballroom, made her way quickly to the library, and stepped gratefully into its dim coolness, thinking herself alone. The next second she recoiled convulsively, heart lurching and scalp prickling. Outlined in a circle of light, "the face of a demon" hung in the gloom as if disembodied—craggy, sardonic, and blue-eyed, like all orthodox Eastern devils. For a dry-mouthed instant Ms. Araki stood rigid with panic.

Then humor boosted sanity back to its throne. It was only Richard Sorge, sprawled out on a sofa under a lamp, book in hand. Ms. Araki knew that Sorge, a poor dancer, sat out every turn he could escape without discourtesy, to hold a knot of amused listeners captive to one of his stories, to engage a knowledgeable guest in earnest political discussion, or to indulge in a few moments of refreshing study. "I was horribly frightened," admitted Ms. Araki years later. "But that was just like Sorge, reading and studying all the time and soaking up his surroundings like a sponge does water. This was his genius—to learn about everything around him.''

Ms. Araki and Sorge exchanged the smiling greetings of old acquaintances, for she had been a favorite in the embassy since Dirksen's time, when Frau Dirksen treated her like a daughter.[1] Ms. Ott, too, was so fond of her that she, like Sorge, was virtually a member of the Ott household.[2] On this occasion, despite her half-humorous, half-annoyed relief at realizing that she had mistaken a German reporter for a demon, Ms. Araki suddenly lost her taste for the library and hastened back to the dance floor. She was not one of Sorge's conquests. Thoroughly feminine, she felt the pull of his virile magnetism, but to her fastidious senses it held the taint of evil.

Nevertheless, as an amateur painter she longed to paint Sorge's portrait. To capture those Luciferian features, to catch the essence of that intriguing mixture of scholar and Tatar would be the ultimate challenge to her skill. For several years she had been coaxing Sorge to sit for her and even wheedled Ott to intercede on her behalf; however, Sorge proved elusive. He would appear to agree, then cancel the sitting when the time came.[3]

Sorge seldom turned down the chance of better acquaintance with an attractive woman, but he seemed content to let relations with Ms. Araki remain distant rather than cordial. Her popularity in Japanese Army circles—"Tojo always made a fuss over me"[4]—might have caused him to wonder if she was not herself a spy, as was later claimed. The prevalent rumor that she and Mirbach were conducting a liaison[5] certainly would not have held Sorge back. Most likely he realized that Ms. Araki could be dangerous to him. Behind her smooth brow worked a mind as clever and as carefully cultivated as his own. Any one of the slips that almost daily sailed into Hanako's right ear and straight out the left would have sent Ms. Araki's incisive brain into action with swift, impersonal logic.[6]

In any case, Sorge disliked posing for a portrait. While a number of likenesses of him exist, most are casual snapshots. At Hanako's request he had his photograph taken but charged her emphatically to keep the result to herself. "I do not like showing my picture to other people," he told her.[7] Naturally he did not want his likeness in circulation in case some visitor from Germany recognized a former Communist agitator and party stalwart. By the same token he could not risk having his features transferred to canvas. A portrait is essentially a distillation of the sitter's most striking characteristics. Even Ms. Araki, who would be the first to admit that she was no Rembrandt, might transmit more than Sorge cared to reveal. So he always returned a smiling but firm refusal to all her petitions, claiming the press of business.[8]

This was true enough because the outbreak of the war in Europe gave added meaning to Sorge's mission. The very day that Hitler's panzers crashed over the Polish border—September 1, 1939—the Fourth Department sent Sorge a panicky message: "Japan must have commenced important movements (military and political) in preparation for war against Russia, but you have not provided us with any appreciable information. Your activity seems to be getting slack. You should utilize all the capacities of Joe, Miki and Otto to the fullest extent."[9]

This was most unjust to Sorge and his hardworking crew. Throughout the summer Sorge, Miyagi (Joe), Koshiro (Miki), and Ozaki (Otto) had knocked themselves out gathering intelligence. Sorge had sent word that the Japanese were not plotting war on the Soviet Union, at least at this time. Why did Moscow keep insisting on the contrary? In view of the fact that Zhukov was mopping up the floor with the Kwantung Army, the Fourth Department certainly seemed to be overreacting. But perhaps his superiors thought that it would do no harm to remind Sorge of his primary mission.

Throughout the autumn he supplied Moscow with information about the Abe government and its attitude toward the conflict. On September 4 Japan formally announced a policy of nonintervention, and Sorge passed on Ozaki's opinion that the Japanese would join the war, if at all, on the side of the perceived winner.[10] The Kremlin did not need to maintain a spy ring in Tokyo to state what was only too obvious.

During the first months of World War II Sorge had as much as he could handle. ". . . the German Embassy no longer had the hollow expectation that Japan would actively participate in the war," he said. Therefore, his German cronies began an exhaustive survey of the attitudes of different classes and groups toward the war, interviewing influential people in various fields.

On the basis of these findings Ott sent many detailed reports to Germany.

Sorge saw all of them. Whenever he thought it worthwhile, and that was often, he wired the information to Moscow. The general trend of these surveys was very unfavorable to Germany. Aside from parts of the army and certain factions led by such firebrands as Suetsugu, Oshima, and Shiratori, Sorge found no inclination to join the war, thanks to the hostile reaction of the Japanese to the Russo-German Nonaggression Pact. Sorge also noted that in the lull after the blitz against Poland "in Japan pro-British and U.S. groups successfully turned the feeling against Germany, and the German Embassy was possessed by anxiety that the Japanese Government might directly turn into the British and U.S. side. . . ."[11]

The outbreak of hostilities caught a number of German ships in Japanese ports, and their disposition became a "problem." Talks on this subject continued for some time between Naval Attaché Leitzmann and the Japanese Naval High Command. The Japanese were eager to purchase some of the stranded vessels, "but the German side wanted to use these ships as suppliers to three light cruisers which were very active at that time in the Pacific Ocean." The Germans had their way without too much difficulty.

Then came the more knotty question of "the repair of these ships and how to load petroleum and other cargo." As Sorge observed, "Ten thousand tons of petroleum and a great amount of other goods were necessary in order to operate all of these ships." To let that much fuel get away from its own navy was no small matter for resource-poor Japan. Long discussions ensued first in Tokyo, then in Berlin between Japan's naval attaché and the German naval command.[12]

The real crux of the negotiations, however, was whether or not Japan would permit the Germans to use Japanese bases. These naval discussions dragged on throughout the autumn and winter and well into 1940, but in the end Japan decided not to compromise its neutrality to that extent. "Thus a few German ships loaded petroleum, food, beer and other items in Japan, set sail, and went out to the southern Pacific." There Japanese vessels gave them some assistance, such as telling the whereabouts of British warships. They also rendezvoused with the

German cruisers, supplying them with goods and picking up sick seamen. "Several other German ships loaded goods in Japan, made their way through the British blockade and went back to Germany around the Cape of Good Hope in Africa."

As a side issue in these talks Japan agreed to supply Germany with tin, zinc, and other items and on the economic front set up companies of joint Japanese-German ownership. Sorge kept on top of these negotiations because "Russia was interested to know to what extent and in what method Japan assisted Germany." He "heard in detail about the talks in the embassy from Naval Attaché Leitzmann and later Wenneker, who participated in the talks."[13]

Although Miyagi found twenty-four items worthy of his attention between June and December 1939,[14] not until November did action for the ring again pick up real momentum. On the twenty-fifth, Moscow finally sent instructions for courier contacts in Tokyo. Under the circumstances the Red Army had no choice but to use couriers and Russian Embassy clerks to contact the Sorge ring.

This imposed a serious double risk. No foreigners in Japan were more closely watched than the Russians. Any linkage visible to the Japanese or German eye between the Soviet Embassy and Richard Sorge, confidant of Hitler's ambassador, absolutely must be avoided. For the time being, however, all concerned had a brief respite from this particular peril, for the first contact was not scheduled until January.[15]

The most important change for Sorge was his altered status in the German Embassy. For months Ott had been urging Sorge to become an official member of the staff, but the spy had managed to put him off without giving offense.

Then the German Foreign Ministry through Ott seconded the offer, with the promise of "a considerably high position to administer activities related to information and newspapers in the embassy." This development placed Sorge in a quandary. Moscow probably would have welcomed this opportunity to plant a trusted agent within the German governmental gates; on the other hand, an official position would have seriously cramped his style as a spy. He could fit his newspaper work and free-lance writing into his schedule, but espionage came first with him. A formal job meant regular hours and a desk piled with papers, many of which would be stereotyped handouts. Sorge feared that under these circumstances he would be able neither to spy on his own nor to coordinate the activities of his subordinates smoothly.

The principal stumbling block was that following the Nazi takeover the Foreign Ministry put all applicants through a rigid security check. "Since they strictly investigate identification cards, if I had accepted the position I would have had to present my identification," Sorge explained. "Then I would have had to change this identification card and what I am could have been discovered after checking my past career."[16] No doubt he was correct, to judge by the ease with which the German police turned up his records when a question about his bona fides arose.

After weighing the pros and cons, Sorge refused Berlin's offer with thanks, although he was flattered and honestly grateful for this evidence of Ott's high regard. When Sorge turned down the proposal, at last Ott became angry with him. To pacify his irate friend and maintain this priceless contact, Sorge arranged a compromise. He still refused to become a government employee, but he agreed "to maintain continuously the role as a private collaborator to ambassador Ott" and further "promised to arrange various information flowing into the embassy in the Information Section." To keep the record straight, he signed a formal contract with Ott along these lines. So both men were happy; Sorge dodged a security check, and Ott continued to avail himself of his experience and advice.

Sorge chose to put in his daily four-hour stint at the embassy's Press Section beginning at 6:00 A.M.[17] That early in the day he had the offices practically to himself. With no telephone to jangle his nerves, no interruptions to break his thread of concentration, the spy had a perfect opportunity to rummage through desks and file cabinets, to examine at leisure an interesting-looking document. Sorge needed privacy for his first task of the day, which was to select "important items out of various information from the ring and arrange them so that higher members of the embassy could look at them immediately."[18] He wanted no one suddenly looming up at his shoulder while he screened a report from Miyagi or Ozaki.

Normally Ott rose early, and by the time Sorge had been

at work for an hour or so he was ready to hear his friend's report. The two men sat on the veranda behind Ott's office and breakfasted together almost every morning. Sorge was jealous of his breakfast spot and told off any journalist he suspected of trying to force him out of it.[19]

At times, however, Ott would awaken stiff and sore, plagued by chronic rheumatism in his shoulders. Then he remained in his warm bed until his circulation returned to normal and he could move about with no more than the usual mutter of pain that formed a continual, nagging background to his days. Sometimes he worked in bed, and on such occasions Sorge would sit at his bedside, running over the latest political and military developments in Asia and Europe.[20]

After his official briefing Sorge collected his notes and returned to his office. There his second order of business was to organize "for the Japanese newspapers and for Germans staying in Japan that part of the information that could be made public." Thus he performed a dual chore. He separated the sheep from the goats, and he tanned press releases from the goat hides. The news suitable for the German community, including members of the embassy, went into the *Deutscher Dienst*, the embassy's news booklet of which Ott had appointed Sorge the editor.

Promptly at 10:00 A.M. Sorge headed for the courtyard, where his tiny car awaited him. A quick whir of the motor, a crunch of gravel, and he was off to his true loves: his *apparat* and his typewriter.[21]

It behooved Sorge to spend considerably more time at that useful instrument if he wanted to maintain the reputation he claimed as the best reporter in Japan,[22] not to mention his fees for the articles he sent to Germany. Despite his accident in 1938, during that year he had polished off thirty-two newspaper articles, plus two for the *Zeitschrift für Geopolitik*. During 1939 he kept up the pace for Haushofer, sending in two solid articles. But his newspaper output dropped dramatically. In all 1939 he published only six times.[23]

Back in 1936 the *Frankfurter Zeitung* had agreed to receive contributions from Sorge but could not sign him on until he joined the German Press Association. This organization fully accepted Sorge early in 1940, but he never became a correspondent for the *Frankfurter Zeitung*; he remained a stringer. The arrangement was advantageous to both. The newspaper obtained as a regular contributor "a most serious and thoughtful person, gifted with both an understanding of a newspaperman's job and political insight" and wrote him several times that it valued his work highly.[24]

Sorge confirmed that the *Frankfurter Zeitung* "often praised me on the ground that my articles elevated its international prestige." He was genuinely proud of his association with a newspaper that "represented the highest standards of German journalism."[25] Becoming a formal employee might have enhanced Sorge's reputation even further, but he would have been at the newspaper's beck and call and would have compromised the independence so necessary for his espionage. So his relationship with the *Frankfurter Zeitung* was analogous to the one he maintained at the German Embassy—close, mutually profitable, but informal.

Just how good a reporter Sorge was is a matter of subjective judgment. Anyone visualizing a reporter as an eager individual, notebook always ready, first at the scene of action, asking questions, scribbling answers, then racing off to scoop his rivals, would deny that Sorge was a reporter at all. Nor was he an investigative reporter in the Watergate tradition, although he did like to check up for himself when this was possible. Thus, primarily, he was a commentator.

The *Frankfurter Zeitung* thought enough of Sorge to accept 163 articles from him over a period of six years[26] and to send him letters of praise. Yet the famed German journalist Margret Boveri claimed that many of his articles were difficult to read and understand and that writing did not come easily to him.[27]

An article which appeared in the *Zeitschrift für Geopolitik* in the late summer of 1939 offered an example of Sorge's style at its best. It was formal, somewhat stiff, but it revealed the author as a man of education, experience, and considerable insight. After the interesting remark "The Japanese is a conqueror but not a colonizer," Sorge continued: "They want raw materials for their war industries and formulate the boundaries of their conquests in accordance with strategic points of view. In this policy of limited objectives lies the strength but also the weakness of the Japanese continental expansion. For as sharply delineated as 'autarchy' and 'strategic needs' may appear, in practice they are boundless and undefineable. Just as boundless as the term 'Asian Continent' is."[28]

Mirbach, chief of the embassy's Press Section, used to complain about Sorge's being "such a mediocre press correspondent."[29] As was evident from his early but short office hours, Sorge did not exactly wear himself out as an embassy official. Indeed, his job was merely a convenient pigeonhole for him, giving Ott a plausible explanation for his presence should any German snooper question the daily appearance of a newspaper reporter at highly classified meetings and discussions. Certainly Ott had better uses for Sorge than piecing together press releases, a job any third secretary armed with scissors and paste could do just as well.

At first Sorge found these new, closer ties with the embassy something of a nuisance, or pretended to. "I have to be here every night. When am I going to have time for drinking and doing my own work?" he complained to Morin of the Associated Press.[30] But he soon found his additional workload well worth the trouble. "Needless to say, this kind of work had an extremely important meaning to my secret activity," he remarked. "I used it for my espionage. In addition, after I engaged in this work, I came to be able to see various secret papers in the embassy more freely in my special office."[31]

After the war had begun, Ott no longer sent lengthy reports to Berlin, in general only telegraphing brief dispatches. No more did Sorge have to photograph documents in the embassy; that removed one danger of detection.[32] Nevertheless, he noted a gradual tightening of military information. In the past military data from the embassy were more valuable and accurate than the items Miyagi and Ozaki rounded up. Information Sorge obtained at the embassy was "collected and organized by brilliant and well-informed attachés who were sent from staff headquarters in Germany and whose names were known even in Russia."[33]

Periodically Sorge had offered to the military study group bits of information submitted to him by Miyagi, the accuracy of which he questioned—in effect, trying it out on the dog. Either Schol or Ott would look into the matter he had raised and inform him whether or not it was true.[34] Thus Sorge both checked up on Miyagi and put himself in a position to give him a tactful push in the right direction when the official information from his obliging German friends disclosed that Miyagi had been on the wrong track.

With the start of the war, however, this situation gradually reversed, and "the military information from Miyagi and Ozaki seemed to have become more valuable than the information from the embassy." Matzky's offerings were brief, and Gronau and Nehmiz reported only monthly.

Later Sorge claimed the data he obtained at the embassy "were not obtained by means of plot, conspiracy, or violence. I was shown them by Schol and Ott, who asked for my cooperation. . . ."[35] This is a choice bit of Alice in Wonderland reasoning. Naturally Sorge did not demand information at the point of a pistol, but his very presence in Japan and his infiltration of the embassy were the essence of conspiracy, carefully and deliberately plotted.

CHAPTER 35

"CLAUSEN HAS HAD A HEART ATTACK"

Once more the wheel of time brought the Year of the Dragon. For the mercurial, loquacious, and malleable Voukelitch, 1940 was to be uniquely his year: "Dragon-year people . . . are quite softhearted and are taken in by any sort of line. This gives other people tremendous advantage over them. . . . Yet other people love them. . . . Dragon people do have big mouths. . . . The dragon symbolizes life and growth and is said to bring the five blessings: riches, harmony, virtue, longevity, and finishing the allotted life span."[1]

This sampling of Dragon Year characteristics gives a surprisingly accurate picture of Voukelitch. The two preceding Dragon years had found him a student, and during his early, lean years in Tokyo he had eked out his income by tutoring in languages.[2] Perhaps nature intended this master of many tongues for a university. Such a path might have led him to riches of the spirit, if not of the purse, as well as brought him his "allotted life span" instead of an early death in a freezing Japanese prison.

On December 18, 1939, his divorce from Edith became final.[3] While originally Edith had no regular salary from the ring, to help support her and her son and to compensate for the use of her home as a sending station Sorge made her an allowance when she established her own residence in March 1939.[4]

Clausen soon found that "when she had a date with a man, that date was more important to her than providing me with her home for wircless work." When he gained admittance,

Edith's housekeeping horrified his neat German soul to such an extent that "after I worked in her home I did not feel like eating anything at all."[5]

However, Clausen overcame his repugnance to a degree. In explaining why, after her move, Sorge paid Edith 400 yen, plus another 100 for expenses, he said, "I had recommended to Sorge that we make this generous payment to her because she and I were having illicit relations and she was like a prostitute in a way, because she was permitting me the use of her house for radio work, and because she had a child to support."[6]

He was sorry for Edith. "Men simply used her body and soon went away from her. Thus she deteriorated gradually through her sexual life." He knew that Edith continued to cooperate with the ring because she needed the money, not because of Communist commitment or even loyalty to her friends. However, he took the knowledge philosophically. "But like most other women she is a woman," he mused profoundly. "Although she was not bright she had sense enough to be able to use other people for herself. . . . If she had had a stronger man than Voukelitch she might have been different. She cannot be said to be bad in everything. Simply her living conditions made her what she is."[7]

Voukelitch himself was supremely happy, unwinding the legal red tape so that he could marry his Yoshiko. For five years he had carefully concealed from her his real business in Japan. Now, shortly before their wedding day, he unburdened his soul of its secret: He was a Communist; he belonged to a spy ring headed by Richard Sorge.[8]

What motive drove Voukelitch to take this irresponsible step remained buried within his bald skull. Possibly he wanted to start his new life with no secrets or misunderstandings between man and wife. Perhaps he succumbed to a human urge to drop his burden on another pair of shoulders. Very likely Clausen was correct when he stated that Voukelitch just could not keep his mouth shut. It may well be that in some remote corner of his psyche Voukelitch hoped his sweetheart would blow the whistle on his clandestine career, demanding that he choose between her and the spy business, or even would turn him over to the police.

Whatever his reasons, the secret was not his to disclose.

In laying down his hand for Yoshiko's inspection, he jeopardized the mission of the ring and the lives and liberty of his colleagues. Fortunately for them, Yoshiko was interested in her man, not in his politics, and accepted the situation. She kept the secret so well that the police never once suspected that she had the slightest inkling her husband was a spy.[9] Safely around this corner, Voukelitch married Yoshiko on January 26, 1940. After a duly conventional lapse of time she could whisper that another Voukelitch would be delivered in a Year of the Dragon.[10]

Voukelitch refrained from telling Sorge that his new bride knew of their activities, so he made no effort to involve Yoshiko as he had Anna and Edith. No doubt Voukelitch was well content that this should be so. Why expose one's lovely wife unnecessarily to the potent charms of one of the most fascinating men in Tokyo?

Sorge came no more to Voukelitch's house. When the agent in the Western camp had anything to tell Sorge, he phoned him and arranged a meeting at Sorge's home. The two men never got together in a public place, for Sorge preferred to keep secret how often and where he met with the Havas representative. He disarmed possible suspicion in the German Embassy by occasionally mentioning to Ott that as a German newspaperman he "was purposely maintaining a fairly tenuous contact with the office of the French news agency Havas in order not to sever all connections with reporters representing enemy countries and countries unfriendly to Germany."[11]

Meetings with Clausen presented no problem to Sorge, both being prominent in the German community and members of the German Club. Ever since Clausen had taken such good care of him at the time of his motorcycle accident, Sorge had allowed the acquaintance to ripen publicly. They "telephoned each other's homes directly, heedless of whether or not the telephone lines were tapped." Clausen visited Sorge's home often, and Sorge dropped in on the Clausens, although somewhat less frequently.[12] "Clausen had free access to Sorge's upstairs room at any time," Hanako recalled. Nevertheless, when they happened to run into each other at the Rheingold, they never drank together. "They acted almost like strangers, only nodding to one another."[13]

Clausen kept careful track of the portion of the ring's funds Sorge had entrusted to him. At the end of each month he gave an accounting to Sorge, who combined Clausen's figures with his own and sent a financial statement to Moscow. At first this was required twice a year; in later days, annually. Clausen never knew Sorge's salary or the total amount available, assuming that the chief used his own judgment in these matters.[14] He was much more conscientious in his accounting than Sorge. "I kept records once in a while, and often did not," the latter remarked cavalierly. This was a slipshod way to do business, but money as such meant little to Sorge. When for a long period in 1939 no courier contact was made, he went into debt to cover the ring's expenses.[15]

The tremendous events of late August and early September 1939 forced the spy ring to alter some of its operating procedures. As a German national Clausen no longer could use the facilities of the British and American banks. Thenceforth he dealt with Japanese banks exclusively.[16]

It had become impractical for Germans to make courier contacts in Shanghai, so Sorge asked Moscow to change the liaison site to Tokyo, but no meeting could take place under the new arrangement for some months. Radio output and intake, however, stepped up considerably. Clausen transmitted to the mainland fifty times in 1939. Sundays became normal radio days.[17]

On the side, Clausen's cover business steadily improved. Trade was so brisk that during 1939 he opened a factory. Even with this outlay, when the accountants added up the books at the end of the year, Clausen could congratulate himself on a net profit of 14,000 yen, a tidy sum.[18]

One day early in 1940 Clausen suddenly asked Anna to go with him to the Teigeki, as the Imperial Theater (*Teikoku Gekijo*) was popularly called. Curious and a little suspicious about what lay behind this unexpected burst of husbandly generosity, Anna asked why.

"I'm supposed to meet a friend," Clausen told her. Immediately and correctly Anna concluded that this theater party was being organized to cover a courier contact and that her husband wanted to take her "because it was unnatural for a European man to go to a theater alone."[19]

Clausen had been nervous for some time waiting for this encounter. Moscow's message agreeing to courier meetings in Tokyo had arrived in November. The ring had anticipated an early rendezvous, but the first set of theater tickets went astray because the go-between made a mistake in the number of Clausen's post office box. Then instructions arrived by radio that Clausen would receive two tickets for the Imperial Theater and the man next to him would be the courier. Shortly thereafter tickets for the performance on January 27 appeared in Clausen's box.[20]

When he and his wife settled into their places in the balcony, a man whom he rightly assumed to be his contact occupied the seat on his right. After some fifteen minutes, the man slipped from his left hand into Clausen's right about 5,000 yen wrapped in a white cloth.[21] In exchange Clausen passed over his small packet of thirty-eight rolls of microfilm.[22] An experienced agent, he knew that the fewer questions he asked, the longer would be his life-span, so he made no attempt to identify his new acquaintance. Not until the police showed him a photograph did he discover that the man was a consul named Vutokevich from the Soviet Embassy.[23]

Successful as he was in business and as a radioman, physically Clausen was not at all well. His heart had been tricky since 1932, and the condition had steadily worsened during his stay in Tokyo. He blamed the trouble on the chemicals he had breathed when he "made a fluorescent board" for lighting as well as on his "irregular spy life, that is, drinking."[24] Even without those factors, Clausen was the type at the sight of whom insurance agents automatically double their premium rates. He had the lusty German appetite for heavy foods washed down by drafts of foamy beer. Had he remained a merchant seaman or stayed on the land, he might have thrived on this diet, burning the calories into hard muscle. But having taken to the underground, Clausen had passed successively through the stages of pleasingly plump and stylishly stout and by early 1940 was frankly fat. He took no physical exercise, and what little recreation he had consisted of listening to his collection of phonograph records or sitting in a German bar.[25]

By day Clausen ran a prosperous business, and such hours as he did not spend at his desk at his office he passed in his room at home, encoding and decoding a never-ending stream of documents, using a fearsomely complicated system, or else he was readying his stations for transmitting sessions two or three times a week. Sometimes in the late afternoon, but more often from 3:00 to 6:00 A.M., he set up his receiver and transmitter, patiently clicking off his messages and straining to pick up the faint crackles from the Siberian station at the other end.[26]

Always he lived with the fear of discovery. Fear kibitzed over his shoulder at coding desk and radio set. Fear walked the streets with him and rode beside him in the car as he carried his machine to and from his home. Fear answered every knock at the door, every ring of the telephone, grinned at him from behind every policeman. One week of this nerve-racking routine would have sent the average man climbing the walls; Clausen had taken it for almost four years. Thus far dedication to his work, an optimistic nature, and a happy marriage had kept him mentally on an even keel, but now outraged nature took its revenge. April 1940 found him under the care of a Dr. Wirtz, a German physician, and undergoing periodic hospital checkups.[27]

Amid this troubled domestic picture, on April 18 Clausen made another contact, this time at the Tokyo Takarazuka Theater. The Russian courier slid Clausen a package wrapped in green paper, which proved to contain $2,000 in American money and 2,500 yen. Clausen presented the courier with about thirty rolls of film, which he had received from Voukelitch. The Russian mentioned that he was going home before long, so Clausen would soon have a new contact, and suggested that they meet again shortly at the Suehiro Restaurant in the Ginza. But Clausen's heart being in bad shape, he proposed Sorge in his stead.[28]

Not long after this Dr. Wirtz ordered Clausen to bed for three months with the recommendation that he forget about his business for that time. He could do so, for M. Clausen Shokai was operating smoothly with dependable employees. But Sorge made clear that he expected him to continue operating the radio,[29] so he improvised a slanted bed table, ostensibly to enable him to read in bed, in reality for coding and decoding.

With Clausen bedridden, Anna played an important role. When the time came to transmit his messages, Clausen directed

operations from his pillow while she assembled the transmitter,
attached the antennas, and placed the apparatus on two chairs
near the bed so that Clausen could send without getting up.
Then she took her usual vantage point by the second-story
window.[30]

This regimen was not exactly what Dr. Wirtz meant by
bed rest. Much of Clausen's sending took place at night, but
he had to be alert against interruptions while coding in the
daytime. Several times one of his Japanese employees came in
before he could hide all his documents, which did not worry
him because the man paid no attention to the papers, but he
did have a scare when Dr. Wirtz, whom the maid usually
announced, walked in without notice and looked inquiringly at
the littered bed table. The doctor merely said, "Don't write
when you are sick," gave Clausen his regular checkup, and
left without further comment. For several days his patient worried that the doctor would report the incident to the police, but
nothing happened.[31]

Not until July 12, after Clausen had been bedridden for
two months, did Sorge finally advise Moscow, "Clausen has
had a heart attack. He operates the wireless lying in bed."[32]

There is nothing like a heart attack to make a man take
stock of himself. His illness gave Clausen plenty of time to
become acquainted with the inner man and to mull over hitherto
unformulated ideas. Pumped full of Communist propaganda,
he had come to Japan eager to improve the lot of the suffering
Japanese masses.[33] As he lay propped up in bed with only his
thoughts and memories for company, a little mouse of doubt
began to nibble at the foundations of his dedication. His practical mind contrasted the living conditions in Moscow and the
Volga Republic with those of Japan. By Western European or
American standards, police-haunted, militarist-ridden Suzuki-
san was pitiable, but it seemed to Clausen that the Japanese
townsman was better off materially than his Russian counterpart. This was what impressed him. Because he was accustomed
to a police state, the lack of freedom did not worry him.

By the same token, Germany's economic upswing under
Hitler caused Clausen "to have a very favorable attitude toward
Hitler's way of doing things." Always a pushover for propa-
ganda, Clausen felt a remote stirring of latent nationalism,

which brought in its wake a ripple of unease about his spying activities.[34] As soon as he could leave his bed, in his confusion he threw himself into his legitimate business, which under his personal touch thrived anew. Outside the office he sought comfort in the sake bottle.[35] All this helped neither his physical nor his mental well-being. But at this stage he kept his doubts to himself and continued to operate his sets at his usual level of efficiency.

CHAPTER 36

"THE FLOW OF INFORMATION"

For Sorge the year 1940 opened with orders from the Fourth Department formally extending his tour of duty in Japan. He acknowledged these instructions in a note dated January 1940: "My dear Comrade, I have received your order to remain another year. No matter how much we may wish to go home we shall carry out your order and continue with our difficult work here. I accept your regards and best wishes for a good holiday with gratitude. If I should take a holiday, however, it would immediately stop the flow of information."[1]

Indeed, much with which the Soviet Union had to remain *au courant* was happening in Japan, and no one but Sorge and his efficient assistants could have kept the Kremlin posted so well and so authoritatively.

One such project was the Japanese effort to establish a puppet regime in China under Wang Ching-wei. Negotiations to that end had proceeded throughout 1939. Ozaki duly reported to Sorge any developments, such as Wang's visit to Tokyo in June 1939 to confer with Konoye and Hiranuma.[2] These negotiations were supposed to be highly confidential, but Sorge heard about them from the German Embassy and even from the newspapers.[3]

The outcome of this maneuver was extremely important to the Soviet Union. Suppose the Japanese succeeded in setting up a Chinese government separate from Chungking, then retired into the wings long enough for Wang to establish himself publicly as a bona fide Chinese yet willing to negotiate peace at a reasonable cost. This would seriously embarrass Chiang Kai-shek. Many Chinese had no love for the Kuomintang but supported Chiang as the only choice between resistance to Japanese aggression and abject surrender. A face-saving compromise would hold considerable appeal for these people. Once the Chinese had accepted him, Wang could open talks with Tokyo. Then, if the Japanese kept their demands within bounds, there was at least a chance that Chiang might have to accept a compromise peace.

Obviously the Soviet Union would profit by a continuation of the China Incident. Peace in China would free the Japanese to turn their undivided attention to Russia. From the Soviet point of view, therefore, much depended upon the terms Japan proposed to extend to Wang as the price of setting him up in business. If they were reasonable, then the Soviet Union must strengthen the Siberian army and be quick about it. From the Japanese viewpoint, secrecy was vital. If the Chinese caught wind of the terms, which, in fact, were unreasonable, Wang would stand revealed as a contemptible puppet of Tokyo. Therefore, the draft, completed in 1939, was as highly classified as a document could be.

Drafter of the treaty was Ken Inukai, chief negotiator with Wang. Inukai hurried home to Tokyo with his masterpiece in December 1939 and shortly thereafter showed it to Kinkazu Saionji. What is more, he allowed Saionji to copy it on the spot.[4] This was an astounding breach of security. If Saionji needed to study the draft, he should have received an official copy properly marked with its classification, and he should have signed a receipt for it.

Saionji now had an illegal, unregistered handwritten copy of a secret state document. As one might expect, one indiscretion led to another, if indeed, Saionji's actions were mere indiscretions. Ozaki told a circumstantial story of what happened next: "Before long . . . Saionji agreed that he would show me the copy of the draft of the Japan-China Basic Treaty and its attached exchange documents. On the appointed day soon after I was given that promise, I arranged things on telephone, and since he said that he was going out on that day, but that he would have his gatekeeper in charge of it, I went to the Saionji residence . . . [and] borrowed from the gate-keeper what he had left for me. . . ."[5]

What can be said of a man who would leave such a document with his gatekeeper to pass to a third party—and a third party with no authority to see it? If Saionji's succeeding activities showed him as a patriotic Japanese, one might give him the benefit of the doubt and consider him no more than careless, even if almost criminally so. But in view of his later career Saionji's action smells very much like collusion rather than folly.[6]

Ozaki scurried home, clutching his prize, and copied the entire four-page treaty. A day or so thereafter he returned Saionji's copy and handed the new copy to Miyagi, who in turn gave it, with an English translation, to Sorge.[7]

This draft treaty included among other things provisions concerning certain zones in China, customs duty, the stationing of troops, and their withdrawal.[8] Ozaki admitted, "I knew thoroughly . . . that the content of the draft of the Japan-China Basic Treaty and its attached exchange documents, which I obtained from Kinkazu Saionji about December of 1939, copied down, and reported to Sorge . . . through Miyagi . . . belonged to secrets from the military viewpoint, not to mention the political viewpoint."[9]

Two Chinese members of the negotiating committee released the draft, and it appeared in the Chinese, British, and American press. This published draft "was not complete, but ninety percent complete," said Sorge.

"What was important to me," he continued, "was whether the draft thus announced was a real one or not." Information from the German Embassy as well as Ozaki indicated it was bona fide. Later Sorge read the released content in the January issue of *China Weekly* and was able to confirm that Ozaki's data were factual.[10]

So, thanks to Sorge, the Soviet Union knew the contents of this treaty many months before its final version was signed and could plan accordingly.

As the speed and complexity of international events increased almost by the hour, Ozaki found his restaurant rendezvous with Miyagi more and more expensive and inconvenient.

He cast about for a way of bringing Miyagi to his home in a natural manner, and while he cudgeled his brain for a legitimate excuse for frequent and regular visits with his fellow conspirator in his own home, his wife said she would like their daughter, Yoko, to learn to paint.

Ozaki jumped at the opportunity. With Sorge's approval he arranged for Miyagi to come every Monday morning to teach her and they transacted their business before and after each lesson. Although many visitors to the Ozaki home saw Miyagi, "since he was Yoko's painting teacher, no suspicion was aroused."[11] If Ms. Ozaki wondered about these private weekly twosomes between her distinguished husband and a rather seedy artist, she said nothing.

By this time *distinguished* was indeed the word for Ozaki. As consultant to the South Manchurian Railroad he received an excellent salary of 500 yen per month, plus a bonus of 2,000 yen paid in semiannual installments. In addition, he scooped in approximately the same amount from royalties, articles, and lecture fees. Thus he could count on a monthly total income of some 1,000 yen—almost four times that of the average Japanese of the day. On this sum Ozaki could live very well indeed—and did.[12]

Although Ken Inukai spent most of his time these days in Nanking and Shanghai, working to establish the puppet government, he came to Tokyo once in a while and kept up his membership in the Breakfast Group. On such occasions Ozaki "met him frequently and exchanged opinions," Ozaki briefing Inukai on the Japanese internal situation and Inukai keeping Ozaki informed about current developments in China. Inukai also replaced Kazami as patron of the China Research Office, and Ozaki received 200 yen from him as maintenance expense funds for that organization.[13]

As the Abe government tottered to its close, Ozaki informed Sorge that the cabinet was on its last legs because of its own weakness and the deadlock of the European situation, which had stirred up the activists. But "the military had not yet come to the surface." Sorge wired Moscow that the lack of confidence in the Abe government in the Diet reflected popular opinion and was dangerous to a military regime.[14]

Japan's situation was complicated. It was waiting to see which side in Europe looked like a winner before committing itself. Ribbentrop labored mightily to remove the bad taste the Hitler-Stalin agreement had left in Japanese mouths and to convince them that the pact would operate to Japan's advantage, freeing the Germans to smash Britain and leaving the South Pacific up for grabs. Of course, the war in Europe so far showed no signs of a quick German victory or indeed of any particular effort on Hitler's part to obtain one. Yet Ribbentrop's line had its effect. On January 12 Japan notified the Netherlands it was terminating their treaty whereby each party agreed to settle all disputes by peaceful means.[15]

At the same time the German Embassy believed that the British had enormous influence over Japan and "Germany was very angry, particularly over the unreliable attitude of Japan."[16] Ott's irritation over Japan's disinclination to pull German chestnuts out of the Asian fire could not have been soothed when the Abe cabinet fell in late January and Admiral Yonai, the outstanding opponent of full alliance with Germany, came to power.

Yonai was a popular figure with an excellent record of public service, first in the navy, then as a Diet member and as navy minister. A handsome man of pleasant disposition, he could deflate potentially explosive situations with a well-timed word or two.[17] His selection reflected the wish of the more level-headed civilian statesmen to remain on at least speaking terms with Great Britain and the United States. He appointed as his foreign minister Arita, who had held the position during a previous period of tension with those powers and was cautious about closer ties with the Axis.[18]

But the pro-Nazi group was too strong to be counted out. Even Kazami, Ozaki's patron, "thought that, as political necessity, 'strike down Britain' should be made a slogan for the time.''[19] So the German Embassy, if annoyed, had no reason to be overly discouraged.

In the early spring, Ozaki became a member of the Foreign Policy Department of the Showa Research Association. The department's director was first Teikichi Yabe, followed by Morio Yukawa of the Foreign Ministry. The members included, among others, Ozaki's friends Hiroo Sassa and Ushiba. During the spring, too, along with Shigeharu Matsumoto* and other members of the Breakfast Group, Ozaki met with Konoye at the prince's invitation. Although Ozaki did not recall any specific details of the conversation, the ex-premier renewed his personal contacts with his faithful kitchen cabinet.[20]

In March Ozaki traveled to Shanghai to attend the second conference concerning the "Chinese resistance capacity" sponsored by the Shanghai Office of the South Manchurian Railway.[21] Sorge saw him go with mixed feelings. On the one hand, Ozaki's absences inconvenienced him;[22] without Ozaki's advice and counsel, he had difficulty in maintaining his reputation for omniscience in matters Japanese, and he did not trust Miyagi's information without Ozaki's confirmation. "If Ozaki says so, it must be so."[23]

On the other hand, Ozaki's usefulness to Sorge depended largely upon just such contacts as these important conferences. Such trips proved most profitable, and whenever Ozaki took to the road, Sorge "asked him to observe carefully anything interesting."[24] The value to the spy ring of the information Ozaki secured at these conferences varied according to the nature of the meetings. "Generally speaking, conferences seemed to be a fad throughout Japan after the China Incident . . ." Ozaki explained. For practical purposes he found them somewhat ineffectual.[25]

However, they gave Ozaki the opportunity to hear speeches by experts in their field, to collect on-the-spot observations, to make and renew valuable contacts. Perhaps most important of all, he could enhance his reputation as an authority and make himself known far and wide as a respected, trusted representative of the powerful South Manchurian Railroad and a member of Konoye's brain trust.

Ozaki was in Shanghai on March 20, when Japan officially established the Wang Ching-wei puppet regime. He obtained some on-the-scene information about "the reputation of the Wang government and its condition of maneuver."[26] Typically he could not resist the temptation to share a few drinks

---

* Chief of the editorial bureau of the Japanese news agency Domei.

at the Palace Hotel in company with Yikuhiro Sekine, an old buddy from the days of Sorge's Shanghai ring. Sekine had fled Japan for Shanghai after being arrested for leading labor disputes and "resorting to terrorism" and then been released. In Shanghai he had helped Ozaki gather information for Sorge's *apparat*.

Ozaki never told Sekine the details of the Shanghai ring's operations, but he thought Sekine understood that its work "was spy activity related to the Chinese Communist Party." The two men had met occasionally since Shanghai days, but Ozaki never used Sekine in connection with the Tokyo ring.[27] Nevertheless, Sekine was an unwise choice in drinking partner for a man who had every cause to be cautious in choosing his friends.

As soon as the Shanghai conference ended, Ozaki returned to Tokyo and met Sorge at a restaurant to report his findings, particularly those concerning the Wang government. Ozaki doubted exceedingly that it would do any good for either China or Japan. The Chinese did not trust it, and opposition to it existed within the Japanese government and business world. Ozaki had discovered that plots were afoot for direct negotiations with Chiang Kai-shek.[28]

Ozaki might have been a little less pleased with himself and a little more careful about drinking with such men as Sekine had he realized just how much interest both the Tokko and the Kempeitai were taking in him. They were trying to plug some security leaks in the South Manchurian Railway. While they did not suspect that Ozaki was a deliberate leak, they did consider that this convivial soul might be an unwitting source of information for subversive elements. So the police were going over Ozaki's writings with a curry comb, the Tokko looking for questionable ideas that might corrupt the national spirit, the Kempeitai seeking concrete evidence to justify forcibly retiring Ozaki to private life.

Ozaki's books and articles had to run through the censorship mill before reaching the printing press.[29] Nevertheless, more than one Japanese had been hauled in for questioning on less cause for suspicion than Ozaki had given. His published double-talk, his championship of such known left-wingers as Shin'ichi Matsumoto and Mizuno, and his persistent association with old cronies with police records were enough to label him a prime security risk.

The fact that Ozaki still roamed at large in the spring of 1940 cast no reflection on the zeal and efficiency of the Japanese police. Certainly it was not due to any precautions of his own. His freedom was a tribute to his public stature as one of Konoye's select group of advisers. And he was so friendly, so openhanded, so humorous! These were disarming virtues, and Ozaki possessed them in abundance.

CHAPTER 37

"AN OVERCOAT FOR A VERY COLD COUNTRY"

In the early months of 1940 Sorge was by no means entirely dependent upon Ozaki's valuable connections. His own supply of influential friends was never more abundant. His old comrade Wenneker returned for a second tour of duty as naval attaché, bringing with him two new items: the rank of rear admiral and a pretty bride.[1]

Sorge made a smooth transition from bachelor drinking buddy to family friend.[2] The admiral took up the threads of his friendship with Sorge most opportunely, for Moscow, unconvinced of Japan's friendly intentions, requested substantial evidence of a military nature. "Investigate the production capacity of the Japanese Army and Navy arsenals and civilian factories about cannon, tanks, airplanes, automobiles and machine guns," the Fourth Department ordered Sorge briskly on February 19, 1940.[3]

Much to his annoyance, the same day's batch of messages included a reproof. Sometime previously he had sent to Moscow by courier an army manual obtained through Koshiro. Now, in Clausen's words, ". . . Moscow expressed its dissatisfaction, saying that such publications did not need to be bought secretly." Sorge was furious, not only at the disapproval but also because this official skinning proved that the Fourth Department had not paid proper attention to his material. The first part of the publication was not classified, but the second section was. In the sulks, he replied promptly that the information contained in the second part of the manual could not be bought legally. "If you think it can be, why don't you use your legal agency and let them buy it?"[4]

His superiors sensibly ignored this somewhat childish reaction, and instead of a scolding, the Fourth Department sent gracious but belated salutations on March 3 in honor of Red Army Day.[5]

Then, on March 7, Moscow inquired, "In the division formation of the Japanese Army, do divisions 106, 109, 110, 114, and 108 really exist? If they do, investigate and report their stationing places." This sort of message came frequently.[6]

Years later Goriev, who had met Sorge in Berlin when he was on his way to Japan, claimed that Sorge warned the Soviet Union of Germany's intention to strike in the West and the date of Hitler's offensive against France, going into some detail concerning the strategic orientation of the principal German troops.[7] The surviving message which most closely approximated this went out on March 7 and read in part somewhat as follows: "Germany means to conquer France, Belgium and the Netherlands, but if she does, the United States will probably come in. Of two plans for German self-sufficiency from the U.S., the USSR and remaining economic areas, the first plan probably will be implemented."[8]

No matter what might be going on in Europe, the Kremlin never lost its keen interest in Japan's military intentions and capabilities. So on March 25 Sorge advised the Fourth Department about the reorganization and mechanization of the Japanese Army which had been going on as a result of lessons painfully learned at Nomonhan.[9]

A symbolic little interlude took place about this time. At dusk one evening Sorge showed Hanako a brown overcoat, not new but of excellent quality. Throwing it open to reveal its fur lining, he informed her that Ott had given him the coat.

"Mr. Ott," she repeated, examining the garment with interest. "This is an overcoat for a very cold country," she went on. "Are you going to wear it?"

"No, I won't. It's not very cold in Japan."[10]

Even so, Ott could not have given him a more symbolic gift. After all, Sorge's entire mission was in effect to provide "an overcoat for a very cold country"—a protective armor of knowledge for Russia.

In April Sorge sent off his annual birthday telegram to his mother in Berlin and also dispatched a box of soap to his sister. "My sister in Berlin has a baby," he explained to Hanako. "She needs to wash the baby's things, but soap is very scarce in Germany."

"Does your mother live with your sister and the baby?" Hanako asked.

"She lives alone in an apartment," replied Sorge. "Occasionally she gets together with my sister and the baby."

Hanako worried to think of this elderly woman, all alone with nothing but letters, an annual telegram from her son, and occasional glimpses of her daughter and grandchild. Sorge brushed aside her anxiety. "Western people often live by themselves," he said. ". . . I like solitude. Being with others all the time is not good."[11]

His claim to be a solitary spirit did not prevent him from appreciating kind words from Moscow, such as "Director's" message which arrived on May 4: "I would like to celebrate May Day International Memorial Day with you and your group. I shall be praying for your health and success in your work."[12] Both Moscow and Sorge had reason to pray for his success, for a message of May 2 had demanded specific information about Japan's military production: "It is very essential to have details about aircraft manufacturing plants. Also it is necessary to estimate the actual 1939 production totals in cannon manufacturing arsenals and factories. What measures are they taking to expand cannon production?"[13]

This assignment started Sorge on a continuing project investigating production in the Mitsubishi Aircraft Factory in Nagoya, the Aichi-Tokei Company, and Nakajima Aircraft, which he accomplished by borrowing from the German Embassy information the air attaché and his subordinates obtained during visits to factories. Sorge copied and photographed this information over a period of several months.[14]

While Sorge was thus engaged, on May 10 Hitler launched the anticipated blitzkrieg in the West. "It goes without saying that in view of the military situation we are putting off the time of our return home," Sorge advised Moscow. "Allow me to assure you once again that this is not the time to bring up the question."[15] His nobility in delaying his return because of the international crisis is slightly diluted by the fact that the Fourth Department already had extended his tour of duty for another year and he had acknowledged its order. He was absolutely correct about one thing: May 1940 was the worst possible time for the Red Army to disrupt a seasoned, functioning *apparat*.

Miyagi offered his opinion on the possible effect on Japan and China of Germany's strike in the West: The "United States will become involved in the war, joining the side of Britain and France to protect its capitalists. United States participation in the war will make the European chaos into a Second World War and as a result less attention and effort will be placed on Far Eastern affairs. So it will be possible to find a clue to solve the China Incident."[16]

In expecting the United States to join the European conflict immediately, Miyagi overlooked the fact that 1940 was a presidential election year, and nothing would have ruined a candidate's chances more surely than a foreign policy platform of intervention in Europe. Furthermore, Miyagi was mistaken in anticipating a slackening of official interest in the Far East. Anxiety may have fathered the thought. If the United States withdrew support from Chiang, Japan might be able to close the China Incident and be free to look around for other, and presumably Russian, worlds to conquer.

Japan was more than willing to profit by the turmoil in Europe. On May 18 it presented demands to Batavia that included a new basic treaty, raw materials, and a written agreement against interfering with such export. Four days later Ott passed the word that the German government was "not interested in the problem of the Netherlands East Indies." Tokyo correctly interpreted this as the Nazi blessing on extension of the Greater East Asia Co-Prosperity Sphere to the Southwest Pacific.[17]

The German Army reached the French coast on May 27. While every available Channel-worthy craft hauled troops out of Dunkirk, the British sent a mission to Moscow under Sir Stafford Cripps. Schulenburg wrote to Berlin on May 29: "There is no reason for apprehension concerning Cripps's mission, since there is no reason to doubt the loyal attitude of the Soviet Union toward us, and since the unchanged direction of Soviet policy toward England precludes damage to Germany or vital German interests. There are no indications of any kind here for belief that the latest German successes cause alarm or fear of Germany in the Soviet Government."[18]

But the Soviet Union was alarmed. Surrounded by icons, carpets, and intrigue in Moscow, Schulenburg had no way of knowing that on May 25 a German in Tokyo, propped up in bed with a receiving set beside him, was absorbing urgent directions from the Red Army's Fourth Department:

> Your next necessary assignment, second only to the primary one, is as follows: We need information and materials concerning the Japanese Army's reorganization, from what troops this reorganization is based on, title of these troops and names of the commanders. We are concerned with the collection of detailed information in problems concerning the trend of foreign policy by the Japanese Government. The information must be obtained in advance. To report after-the-fact information is not good enough.[19]

On June 14 Hitler entered Paris. The British evacuated Norway, and Mussolini finally decided it was safe to join the war. The "corpse-robbers," as Sorge called the Nazis,[20] had reached the apex of their power. As bodysnatchers they were joined by the Soviet Union, which invaded Lithuania, Latvia, and Estonia on the fifteenth and installed puppet governments four days later.

In the meantime, Japan demanded of France that it cease traffic in munitions from Indochina to Chungking and accept Japanese military observers to be sure the agreement stuck. To prod matters along, it offered congratulations on Germany's great victory, then asked for a free hand in Indochina such as that already received for the Netherland East Indies.[21]

Japan approached Germany, because as Sorge radioed the Soviet Union, Germany had guaranteed French territory when the two countries had made a truce. He added on information from the embassy that the German government was recommending that France accept the Japanese demands.[22] When France signed an armistice with Germany a few days later, the Japanese reverted to dealing directly with the French government.[23]

Sorge talked over with Miyagi the implications of Japan's increasing boldness. "If the army gets cooperation from the navy," the artist opined, "the army will march into not only Hanoi but also Saigon."

"British and American strength is dominant in southern Indochina, and Japan can't go that far," Sorge objected.

But Miyagi stood his ground. "It is natural for Japan to shift her troops from southern China into French Indochina, particularly if they cannot solve the China Incident. The army alone can go only as far as Hanoi, but with the cooperation of the Navy it will go as far as Saigon."[24]

Ozaki confirmed Miyagi's opinion by informing Sorge that the new treaty of friendship with Thailand strengthened Japan's foothold for an advance south, especially inasmuch as the current Thai prime minister was pro-Japanese.[25]

While the Germans were working out the armistice with the French government, the Russians moved in strength into the Baltic states and Poland and demanded Bessarabia and northern Bukovina from Rumania. Not yet ready to cross swords with Stalin, Hitler advised the Rumanians to yield. Any thoughtful observer watching the red stain spreading out from Moscow and the black one extending from Berlin could tell that it was only a question of time before the two met. Something then would have to give, nonaggression pact or no. Sorge had never doubted it since the beginning of the war, when he had heard through his Nazi Party associates in Tokyo that "even though Germany had come to terms with Russia, anti-Soviet feeling in the Nazi Party ran high. . . ." Henceforth he "was of the opinion that, despite the existence of the pact, sooner or later a break with the Soviet Union would inevitably occur."[26]

CHAPTER 38

"KONOYE CAME UP AGAIN"

Japan hissed with rumors of assassination plots that summer of 1940. Like so many Japanese rumors, these had a foundation in fact. An extreme segment of the military was planning to kill all the key exponents of good relations with the United States and Great Britain, including Yonai. Fortunately the government received a tip-off in time to round up the conspirators and crush the rebellion.[1]

But Yonai was swimming upstream. His policy of conquering China before venturing farther afield did not commend itself to the army, which saw the fall of France as an invitation to take over French possessions in Asia. Inevitably it was the war minister, General Shunroku Hata, who precipitated the crisis. Following various ritual preliminaries, he gave Yonai his written statement of what the army wanted: a Nazi type of state and an all-out alliance with Germany. Yonai disagreed, Hata resigned, the army refused to name a successor, and Yonai had no choice but to resign.[2]

Sorge knew that the Yonai cabinet had fallen because the military preferred Konoye and that if Konoye did become prime minister, Japan undoubtedly would join the Rome-Berlin Axis.[3]

He was absolutely right. The Privy Council met on July 17 and recommended Konoye to the Emperor in record time. It did not seriously consider any other candidate.[4] Ozaki told Sorge, "Although it was reported that the prince made 'complete understanding with the military' " as his condition for acceptance "and that he was determined strongly to check political intervention by the military, the prince's conference with the military was simply like 'tuning the talk to the company.' "[5] Ozaki was happy to ride on Konoye's coattails, but he had no illusions about his eminent patron. The aristocrat had made a career of speaking against political intervention by the military while in practice doing its bidding.

Miyagi's opinion marched in step with Ozaki's. "Since the army wanted to have a strong cabinet, Konoye came up again," he reported to Sorge at one of their restaurant meetings. "But by this time Konoye has made close friends of the capitalists. Konoye himself knows that he does not have the ability to solve the problems of Japan and China, and yet the general public holds expectations or hopes from him."[6]

The new prime minister's cabinet selections painted the ideographs on the wall with painful clarity. He chose Yosuke Matsuoka as foreign minister. Erratic, garrulous, and untrustworthy, with close ties to the Kwantung Army, Matsuoka had strongly supported Japan's Manchurian policy and had led the Japanese delegation out of the League of Nations.[7]

Ozaki predicted that Matsuoka was likely to take "some big, unexpected diplomatic step."[8] Ozaki never spoke more truly.

Miyagi, too, took Matsuoka's measure and delivered his opinion to Sorge: "By this move Japanese diplomacy hopes to strengthen the German-Italian Axis, exclude or boycott United States and British power from the Orient, solve the China Incident and establish a self-sufficient East Asia and new order in East Asia." Such an all-encompassing program would have taxed the combined powers of Napoleon, Bismarck, and Peter the Great.

Miyagi continued with his usual common sense. "But the fact that Matsuoka fired so many pro-United States and British groups will surely cause a reaction, and Matsuoka himself will be attacked. His political life will not be long."[9] In fact, he lasted almost exactly one year, not bad in the free-for-all of Japanese politics.

For the key position of war minister, Konoye called upon General Hideki Tojo. Popularly known as Razor Brain, the general was indeed as sharp as a razor blade but considerably less flexible. He represented the hard-core army interests, and his presence in the cabinet was visible proof that Konoye was not his own master.[10]

Konoye's accession to power meant dusting off the New Structure (National Reorganization) Plan. Ozaki had been working on it for about a month when the new cabinet took office on July 22. Sorge asked him for a report on what Konoye thought about the New Structure and just what form it would take. This was more easily asked than answered, and more easily answered than understood.

"Konoye thinks that since conducting Japanese politics depending upon the political strength led by the old parties would be a very difficult situation now, he must organize a nationwide political system based on new strength in order to aim at national unity," Ozaki told his chief. "He wants to establish a political system which gives unanimous support of the whole nation to his policies."[11]

Yet Konoye was not the stuff of which dictators are made. He lacked the flamboyant showmanship of Mussolini, the single-minded fanaticism of Hitler, the lust for power of Stalin. As was implicit in Ozaki's briefing of Sorge, the prince wished to establish a totalitarian regime principally because he was neither clever nor strong enough to handle a multiparty system.

For Sorge and Ozaki, a one-party government would be most desirable. If Konoye had succeeded in establishing such a system, he would have accomplished a good three-quarters of Moscow's work for it. From such a setup to full communism was a step which to Sorge and Ozaki seemed natural and inevitable.[12]

But then Konoye announced that Japan must avoid a shogunate form of government. Immediately Sorge and Ozaki tried to interpret his meaning. It was generally reported that his statement was made as the result of the check by the right wing in Japan.[13]

The New Structure matter always puzzled Sorge, and now he was more perplexed than ever. Ozaki probably meant that Konoye's fellow aristocrats had put on the brakes to protect the imperial system and to avoid any risk of Japanese industry, vital to the national life, falling into the hands of the government, which in turn was at the mercy of the army. In any case Sorge threw in the sponge. He had intended to report the New

Structure to Moscow but gave up the idea "because the problem became obscure."[14]

Ozaki continued to pour in reports on other aspects of the domestic situation, such as Japan's annual trade balances, the rice and grain situation, and inflation.[15] He seldom told Sorge just where and from whom he received his information, using some such phrase as "the Konoye group" or "Konoye's attendants." This designation lumped together such sources as Saionji, Ushiba, Kishi, Matsumoto, or Inukai. He did not include Kazami in the overall category, doing him the honor of always citing him by name.[16]

This discretion was just what Sorge wanted. He preferred not to know the names of his colleagues' sources "so that if I were questioned about them, I would know very little likely to get them into trouble. This is a traditional principle for illegal activity."[17]

Immediately upon formation of the second Konoye cabinet, the Breakfast Group began to gather at the official residence of the chief secretary, Kenji Tomita. This group, which Ozaki called the Tomita *Asameshi-kai* (Breakfast Group), he considered "not so important for my spy activity." He attended only three sessions, and the group "dissolved by itself about October."[18]

Ozaki obtained most of his information on military subjects through the South Manchurian Railway. He always told Sorge that his source of such items was either the military or a source related to the military, never mentioning the railroad by name.[19] In his year of employment there Ozaki had developed a curious pride in it. He thought that in his own department talent was going to waste. There seemed to be too much gathering of data for their own sake without any thought of practical application—an inevitable development in a statistical and evaluation office unless sternly controlled. Ozaki later told his prosecutors: "It may be very insolent for me who have given much trouble to this organization to say this, but I think that if I had not been in such a double-crossing position, I would have made efforts to enhance the function more than for the sake of the Manchurian Railroad. I think that such a huge organization with men and capital will be evaluated more highly in the future from the national point of view."[20]

These are the words of a man who has become interested
in his firm. Not that Ozaki thought of switching priorities. For
him, the railroad's value was as a source of information for
the Soviet Union. But being a man of intelligence, he itched
to clear away inefficiency whenever he found it.

Such was Ozaki's situation when Kawai returned permanently to Japan in August 1940. Since his release from the
hands of the police he had been lying low in North China,
visiting Japan from time to time to bring Ozaki bits and pieces
of information, which were not of much use to the ring.[21]

Despite Kawai's questionable value as a spy, Ozaki had
kept up the acquaintance and helped him out financially.[22] So
now, having come back for good, the little *Shina ronin* lost no
time in paying his respects to his patron. He wanted to turn
over his latest report on China and in return discover, if he
could, the latest Japanese policy toward China.

In this respect he had little luck. "At the moment I cannot
get close to Konoye," Ozaki replied. He informed Kawai that
he had advised the government to pull the troops out of China,
but the army was dead set on taking over the whole country.
Ozaki was thoroughly out of patience. "They are all a bunch
of fools," he snapped. His face grew suddenly haggard. He
could not stand the thought of war's carnage, he told Kawai,
of the thousands dying on the battlefield. Then his natural
optimism, never long submerged, bobbed to the surface. A
Communist revolution was sure to sweep over Japan and carry
the militarists before it into the sea.[23]

Kawai surveyed him with a mixture of affection and
annoyance. He had none of the intellectual power and vast fund
of knowledge that had lifted his patron into the very shadow
of the prime minister, but he had all the down-to-earth shrewdness of the soldier of fortune.

He asked himself if Ozaki really knew what communism
was all about. Ozaki had no direct knowledge of the party's
rules and regulations, no experience of life as a party member.
His lofty perch on the intellectual and political heights, precluded contact with the rank and file. While he felt genuine
compassion for the Chinese, he had little interest in and less
understanding of his own countrymen.[24] So Kawai, who, de-

spite his years in China, had kept his roots in the soil of Japan, contradicted Ozaki respectfully but firmly.

"No," Kawai replied, "it is not in the nature of the Japanese to have a proletarian revolution. The Japanese are traditional laborers."

The scarred adventurer and the smooth scholar argued the point for some time. "Yes," Ozaki insisted, "as long as we have a leader, we can have a Japanese revolution."

"No," said Kawai with quiet finality, "not even with a leader will we have one."

Ozaki's eyes clouded as he closed the subject somberly. "Then we will have to die."[25]

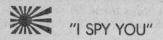

CHAPTER 39

"I SPY YOU"

Early in 1940 Sorge informed Hanako that he was going to Manchuria. She coaxed him to take her along, but he could not because she had no passport. His aircraft had scarcely left the runway when a Kempeitai agent visited Hanako at her home to ask where Sorge had gone and when he would be back. Miserable with a cold, she did not ask him to come in, and the military policeman made no attempt to do so. He asked his few questions and departed within minutes.[1]

For some time Sorge had been the object of routine surveillance by the Kempeitai—which had first contacted Hanako in the autumn of 1938—as well as by the Tokko. Of the two, the former posed the greater danger. It was notorious for its far from gentle ways with prisoners, and in the future Sorge would go to considerable trouble to keep his case out of its jurisdiction. The Kempeitai concerned itself with known or prospective risks to national security and the war effort, whereas the Tokko dealt with questions of subversive ideologies on the home front.

Thus it happened that the Tokko rather than the Kempeitai was busily but unwittingly twining the rope that eventually would hang Sorge and Ozaki. In November 1939 it arrested an employee of the South Manchurian Railroad's Investigation Department named Ritsu Ito. The reason for his apprehension was vague.[2] Probably the Tokko snagged Ito when it flung out its net in one of its periodic sweeps of known and suspected leftists. These sweeps picked up informers as well as Communists and provided excellent cover for extracting information from the informers without arousing suspicion.

Whether or not Ito had already become an informer when the police picked him up in November 1939 is not known, but in any case, he was a peculiar choice to be working for the South Manchurian Railroad. At twenty-six, Ito was no stranger to the inside of a jail, having spent some two years from early in 1933 as the reluctant guest of His Imperial Majesty. This gave him plenty of time to weigh the merits of his membership in the Japanese Communist Youth League, and he renounced communism before his release. Reformation did not last long. He was soon back in stride as an agrarian agitator, and at the time of his second arrest he was an active member of the Preparatory Committee for Rebuilding the Japanese Communist Party.

Yet with this background the South Manchurian Railroad, which placed the resources of its very efficient Investigation Department at the disposal of the military for highly classified projects, hired Ito in August 1939. More than that, they placed him in the Investigation Department and, to top off the jest, gave him to Ozaki as an assistant.

With his talent for associating with the wrong people, Ozaki made the young man his trusted aide and personal friend.[3] If Ozaki's employers felt any alarm at his close friendship with Ito, a known Communist and jailbird, they kept it to themselves. In later days Kawai was certain that the police had placed Ito in that particular office as a spy. Be that as it may, after his arrest in November Ito reposed in a Tokyo jail for many months.[4]

During that period the Tokko was giving very special attention to Japanese being repatriated from the United States. It took an interest in these people for two reasons: American agents might be among them, and Communists might thus infiltrate the sacred soil. Of the two, the Japanese took the second much more seriously. They knew that Moscow channeled its propaganda material and its agents into Japan by way of the United States, for the war in China and Manchuria seriously cramped its style in Asia.[5]

So the Tokko earnestly besought Ito to reveal the names

of any members of the Communist Party of America (CPA) known to him. As the official report expressed it delicately, "A sharp-minded, die-hard communist, Ito refused to confess his guilt for several months after his arrest, but, after much difficulty, the severe but considerate attitude of the police led him to renounce Communism and confess his crimes." In May 1940 Ito remembered that his housekeeper had an aunt who had come home to Japan a few years ago and occasionally boasted of her connections with the party across the Pacific. Ito put the finger on this woman as a former CPA member. His target was none other than Tomo Kitabayashi.[6]

Why did Ito betray her? The guesses have been many and varied. A certain amount of evidence hints that he had known her in California.[7] The U.S. Army Far East Command's report on the Sorge case observed that Ito "had noted that since her return to Japan she had refused to have any intercourse with Communists and appeared to have become an apostate. But she continuously asked questions on all sorts of matters."[8] Ito may well have suspected that the woman had become an American agent and that he was doing the Communist cause a favor by bringing her to the Tokko's attention.

There is no evidence that Ito knew Ms. Kitabayashi had any connection with the Sorge *apparat* or even that such an organization existed. Nevertheless, in view of their friendship, one must wonder just how deeply the expansive Ozaki had taken Ito into his confidence. Ozaki's young half brother believed that Ito might have worked for the elder Ozaki in the ring.[9] In that case the most charitable explanation of Ito's behavior might be that knowing Ozaki was engaged in espionage, Ito used Ms. Kitabayashi as a decoy to direct attention away from his benefactor.

But probably the simplest theory is nearest the truth: Ito was either already a police spy or in the process of becoming one. He badly wanted to get out of jail with a whole skin. At the same time he remained a Communist at heart. So he tossed this minor comrade to the wolves. As a former member of the CPA she was exactly what the Tokko wanted but was no great loss to communism.

Almost immediately upon Ito's dropping her name, a question arose of whether her case properly fell within the purview of the Foreign Section because of her American background or within that of the First Section because of her leftist activities. For the time being, the Foreign Section received the official nod, for the possibility always existed that Ms. Kitabayashi might be an American agent, planted among the repatriates with a carefully nurtured Communist background as a cover for her real allegiance.[10]

Accordingly the Tokko dispatched two of the Foreign Section's crack inspectors to take a look at her and her surroundings. No one could have been more polite than these two young men, smart in their uniforms, notebooks in hand, who stood on the threshold of the Los Angeles Dressmaking School at 2–74 Onda, Shibuya-ku. To the unobtrusive little woman who opened the door they introduced themselves as representatives of the nearby police station. So sorry to trouble her, but they were making a periodic household survey.

The woman answered their questions with patient resignation. Her name? Tomo Kitabayashi. Occupation: She taught dressmaking to the young girls living in the neighborhood. Residence? She lived on the premises. Husband? Yoshisaburo Kitabayashi. His present whereabouts? He was in the United States but would return to Japan very soon. His permanent address? Kokawa, a small town in Wakayama Prefecture. The men noted the answers in their conspicuous household survey notebooks, thanked her, and took courteous leave.[11]

The Tokko had no intention of arresting and questioning Ms. Kitabayashi at that time. For the moment she was much more useful as bait for a bigger catch than wriggling in the creel herself. The Tokko had received a tip that a key liaison man from the Japanese Department of the CPA was making frequent trips between the United States and Japan. The possibility that this man or some other important Communist might get in touch with Ms. Kitabayashi justified the Tokko in assigning several detectives to keep an eye on her. As the first step they rented a second-floor front room in the house opposite the sewing school. From this observation post agents watched the school entrance night and day. They trailed Ms. Kitabayashi whenever she went out, with no results whatever.[12]

This little woman must have been more adroit than she looked, for she was in touch with Miyagi and his subring at this time and would continue to be for more than a year without bringing the slightest suspicion of such activity to the attention of her unseen chaperons.[13]

Shortly after the Tokko had set the watch, her husband returned to his native shores, gathered her up, and moved to Kokawa. The unhappy Tokko detectives had to leave the metropolitan joys of Tokyo and follow the couple to the sticks. In Kokawa they adopted their former procedure—no one ever refused to rent a room to the Tokko—and continued the surveillance, with no inkling that by tugging gently at this slender thread they might unravel an exceedingly intricate web.[14]

After Ritsu Ito disclosed the name of Ms. Kitabayashi, the Tokko held him for a while. In August 1940 they turned him loose, officially because he had developed tuberculosis and no longer could stand the rigors of prison life. Ito did have tuberculosis; however, such solicitude was uncharacteristic of the Tokko. But the story served for the record. The cage door open, Ito flew back to the South Manchurian Railroad, which welcomed with open arms this security risk fresh from jail.[15] Once more roosting in that key organization, Ito could peck about for crumbs and be in a position to sing if the occasion arose.

Whatever doubt may have existed about Ito's status at the time of his previous arrest, when he emerged from his cell, he was definitely a police informer.[16] In the context of Japan in that year, when he returned to his desk in the Investigation Department, it should have been obvious to anyone not mentally retarded that he was either a police spy or a Communist who had wormed his way out of jail. In either case he was no suitable friend for Ozaki. Yet Ozaki picked up his friendship with Ito right where it had been interrupted so rudely. Ito was a frequent guest in the Ozaki home, and Yoko called him Uncle Ito.[17]

Kawai met him there once, and Ozaki introduced him: "He is Ito of the South Manchuria Railway Company, but he is like a right arm to me." This comment dampened Kawai considerably. "I had previously considered myself to be Ozaki's right hand man, but I now realized that such was not the case." From Ozaki's conversation Kawai gathered that Ito "was a leftist out on parole." To complete the gathering, a little later

Shin'ichi Matsumoto "came over in response to a call from Ozaki. He appeared to be an old friend of Ito."[18]

The stupidity of the intelligent can be awesome. Ozaki was especially foolish because he had gradually come to realize that he had attracted official attention. When he first noticed this interest, his initial reaction was incredulity. He was pleased with his own cleverness and positive that he had buried his trail too deeply for the bloodhounds to track him. His irrepressible optimism preserved him from alarm. He was confident that the police were checking on Ozaki the intellectual, not Ozaki the spy.[19]

About a month before the Tokko released Ito, a cause célèbre gave abundant reason for any foreign correspondent such as Sorge to be exceedingly circumspect. Japanese newspapers proclaimed that a large British espionage ring had been brought to light. One of those rounded up was James Melville ("Jimmy") Cox, the Reuters correspondent in Tokyo. What could have been just another bizarre example of Japanese spy mania turned tragic when Cox jumped, fell, or was pushed out a fifth-floor window of the military prison where he was being questioned. The Japanese claimed it was suicide, hence proof of his guilt.[20] British Ambassador Sir Robert Craigie later wrote that the Japanese gave the British Embassy every facility to investigate, and no evidence of foul play developed.[21] Others were not so sure, and a really satisfactory solution has never been forthcoming.

Sorge said he had always thought Cox simply "a happy-go-lucky, completely naïve reporter."[22] Sorge's American friend Morin of the Associated Press believed that the Japanese had cooked up a spy scare to rouse public opinion against Britain. And apparently not just Britain, for when Morin returned from Cox's funeral, the Kempeitai scooped him in. Although they used no physical torture, he underwent a long, hard grilling. He signed what they told him was a statement that he had not been mistreated and had answered questions without coercion. The next day newspapers reported that he had confessed and fingered the British Embassy as a center of espionage.[23]

Sorge was under a double, if still somewhat desultory, watch. The Tokko's incisive young agent Saito periodically turned his handsome face in Sorge's direction, while Aoyama, the spy's near neighbor at the Toriizaka Station, was virtually part of the local scenery. Sorge may have been and probably was unaware of Saito's surveillance, but he could not have overlooked Aoyama. If Sorge knew what was good for him, from now on he would walk delicately. Yet amid these dangers he made a move that could be interpreted as an attempt to expand his group of espionage assistants.

One afternoon he found Hanako pecking at his typewriter, trying to copy a German song. Sorge obligingly added the umlauts and translated a difficult phrase or two. Watching Hanako's slim fingers playing over the keys, he conceived an idea.

"I could work faster if you could type English copies for me," he said. Bestowing upon her his most charming smile, he asked winningly, "Would you like to help Sorge?"

"I will be glad to help you," she replied, enchanted to be of service. "But I don't know English very well. I read only German."

Sorge brushed aside this minor obstacle. "You will study English a little, won't you?" he coaxed. Hanako would have studied Sanskrit if Sorge had asked her, so she arranged for lessons twice a week with the minister of a nearby Christian church.[24]

The only work for which Sorge used English was his documentation for the Fourth Department. The conclusion is inescapable. He intended to use Hanako in his spy business. That in doing so he risked her liberty, if not her life, did not concern him. As Clausen observed, "He is a man who can destroy even his best friend for the sake of Communism."[25] To do him justice, Sorge would die himself just as willingly.

Sheer chance aborted this scheme. One day, when Hanako had progressed to the third reader and was stretched out on the couch in Sorge's study mentally reviewing her lessons, she recalled a picture in the first reader of children playing hide-and-seek. Impishly she looked across the room at Sorge's back and chanted, "I spy you!"

Hit right where he lived, Sorge flashed around. "What? Spy?" he barked.

"That means 'I have found you,' " Hanako said falteringly. "Is anything wrong with these words?"

"Something is a little wrong with your teacher," Sorge said slowly. "I don't think he is very good."

What student could resist such a gambit? "That's right," Hanako agreed. "Something *is* wrong with my teacher. We study by ourselves, and he touches my feet under the desk."

This was better luck than Sorge had any right to expect. "Is your teacher a bachelor?" he inquired.

"Yes. He's the minister of the church. He is very kind, but there is something odd about him. I don't like him."

Sorge grinned. "Something is always wrong about a bachelor! If you don't like him, you needn't go there anymore."

"Can you teach me?" Hanako asked eagerly.

"No, I am busy. You study by yourself, and I'll hear your lesson once in a while."

She tried to keep on with her English but found the language difficult. Lacking supervision and guidance, she made no progress.[26] So after all, she was not able to help Sorge with his espionage work, a very fortunate circumstance. Three idle, jesting words may have saved her from a long jail sentence. For had she typed documents in English for Sorge, understanding at least something of their meaning, no amount of fast talking on Sorge's part could have convinced the Tokko that she had not knowingly participated in his espionage.

PART 3

SPINNING THE RING

The house at Adjikent near Baku where Richard Sorge was born.

The Sorge family. Richard, at six months, held by his mother, Nina Semionova Kobieleva Sorge.

Richard at eight years with his father, Adolf Sorge.

Richard Sorge as a young soldier during World War I.

Sorge on his twenty-third
birthday, October 1918.

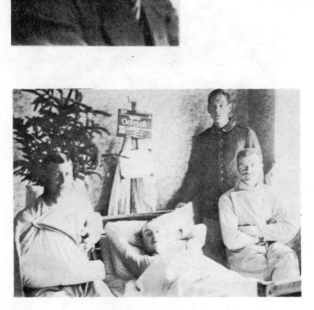

Sorge (at rear) in a hospital during World War I.

Richard Sorge in October 1933 at the outset of his mission in Japan.

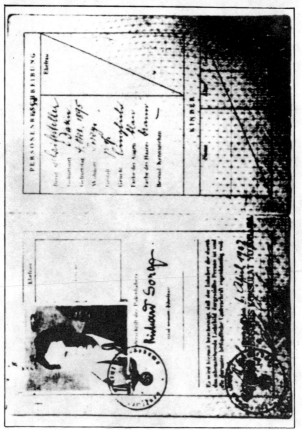

Sorge's passport, 1937.

Sorge during the period of his espionage ring in Tokyo, circa 1937.

Sorge's second wife, Ykaterina ("Katcha") Maximova, standing over her two sisters.

Façade of the German Embassy in Tokyo in 1938.

Seiichi Ichijima, governor of Sugamo Prison.

Anna Clausen.

Max Clausen during
period of espionage in
Tokyo.

Hanako Ishii, Sorge's companion for many years, with Professor
Gordon Prange. Ishii wrote a book on her life with Sorge.

Sample of Clausen's
encoding work sheets.

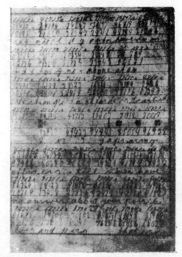

Max Clausen's radio sets: transmitter on left, receiver on right.

Hotzumi Ozaki.

Branko de Voukelitch.

One of the last pictures taken of Richard Sorge.

CHAPTER 40

"RUSSIA WAS EXCLUDED"

The German Embassy fairly jumped with activity in the late summer and early autumn of 1940. No sooner had Konoye grasped the portfolio than his government came out for the Rome-Berlin Axis. The Japanese and German governments both proposed an alliance. All that remained was to work out the terms.[1]

Not everyone was happy. "The Japanese Navy still opposes sending warships to the Mediterranean and Indian Oceans to help Germany and Italy," Ozaki told Sorge at one of their many tête-à-têtes over a restaurant table, "and sticks strongly to the idea of a conditional military alliance."[2]

Sorge knew these developments would throw a terrific workload on his ring because, as he explained, "to Russia, whether this alliance would be directed against the Soviets or not was most crucial."[3] Therefore, he would have to follow the forthcoming negotiations through every twist and turn. He would need every bit of assistance he could muster to keep on top of the problem.

On August 23 Ribbentrop sent Sorge's old acquaintance Heinrich Stahmer to Japan as an envoy to determine this potential ally's desires and, more important, what the Nazis could expect in return.[4] Sorge knew of Stahmer's mission almost as soon as Ribbentrop, for the South Manchurian Railroad arranged all the details of his visit to Tokyo, and Ozaki immediately spread the tidings.[5]

The moment seemed propitious for Japan to climb aboard the Nazi bandwagon. Britain alone stood in its path, and Ger-

man bombers were pulverizing its industrial and military centers.
Soon they would begin the indiscriminate bombing of London.
Across the Channel German vessels awaited the signal for invasion. Daring indeed was the bookie who gave more than even
odds against Hitler's becoming undisputed master of Europe.

Konoye's cabinet had no sooner been seated than Japanese actions began to point unmistakably to preparation for
close ties with Germany. Matsuoka cleaned house in the Foreign Ministry, the so-called Matsuoka cyclone whirling away
diplomats and other officials not to his liking, especially those
who favored cooperation with the Western democracies.[6]

Eager as the Japanese were to line up on what looked
like the winning side, they did not intend to become tools of
German interests. On September 4 the four principal ministers
met to establish guidelines for the negotiations. Inasmuch as a
record of the official texts appeared in a Foreign Office memorandum prepared by Shin'ichi Matsumoto,[7] it is a fairly safe
bet that Ozaki knew about it almost before the ink was dry.

According to this guideline, Japan, Germany, and Italy
would cooperate in the "new order" and assist one another
politically, economically, and if necessary militarily. Japan's
sphere would encompass the former German mandated islands,
French Indochina and the Pacific islands, Thailand, British
Malaya and Borneo, the Netherlands East Indies, Burma, Australia, New Zealand, and possibly India, with Japan, Manchuria, and China as the hard core. India could be considered
within the sphere of the Soviet Union, at least temporarily.

The four ministers agreed that Japan should decide independently whether or not to use armed force against Britain
or the United States. If the China Incident should be settled,
or nearly so, Japan would take up arms if a favorable opportunity presented itself. If the incident remained unresolved,
Japan would prefer to act short of war but, if necessary or
desirable, would fight anyway. This document was entirely for
home consumption. The Japanese did not care to tell the Germans just how big a slice of cake they planned to cut for
themselves.[8]

Stahmer declared that his country did not want Japan to
join in the war on Britain. Germany planned a quick end to it
and had no desire to extend it. What it wanted from Japan was

to keep the United States from intervening. A solid military alliance of the Axis powers should do the trick. Stahmer also hinted that more cordial relations between Japan and the Soviet Union would help the good work along.[9]

So Matsuoka packed off General Yoshitsugu Tatekawa to Moscow as Japanese ambassador. Miyagi docketed him for Sorge's benefit: "General Tatekawa has the right industry men in Osaka as supporters. He is large-minded and has the features of a big boss, but he does not have any political background. He comes from the cavalry. . . . As a diplomat we cannot expect much from him. This was the reason he was sent to Moscow—because Japan did not intend to inaugurate anything new with Soviet Russia."[10]

Matsuoka and Stahmer, reaching a general agreement in an amazingly short time, decided upon the alliance on September 13. All the negotiations as well as the discussions that followed the initial agreements were top secrets from the rest of the world, but not from Sorge. Ott and Stahmer told him of each development as soon as it happened, and he saw all of the German government's wires of instruction to Stahmer. Sorge radioed progress to the Fourth Department every step of the way.[11] Aside from Tokyo and Berlin, Moscow was probably the best-informed capital in the world concerning the Tripartite Pact, thanks to Sorge's privileged position at Ott's right hand.

Despite the early agreement upon basic treaty provisions, Konoye, Matsuoka, and Ott met repeatedly to haggle over the question of the circumstances under which the alliance would become operative. Sorge's explanation of the problem and its solution was lucid: "The German side wanted a narrow interpretation; on the other hand, the Japanese side wanted a somewhat vague interpretation. Finally, they agreed that the alliance would become effective in the case of attack. The decision of which country attacked was up to each allied country."[12]

With official attention thus focused on the diplomatic front, the Japanese decided to sneak an end run. They did not catch Miyagi and Sorge napping. Sorge radioed Moscow toward the middle of the month: "The Japanese Army may land in Indochina soon. The troops seem to be transported from Taiwan on board the ships of big companies such as Nihon Yusen, Nippon Yusen Kaisha and Osaka Shosen. This force is made up of two or three divisions. The purpose of this landing is to stop the transportation of ammunition and other goods prepared to be sent to Chungking.''[13]

Sorge later claimed that Clausen had to be mistaken; at that time the Japanese ''used to advance there [Indochina] on land through China, and did not have sea transportation. . . .''[14] But the meat of the message was accurate, for on September 19 the Japanese notified Indochina that their forces would cross the border. The same day Tokyo decided that it would move to separate the Netherlands East Indies from Holland, then obtain recognition from Batavia of Japanese ''special interests.'' In this maneuver the government planned to use oblique means rather than direct military force, in case the Dutch blew up their oil wells and refineries, which were Japan's chief objectives.[15]

The Japanese marched into Indochina on the twenty-third and took Tonkin Province after a brief skirmish. The Germans were not pleased with this move. As conquerors of the Netherlands and France they considered they had what Sorge termed ''a sort of ethical right'' in those territories. Sorge said that this matter was not discussed during the Tripartite Pact conversations but that it was tacitly assumed that Japan had an obligation to inform Germany when its troops moved into Indochina.[16] Japan, then, had begun to flex its muscles independently of its partner even before the pact was signed.

The formal signing took place in Berlin on September 27. Both British Ambassador Craigie and U.S. Ambassador Grew noted that the alliance had a mixed reception in Japan. The press sang its praises, but behind the scenes they scented what Grew called ''a marked lack of enthusiasm.''[17]

Miyagi gained a slightly different impression. ''The Japanese as a whole showed a favorable reaction since the policy of Japan has been set,'' he told his chief. ''But it is doubtful whether this new treaty will help to settle the China Incident and the Japanese intelligent classes do not seem to be friendly to Germany and Italy.''[18]

Murmuring against the pact ceased, at least on the surface, when the Emperor issued the first imperial rescript since Japan had left the League of Nations in 1934: ''It has been the great instruction bequeathed by our imperial foundress and other imperial ancestors that our grand moral obligation should be extended to all directions and the world be unified under one roof.* This is a point we are trying to obey day in and day out."[19]

Many, perhaps most, Japanese of the day truly believed themselves thus divinely commissioned to bring the whole world under the imperial roof. The question was: How could the Tripartite Pact possibly forward this objective? No nation had ever profited by allying itself with either Germany or Prussia, which veteran diplomat Viscount Kikujiro Ishii courageously pointed out to the cabinet.[20]

Some have credited Sorge with being a primary architect of the pact, claiming that it was he who arranged for its target to be the United States.[21]

Sorge himself claimed no such major role. His words concerning the treaty's object are crisp: "In this alliance treaty Russia was excluded from the beginning because of the Russian-German friendship treaty. The treaty was directed mainly toward Britain and was to be used against the United States if the U.S. joined the war against Germany."[22]

Articles I and II committed Japan, on the one side, and Germany and Italy, on the other, mutually to "recognize and respect the leadership" of the other in establishing a "new order" respectively in Europe and Greater East Asia. The meat of the treaty was in Article III: "Japan, Germany and Italy shall agree to cooperate with one another in carrying out the aforementioned policy; and, further, if and when any one of the signatories be attacked by any third power not presently engaged in the present European war, or the China Incident, the other two shall aid her in any way political, economical or military."[23]

With the Soviet Union specifically ruled out, the target was obvious. The parties hoped that the prospect of being

---

* Hirohito referred to the principle of *Hakku Ichiu,* as expressed by Jimmu Tenno, the founder of the Japanese imperial house: "Therefore let the capital be so extended so as to embrace the six cardinal points and let the right corners of the world be covered so as to form a roof. Will this not be good?" (quoted in Joseph Newman, *Goodbye Japan* [New York, 1942], p. 43).

pounced upon from both east and west would keep the United States out of the conflict and modify its disapproving attitude toward Japan.

These were matters over which Sorge had no control. He exerted a certain influence over Ott, who in turn carried some weight in Berlin by virtue of his position. But Ott's was only one of many voices heard in the Wilhelmstrasse and a long way from the most influential. He was outside the Nazi inner circle, and in any case Hitler took his diplomats' advice only when it pleased his capricious fancy to do so.

Undoubtedly Sorge played an indirect part in this drama. That both Ott and Stahmer discussed progress with him and showed him the messages to and from Berlin indicates that Sorge was deeply in their confidence. But his hand did not steer the German ship of state away from Soviet shores. Since signing the Nonaggression Pact with Hitler, Stalin had cooperated with Germany. The Soviet Union was providing the Reich with much-needed food and raw materials, while Russian newspapers fulminated with satisfactory virulence against the British capitalists and warmongers. For the moment Hitler was content.

However, the unexpected endurance of Britain, which necessitated indefinite postponement of Hitler's projected invasion, threw off his timetable and wounded his self-esteem so deeply that swallowing Rumania the same month did not assuage his wrath. Frustrated, Hitler would turn hysterically on someone, and it was not difficult to guess on whom. Article V of the Tripartite Pact would be valid just as long as it suited Hitler, and not one second longer. No one should have known this better than Stalin.

The saga of Sorge and the Tripartite Pact is not that of a puppet master but that of a spy. To be kept informed day by day from within the very walls of the German Embassy in Tokyo, to receive each day's tip on the races straight from the stable—this was all his country could ask of him.

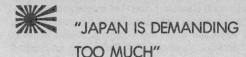

CHAPTER 41

"JAPAN IS DEMANDING
TOO MUCH"

"It is said that the Japanese Army is carrying out a nationwide general mobilization of reserve soldiers. ind out the purpose and report the result."[1] Thus Moscow directed Sorge on July 4, 1940. If the Japanese Army were conducting a general mobilization, he would not need the Fourth Department to point it out to him. He answered promptly and briefly that a partial, small mobilization was being held.[2] He had more important matters on his mind.

Japan was bullying the Dutch, French, and British. Badgering of the latter centered on the Burma Road, Tokyo exerting pressure to seal off this lifeline between Chungking and the outside world. During these discussions Sorge wired Moscow to this effect: "Japan is negotiating with the British Government concerning the demand to close the Burma route. . . . However, Britain has no intention of closing the route, so the negotiations cannot produce any results."

This information, which came from Ozaki,[3] was far off course. On July 17, as almost the last official act of the Yonai cabinet, Arita signed with Craigie the agreement ceasing traffic in war matériel among Chungking, Hong Kong, and Burma for three months.[4]

Sorge hurried to correct his mistaken estimate by advising Moscow that the cutoff was temporary.[5]

The Japanese government was testing how far it could go. On August 1 Tokyo demanded of France the right to transport troops across Tonkin as well as control of the airfields. Matsuoka had already asked Germany to put the squeeze on

France to comply. With the Dutch he was having less luck. The original selection to head the large Japanese mission to Batavia was General Kunishi Koiso, but a combination of indiscreet public utterances and unreasonable personal demands from the self-important Koiso led Konoye to relieve Koiso as chief of the mission in favor of Ichizo Kobayashi, his minister of commerce and industry.[6]

Sorge proudly confided to Clausen "that he met this Kobayashi at the Imperial Hotel and that he was a very good source of information."[7] This was a connection very much to Sorge's liking, for he closely followed Japan's machinations in Southeast Asia. Every step south was a step away from the Soviet Union. To keep on top of the Japanese negotiations with France and the Netherlands was a crucial part of Sorge's primary mission of detecting Japanese intentions and abilities vis-à-vis the Soviet Union.

Ozaki was not optimistic about the Kobayashi mission's chances. Its object fundamentally was to get as much petroleum as possible, but he thought the negotiations "may end without any result at all, because the Netherlands Indies is being backed by the United States and by Britain and Japan is demanding too much."[8] In any case the Japanese Navy was not yet ready to fight,[9] so for the time being the Dutch fared better than the French, who danced to Hitler's tune.

On this particular front Sorge had to rely heavily on his Japanese assistants. So when Miyagi came to him with a suggestion about Kawai, Sorge was in a receptive mood. Since returning from China, Kawai had fallen into his old routine of sponging off Ozaki, and occasionally he touched Miyagi for pocket money. Miyagi took a dim view of this situation. "I don't know exactly whether Kawai was really getting living expenses from Ozaki," he said, "but . . . he went to Ozaki's place anytime his money for drinks was exhausted. . . . Ozaki's home was visited by considerably prominent people frequently, and if a man like Kawai visited Ozaki's place very often, that might be troublesome to Ozaki himself and interfere with his work." So Miyagi offered to take care of Kawai.

"As a matter of fact, Ozaki asked me about this matter," replied Sorge, "so would you take care of Kawai hereafter? Teach him the nature of the work and let him help you."

Miyagi took Kawai under his wing and paid him from 60 to 100 yen a month. He interpreted Sorge's instructions to "teach him the nature of the work" to mean not only instructing his recruit in the job of spying but also "stimulating a communism consciousness in Kawai and also making him realize the importance of the situation."[10]

Miyagi ran Kawai's catch through a fine mesh. Of five papers Kawai submitted at this time, Miyagi considered only one, which concerned the activities of the commander of the North China Army, sufficiently important to pass on to his chief.[11]

Ozaki had been in Hsinking, Manchuria, since late September as an observer at the Sixth Conference of the National Council of the Concordia Society *(Hsieh Ho Hui)*.[12] He was interested in this society as a model for the Imperial Rule Assistance Association being formed in Japan to carry out the New Structure concept.[13]

In this connection Grew had noted in his diary on September 1, "There is to be no single political party, as in Italy and Germany, but rather an absence of all parties, the whole country being held together in individual loyalty to the Emperor."[14] That concept was implicit in the title, for in that period the word *assistance* (*yokusan*) often signified the supporting role the subject played in relation to his Emperor. This nebulous project soon fell prey to factionalism and irresponsibility.[15] Inevitably the ultranationalists and the army took it over.[16] Meanwhile, the meeting in Manchuria gave Ozaki the always welcome opportunity to meet other influential conferees. He imparted his gleanings to Sorge.[17]

Not long after his return from Manchuria, Ozaki had another scoop for his chief. The leaking of the terms of the proposed Tokyo-Nanking treaty in late December 1939 and early January 1940 had necessitated rushing through a new treaty. Inukai participated in the negotiations, and when he returned to Tokyo, Ozaki visited him at his residence, to determine the content and secret provisions of this revised draft. Inukai obligingly handed over a printed copy of the basic treaty and its secret protocol. Hastening to his office, Ozaki armed himself with pen and small loose-leaf notebook and hastily copied the subject and essentials of each provision. The same afternoon he returned the borrowed document to Inukai at his home. Ozaki considered this material so urgent that instead of waiting for his weekly date with Miyagi, he summoned the artist to come that same day to the China Research Office. There he gave Miyagi the notes to translate.[18] Miyagi delegated this chore to Akiyama.[19]

When the translation was ready, Ozaki took it to Sorge's home. By late 1940 Japan had fallen so deeply into xenophobia that for a Japanese to be seen too often in public with an Occidental was dangerous. Both Ozaki and Miyagi informed Sorge that after each of their meetings even the bartenders and waitresses quizzed them. Knowing that from motives mercenary or patriotic many of these people promptly informed the police of any suspicious contacts noted in their daily work, Sorge arranged that for the most part his right- and left-hand men should come to his home after dark, although once in a while he and Ozaki continued to get together in restaurants.[20]

On this occasion, Sorge conceded that Ozaki had brought him "a fairly important report." That he was keenly interested is clear from his detailed memory of the briefing. "Of course," he remarked, "this information was important to the Russian side, which had an interest in Japanese policy toward China." Immediately he relayed Ozaki's information to the Fourth Department.[21]

The treaty was very broad in scope, and a number of major items were of particular interest to Sorge: "The Japanese Army had no intention of evacuating China permanently, but since this could not be stated openly, a very roundabout expression was used, saying 'two years after peace and order in China are restored.' In a place such as China," Sorge continued cynically, "the problem of restoring 'peace and order' itself is very general and obscure, and can be interpreted in any way. I thought that this expression was very interesting." He was also acutely alert to the areas of China in which Japanese troops were to be permanently stationed because Inner Mongolia and North China were named but not delineated precisely. The treaty also stipulated that Hainan Island, that jumping-off place to the south, be a permanent Japanese base.[22]

Sorge especially noted the political provisions. "The independent suzerain rights of China were allowed as a matter of formality. But practically, it was so arranged that Japanese leaders and advisers got into all fields of the Nanking government and they would lead the government. . . ."[23] In short, if the Wang Ching-wei regime took root, Japan would have won the China Incident by default.

Such machinations as the Wang Ching-wei treaty, the bellicose moves toward the nations of Southeast Asia, and Japan's tightening ties with the Nazis brought with them intensified security measures. Strolling toward Ozaki's home in late October, Kawai sensed the added tension in the air. He decided that the change dated from the signing of the Tripartite Pact. Having been away so long, Kawai noticed the altered atmosphere more clearly than those who lived with it day by day. He knew that Ozaki was scheduled to return to China for another conference in December. Privately he hoped that his patron would stay there because Japan was becoming too dangerous.[24]

Arriving at his destination, Kawai encountered Miyagi, just finishing his weekly painting lesson with Yoko. They left the house together. As they paused in the doorway to put on their shoes, Kawai spotted a passerby glancing in their direction. Ozaki's residence was on a narrow street with little pedestrian traffic, so Kawai mentally tagged the stranger as a plainclothesman. He whispered to Miyagi that they were being watched and should not leave the house together. They should go separate ways and meet at the railroad station. When they met at the depot, there ahead of them was the same stranger. This really jolted them. Again they divided forces. Miyagi took a bus. Kawai swung aboard the train, the plainclothesman close on his heels. At the last possible second Kawai jumped off, losing his shadow but not his uneasiness.[25]

Reminded of his duty to put Kawai to use, Miyagi had an idea. The ring should place someone in Nagoya to investigate production in the important aircraft factories there. Why not Kawai?

"That's a good idea," agreed Sorge. His mind slipped into a well-worn Communist rut. "If Kawai will open a bookstore in Nagoya, we will supply the necessary capital for it."[26]

Miyagi hurriedly rounded up Kawai and put the proposition to him. "We don't have any members to cooperate with us in the Nagoya area, but that area is very important, so can you go there?" he asked. "Can you open a bookstore in Nagoya?" Kawai had had his fill of this bookstore business. Moreover, he suspected—correctly—that Miyagi was trying to get rid of him. So he did not answer in words but made a face that Miyagi deduced signified disapproval.[27]

Miyagi was not yet beaten. Hearing that Kawai had a relative in Nagoya, he thought that sending him on a trip to that city might change his mind and induce him to set up shop there. So he sent him on a swing around Gifu and Aichi prefectures with Nagoya as a central point.

"The most important problem in the Nagoya area is that of aircraft production," he instructed his pupil. "There manufacturers are Mitsubishi, Aichi-Tokei, and also there seems to be a manufacturer by the name of Okazaki." From this starting point the conscientious Miyagi launched into a detailed briefing and hopefully sent Kawai on his way. "But his report after coming back said only that there were Mitsubishi and Aichi-Tokei," Miyagi summarized gloomily. "And he had even forgotten the preliminary review I had given him."[28] One suspects that Kawai was far too smart to turn in an excellent account, which would have condemned him to Nagoya forever, out of touch with Ozaki.

The latter encountered a setback that autumn. The Showa Research Association closed its doors, depriving him of a fertile source of information. But the Breakfast Group continued to flourish, now meeting in the prime minister's official residence.[29] Thus Ozaki edged yet a little nearer to the seat of government.

CHAPTER 42

"SICK AND TIRED OF SPY WORK"

"Max is unfortunately so seriously ill that a return to his former work capacity cannot be counted on. He has been working here five years, and the conditions here would undermine the strongest constitution. I am learning his job now and will take his work on myself." After that falsehood Sorge turned to himself:

> As for me, I have already told you that while the European War is still in progress I shall remain at my post. But since the Germans here say the war will soon be over I must know what is to become of me. May I count on being able to return home at the end of the war? I have just turned 45 and have been on this job for 11 years. It is time for me to settle down, put an end to this nomad life, and utilize the vast experience I have accumulated. I beg you not to forget that I have been living here without a break, and unlike other "respectable foreigners" have not taken a holiday every three or four years. That may look suspicious.
>
> We remain, with health somewhat undermined, it is true, always your true comrades and co-workers.[1]

Sorge affixed his small, neat signature. Even if he believed the war was nearly over, his primary mission remained what it had been from the beginning: to keep the Russians posted on Japanese intentions toward their country.

His letter to his Fourth Department chief would be en route to Moscow sometime in September, if nothing interfered with Clausen's scheduled rendezvous with the courier. For, contrary to Sorge, at the time he wrote this letter, Clausen was out of bed and back to his usual routine. Although the radioman had to be careful about undue exertion, Sorge had no overt reason to hint at a future drop in radio volume. He had not demonstrated concern for his co-worker when Clausen really needed it, a sore point with him, not overlooked in his list of grievances.[2] Sorge did not learn and perform Clausen's work, nor could the Red Army expect him to take on those tasks, for which he had neither the time nor the technical qualifications.

Seven o'clock in the evening of September 19 found Clausen patiently waiting at the Suehiro Restaurant in accordance with recent instructions from Moscow to "meet the man you met before." But Vutokevich was nowhere to be seen. Clausen lingered in the restaurant until further waiting would make him conspicuous, then made his way home. At his next radio contact the Fourth Department admitted to a mistake; the correct date was October 20.[3]

Only recently discharged from his bed, Clausen was still shaky, and exertion brought on dizzy spells. Henceforth he no longer carried from place to place the heavy black bag containing his radio set. Voukelitch and his former wife, Edith, did it for him, while Anna made certain that her maid was occupied elsewhere.[4] When Edith came to pick up the set, Anna had no particular problem, for the maid knew Edith as a friend of the family. However, when she returned the bag wrapped in a *furoshiki*,* Anna feared that the maid would become suspicious, so Edith telephoned in advance when she was on the way, and Anna hovered near the door to answer the ring herself. Voukelitch never concealed the bag, but usually he timed his visits for late evening when the maid had gone for the day.[5]

For his next courier contact Clausen went to the Suehiro Restaurant again and found Vutokevich already there, seated at a downstairs table with a round-faced, broad-shouldered man

* A kerchief which was the Japanese woman's equivalent of a shopping bag.

of some thirty years. "This is Serge," said Vutokevich as Clausen took his seat, "whom you will contact hereafter."[6]

From comments his new contact made, Clausen correctly deduced that he belonged to the Soviet Embassy. For Serge was Viktor Sergevitch Zaitsev,† second secretary and consul at the embassy. Clausen gave him a ride as far as his office in Shimbashi, and Vutokcvich to an address in Azabu ku, arranging to meet him at the Ota beef store in Shimbashi a week later. At that time Clausen handed over twenty rolls of film, receiving $500 in exchange. This was his last meeting with Vutokevich. Henceforth he contacted only Zaitsev.[7]

The last straw for Clausen came in the form of an order from Moscow in November: "Because of the war, foreign exchange has become difficult and remittance has become troublesome, so remittance from us will be reduced to about 2,000 yen a month. The rest of the money needed should be taken out of the profits of the Clausen business." The Soviet Union had put up capital for M. Clausen Shokai[8] and now wanted to receive some dividends.

Though Clausen's firm was a cover operation, it had taken root and grown, and he was understandably proud of it. True, Moscow had put up the initial funds, but a capital investment cannot ensure success. Had Clausen merely played at his business, he would have run it into the red, and no one in Moscow could have done anything about it except pour in more money. So he considered the firm his own.

He genuinely enjoyed his work as a businessman, experiencing the satisfaction of pulling his weight as a productive member of a community. Then, in late 1940, "as I became disinterested in spying work and as my belief in Communism became shaky, I came to devote myself seriously to this business. I put all of my money into this business and worked as hard as I could. . . ."[9]

Cause and effect were interwoven, and perhaps Clausen himself could not have said which came first, the chicken or the egg. His disenchantment with communism aided his firm,

---

† To avoid possible confusion between "Sorge" and "Serge," the text will refer to the contact man as "Zaitsev," although he appears in the testimony almost exclusively by his code name.

but how far was his life responsible for his disillusionment? It is a bit difficult to remain a fire-eating revolutionary while running a successful business and driving a good car, seated beside a wife swathed in furs.

The transition of a "100 percent Communist" who "thought that the work of secret spying was sacred and important work" into a man "sick and tired of spy work" did not take place overnight. Many factors entered into it. Clausen had come increasingly under the spell of Nazi propaganda. A German by birth, in constant association with his fellow countrymen at the German Club and at social functions, he devoured German newspapers and decided that this man Hitler had something.[10] The Nazi propaganda sheets gave the impression that the Reich was a Valhalla of stalwart heroes, beautiful maidens, humming industry, and starched, pigtailed little girls offering bouquets of wild flowers to a beaming *Führer*. It turned many a head in those days.

Clausen's musings did not go deep enough to effect any genuine change in the nature of his beliefs. He came to have "a favorable feeling about Hitler's policies in Germany."[11] Thus he did not transform himself from a Communist into an apostle of freedom. He still thought in the totalitarian pattern and merely shifted gears with no noticeable grinding from one dictatorship to another.

Realizing "for the first time that I am a German," he pointed with pride to Hitler's elimination of unemployment, not noting that Germany had purchased full employment with war, genocide, and mass exile. In the past he had simply become a Communist "because all of the people could not find employment." Now Germany had put everyone to work without communism. His Japanese friends, too, seemed quite content. Evidently "this country does not need communism."[12]

Although he clung to his belief in a planned economy, he began to wonder whether the communism to which he had given his allegiance was not an impossible dream, that to achieve a world of peace and plenty for everyone would require a major change in human nature. And with a flash of insight, he had come to see that if the new masters of the Kremlin had ever shared that dream, they had sacrificed it to Russian national interests. Thus Clausen began to feel "that my spying work was nonsense." It was all very disconcerting and filled him with unease.[13] So, as he wrote, "I have been wandering between my old communist ideology on the one hand and the newborn Germany and the patriotic Japanese people."[14]

Beyond politics lay a personal resentment toward Sorge that the latter had brought on himself. He had sown the wind of arrogance and rudeness and now reaped the whirlwind of disillusionment, even sabotage. Brought up in Kaiser Wilhelm's Germany, Sorge and Clausen were prototypes of their classes—Sorge the bourgeois intellectual; Clausen the small-town mechanic. Each was incapable of understanding the other or fully appreciating his virtues, although they could unite in a common cause or in the face of a common danger. Usually Clausen's good nature overcame any incipient personality clashes. His descriptions of most of the members of the ring make clear that he was a sunny individual who in general liked his fellow-man. Yet his written account of Sorge is smoky with anger.

Clausen's statement, written in English,[15] conveys a stark conviction lacking in Sorge's baroque flow of words. Clausen reveals himself plainly, hiding none of his doubts, fears, and mistakes, never attempting to make himself the hero of his narrative. For this reason, his comments about Sorge, although lengthy, deserve consideration:

> It is very difficult to explain Sorge's personality. He has never shown his true self. But he is a true Communist. . . . He is a man who can destroy even his best friend for the sake of Communism. But judging from what I have observed, if he were in a different position he would be a miserably small-minded person. . . . [He] did not need to have much courage in working in the Embassy. On the other hand . . . he collected all information from his spy ring members and he himself tried to stay away from danger. About this point I know something. He sometimes became slightly sick and on these occasions I had to be always beside him because he was very afraid of being alone by himself. At that time I myself was seriously ill and was being told by the doctor not to work but Sorge

requested me to work the same as though I were
well.

Therefore he may be said to be inconsiderate
of other people. . . . [He] does not give money
even when necessary but at the same time he spent
money as though he were throwing it away. Thus
his character cannot be said to be ideal . . . [He]
always treated me as a kind of a boy* . . . But he
always treated women well. However, he did not
like my wife. . . .[16]

That was Clausen's evaluation of the man he worked
with closely for six years. Confirming evidence about their
relationship came from Hanako, who frequently saw them together. Because she cherished Sorge's memory, any hint from
her that he was less than perfect must command attention.
"Sorge showed no smiling expression toward Clausen," she
said. She summed up the situation in one sentence: "Sorge did
not feel any necessity to be amiable to Clausen."[17]

Clausen struck back at Sorge. Even before the cheese-
paring message from Moscow, he had begun to destroy some
of Sorge's material without sending it to the Fourth Department.
At the time he did not think of this as sabotage. He rationalized
it as neglect because of his being "bored with this spying
activity."[18]

Inspecting the order to help finance the ring, Clausen
was acutely conscious that he "wanted to stay out of involvement with Moscow. . . ." Seizing his courage in both hands,
he declared to Sorge that he "could not accept such instruction. . . ." He made out a report explaining the reason why,
but he did not give this to Sorge until January 1941. How could
Clausen explain his refusal to obey Moscow's orders? He could
not honestly claim financial disability, for "the business at that
time was very good and the net profit amounted to 14,000 yen
a year."[19]

Nevertheless, despite Clausen's personal problems, during 1940 he transmitted about sixty times, ten more than in
1939, for a total of 29,179 words, or 6,040 more than in the

* That is, a servant.

previous year. As Clausen employed the term in this context, a *word* meant a code group of five letters.[20] Although under the doctor's care for the entire year, confined to bed for three months, and in the final quarter wrestling with qualms of conscience, Clausen made 1940 a banner year in wireless volume.

CHAPTER 43

"MANY ANXIOUS MOMENTS"

Sorge and Ott were never closer than during this period when both were mutually dependent. Sorge was a regular visitor at the Otts' summer villa at Akiya, about thirty kilometers south of Tokyo, where the two men prowled about the countryside together, Sorge snapping pictures of peasant life. On one such occasion Ott had to invoke his diplomatic status to prevent a military policeman from arresting Sorge.[1] Ms. Ott was endlessly kind. When Sorge had a sick spell— and for all his muscular strength he was not too healthy—she brought him nourishing soups and German tidbits to tempt his appetite.[2]

He had a good deal of regard and respect for Ott, who had developed into an effective ambassador. Grew confided to Sieburg that "of all his foreign colleagues only Ott had real access to Japanese politics and the holders of power, and that was due more to Ott's human qualities than to German policies."[3] Nevertheless, Ott insisted that his daughter join the Nazi women's organization, and although a convinced Catholic, he went to church only on Christmas lest someone tip off the Foreign Office that he had attended mass.[4]

Sorge's embassy contacts and Ozaki's many reports on Japanese social and economic conditions reinforced Sorge's already formidable storehouse of knowledge about conditions in Japan, hence helped him maintain his prestige as a journalist. With the outbreak of the European war in 1939 Sorge had ceased to write for the *Zeitschrift für Geopolitik*. But his appearances in the *Frankfurter Zeitung* increased dramatically over 1939. No fewer than forty-three of his articles appeared during 1940, most of them on the front page.

This coverage is all the more remarkable in view of the fact that the wartime issues of the *Frankfurter Zeitung* seldom exceeded six pages. The quality of Sorge's writing varied, at its best reading like well-informed political commentary. Naturally he usually expressed the German point of view, and the very titles of his articles testify to his debt to Ozaki.[5]

During the summer General Thomas sent a request through Matzky for an essay "on the problems of Japanese wartime industry." Relying almost solely upon data Matzky furnished, Sorge wrote a detailed essay, consisting of "specific studies on aircraft, automobiles, tanks, aluminum, artificial petroleum, iron and steel among Japanese wartime industries from 1938 through 1939." Matzky being ready for reassignment to Germany, Sorge entrusted him with this essay for Thomas.[6]

Matzky's replacement was Colonel Alfred Kretschmer. As "army executives" had told the new military attaché "he could trust Sorge," the letter's unofficial supervision of the embassy continued without a hitch.[7]

He had his hands full on two fronts. Japan began determined efforts to end the undeclared war in China. Berlin bore down on Chiang through the German ambassador in Chungking, who urged the generalissimo to make peace with Japan and take his losses. Soon, the ambassador argued, the European war would end and China would no longer be able to count on British and American assistance. Germany would guarantee Japanese good faith. In Berlin Ribbentrop played out the same line to the Chinese ambassador, adding that the Soviet Union, too, might cease to give aid and comfort.[8] Japan also tried an indirect route, appointing Admiral Nomura ambassador to the United States. Ozaki had the inside story. Nomura had many acquaintances in the United States, Roosevelt among them. His appointment suggested that Matsuoka hoped to end the war in China by a compromise with the United States.[9]

Meanwhile, Ott and his service attachés were working on a top secret project. "Around that time the German side thought that if Japan should stand up and attack Singapore, Germany could subsequently cut down the British power in the Mediterranean and in the Atlantic and therefore would be able to carry out the landing operation on Britain. So through the German Embassy, Germany propagandized to the Japanese military and Government to open an attack upon Singapore.'' Thus Sorge set the stage.[10]

Accordingly Ott, his service attachés, and his chief of the Economic Section, Alois Tichy, prepared a study of the problems the Japanese Army would face in an attempt to take Singapore. Before the end of January they decided that, in Sorge's words, ''it would be possible to conquer Singapore if Japan would attack from the direction of the Malay Peninsula. But in order to do so, a sudden attack should be the first condition and at least three months would be necessary for the conquest and that Germany would assist Japan indirectly by taking the offensive in the Atlantic during the period and by thus drawing British forces there.''[11]

Gathering up the results of their labors, the attachés visited the Japanese General Staff and tried to sell the idea. ''But they were welcomed only with smiles and did not get any answers from the Japanese side.''[12]

Sorge took no part in this exclusive study circle, but he saw all the materials. Observing them, he wondered why Germany should be so hell-bent to bring Japan into the picture by way of Singapore. As became clear later, this was because ''Germany at that time was already determined to have a war against Russia,'' explained Sorge. ''And since she could not give any time to Britain, she was eager for the Japanese to join the war against Britain.''[13]

While this was going on, Japan attempted to force arbitration of their disputes down the throats of Thailand and French Indochina. Following the course of these proceedings, Ozaki came to some accurate conclusions: ''. . . that Japanese basic policy was to assist Thailand and subdue Indochina; . . . that if Indochina would not accept Japanese demands in the case, Japan would try to advance by force and at the same time ask Thailand to offer military bases as compensation.''[14] This was exactly what Japan planned and what in the end it did.

Sorge set Ozaki, Miyagi, and Voukelitch on the trail of these mediation maneuvers, for he thought there might be ''a secret treaty behind the treaty.'' Their efforts turned up nothing of this nature.[15] On January 31, 1941, in his role as foreign journalist Sorge attended the formal signing of the armistice between Thailand and Indochina.[16]

In this same period Sorge was keenly interested in an economic mission from Germany headed by a man Sorge identified only as Wohltat.* The arrival of the mission was made public, but the details of the negotiations were kept secret. From Tichy and members of the mission, Sorge learned the nature of the negotiations and something of what Japan and Germany desired of each other. Japan wanted parts for machines, tanks, submarines, and antiaircraft guns, assistance in mass production of war matériel, and patent releases on such items as artificial petroleum and airplanes.[17]

German demands included 60,000 tons of rubber a year, beans, whale oil, various minerals, a guarantee of German rights in China, and agreement on the method of payment for exports.[18] In view of Wohltat's background, oil may well have played a more important role in these negotiations than Sorge knew. He kept the Kremlin *au courant* of the proceedings until the opening of the Russo-German war in June 1941 brought the negotiations to an end.[19]

While Sorge spent his mornings in the German Embassy and his afternoons reading, writing, studying, or clattering away at his typewriter, Hanako found herself left very much to her own devices. Fortunately for both of them she was neither demanding nor restless and was far too much in awe of Sorge to distract him at work. Even during his free time the language barrier precluded conversation in depth. Her attempts to teach Sorge the Japanese vernacular dropped with a thud before a wall of literal-mindedness. He rendered every word with pedantic precision, sometimes with comical results.[20]

Surrounded by volumes in several languages as well as an ever-expanding collection of classical records, Hanako asked Sorge which language he found most pleasing to the ear. Not at all unwilling to display his talents, he tested one language after another on his tongue—German, Japanese, English, Italian, French, Chinese. "Italian is the worst for speaking," he

* Probably Helmut Wohltat, a Finance Ministry official who specialized in matters relating to oil (Curt Reiss, *Total Espionage* [New York, 1941], pp. 203–04).

declared. He uttered a few more words as if he found the sensuously flowing syllables difficult or distasteful.

"Italian songs sound beautiful," protested Hanako.

Slightly annoyed at this hint of mutiny on the part of his usually compliant audience, he narrowed his eyes. "Russian songs are the most beautiful," he announced in a voice laden with emotion.

Hanako retreated tactfully. Sorge must have a deaf ear for Italian vocalizing; he had given her all the Gigli and Caruso records from his collection. But she loved her recordings of Russian folk songs sung by the matchless Feodor Chaliapin, so she could agree with Sorge without undue wear and tear on her conscience.[21]

Some of Sorge's dislike of the Italian language may have been political. To Morin he frankly revealed his antipathy to Mussolini's Italy. The head of an Italian economic mission to Tokyo had held a press conference in the Imperial Hotel in 1938. This "pompous little man . . . evaded questions about his negotiations with the Japanese by long digressions about the glory of Mussolini and the Fascist regime in Italy." After a few samples of this oratory Sorge whispered to the American, "Let's get out of here before I lose my temper and hit this oilcan on the spout." Outside the hotel Morin kidded Sorge for talking so disrespectfully about his "loyal allies." Usually Sorge laughed off Morin's needling comments, but this time he reacted violently. "Bad people, the Fascists. They are worse for the Italian masses than the old monarchists." So venomous was his tone that Morin forbore to comment on the difficulty of telling the difference between Fascists and Nazis.[22]

Either by direct suggestion or indirect influence, Sorge largely guided Hanako's reading. Once he questioned her about Margaret Mitchell's *Gone With the Wind,* which Sorge considered "magnificent." She chattered about the best seller and its colorful characters. When she said, "I like Captain Butler," Sorge asked, "Do you think I am like Rhett Butler?"

Sorge might well have experienced a fellow feeling for Clark Gable's film interpretation of Butler—the sardonic intelligence, the virile magnetism, the cynicism about war. But Hanako could see no real resemblance between Sorge and a war profiteer like Butler, and Sorge agreed with her. He thought

Scarlett O'Hara a much stronger character.[23] Strength and size were the yardsticks by which he measured worth in his conversations with Hanako.

With the world ringing with the name of Hitler, she read *Mein Kampf*. "Why does Hitler say that Jews are bad and dirty?" she asked her personal fount of wisdom. "I don't understand. Many Jewish people have been excellent artists. Sorge, what do you think? Are the Jews dirty?"

"No, I don't think they are dirty!" snapped Sorge. "Jewish girls have black eyes, melancholy and very beautiful. I like them." Then the voice of experience told him that it would be tactful to change the subject. "Hitler stands for fascism. He is not a very big man."

"Is Mussolini the same?" asked Hanako.

"That's right. Mussolini is a little man."

"Who is the greatest man?" she inquired, curious about Sorge's opinion.

"Stalin is a great man, I think!"

"Is that so?" exclaimed Hanako, surprised.

"Yes," Sorge repeated. "I think Stalin is a great man."[24]

"By the end of 1940," Hanako said, "Sorge had the conviction that someday Germany and Russia would fight. Sorge was deeply troubled by this prospect. It gave him many anxious moments." At the time Sorge's attitude puzzled her; later she looked back and understood his anxiety: "He had a deep inner conflict. He spied for the Russians, but he both liked and respected the Germans and he did not want to see Germany and Russia fight."[25]

Goriev claimed that Sorge's first notice to Moscow about German plans for war against the Soviet Union was dated November 18, 1940, and that Sorge obtained his information from "a man who had succeeded in fleeing Germany."[26] It is difficult to accept that even Sorge, well connected as he was, could have obtained that information a full month before Hitler issued Directive 21, dated December 18, 1940, spelling out Operation Barbarossa, the code name assigned to the projected campaign against the Soviet Union.[27] It equally strains the credulity that a man would flee Nazi Germany only to appear in Tokyo, with its close diplomatic ties with Berlin, its flourishing German community, and its many German agents, am-

ateur and professional. Moreover, Clausen declared that the
ring knew nothing about the projected German attack on Russia
until "two or three months before the opening of the war."[28]

Sorge never claimed such a coup, as undoubtedly he
would have had he been in a position to do so. He was never
shy about giving himself credit, for he was proud of his exploits—and justifiably so.

CHAPTER 44

"CONTINUE TO BE ON THE LOOKOUT"

By far the most important project simmering at the German Embassy during the autumn of 1940 and well into 1941 started when Ribbentrop invited Matsuoka to visit Berlin. Both the Japanese foreign minister and Ott thought this was a fine idea and decided they should go together. It would be difficult to improve on Sorge's own account of the background:

> . . . Germany was somewhat disappointed by the Japanese attitude after the conclusion of the three-country alliance, for Germany expected that Japan would by this alliance take a more aggressive attitude toward the United States and Britain. But all that Japan tried to do was to bring Indochina into the Greater East Asia Co-Prosperity Sphere. . . . And if Japan should take Indochina into the Greater East Asia Co-Prosperity Sphere, the materials Germany would get from Indochina would be reduced correspondingly. So Germany worried about this point, and yet since Germany accepted the Japanese Greater East Asia Co-Prosperity Sphere she could not protest against it officially. . . . Thus this diplomatic game ended with a complete Japanese victory.[1]

Sorge watched with intense interest as this little chess match moved across the Far Eastern board and reported frequently to Moscow.[2]

Ott did not take his diplomatic skinning at Matsuoka's

hands lying down. He continued to work on the elusive foreign minister and "kept a close contact with various organizations in Japan insisting on action to smash Britain. . . ."[3]

Through these shenanigans of late 1940 and early 1941, Sorge kept his gaze firmly on two points: "(1) How relations between Japan and Germany after the conclusion of the alliance would actually develop; (2) The fact that Japan's eyes were gradually shifted to the south and its interest in the north gradually decreased. From this standpoint, the German-Japanese relation . . . was very important. So I reported its development to Moscow consistently."[4]

On the Berlin front Hitler played a dangerous double game. He had already decided to strike at the Soviet Union, but in early November he offered to deal Stalin a hand in dividing the Eastern Hemisphere. This move was section one of a two-part sleight of hand trick. The second section was the infiltration of the Eastern European countries, which would explain large German troop movements eastward.[5] Like Sorge's career in journalism, which both covered and assisted his real objective, Hitler's operations in late 1940 were intrinsically valuable to him as well as being effective smoke screens. If some unforeseen development interfered with the Russian campaign, he had nothing to lose by following through on his diversionary tactics.

So Hitler notified Japan that Germany was proposing an agreement between the Tripartite Pact nations as one party and the Soviet Union as the other. Japan interposed no objections, and Stalin dispatched Molotov to Berlin.[6]

In talking with Hitler and Ribbentrop, Molotov indicated that his country's participation in the Tripartite Pact was acceptable in principle, provided it would be a genuine partner. Before formal agreement, however, Moscow wanted certain things spelled out, especially the extent of the nebulous Greater East Asia Co-Prosperity Sphere. When he left for Moscow, Molotov had neither definitely accepted nor rejected the proposed alliance. However, he made clear that until the Russians found out what was in this four-partner deal for them, they would keep the line free to China, hence by extension to Britain and the United States.[7]

In the meantime, Ribbentrop submitted to Japan a draft

of the proposed four-power agreement. The Soviet Union recognized the leadership of Germany, Italy, and Japan respectively in Europe and East Asia. They in turn agreed to respect Soviet territory. All pledged to give no assistance to the other's enemies. A secret protocol assigned areas of influence: The Persian Gulf and India were within the Russian sphere, Japan got the South Seas, Germany was to scoop in Central Africa, and Italy fell heir to northern Africa. In his talks with Ambassador Schulenburg in Moscow Molotov kept demanding more and more for the Soviet Union and less and less for Japan and Germany. As a result, the negotiations broke down, and Russian-German relations took a marked turn for the worse.[8]

Oddly enough, possibly because Tokyo did not know of Molotov's demands at Japan's expense, the Japanese became better disposed toward Russia. Matsuoka decided that when he went to Berlin, he would go by way of the Soviet Union.

Throughout this period Matsuoka and Ott prepared for the long-postponed official visit to Berlin. On February 3 a liaison conference established guidelines for the foreign minister. These boiled down to securing a firm recognition of Japan's supremacy over the Greater East Asia Co-Prosperity Sphere and to coming to an agreement with the Soviet Union within the spirit of the Tripartite Pact.[9]

Saionji, who was to be one of Matsuoka's party, believed that the foreign minister had no special mission. He merely wanted to find out if Germany was going to invade Britain and incidentally to make the acquaintance of Hitler, Ribbentrop, and Stalin. "It goes without saying that a person who has assumed responsibility for a nation's foreign policy should know the face, character, and way of thinking of the negotiator on the other side of diplomatic discussions," Saionji explained to Ozaki when the latter sought out his friend to pump him.[10] Hence Ozaki expected no world-shaking results from Matsuoka's visit and at the end of the trip had to admit that for once events had caught him and Sorge off base.[11]

On February 10 Ott telegraphed Ribbentrop that the mission had been approved, and Matsuoka was very happy about it. He planned to talk with Hitler and Ribbentrop about their joint policy toward the United States, if possible to keep that country neutral by diplomacy. If necessary, Japan would attack

Singapore. He promised that Japan would make no decisions without German concurrence but in the meantime would prepare for war. He hoped to reach agreement with Russia and China.[12] Such a self-contradictory program was typical of Matsuoka.

Ribbentrop met with Oshima on the twenty-third and pressed for Japanese entry into the war as early as possible. He implored the Japanese to keep hands off the Philippines. If they struck Singapore and presented the United States with the *fait accompli,* it probably would accept the situation rather than go to war over territory not under its own protection. In return, Oshima probed Ribbentrop about German relations with the Soviet Union. The German foreign minister sidestepped. Discussions with Moscow were "still in the balance."[13]

Miyagi was skeptical of any good resulting from Matsuoka's big-game safari. ". . . I do not think visiting the Soviet Union will improve Russian-Japanese relations," he told Sorge pessimistically. "As for German relations, Matsuoka probably will not exert any influence on Hitler."[14]

Miyagi held both Matsuoka and Oshima, the Japanese ambassador to Germany, in low esteem. "Ambassador Oshima," he continued contemptuously, "is a hero type. He does not have an opinion of his own."[15]

Naturally the Matsuoka odyssey and its results, if any, were of considerable interest to the Soviet Union, and Sorge kept Moscow posted by radio and courier.[16]

On March 13 Matsuoka, accompanied by Ott, set forth on his journey to Europe via the Trans-Siberian Railway.[17] Matsuoka stopped off in Moscow, where he offered Stalin and Molotov a nonaggression pact. Molotov suggested a neutrality agreement instead, but Matsuoka deferred his answer until his return from Germany. Why involve Japan with Moscow until he saw what Berlin had to offer? He did not know that the German bigwigs were debating how much, if anything, to tell him about Operation Barbarossa. Some argued that he should know the truth to be able to negotiate intelligently and so that Germany might use him to control Japanese policy. However, Hitler decided to play his cards close to his chest in fear of the Japanese's selling the knowledge to the Russians, the British, or the Americans for a quid pro quo.[18]

In the course of lengthy discussions among Matsuoka,

Hitler, and Ribbentrop, the German foreign minister pressed for a commitment that Japan would attack Singapore, an action which, he stressed, probably would finish the British in Southeast Asia and ensure Japan's dominance. Despite Hitler's veto, Ribbentrop gave Matsuoka any number of broad hints about the true state of German-Russian relations, so broad indeed that if Matsuoka misunderstood him, it was because he wanted to do so. He fairly bubbled his thanks and personal agreement with everything Hitler and Ribbentrop said. But shorn of its diplomatic language, his reply clearly showed that he had neither the authority nor any particular wish, at least for the moment, to commit his country to war with Britain.[19]

Matsuoka might not have found it so easy to squirm off the German hook if Hitler and Ribbentrop had been able to give him their full attention. But on March 27, the very day Matsuoka arrived in Berlin, Yugoslavia kicked out Prince Paul, who had taken his country into the Axis two days before, and refused to acknowledge his signature. This unexpected defiance changed the entire picture in Eastern Europe. Much too small-minded to ignore the revolt and go on with his grand design, Hitler decided upon a quick punitive campaign. On March 27, he postponed Operation Barbarossa to June 15, and a little later for another week.[20]

Matsuoka returned to Moscow, where he spent a week and had several interviews with Stalin and Molotov.[21] To American Ambassador Laurence Steinhardt he remarked on April 8 that Hitler and Ribbentrop had urged him to make friends with the Soviet Union; he would be pleased to do so, but Japan could not afford that luxury in view of Molotov's excessive demands. Yet to German Ambassador Schulenburg, on April 13, Matsuoka claimed that he was not at all eager to sign up with the Soviets but would have no choice if Moscow met Japanese terms. Before he left, he and Molotov signed a neutrality pact.[22]

Well pleased, Sorge accepted this unexpected development "as a success in Russian diplomacy, in that by formation of this Japanese-Russia Neutrality Treaty Russia successfully separated Japan from Germany for the time being."[23] Ozaki believed that the action "resulted from the tension between Russia and Germany caused by the excessive foreign policy of Russia in the Balkan Peninsula" and so informed Sorge. The latter requested Ozaki to bring him tidings of the impact of the treaty on public and government opinion.[24]

Interpretation of how, if at all, this new accord would affect the Tripartite Pact became an immediate subject for discussion at the Breakfast Group, so Ozaki had no trouble in obtaining the opinions of his fellow members as well as the interpretations of the South Manchurian Railroad's experts. He briefed Sorge several times between April 13 and the beginning of May.[25]

Ozaki advised that in general the political world approved the agreement. Even the military had no overt objection. There was some right-wing opposition, but not much. The citizenry, too, was pleased to be released from the fear of a war with Russia.[26]

The politicians were split into two camps about the relationship of the treaty with Russia to the Tripartite Pact. The Axis Faction insisted that the new Japanese-Russian treaty could not change the basic relation between Japan and Germany because the Tripartite Pact had been established by imperial rescript. The other school of thought argued that the Tripartite Pact specifically excluded the Soviet Union as its object, and moreover, the new treaty postdated the old one.[27]

The Breakfast Group agreed with the second interpretation, but Ozaki was uneasy. He knew that "the Japanese attitude might change in any direction according to the situation of the time." So he warned Sorge bluntly, ". . . we should continue to be on the lookout for Japanese preparations to attack Russia."[28]

To add to Sorge's discomfort, Miyagi informed him that General Araki's powerful faction in the army "was not happy and took an opposing stand." Sorge summarized these findings and interpretations for Moscow.[29] He emphasized to Miyagi in words that much impressed him:

> . . . if we can predict the Japanese attack on Russia two months in advance, that attack can be avoided through diplomatic negotiations; if we can tell one month in advance, Russia could move major military forces to the border and could make complete defense preparations. If we can warn two weeks

in advance, Russia could at least make defensive preparations at the front line. And if we can advise a week in advance, that should help minimize the sacrifice.[30]

Sorge and Ozaki gave the impression that if the Russo-Japanese Neutrality Pact were broken, the break would be of Japan's doing. Clausen, however, pointed out that it was "contradictory to the principle of communism based on the class struggle that Russia would seriously have a friendly relationship such as this with a capitalist nation."[31]

Naturally Sorge wanted to hear Ott's views and asked his friend point-blank for the story on the Japanese-Russian treaty. Ott "said clearly that he never expected it and that such a Japan-Russia Neutrality Treaty was far from a happy thing for Germany. . . ."[32]

Ott was much discomfited, especially when he discovered upon his return that "the idea of attacking Singapore had died and disappeared completely." Sorge remembered that Ozaki asked Konoye, "What happened to Singapore?" and the prime minister replied, "Only Ambassador Ott played with that idea."[33] That statement is patently false, and Konoye vigorously denied ever having said anything of the kind.[34]

Altogether Matsuoka had proved fully as adept at the art of the double cross as Hitler and Stalin and, incidentally and unknowingly, made Richard Sorge a very happy man—at least temporarily.

CHAPTER 45

"DIFFICULTIES FOR SORGE"

Amid the thunder of war already in being and the threat of worse to come, Voukelitch ended his Year of the Dragon in the company of Clausen. The two men were chugging home in Clausen's car at about eight o'clock one December evening after a transmitting session. Voukelitch held the black bag carefully on his lap. As the car neared a police box, the policeman on duty emerged and signaled the automobile to a halt. "Where are you going?" he inquired.

Clausen "felt shocked, being afraid that our work had been detected at last." But to his mystification and relief the officer did not check the car's contents. "Your car's headlight is off, so drive carefully!" he warned Clausen politely, and popped back into his box. Clausen and Voukelitch exchanged sickly smiles as they drove into the night.[1]

Japan ushered in 1941, the Year of the Snake, with a full measure of color, firecrackers, poetry contests, and political bombast. New Year courtesy calls upon friends being in order, Kawai went to wish Miyagi the compliments of the season. Relations between these two men were peculiar. There had been some unpleasantness around the end of 1940. Miyagi had pigeonholed Kawai as being not of the pure faith, too bohemian in his personal life to be a credit to the party. Kawai respected Miyagi's inner strength and gentleness but found him morbid, obsessed with the fear of discovery. Each thought the other drank more than was good for him.[2] Yet quite aside from Miyagi's tutoring Kawai in espionage, they seemed drawn together, perhaps by sheer loneliness. Neither had anyone else with whom he could talk freely as an equal.

But when Kawai reached Miyagi's boardinghouse to pay his New Year's call, he found it closed and locked. No one answered his knock. Then he noticed a banana peel hung on top of the gate. Kawai's sensitized mind read into this odd circumstance only one possible explanation: a signal between Tokko agents. So he retraced his steps, much troubled in spirit.[3]

So far there is no evidence of police interest in Miyagi at this time. They had almost decided to call off their surveillance of his Achilles' heel, Ms. Kitabayashi. Six months of investigation had developed a picture of a woman scurrying about her housewifely errands, once in a while wistfully recalling old times in the American Communist Party—the only exotic note in the plainsong of her days.[4] The Tokko had nothing more concrete against her than past associations thousands of miles away and Ito's accusation. And the Tokko had no reason to trust Ito further than any police force trusts any informer. Ito might be honestly mistaken, but he would not be above baiting the police hook with a lure.

No big fish had thus far swum near to snap at the bait, and the Tokko agents had better things to do than to stalk an inoffensive seamstress. About this time, however, they made another routine sweep of known Communists. There is some reason to believe they picked up Ito again briefly, but if he parted with any more tip-offs, they were not germane to the Sorge case. In the same catch the Tokko hooked Kikuyo Aoyagi, who was both Ito's housekeeper and Ms. Kitabayashi's niece.[5]

Member of an all-female Communist cell, Ms. Aoyagi was at first reluctant to discuss her left-wing associates but soon changed her mind. The police used no force on her, nor did they have to. A Japanese prison of the early 1940s was not a pleasant place, and Ms. Aoyagi earnestly desired to be elsewhere. Among her revelations she mentioned a woman who had been a member of the American Communist Party. This woman had returned to Japan and now taught sewing in Wakayama Prefecture. Ms. Aoyagi told enough about the current activities of the Japanese Communist Party to revive the Tokko's interest in anyone connected with her.[6]

The Tokko raised its collective eyebrows. There could hardly be two former CPA members who earned a living by the needle in Wakayama Prefecture. On the verge of expiring the Kitabayashi investigation received a stiff shot of adrenaline. Kiyoshi Miyayashi, an agent of the Tokko's Foreign Section, went to Wakayama and rented a room next door to the Kitabayashis. He watched Ms. Kitabayashi's comings and goings for a month, as she plied her trade on weekdays and ventured forth to the nearby Seventh-Day Adventist church on Saturdays. A less subversive program could scarcely be imagined, and Miyayashi returned in disgust to headquarters.

There the Tokko chiefs once more reviewed the question of jurisdiction. Since the inquiry had produced no evidence of espionage, the prevailing opinion was that the woman's only interest to the authorities lay in her ideology; hence she fell within the purview of the First Section. This department specialized in Communists and was better qualified to deal with her than the Foreign Section. The Foreign Section, heavily undermanned in ratio to the number of foreigners it had to survey, was not sorry to be relieved of this troublesome investigation and retired from the case with satisfaction.[7]

The Tokko could anticipate a rush of business in the very near future, for Japan was putting teeth in its anti-Communist drive. On March 10 the Diet passed a modification of the Peace Preservation Law, giving wide powers to the Tokko and making a criminal offense of any attempt to change the *kokutai* ("national polity") or the private ownership system.[8]

Miyagi was deep in the dismals at this time, as Kawai noticed, and sought comfort as well as livelihood in his palette and brush. Although he was gifted in working in pastels, the soft delicacy of that medium did not satisfy him, so he worked mostly in oils and in the Western rather than Oriental style. His canvases were large and a bit on the melancholy side when he painted to suit himself. But he liked to please his friends, and preparing a picture for someone of less sober tastes than his own, he lightened his touch accordingly. Kawai treasured a portrait of a geisha, the jolly, roly-poly type Miyagi preferred.[9]

But Miyagi was in no mood for the glowing end of the spectrum one day early in 1941, as he selected a piece of canvas some two and a half by three feet in size, stretched it, and set it on his easel. Miyagi was not a great artist, yet on this day something akin to genius touched him as he worked. A few days later he showed the result to Kawai, and the two men sat down before it, sipping sake. Kawai stared at the work in mingled fascination and repulsion. Bareback on a white horse under a harsh sky, a Japanese man wearing a blue kimono rode as if to execution, his hands tied behind his back. In the upper corner, backed by a blazing sun, a disembodied head looked down, impersonal, judging.

Kawai felt the power of the painting, but it smelled of fear, and his hackles rose in protest. Suddenly it came to him that the rider, dressed in Miyagi's favorite color, was the artist himself. When the sun of truth came out, revealing Miyagi's treason to the dispassionate eye of justice, he would go to his death.[10]

Kawai remembered this unnerving incident when, on May 10, Miyagi picked him up at his home and took him to the Ueno Zoo. Although they had nothing secret to discuss at the time, they had fallen into the pattern of meeting in public parks, safe from prying eyes and pricked-up ears. They discussed the National Defense Security Law, which became effective that day and agreed that it would impose great difficulties on their work.[11] It did indeed, for it provided penalties running from death down to a minimum of three years' penal servitude for disclosing state secrets to any foreigner. State secrets encompassed diplomatic, political, and economic information such as, among other things, decisions or proceedings of cabinet meetings or imperial conferences. The new legislation made no mention of military secrets, those being more than adequately covered by earlier laws.[12]

Miyagi had read about this legislation in the newspapers and also had examined the official report on it.[13] As a result, his morale was dragging. He had spent years conspiring against his own race and collecting information that, so far as he knew, might have been totally useless. Why not leave Tokyo? He unburdened his soul in this vein to Kawai. The ever-present possibility of arrest haunted him, for he knew his weak lungs would not carry him through a long prison term. Well, the police would not take him without a fight! He was something of an adept at *Zu-Tsu-Ki*, an Okinawan form of self-defense, which utilized the head as well as the hands. "If I ever get caught, I'll butt them with my head," Miyagi told Kawai with a flash of spirit. Perhaps he would chuck the whole spy business and retire to Wakayama to start an agricultural reform movement.[14]

Kawai diagnosed his companion's bleak mood as a combination of poor health, a sense of inferiority, and the blues, complicated by the day's headlines. Perhaps his sudden interest in agricultural reform was the pull of the land. Miyagi loved flowers and had a green thumb. Kawai saw him as a tragic figure, who with his tuberculosis and inferiority complex was unsuited for the life of an underground agent.[15]

On his next visit to Ozaki Kawai reported that Miyagi was in a dangerously depressed state. Ozaki responded with the comfortable platitudes of a man hearing about someone else's problems. "Well, there are sunshiny days and cloudy days," he observed philosophically. Kawai pointed out that with the whole trio—himself, Ozaki, and Miyagi—under observation, they had reason to be on their guard. But Ozaki refused to be dampened. "Don't worry," he said with a smile. Seeing that he could not penetrate the smooth armor of Ozaki's self-confidence, Kawai departed in some little irritation. To him Ozaki would always be the great man who had befriended him and helped him keep his head above water financially, but under the circumstances his perpetual good cheer got on Kawai's nerves.[16]

While the Japanese tightened their already formidable security laws, a sharp danger had been threatening Sorge in the very place where he felt most secure: the German Embassy. By 1940 certain elements within the Nazi Party had begun "creating difficulties for Sorge because of his political past." The chief of the DNB, Wilhelm von Ritgen, had been receiving a steady flow of personal mail from Sorge. These letters contained obviously authoritative reports on political developments in Japan for Ritgen's use as editor of the *NS Partei-Korrespondenz*, the Nazi Party's official newspaper. Ritgen considered these reports well-nigh indispensable, so he went to Walter Schellenberg, chief of the Foreign Intelligence Section of the *Reichssicherheitshauptamt* (RSHA) or the Reich Central Security Office. Would Schellenberg arrange for a thorough check of the Gestapo files on Richard Sorge and see if some way could not be worked out to continue making use of him?[17]

Schellenberg could and did, with results so interesting that he and Ritgen immediately went into serious conference. While Sorge's file did not contain proof that he was a Soviet agent, it held enough to make this a distinct possibility. Ritgen reacted as a newspaper editor rather than as a party functionary. In his opinion Sorge was a source much too valuable to lose. Somehow they must keep him in action. After some hesitation Schellenberg agreed, so the two men pondered ways and means. Finally Schellenberg stated his position: He would keep the party ferrets off Sorge on the condition that henceforth he must include in his letters to Ritgen intelligence on the Soviet Union, China, and Japan.[18]

Then Schellenberg carried the case upstairs to Reinhard Heydrich, who added his contribution: Sorge's material must be thoroughly screened before going into the *NS Partei-Korrespondenz* mill, and Sorge himself placed under personal observation. This posed a problem. Schellenberg had agents in Tokyo, but most of them were young and inexperienced. Then suddenly the answer came to hand. Gestapo Colonel Joseph Meisinger had just been ordered to Tokyo as the embassy's police attaché.[19]

Schellenberg despised Meisinger as "one of the most evil creatures among Heydrich's bunch of thugs." Schellenberg's file on Meisinger's activities in Warsaw "proved him to be so unutterably bestial and corrupt as to be practically inhuman." His record had shocked even Heinrich Himmler, who ordered him court-martialed and shot, but somehow Heydrich had saved his neck. Tokyo being about as far as one could travel from Berlin, thither Meisinger was dispatched. Schellenberg told Meisinger something about the Sorge situation and instructed him to keep the journalist under observation and advise Berlin regularly by telephone.[20]

So the Gestapo colonel sped to Tokyo, where he and Sorge promptly established a friendship of sorts. Each had good reason for cultivating the other. Meisinger had his job to do, and Sorge had to keep a close eye on whoever became police attaché. Then, too, coming on the heels of Ritgen's request that he add intelligence about Japan, China, and Russia to his political analyses, the arrival of so notorious a Nazi as Meisinger was a disquieting development.

Sorge turned the full voltage of his charm upon the newcomer. Erich Kordt, recently assigned as the embassy's minister, later recorded that Meisinger "seemed to feel honored that Sorge often heartily helped contribute to the demolition of his whiskey stocks even though on those occasions Sorge made great fun of the portly Meisinger."[21]

Rummaging through his predecessor's files, Meisinger came across a paper signed by Sorge acknowledging receipt of certain funds.[22] This might indicate that Sorge was actually in the pay of some German agency, in which case it behooved Meisinger to tread lightly. On the other hand, the receipt might cover reimbursement to Sorge for some legitimate expense incurred on behalf of the embassy. Whatever his reason for so doing, Meisinger informed Schellenberg that Sorge enjoyed the favor of the embassy and also had excellent connections with the Japanese government.[23]

Shortly after Meisinger had taken up his duties, Schellenberg was badly rocked when a visiting Japanese police commissioner asked him whether or not Meisinger had some of his fellow Germans under observation. Schellenberg jumped to the conclusion that he was alluding to Sorge. Because that journalist's information was of increasing importance with zero hour for the German invasion of the Soviet Union approaching, nothing must arouse his suspicions, so Schellenberg had enjoined the strictest secrecy upon Meisinger. But intentionally or not, Meisinger must have tipped his hand to the police.[24]

The military police, the Kempeitai, were not slow to snap up any hints Meisinger may have dropped and quietly began to collect information about Sorge and his associates, with extra emphasis on any Japanese seen in his company. The Kempeitai had little to go on—just the shadow of a suggestion that Meisinger had Sorge under observation. But if the Gestapo was so interested in a man as to put a full colonel on his tail, the Kempeitai should keep an eye on him. The Japanese always considered the possibility that the whole business might be a Nazi setup. Indeed, Sorge might be a Nazi agent.[25]

Quite aside from Meisinger, the embassy compound was

virtually a fortress beneath its placid surface. Over the years the staff had mushroomed far beyond the modest handful of Dirksen's day. In addition to the embassy personnel, more than 100 German reporters swarmed over the place individually or in groups, reporting their findings to the ambassador in accordance with his instructions. Ott posted storm troopers festooned with hand grenades on twenty-four-hour-a-day guard and even set up a shortwave station on the embassy roof.[26]

Sorge's special pass enabled him to come and go without hindrance, but once inside, he was somewhat handicapped. As more and more offices became jammed to capacity, less and less often could he find a secluded nook to photograph borrowed documents for his Soviet masters. Fortunately for him, as the year progressed, the Fourth Department became too busy to pore over large, detailed documents, so he was able to curtail this delicate portion of his work without impairing his mission.[27]

CHAPTER 46

"THE SOVIET UNION IGNORED OUR REPORT"

By early spring of 1941 the question that haunted Sorge—whether or not Germany would strike at the Soviet Union—was no longer so much "whether" as "when." According to later Soviet releases, Sorge dispatched a message sometime during March: "The German military attaché in Tokyo has declared that immediately after the war in Europe is over, war against the Soviet Union will begin."[1] This makes little sense in the context of March 1941, seeming to indicate that Hitler would not attack the Soviet Union until Britain was subdued, in which case there was no immediate urgency.

But change the date from March to April, transform "war in Europe" into "war in the Balkans," and it not only makes sense but bears a remarkable resemblance to a message Steinhardt sent to the State Department on April 18. Ryuki Sakamoto, director of the Japanese Foreign Office's European Department and a member of the Matsuoka party, had informed the Slovak minister in Moscow that he thought Germany "wished to and was capable of destroying the Soviet Empire" and might well attack when the Balkan campaign ended.[2]

When Saionji returned from his trip to Europe, Ozaki got together with him and casually dropped the question "Is Germany intending to fight with Russia at all?"

"The relationship between Germany and Russia is very tense," replied Saionji. "But it cannot be thought that a war with Russia will benefit Germany. So probably Germany will not, after all." Ozaki passed along this view to Sorge.[3]

From other quarters, however, Sorge gained no such

optimistic appraisal. Among his very important sources of information were the German officers who accompanied the diplomatic couriers who came from Berlin to Tokyo weekly. Such a courier was Colonel Oskar Ritter von Niedermayer, an old friend of former Ambassador Dirksen, who had given Niedermayer a letter of introduction to Sorge. His mission to Tokyo was "to investigate to what extent Japan would be able to participate" in the forthcoming war.[4] Waxing confidential under the spell of Sorge's genial hospitality, Niedermayer confided:

> that opening of a German-Russian war was already a determined fact and that Germany had a three-fold objective: (1) to occupy the European grain area of the Ukraine; (2) to obtain at least a million or two million captives to supplement the German scarcity of labor and use them for agriculture and industry; (3) to eliminate completely the danger existing at the eastern border of Germany. Hitler thought that probably he could not find another chance if he should pass this one up. . . .[5]

Bits and pieces of information from other couriers and escort officers helped round out the picture. German forces had been mobilized on the eastern border, some having been transferred from France. German fortifications were completed on the eastern border. At the same time, Berlin instructed Kretschmer, the military attaché, "to inform the Japanese military that since Russia was mobilizing troops on its western border, Germany would have to take measures to cope with it." Said Sorge: "This instruction was in detail and showed by map the specific mobilization conditions of the Russian Red Army."[6]

Kretschmer told Sorge that the Germans had completed large-scale preparations, although war was not yet certain. Germany might use this display of power to force the Soviet Union to accept its demands. No one seemed to know just what these demands comprised. But the question was academic for, said Kretschmer, ". . . starting a war or not was solely dependent upon Hitler's intentions, and would be decided without reference to Russia at all."[7] So what with Kretschmer, Niedermayer, and a bevy of anonymous transients, Sorge had a heavy load of bad news to furnish the Fourth Department as quickly as Clausen's fingers could click it off.

On May 6[8] Clausen sent out eight messages, among them the morsel dated only "May 1941" which the Soviet Union later released for publication: "A number of German representatives are returning to Berlin. They believe war against the U.S.S.R. will start at the end of May."[9]

In view of all Sorge had to offer, why was such a short and general message the best the Soviet Union could produce to support Sorge's secular canonization? Clausen supplied at least a partial answer. He claimed that Sorge gave him "very many informational manuscripts" during the spring of 1941. After listing certain types of intelligence, Clausen continued: "However, I already had doubts about communism at that time and so I sent just a little out of the above to Moscow. Most of the manuscripts given to me by Sorge were torn up." He may have exaggerated his conversion, but the amount of information that died in his trash basket substantiates his claim to a certain degree. And he pointed out his diary would support his statement.[10]

Since the beginning of 1941 Clausen had been systematically sabotaging the ring. A careful reading of his testimony and a comparison of transmission figures make evident that in 1941 between one-half and two-thirds of the material Sorge gave him to send never reached the airways. Some manuscripts Clausen culled before destroying a part or the whole; others he did not even bother to read. Of what he screened, he did not weed out what he considered nonessential; he skimmed off the cream. Of the more important material, he coded and transmitted what for one reason or another he dared not suppress. He dispatched just enough to keep the Fourth Department from suspecting subversion.[11] The apparent drop in Sorge's efficiency should have puzzled and disappointed his superiors in Moscow.

Unaware of this development, Sorge listened with outstretched ears to the fascinating saga of an old friend. Lieutenant Colonel Schol, en route to Thailand as German military attaché, "stopped at the German Embassy and orally transmitted to Ambassador Ott special, highly secret instructions concerning the coming German-Russian war." Sorge's statement makes clear just how exceedingly classified they were: "Ott hid as much as possible the secret instructions he received from Schol and did not tell even me. And he did not even give any warning to those Germans who were going home via Siberian Railroad. . . ."[12]

But Schol had no such inhibitions and gave Sorge many details. Sorge summed up Schol's information concisely:

> The German-Russian war will be opened on the coming June 20th; it may be postponed for a few days but the preparation is already completed. At the eastern border the German Army of 170–180 divisions are concentrated, and all these divisions have tanks or are mechanized. The German attack will be made on the entire front line and its main force will be directed to Moscow and to Leningrad and later to the Ukraine. With this much force Germany can break into the Russian Red Army all at once and capture it. For opening the war, they would not send an ultimatum but declare war after starting the battle. Within two months the Red Army may collapse and the Russian government may fall. And in the winter the Siberian Railroad will be opened and contact with Japan will be made possible.[13]

What a consummate actor Sorge was to receive this hair-raising information with no outward sign of more than the friendly interest of a politically keen newsman! Schol may have had a quid pro quo in mind, for he asked Sorge to come see him in Bangkok in the autumn, saying that there was a job for him.[14]

Sorge wasted no time in getting Schol's information to Clausen and ordered him to send it at once. Unfortunately for Sorge, he did not stand over Clausen while he coded, and Clausen did quite a job of abridging. The information that "German troops had already started to gather near the Russian border in preparation for the attack on Russia" was one item that fell by the wayside. "I thought it was a very important subject," said Clausen, "but since I had a favorable attitude already at that time toward Hitler's policies, I did not send out this information." He did transmit data that he attributed to Schol but that seem to have reached Sorge through one of the couriers: "Of the German Air Force, those which had been at the Western Front for the battle against Britain are now being sent to the Russian border." He censored the detail that "these troops were sent to Katowitz and that the units are made up of ninety airplanes."[15]

Moscow claimed to have received a message dated May 19 reading, "Nine armies of 150 divisions will be concentrated against the U.S.S.R."[16] If Moscow thought this skimpy document was a big fish, it should have seen the ones that got away! Clausen actually went on the air on May 21 Tokyo time, sending eight messages totaling 797 word groups, a goodly crop considering his estimate that he dispatched only one-third of all of Sorge's manuscripts during 1941. The figures in his diary support this, showing a drop from a peak of 29,179 word groups in 1940 to 13,103 for 1941. Clausen was on the air only nine months of 1941, but a little figuring shows that if he had kept up his monthly average of roughly 1,465 word groups, his output for the entire year would have been only 17,472. Yet by Clausen's estimate, Sorge gave him approximately 40,000.[17]

Believing his detailed warning messages to be safely in Red Army hands, Sorge waited impatiently for some indication that Moscow was making use of its month's warning. But nothing happened—no diplomatic checkmate, no significant Russian troop movements, not even a request for details, much less a grateful acknowledgment. Instead, there arrived "a funny sort of telegram," saying, in effect, "We doubt the veracity of your information." Sorge was with Clausen when this brusque message came in, and he flew into a rage. He sprang to his feet and strode to and fro, clutching his head as if fearing that he might actually blow his top. "Now, I've had enough of this!" he shouted. "Why don't they believe me? Those wretches, how can they ignore our message!" Clausen recalled, "This was the only time when both of us were beside ourselves."[18] No doubt! Suppose Sorge had demanded a recount, asked the Fourth Department to play back his messages sent thus far in May, or even asked for a report of the number of word groups received. What would the harvest have been?

But Sorge was in no state to take such a simple, logical course. One can readily picture him as beside himself with wounded vanity and vexation of spirit as well as with genuine fear for his beloved adopted homeland. Was it for this that he had poured out the best years of life at its feet? Was this all the thanks he and his faithful coterie received for their toil at the risk of their lives? For the time being, it was. As Miyagi bluntly observed later, "The Soviet Union ignored our report and did not prepare anything."[19]

No wonder that Sorge's nerves were jagged and continued that way until the end. The strain of his way of life took its toll. Even so minor a detail as his new maid's voice grated on him. Late in the winter Ms. Fukuda had suffered a heart attack, which required him to hire a servant to assist her. Sorge had grown accustomed to Hanako's cello tones and the Amasan's violin murmur. The new woman had a high, shrill voice that went through his ears like the squeal of a fife.

He drank even more heavily than usual and at times came home drunk. On one occasion he lurched into his study, where Hanako was reading, seized her, and made love to her so violently that she buried her face in her hands with embarrassment. Sorge was a considerate lover, so this departure from the norm puzzled and alarmed her.[20]

One day at the height of this prewar crisis she halted abruptly on the threshold of the study, almost paralyzed with amazement. Sorge lay on the couch, his hand over his forehead, tears slipping down his craggy face. She had never imagined that he could cry. "Why do you weep so?" she asked softly.

Sorge turned tear-wet eyes to her and answered, "I am lonely."

"How can this be," she inquired, "when you have so many German friends here in Tokyo?"

Sorge replied with despair in his voice, "They are not my true friends."[21]

Loneliness had always pressed upon him with a special weight. A fragment survives of a poem he penned in Germany: "Forever a stranger, fleeing from himself . . ."[22]

In those dreadful weeks of May and early June he was indeed alone. That cold, almost contemptuous slap in the face from Moscow must have left him feeling utterly rejected. Hanako knew that Russo-German matters nagged at Sorge like an aching tooth. Not realizing that he was part Russian, believing him "German to the last drop of his blood," she ascribed his agitation to his hatred of war in the abstract and to the loneliness of a stranger in a strange land.[23] She had no way of knowing—and perhaps Sorge himself did not fully realize—that his personality and way of life almost inevitably made his ego structure the arena of a symbolic Russo-German war.

Long ago he had cast his lot with his distaff side, becoming a Russian by inclination and citizenship. The Russian river ran deep in Sorge; the very soul of Russia—in all its tragic hilarity, its rigid profusion, its ruthless charm—looked out from behind his eyes. He worked for Russia with his whole force all his adult life. The rise of Hitler and nazism solidified an already firm commitment. He had sealed over the German stream, but still it flowed. To all but the most perceptive observers he presented the appearance of a typical German—the punctilious formality to strangers; the jovial conviviality with friends; the arrogance to juniors. The picture may have held a hint of caricature; sometimes Sorge overdid things—itself a very German characteristic. The inner Sorge, too, held much of the Teuton. His capacity for hard work; his respect for the world of the mind and his love of study; his mental orderliness so at variance with his personal untidiness; his meticulous attention to detail—all these he owed to his father. A less worthy inheritance was an insensitivity born of self-satisfaction, which caused Sorge to evaluate everyone who crossed his path in terms of that person's usefulness to him.

If the Kremlin had decreed that he should live and work in Russia, the German current might have remained quiescent. But for almost a decade Sorge had assiduously cultivated his German heritage. He had not set foot on Russian soil since 1935, and then only briefly. During his entire stay in Japan he worked, wrote, spoke, even thought in German. His associates were Germans; he ate in German restaurants; he drank in German bars.

This necessary masquerade held its dangers. No man can live for years in a particular environment, deliberately steeping himself in its ways, without taking on some of its color. Sorge might hate everything his Teutonic associates stood for, he might like or dislike them as individuals, but he could not deny them, although he betrayed them every waking hour. He was not lonely because he had no true friends but because the nature of his mission made it inevitable that he could be a true friend to no one.

CHAPTER 47

"ATTACK SOVIET RUSSIA"

As the tension preceding the outbreak of the Russo-German war mounted, the strain from which Sorge obviously suffered reached such a pitch that his friends in the embassy seriously worried about his physical and mental health. Ott confided his uneasiness to Prince von Urach, who was in Tokyo during May and June 1941, staying in Ott's residence.[1] His mission was "to arrange a newspaper pact between the Japanese and German Ministries of Foreign Affairs," Sorge recalled. "However, behind it he was given a secret mission from the German Government. He brought to Ambassador Ott the mission to investigate whether Japan would be able to attack Singapore and whether Japan would be able to join the war against Russia in cooperation with Germany."[2]

Ott wanted Urach to persuade Sorge to return with him to Germany, where he would try to arrange a good press job for Sorge in Berlin. Recently "Sorge had become increasingly nervous and was drinking hard." Ott "had some evil premonition that something unpleasant might happen. . . ." Urach had no hope of success: Sorge hated the Nazis and enjoyed his untrammeled life overseas. But he promised to try, and Ott donated as much whiskey as he might need to lubricate Sorge into acceptance.[3] But even totally drunk, Sorge refused: "At home he was just another journalist, while here he was Sorge, who knew what was going on. What would he want in 'Germany, the great concentration camp'?"

Urach pointed out to the keenly disappointed ambassador that as Sorge's "day-in, day-out friend," Ott could think up more potent arguments than he could. And why did he not simply send Sorge back to Berlin? "That won't do," replied Ott. "I'm his friend!"[4]

Had Ott followed Urach's advice, he could have saved his friend's life. But Sorge would have resisted the move at the last ditch. Who but he could so well serve Russia in Tokyo?

His good left hand, Miyagi, visited his subring agent Ugenda Taguchi to solicit his views concerning the inevitability of a German attack on Russia. Taguchi took a pessimistic view. He also informed Miyagi that if the Nazis struck and routed the Russians, the Germans might establish a White Russian government in Siberia.[5]

On the basis of his research Miyagi was certain Germany would attack within the month. As he saw it, Germany faced a shortage of food and petroleum as a result of the Balkan campaign and the delay in attacking Britain. "So there is nothing else to do but attack Soviet Russia. Also, as a domestic policy the attack on Russia is inevitable in order to maintain the people's enthusiasm for victory," he told Sorge. "The rumor that Germany is mobilizing her forces against European Russia is floating around Japan." The second portion of Miyagi's recital dealt with the Japanese position: "The Japanese people are already tired of war, and they are not enthusiastic about launching an attack on Russia. Also, the capitalists do not want an attack on Russia because of the difficulties of developing Siberia and the difficulties of a permanent occupation. Especially the navy will not support the ideas of the aggressive groups in the army."[6]

Of the major members of the ring Ozaki was the last to admit the inevitability of a Russo-German war. Throughout May he would concede only that "if German strategy in Crete is successful and if the battle in the Balkans is prolonged, then Germany will probably attack the Ukraine and Caucasus areas."[7]

Ozaki could not believe the worst until it fell upon him, as Kawai was reminded when he visited his office to pay his respects. To his surprise a reception desk barred the way. Kawai did not like the look of this. Anyone wishing to see Ozaki had to pass inspection and sign a form. While Kawai scrawled his name, the receptionist informed him that Ozaki was out. "Then there is no need to hand in this form," remarked Kawai, starting to stuff it into his pocket. But the man leaned over the desk and yanked the paper from his hand. Kawai walked away, seemingly indifferent but inwardly much troubled. On his return visit he mentioned the incident to Ozaki. "They are even watching you inside your own office," he warned his patron, "so you have to be careful."[8]

"They are watching me closely because I am one of Matsuoka's boys," replied Ozaki easily. At this point he did not doubt his ability to ride the sea of troubles on the surfboard of his own cleverness and prestige. The worst that could happen to him, he told Kawai, would be a month or two's detention for questioning. Moreover, Ozaki believed in an impending Japanese revolution as unquestioningly as a child believes in Santa Claus. "Our age will come soon when you will be well repaid for all your trouble," he assured Kawai. That practical soul did not try to argue. If Ozaki got any satisfaction from his delusion, more power to him.[9]

Ozaki may have refused to worry over his own safety, but he was exceedingly concerned about that of the Soviet Union. He informed Sorge that Konoye did not want war with Russia, being "up to his ears with the China Incident" and with the future of Japanese-American relations unpredictable. He added, however, "If Prime Minister Konoye has to choose between a war with Britain and the United States or a war with Russia, he would rather choose Russia, because he doesn't like Russia."[10]

The immediate problem, however, was not Konoye's likes or dislikes but Hitler's obvious animosity. "Flanking maneuvers and efforts to encircle and isolate separate groups are to be expected from the Germans." According to the Russian press, this message from Sorge was dated June 1.[11] Clausen went on the air the last of May. One of his messages read: "Germany will attack Russia most heavily on the left wing war front. This needs special attention."[12] The Soviet press release may well represent the best sense the puzzled Fourth Department could make of Clausen's cryptic bit of intelligence.

"The words 'left wing war front' . . . refer to White Russia and the Baltic area," Clausen explained. "I intentionally obscured the meaning of this and sent the information out after keeping the manuscript with me for a week or two. So

Moscow repeatedly sent us questions, asking 'What does the left wing war front mean?' " By the time his radioman showed Sorge the Fourth Department's query events had overtaken it.[13]

With the dateline Schol had given rapidly approaching, the Soviet Union's days of grace were almost at an end. Sorge could only hope that by some mental miracle he could drive home the danger in time to save a few lives. Then he would turn his full attention to keeping Japan off Russia's back, if possible, and, if not, would once more go through the excruciating business of warning and rewarning, again with a good chance of being disbelieved. That duty done, there would be nothing to hold him in Japan.

Perhaps that thought was on his mind one day when he abruptly told Hanako that she should get married. "Who should I marry?" she asked somewhat blankly.

"Don't you have a friend?"

The question cut her cruelly. "I have no friend," she replied quietly. "Always and only you."

Sorge prowled restlessly around the study. "I may not be in Japan much longer. Your heart will ache if you keep thinking about me. If you marry a wise Japanese man, you will make a fine wife. A wife has no worries. Yes, I think you should marry."

"If I must, let it be one of your friends," she answered.

Sorge brooded. "I don't know many Japanese men. Let me see." Light dawned, and his face brightened. "I have a friend who is an adviser to the Manchurian Railroad."

Having settled upon Ozaki and assuring Hanako that he was a kind, intelligent man who could make her happy, he bustled off to break the news to him.[14] In all his years of close association with Ozaki, he had never discovered that his esteemed colleague already had a wife, a tribute to both Sorge's absorption in his work and his indifference to his co-workers as people. Even more significant, it did not occur to Sorge that Ozaki might object to this arrangement.

A few days later Sorge, looking worried, told Hanako, "I have found out that Ozaki-san is already married. Too bad! I don't know of anyone else." He dropped down at his desk, scratched his head, then turned back to his work.[15]

According to Urach, Sorge offered to sell Hanako to him,

saying that their affair was over. Hanako's memoirs relate a different story: Urach told Sorge that he wanted to take her to Germany with him, but Sorge refused, saying that without her "it would be difficult for me to live." Sorge's relationship with Hanako continued until prison gates parted them.[16]

Events inexorably pressed in on Sorge. The Soviet press stated that on June 15, 1941, Sorge sent off a dispatch reading, "The war will begin on June 22."[17] Clausen broadcast on the eleventh,[18] and Sorge never claimed to have pinpointed the exact date of the attack. If one credits him, Schol's estimate of June 20 was the nearest the spy came. Granted Hitler's taste for blitzes, the twenty-second was the more likely date. "I received many manuscripts from Sorge saying that war would undoubtedly break out," Clausen said. "But I sent out only a little from those manuscripts. I don't remember sending a message foretelling the time of the outbreak of the war."[19]

Russia gave no public intimation that relations between it and Germany had altered. On the contrary, on June 14 a dispatch from Tass, the Soviet news agency, bewailed rumors of intensified German demands and troop concentrations by both countries near the border and termed them "clumsily concocted propaganda by powers hostile to the U.S.S.R. and Germany, who [sic] are interested in a further widening and unleashing of the war."[20]

Ozaki worried over press releases indicating that Germany's shortages of petroleum and grains were leading up to demands on the Soviet Union. "Russia should avoid a war with Germany by all means," he said to Sorge. "Why does she not make decisive economic concessions to Germany?"

"Leaders in our country clearly have that in mind," replied Sorge impatiently. "But since Germany intends to smash our military force willy-nilly, there is no ground for compromises."[21]

Comparing the military strength of Germany and the Soviet Union, he said pessimistically, "If this year would only pass by, Russia would be better off."[22]

Considering the intense stresses to which Sorge was subject during the spring and summer of 1941, his press output was astounding. From January through July 1941 the *Frankfurter Zeitung* published fifty-one articles with his by-line, most of which rated the front page. None were the generalized superficialities a clever journalist could toss off with little trouble. They were solid, thoughtful efforts, many dealing with Japan's foreign policies and its voluble foreign minister.[23]

His reputation as a journalist had reached Kordt's ears even before he joined the German Embassy staff. Kordt was close to Ribbentrop and brought letters of introduction to Sorge from Etzdorff and Urach, so Sorge added another valuable contact to his catch.[24]

Kordt had heard of him as "the intelligent German journalist who supposedly was more knowledgeable about Japan's complicated political conditions than anyone else." He also knew Sorge's reputation as being "decidedly bohemian, very receptive to feminine charms and more than willing to partake of a good drink." So Kordt looked forward to meeting a man both amusing and well informed.[25]

Typically, midnight had struck when a friend of his introduced him to Sorge at the Imperial Hotel. Sorge impressed him as "bizarre" and "in a belligerent mood." He declared flatly that the Japanese were pirates but that they would never oblige the Germans by striking Singapore. Another week should decide whether or not the Japanese would get back together with the Americans.[26]

Impelled by an understandable desire to pique this argumentative newspaperman, Kordt remarked that he could not imagine that Tokyo would deal with Washington behind Hitler's back.

"Yes, that's beyond you," retorted Sorge, "but in two weeks I can get you all the details." He explained that currently a spy week was in progress. Every city block had to report to the police anyone who contacted any foreigner living in that block. By next week all this should have blown over, and his friends would be able to visit him once more.[27]

Having killed off a bottle of brandy, Sorge departed around 3:00 A.M., leaving Kordt disappointed. The famous Sorge was "a real braggart." But his friend cautioned him against underestimating his new acquaintance. Sorge's rudeness was a pose; at their next meeting he probably would be well mannered. He was "very knowledgeable about Japan," also "cultured and talented," and fundamentally "a nice and respectable man." Moreover, while he openly disliked national socialism, he was a favorite with the ambassador, and even the AO* functionaries did not take his anti-Nazi comments seriously.[28]

All of this indicates that Sorge had disarmed suspicion in one of the cleverest ways possible—by making himself a character in his social and professional circles. Even outspoken anti-Nazi comments that would have brought the Gestapo down on anyone else were shrugged off. It was just Sorge, who liked to be different and to stir up the dust.

---

* *Auslands-Organization*, the league of Germans living abroad.

CHAPTER 48

 "SOME INFLUENCE ON JAPANESE POLICY"

Sorge never spoke to his Japanese interrogators of the anger, frustration, and pain that filled him almost to suffocation at the German invasion of the Soviet Union of June 22, 1941.

With his German associates at the time he was much less guarded. One somewhat lurid account relates that he was drunk the entire day and by telephone severed relations with the Mohrs, claiming he wanted nothing further to do with "rich, corrupt people." The only one of the whole crowd with a heart was Ott, although he could do with "a little bit more character." Beating on the table at the Imperial Hotel, he shouted, "These swine!" But the next day he had pulled himself together and was back on the job.[1]

Kordt noticed how deeply the outbreak of the Russo-German war affected Sorge. He gave a harsh rebuff to a lady who expressed satisfaction over one of the early German victories. According to Kordt, Sorge confided to him that he felt particular sympathy for the Russian people, having been born in Russia of a Russian mother.[2]

In view of Sorge's long effort to conceal his Russian connections, this is difficult to swallow. Unless Kordt was pulling a long bow with the advantage of hindsight, the alcohol may have been talking, or Sorge may have felt he might as well forestall an inevitable revelation.

One night Sorge cried despairingly to Clausen, "Why didn't Stalin react?"[3] Why indeed? No ruler in history had ever received so many and such explicit warnings of a planned

invasion. The Americans and the British repeatedly sounded
the alarm, as did a number of Soviet attachés in Western Europe. All these predictions bounced off the Kremlin walls without making a dent. The American and British warnings? A
sneaky capitalist trick to drive a wedge between Moscow and
Berlin. Russian reports from Europe? Forget them. Stalin knew
best.[4] Sorge's messages? Filed away, labeled "doubtful and
misleading information."[5]

If Stalin ignored words, what about deeds? Why did the
Russian dictator not see the cut-and-dried pattern Hitler had
applied in the West going into effect in the East? The Nonaggression Pact, the exchange of missions, the border violations, the protests, the escalating economic demands, finally
the surprise attack over the weekend?[6]

Why the Soviet Union had set up the Sorge ring in Tokyo
only to distrust the intelligence it collected remains one of the
many secrets Stalin took to his grave. But one may hazard a
guess or two.

It is a historical cliché that dictatorships are supposed to
be more efficient than democracies, yet a dictatorship has certain built-in weaknesses. Stalin had made a monumental blunder in tying himself to Hitler, in pouring into Germany food,
fuel, and matériel his own nation needed urgently. To believe
warnings of imminent war, Stalin would have had to admit to
himself and to the Russian people that he had been a fool to
trust Hitler. This he lacked the moral stature to do. A dictator
must appear omniscient.

There is yet another aspect to this complex situation.
Sorge never doubted that his lofty position on Tokyo's diplomatic and journalistic heights automatically made him among
the most, if not the most, credible of Soviet spies. This was
not necessarily so. In fact, J.C. Masterman has stated it well:

> It is a mistake to suppose that the well-placed per-
> son, friendly, let us say, with a Cabinet Minister
> or an official in the Foreign Office or a highly-
> placed staff officer is necessarily in the highest
> grade of agents. The individual remarks of min-
> isters or generals do not carry much conviction,
> and it is a truism of historical research that when

dealing with diplomatic conversations and the rumors of embassies we are in the very realm of lies.

Masterman has pointed out further that the recipient needed facts, so that ''he could make his own appreciations.''[7] Perhaps if Clausen had transmitted all the material Sorge gave him to send, Moscow might have been more disposed to pay attention. But that must remain problematical, for Sorge was not in a position to give the Kremlin logistical facts concerning the Russo-German situation. In far-off Tokyo he could glean only secondhand information, and with the future of the Soviet Union in the balance, Stalin and his advisers may not have considered this good enough to form a firm judgment. What the pragmatists in the Kremlin required was not what someone said about German intentions; they needed such information as this: Were German troops massing in Eastern Europe? If so, in what numbers, with what equipment, under what leaders, with what instructions?

But even after making all due allowance for Stalin's personal and political limitations, the fact remains that if genuinely taken by surprise when Hitler attacked on June 22, he was almost the only European statesman of any stature who was.

Sorge and his men swung into action immediately. As Ozaki put it, ''. . . the spirit of the Japanese Army was directed to conquest of the continent, and since it was needless to say that realization of such a purpose necessitated destruction of Russian strength, the danger of Japanese assault upon Russia always existed.''[8]

During the summer of 1941 Sorge assured Moscow on more than one occasion that Japan would not attack the Soviet Union.[9] Yet in the period between the actual outbreak of the Russo-German war and the imperial conference of July 2, the spy genuinely feared that Japan would consider the opportunity too good to miss. Miyagi predicted that ''it would take a month for Russia to recover from the damage at the outset and so, in the meantime, the Germans will advance far into the interior of the country.''[10] Sorge was not content to report progress to Moscow from the sidelines without taking a hand in the situation.

He poured cold water over any expectations of Japanese intervention that Ott or Kretschmer might entertain. He did not have to worry about Wenneker, who felt certain Japan had no such intention. "Japan not only is emphasizing its relations with the United States rather than the German-Russian war, but also does not see why Germany started a war against Russia. The Japanese people wonder why Germany attacked Russia after having been supplied with grains and petroleum from Russia for a year and a half. Japanese people who are my acquaintances find it especially difficult to understand why Germany concluded the nonaggression treaty with Russia, broke it off immediately afterwards and started a war."

His pessimism somewhat dampened Ott, or so Sorge thought, although the Germans continued to urge the Japanese to join the fray.[11] Indeed, Ozaki said that Ott boasted "that if Japan would not stand up, Germany would carry out the war with Russia alone and would reach Vladivostok after three months."[12]

Ozaki longed to follow Sorge's example and dip his fingers in the political stew. Once before, in 1939, he had suggested to Sorge that since he had "a considerable persuasive power socially as an expert on Chinese problems and contact politically with influential people," he might indulge in some discreet propaganda for the protection of Russia, to which Sorge had replied that the ring's fundamental duty was in spying and political work was outside their assignment.[13]

Now, with the Soviet Union under attack, Ozaki tried again. The Konoye group's "attitude toward Russia was considerably flexible," so "there was some ground to enable my political maneuvering."[14] He further informed Sorge that his, Ozaki's, opinion "was evaluated fairly highly, and this was a chance for him to disclose his opinion about the current crucial problem of whether Japan should join the war against Russia or not and asking what he should do."[15] This time Sorge jumped at the chance. Immediately he radioed Moscow, "saying that we had a possibility of carrying out a positive political activity and asking whether we should go ahead and do it."[16]

While he waited for an answer, Miyagi came to his home, bringing with him a long, important report covering two official conferences held on June 19 and 23. The first of these was an army-navy executive meeting held in view of the then impending German attack on Russia. The top brass had decided to abide by both the Tripartite Pact and the Japan-USSR Neutrality Pact and see how the forthcoming war developed. The civil arm attended the conference of June 23. This gathering confirmed and amplified the previous one. The most important decision was that the military would adopt "a north-and-south integration strategy . . . in accordance with the future changes in the international situation."[17]

As both Ozaki and Miyagi explained to Sorge, this meant that Japan would be ready to move in whatever direction that events seemed to indicate most profitable and, if necessary, in both directions at once. This represented a compromise between the army and the navy, which called off their long feud to cooperate, a fact that Miyagi considered extremely important and significant.[18]

Miyagi further informed his chief that the Japanese government had heard that "Germany intends to clean up the Russian Army, occupy European Russia, establish a pro-German Government, keep important areas under military control, allow unimportant areas self-government, and then probably will leave Russia." In this connection, he told Sorge about the scheme to establish a White Russian regime in Siberia.[19]

Miyagi continued that, with the overland route severed, Japan no longer could import military supplies from Germany, so had to obtain them from the United States. Therefore, Japan must "take a compromising attitude toward the United States." In general, the business community supported easing relations with Washington and maintaining neutrality toward Russia. But General Araki had stated in a news interview, "Our national policy is advancement to the north and this is the time to destroy Soviet Russia."[20]

Sorge sent nothing of this interesting report to Moscow except the tidings about Araki, for the spy "did not trust the information immediately, and waited for Ozaki's report . . ." As for the portion concerning German plans to crush Russia and establish a Tsarist government in Siberia, Sorge remarked disdainfully, "I did not take it up because of its absurdity. I knew better than Miyagi what Germany intended to do with Russia."[21]

Yet, except for Miyagi's optimistic suggestion that the Germans might leave voluntarily, the pattern he reported was Hitler all down the line—strike without warning, crush military opposition, occupy the strategic territory, set up a puppet government in the rest.

Ozaki had little to add to Miyagi's report, although he reminded Sorge that these two conferences were scarcely more than dress rehearsals for a forthcoming Imperial conference.[22]

Sorge soon heard from Moscow about his request for permission to become politically active. "Moscow did not reject it particularly but answered that we did not need to do so." Sorge interpreted this mild negative as a green light, continued his own political activity, and immediately put Ozaki to work in the same field.[23] The two agreed that Ozaki should hold forth as follows:

> In the first place, there would never come a positive danger to Japan from the Russian side; secondly, Russia is in a defensive position, and she is very strong in a defensive war; thirdly, the traditional political and economic inevitability and interest of Japan is in the south, not in the north. Japan has to acquire natural resources such as rubber and tin by advancing to the south instead of carrying out the difficult undertaking of a winter war in Siberia.[24]

This assignment was very much to Ozaki's taste, for as Sorge said, "Ozaki himself had the opinion that it would be a crazy matter for Japan to go to war against Russia. . . ."[25] Soon he had the opportunity to expound his beliefs.

The Breakfast Group met very shortly after the invasion had begun, devoting an entire session to discussing the possibilities inherent in it. The participants viewed the situation with mixed feelings. Germany seemed well on the way not only to overrun western Russia but also to take Leningrad and Moscow. To some of the more jittery spirits it appeared that the Soviet Union must collapse in three to six weeks.[26]

There might even be a German threat to Siberia, a prospect that did not particularly cheer them. Allies or not, the Nazis were not comfortable neighbors. "Ozaki was very much concerned about this possibility," said Shigeharu Matsumoto. On the whole, the voice of common sense prevailed. Matsumoto doubted that Moscow would fall, and the whole group recalled Napoleon's failure of 1812. Still, the Nazis had upset any number of fixed ideas, and one could not be sure where their latest campaign would end. Conceivably the Germans might profit from Napoleon's mistakes.[27]

Inevitably the group discussed how this new development would affect Japanese interests. Could this not be a heaven-sent opportunity to strike the Soviet Union, claim a slice of territory for the Rising Sun, and perhaps get rid of the Russian menace once and for all? The consensus was negative. "Even if Japan had joined Germany in the war against Russia, it would have been very difficult to defeat Russia" was how Matsumoto recalled the gist of the final decision. And why attempt a territorial grab to the north? "Only the Russians can survive in Siberia," Matsumoto pointed out. "It is much too cold there for Japanese." He further remarked, "All members of the Breakfast meeting were against such a move, especially Ozaki."[28]

If Japan struck in full force so nearly in concert with Germany, the Soviet Union would be in sore straits. Its vast stretches and freezing winter might protect it as so often in the past, but for a double invasion there was no precedent in its history, hence no valid conclusion to be drawn. One thing was certain: The masters of the Soviet Union contemplated this possibility with something verging on panic. Hence the steady pressure on Sorge to discover and report Japanese intentions. In this crisis he could play only a passive part, a sort of Greek chorus commenting upon the drama. Ozaki, however, could take an active role.

So whenever Ozaki had the opportunity, throughout the summer of 1941, he argued with his colleagues in the Breakfast Group and in the South Manchurian Railroad, as well as with anyone else with whom he came in contact, against war with Russia. He admitted that the Soviet Union might suffer military defeat but that it would not necessarily entail internal collapse—"on this point Germany is making a big miscalculation." Slyly he remarked, "If Germany should defeat Russia and Russia should eventually collapse, Japan would be able to obtain Siberia automatically, so is it necessary for Japan to send troops to Siberia in such a severe coldness?'' In any case Siberia would be a drag on Japan. Traditionally it could not survive independently. More to the point, ''From the standpoint of natural resources, neither petroleum nor rubber, which Japan wants to have now, exist in Siberia; therefore, Japan should advance to the south.''[29]

Such was Ozaki's rather mild version of his activities. But Sorge drew a much sharper picture of Ozaki's propagandizing: The Soviet Union did not want war with Japan and, ''even if Japan should invade Siberia, would simply defend itself.'' Japan would be shortsighted and mistaken to attack Russia ''since she cannot expect to gain anything in Eastern Siberia or to wrest any sizable political or economic benefits from such a war.'' A Japanese-Russian conflict would play into the hands of the United States and Britain, which very likely would strike Japan ''after her oil and iron reserves were depleted. Moreover, if Germany should succeed in defeating the Soviet Union, Siberia might fall into Japan's lap without her raising a finger.'' Southeast Asia was the only worthwhile target for expansion, ''for there Japan would find the critical resources so essential to her wartime economy, and there she would confront the true enemy blocking her bid for a place in the sun.''[30]

Ozaki hoped that his opinions would reach Konoye through Ushiba or some of their colleagues ''and would have some influence on Japanese policy toward Russia. . . .'' Still, he realized that his influence had a natural limit because the military, not the government, would decide Japan's war policy.[31]

Thus the Breakfast Group was treated to the incongruous spectacle of Ozaki, the pacifist and international Communist, urging the cause of Japanese imperialism. From the immediate viewpoint of Japanese nationalism he made a good case, but for Ozaki logic and consistency, not to mention patriotism, were irrelevant. He urged this course because ''doing so amounted in effect to defending Russia. . . .''[32]

Yet in a queer little flash of revelation, he later admitted that his ''main motive was caused by my feeling of repulsion because my opinion was being opposed strongly by these people.''[33] How dare his colleagues disagree with the great Hotzumi Ozaki? So a stain of vindictiveness tainted Ozaki's devotion to the Communist motherland, at least in this instance. But however mixed his motivation, he not only deliberately and voluntarily betrayed the secrets of his nation and the confidence of its inner councils but also worked actively to send millions of his countrymen to kill and be killed, maim and be maimed, for the benefit of a foreign power.

CHAPTER 49

"A FATEFUL DAY"

On three broad fronts Hitler's armies tore into the Soviet Union. Those first five days carried the Germans halfway to Leningrad. With Russia's very life at stake in the West, Stalin and his colleagues continued to ask themselves whether Japan would take advantage of their plight and stab them in the back. On June 27, the day the Germans reached Minsk, an urgent message from "Organizer," as Dal now signed himself, reached Sorge. "In connection with the German-Russian war, what decision has the Japanese government made about our country? I want you to inform us about that. I also want you to inform us about the movement of troops to our border."[1]

"About this problem, Sorge brought many manuscripts to me," said Clausen, "telling me to send them to Moscow. However, I sent out just a little out of these and tore up most of the parts." He explained, "The reason why I sent out a little instead of tearing up all of the manuscripts was that if I tore them all up, there would be no reports or messages reaching Moscow. In that case they would surely telegraph the Russian Embassy in Japan asking about it, and Sorge would come to my place to question the reason why. So I sent out only a few and unimportant ones."[2]

The decrease in the volume of their Tokyo agent's reports did not go unnoticed in Moscow, and the Fourth Department expressed dissatisfaction to Clausen. But he smoothed this over by advising that he "could not send out because of bad air conditions."[3]

On June 29 Clausen went on the air for a lengthy broadcast. Among other things he advised Moscow, "The Japanese army is having a big mobilization in preparation for the possible attack on Russia. The Japanese army wants to have a war against Russia." This information came from Miyagi, as Clausen recalled. In the same message he included word from Ozaki: "However, Prime Minister Konoye is still trying to delay the outbreak of Japan-Russian war."[4]

While Clausen was in the act of transmitting, a Kempeitai agent dropped in unannounced. Hastily having cut the power and locked the second-floor room, Clausen received his caller in the downstairs living room. The military policeman made no attempt to search the house and went away satisfied, leaving Clausen with a few more gray hairs.[5]

That week was a momentous one in Japan. Sorge and Ozaki awaited with the keenest interest the scheduled imperial conference of July 2, 1941. The very fact that the crisis called for such a conclave stressed the seriousness of the hour. There was no such thing as a routine imperial conference.

"July the second was a fateful day in the history of Japan," said Matsumoto.[6] It was indeed! The path established in "An Outline of the Policy of the Imperial Government in View of Present Developments" was both specious and belligerent. Japan was to "continue its effort to effect a settlement of the China Incident and to establish a solid basis for the security and preservation of the nation. This will involve an advance into the Southern Regions and, depending on future developments, a settlement of the Soviet Question as well." A seven-part summary of actions to be taken to implement this policy included "preparations for a war with England and America" if diplomacy failed. Japan would not enter the Russo-German war immediately, but in case that conflict "should develop to our advantage, we will make use of our military strength, settle the Soviet question and guarantee the safety of our northern borders."[7]

This document was so comprehensive that no faction could feel definitely rejected. The meat of it was simple: Japan had officially adopted a policy of expansion, and if it could not obtain what it wanted by diplomacy, it would take it by the sword.

Needless to say, Sorge longed for a glimpse of this paper or reliable word of its content. So did every other foreign correspondent in Japan, if for somewhat different reasons. Almost before the last statesman had bowed out of the conference room, Tokyo's newshounds were baying.

The Japanese press of the day was the creature and mouthpiece of the state, printing only so much of the news as the government considered harmless or useful. But hope sprang eternal in the reporters' breasts, so newsmen besieged Matsumoto's office in Domei in person or by phone all day, each hopeful that his might be the ear into which Matsumoto would drop some word beyond "No comment."

Matsumoto expected the bombardment and took it in stride. What did surprise him was a phone call from Ozaki. Domei worked far into the night on July 2, and the office clock showed just past ten when Ozaki telephoned to ask him what decision had been reached in the imperial conference. Ozaki had no legitimate reason to be concerned about the matter, and fellow member of the Breakfast Group though he was, Matsumoto would not betray his official trust by giving Ozaki any personal tips. So Matsumoto responded to his colleague's queries with his laconic "No comment."[8]

Ozaki accepted the implicit rebuke in silence. After a few polite phrases he hung up. Matsumoto replaced the receiver, wondering why Ozaki should have called him at such a late hour, when he would discover all that was good for him to know at the next gathering of the Breakfast Group. Furthermore, Ozaki's voice had revealed a degree of personal interest uncalled for in one who had no official place in the government. "To call me at ten P.M. at night and with a sense of urgency—I thought that was somewhat strange," Matsumoto said reminiscently. "That was the first time that I pricked up my ears. Not that I was suspicious of Ozaki; I was not." Then the organized bedlam of his office closed in on Matsumoto again and drove Ozaki from his mind.[9]

Others were not as discreet as Matsumoto. Ozaki had a fairly good idea of what would come out of the imperial conference, basing it on his experience of Japanese politics and his information about the preliminary meetings of June 19 and

23. The south-and-north strategy had already been determined. If the Soviet Union fell shortly, as was the military forecast both at the Breakfast Group and through the South Manchurian Railroad, obviously Japan must establish guidelines for such a contingency. Moreover, "negotiations with the United States were in such a state that no optimistic view could be allowed, and Japan had to have a prepared policy to take in case of failure of the negotiations." Having reached these conclusions, Ozaki set about securing confirmation by pumping such willing associates as Saionji.[10]

In the meantime, Miyagi hurried to Sorge's house to ask whether he had learned the decision of the conference. "I have not found it yet," replied Sorge, "so I would like you to investigate the problem."

The next day Miyagi visited Taguchi's home, for the "man from Hokkaido" had excellent sources of information. But Taguchi still had no word of the conference. Immediately upon leaving Taguchi, Miyagi went to Ozaki, and for the third time put his question: "Do you know the decision of the imperial conference?"

"Yes, I do," replied Ozaki.

"Wasn't it about the Japan-United States treaty and the south-to-north integration strategy?" asked Miyagi shrewdly.

"You're right." Ozaki nodded. With that, he opened a pocket-sized notebook and showed Miyagi four penciled entries. As Miyagi read them, Ozaki gave him a brief explanation.[11] On July 10 Miyagi wrote his report in Japanese and, as he finished each page, gave it to Akiyama to translate into English. The same evening he took Sorge both the Japanese and the English documents.[12]

Ozaki briefed Sorge in person.[13] Sorge had already heard one version of the conference decision from Ott, who had received it from Matsuoka. The foreign minister's version was: "(1) Japan would expand her military preparations for the north and make every possible preparation to crush bolshevism. (2) Japan would continuously advance actively in the south."[14]

Listening to Ott's account, Sorge thought "that Foreign Minister Matsuoka told such a story to Ambassador Ott in order to please him, but the truth might be different."[15] What Matsuoka told Ott was not untrue in itself, but it was not the whole truth. As Sorge expected, Ozaki's story "was somewhat different. . . . Ozaki rather emphasized the second point, and his report was more accurate."[16]

As Ozaki understood it, the policy decided upon was as follows:

1. Japan would press on in China but would prepare to cope with any new development in the Russo-German war, such as internal unrest in Russia. Meanwhile, Japanese-American relations were growing more and more strained. Therefore, Japan would mobilize and send soldiers both to the north and the south.

2. Temporarily at least Japan would maintain neutrality in the Russo-German war.

3. Tokyo would continue the discussions with Washington, "with the determination to resort to force" in case diplomacy failed.[17]

Had Ozaki and Miyagi never performed another act of espionage, their giving Sorge information about the decision of the imperial conference would have been enough to seal their fate. The National Defense Security Act of May 10, 1941, specifically provided that disclosing the decisions of an imperial conference to a foreigner merited the death penalty.[18]

Before reporting to Moscow, Sorge compiled and evaluated carefully all information from his various sources about the decision of the imperial conference. And for good reason: ". . . the spy activity concerning the problem was extremely important and we did not touch any information unless it was absolutely accurate."[19] He admitted that "it was a very difficult problem to interpret what the content of the imperial conference meant."[20] He finally concluded that Japan definitely would advance into southern Indochina and would mobilize in the north but defer action there.[21] His message to the effect went out on July 10.[22]

Despite his emphasis on Japan's southward orientation, Ozaki was deeply troubled on the Soviet Union's behalf. "Judging from the previous basic attitude of the Army, I observed at that time that an assault upon Russia was almost definite," he asserted. "Although undertaking an attack against Russia was difficult from the practical point of view because of the Chinese Incident, a good chance to strike Russia came as a result of the opening of the German-Russian war," he continued, "so I judged that . . . the army, without waiting for the fall of Russia, intended to start a war by taking advantage of some German military success."[23]

Spurred on by Matsuoka's information about the imperial conference, coming on top of orders from Ribbentrop, "the German Embassy began to develop more active and systematic political measures to have Japan join the war against Russia."[24]

Before the German attack on the Soviet Union Ott had been concentrating on persuading his Japanese friends to hit Britain through Singapore.[25] On June 28 he had cabled Ribbentrop, asking if his instructions to ignore the Soviet Union and steer the Japanese southward were still in effect. Ribbentrop wired back the same day, squelching this idea firmly. Japan had to "solve the Russian problem" at its rear before moving south. If it delayed until the Russians were flat on their backs, Japan would prejudice its "moral and political position." This meant that unless Japan helped Germany now, it could not expect assistance from Germany at some future date.[26]

On instructions from Berlin, Kretschmer propagandized to the Japanese military "Germany's unprecedented success in the German-Russian war." He claimed that "Moscow should fall within two months, and that since Germany would destroy the entire Russian Army in six weeks," the Soviet Union would have no more than sixty divisions to fight Japan or anyone else. He even drew up a plan for a Japanese attack on Siberia and Vladivostok.[27]

But Matsuoka, as well as Ott's Japanese Army friends, asked him to lay off until completion of the big mobilization, begun as a result of the imperial conference. According to Sorge, these Japanese "stated that Japan would join the war when the German Army occupied Moscow and advanced at least to the Volga River line." By this standard, Ott and Kretschmer believed that "Japan would join the war within two months," while Wenneker and Sorge "were of the opinion that Japan would not join the war during the year."[28]

Sorge continued to throw wet blankets on Ott's hopes. When he "obtained various information items from Ozaki and Miyagi," he "distorted them conveniently, propagandized them, and worked so that the German side should not have a hope that Japan would join the war." He argued to Ott and Kretschmer along much the same lines that Ozaki used in the Breakfast Group: Why should Japan engage in a costly war with the Soviet Union when it could secure whatever it wanted through a German victory? In view of their current "very tense situation" with Washington and London, why should the Japanese allow their country "to be made a cat's-paw of Germany?" Why sacrifice "several hundred thousand men for Hitler's sake" when Japan's economic interests pulled it southward? If Japan had any real intention of fighting the Soviet Union, why had the major part of the currently mobilized troops been sent to China and the south instead of to Manchuria? And Sorge ended rather academically, "From the standpoint of my study of Japanese history, Japan has always tried to advance to the Chinese continent through Korea and has never tried to advance through Siberia."[29]

Sorge sounded convincing, but in his heart he was not quite sure of his own logic. Clausen said, "Immediately after the outbreak of the Russian-German war, Sorge seemed to be also thinking Japan would open war against Russia in the same way Germany had."[30] Miyagi brought the disconcerting news that at Japanese Army headquarters it was even money that the Germans would soon overrun Moscow, that in the War Ministry the odds were seven to three in favor of the Wehrmacht. The staff prediction was made on purely strategic considerations, as Miyagi pointed out, but the War Ministry bookmakers took political matters into account to some extent. He heard on the street that Sugiyama was promising Japan would attack between July 15 and the end of the month.[31] Miyagi gave Sorge a map of Hokkaido and Karafuto, so near to Soviet territory, having marked it with air bases and important ports.[32]

Clausen sent a message that month that Konoye would have to resign unless he started a war with Russia.[33]

Around this time Clausen received instructions for his next meeting with Zaitsev. This directive began with "a portion expressing their gratitude for our previous information."[34] At last the Soviet Union thanked Sorge for his warnings of the impending German strike. Appreciation for past services was all very well, but for Sorge the question was: Would Moscow believe him in this latest crisis?

CHAPTER 50

 "TOO EARLY TO MAKE A FINAL JUDGMENT"

Even while Sorge had been trying frantically to waken his superiors in Moscow to the danger threatening from Germany, the Fourth Department continued to press him for details about Japan's armed forces. In March Ozaki had secured from a colleague at the South Manchurian Railroad a list of the new Japanese Army divisions stationed in the home islands; Korea; Formosa; North, Central, and South China; and Manchuria. The list was typewritten in Japanese on the railroad's own rice paper. Ozaki considered the information so important that he personally translated it into English on Western-style paper. His prize securely in hand, he hurried to Sorge's home instead of going through Miyagi, as he usually did.[1] It was important information and helped Sorge satisfy the Fourth Department's demands for details about the Japanese Army's organization and stationing.

In May Miyagi had kept busy correcting and updating for presentation to Sorge later in the month Ozaki's listing of army divisions.[2] He met with Koshiro and secured a report that the Fifteenth Regiment in Takasaki would be made up of new draftees who had been whisked off to Manchuria just a few days after registration.[3] Another of Koshiro's invaluable reports provided the basis for a sketched map of troop allocations along the eastern border of Manchuria.[4]

The same month Moscow had reminded Sorge that it wanted current information about the Japanese Army reorganization.[5] As Ozaki said, this "was an important military secret hard to be obtained."[6] He and Miyagi pooled their resources.

400

Sorge secured some facts from the German service attachés, but Miyagi, bringing his own as well as Ozaki's findings, contributed the bulk. First they made a rough table based on Miyagi's data.[7] On the first two pages they listed recent army personnel shifts, then tabulated the divisions and their chiefs, broken down into five main parts: Japan including Korea and Taiwan; North China; Central China; South China; and Manchuria. This initial layout revealed fifty divisions already completed.[8]

Certain pesky questions kept coming up. If a division was garrisoned in Japan, yet one of the same name appeared in Manchuria, should it be counted as two divisions or as two parts of one division? While the Fiftieth to Fifty-ninth divisions were manned, the Fortieth to Forty-ninth were not. Did this mean the Fortieth to Forty-ninth existed in cadre and would be fully manned later, or were they shams? Then, too, the Konoye Division in Japan consisted of six regiments, making it the equivalent of two divisions. This was complicated enough, but yet another Konoye Division was in Indochina. For the Soviet Union's purposes, did they count as one, two, or three divisions?[9]

Gradually the two men ironed out these wrinkles. Although they could list only ordinary divisions without artillery, tank, or air regiments, Sorge decided that "we could not make anything better than this." He scribbled a note advising the Fourth Department that this list was unofficial, so he could not guarantee its accuracy and that even the German Embassy could not ascertain this information. Thereupon he photographed the package.[10] It was ready for Zaitsev in exchange for currency when he visited Clausen on May 23. Once more Clausen fended off Sorge's request for a financial accounting, which he had let slip that year. In fact, he never got around to adding it up.[11]

One of Sorge's major bits of intelligence was his coverage of the so-called Big Mobilization of the Japanese Army. This consisted of three mobilizations, starting in July and continuing for more than a month. Sorge's main concern was whether or not the German Embassy was interpreting the repercussions correctly. Ott and his colleagues believed that once the mobilization was under way, matters could not remain as they were: The Japanese "would surely advance toward Russia."[12]

In other words, if the Japanese Army got its hands on so much manpower and matériel, it would do as it pleased and present the government with a *fait accompli*.

For once Sorge was disappointed in Ozaki, whose report "was of almost no value," for it contained details which he could have obtained from Miyagi. What Sorge wanted from his esteemed colleague was "information from a general viewpoint, such as how many forces went to Manchuria and to what extent the preparations there were progressing." Ozaki thought that the army alone had arranged the mobilization, and "even Prime Minister Konoye was reportedly astonished by it." Therefore, as Sorge said, "I, Ozaki, and Moscow were caught by a great uneasiness for a while. . . ."[13]

Meanwhile, Miyagi brought in details, which Sorge screened thoroughly, picking out the fairly important items and sending them to Moscow by radio. There had been a call-up of soldiers between the ages of twenty-five and thirty, including many recently returned from China. Many students had been called to the colors and had been spread through small units instead of being lumped into big ones. Miyagi even noted the type of uniform issued because that helped indicate how many soldiers were going north and how many south.[14]

He often went to Utsunomiya, which is about seventy miles from Tokyo, to visit Koshiro. Recalled to active duty in July, Koshiro was serving with the Fourteenth Division there. He told Miyagi "that the division was preparing to call out the reserve and send it to the continent," probably to Manchuria; a new infantry regiment was stationed near Utsunomiya, and several drill grounds for infantry and tanks had been constructed in that area. According to Koshiro, only a relatively small number of those mobilized had gone to Manchuria; most stayed in Japan, to be fed gradually into China or southern theaters.[15]

Koshiro himself transferred to Manchuria, whence he wrote briefly to Miyagi, saying that there would be no war against the Soviet Union that year and he was optimistic that he might return to Japan fairly soon.[16] So Koshiro continued to participate in the spy ring even after going on active duty.

Sorge's second major concern with the mobilization was the speed with which it might be carried out. On this score he felt a surge of anxious hope "because if the war were not started by a certain time, i.e., the middle or end of August, winter would come, which would make it impossible to have a war against Russia during that year."[17]

Ott continued his efforts to induce Japan to join the great crusade. Sorge saw two plans, one drawn up by Kretschmer, the other by Assistant Air Attaché Nehmiz. The content of Kretschmer's plan was childish, in Sorge's opinion. It called for only thirty divisions to attack the Soviet Union. Obviously these could not be enough. Sorge dismissed just as contemptuously the air report, which attempted to convince the Japanese that the Soviet Union had only about fifty modern planes capable of bombing Japan and that therefore, no danger existed of air attacks from Siberia.[18]

In the midst of all this activity France yielded to Japanese demands concerning Indochina on July 21. On the twenty-fourth Japanese troopships left Hainan Island and warships appeared near Camranh Bay. Miyagi had excellent intelligence to submit on this venture, passing each completed page of his report to the ever-ready Akiyama for translation:

> The major target for Japan to attack will naturally be Singapore, which is the most important base for England in the Orient. So it is necessary to have Thailand as a stepping-stone. . . . The army may attack Singapore from the north and the navy from the south. The best season for advancing into Thailand is around October; that is, after the rainy season. Needless to say, in a war in the south, it is strategically advantageous to occupy navy bases, i.e., Singapore.
>
> The navy's younger officers have considerable confidence in their southern strategy. Recently many passenger ships of thousand ton classes have been requisitioned in great numbers.[19]

Sorge claimed to have forgotten about most of this because the report represented Miyagi's "summarized opinions and judgment of some other people."[20] But Miyagi told another story. When Akiyama had finished the English version, Miyagi carried it to Sorge and explained it to him. Sorge was incredulous. "If we send out this sort of information to Russia, you will be called crazy!" he exclaimed. "When Japan is increasing soldiers in the north, it is impossible to think of strategy in the south."

Patiently Miyagi explained all over again, and still Sorge did not understand.[21] His unwillingness to accept Miyagi's information and interpretation reveals that however he might propagandize in the German Embassy, he remained far from convinced that Japan would not attack the Soviet Union.

Then, too, Miyagi's prophecy had its paradoxical aspects. For months Ott had been entreating the Japanese to hit Singapore, only to be fended off. Now, if Miyagi was to be believed, when Ott had switched directions and was urging them to hit Russia instead, the Japanese were taking the Singapore project seriously.

On August 7 Clausen went on the air, sending only three messages totaling 258 word groups. These were about the Big Mobilization.[22] Sorge had given him a long report concerning the status of the mobilization as of the end of July, including the destination of the soldiers, the purpose and meaning of General Tomoyuki Yamashita's transfer to Manchuria as commander of the National Defense headquarters instead of the Kwantung Army, Germany's concern, and the Japanese Army's intentions in the field of Japanese-Russian relations. Of this report Clausen sent out only a part.[23]

Sorge, Ozaki, and Miyagi would have been distressed to know that Moscow would never see their information about Yamashita. They believed this firm friend and supporter of Ott and Oshima to be an excellent weathervane to the direction of Japanese foreign policy; consequently, they devoted time and pains to their reports about him.[24]

Just how clear a picture reached Moscow at this time is a question because Sorge gave Clausen a number of significant messages that never saw the light in the Soviet Union, including the following:

> Germany is trying to induce Japan to enter the war. There was a request to Ambassador Ott to send to the home government materials on which judgment could be made whether Japan would attack Russia or not during the winter time. The fact that Ger-

many could not occupy Moscow on the previous Sunday cooled down Japanese enthusiasm for a Japan-Russian war. And the Japanese Army was impressed by the fact that the German-Russian War might turn out to be a second Chinese Incident.[25]

At this time "Moscow took a suspicious attitude" toward Sorge's reports,[26] which, thanks to Clausen, were neither so plentiful nor so explicit as the Fourth Department could have wished. Perhaps, too, the Russians questioned Sorge's conclusions, as they had earlier in the year. Only bit by bit did Ozaki obtain information contributing to an optimistic point of view. Knowing weather conditions in Siberia, he believed that if the Japanese planned to attack the Soviet Union during 1941, they would have to do so no later than the end of August, so that the bulk of the operation would be completed before winter set in. In view of this, rumors circulating in late July that a war with Russia was inevitable and probably would start on August 15 genuinely worried him.[27]

He quizzed his friend Shintaro Oda, vice-chief of the Shipping Department of Mitsui Bussan. "It looks as if Japan is working toward the north," he said in effect. Oda fell into the trap and met one statement with another. "News coming to my place shows that more soldiers went to the south, and a smaller number to the north." Ozaki asked for specifics and learned: "250,000 went north, 350,000 south, and 40,000 remained in Japan." This being directly contrary to Ozaki's expectation, he "was more or less suspicious of these figures."[28] Correct or not, they probably never reached the Soviet Union. Clausen did not remember receiving such a report from Sorge, and remarked that if he had done so, most likely he tore it up without sending it.[29]

Ozaki's unhappiness was by no means allayed at a meeting which he attended at the invitation of Ryunosuke Goto, founder of the Showa Research Association. Guests included several veterans of that organization and Colonel Kenryo Sato, who held the key post of chief, Military Affairs Section, War Ministry. He "was famous for his scolding of Diet members at the Congress."[30]

As might be expected, the colonel had much to say. His

discourse ran along the well-worn groove of Japan's encircle-
ment. "Just looking at the squeeze without doing anything
about it is most stupid from the strategic point of view," he
said. "We must find a way somewhere to break off the strangle-
hold. It is our duty to think about military strategy, but I want
you people to consider diplomatic methods. . . ." Then he
added the words that made Ozaki prick up his ears: "If Russia
should be defeated in her fight with Germany and some internal
collapse or chaos should take place, Japan should naturally
send troops to Siberia. There would not be a single Japanese
who would stand by and watch the situation. It is ridiculous
not to eat the food being set before you."

"This," thought Ozaki, "is a very interesting opinion."[31] A real understatement particularly because he knew
that the Kwantung Army had alerted the South Manchurian
Railroad to expect a sudden heavy call upon its services.[32]

Then for the first time the friends of the Soviet Union
had some relatively good news. Hitler had not reached Moscow,
and the attack on Smolensk, begun on August 7, hit a snag.
The Germans had begun to feel the strength of their second
real enemy on the eastern front—geography. The German slow-
down, plus the worsening of relations with the United States
following the economic freeze, gave Ozaki hope that Japan
would indeed turn south and ignore the Soviet Union. He lined
up his collection of opinions and presented the result to Sorge:

> The top class which supported the mobilization,
> anticipating that Russia would collapse as a result
> of the opening of the German-Russian war, was
> generally reported to have started to reveal hesi-
> tation about the attack upon Russia. In the military,
> which believed in Russian defeat at the beginning,
> there appeared some different opinions, and some
> have come to think that Russia may endure the
> war. In the Manchurian Railroad an opinion arose
> that . . . the General Staff headquarters was taking
> a cautious attitude. On the other hand, the navy
> did not want to use its aircraft carriers, which were
> built for sea operations, in a war with Russia.[33]

The navy had other plans for those carriers—a little cruise in Hawaiian waters—of which Ozaki had no inkling. "Also from the economic standpoint," he continued, "Siberia would not be a target for procuring the necessary resources to rid Japan of her prevailing economic adversity. And although the Kwantung Army ordered the Manchurian Railroad to have its employees ready, it did not use them." For these reasons, and because of the time element, Ozaki forecast that "there almost surely would not be a war with Russia." But Sorge continued to take a cautious attitude. "It is still too early to make a final judgment,"[34] he told Ozaki somberly.

CHAPTER 51

"JAPAN—UNITED STATES NEGOTIATIONS"

A subject to which hitherto Sorge had paid little attention began to assume a certain importance in the spring of 1941. This was the discussions under way in Washington between Secretary of State Cordell Hull and Japanese Ambassador Nomura.[1] The nature of the points under discussion, not to mention the rights or wrongs of the issues involved, concerned Sorge much less than the fact the talks were going on and their possible implications for the Soviet Union.

When Matsuoka and his entourage returned to Japan on April 22, the foreign minister was very much upset to be confronted with the decision of the liaison conference held on April 18 that although Japan would do nothing to jeopardize the Tripartite Pact, neither would it do anything to interfere with Nomura's efforts in Washington.[2]

As Ozaki understated to Sorge, "Matsuoka was very offended by the opening of negotiations ignoring him."[3] Already he had antagonized Germany by signing with Stalin. The Hull-Nomura talks, if successful, almost certainly meant alienating his Nazi friends beyond reconciliation.

Germany wanted to know the scale of these talks and, in Sorge's words, "to what degree the negotiations were advancing from the standpoint of the three-country alliance."[4] Ott informed Sorge of Matsuoka's assurances: The Japanese-American talks would be held within the framework of the Tripartite Pact, by which Japan would abide. "Also, Foreign Minister Matsuoka stated clearly that if the United States should implement the escort system of escorting merchant ships by warships, Japan would interpret it immediately as an attack." He further asserted that his government would put these two points to Washington in writing.[5]

This was an extreme position, even for Matsuoka. Understandably Ott was suspicious. "He asked Matsuoka what the truth was," Sorge said, "saying that he had heard that Japan was requesting the United States to mediate between Japan and China. Foreign Minister Matsuoka denied this, saying that there was no such thing."[6]

Ott seized upon this matter of possible American mediation as a touchstone of Japan's good faith. He knew that the army was the real arbiter of foreign relations; hence the Japanese occupation forces on the mainland could give him the most valid intelligence about how the Japanese government would react to a U.S.-mediated settlement in China. Ott asked Sorge to investigate on the spot.

The commission was advantageous for Sorge for a number of reasons: It gave concrete proof that Ott's absence had not weakened his trust or dependence; the *Frankfurter Zeitung* had instructed Sorge to report on the Japanese-American talks, especially on any American mediation between Japan and China;[7] and the pattern of his espionage mission no longer could be separated into neat units. Back and forth wove the diplomatic shuttle in the intricate design of twentieth-century statesmanship. The Japan-China-United States discussions touched the Soviet Union, too.

Ozaki asserted that the ring's interest in the Hull-Nomura discussions was twofold: "On one side, if Japan-United States cooperation is achieved, Japan will break with Germany—and therefore relations between Japan and Russia will be softened; on the other side, if Japanese negotiations with the United States should break down, Japanese advancement to the south will be inevitable, and in that case Russia will not be attacked."[8] Put in these terms, which held considerable common sense, the Soviet Union had nothing to lose however the discussions turned out, and Sorge's intense interest in Japanese-American relations would be unjustified. But he shared Moscow's obsession that the capitalist nations would settle their differences long enough to jump en masse on the Communist motherland. He explained that the Washington-Tokyo discussions were "extremely im-

portant and significant to Moscow because (1) . . . in case
Japan-China relations are improved by the Japan-United States
negotiations, Japan will eventually have more leeway in military force and other areas . . . ; (2) if the Japan-United States
negotiations become successful, Japan and the U.S. may conclude a friendly relation and might take an anti-Russian policy
hand in hand. . . ."[9]

Sorge's mission in Shanghai was to determine for Ott
"what attitude and feeling different classes of Japanese in China
had about this rumor of peace mediation." He first stopped at
the German Consulate General, which put him "in touch with
various classes of Japanese" in Shanghai, including "the Consul General of Japan, personnel in the Foreign Ministry, a few
businessmen, local executives of the army and navy . . ."[10]

Sorge required very little time to discover that "about
90% of these people were absolutely against peace mediation,
and said that if Prime Minister Konoye and Foreign Minister
Matsuoka should try to force it, they would come across strong
opposition." From Shanghai he sent Ott a coded telegram covering his findings and discovered when he returned to Tokyo
that Ott had sent it to the German government "without correcting a single word or phrase." Sorge drafted a second message to go to Moscow on the next transmission date.[11]

For some time the events prior to and after the German
invasion of the Soviet Union pushed the Japanese-American
situation into the background of Sorge's consciousness, but
Ozaki still gave him anything he could find or surmise about
whatever deal Konoye might be trying to arrange with the
Americans.[12]

Around the middle of July Sorge caught a breath of
optimism, informing Moscow that Ozaki had heard that the
Konoye cabinet was facing another crisis and whether or not
Konoye compromised successfully with the United States, he
would have trouble politically.[13]

However, the cabinet dissolved simply to be rid of Matsuoka.[14] Face must be saved at all costs, so Konoye could not
fire his foreign minister alone; the whole cabinet resigned on
July 16. Once more Konoye was the only person acceptable to
both military and civilian circles. Two days later he became
premier again, with Admiral Teijiro Toyoda replacing Mat-

suoka. To Sorge the change made little difference, but Toyoda "took a very cold attitude toward the German side," so Ott was not at all happy.[15]

He and the new foreign minister were not close. Ott even feared that Toyoda might break up the Tripartite Pact. So he asked him about it. Toyoda replied "that the Three Country Alliance would continue to exist, but this answer seemed very vague to Ambassador Ott, and Ott looked all the more worried and impatient."[16]

One event caught both Sorge and Ozaki unawares: the economic freeze of July 26 (Japanese time) on the part of the United States, Great Britain, Australia, and the Netherlands East Indies. Sorge claimed that he had engaged in no espionage in regard to the background of the move but that either Ozaki or Miyagi—he could not remember which—informed him "that the steps taken by these countries was quite unexpected to Japan, and Japan had not foreseen this at all."[17]

Japan's troubles with the United States pleased Sorge, for they meant that "the possibility of a Japanese war against Russia decreased." He explained, "I thought basically that whether Japan would yield to the United States or resist against it was not a choice given to Japan, but was rather dependent upon the attitude of the United States. In other words, it depended on whether the Americans were clever or stupid."[18]

In early August Ozaki checked into the state of Japan's petroleum reserves "as an issue directly related to the forecast of the Japan-United States negotiations." If the stock fell low enough, Japan would have to forget about the north and head for Southeast Asia. As usual Ozaki utilized indirect methods with outstanding success. One Yoshio Miyanishi addressed a meeting of the Tokyo branch office of the South Manchurian Railroad preparatory to a conference "to investigate the influence of the new situation on Japanese politics and economy." Ozaki seized upon Miyanishi and lectured him gently.

It was wrong, he pointed out, "to determine the international movement of Japan only from economic information, for the economic power of the army and the navy and its proportion to the entire society must be taken into account. . . ."[19] This concept of the Japanese military as a subsociety with an economy and resources of its own was one of Ozaki's pet theories, and indeed, it held considerable truth.[20] "For instance," he continued, "one should not judge the international attitude of Japan only by the fact that stock and production are low, but should judge after taking into consideration those amounts possessed by the military; otherwise, the judgment cannot be correct."[21]

Miyanishi took his lesson to heart. Several days later he told Ozaki, "Since you advised me the other day, I checked up on this. This is the result." He proffered a paper listing tons of petroleum, including naphtha, heavy oil, crude oil, and lighting oil, available for use—2 million tons for civilian purposes; 2 million tons for the army; 8 or 9 million tons for the navy. Ozaki suspected that the navy might have about 2 million more stashed away.[22]

Ozaki showed these figures to Sorge and Miyagi, explaining that since normal civilian consumption was 4 million tons a year, "there would not be a drop of petroleum for civilian use in Japan after half a year, according to this figure, and an examination of the oil condition would reveal that Japan is placed in a position of choosing one out of two solutions: advancing to the south and acquiring oil in the Netherlands Indies, or yielding to the United States and receiving a petroleum supply from her."[23] This was a masterly job of research and evaluation.

A little later that month another problem with the United States arose. American tankers carrying oil to the Soviet Union had been moving through Japanese waters on their way to Vladivostok. Sorge had his eye on this ticklish situation, which Ozaki had brought to his attention. Ozaki pointed out that these shipments indicated "that the United States showed outright distrust of Japan by supplying petroleum to Russia while forbidding export of petroleum to Japan." He added that public opinion against both the Soviet Union and the United States was embittered, and some dissatisfaction arose with the government, "which tended to overlook the fact. . . ." This the government was trying to squelch by banning the subject from the newspapers.

"Japan will probably present a protest to the United States and Russia about this," observed Sorge. "We must pay attention to this because it will become a great problem if Japan should go one step further and catch or sink the ship.'' Ozaki thought Tokyo would not permit matters to go that far because ''if Japan should resort to such measures, she would have both the United States and Russia as enemies. . . .''[24] In fact, Japan owed the United States a spot of ignoring in exchange for Washington's overlooking the Japanese bombing of the U.S. gunboat *Tutuila* in the Yangtze in late July.[25]

On August 28 a new story broke that Konoye had sent a personal message to Roosevelt. While the contents were not divulged, Ozaki correctly assumed that among them was a suggestion for a summit meeting between the President and prime minister.[26] Kawai believed that it was Ozaki who first proposed a Konoye-Roosevelt conference. Furthermore, in one of Kawai's last meetings with Ozaki, the latter expressed the opinion that Japan would never attack the United States; it would have to bow to American will and superior power.[27] This despite the fact that Ozaki had been working with all his might to steer Japan southward, where inevitably it would challenge American interests.

Sorge sent to Moscow a long message obviously based upon information from Ott. The ambassador had visited Toyoda, the new foreign minister, who informed him that Konoye had merely requested reopening the negotiations that had broken down under Matsuoka. Roosevelt had agreed, and negotiations had started up again. Toyoda did not give Ott any of the details, beyond assuring him that no provision that would harm the Axis was involved. Ott was suspicious. Toyoda remarked that ''since Japan gave up hope of reopening the Siberian railroad in the near future, Japan was compelled to try to reach some agreement with the United States.''[28] In other words, the Wehrmacht's failure to conquer the Russians had left Japan isolated from its European allies, so it must look elsewhere.

To determine cabinet thinking about the possibilities of agreement with the United States, Ozaki kept in touch with Saionji.

''Japan is suffering from the freezing of assets,'' observed Ozaki. ''It is not good to proceed with negotiations while squeezing the partner's neck. Why doesn't Japan get them to release the freezing of assets and then proceed with the negotiations?''

"Don't you see that Japan hasn't the strength to do that?'' replied Saionji somewhat impatiently. "This is their trump card. Naturally they say that they will quit freezing if an agreement is reached in the negotiations.''

"What the United States really wants is Japanese secession from the Triple Alliance, isn't that right?'' asked Ozaki.

"For domestic and other reasons Japan can't come out with any idea of leaving the Tripartite Pact, but of course, the negotiations more or less contain that implication,'' admitted Saionji.

"What will they do if Chiang Kai-shek doesn't listen to the Japanese terms for solving the Chinese problem?'' inquired Ozaki. "Surely there is a possibility that China wouldn't listen even if the United States tried to mediate.''

"We aren't as soft as that!'' Saionji said with a smile. "If the United States should accept that role, she has to make Chiang Kai-shek obey even through pressure; otherwise it would be meaningless.''[29]

The whole sorry mess intensely gratified Sorge and Ozaki. The worse the relations between Japan and the United States, the better for the Soviet Union.

CHAPTER 52

"WORRIED ABOUT MIYAKE-SAN"

As the full heat of midsummer blazed over Tokyo, Clausen was acutely aware of the interest of Shigeru Aoyama, Sorge's neighbor from the Toriizaka Police Station. Aoyama frequently dropped in at the Clausen house when he was out. Usually Aoyama contented himself with speaking briefly with the maid, who dutifully reported the circumstances to her master. Once, however, he asked her to have Clausen send a photograph of himself to the police station, claiming that someone had spilled ink on the file copy. Clausen complied, then waited fearfully lest the police send the picture to China or Manchuria for comparison but heard no further word on the subject.[1]

Curiously enough, Clausen first came to Aoyama's attention innocently. Aoyama had questioned Clausen's maid in the course of investigating a French officer who had become involved in some "woman trouble" and who happened to live next door to Clausen. He listened with only half an ear while she chattered about her own employers but did not arrest the flow in case she took offense and clammed up. Then one day she uttered a sentence that riveted his attention: "My master gets up in the middle of the night and fiddles around with a machine with shiny knobs."

Himself a ham radio operator, Aoyama recognized the description and had a flash of recollection. About ten days before, an official of the Ministry of Telecommunications arrived at the Toriizaka Station and asked him if he knew of anyone in the Azabu area sending out unregistered shortwave messages. So Aoyama wondered if it was possible that thus casually he had hit the jackpot.[2]

A young policeman could not arrest a prominent German businessman without very good reason, so Aoyama cultivated the Clausens unobtrusively. In conversations with Anna he formed the impression that the Clausens "were a very close and intimate man and wife." But Anna told Aoyama that if she asked her husband what he was doing after midnight, he "would get very angry and scold her severely." Of course, Anna knew exactly what her husband was doing.[3]

During his investigation of the Frenchman for the first time Aoyama found out that Clausen was connected somehow with Sorge. "Sorge is a bad influence on my husband," Anna told him. "He takes my husband who has a very bad heart to all sorts of outlandish places at ridiculous hours, such as Kunenuma to go fishing. So please, Mr. Aoyama"—Anna dimpled—"when you next see Sorge, please scold him for me." Aoyama assumed that if Clausen had any questionable relationship with Sorge or had been sending out illegal messages, Anna knew nothing of it; otherwise she would never have spoken in that manner.[4] Actually she could not have given Aoyama a broader hint.

Nonetheless, Aoyama did not neglect Sorge. One day in August he decided to visit his neighbor. No one answered his knock, so he assumed that both Sorge and Ms. Fukuda were out. Suddenly overcome by curiosity to check on Sorge's study, he tried the door, which opened at his touch. He mounted the stairs and entered the study without knocking. There sat Sorge at his typewriter. Naturally furious, Sorge yelled that he was trespassing; knowing himself in the wrong, Aoyama was much embarrassed. However, Sorge's anger evaporated almost immediately, and the men parted amicably.[5]

In addition to Aoyama's vague suspicions, Sorge was again under the eye of Saito, who had been off the case temporarily on a special mission in China. To the best of Saito's knowledge, nothing new had developed in connection with Sorge during his absence, but he considered continued surveillance of this German newsman natural and proper.[6]

About the time that Saito resumed his watch on Sorge, the Tokko decided to pick up Tomo Kitabayashi for questioning. To this end they approached Mitsusaburo Tamazawa of the Thought Section, the official who authorized and issued warrants. He pointed out that they had no concrete facts to back up their suspicions and the matter was not urgent. Why not wait until September? Ms. Kitabayashi might well prove to be no more than the honest sewing teacher she seemed, so she should be spared a spell in prison during the hottest months of the year—an experience sure to be exceedingly uncomfortable, perhaps even dangerous, for a woman of such advanced years. To these policemen in the full flood of young manhood, Ms. Kitabayashi at fifty-six seemed to be on the brink of the grave. They agreed to Tamazawa's proposed delay. Thus the break in the Sorge case waited upon chivalry.[7]

But another and much younger woman might repay official attention, although no action so drastic as arrest. First the police summoned Sorge's new maid to the Toriizaka Station in an attempt to secure Hanako's address. The maid told them truthfully that she had not worked for Sorge very long and did not know where Miyake-san lived. Her questioners turned nasty. "You had better let us know the next time Miyake-san comes, or we won't put up with it!"

The little woman bristled. "I cook my master's meals and get paid for it!" she shouted. "There's no reason why you people should push me around!"

More amused than annoyed, the policemen cried out, "This old bitch is fresh!" and smacked her behind.

Weeping with rage and mortification, she sped back to Sorge's kitchen.[8]

So she viewed Aoyama with no friendly eye when he presented himself at Sorge's door amid the violet shadows of an early August dusk.

"I'm from the Toriizaka Police Station," he introduced himself when Hanako came at the maid's call. "The chief wants to talk to you. Could you come along with me, please?"[9]

Vaguely disturbed, Hanako accompanied Aoyama on the two-minute walk to the station and upstairs to a narrow room with windows that faced the street. There sat the chief, a severe-looking elderly man in plain clothes, whom Hanako thereafter referred to as Mr. M. He picked up a pencil and filled in a form as she replied to his routine queries on name, age, address, education, etc. Gradually he varied the questions with rude remarks about her relationship with Sorge. "I don't see why an educated woman like you . . . lives with a foreigner," he declared. "Aren't there enough men in Japan?"

Longing to escape, Hanako tried a bit of fiction. "I've been separated from Sorge for a long time," she said, "and there is nothing between us now."[10]

The chief grunted skeptically. "If you have nothing to do with him, why do you go there all the time?" Somewhat weakly Hanako responded that he must be mistaking her for someone else. "Stop lying!" he barked. "You're the only Japanese woman who visits Sorge. I know exactly when you get there and when you leave. Bah! From the window here I can see you lying in bed with your rear bare!" Hanako's fear dissolved in a wave of angry disgust.[11]

The chief continued. "We think you should separate from Sorge, leave him."

Hanako retorted that Japan's policy of breaking up mixed unions, legal or not, between Japanese and foreigners was silly. It made some sense to separate Japanese from Americans, she pointed out, but why discriminate against Germans, who were Japan's allies?[12]

"You know that a Japanese woman who lives with a foreigner is not considered a Japanese national" came the reply. Hanako spluttered with fury. Taking advantage of her momentary disadvantage, Mr. M. pressed on. "Don't live with him," he urged. He added helpfully, "We will get severance pay from him. We will take care of the details."

This calm assumption that she lived with Sorge only for money stung her into open revolt. "What will you do about it if I refuse?" she inquired. Unaccustomed to having the war carried into his own country, the officer glared at her. Hanako glared back, then, overcome, turned toward the window to hide tears of anger and humiliation.

"What do you see in these hairy *Ketto*?" the chief asked scornfully. Receiving no reply but a disdainful sniff, he sneered, "We cannot compete with these hairy foreigners. They are so sweet and nice to our women."[13]

Gibes had no more effect than wheedling, only drying Hanako's tears and stiffening her resistance. Facing her tor-

mentors, she asked with dangerous quiet, "May I leave now
if you have no more questions?" The men had no reason to
detain her. But they told her to come back when next she visited
Sorge, at which time she must sign a written transcript of their
interview to be used as the basis for a report on her to the
Ministry of Home Affairs. Deigning no reply, Hanako departed.[14]

She allowed herself a few days' cooling-off period before
giving Sorge a spirited account of the occurrence. Blood flooded
his face. "Did they use violence against you?" he demanded.

"No," she replied, "but they abused me with degrading
words." She cited as an example the statement that a Japanese
woman who lived with a foreigner was considered no longer
a daughter of Dai Nippon.

Sorge bounced up and stamped about the room, fulmi-
nating, ending up with "If Japan takes you away from me, I
will have Germany take all German girls away from their Japanese men. I can do it! I'll send a telegram to Germany!"
Then, as if amused at his childish outburst, he patted Hanako's
hand and said lightly, "I'm strong. You needn't worry." With
that, still somewhat flushed with excitement, he turned back
to his typewriter.[15]

The next evening, after Hanako had gone home, Aoyama
knocked at Sorge's door again. Hearing a familiar voice talking
to his maid, Sorge strode out to the dining room to see what
was up. Aoyama asked for Miyake-san. "What do you want
with Miyake-san?" demanded Sorge harshly. "Anything concerning her I'll answer."

Intent on his errand, Aoyama said, "You don't understand." He started to push past Sorge, asking the maid, "When
Miyake-san comes back, please send her to the police station."[16]

Even as he spoke, a short uppercut struck with the speed
of a snake. Aoyama crashed to the floor in a heap, suffering
as much from astonishment as pain. Between Sorge and his
police neighbors an easy camaraderie had always existed. When
they checked at his house, he received them as honored guests,
giving them tea and small gifts. So this outburst was completely
unexpected.

Sorge hastened to repair the damage. He could not afford

to antagonize the police. Summoning his most charming smile, he helped Aoyama to his feet. "I am very sorry about this," he apologized. "I did not think. I was so worried about Miyake-san." He instructed the maid to bring a pair of his best shoes, which he presented to his victim with a bow. Aoyama accepted both apology and shoes and went his way.[17] To the maid who grimly escorted him to the door he murmured, "I didn't think Mr. Sorge would get so angry. He is touchy! It will be awkward for me to try to reach her here."[18]

The sudden blow was evidence of the turmoil Hanako's interrogation had stirred up in Sorge's mind. His agitation indicated that he realized, perhaps for the first time, that Hanako was a possible source of danger. His attitude toward her had been that of a kindly owner toward a pet cat. He was fond of the little creature, in fact very much attached to it. He would be good to it, responsive to its moods, attentive to its wants. He would play with it, stroke it, feed it well, and keep its coat groomed. He would respect its beauty, its fluid grace, its cleverness. He would even muse aloud to it. But he would not admit it to his own status as *homo sapiens*. However, the Japanese police regarded Hanako as a human being with eyes to see, ears to hear, and a tongue to speak, so it behooved Sorge to do likewise.

Sorge had violated one of the basic commandments of espionage: Thou shalt not become involved. The dedicated spy must walk alone, "forever a stranger," through the shadow world he has chosen. Sorge had lectured Hede Massing—how many years ago?—on "how lonely and ascetic the life of an *apparatchik* must be, with no attachments, no strings, no sentimentalities."[19] Through Hanako, he was vulnerable because he had failed to apply his own precepts. Hanako could tell the police a good deal if she wanted to—his hatred of war in general and his particular abhorrence of the Russo-German conflict; his contempt for Hitler and his admiration of Stalin; his tolerance toward the Jews; his criticism of Japanese aggression.

Of course, such a small fish might slip through the official net. Sorge fervently hoped so, for danger and distraction at home could interfere seriously with his activities abroad in the land. In fact, in July and early August Sorge's espionage career could have come to a screeching halt through at least six channels: the Tokko, the Kempeitai, the case of Ms. Kitabayashi, Meisinger and the Gestapo, Aoyama's checkup on Clausen, or even the questioning of Hanako. But the fates had not yet finished with him.

CHAPTER 53

"SORGE WILL BECOME A GOD"

About a week after her first interrogation, Hanako passed the Toriizaka Station on her way home. She tried to slip by unnoticed, but sharp eyes had been watching. "Miyake-san, Miyake-san!" Looking up, she saw Aoyama beckoning from a window. Reluctantly she turned into the building and into the presence of the chief, who demanded sharply, "Why did you not come back when we asked you to?"[1]

Having no answer, Hanako attempted none. Several seconds ticked by as they took each other's measure. "Mr. Sorge struck our Mr. Aoyama," observed Mr. M. suddenly. He tsk-tsk'd solemnly. "A terrible thing!"

"That's right," interposed Aoyama. "He knocked me down with a quick uppercut with that arm of his. That was too much for me! Tremendous power! Mr. Sorge is tough when he's angry, isn't he?"

To her blank amazement, Hanako saw that both men were grinning. Some alchemy of masculine psychology had transmuted Sorge's blow into a matter for amusement and, yes, admiration. What a difference their good nature made! The chief's smile flooded his face with kindliness. Obviously somehow—perhaps by her loyalty to Sorge—she, too, had won their respect, for they spoke to her frankly, without threats, sneers, or condescension.

Mr. M. picked up a thick bundle of papers and balanced them thoughtfully. "These are all files of Japanese women of Chinese and Koreans," he said. Every one of them, he told her, had broken off the affair when enough money was offered. "Not one of them stuck to her man like you."[2]

Again he urged Hanako to leave Sorge; they would arrange a substantial cash settlement. But she would have none of such an arrangement. In the end he brought out rice paper and noted her answers to questions that were much the same as those he had asked during their previous session. When he had finished, he handed her the document, which she read and signed without protest, authenticating her signature with her thumbprint. This ceremony over, the men bowed her out politely.[3]

When she next visited Sorge, she recounted the story of this second interview, stressing the signing of the affidavit. Sorge strode up and down the room, his eyes narrowed and intent. Hanako recognized the symptoms of deep thought and watched him anxiously.[4]

This second questioning removed whatever doubt Sorge entertained that he had attracted more than casual official attention. He was the only factor in Hanako's life of any possible interest to the police. So it would be best to remove her from the scene. He stopped his tigerish pacing and faced her abruptly. "It is not good for you to have so many worries. You have your mother and your young niece to consider. I think you ought to send them both back to the country. And you had better go to Shanghai because I have lots of money in the bank at Shanghai."

"Are we going to Shanghai together?" she asked.

"Not now," he replied. "But my work here will be finished soon. Then I will join you in Shanghai and we will live together there." He smiled down at her. "Is this agreeable to you?"

She assented, and Sorge went back to work. Hanako curled up on the bed and tried to read but soon cast the book aside. Caught up in a premonition of disaster, she wept a little, silently, so as not to disturb him. Presently she drifted into light sleep.[5]

She awoke to the chill of dusk, to hear Sorge suggesting dinner. Clausen would come with them.

Clausen came in bubbling with jokes and chuckles. He sobered when he saw traces of tears on her face. "The Japanese police made M'yoke cry," Sorge explained in answer to his unspoken query. "They always bully women and I'm worried."

"Don't worry!" Clausen flapped his big hand impatiently. "The Japanese police are nothing but a bunch of fools."[6]

Then the two men conferred in such rapid German that Hanako could catch only an occasional word or two. One of these was passport. Evidently Sorge was explaining the situation to Clausen, along with his plan to hustle Hanako out of the country. Down-to-earth Clausen pointed out the flaw: Hanako had no passport, and in the circumstances the government would not issue one to her. Sorge's face clouded, and Hanako's heart sank.

Glancing at her, Sorge said, "Since you do not have a passport, it will be difficult to go to Shanghai. I don't know what I shall do." He fell into a brown study for a few moments, then resumed, "I think we probably won't get into trouble by staying together in Tokyo. Are you worried?"

Not entirely honestly, Hanako disclaimed worry. She added wistfully, "It is always best to stay beside you."[7]

While Sorge prepared to join them for dinner, Clausen told Hanako that she did not need Sorge; he himself would be her sweetheart. This was probably no more than a rather ham-handed effort to cheer her up, but Hanako took it for a genuine attempt to make time with her, and he had some little difficulty in smoothing down her ruffled feathers.[8] Then he shepherded his boss and the woman into his car and drove to a little Japanese restaurant.

Once more the two men fell into long, earnest conversation over Hanako's head. Toward the end of the meal Sorge addressed her with the air of one determined to shake annoying matters out of his mind. "I feel very depressed," he told her. "Tonight I am not going to work." Hanako's eyes widened in surprise, for almost invariably he put in a few hours' work in the evening. "Tonight I am going to get drunk," he announced firmly. This, at least, was standard procedure.

"You drink, too," he ordered his companions. All three tried hard to make their dinner a festive occasion.

Back home together, Sorge and Hanako played some of the German classics he loved. But the floods of gorgeous sound failed to buoy up his spirits, and he was still depressed when night closed over them.[9]

He was also drunk and on a talking jag. "I don't know what to do. . . . When Sorge is gone, you will think, 'Sorge is a great man!' . . . Would you like to die with Sorge?"

This was too much for Hanako. "I'm scared of dying!" she declared frankly.

Sorge mumbled on. "Well, everybody is afraid of dying. . . . Sorge is a strong man . . . I will never talk . . .

"I shan't forget you, but now I can do without you . . . I will write many good books. You will find out later. Oh, dear, Sorge is great! Let's sleep together . . . I will die soon. . . . Something is very wrong with me today. . . ."[10]

The next morning Sorge had to face the work he had neglected the preceding night, and suggested to Hanako that she go home. But before she left, he made her take $2,000. Then he phoned the German Embassy, requesting that the official Japanese interpreter meet him and Hanako for dinner the following Wednesday.[11]

When Sorge and Hanako alighted from his Datsun in front of a restaurant in Nihonbashi on Wednesday evening, a tall, thin Japanese in his middle thirties moved toward them expectantly. This was Mr. Tsunajima, the interpreter from the German Embassy. Sorge performed the necessary introductions, and the three entered the restaurant.

Within a few minutes a waitress ushered in Mr. M. and Aoyama.[12] Hanako knew that something was up. In fact, Sorge was counting on his powers of persuasion to talk the chief into destroying her affidavit.[13]

No one dreamed of coming to the point directly. Japanese suavity vied with German punctilio; sake and beer were plentiful. Mr. M. smiled at Hanako. "Miyake-san, you are very attractive in kimono. Aoyama can't talk about anything but 'Miyake-san, Miyake-san.' "

As Aoyama put his hand over his face in mock embarrassment, Hanako noticed something different about him. "Mr. Aoyama, why did you shave off your mustache?" she exclaimed. "You look much younger."

"I shaved it off after Mr. Sorge hit me, to make a new man of myself," he said grinning.

Well pleased, Sorge observed to Hanako sotto voce, "He likes you. You will be his wife. That makes me happy."

"He has a wife," she snapped. "I don't want a married man!"[14]

After a bit more badinage Sorge began a long conversation among himself, Mr. M., and Tsunajima, too low-pitched for the others to hear. Night had fallen when the two policemen took their leave, but Sorge and Tsunajima talked awhile longer, Sorge looking displeased. As the three left the restaurant, the interpreter whispered to Hanako, "The police are keeping an eye on Mr. Sorge because he is single. I think you had better not go to his place for a while. I don't know just what the trouble is, but as a Japanese I'm on your side."[15]

Sorge seemed discouraged, evidently not sure he had attained his objective. After dropping off Tsunajima, he warned Hanako, "The police are still watching you. Would you like to keep on coming or not? Whatever you want will be all right with me."

"I'm not afraid," she replied proudly. "If the police watch me, I know other ways to get there." This remark hints at a means of entry to and exit from Sorge's house beyond police observation—a subject soon to have a practical application. Hanako reverted to the problem preying on her mind. "I don't want a Japanese husband," she said earnestly. "I don't like Japanese men."[16]

The official attitude that a Japanese woman who lived with a foreigner compromised her birthright held a core of truth. Five years with Sorge had spoiled Hanako for life with one of her own countrymen. In a large measure Sorge had made a stranger of her, too.

Shortly after their dinner with the police Sorge and Hanako dined at Lohmeyer's, the scene of their first date. The restaurant was bright, crowded, and noisy. Sorge held something of an impromptu reception, nodding affably from side to side as he guided her to a place. During their meal many of his European acquaintances made a special point of coming to his table to speak with him.

After dinner, at home again, Sorge extracted a bottle of vermouth from his liquor stock and put Edwin Fischer's recording of Beethoven's *Fantasia* on the record player. Fischer was Sorge's favorite pianist, and he told Hanako proudly that as a little boy he often visited his home.[17]

The association and the vermouth evidently loosed the floodgates of memory, for he rambled on at length about his war experiences. "War has no voice," he said. "If people understood it, there would be no more war. I know what to do about it. . . . I'll write a book, a good one. . . . You will find out later what Sorge has done. I won't tell."

"Why?" asked Hanako.

"You should not know," he replied with preternatural solemnity born of the vermouth. "I don't think it is good for a girl to be always in danger, so Sorge will work alone.[18] You will find out later what Sorge has done. Sorge is wise, strong, he doesn't worry about danger . . ." he continued in a paroxysm of self-admiration. ". . . Sorge is ready to die for the cause. . . . If I die, later on the Japanese people will be happy. . . . Do you think it is good that people live happily?"

"Yes," she answered hesitatingly. "I think so."

"You are wise," replied Sorge profoundly. Then he flared into anger. "The Japanese government is stupid, stupid! . . . But Sorge won't be defeated. Sorge is wise. I will work and work; I will put an end to the war. . . .[19] You will understand later. What has Sorge done? I have done something good. People will find out what Sorge has done, and if they understand, they will not be angry." He paused, shifting gears. "What would you like to have?"

Hanako could make but one answer. "I want Sorge."

He shook his head dismally, all his Russian blood sweeping him on in a fatalistic spate that at last broke the barriers of secrecy. "You can't have Sorge. Sorge is going to die. . . .[20] If we go back to Russia together, who will do the true work? . . . I want to live! It would be wonderful if both of us could go back to Russia together. . . . You would like to go to Russia with Sorge?"

"Yes, I would like to." With Sorge—that was the magic phrase. What matter where?

"If you and I return to Russia, Japan will be in bad shape. Everyone will die. I know it. The United States is very strong. Japan can't win. Russia won't fight the United States. I told Stalin that Russia could not fight against America. Do you know who Stalin is?'' he interjected.

"Yes, of course.''[21]

"You please write what Sorge has said and what Sorge has done,'' he directed, forgetting that he had just refused to tell her what that was. "Sorge is a big man. He does good things all the time. Do you know what Sorge is? Sorge is a god. . . . God is always a man. . . . Christ is not God. Christ is not man. Man created Christ. . . . Men thought and thought until at last Christ was created. . . . Had there not been Christ, man would have been worse. . . . Men think more, and that is the end of Christ. . . . People need more gods. Sorge will become a god. . . .[22]

"Do you know what Sorge has done? I have arranged that the Japanese government will be defeated soon. . . . I thought it over!'' he assured Hanako. "The Japanese people are a little weak. . . .'' he observed critically. "French and American men are not strong, but Russian men are strong. Why, I don't know. Even the Russians don't know. . . . If Japan is to fight against the United States, Japan will lose. . . . Russia will never ask Japan to fight with her. I guarantee it.''[23]

This conversation must have cleared up many things in the woman's mind. Obviously her man was devoted heart and soul to the Soviet Union, was in Japan to work Moscow's will, thought of Mother Russia as the home to which he longed to return. If the fragile house of cards he had built in the German Embassy fell, would not others fall with it?

"Aren't your good Japanese friends in danger?'' she asked fearfully.

"Japan won't kill Ozaki-san,'' he declared confidently. "If I thought they would, I wouldn't have thought of your marrying him. . . . They will only kill Sorge. . . . Well, I may be able to end the war soon. Sorge is a strong man. I am not frightened. . . . I don't need to tell you any more. . . . Let's drink together, then let's sleep together. . . .''

The next day Sorge suggested that she take her things to her mother's. And this time she made no objection.[24]

CHAPTER 54

"GETTING INTO DANGEROUS GROUND"

By the end of September the heat of summer had moderated, so the Tokko reminded its Thought Section of the postponed arrest of the Kitabayashis. This time Tamazawa made no objections, although nothing material had developed against the pair as yet.[1] Armed with Tamazawa's warrant on the basis of the National Defense Security Law, on September 28 Tokko agents arrested the Kitabayashis at Wakayama and transferred them to Tokyo. By sheer chance the police station selected was that of Ròppongi, the one nearest Miyagi's residence.[2]

The Tokko agents soon convinced themselves that Mr. Kitabayashi's value to them was nil.[3] In this Japanese family the wife could not be dismissed as a carbon copy of her husband. Yet he did not come across as a henpecked nonentity. Mr. Kitabayashi emerges clearly from the few references to him in the records as an indulgent husband who wanted his wife to enjoy herself and, what is much rarer, was willing that she do so in her own way.

Ms. Kitabayashi was a tiny woman, looking old beyond her years. Her most distinguishing feature was that she had absolutely no distinguishing feature.[4] She could have posed as the prototype of every Japanese middle-aged lower-middle-class woman. Nothing less like a dangerous subversive could be imagined. The police had no wish to harm her or to alarm her unduly. They had arrested her with little hope of any really useful revelations but kept her in custody and questioned her at length because of her Communist background.[5] Inasmuch as twelve days passed before anything further happened, obviously the Tokko did not lean on her very hard.

Even without the jailing of this fringe helper, the Sorge ring had been breaking up gradually. It is doubtful if Sorge noticed the slow disintegration, preoccupied as he was with urgent matters of international import. Yet he himself led the slide downhill. His drinking had reached the point where his friends feared that he was on the verge of a breakdown. His mumblings to Hanako that he would personally end the war and become a god hinted that his self-confidence had expanded into egomania.

In the spring of 1941 Miyagi and Kawai lost touch with each other. Abandoning hope of ever pressing Kawai into the orthodox Communist mold, with Sorge's permission Miyagi returned him to Ozaki, who found him a job with a paper factory. Miyagi had no further contact with Kawai except once, when the *Shina ronin* came to his home drunk. Since Miyagi was very busy, he "asked him to go home right away."[6] It was a sad note on which to part forever.

Occasionally Kawai dropped in on his patron to pay his respects. On one such day he went to Ozaki's home instead of his office as he customarily did. He brought a box of sushi for Ms. Ozaki. Her husband was not there, but Ritsu Ito was— and very much at home. Ms. Ozaki received Kawai graciously, and the three visited for a while, nibbling the little cakes and exchanging small talk.

Ito bore himself with the unmistakable air of a frequent visitor on intimate terms with his host's family. Kawai was not at all pleased with this atmosphere. He had no way of knowing that Ito had handed the Tokko the key to the Sorge case, but the man's plastic features and cobra eyes gave him an uneasy feeling of distrust.[7]

Early that autumn Ozaki took a business trip to the northern islands. While he was on the way to Ueno Station by streetcar, Kawai swung aboard and dropped into the seat beside him. Ozaki told Kawai that he was just leaving for Hokkaido and Karafuto, so Kawai accompanied him to the station. There the two men wandered into the beer hall to kill time before the train arrived, and over their glasses Ozaki confided that he was still being followed and had been for some time. This was no news to Kawai, but he gained the impression that Ozaki expected to be arrested in the not too distant future.

Soon afterward Yoshiharu Makino, the well-known novelist, who accompanied Ozaki on this trip, told Kawai that when they returned to Tokyo, Ozaki invited him out for an evening of drinking and became extremely drunk. This was so unusual, for Ozaki could hold his liquor, that it was another indication that something was preying on his mind. Kawai never forgot that chance encounter with his patron, but no premonition of the truth troubled him. He and Ozaki had shared their last bottle together.[8]

Meanwhile, Voukelitch had been making himself useful as Sorge's eyes and ears in the American and British camp. He cultivated Joseph Newman, the New York *Herald Tribune*'s Tokyo correspondent, who worked in the same building and who innocently discussed with him items he picked up at the American Embassy, chiefly from Counselor Eugene H. Dooman. Voukelitch also supplied information on the agricultural and food situation in Japan, always interesting to Sorge.[9]

The chief of the United Press Tokyo office, Harold Thompson, had been paying Voukelitch for bits of information. Thompson liked Voukelitch, who had been helpful on several occasions. At some point in their association, Voukelitch asked Thompson if he would like to know how the Japanese intended to capture Singapore. The startled American warned him "that he was getting into dangerous ground, that he was getting into the field of espionage and away from news." Voukelitch only laughed and remarked that he had good friends in the Japanese military. Mindful of that border between journalism and espionage, Thompson refused to listen to Voukelitch about Singapore and, after warning him yet again, informed him that under the circumstances he "could not use his services any more. . . ."[10]

There is no evidence that Voukelitch ever submitted the Japanese plan for the conquest of Singapore where it would do the most good—namely, to his friends at the British Embassy. So he must have offered his find to Thompson for whatever financial profit he could reap. He could have used the money, for he had a second son to support. The baby born in the autumn of 1940 bore up nobly under the awesome name of Kiyoshi

Jaroslav Yamasaki-Voukelitch, mercifully shortened to Yo by his doting family and friends.[11]

Sensitized by his own growing disillusionment, Clausen noticed that Voukelitch "was going away from communism." Around mid-summer of 1941 he confided to Clausen "that communism would be defeated anyway and that therefore it would be useless to work for the principle any longer."[12] Privately Clausen agreed, but he said nothing, for he could not trust Voukelitch to hold his tongue in Sorge's company. Once when Clausen brought a document to be photographed for Sorge, Voukelitch remarked that he did not have time to do it because he had to go to his office. "And yet he stayed at home another two hours and read a book he liked." This and many similar incidents fed Clausen's opinion. He noted that at times when Sorge wanted to see Voukelitch, he would disappear for a whole week. Clausen did not blame him. "He had a good wife and child and loved them from the bottom of his heart." And Voukelitch had built up a successful career as a newspaperman. "So it was natural for him to turn away from this adventurous and dangerous life."[13]

This slackening off took some courage, because Sorge had "a very strong personality and demanded absolute obedience from his men."[14] Sorge had worked with Ozaki, his closest associate in espionage, for years before he discovered that Ozaki was married. So it is not surprising that he failed to scent the disaffection—active on Clausen's part, passive on Voukelitch's—going on under his nose. He did note that Voukelitch was less than eager. He compared him to himself: ". . . I came here for the purpose of this spy activity, and was a journalist to disguise my true work, and my work as a journalist was rather bothersome to me. As for Voukelitch, however, journalism came to be as if it were his true profession and doing spy activity as if it were his part-time work."[15]

Edith Voukelitch, too, was preparing to cease playing her small but useful role for the ring. Sorge drafted a request that Moscow allow her and her son, Paul, to leave Japan for Australia, where Edith's younger sister had offered her a home. He asked for $400 to cover her travel expenses. To Clausen $400 seemed ungenerous. With a firm pen he altered the 4 to a 5 and sent off the amended message on August 21.[16]

Edith's departure was a setback for the ring because it meant the loss of a broadcasting site as well as of a woman who knew too much about the operation for comfort. But for some time Voukelitch had been trying to persuade his ex-wife to leave the country. She and Paul sailed to Australia on September 25.[17]

Clausen had almost totally reversed his priorities. Now he was a full-fledged capitalist. With war imminent, Japan's industries were booming and provided a ready market for his blueprint machinery and reproduction services. He incorporated M. Clausen Shokai as a joint stock company capitalized at 100,000 yen, of which 85,000 yen represented his own investment. He opened a branch at Mukden with 20,000 yen. These were goodly sums in the Japanese economy of February 1941. He employed a total of fourteen individuals. His customers included the War and Navy ministries, the Mitsubishi, Mitsui, Nakajima, and Hidachi firms, and the army's medical schools. The enterprise poured a steady stream of yen into Clausen's bank account. Had he been so inclined, he could have obeyed Moscow's order to pay the ring's expenses over and above Moscow's proposed 2,000 yen a month.[18] But he was not interested in such altruism.

So the ring continued to depend upon Moscow to take up the slack financially. Zaitsev met with Clausen approximately once a month to deliver money and receive film in exchange. At times, because of the curtailment of Sorge's photography in the German Embassy, Clausen had nothing to submit. In this respect he continued to serve the ring faithfully. In February he arranged the contact for his own home. Zaitsev visited there twice that month, the first time receiving some film in exchange for 2,000 yen and the second time bringing 2,500 yen.[19]

When, on August 6, Zaitsev came to meet Clausen in his office, Sorge was also there, and the two discussed the war briefly. Zaitsev remarked that he recognized Sorge from a photograph he had seen in Moscow.[20] Later Sorge professed to find the Russian "in every respect a typical professional courier, traveling from country to country,"[21] although he must have known who he was. At this meeting, Zaitsev gave the ring's expense money directly to Sorge, who passed $500 of it to

Clausen, who had no film to turn over in exchange.[22] In those urgent days, most information worth gathering was important enough to go by radio. That fact makes the sharp drop in transmissions during 1941 all the more significant.

For this, the radio operation, was the field of Clausen's major defection. Higher and higher grew the stack of untransmitted material in his possession, an ever-increasing security hazard.[23] Moscow had established a new station in July, but Clausen ignored the directive to use it.[24]

Radio was also the area of his greatest fears. Ever since the incident of the Kempeitai agent, his jumpiness had increased by leaps and bounds. Once a repairman from the city electrical bureau knocked on the door of Voukelitch's home and asked him to cut off the power because he was working in the neighborhood. Clausen had just set up his portable transmitter and perforce shut off the juice. During one of his broadcasts from Edith's house a roofer climbing up to start work looked in the window of the room where he was busy with his apparatus.[25] Clausen received a severe jolt when the laborer appeared as if by levitation at the second-floor window.

Thus, of Sorge's major assistants, only Ozaki and Miyagi continued as functioning, productive agents to the day of their arrests.

CHAPTER 55

☀️ "RELEASED FROM A HEAVY BURDEN"

In early August Sorge heard interesting tidings of Manchuria from Kretschmer and Ott: Transfer of troops and transportation in that area were going slowly because of food and coal problems. Also, a "considerable number of Japanese troops were sent to China, which made the embassy uneasy."[1] Sorge incorporated this information into a draft for Clausen. It read somewhat as follows:

> . . . Already six divisions of the Japanese Army are in Korea. They may stay in Korea in preparation for a possible attack on Vladivostok. In Manchuria already a reinforcement army of four divisions has arrived, and Kretschmer heard that Japan is going to strengthen the army in Manchuria and Korea into thirty divisions. Reinforcements are arriving one after the other, but completion of the preparations will be between August 20 and the beginning of September.
>
> Kretschmer wired Germany . . . that the completion of this preparation does not necessarily mean that Japan has decided to attack Russia immediately. According to this attaché's observation, the first target of the Japanese attack would be Vladivostok; . . . only three divisions would go to Blagoveshchensk.
>
> . . . Ambassador Ott became sure that Japan would delay the possible attack until the Red

Army weakened and the Japanese attack would not be dangerous for Japan. This conviction was reached after Ambassador Ott conferred with General Doihara and General Okamura.* Doihara said that Japan cannot afford a long-term war and that since the petroleum stock in Japan is getting very low, Japan would not attack until it became clear that the war would not last long.[2]

This report was before Clausen when he established contact with the Fourth Department on August 21.[3] He dispatched only the first two paragraphs, omitting the parts about the German political moves and the petroleum shortage. His explanation was a typical example of his shrewdness:

> . . . The reason why I did not send the latter portion of the manuscript is this: The portion read that the stock of petroleum of the Japanese army was decreasing very much. This was very important to Japan and nobody else knew that sort of thing except us. As for me, whose way of thinking was changing at that time, it was unbearable to send such information to Moscow.
> The trend of the Japanese army in Manchuria was similarly important. However, there are lots of Russian spy groups in Manchuria, so I sent out the information thinking that Russia might know such information already.[4]

A number of other significant drafts sped out beneath his skillful fingers. One indicated that the navy's leaders did not want war with Russia.[5] As Sorge explained, Wenneker had heard through a navy man that "the possibility of a Japanese war against Russia had disappeared. . . ." The army, especially its Young Officer element, was "absolutely dissatisfied with the decision" but could not start a war totally ignoring the navy and the government. This decision would not be official until sometime between August 22 and 25.

---

* Probably Lieutenant General Yasuji Okamura, another "old China hand."

Sorge heard the same news from Ott and Kordt, "the right arm of Ott."[6] It was unfortunate for Moscow that they did not postpone the contact date of August 21 for a few days. The reference to August 22 and 25 pertained to a conference held from August 20 to 23 between the High Command of the Japanese Army and the top brass of the Kwantung Army. Ott and Kretschmer watched eagerly for news of this conference, but knew only that "some important discussion was going on concerning the Japanese army's mobilization."[7]

Ozaki had better luck. While the conference was in progress, a fellow employee of the South Manchurian Railroad advised him, "The Kwantung Army has decided not to have a war with Russia. That is why its representatives came to Tokyo and are now talking with the central authorities."[8]

On August 25 or 26 Ozaki sought out Saionji to confirm the cabinet's attitude. "They say that some people came over from the Kwantung Army and are discussing about whether Japan should have a war with Russia or not. Is that right?" Ozaki asked.

"Well," Saionji replied, "the government and the military have already decided not to have a war."[9]

Further confirmation came from Miyagi, who heard the news from Kikuchi that officers from the Kwantung Army headquarters were coming to Tokyo and from Taguchi that the Kwantung Army had planned an attack on the Russians but had called it off because Japan was not prepared and the Russians were. Miyagi put two and two together and advised Ozaki, who replied that he already knew about it.[10]

Ozaki hurried to bring the glad tidings to Sorge, but he added a warning or two. First, he gave his own evaluation that "Japanese policy may be changed again . . . in case the German war should show unexpected development, signs of [Russian] collapse should become clear, and some huge unrest should take place." He added more specific information, which he had learned from military sources: "The Japanese Army intends to open an assault upon Russia . . . (1) when the Kwantung Army's strength triples that of the Red Army in Siberia, (2) when . . . Russia should be defeated, and should signs of internal collapse in the Red Army in Siberia become clear." He added his opinion that in any case, "if such a situation does not occur by the middle of September at the latest, the Russian problem will be left over definitely until next spring's snow-melting . . . at the earliest. . . .''[11]

At this word from Ozaki, Sorge ''looked as happy as if he had been released from a heavy burden.''[12] Sorge's own conviction had been moving in this direction, and Ozaki's con-tribution tied it up. The factors entering into Sorge's gradual belief that the danger of his country had virtually passed were the comparative slowness of the mobilization, the relatively small number of troops sent to Manchuria, the movement of some Japanese forces from the northern border of Manchuria southward, and the fact that ''uneasiness in the German Em-bassy increased more and more day by day—especially Kretschmer said that Japan must have decided not to have a war, judging from the fact that the Japanese military gave obscure explanations about the results of the conference. . . .''[13] Having just missed Clausen's August contact, Sorge was unable to convey this vital information to Moscow immediately.

Ozaki was scheduled to leave on September 2 for two weeks in Manchuria on an assignment from the South Man-churian Railroad, and Sorge had special instructions for him. Both men were pleased about this trip. Ozaki believed that to predict Japanese relations with Russia, he needed an on-the-spot inspection of Manchuria.[14]

Sorge told him to investigate two main areas: ''(1) to what extent the preparation of the Japanese Army in Manchuria has been progressing, and (2) what divisions of the Japanese Army have arrived in Manchuria.'' In addition, if breakout of a Russian-Japanese war seemed imminent, Ozaki should so notify Miyagi by telegram, and Miyagi would pass the word to Sorge.[15]

In Dairen Ozaki was in his element, knee-deep in VIPs, an expert among experts.[16] From there he went to Hsinking and Ho-t'ien, observing rail movements carefully. He was gra-tified to note no large movements of troops or matériel.[17] In Ho-t'ien he had luck. A reference to ''preparations for military transportation'' in the report of Kensho Goto, the statistics director of the Ho-t'ien branch's General Bureau, struck Ozaki's sensitive ear, so he looked up this gentleman and some of his executives. After Ozaki at his most persuasive had ''explained about the political situation Japan was facing," these men agreed to tell him "secret information of the military order as token of their gratitude. . . ."[18]

Goto explained that just before the start of the mobilization in July, the Kwantung Army had suddenly ordered the railroad to be prepared to handle 100,000 tons of military freight per day for forty days. To meet this demand, the railroad brought 3,000 freight cars from northern China; however, "although the transportation order was carried out as scheduled at the beginning, later the transportation decreased gradually."[19]

At the same time, from various people present at the conference in Dairen, Ozaki learned that the Kwantung Army had alerted the railroad "to prepare 3,000 well-experienced railroad workers and wait as preparation for an assault upon the Red Army." This number gradually had dwindled to 1,500, then to 1,000, then to 150, and by the time Ozaki heard the story "only ten or so have been used."[20]

The significance of this information cannot be exaggerated. Here for the first time, straight from the source, were cold, hard facts that a massive operation had been planned against the Soviet Union and been abandoned. This was the sort of genuine evidence, not mere educated guesswork from Sorge, that the Fourth Department could sink its teeth into.

But the Ho-t'ien branch had some disquieting information, too. A young man in charge of railroad construction planning showed Ozaki how "in the past the railroad construction plan of the Manchurian Railroad centered on Vladivostok." Now the ever-eager Kwantung Army had given the organization a secret order "to construct a new railroad and highway which will lead to Khabarovsk at the Russian border." The sole reason for this new hookup was "military necessity in case of Japanese assault on Russia." While no attack was planned for the remainder of 1941, the Kwantung Army was "trying to make this place into an offensive base considering a war which might break out next year [1942]. . . ." Ozaki also discovered during his travels in Manchuria that frontline troops from northern Manchuria were to winter in the south and that the railroad had been alerted to house these men in their company residences "and other public buildings."[21]

While awaiting Ozaki's return, Sorge sent the word, based

upon his own August research, that Japan would not strike
Russia. The Moscow version of this message read: "The Japanese government has decided not to advance against the U.S.S.R.
Armed force, however, will be left in Manchuria. Military
action may start in the spring of next year if the U.S.S.R. is
defeated."[22] Clausen's recollection was more detailed, and represented a severe boiling down of several manuscripts from
Sorge:

> It seems that Japan has decided not to open war
> against Russia at least during this year. If Japan
> does, it would be some time after the snow-melting
> season. However, Japan has decided to be ready
> for an attack on Russia at any time, in accordance
> with the situational changes. Japan may attack Rus-
> sia if any one of the following should happen: 1.
> Breakout of civil war in Siberia. 2. Occupation of
> Moscow by Germany. 3. When the Kwantung Ar-
> my's force doubles* that of Russia's Far Eastern
> Army.[23]

This was one of eleven messages Clausen sent on Sunday,
September 14—very heavy traffic indeed.[24]

Ozaki's swing around Hsinking and Ho-t'ien added almost a week to his schedule. Not until the nineteenth did he
return to his desk in the railroad building.[25] This was the same
day the Germans captured Kiev. However, Leningrad still held
out, so the Nazis had not yet breached the Leningrad–Moscow–
Volga line of which Sorge had spoken. Miyagi submitted to
him a written study entitled "Movement of the Japanese Military Forces," in which he observed in part:

> . . . in the Japanese military there is excitement
> concerning Russian problems since it obtained the
> information that the German Army will advance
> swiftly into European Russia as soon as it takes
> Kiev. As a result, among the Japanese people there
> is an opinion that the Japanese Army might start
> a winter campaign against Russia. But according

---

* A slip of Clausen's memory; *triple* was Ozaki's estimate.

to the statement of considerable important figures
in the Japanese military, the intention of the highest
military executives is to watch the present situation
as a bystander.[26]

Attempting to pin down Japan's future moves before
submitting his findings to Sorge, Ozaki pumped one of his co-
workers in the Investigations Department, Takeo Sakai, a captain in the naval reserve. "Isn't the navy ready to advance to
the south?" he inquired.

"I heard that the navy is all set, but the army isn't ready
yet," replied Sakai. "Advancing as far as Singapore may require many times the number of soldiers now stationed in southern Indochina."

"Will three hundred thousand be necessary?" asked Ozaki
casually.

"Probably about that many," Sakai agreed.[27]

While Ozaki added this item to a long report he was
preparing for Sorge, Clausen tried to contact the mainland on
Saturday, September 27, but had to give up because of poor
atmospheric conditions.[28] "Organizer" may have been able to
reach Clausen, however, for this interesting message from the
Soviet Union is recorded as having been received toward the
end of September:

> Around Kobe on what island are there places to
> keep petroleum and docks? How many new tank
> troops were established in Japan? How many eigh-
> teen-ton trucks are there? Where is the air defense
> command of Tokyo? Also where are anti-aircraft
> bases to be established? From what troops is each
> new division command organized? We obtained
> information concerning the reorganization of the
> Army and the modernization of military equipment
> in 1940 and 1941. So try to clarify production
> expansion policies of these, specific analyses of all
> kinds of troops and their size.[29]

Sorge claimed that not until the end of September did
Moscow finally believe his report that Japan had no immediate
lethal intentions, and "around that time they sent me a special

telegram of their appreciation for this report.''[30] Perhaps the Fourth Department's words sufficed to lighten the fearful shadow in which Sorge was struggling. He had few enough happy moments left.

On the twenty-second Ozaki briefed Sorge at length about his visit to Manchuria, using a map to pinpoint the places in question. He emphasized the new rail construction near Khabarovsk and its military implications. "Utmost caution is necessary about this point," he insisted.[31]

"It is difficult to know the number of divisions being sent to Manchuria," he explained, "but we must remember that the same division as one existing in Japan may be formed in Manchuria. All the military organizations have the name of their division chief and can be identified as a regiment, brigade, or division only by the rank of the chief. Reinforcements are recruited from soldiers mobilized in various parts of Japan. . . .''[32]

"How many soldiers are there now in Manchuria?" Sorge asked.

"We can estimate that the Japanese troops normally stationed in Manchuria are four hundred thousand, and reinforcements over the last two months since the Big Mobilization may be between three hundred thousand and three hundred fifty thousand," replied Ozaki. By comparison with the rest of his report, this was poor intelligence, based entirely upon an arbitrary rule of thumb, 400,000 being the "common-sense figure" the survey staff used when considering the normal troop complement in Manchuria.[33]

Before Ozaki's next meeting with Sorge, scheduled for Monday, September 29, he cleared up a few points with Saionji about a related subject: Japanese-American relations.[34] "Even if the negotiations should reach some agreement, it does not mean that this would solve the Chinese problem immediately," Ozaki told Saionji. "In contrast with the attitude of the top level of Japan, the masses are against Britain and the United States, and it seems that the top level is taking this general mood lightly. If this is true," he continued, "a great political difficulty may come about. Japan should go to the negotiation with wisdom enough to have the United States release the of assets.'' Ozaki still harped on that string, although doubtful of success.

But Saionji believed the talks could succeed. He promised to show Ozaki the proposals made to the United States. Ozaki mentally filed this away for action at the earliest possible moment.[35]

A few days later they got together again at the Kuwana assignation house, where Saionji was expecting guests. He pulled a file from his briefcase and handed Ozaki a document ''written with a fountain pen on a few sheets of foolscap, containing about six major items, and corrections and editing work could be seen from the addition and deletion of words and phrases. . . . '' Ozaki claimed that he only glanced at it, but if so, he remembered the contents amazingly well. Roughly the points were: conclusion of a comprehensive Japanese-American peace treaty, a new commercial treaty, adjustments of Sino-Japanese relations (including withdrawal of troops from certain locations), Japan's special position in the Pacific and relations with the Axis countries, resources in the South Pacific, and the format of the proposed treaty.[36]

''I see,'' Ozaki said. ''I thought that it would be like this. It is pretty well organized, isn't it?'' Just as he finished reading the document, Saionji's guests arrived, so Ozaki hurriedly handed it back to its indiscreet owner.[37]

Thus at their rendezvous Ozaki was able to give Sorge a long briefing concerning the Japanese-American talks and the Southern Operation, two subjects inextricably entwined. The timing was of particular interest to them because, in Ozaki's words, ''it seems that naturally there was a time limit attached'' to the discussions. They had previously hit upon the end of September as the deadline, but when Ozaki returned from Manchuria, he had decided on the end of October.[38]

When Ozaki suggested this idea to Sakai, however, he disagreed. ''As far as the navy is concerned, we cannot wait until the end of October,'' he declared. ''It must be the beginning of October.'' Ozaki told Sorge that this was the navy's view.[39]

At the time both men were correct. An imperial conference held on September 6 committed Japan to a very tight schedule of deadlines. The nation would decide upon war with the United States if Washington did not agree to Tokyo's demands by early October. Meanwhile, Japan would go on with war preparations, with a target date of the end of October.[40]

At their weekly rendezvous on Monday, September 29, Ozaki informed Sorge of the contents of Saionji's draft. He explained that he did not know whether it had been sent already or was to be sent in the future but that it represented current Japanese thinking. "The negotiation with the United States is taking a quick turn now," he said. "This can be seen from the fact that . . . Wakasugi* returned to Japan in a hurry, talked with the government and the military, and then went back to his post. It seems that Wakasugi has some concrete compromise suggestions. . . . This compromise plan seems to contain acceptance of withdrawing troops from central and southern China and the southern part of Indochina. . . ." Ozaki continued. "As to this, however, agreement seems to have been reached between the military and the government determining that the army and navy will execute military operations jointly in case the compromise cannot be reached.

"Compared with the tension in Japan, the attitude of the United States is somewhat self-possessed. Although the United States, of course, desires to reach agreement in the negotiations, there is a great gap between her and Japan in the conditions and enthusiasm for the negotiations."[41]

Using a map of Southeast Asia, Ozaki explained that "to conquer Singapore, probably Japan will go south from Indochina to Thailand and further to Singapore through the Malay Peninsula. . . . The purpose of the Japanese assault will be Sumatra and Borneo. Sumatra is far richer in petroleum resources.

"Japan considered taking over only the Netherlands East Indies . . . excluding Singapore," Ozaki added. "But this method was abolished as impossible, because from the strategic point of view there would be Singapore and Manila, which are military positions, at both wings."[42]

The illness that was to strike Sorge shortly may have

---

* Kaname Wakasugi, minister of the Japanese Embassy in Washington.

been working on him already, for he mixed up this clear-cut information when he prepared the draft for Clausen to send to the Fourth Department.[43] Possibly, too, his morbid obsession with personal disaster prevented his concentration on business. Sorge was a brave man, but his maudlin wails to Hanako about dying for the cause and his panicky reactions to the interest of the police in his sweetheart tell a story of fatalistic awareness of an ever-increasing danger.

CHAPTER 56

"GUARANTEED AGAINST
JAPANESE ATTACK"

Saturday, October 4, 1941, Sorge's forty-sixth birthday, was the occasion of Clausen's last transmission to the Fourth Department. He set up his machine in Voukelitch's house and arranged the six messages he had selected. Some ended with the figure 6, which indicated that he had coded them on September 26, intending to radio them the next day. But because of atmospheric conditions, the messages had to wait another week.[1]

At last he was ready to give the Soviet Union Sorge's firm, final assurance that the Communist homeland was safe, at least temporarily, from a two-front war. "The Soviet Far East may be considered guaranteed against Japanese attack."[2] This laconic item dated at the end of September is all the Soviet Union released. But Clausen remembered a more detailed version:

> According to the careful judgment of us, Kretsch-mer, Wenneker and Ambassador Ott, it has be-come certain that the possibility of a Japanese attack is small, and the period to the end of the coming winter is guaranteed. There is no doubt about this point. A Japanese attack will take place when you repatriate most of your soldiers from Siberia (to the western front of Russia) and when civil war breaks out in Siberia. Now there is developing a responsibility problem about the hasty large-scale mobilization already carried out (in Japan) in the

Japanese Army, because maintaining the big Kwantung Army will generate various economic and political difficulties.[3]

This message bore a marked resemblance to the one Clausen sent on September 14 but was considerably more forceful. The last sentence reflected the shift of emphasis from north to south. Japan could not maintain the Kwantung Army in the style to which it had become accustomed and at the same time beef up the southern armies and the navy. Southward lay the petroleum and other products it needed; southward it would go.

The praise which the Soviet press heaped upon Sorge in 1964 included a measure of credit for his final messages:

In this grave hour for our country . . . Richard Sorge and his fearless comrades once again rendered invaluable service to the Soviet people. They reported that the Japanese militarists, confident that the Hitlerites would cope with the Red Army, were concentrating forces for unleashing war in the Pacific. This information made possible the transfer of Soviet divisions from the Far East, although the presence of the Kwantung Army in Manchuria necessitated the Soviet Union's keeping a large number of troops on the eastern borders. . . . [4]

Others have pointed out that the High Command began moves from the Far East as early as May 26, 1941, almost a full month before the Russo-German war broke out.[5] Nevertheless, one cannot doubt that the intelligence emanating from Sorge's *apparat* entered into top-level Russian thinking. Sorge's was the only known undercover group in Tokyo, and his information carried weight. It was very different from his warnings that Germany was going to attack the Soviet Union. Then he could offer only hearsay, however knowledgeable; now his information came as straight from the stables as Moscow could expect.

On September 14, Sorge had told the Soviet Union that the Japanese would strike Russia when the Germans took Moscow, when the Kwantung Army reached triple the size of the Russian Far East forces, and when civil war broke out in Siberia.

The Kremlin could discount the last condition. Siberia had never bred a tradition of freedom, and Stalin's purges had, to say the least, discouraged any such tendency anywhere in the Soviet Union. Furthermore, the Russians' heroic defense against the Germans had proved that their one aim right now was to repel the invaders.

The Kwantung Army's star was sinking. It could be three times as strong as the Soviet Union's Far East forces only by Stalin's moving the vast majority of his troops westward, not by its own expansion. The initiative was Stalin's.

Only one condition remained worth considering. The Japanese might be tempted to strike should the Germans smash the Leningrad–Moscow–Volga line and race toward the Urals. This was a real possibility. Soon Stalin would proclaim Moscow under siege and move the diplomatic portion of the government to Kuybyshev, more than 500 miles southeast of Moscow. So he had a very limited range of choice.

Paradoxically, according to Sorge's information, the best way to protect against Japanese attack in the East was to beat off the Germans in the West. To put it brutally, the Japanese were after easy pickings; they would hit the USSR only if Hitler did most of the dirty work for them.

So for a number of cogent reasons, an important one being Sorge's information, by the end of 1941 the Soviet Union had released about half the division strength of its Far Eastern armies to fight in the West. This was enough to do the job but not enough to tempt the Japanese to hit Siberia. On November 27, 1941, the U.S. War Department G-2 advised in a memorandum for the chief of staff: "1. It has been reported on good authority, that between 18 and 24 Infantry Divisions and 8 Armored Brigades from the Russian Far Eastern Army have been identified on the Western front. If this is true, between 24 and 18 Divisions and 2 Armored Brigades remain in Eastern Siberia. . . ."[6]

The best available evidence is that the transferred troops constituted the following:[7]

From	Infantry Divisions	Calvary Divisions	Air Divisions	Tank Brigade
Outer Mongolia	1			2
Trans-Baikal area	7	2	3	2
Amur area	2		1	1
Ussuri area	5	1	–	3
Totals	15	3	4 (1,500 aircraft)	8 (1,700 tanks)

If these figures reflect the truth, the American estimate was astonishingly accurate. By way of an odd little coincidence, the G-2 memorandum was signed by Colonel Rufus S. Bratton, who had been acting U.S. military attaché in Tokyo on the day Sorge landed at Yokohama to begin his task.

On October 4, Clausen also dispatched the gist of Ozaki's report from his Manchurian trip, with its implication that "war will not break out during this year." He showed the Fourth Department the reverse of the coin: ". . . in case Japan should attack Russia, the first attack would be on the eastern border (of Manchuria), that is, near Vladivostok. At the same time there would be attacks at other places—at the northern border and there the Japanese Army may try to close the Siberian Railroad to stop transportation of war matériel."[8] Undoubtedly this warning was based on Ozaki's intelligence concerning the buildup near Khabarovsk.

Another of Clausen's transmissions of October 4 holds a special interest for Americans. It was the gist of the report Ozaki had given Sorge at their last meeting, on September 29, about the probable course of the Japanese campaign south if the U.S.-Japanese negotiations broke down, but Sorge had garbled it. Though Ozaki had not mentioned an attack on the United States, part of Clausen's dispatch read: "Japan will first attack the United States, then Malaya, Singapore and Sumatra."[9] Stories that Sorge pinpointed the date of the Pearl Harbor attack, informed the Soviet Union of it, and in turn Moscow warned Washington, which ignored the tip-off, have circulated for years. Nothing in the entire testimony of the Sorge case backs up this fascinating myth.

Like most such legends, its public career began innocuously enough. On August 29, 1949, a *Chicago Tribune* article discussed a telegram which Chiang Kai-shek allegedly sent Roosevelt in November 1941, warning of Pearl Harbor. Almost casually the writer, correspondent Willard Edwards, remarked that the "Chinese government obtained the same information regarding Japanese plans for the attack which was gained by Dr. Richard Sorge . . . and given to Moscow at the time. . . ." He did not mention any tip-off from Moscow to Washington.

Columnist John O'Donnell was not so circumspect some two years later. He proclaimed in his column "Capital Stuff" that amid a treasure trove of documents which Major General Charles A. Willoughby, G-2 of the Far East Command, had collected in Japan were papers revealing "that Moscow spies knew in advance of the fixed date of the Pearl Harbor assault . . . ," as did U.S. State and War department officials. What is more, "somebody in the Pentagon" deleted from Sorge's confession his statement "that he had informed the Kremlin in October 1941, that the Japs intended to attack Pearl Harbor in 60 days and that he had received thanks for his report and the notice that Washington . . . had been advised of the Japs' intentions."[10]

Willoughby inadvertently forwarded this lurid concept when he testified before the House Un-American Activities Committee on August 22, 1951. Asked if the Russians did indeed know of the proposed attack, he answered, "Yes. They did get the information." However, he pinned down his testimony the next day, explaining, "Pearl Harbor is a fixed date and did not appear in the Sorge message. But that was not important—the important thing was that the Japanese were aiming South into a collision with the United States and Britain."[11]

Then in *Spies, Dupes, and Diplomats*, Ralph de Toledano asserted that Sorge had unearthed this secret and so advised Moscow.[12] In an article in June 1952 he stated only that Sorge had reported that Japan would attack the United States and Britain in December 1941, perhaps early in January 1942.[13]

Four months later, in a campaign speech, Adlai Stevenson, Jr., credited the Russians with having penetrated the Japanese government so successfully that they had learned about Pearl Harbor in advance.[14]

Rear Admiral Robert A. Theobald, in *The Final Secret of Pearl Harbor*, swallowed the Sorge line from bait to reel.[15]

Sorge's acquaintance at the German Embassy, Hans-Otto Meissner, made this tale the climax of his book, publishing what he purported to be Sorge's exact message: "JAPANESE CARRIER AIR FORCE ATTACKING UNITED STATES NAVY AT PEARL HARBOR PROBABLY DAWN NOVEMBER SIX [sic] STOP SOURCE RELIABLE STOP JOE."[16]

All this is an entertaining example of how a tiny seed of truth can grow into a jungle of innuendo and legend. Far from claiming that he had tipped off Moscow to the Pearl Harbor secret, Sorge wrote in his memoir: "The Russians were so prone to suspect that the Japanese and German foreign policies were aimed against the U.S.S.R. that in 1941, when Japan took the last great turning in her career, Moscow was taken completely by surprise."[17]

His single sentence, tucked away in a long and not too accurate dispatch, is the closest this spy ring came to scooping the Pearl Harbor story. And even this much one must accept for what it may be worth on the basis of Clausen's memory, for Sorge never mentioned this item.

As for the Southern Operation, Clausen recalled sending information that "for Japan to start military action in Thailand and Singapore at least 300,000 soldiers are necessary, and since only 40,000 are stationed in southern Indo-China, a big increase of soldiers would be necessary to start action and this will be immediately detected by the United States and Britain."[18] So Japan was sailing south straight into the sort of trouble that would free Russian hands in the north.

Sorge's last and best service to his country did not consist of one message guaranteeing Russian immunity for the remainder of the calendar year. This particular dispatch was just a statement of opinion, as Sorge admitted in the text of the message. What gave it weight was the other intelligence that accompanied it: the increasing factual evidence of preoccupation with the south; the gathering storm clouds over the United States; even the suggestion that Japan planned to attack the United States before moving south.

Clausen did a bit of editing in these final transmissions, omitting among other things important advice from Wenneker:

[The] Japanese Navy has completed its preparations to start action to the south. However, it has
delayed the opening of action and permitted Konoye to try negotiations with the United States
because the Red Army . . . was unexpectedly strong
and because the preparation of the Japanese Army
was not sufficient . . . and because economic conditions in Japan were difficult. If the negotiations
should break off, Japan could not help opening
action to the south, thus risking the danger.[19]

This batch of messages on the way, Clausen dismantled
his apparatus and placed it in the battered suitcase. The faithful
little machine had crackled off its last dispatch and now was
to enter upon a brief retirement before it emerged as a prime
exhibit in the Sorge trials.

October 4 was not only the last transmission date and
Sorge's birthday but the sixth anniversary of his meeting Hanako. So he escorted her to Lohmeyer's, where they stayed
only long enough for a drink. That evening she wore Western
clothes, very becoming to her height and slimness. She was
feeling somewhat relieved because Mr. M. had visited her a
few days earlier and had burned her signed statement in her
presence. Sorge ushered her to a table near the center of the
room, remarking upon the number of police around.[20]

While they sipped their cocktails, Sorge asked Hanako
what her brother, who had recently visited her from the country,
thought of the dangerous situation between Japan and the United
States. Her brother took an optimistic view. But Hanako's
thoughts were pessimistic: The Japanese militarists were too
aggressive to permit settlement of the differences between Japan
and the United States.

"The Japanese government is always a burglar," Sorge
agreed. ". . . America is strong, she is big, she produces many
good things," he continued, Sorge sober confirming Sorge
drunk. "If Japan fights with America, Japan will never win;
she will be defeated over and over. . . ."

"Perhaps Japan will imitate Germany and try a blitzkrieg," Hanako suggested, and Sorge soon turned the talk into
lighter channels.[21]

As he prepared to pay the check, he asked Hanako to wait for him outside. It was barely six-thirty and dusk was just settling over Tokyo when he joined her on the sidewalk. "I don't think you should come home with me tonight because the secret police are following me," he told her. "I think you should stay at your mother's tonight. And when things look bright, I'll send you a telegram."

Hanako's eyes searched his face. "You won't be lonely?"

"Even if I am, it will be all right," he replied. "You had better go home now." Courteous as always, he added, "Please remember me to your mother." With a casual good-night and clasp of the hands they went their separate paths, Sorge with his loose stride toward Shimbashi Station, Hanako picking her way daintily toward the Ginza. After a few steps she turned to look after Sorge, but the mellow evening had already hidden him. That backward glance held no special meaning; no dark intuition told her that she had seen him for the last time.[22]

Sorge's evening had not ended. He moved on to Kordt's home, where the Otts and the Mohrs joined them for a birthday party. He made himself so thoroughly obnoxious that his companions were delighted when he rudely departed at around nine, although the party had been arranged in his honor. He moved on to Weise's, where he drank with the DNB chief until morning.[23]

On October 6 Sorge met with Ozaki rather briefly. The latter had heard a rumor that Konoye would resign, but its reliability was difficult to assess. Someone might have started it deliberately in the hope it would become a self-fulfilling prophecy. Ozaki thought that Konoye had boxed himself in hopelessly: If the Washington talks failed, he would have led his country into war again; if they succeeded, "it would mean failure of the Chinese Incident and submission to the United States." He told Miyagi as well as Sorge the same day that he expected the discussions to fail and the cabinet to fall, but "after some more complications," not just yet.[24]

He also pointed out to Sorge that October had begun with no sign of "advancement to the south by force." The "Japan-United States negotiation was still in a floating condition." Therefore, he assumed that Japan had extended the deadline, and "it might not be too late at all to have the end of December as the time limit."[25]

As the two comrades parted, they made an engagement to meet the next Monday in the Asia Restaurant. But Sorge, his mind blurred with fever and worry, mixed up his dates. When Ozaki slipped on his shoes and bowed himself out the door and down the path, he, too, walked out of Sorge's life.[26]

Ms. Araki noticed that during this period Sorge was given to fits of weeping and seemed to be on the verge of a nervous breakdown. He disappeared from his usual haunts for several days in October, spending them in the home of a Mr. Schneider.[27]

On October 7 Sorge took to his bed with a feverish cold. He was quite ill, and the German Embassy sent a nurse to attend him. First Clausen, then Miyagi came to his bedside. Miyagi brought a long treatise on the "South-to-North Integration Strategy." Later Sorge could not recall much of it either because it was not clear or because he "was unable to understand it because of fever. . . ."[28] There can be no doubt that in October 1941 Sorge was a sick man. Because he was so ill, he asked Clausen to receive Miyagi's material—which included a report and map showing antiaircraft gun emplacements in Tokyo—on his behalf. This constituted Clausen's only official spy contact with Miyagi.[29] In spite of his fever, Sorge recalled these documents very well. As usual he deprecated Miyagi's effort, saying that "these places were those which an average citizen could witness, like a park . . . needless to say these could be found through inspection, by walking and visiting."[30] But the Moscow authorities could do no "walking and visiting" in Tokyo; that was precisely why they had planted a spy ring in the Japanese capital. Moreover, the gun sites were part of the air defense system concerning which the Red Army had specifically asked.

A day or so following his meeting with Clausen and Miyagi, Sorge had a last item from Voukelitch to mull over. Voukelitch had learned from American journalist Newman that at a recent gathering in the American Club, U.S. Ambassador Grew had expressed his personal opinion of official Japanese reliability. He told his compatriots that "the Japanese military does not feel any obligation to the promises which the Japanese Government made. . . . [Under] such conditions it is impos-

sible to trust the promise of the Japanese Government no matter
under what Cabinet it was made." According to Voukelitch,
Newman believed that as long as the American ambassador
held such views, "there would be no hope for the Japan-U.S.
negotiations to come to an agreement."[31] This story may have
gained in strength during its travels, as such tales will, because
Grew's diary told a much milder story.[32]

Sorge said that he considered this Voukelitch's most important coup.[33] If indeed this was the best he could do, small
wonder that he took a dim view of Voukelitch's prowess as a
spy. Certainly the situation, whether remarked upon as Voukelitch reported or more discreetly in accordance with Grew's
diary, was no secret from anyone acquainted with Japanese
politics, Sorge very much included. So he did not bother to
prepare a report of Grew's remarks for Moscow. He was quite
sure that the American ambassador "gave the address desiring
to let Japan and the embassies of other countries know about
the content indirectly." The German Embassy "knew about
the content and therefore the Russian Embassy must have known
it, too."[34]

Sometime during the week Ott visited Sorge's bedside
and briefed him on the German Embassy's information concerning the Japanese-American talks. These talks worried him
exceedingly. He had heard that "if the United States should
make a considerable concession to Japan at this time, Japan
would reciprocate and the Tripartite Alliance may become nom-
inal, even if it were not demolished officially."[35] This was the
last time Ott and Sorge talked together as friends, although a
brief, searing encounter lay in the near future.

Clausen's sands had not yet run out. He met with Zaitsev
in his office on October 10, giving him Miyagi's maps and
reports and receiving $500 to reimburse him for Edith's travel
expenses. Zaitsev instructed Clausen to meet him at the same
place on November 20, but on that day Clausen was very much
otherwise occupied.[36] As he talked with Zaitsev on October 10,
he was living in freedom on borrowed time, for that very
morning the Tokko snapped its trap over Miyagi.

PART 4

BREAKING THE RING

CHAPTER 57

"HE HAD CROSSED THE BARRIER
OF DEATH"

Fully ten days passed before the Tokko agents took up with Tomo Kitabayashi the one item that really interested them. When arrested, she carried a sum of American money. This was not surprising in view of her past, and the dollar was a coveted medium of exchange. What concerned the Tokko was who had given the dollars to her, and why. She replied to these questions with the truth as far as it went. Her friend Yotoku Miyagi sometimes gave her money. At one time he had boarded in her home in California, and they had resumed the acquaintance in Japan.[1]

The name Miyagi was a new one to her questioner, and the policeman was excited at receiving an unexpected lead. But he kept a poker face and replied, "Miyagi didn't say that. Don't tell lies!"[2] Ms. Kitabayashi swallowed the bait. Resignedly she admitted that she and Miyagi had been members of the American Communist Party. She denied having engaged in any Communist activity since her return to Japan but said that Miyagi had done some spying.[3]

This was enough to slip the Tokko's leash and send the hounds on Miyagi's trail. The Tsukiji Police Station already had Miyagi under investigation; now the Tokko decided to bring him in for questioning.[4]

A subdivision of the Tokko's First Section covered the theatrical world and went into action whenever the search crossed the borders of Japan's bohemia. As an artist Miyagi fell within this jurisdiction. Once given the nod, its chief, Noboru Takagi, lost no time. On the very day after Tomo dropped Miyagi's name, Takagi, with two of his best detectives, Tamotsu Sakai and Jimpei Tsuge, set forth to pick him up.[5]

Sakai was a dedicated policeman of eighteen years' service. No soldier or sailor of Hirohito's armed forces was prouder of his position than Sakai protecting the very spirit of Japan against contamination as a Tokko detective. Sturdy of body, earnest of mind, he had a round, forceful face that frequently split into a good-natured grin.[6]

The morning of October 10, 1941, was newly minted when the three men gathered at the Roppongi Station and piled into a police car. Tokyo's clocks had not yet chimed seven when the car drew up before Miyagi's house. When the landlady answered the knock at the door, Sakai and his associates bowed politely and extended business cards, like all other Japanese gentlemen making a formal morning call, and asked to speak with Miyagi-san. Seeing the ominous ideographs of the Tokko, the woman immediately protested, "Miyagi is not a bad person!" Clucking with agitation, she turned toward the stairs, the three agents hard on her heels. Evidently Miyagi's landlady was fond of her boarder and, if left alone with him, would have warned him of what lay in store.

They found their quarry sleeping soundly. He blinked himself awake as Takagi said, "We have a few things to ask you. Will you come with us?" Miyagi yielded to arrest with stoic dignity.[7]

While he dressed, the detectives searched his room. It was not a really thorough job, but a number of documents lay in plain sight. At least one of them was of a kind only a few in the government should have seen. As Yoshikawa later testified, "We thought it strange that an artist had such kind of document." Takagi and his men found a complete study of Japan's oil stock level in Manchuria. Oil, the very lifeblood of empire; oil, the Pied Piper luring Japan outward and southward! How much of the precious stuff Japan had and where it was stored were the highest of top secrets. Yet here under the policemen's dazed eyes was this information not only in Japanese but also in typed English translation. In that moment something of the true nature of the case came to the Tokko: They had gone fishing for a minnow and hooked a shark.[8]

As Miyagi seated himself beside his captors in the police

car, he showed no sign of inner turmoil.[9] But who can doubt that powerful emotions gripped him as the car threaded its way to the Roppongi Station? It is no disrespect to his memory to picture him on this short ride as racked with fear and despair. Only an insensitive brute could have faced this moment of truth with inner equilibrium.

After the party had trooped into the Roppongi Station, a question arose. The station being very small, Miyagi and Ms. Kitabayashi might find some means of communicating with each other. Much better to isolate the two until the police had the opportunity to question Miyagi. Tokyo had few vacant cells in those days, but after a number of telephone calls the Tokko decided to take Miyagi to the Tsukiji Station, which already had a proprietary interest in him. So the next day, October 11, the same three agents drove with Miyagi to downtown Tokyo and entered the Tsukiji Station, there to enact a more bizarre drama than any gracing the boards of the Kabuki Theater across the street.[10]

The detectives escorted Miyagi upstairs, deposited him in a room, confronted him with the documents confiscated from his room, and began a long interrogation. Pressure of business soon summoned Takagi to his office. Then Tsuge was called away, leaving Sakai face-to-face with Miyagi. By circumstances and tacit agreement, therefore, Sakai inherited primary responsibility for the unhappy artist. He put Miyagi through three solid hours of questioning, at the end of which both men were exhausted. Although Sakai suspected Miyagi of espionage, he did not dig into the matter at this first session. Miyagi admitted that the documents were his. Having obtained this much, Sakai decided to wait before pursuing this line. With typical Japanese thoroughness and circumlocution, he first wanted a full picture of Miyagi the man.[11]

Sakai returned to his office to find that he had suddenly acquired a new boss. The Tokko had put Takagi on another case, and Yosuke Takahashi had taken over Sakai's subdivision. So Sakai went immediately to Takahashi's office to brief him on the Miyagi case and explain just where it stood to date. Takahashi was extremely interested and inclined to agree that in Miyagi they had landed a rare fish. "From today we will really check into him," he assured Sakai with satisfaction. Then he, Sakai, and four lesser lights of the Tokko met with Miyagi in a large room on the second floor. They seated themselves around a long table, Miyagi with his back to the window. Takahashi faced him across the table, while Sakai occupied the place of honor at Miyagi's right. They caught the prisoner in a crossfire of questions. Inquiries of a general nature he answered without protest, but any matter remotely touching upon espionage froze him into obstinate silence.[12]

Some students of the Sorge case assume that the Tokko tortured Miyagi at this session.[13] The Tokko men could be absolutely ruthless when they considered this in the best interests of Japan, but Sakai and his like were not sadistic for the fun of it. Long experience had given them a fairly shrewd idea of what type of man responds to what type of pressure. Something about this prisoner told them that extreme measures would not work; they might kill their man with his story still untold. Mitsusada Yoshikawa, chief prosecutor in the Sorge trials, denied that the Tokko used torture on the artist. "Miyagi was not the type to break under torture," he added. "Miyagi was not the type to confess unless he wanted to."[14]

However, the Tokko agents were far from gentle with Miyagi. They threatened him, yelled at him, poured over his defiant head all the picturesque invective of which the Japanese tongue is capable, to no avail. They cajoled, wheedled, implored, with no better result. By noon all concerned felt battered and baffled, so they called a halt for lunch. Takahashi and Sakai retired to a room across the hall with two of the others to eat and to discuss the case. They left two men behind to guard Miyagi and ordered lunch for him, but he refused to touch it, claiming he was not hungry.[15]

Sakai and Takahashi agreed that they were getting nowhere with him, and decided on a strategy. They would set a watch on his home to check out his visitors and mail. Perhaps these measures would turn up some of his associates. Because Sakai knew the general layout of Miyagi's neighborhood and by now knew quite a bit about the man as well, Takahashi told him to take two assistants and start surveillance the next day.[16]

They also discussed certain letters found in Miyagi's room, which had disturbed Sakai more than he would care to admit, love letters penned by a Ms. Kimiko Suzuki. Ms. Suzuki was an interpreter in the Tokko's American-European Division under Tomiki Suzuki.* She was a divorcée, thirty years of age, with a child to support, whose marriage had foundered on the reef of communism. She had left the party, but her husband had refused to follow suit. The Tokko employed her gladly, for she spoke fluent English and typed well in addition to knowing a good deal about her former associates in the party.

So the little bundle of love letters shocked the Tokko, which did not shock easily. Her private life was her own business, but if Kimiko Suzuki should prove to be a traitor, whom could they trust? Had Miyagi infiltrated the Tokko itself? The two men agreed that they had to tell Tomiki Suzuki about this. Subsequent investigation produced nothing to connect Ms. Suzuki with Miyagi's spying. Shortly before his arrest he had discovered that she worked for the police and had broken off the friendship. She was guilty of nothing worse than a tendency to fall in love with the wrong man.[17]

Swallowing the last crumb of food and sip of tea, Takahashi and Sakai crossed the hall to return to their interrogation of Miyagi and to bring lunch to the two guards. As Sakai opened the door, both guards instinctively looked up inquiringly. In that split second Miyagi sprang to his feet, whirled about, plunged for the open window—the casement type, which opened outward—and dived out of it headfirst.[18]

The thought flashed through Sakai's mind: "I must not let Miyagi get away. He is our star witness." He shouted a command to surround the building, then with a bound jumped right out the window after Miyagi. Pursuer and pursued hit some shrubbery near the edge of the street. Sakai struggled to rise but could not and for a sickening moment thought he was paralyzed. Policemen stampeded out of the building, and someone called for a police car to take the shaken men to a hospital.

When the car drove up, Miyagi, the less hurt of the two men—he happened to fall on some thick shrubbery, escaping with a few wrenched muscles in his thigh—refused to get in until Sakai had been settled comfortably. This matter resolved to Miyagi's satisfaction, they all sped to a navy hospital located

* The two were not related. Suzuki is perhaps the most common family name in Japan.

directly behind the police station. There the doctors discovered that Sakai had hit the ground so hard that both his shoes had split open, but miraculously, in view of the two-story drop and the force of his fall, he had escaped with nothing more serious than a badly wrenched back. The injury took him off the case; he was not to return to duty for three weeks.[19]

The parallel between Miyagi's jump and that of the English reporter, Jimmy Cox, is striking. Could the thought of the tragic Englishman have crossed Miyagi's mind? But while a question remains whether Cox fell a victim to murder, accident, or suicide in the course of his interrogation by the Kempeitai, there is no doubt that Miyagi intended to kill himself. With one stroke he would have been able to end his lonely, disease-ridden existence, the unbearable pressure of spying with its relentless fear of discovery, and to spare himself the humiliation of breaking down and betraying the ring.[20]

Significantly Miyagi did not poise on the windowsill and leap out feet first, the instinctive way of jumping when one hopes to walk away intact. He dived out headfirst and survived by mere chance. A streetcar clanged past as he shot out the window; if his momentum had carried him a few yards farther, he might have landed on the street directly in its path. Having ascertained he was not much hurt, his captors hustled him back to the station and his interrogation.

They found him a changed man.[21] He had leaped from the prison casement in the Japanese tradition of honorable suicide, but death had not accepted him, and he had been severely shaken in mind as well as in body. Any dramatic gesture that fails to come off leaves the actor feeling rather let-down and sheepish, and Miyagi came back to earth with a psychological as well as physical thud. Sakai's hazarding his life in pursuit impressed Miyagi deeply. An agent of the hated Tokko had risked his neck in line of duty. Later he told his captors how much he admired Sakai's devotion.[22]

Beneath these surface reactions ran something deeper. As with a cleaver, Miyagi had severed himself from his past. Yoshikawa expressed the situation thus: "He had crossed the barrier of death and had come back to life." Miyagi had experienced no less than a resurrection, and what life remained to him he must live with clean hands. He must make a general confession and start over with an unmarked slate.

So back in the conference room Miyagi talked. And talked and talked and talked. It was like drawing the cork of a champagne bottle: The whole broad outline of the Sorge ring burst out in a heady foam. When Miyagi paused for sheer lack of breath, he had rocked the Tokko as it had never been rocked before. The tremendous scope of the operation, the social status of the two principals, and the international complications—all sent the Tokko into a state verging on shock. The confession that Miyagi spied for the Comintern—which is what he believed—was "a terrific revelation." The involvement of Richard Sorge, prominent journalist and confidant of the German ambassador, was an astonishing circumstance. But to the Japanese authorities the real stunner was Ozaki.[23]

For more than a year the police had been screening his writings for any signs of political heresy and had found no subversion in his published works because there was none to find. The views he expressed parroted neither the supernationalist line nor Communist propaganda; they were the ideas of a thoughtful, well-informed scholar with a certain originality of mind.

Ozaki's very authenticity gave the Tokko pause, for the scholar enjoys great honor in Japan. Despite their long surveillance of him, they could not really believe he was a spy. Now that their nebulous suspicions seemed confirmed, they backed away in incredulous horror. The Tokko reacted like a group of dabblers in black magic who, testing an ancient incantation, hear a clap of thunder and find that they have actually conjured up a demon.

It was all too much for the agents, well above their level of operations and authority. They almost fell over themselves in their haste to drop this ticking bomb into some other lap and rushed to the office of Mitsusada Yoshikawa as soon as Miyagi had finished his confession. As Yoshikawa explained, "The arrest of a group of underground Communists was a routine business in Japan at the time, but the discovery of such a high-level spy ring was an altogether different matter."[24]

Yoshikawa was a procurator of the Tokyo District Criminal Court and as such under the Justice Ministry rather than the Home Ministry, as was the Tokko. Procurators were attached to the Supreme Court and the district and appeals courts. A procurator was somewhat like a district attorney in the United States but had rather more power.[25] His duties were formally defined thus: "To conduct searches, institute prosecutions, and supervise the execution of judgments in criminal cases, and to act as representative of the public interest in civil cases of public concern."[26]

Yoshikawa, whose bright eyes, alert expression, and agile movements made him resemble a highly intelligent, horn-rimmed chipmunk, was eminently qualified by experience and temperament to carry out these duties. Dynamic, efficient, and organized, he seized upon this strange case with all its built-in headaches as a chess master welcomes a championship match.[27]

A group of prosecutors was assigned to investigate and prosecute the entire case under Toneo Nakamura, chief of the Prosecution Bureau of the Tokyo District Criminal Court. Under Nakamura, Yoshikawa had primary charge of the prosecution, with several prosecutors under him. He personally conducted the investigation and also instructed the police to assist.[28]

So fraught with complications was the case that Yoshikawa decided to seek another opinion and called in Mitsusaburo Tamazawa, a fellow prosecutor. "I wanted a fresh mind to come into the case with me," he explained.[29]

Tamazawa immediately went to the Tsukiji Station to question Miyagi in person. "He had calmed down sufficiently to give a coherent account of the details of his crimes. . . ." Miyagi implicated not only Sorge and Ozaki but also Clausen, Voukelitch, Mizuno, and Kawai among others. The magnitude of the case astounded Tamazawa.[30]

When he returned to Yoshikawa's office, the two compared notes. They could see even more clearly than the Tokko detectives the ugly labyrinth to which Miyagi had opened the door, if he was telling the truth. Sheer practical politics made dealing with Sorge a nightmare. This swashbuckling journalist was a prominent figure in the capital, and behind him loomed powerful forces in Berlin. In fact, at first the Foreign Section of the Tokko refused to touch him, declaring "that Sorge was an influential assistant to German Ambassador Ott in matters related to information and that it was unbelievable that he was a Soviet spy."[31]

Not mentioned officially but undoubtedly very much in the minds of these intelligent men was the fact that Sorge stood accused of spying for the Soviet Union, technically a friendly nation; Japan was more than satisfied to keep it so. Already mired in China, Japan was heading for war with the United States, Great Britain, and the Netherlands. A flaming scandal involving a Soviet espionage ring would not exactly endear Japan to Russia. In short, Sorge was under the protection of both Japan's ally Germany and its restive friend the Soviet Union. A mistake about such a man could leave Yoshikawa and Tamazawa facing professional and personal ruin.

And Ozaki, whom Yoshikawa described as "one of the most brilliant advisers of Konoye"! Could the Tokko and the procurators afford to proceed against such a well-known, highly placed intellectual as Ozaki on the word of a self-confessed Communist agent? Obviously the investigation required that Miyagi's confession be either confirmed or disproved. Yoshikawa decided to pull in some of Miyagi's assistants. Reviewing the long list of names gleaned from Miyagi's statement, he checked two as likely prospects for Tokko grilling. So on October 13 the police swooped down on Akiyama and Ms. Kuzumi.

Confronted by a battery of grim detectives, Akiyama lost no time in parting with information about Miyagi and his activities. "Akiyama told everything he knew when questioned," said Yoshikawa. "He did not deny anything." His statements checked with what Miyagi had told. Furthermore, a search of his home unearthed a quantity of material relative to the South Manchurian Railroad as well as military information, evidently awaiting translation into English.[32]

Satisfied that they had milked Akiyama dry, the Tokko turned its attention to Ms. Kuzumi. Although of a very different type from Akiyama, she was not proof against the Tokko's expert questioning, and indeed, Miyagi having already confessed, there was little point in her not following suit. Her evidence dovetailed with his and left the police with virtually no doubt that they had heard the truth.[33]

But in this case "virtually" was not good enough; they had to be absolutely sure. So once more the Tokko detectives put Miyagi through his paces. They now had more facts upon which to base their questions and went into exhaustive detail. "Miyagi spoke with conviction concerning his relations with Ozaki," said Yoshikawa. "Still, the police doubted him."

No better proof could be found of Ozaki's prestige than this: The prosecutors and the Tokko men, all with long experience in criminal investigation and with few illusions left, continued to cling to belief in his innocence despite the testimony of three independent witnesses. One after another his inquisitors demanded of Miyagi almost pleadingly, "Is this the truth?"

And wearily but staunchly he replied, "Yes, it is the truth." Finally, like it or not, they had no choice but to believe.[34]

CHAPTER 58

  "A VERY QUIET ARREST"

At noon on Tuesday, October 14, Ozaki left his office and strolled along to the Asia Restaurant which was in the same building. As he walked in, almost the first faces he saw were those of an interesting trio: Goro Murata, chief of the Security Section of the Home Affairs Ministry; Kentaro Nomura, a division chief of the Tokko; and another Tokko representative, Keijo Okazaki. Ozaki hesitated, then walked up to these men, whom he knew slightly, and exchanged greetings.

What impelled this action? Kawai thought Ozaki sensed that his arrest was at hand and wanted to see if he could read any meaning in the expression on their faces.[1] Yet Ozaki's testimony later indicated no presentiment of arrest. He had been no more than faintly surprised when Miyagi had not shown up on the previous Sunday to give Yoko her weekly painting lesson and not at all disturbed that Sorge had missed an appointment with him in that very restaurant yesterday, Monday, the thirteenth,[2] Monday being the usual day they met. (Sorge turned up for the meeting that Tuesday evening.[3] Nothing could reveal more clearly the extent to which Sorge was rattled at this time.) Ozaki did not even bother to call Sorge to check into the matter.[4]

By this time the only question remaining for officialdom was not whether to arrest Ozaki but when. One school wanted to scoop up all the principals at once. Sorge kept in frequent touch with Ozaki, and if the contact were broken, he might sense danger and seek asylum in the German Embassy or otherwise escape, perhaps even commit suicide. The other view was more political. Japanese-German relations had to be considered; in particular Sorge's relationship with Ott constituted "a hidden sword." Therefore, Ozaki had to be arrested first. If he gave the authorities strong confirmation of Miyagi's story, they could proceed against Sorge and the other foreigners. This strategy prevailed.[5]

In accordance with his custom, Ozaki rose early on the morning of October 15 and went to his library for a brief period of reading before setting out on the day's business. As he did so, a black automobile stopped before his house and disgorged several plainclothes policemen, who gained admittance to the house by presenting business cards. Ozaki was not aware of them until they entered the library at about six.

When they showed him the warrant for his arrest, a shadow of disquiet touched his face but departed just as quickly. To struggle or attempt escape was beneath his dignity. Even at this late date he believed he was being arrested because of his writings and liberal tinge, not for espionage. Calmly he told his family what had happened and went along impassively with his captors to the Meguro Police Station. It was "a very quiet arrest for such a big figure."[6]

As Ozaki sat in the station surrounded by plainclothesmen, he had no idea that Miyagi had been arrested and that the Tokko already knew much about Sorge's spy ring.[7] Contrary to Ozaki's belief that he would be questioned about his writings, the first police questioner told him bluntly, "I am going to examine you on the suspicion that you have believed in communism for several years, supported the Comintern and the Japanese Communist Party, spread propaganda for communism through writings and other methods, and thus have worked for the Comintern and the Japanese Communist Party." The agent looked up from the charge sheet into Ozaki's dark eyes. "Do you have anything to say?"

Arrogantly confident, Ozaki met his interrogator's stern regard. "Consciously or specifically I have never done such activities as you are asking about," he replied.[8] But when at last he realized that the police were concentrating on his spying, "his inner unrest clearly manifested itself on his face."[9] Although informed of Miyagi's arrest, Ozaki continued to resist. Whereupon Hiroshi Miyashita, an assistant section chief of the

Tokko, peeled off the kid gloves. Pounding on his desk, he shouted, "We're not examining you as a Japanese but as a spy for the Comintern or the Soviet Union. When Japan is at war, spies can't expect any mercy."[10]

This laid it on the line. Obliquely Miyashita had told Ozaki that he could no longer rely on his contacts and influential friends; as a Comintern or Soviet spy he had forfeited consideration as a son of Dai Nippon. No wonder Ozaki turned pale. But he insisted, "I'm not a spy but just an expert on political affairs."

"I don't know your mind," growled Miyashita contemptuously, "but you're not being investigated for being a political scientist. You're charged with breaking the Peace Preservation Act and the National Defense Act."[11]

For the time being Ozaki maintained his silence. Although this was only to be expected, his recalcitrance threatened to throw a monkey wrench into the finely meshed gears of the schedule for cleaning up the Sorge ring. Without Ozaki's confession the authorities could not proceed against the three foreigners. With Sorge's arrest programmed for the early morning of October 18, the Tokko needed Ozaki's story by midnight of the fifteenth or early on the sixteenth; otherwise Yoshikawa would lack sufficient evidence to obtain the consent of the Ministry of Justice to round up the foreign members of the ring.[12]

Ozaki's questioning was in Miyashita's capable hands. He enjoyed the reputation of being the most skillful interrogator in the police and set about the task with all the dexterity and experience he could command. But his opponent was a master of the Japanese language and fighting for his life. Morning wore into afternoon, afternoon into evening, and still it seemed that the irresistible force had met the immovable object. Miyashita's task was not made any easier by the incessant phone calls from the police and the procurator's office asking if Ozaki had confessed and, if not, when they could expect him to break down.[13]

At about 10:00 P.M., unable to bear the suspense any longer, Miyashita's chief dashed out of police headquarters and plunged into the Meguro Station just when Ozaki's composure showed signs of cracking. His resistance ended with the day.

On almost the stroke of midnight he said, as if released from unbearable tension, "I will tell all the facts, so let me take a rest today and let me think a little." His secretly relieved interrogators agreed, for by this time they needed rest almost as much as the prisoner did. Now that they had jumped the main hurdle, details could wait for the morrow.[14]

In the meantime, Ms. Ozaki was trying distractedly to find out what her husband's arrest was all about. The officers gave her no clue, so she was thoroughly distressed and bewildered. She hastened to phone Michizo Kishi, one of Konoye's private secretaries and a good friend of her husband's, to ask if he knew what was going on. In turn Kishi contacted a friend in the Home Ministry, who informed him only that this was a Communist case.[15]

Ms. Ozaki was fortunate to reach Kishi, for he was a member of the Breakfast Group, which met that very day. Flinging his morsel of information to Ms. Ozaki, Kishi sped to the prime minister's official residence as fast as feet and wheels could carry him. The group was already in session, deep in a discussion of how to extricate the Japanese Army from the Chinese bog. Ushiba, Kazami, Matsumoto, and a few others were in place, thrashing out their problem with the brisk informality of men who are friends as well as associates. Into this assembly Kishi burst with the amazing news of Ozaki's arrest. They said no more that day about the army or China; they turned their undivided attention to this incredible development. It was beyond their comprehension, and they took refuge in baffled incredulity.

The Breakfast Group dubbed Ozaki *tanuki* ("badger"), alluding to the belief in rural Japan that a badger could deceive a farmer. "Ozaki fooled us so completely," Matsumoto observed ruefully. Ozaki continued to do so for years after his death. "Still now to this day we cannot clearly figure out Ozaki's involvement completely."[16] Yet the record is plain. Ambiguity existed only in the minds of Ozaki's loyal friends and admirers.

While these dramatic events were being enacted, Sorge was winding down his affairs in Japan. On October 15, while Ozaki was undergoing his initial questioning, Clausen came to Sorge's house. Sorge had a sheaf of manuscripts for transmission. If all went according to his plan, one of the messages would be the last official wire concerning his mission in Tokyo. He claimed to have felt no particular sense of danger but had concluded that the ring had completed its task. Sorge wanted a change of scene and new work in either Moscow or Europe. So along with routine data, he intended to request new instructions. Should the ring return to Russia or start a new activity in Germany?[17]

Clausen hastily skimmed through the papers, then handed them back to Sorge. "It is a little too early to send these," he objected. "So I want you to keep them for a while."[18]

Hitherto Clausen had never refused to accept drafts, only taking it upon himself not to encode and transmit all of them. To reject an assignment outright, coolly telling his chief that the time was not ripe, was a very bold thing to do. But for months he had been tasting the heady wine of editing and exercising independence, and his courage grew by what it fed on.

Clausen faced some unpleasant conclusions. If the request for reassignment went out and the Fourth Department ordered the ring back to Moscow, he would have to pay the piper for his months of dancing. Red Army Intelligence would demand of Sorge a full explanation of the amazing drop in the quantity and quality of the information he had furnished throughout 1941. Outraged and astounded, Sorge would compare the messages Moscow had received with his record of drafts given to Clausen for transmission, Clausen's insubordination would stand revealed, and the Day of Judgment would be at hand. No, very definitely he could not bring himself to send that message. He would postpone the evil hour as long as possible.

That Sorge did not blast him to a cinder for his presumption indicates in itself that he was not in his usual form. His health was below par, and the unexpected absence of Ozaki and Miyagi worried him. He unburdened himself to Clausen, remarking that Miyagi was a punctual man; since he had not shown up, perhaps he had been arrested. He also referred to the failure of Ozaki to meet him at the Asia Restaurant. At this Clausen felt uneasy. Sorge tried to telephone Ozaki but could not find his number, no astonishing circumstance in view of the usual clutter surrounding him. He abandoned the search, saying, "Let's wait for a couple of days anyway, and if he does not show up, I will call him on the telephone." This had been his usual custom when Ozaki or Miyagi had not kept a rendezvous.[19]

But Sorge knew that his drama would have no happy ending. His sense of doom emanated from him in an almost palpable net which caught the impressionable Clausen in its meshes. He left Sorge's house that day feeling "that the time of arrest was approaching."[20]

As more and more evidence came out in support of Miyagi's confession, the word passed through Tokko channels for Saito to intensify his surveillance of Sorge. Suzuki personally instructed him. He was to keep a close watch on Sorge, make sure he neither escaped nor committed suicide, and at the same time give him no inkling of imminent arrest. How to do this his supervisors left to Saito's initiative, a quality he possessed in abundance. Since his return to the job in July he had rented a second-floor room in a house across from Sorge's. From this vantage point he could see the entrance to Sorge's house, although not the alley behind it. This passage was too narrow to admit a car. So upon receipt of his new orders, Saito established himself in his rented room, from which he watched Sorge's house intently. Having ascertained that these days Sorge slept late, not rising before 9:00 A.M., Saito had plenty of time to breakfast, take the hour-long trolley ride from Ueno to Azabu, and reach his rented perch before his quarry was up and stirring. Not until Sorge's last light went off at about 11:00 P.M. did he abandon his watch and return to his home.[21]

From its inception the Tokko's watch on Sorge had been inadequate. Even with the task fined down solely to the three days of October 15, 16, and 17, the net was still much too wide-meshed for efficiency. Saito had no relief while he slept, ate, and answered the call of nature, and of course, he could watch only one side of the house at one time. At night he had to trust to luck.[22] In one sense a tighter surveillance was unnecessary. Sorge could not leave Japan, with every harbor and airport on the lookout. Nevertheless, a great many things could go on across the way without Saito's knowing anything about them, and plenty did.

Even as Saito set forth to keep an eye on Sorge's ramshackle residence on October 16, Yoshikawa was en route to the Meguro Station. When he arrived to secure Ozaki's promised confession, he found the prisoner pale and tense. To clear the decks for action and remove any possible cause for misunderstanding, Yoshikawa frankly told Ozaki all he knew from the interrogations of Miyagi. Ozaki listened gravely without interpolation. At the end of Yoshikawa's recital he nodded his head submissively and spoke one word: *"Wakarimashita* [I understand].''

Then Yoshikawa questioned Ozaki thoroughly. He no longer attempted to deny the charges. He spoke freely of his espionage activities, his work in China, his subsequent meeting with Sorge in Japan, his agreement to cooperate with him, his relationship with Miyagi. He admitted to Yoshikawa that his arrest had greatly shocked him. Indeed, on a man so pleased with himself, so sure of his position, it must have descended like an avalanche.

Oddly enough, no member of the ring had prepared or evidently even considered a story to cover his activities in case of arrest.

One question still roused Ozaki to resistance. "Who will succeed you?" asked Yoshikawa. So cleverly did Ozaki parry this query that a full thirty minutes elapsed before Yoshikawa extracted the name of Shigeru Mizuno. Then, resigned, Ozaki continued that Mizuno had worked closely with him in a number of capacities and was his direct assistant.

Ozaki's statement having laid to rest the last of Yoshikawa's lingering doubts, he went about compiling the evidence he would need to present to Michiyo Iwamura, the minister of justice.[23] Iwamura had to approve the arrest of any foreigner, and Richard Sorge was far from just any foreigner. Both the Foreign Section of the Tokko and the Kempeitai hesitated to take Sorge into custody, for the truth about his espionage still remained locked in the brains of the Tokko's First Section and Yoshikawa's office. In view of Sorge's close connection with the German Embassy, the reaction of the Kempeitai and the Foreign Section could be summed up by "Include me out."[24] So if Yoshikawa expected the minister of justice to act, he would have to have ample proof to lay before him.

He put his stenographers to work, making copies of all

the affidavits and confessions so far obtained in the case. Yoshikawa and Tamazawa went over them line by line and discussed
every point exhaustively. Painstakingly Yoshikawa underlined
in red ink the parts he considered vital for Iwamura to read.

As he worked over the documentation, Yoshikawa's brain
systematically dissected the questions and implications of the
case. He was by no means sure that the Justice Ministry would
go along with having Sorge, Voukelitch, and Clausen arrested.
Konoye's government hung on by its fingernails and would
drop at any minute. In the circumstances it was almost too
much to hope that the rapidly expiring administration would
approve airing a scandal certain to snuff out the tiny flicker of
life remaining.

Would the top brass of the Japanese Army stand still for
an arrest sure to trigger one of the most spectacular cases of
all time and cause its German allies to lose face? On the other
hand, the very word *Communist* set General Tojo off like an
alarm clock in a chattering rage. If Tojo had to choose between
clearing out a Soviet *apparat* and inconveniencing Germany,
Yoshikawa was fairly certain he would pick the former.[25]

What really plowed furrows across Yoshikawa's high
forehead was this question: Is Sorge a double agent? Was he
spying for both the Russians and the Germans? So far Yoshikawa had no proof that Sorge or anyone else had in fact sent
secret materials to Moscow. He knew that the ring sent documents to Russia by courier, but what sort of documents—real
classified material or examples of the impressive-looking but
innocuous junk that every government agency turns out? Was
Sorge really serving the Soviets, or was he feeding them just
enough to keep them happy and himself in their confidence,
the better to serve his real master, Hitler? Sorge and his men
used radio and sent dispatches in code, but so far the code
remained unbroken. Of course, Yoshikawa did not know at
this time that Sorge indeed supplied information to Schellenberg
and Ritgen in Berlin, information valuable enough to persuade
Schellenberg to go along with that cozy but delicate arrangement.

Nevertheless, a good bit of surface evidence lent credence
to the possibility that Sorge was playing a double game: his
close friendship with Ott; his semiofficial position at the embassy; his connection with the *Frankfurter Zeitung*; the man's

whole attitude and personality. If Sorge actually wore two hats, arresting him could strip any number of gears. All in all, Yoshikawa was in a grim mood that October 16.[26]

Sorge no less than Yoshikawa was under tension that day. He had lost touch with his two best agents, and he himself had been ill for the past few weeks, so much so that Miyagi had been worried about him. At his last meeting with Ozaki Miyagi recommended that they try to persuade their chief to enter a hospital.[27]

The police had not neglected Voukelitch during these past few days. His case was under the watchful eye of an inspector of the Tokko's Foreign Section. This man was also chief of the American-European Division. He was none other than Tomiki Suzuki, the same officer Sakai had consulted in connection with Miyagi's ex-girl friend in Suzuki's employ and of his name. Suzuki inherited Voukelitch immediately after Miyagi's confession and set a brace of policemen on his trail. Because Voukelitch had no car, his shadows had an interesting time of it, catching various means of public transportation without giving themselves away. In the meantime, another policeman watched Voukelitch's home day and night, just in case his personal followers lost him.[28]

Voukelitch's usefulness to the ring had almost ended in any case. If Japan were to become embroiled in a full-scale war with the Allies, correspondents of Allied nations automatically would become enemy aliens. They would be hurried out of the country or clapped into prison. If he were deported, what of his wife and son? Would the Japanese permit them to leave the country with him, or would Tokyo invoke the policy of separating Japanese from foreign spouses? Voukelitch adored his pretty second wife and their baby. Even if the police had never had an inkling of the spy ring, Voukelitch would have been facing vexing personal worries.

Japan no less than Voukelitch stood at a crossroads. At 5:00 P.M. that October 16, Konoye bit the bullet and formally submitted the resignation of his cabinet. The way was clear for Tojo.

That night the moon shone on Tokyo, its beams unnoticed by a variety of people of widely separated conditions and states of mind: On Konoye, probably divided between disappointment at the failure of his government and relief to be rid of the crushing yoke. On Tojo, raring to go. On Voukelitch, wondering how much longer Yoshiko's beloved head would rest beside him. On Tamazawa and Yoshikawa, cocked and primed for battle. On Saito, sleeping the sleep of the tired and bored in his bachelor quarters at Ueno. On Ozaki, stretched out in a prison cell. On Miyagi, by this time no doubt too exhausted to think at all. On a thousand and one Japanese wondering if their sons had lived through the day in China. And on Sorge, sleeping for once alone except for his troubled thoughts.

CHAPTER 59

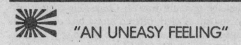 "AN UNEASY FEELING"

With Ozaki's finger pointing in his direction, inevitably Shigeru Mizuno was next on the list for questioning. The Tokko swooped down and returned with him in their talons to the Suganami Police Station. Thither Yoshikawa hastened to question this latest catch personally and encountered no trouble with him. Mizuno talked freely, and since his testimony agreed in all essentials with that of Ozaki and Miyagi, Yoshikawa felt more certain of his position in going to the minister of justice. [1]

The police put Ozaki through a busy day of interrogations, but the atmosphere was much more relaxed than it had been on either the fifteenth or sixteenth. Being the type who would remember a good story and try to tell it if he were up before the recording angel, Ozaki cracked a number of jokes. He was not in the least averse to offering an opinion on the new cabinet. Shown a newspaper story about Tojo's selections, Ozaki remarked, "This cabinet is the one which is going to war against the United States." Knowing every Japanese statesman and politician of any consequence either personally or by reputation, Ozaki needed no tea leaves to read the future in that list.

"If they adopt my idea, the China Incident will be solved in three days," he continued sententiously. Understandably agog to hear a formula that would stop a four-year-old war in three days, the interrogator begged for details. "Of course," replied the prisoner graciously. "If the Chinese Communist Party takes over China and the Japanese Communist Party takes over Japan, then Japan, Russia, and China could cooperate with each other."[2]

Now that the pressure was off Ozaki, his captors permitted him to smoke. A clerk offered him a box of matches, which by chance was decorated with one of the spy warnings in use throughout Japan. "This match has often made me feel bad," Ozaki remarked with a grin. "Once while I was conferring with Sorge secretly, I picked a match out of my pocket to light a cigarette. I don't know where I picked up that match, but the poster on the matchbox read 'Spy springs!' I felt bad at that time," he concluded, still grinning.[3]

While Ozaki wisecracked with his captors, his wife suffered torments over how best to aid him. During the day Yoshizaburo Takane, a judge of the Tokyo District Civil Court, called to offer his services to her husband, an old classmate. Touched by this willingness to help a friend arrested in connection with a Communist case, Ms. Ozaki gratefully accepted Takane's proffered assistance in arranging suitable defense counsel.[4]

How Sorge spent the morning is not known. He had appointments with Clausen and Voukelitch scheduled for the day. In view of the disappearance of his two other associates, he was somewhat fearful that the remaining duo might have vanished in the night likewise, and he was prey to mounting disquiet.[5] But he had no intention of throwing in the sponge. Indeed, he never showed himself more the expert in his trade than on this, his last day of freedom.

Sorge and the members of his ring always entered and left one another's homes as if the places were under surveillance, and they knew how to make unobtrusive entrances and exits. Then, too, Hanako's remark that she knew more than one way to reach Sorge's house if the police were watching her suggests well-concealed approaches. Late that morning Clausen arrived, unnoticed by Saito, on personal business unconnected with espionage. Sorge's little Datsun was in a garage for repairs. Clausen had borrowed it to go to the drugstore after some medicine for Sorge, and driving down a sloping street, he had lost control, and the car had turned turtle. Clausen crawled out, uninjured, and righted the car with the help of a policeman. Sorge had asked Clausen to accompany him to the garage.[6]

Did Sorge know that the Tokko had planted a man opposite him? Possibly. A window that can be looked out of can be looked into, and Sorge knew every trick of the trade. Sorge and his friends were very cagey on this day. Sorge and Clausen left the house, unseen and unheard. They went to the garage, secured the trusty Datsun, and drove to the Minoru Restaurant for lunch. The two spies arrived well after noon and lingered over their meal, for they did not break up until about 4:00 P.M.[7]

Parting from his chief at the restaurant, Clausen wandered to the Ginza. After some shopping, he took in a movie, then returned to the Minoru Restaurant's bar. He knew that he was drinking more than was good for him. Then he went home, where Sorge reached him later that evening.[8]

After the two men had parted company, Sorge drove to the garage near his home where he kept his Datsun. This garage figured prominently in the police net flung around him. Every time he parked his car and left the garage the police walked right in and searched the vehicle. On this occasion a quick check disclosed a sizable amount of money rolled up in envelopes. The searcher counted it, took it to the nearby police station, photographed it, and returned it to the garage owner with instructions to give it to Sorge. If possible, he was to enter the house and report to the police just what he saw.[9] That Sorge should have left a large sum in his car spoke eloquently of his carelessness and waning powers.

With Sorge on his way home that afternoon and Clausen pouring sake down the hatch, where was Voukelitch? His morning held nothing but routine. That afternoon, at the close of the working day, his two shadows saw him leave his office building and stride off in the direction of Shimbashi Station. The Tokko men followed at a safe distance. Near the station Voukelitch paused and stepped into a phone booth. As he closed the door, the agents blended into the shadows so close that they could hear him speaking German. Fortunately, one of the detectives understood that language and caught the words "Boss, may I come to see you now?"[10]

Obviously he was speaking to Sorge; just as obviously

the answer was in the affirmative. Voukelitch hung up, moved briskly down the sidewalk to a trolley stop, and presently swung aboard a car headed for Azabu, the police close on his trail. Somewhere along the line they lost their prey, not too difficult in those days, with little gas for prowl cars and taxis not always available. So the Tokko men were unable to follow Voukelitch directly, but they felt certain that his destination was Sorge's house, which was already under watch. Their man on the spot could pick up the scent.[11]

They were right on one count and wrong on the other. Voukelitch was on his way to report to Sorge, but Saito did not see him.[12]

Sorge's principal motive for summoning Voukelitch was to ask him to try to reach Ozaki the next morning through the South Manchurian Railroad or the publishers of *Modern Japan*.[13]

Deciding to call a council of war, Sorge phoned Clausen to join them immediately. Clausen took off promptly, and in sympathetic consideration of Sorge's illness brought him a one-*sho* bottle of sake—nearly half a gallon. The clock hands hovered between 7:30 and 8:00 P.M. when Clausen appeared, bottle in hand. The contribution was redundant, for Sorge and Voukelitch were already imbibing sake.[14]

No sooner had Clausen dropped into a chair when still another visitor knocked on Sorge's door. How this one arrived without attracting Saito's attention is a real mystery, for he had no reason to be furtive. He was the owner of the nearby garage, come to return Sorge's money, as the Tokko had directed. Sorge invited the man into the house while he counted the bills, peeling off a reward as he did so. The visitor smiled and bowed his thanks, exchanged a polite farewell with Sorge, then scurried to the police station to report that he had seen Sorge, Clausen—whom he recognized—and "a bald man" together in Sorge's house. This intelligence worried his hearers, who feared this gathering meant that the foreigners were plotting escape.[15]

The interruption made no impression on Voukelitch or Clausen, absorbed in their own gloomy thoughts. Sorge spoke a little about the fall of the Konoye cabinet, but obviously his mind was not on Japanese politics. On this, the last time these three spent together, only one subject interested them: the disappearance of their colleagues.[16]

"I have not seen Joe and Otto," said Sorge despondently. "Probably they have been arrested by the police." Sorge was so upset that somewhere in the conversation he referred to Ozaki by his real name. Thus for the first time Clausen learned the identity of Otto.[17]

Fear stood at the elbows of these three as they worried at the puzzle like terriers with a bone from which they had long since chewed all the meat. One member of the inner ring might disappear for legitimate reasons—there were such things as accidents, sudden illnesses, even amnesia—but not two of them in one week. Something had gone wrong. Bleakly Sorge pointed out that if Ozaki and Miyagi had been arrested, "our destiny would be the same." Rousing himself to his duties as host, Sorge said, "I will warm up the sake." He started to open Clausen's bottle, but Clausen had had enough in more ways than one. The whole dismal atmosphere was too much for him, and within ten minutes of his arrival he made his excuses and took off into the night, filled with "an inexpressible uneasiness."[18]

He got no further than Juban-cho when he ran into two detectives from the Toriizaka Station. One he did not recognize; the other was Aoyama. In view of Clausen's jittery nerves and the nature of the discussion he had just quitted, the latter appeared a very figure of doom. After an exchange of greetings Aoyama asked, "Where are you going?"

"I am going home," replied Clausen, trying to sound casual. At that moment a streetcar bound for Furukawabashi rattled to a stop, and he hastily clambered aboard. Sensing Aoyama's eyes burning two holes in the back of his head, he glanced back. Both agents were gazing steadily in his direction. Clausen swiveled his head to the fore, more convinced than ever "that the time of arrest approached."[19]

Once at home he said nothing to Anna of his experience or his fears, but he prowled restlessly about the house, engaged in a heart-to-heart talk with himself. His transmission room fairly teemed with documents, some to be coded, others already sent, their English translations on his table with the originals. His code book, grimy with long use, rested on the bookshelf, and the telltale improvised radio awaited discovery, mute evidence of illegal operations. Should he burn the papers and bury the transmitter? Clausen wandered out onto the veranda and squinted through the darkness into the garden for a suitable place to inter the radio. But he hesitated to act.[20]

It is not too difficult to imagine the nature of his mental questioning. If he destroyed the evidence and the present crisis turned out to be a mare's nest woven of coincidence and fear, he would have to start all over again from scratch, if indeed Sorge were to give him a second chance. His nerves almost shot, Sorge would pour all the vials of his wrath over Clausen's bowed head if he acted prematurely on his own initiative. Yet what if the danger were real? Was it not his clear duty to get rid of the incriminating evidence just in case?

Torn between Sorge and the Tokko, Clausen did what many another has done when faced with an irrevocable choice: He went to bed. Perhaps the next day would bring the answers to all his questions and lift this burden of decision from his reluctant shoulders. Clausen crawled wearily between the sheets, only to heave and toss through the restless night.[21]

While the three remaining major members of the Sorge ring worried and wondered their way through their last day of freedom, Yoshikawa and his office staff labored over their dossier for presentation to the minister of justice. The testimony of Mizuno, arrested that very day, and additional facts from Ozaki kept the papers rustling and typewriters clacking throughout the afternoon. So the evening was well along before Yoshikawa and Tamazawa set out for their appointment with Iwamura. Katsu Ikeda of the Supreme Court as well as the chief detectives of the Ministry of Justice were also present at the meeting, held in Iwamura's office in Suginami.[22]

Fortunately the delegation found the minister in an expansive mood. Tojo had asked him to continue as a member of his cabinet, so Iwamura was pleased with himself and with life in general. While other political heads were falling, his gray-haired, plump-faced one rested firmly on his aristocratic shoulders. He beamed genially on these excellent fellows. Tamazawa and Yoshikawa took in the situation at a glance and sent a silent prayer of thanksgiving winging heavenward. If the Konoye government had to fall, it had picked a fine day. The prince's cabinet had a vested interest in keeping the Sorge case as quiet as possible, whereas undoubtedly Tojo would leap at the chance to embarrass his predecessor. And here was Iwamura in a mood to sign anything without reading the fine print.[23]

But Tamazawa and Yoshikawa laid all their cards on the table. Iwamura was a respected and popular man, a clever and able minister. He deserved the truth, so his visitors dealt him the jokers as well as the aces. They explained that while they had proof of their case, some of the authorities were reluctant to arrest Sorge in view of his high connections and the complex ramifications of his operations. All the procurators wanted from Iwamura was the go signal. They would assume all responsibility if the case blew up in their faces.

Iwamura would not agree to this. "If you have proof, I will take the responsibility," he declared, and forthwith gave his permission for the arrest of Sorge and the other foreigners connected with him. The delegation thanked the minister for his cooperation, bowed their good-byes, and hastened to their respective offices. Tamazawa issued the warrants.[24]

Meanwhile, what of Sorge and Voukelitch, whom Clausen left shortly after 8:00 P.M. nursing their woes and a half gallon of sake? Voukelitch took his departure a while after Clausen, either by good luck or by good management evading Saito's eye. He must have hit more than one bar on his way, for when the silently patient Tokko watch on his house saw its quarry stumble home, the clocks hovered near midnight and Voukelitch was very drunk.[25]

Saito kept his surveillance of Sorge's house. A light still shone, and Saito resigned himself to another hour or so of duty. Presently the sight of a man rapping on Sorge's door rewarded him. Saito recognized the caller as an official from the German Embassy, the third secretary, Embritch—or some such outlandish name and title. Soon Sorge and his visitor appeared in Sorge's second-floor window and perched on the sill. A barrage of German gutturals flew into Saito's willing ears, but he could not make out the meaning. Inasmuch as this was obviously no clandestine encounter, Saito spared them a qualm of sympathy. "Those poor men, talking so loudly and not knowing that I am watching them," he thought.[26]

The encounter was almost aggressively open. Instead of

sitting his guest in a comfortable chair, Sorge made him roost on the windowsill. Was he deliberately underlining his connection with the German Embassy, saying in effect to anyone who watched, "Remember that I, Richard Sorge, stand at the right side of Ambassador Ott"? The secretary did not stay long, leaving at about 10:00 P.M. Within a short time Sorge seemed to settle down for the night. His light blinked off close to 11:00. After waiting awhile longer, Saito called it a day and thankfully sped home, for he anticipated an early awakening with much action to follow.[27]

But, according to a story which a reliable source told in obvious sincerity, Sorge's day had not ended. Well after midnight, he had another caller who remained with him until after dawn—Ms. Ott. One cannot be certain that this is true, for no other source confirmed it.[28] But if so, if this meeting did indeed take place, how dramatically fitting, how typical of Sorge, and what a strange twist of fate! It would mean that destiny willed that the last woman in Sorge's life would be a daughter of the now-despised land of his father, a woman he had ruthlessly exploited for his own purposes, and the wife of a man he had doubly betrayed.

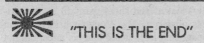

CHAPTER 60

"THIS IS THE END"

The British Embassy loomed dark and silent in the chill predawn of October 18. An employee peering out into the darkness might have observed a number of black shadows converging upon the nearby official residence of the Tokko's Foreign Section chief. This was the rendezvous point of the agents assigned to arrest Sorge, Voukelitch, and Clausen. The aggregation consisted of three squads of about ten men each, clustered together to receive last-minute instructions: Get your man, but be sure no harm comes to him at his own hands or otherwise, and search his house thoroughly. The men then piled into the small fleet of waiting police cars and sped off.[1] The previous day's fine weather had turned in the night. Random drops spattered on the windshields, harbingers of the gray rains that the southerly wind drove across the city intermittently all day.[2]

Darkness still blanketed Tokyo when Tomiki Suzuki and his detachment of plainclothesmen pulled up near Voukelitch's house. They remained at a slight distance, waiting for dawn to lighten the sky. At about six Suzuki silently signaled to his men, and the group moved swiftly upon the little house. Suzuki rapped on the door and inwardly braced himself in case of trouble. A maid answered his knock promptly. Giving the woman no time to protest or cry out, Suzuki charged up the stairs with a few of his men and burst into the second-floor bedroom.

Voukelitch and his wife were fast asleep. Suzuki shook his man awake and hustled him out of bed. Ms. Voukelitch huddled under the covers, her eyes dark with astonishment and horror. Suzuki gained the impression that she knew nothing of her husband's clandestine career and that this unexpected turn of events thoroughly shocked and shook her.[3] In his first assumption Suzuki was mistaken. Ms. Voukelitch knew about her husband's espionage and later stated that his arrest did not surprise her.[4] Still, to have a band of policemen invade one's bedroom, snatch one's spouse from between the sheets, and flourish a warrant in his face is enough to jolt the most blasé person.

Ms. Voukelitch's immunity throughout the investigation is surprising in view of her husband's activities and her membership in the Japanese-American Student Association. But she was a beautiful young woman, well-bred and polished to a smooth patina by an excellent education. Detectives are only human. Later Suzuki questioned her thoroughly and became convinced not only that she was ignorant of Voukelitch's espionage but that Voukelitch had gone to great lengths to keep her so.[5]

Voukelitch struggled out of his pajamas and into trousers and shirt, but Suzuki stopped him from donning his jacket. Jacket pockets might hold guns or knives. Voukelitch made no move to resist and no more than glanced at the warrant. Drugged with sleep and hung-over from the previous night's drinking bout, he was in a somewhat fuzzy state when Suzuki hurried him downstairs and into the police car.[6]

While part of Suzuki's squad accompanied Voukelitch to the Kagurazaka Police Station, another remained behind to search the house and confiscate anything incriminating. The search party paid particular attention to the photographic darkroom. Located on the first floor, it was by far the best room in the small house, and normally would have been the living room. Evidently Voukelitch took his photography seriously to house it so well—how seriously the Tokko agents did not realize until they discovered many pictures of Japanese military installations. Picking up these items, the searchers followed the first contingent back to the station.[7]

Experience had taught the police that many Communists secreted poison upon their persons and managed to swallow it after capture, so the agents stripped Voukelitch and subjected him to a thorough search for hidden poison.

Within the hour the Tokko had spirited him to Sugamo Prison, where they left him severely alone for the rest of the day to nurse the remains of his hangover and give his imagination free rein to consider the interrogation coming up on the morrow.[8]

A second flying squad headed by Aoyama and an agent named Hiramoto, of the Tokko's Foreign Section, descended on the Clausen residence at about the same time Suzuki picked up Voukelitch. Clausen had finally dropped off to sleep after his white night and was still deep in slumber when he awakened to find Aoyama standing in his bedroom doorway. Aoyama moved over to the bed and, looking down at the stupefied Clausen, said pleasantly enough, "I would like to ask you something about an automobile accident that happened the other day. So I would like you to come over to the police station." Clausen later said, "Combining with the incident of the previous night I got a hunch that this was not just a problem of an automobile accident."[9]

Aoyama left Anna alone, their previous conversations having convinced him that she did not understand the true nature of Clausen's activities. In this he had fallen into error, but at this time no one in the Tokko was clear about Anna's part in the ring.

Aoyama and Hiramoto gave Clausen time to dress and have breakfast. He was too upset to think straight. "I made some absent-minded preparations and left my home sandwiched between the two policemen," he recalled. However, he retained enough presence of mind to tell Anna that he was going to talk to the police about his automobile accident. A car containing two plainclothesmen waited in the street outside his house, and he was squashed in between the two agents. When the car moved off but not in the direction of the Toriizaka Station, Aoyama's home base, Clausen suspected that he was in serious trouble and "gave up my destiny with some feeling of doubt and was finally taken to Mita Police Station."[10]

Clausen refused to answer questions on the first day of incarceration, and the police put forth no great efforts to make him. Not until the twentieth did he begin to talk, and by that time he, like Voukelitch, had been hurried off to Sugamo Prison.[11]

The first search of Clausen's premises apparently produced little of importance. The place was so littered that the police could not see the trees for the forest. Fortunately Tamazawa personally supervised the searches at the homes of all three foreigners. Soon after the first sweep he made the rounds to see if the squad had overlooked anything. He found Voukelitch's rooms picked clean; in fact, the well-appointed darkroom was dusty and apparently had not been used for several days.[12]

At Clausen's, however, Tamazawa noticed what looked like a small suitcase resting on the desk in the living room. At first glance he ignored it as being too obvious for suspicion. Then the force of his professional thoroughness took over, and he opened the bag. There in all its glory sat Clausen's do-it-yourself sending set.[13]

Naturally this discovery led to the suspicion that further treasure awaited the searchers. Shinichi Ogata, chief of the Foreign Section, was the next official to tackle Clausen's quarters. He hit the jackpot. He left the premises clutching an armload of messages. Some seemed to be copies of dispatches already sent, others rough drafts. Some of the material was in German, but most of it was in English. Looking at the mass of documents, Ogata reflected resignedly that he had his work cut out for several days and nights to come. So far one thing eluded the seekers: Clausen's code book. While convinced in his own mind that Clausen was a spy, Ogata was not absolutely certain.[14] In fact, a number of the policemen involved did not understand the nature of the case, for the procurators played their cards tight against their chests.

In the meantime, several police cars glided to a smooth halt a little distance from Sorge's house beyond sight and hearing of its inhabitants. Drivers and passengers scrambled out and formed three groups, which swiftly deployed around the building. One section under Saito took the front path, while the others circled the premises. The whole body blended in the shadows to await zero hour.[15]

The time originally scheduled was 6:00 A.M., to coincide with the other two arrests, but circumstances delayed action somewhat. A car from the German Embassy was parked near Sorge's door, and the officers had to wait until his visitor departed,[16] and by general agreement Aoyama had to be present. He was the only member of the select group on the Sorge case who actually knew the man. Sorge liked and trusted Aoyama, while Aoyama, having penetrated Sorge's somewhat forbidding outer crust, found an intelligent man of much charm and humor, what he called "a big man in every respect." The principal fear of the arresting authorities being that Sorge might take fright and kill himself if a strange Tokko agent barged in on him, Aoyama's reassuring presence was necessary.[17]

Yet Clausen, not Sorge, was Aoyama's pigeon. In view of Aoyama's long surveillance of him and the importance of his discoveries about the illegal shortwave operation, it would have offended every Japanese sense of fitness to permit anyone else to make the actual arrest of Clausen. So the squad covering Sorge had to wait for Aoyama. An hour or so one way or the other made little difference.

In command of the group surrounding Sorge's home was Hideo Ohashi, whose division of the Foreign Section had taken over Sorge's case five days before the arrest. Ohashi was short and chunky, built to a cubist pattern—square body; square hands; square face. His sphere of jurisdiction in the Foreign Section covered the Soviets. By strict technicality Sorge, as a purported German citizen, fell within Suzuki's purview, but Suzuki had his hands full. Ohashi had taken over the case because, regardless of Sorge's nationality, this was a Soviet operation and Ohashi had an intensive knowledge of the Comintern.[18]

Everyone in the group wore civilian clothes and was unarmed. Although the Japanese took into consideration the possibility that Sorge might shoot at the arresting officers, their national obsession with suicide and their experience of poison in the possession of Communists made them worry principally that he would kill himself. This fear did not stem from any tender regard for Sorge's skin; the authorities needed every bit of information he had to give so that they might clean out this poisonous growth root and branch.[19]

Their second concern was whether Sorge was in the house. They had no assurance that he had not decamped in the night. So while they waited, the agents cautiously searched the grounds, trying to peer into the windows to discover whether their quarry was or was not still in his den.[20]

Saito had a private worry. Knowing Tori Fukuda's devotion to her master and aware that even at this early hour she would be about her duties, he feared that when she opened the door to a group of Tokko agents, she would rouse Sorge with her outcries, thus giving him the margin of time needed to commit suicide. Even as Saito turned over this possibility in his mind, she emerged from the house, carrying one of Sorge's large shoes.[21] Evidently Ama-san was bound for a shoemaker. With any luck they could finish the whole business before she returned.

As the patter of her feet died away, Aoyama hurried up, having seen Clausen on his way to jail. By this time the embassy car had sped off. Dawn had long passed, although sullen clouds obscured the sun. Ohashi signaled for action. Saito, Aoyama, and another agent, Iida, detached themselves from their cover and advanced up the path. Saito tried the door; it was unlocked. Gingerly he pushed it open, calling out, "Good morning!" No answer. The three men entered the house, and once again Saito sang out, this time somewhat louder,

"Excuse me, good morning!" A wordless grunt from upstairs and a soft padding on the steps rewarded him. An erect figure in pajamas entered, and for the first time Saito stood face-to-face with the man he had come to know so well from a distance.[22]

Although Sorge's hair was tousled, he had shaved. His face was absolutely expressionless. Behind those deadpan features the cool, swift brain must have been clicking like a computer, grinding out the obvious conclusion. But he was not the man to admit defeat until flat on his back. Courteously he invited his unexpected guests into the living room and waited impassively while they removed their shoes. He sat down on the sofa between Aoyama and Saito, Iida lingering near the door. The three men had barely seated themselves when Ohashi bounded in, evidently impatient at the delay. Saito and Iida each seized one of Sorge's arms. Saito cracked out a sharp command, and the police outside the house moved to join their colleagues.[23]

Sorge stood without speaking or moving. He would not demean himself by resisting arrest or arguing with policemen in the execution of their duty. Someone found a topcoat and slipped it over his shoulders. The little procession stopped at the front door, the men put on their shoes, and they all walked off to the Toriizaka Station, Sorge's topcoat swinging with his stride.[24]

Aoyama hung behind a bit. He knew that Sorge, a gallant foe, would hold no malice toward the player across the board. But he also knew with instinctive delicacy that Sorge would not be able to bear having a friend look upon his face in this moment of humiliation. Nor did Aoyama wish to see it. So he brought up the rear, triumphantly miserable and miserably triumphant. It was a great day for a Japanese policeman, but a gray day for a friend of Sorge's.[25]

Ohashi watched the departure, outwardly unmoved, inwardly appreciative of the drama and respectful of a protagonist with such power to hold the spotlight. Then and there Ohashi took a liking to Sorge, which over the weeks to follow grew and was reciprocated. Signaling four policemen to remain with him, he set about searching the house inch by inch. To one accustomed to Japanese interior decoration, with its age-old motto "When in doubt, get it out of sight," Sorge's residence must have looked more like a magpie's nest than a fit abode for a cultured human being. Ohashi had planned to sort out everything on the spot, but one look convinced him that this idea was impractical. He would have to go through file cabinets and boxes full of typewritten manuscript and notes and about 1,000 books. Inwardly groaning at the magnitude of the task, Ohashi sent for a two-ton truck. He would load everything on the vehicle for careful examination at the station. Leaving his assistants in charge, he hastened to the Toriizaka Station to be in on the first part of Sorge's questioning.[26]

Yoshikawa and Ogata, with several policemen, were waiting for the prisoner in a second-floor room. Someone—possibly Ohashi—must have brought clothes for Sorge, for when escorted to Yoshikawa, he wore his customary slacks and shirt. Sorge's eyes roved over the faces before him and came to rest on Yoshikawa's alert features. Some duelist's instinct seemed to tell him that this man was the enemy to be feared.

"Why have you arrested me?" he demanded harshly—his first words since his apprehension.

Yoshikawa extended the warrant and replied formally,

"We capture you on the basis of the National Peace Preservation Law as a spy suspect."[27]

One can almost hear the click as Sorge's steel-trap mind snapped over this bit of information. The Peace Preservation Law, that anti-Communist workhorse, not the new National Defense Security Law. This could only mean that the authorities had not discovered his connection with the Red Army. Obviously Miyagi and Ozaki had talked, and they must have implicated him seriously; otherwise Germany's ally would not lay hands on such a prominent German. But Miyagi and Ozaki believed themselves to be working for the Comintern.

By the time Yoshikawa and Ohashi, who had slipped in, began their questioning Sorge had decided to brazen it out and had determined his line of action: dodge specifics, shout generalities, and, when ideas begin to run out, scream.

"Have you not been guilty of spying for the Comintern?" inquired Yoshikawa.

"No!" roared Sorge, crashing his fist on the table with a force that made everything on it jump. "I am a Nazi! Inform the German Ambassador at once!" He ignored all direct questions with royal contempt. "Has the Japanese Foreign Office informed the German Ambassador of my arrest?" he demanded. "I cannot make any statement unless Ambassador Ott is with me!"[28]

Suddenly he sprang to his feet and paced up and down the room, hands jammed in his pockets, the triangle between his eyebrows sharp with thought. All the while words poured from him in a flood and broke against the walls in a foam of rhetoric. "This arrest will be a reflection on the good relations between Japan and Germany!" he stormed. "I am a correspondent for the *Frankfurter Zeitung* and an information officer in the German Embassy!" Above all, one theme ran through Sorge's tirade: "I am a Nazi!"[29]

Looking Sorge in the eye, Yoshikawa pointed out levelly, "There are also Communists in the German Nazi Party." This home truth flicked Sorge on the raw, and he resumed his pantherish prowling. Calmly appraising his raging foe and not in the least impressed by his histrionics, Yoshikawa packed Sorge off to a cell to be searched and, if possible, cooled off before being sent to Sugamo.[30]

As soon as his cell door clanged shut, Sorge's outraged bellow "AOYAMA!" resounded. No one else would do. One of Sorge's guards besought Aoyama's help to shut up their roaring prisoner. As Aoyama approached the cell, a fascinating sight met his eyes. The guard assigned to search Sorge was cringing at a safe distance, while the prisoner crouched at bay across the cell. It was blindingly clear to Aoyama that the guard would sooner have tried to examine the teeth of a Bengal tiger than search this man with the swinging fists and incandescent eyes.[31]

Several minutes' fast talking on Aoyama's part soothed Sorge to a point at which he agreed to allow the guard to go through with this inevitable formality, but only if Aoyama would stand in front of him as a screen while he undressed. Convinced that Sorge harbored no hidden poison, microfilm, or anything else of interest, the guard departed thankfully. Once more fully clothed and more or less in his right mind, Sorge made ready for the trip to Sugamo. "This is the end," he said before he left his cell. "I shall leave all my possessions to you, Mr. Aoyama. Please discuss this with my lawyer." When Sorge's time came, his will made another disposition of his assets. Probably he intended to charge Aoyama with the care of his worldly goods in his absence. This was the last time the two men saw one another. Not too long thereafter Aoyama was drafted into the army, where he remained throughout Sorge's trial and its grim aftermath.[32]

As soon as the tumult and the shouting had died, Ogata, feeling slightly anticlimactic, went to Sorge's home to follow through on the search. He had no doubt that all three foreigners were Communist spies; the national interest demanded a thorough investigation. He considered that for all of Sorge's bluster the spy knew that he had met his match in Yoshikawa, yet Sorge would be a hard nut to crack, for the man's strong will exhaled from him with every breath. The four agents were still sorting books and emptying file cabinets, so after checking to be sure they had missed nothing, Ogata left the house and went about the ordinary business of the day.[33]

While these dramatic events were taking place, Kawai strolled up to the Ozaki residence for his regular report to his chief. There he found Ms. Ozaki pale and frightened. The grief-stricken lady informed the dismayed and alarmed Kawai that

Ozaki, Miyagi, and Mizuno were in the hands of the Tokko.
She told Kawai that the police had advised her to bring a supply
of warm clothing to the Meguro Station, for her husband's
absence would be prolonged and he did not appear to be in the
best of health. She was preparing a Korean quilted suit for
him.

Kawai expressed his sympathy and shock, then betook
himself off, a badly worried man. With Ozaki, Miyagi, and
Mizuno behind bars, he knew that his days of freedom were
numbered.[34]

That day Ms. Ozaki and Takane consulted with Juso
Miwa, a renowned attorney and friend of Ozaki's, who agreed
to advise them concerning counsel when the case came to trial.
Shin'ichi Matsumoto offered his services too, and became a
sort of ringmaster for Ozaki's defense.[35]

Matsumoto was one of the trouble-prone individuals whom
Ozaki attracted. He was decent enough to be grateful and not
to desert his patron in his hour of need; nevertheless, his record
was not that of the ideal representative for a suspected Communist spy. His long career of close association with the Communist Party had led to three substantial jail sentences. Ozaki
was consistent to the end in his unfortunate choice of associates.

In the days and weeks that followed, Saito went frequently to Sorge's house to search for evidence. There he met
Ama-san, who continued to come to work, as if at a loss to
know what else to do. During one of these encounters she broke
down and begged Saito for the release of her adored employer
and for permission to visit him, weeping with the unabashed
grief of a hurt child. Deeply touched and disturbed, Saito tried
to comfort her but could offer her no hope.[36]

CHAPTER 61

"CLAUSEN'S FATAL ERROR"

Several reasons existed for the hasty removal of the foreigners from the local police stations to a major jail. In the local stations they might possibly communicate with some of their influential friends on the outside. The sooner they were stashed in a maximum security prison, the better. More important, the police at the neighborhood stations at times were none too gentle in their treatment of those coming to their attention. In view of the delicate nature of this case and its international ramifications, Yoshikawa took precautions against physical abuse or undue pressure on his foreign prisoners. "They were too important to leave in local police stations, where they might receive ill treatment," said Yoshikawa. Not that he wasted any sympathy on these three spies, but he did not want their respective embassies beating down the doors of the Foreign Affairs Ministry. At Sugamo they would be both isolated and safe.[1]

For the first day following the arrest of the three foreigners Suzuki had no luck in securing a confession from Voukelitch. Although somewhat nervous, he took refuge in a mask of aloof arrogance. He sniffed contemptuously at all questions, bluntly denied everything, and attempted to play down the entire matter.

However, before long Suzuki obtained results by one of the oldest tricks in the book. He persuaded Voukelitch that Sorge had already confessed. This depressed Voukelitch, who began to tell his story bit by bit. They progressed at a snail's pace. Before answering any query, Voukelitch would ask pa-

thetically, "Has Sorge told you this?" He would not reply until
Suzuki once more patiently, although at first mendaciously,
confirmed that Sorge had indeed told everything.

Thoughts of his wife and little Yo obsessed him. He
required constant reassurance about their health and well-being.[2]
Soon, however, he was in direct touch with Yoshiko, who
wrote to him daily in English, letters that later were translated
into Japanese. In a rather pathetic gesture toward sharing his
deprivations, she gave up drinking tea for the duration of his
imprisonment.[3]

After many weeks of questioning, Voukelitch talked fairly
freely, but at this early stage he parted with every scrap of
information with the reluctance of a miser adding another item
to his income tax return. In the meantime, his feet were cold.
Prisoners in Japanese cells were forbidden socks and stockings
in case they used them to hide sharp instruments such as razor
blades or even to hang themselves. In the chill of Sugamo
Voukelitch suffered so miserably that Suzuki took pity on him
and arranged a special dispensation for him to wear socks, for
which Voukelitch was duly grateful.[4]

The question that the police might have tortured Voukelitch to obtain his confession has been raised.[5] There is no
evidence to support this claim beyond the undeniable fact that
in this period of history Japanese police did resort to torture
all too often. But in the case of the Sorge ring principals, very
good reasons existed why this should not be so. For one, these
men had powerful friends in high places, and a misstep might
have caused a very nasty diplomatic incident.[6]

Eventually Voukelitch was bound to talk, for he was an
incorrigible chatterbox. Possibly the most convincing indication
of lack of undue duress is the cordial relationship that developed
between him and his investigators and prosecutors. Suzuki became very attached to this man, with whom he talked through
an interpreter of French. He found his prisoner not too robust
physically, a man gentle of face and personality. Suzuki's liking
did not rise to the level of admiration. In his eyes there could
be no comparison between Sorge and Voukelitch. "Sorge was
topflight, Voukelitch second-rate." Voukelitch lacked ambition
and fire and seemed to be lukewarm in his convictions. Certainly he did not strike Suzuki as being a strong Communist.[7]

With Ken Fuse, the chief prosecutor assigned to him, Voukelitch was rather more open. Although quiet, he allowed his natural mischief and sense of humor to come through. And Fuse noted that at times his usually gentle eyes could turn very sharp and penetrating. Nevertheless, Fuse agreed with Suzuki that Voukelitch was not in the same class as Sorge.[8]

Both Suzuki and Fuse became respectful admirers of Ms. Voukelitch, whom they obviously considered a good cut above her husband, and not just on racial grounds. Her deep love for and steadfast devotion to him touched and impressed them. Throughout the ensuing years Fuse and Ms. Voukelitch remained close friends;[9] that would scarcely have been the case had he been a party to torturing the husband whose memory she cherished.

For his part Voukelitch seemed glad to leave his cold cell for a warm interrogation room, where Suzuki had cigarettes and sometimes hot soup for him. Questioning took place in a mixture of languages, principally French via an interpreter, with side excursions into Japanese and English.[10] Voukelitch spoke nine languages more or less well: French, German, English, Spanish, Japanese, Russian, Serbian, and Italian in addition to his native Croatian. German and English were his best foreign tongues, so later in his interrogation the authorities agreed that, while his Japanese was good, he should write his testimony in English, which was then translated into Japanese to avoid any possibility of misunderstanding the oral questioning.[11]

Indicative of the secrecy with which the Japanese conducted the Sorge matter is the fact that neither Suzuki nor Fuse knew just what sort of case he was working on, although each was entrusted with the interrogation of a key suspect. The police were surprised when Voukelitch confessed to spying for the Comintern, having gained the impression that Voukelitch worked for either the Germans or the Americans.[12]

The material confiscated from his house included two cameras, a copying camera, four lenses—one of them a high-speed telescopic—and a complete set of films, plates, and other photographic paraphernalia. The police found even more intriguing a copy of the 1935 *German Statistical Yearbook*, which later proved to be the ring's code book. Clausen had the master copy. The haul also dredged up five diaries, which contained some highly interesting entries of contacts with other agents. An empty electric phonograph cabinet presented a puzzle, which was solved when Clausen identified it as having contained Wendt's shortwave set, now at the bottom of Yamanaka Lake.[13]

While Suzuki and Fuse put Voukelitch through his paces, Taiji Hasebe did the same with Clausen. Clausen likewise refused to talk on October 19, and what little he said revealed few, if any, items of interest. Tonekichi Horie, chief of the Asian subsection of the Tokko, participated in this questioning, which took place at a long conference table in a large interrogation room. Conversation was in English, which Clausen spoke fairly well. His inquisitors told him that they already knew the whole story, that both Miyagi and Ozaki had confessed. Although uneasy and nervous, he denied everything. "I know nothing," he repeated sullenly. "To every question put to Clausen concerning any of his activities," said Hasebe, "his answer was always no."[14]

Clausen did not impress his interrogators as the stuff of which heroes are made, although he was a fine man, friendly and easygoing. "He was a good person but not a big person," said Ogata. By this time Clausen was upset, almost distraught.[15] In view of his obvious agitation Hasebe and his associates were sure that eventually he would break down, so they returned to the questioning with renewed vigor. They knew his denials were lies and told him so in no uncertain terms, but he still maintained his stubborn silence. The session continued until 10:00 P.M. By then the police were too tired to ask any more questions, and as Hasebe remarked rather grimly, "Clausen was even more exhausted than we were."[16]

He was indeed worn-out, crushed beneath a burden of long-standing unrest, sleeplessness, and questioning. In view of the state of his health and his disaffection over the preceding months, the wonder is that he did not confess considerably before he did. But he had one overriding motive for stiffening his spine: protecting his wife, who was still free.

The next day, October 20, three occurrences worked together to crack Clausen wide open. First and foremost, Hasebe told him that Anna was in the special women's section of Sugamo. "This disturbed Clausen very much," said Hasebe, "and he broke down and cried when he heard his wife was in prison." Hasebe seems truly to have thought that Anna had been jailed, but the police did not pick her up until November 19. This assertion had the desired effect. Frantically Clausen begged his captors to let Anna go because she had nothing to do with his work. "It was a flagrant lie," said Hasebe, and severely taxed him with tampering with the truth. He told him that they knew Ms. Clausen had acted as a secret courier between Tokyo and Shanghai.[17]

His interrogators also told him that Voukelitch had confessed, so there was no point in remaining stubborn. Although the news of Anna's arrest almost crushed Clausen's spirit, and the reported breakdown of Voukelitch shook his resolution, he might have remained a much less fertile source of information had not the police translators begun to crank out Japanese transcripts of the messages removed from his home.[18] One of these was a manuscript in English of ten typewritten pages plus two pages in pencil. The searchers also came up with two writing pads full of codes and no fewer than ten diaries, which contained incriminating entries about various liaison contacts.[19]

Ogata stayed up all night reading this material. The more he read, the more surprised he became. Among other items he found detailed information concerning the Japanese-American conversations in Washington. At the time these were so highly classified that Ogata knew nothing at all about them. Now he learned of these secret talks for the first time from a Japanese translation of a document written in English by a German for transmission to the Soviet Union. Ogata's eyes popped, and he began to see the overwhelming importance of this case. Among the messages the police found some $800 in American money, a suspicious item to be discovered in the possession of a German merchant in Tokyo.[20]

Hasebe and Ogata agreed that Clausen's big mistake was hanging on to these documents after they had served their purpose, as well as keeping untransmitted messages about in plain sight. "That was Clausen's fatal error," said Ogata. He should have obeyed his impulse to destroy all his papers and bury his set that night of October 17, when he prowled his home in an agony of indecision. Confronted with this concrete evidence and demoralized by his fears for Anna, he began to talk. On only one item did he hold his peace. Soon discovering from their line of questioning that the police had not broken his code, he refused to help them break it.[21]

Within a few days, however, the Japanese forged the final link in the chain of evidence. Yoshikawa, Ogata, and a code specialist went to Clausen's house and searched among the books on his shelves. Three volumes of the *German Statistical Yearbook*, one each for 1934, 1935, and 1936, rewarded their search. Pointing to one black with use, the code man said confidently, "This is the code book."[22] Clausen had employed "The Purloined Letter" technique but spoiled his cleverness by using one copy of the book until its grimy state betrayed his secret.

Armed with the code book, Ogata set his cryptographers to work, and Hasebe went back to Clausen. About a week after his first confession he gave in and explained how the code worked. This solved the problem that had long maddened the Japanese Communications Ministry, which now had the key to that fat collection of mysterious messages known as Dal X.[23]

Next the police brought up the matter of "Clausen's machine," as Yoshikawa called the transmitter, which so far had baffled their best efforts to operate. "We Japanese had tried to reach Harbin with it," said Yoshikawa, "but we had no luck. But once we called Clausen in, he made a few rapid adjustments, turned a few knobs, and he got Harbin in about a minute."[24]

With no further reason to maintain silence, Clausen, like Miyagi before him, seemed eager to tell as much as possible and get it off his mind. All his long-pent-up resentment of Sorge broke in the open. He set about writing a detailed confession. Because the police had only one interpreter of German at this time, and he was having troubles of his own with Sorge, they questioned Clausen in English, and he wrote in that language. Although his interrogators found Clausen's spoken English not as fluent as Sorge's, his written effort is amazingly good—direct, simply expressed, and with no effort to camouflage all his own trials and fears.[25]

Years later the German magazine *Der Spiegel* flatly averred, "His confession is less remarkable for its contents than for the fact that the Japanese created parts of it themselves. From a chunky blockhead like Klausen [sic] one would never have gotten coherent sentences. . . ."[26] Blacksmith's apprentice, merchant seaman, mechanic—Clausen was no intellectual. But he had made himself master of a highly technical craft; had won his way back to acceptance after exile in the Volga Republic; had taught himself Russian, English, and Japanese; was Sorge's personal choice as his colleague in Tokyo; and had built up a cover into a successful business. Chunky, yes; blockhead, no. Clausen was quite capable of writing his own confession, and there is no real reason to believe he did not do so.

According to one account, Sorge was "most contemptuous" when he learned Clausen had become an "informant" and volunteered the opinion that even if Clausen "escaped the noose in Japan if he ever got back to the U.S.S.R. he would be taken care of. . . ."[27] As matters turned out, this prognostication held more irony than prophecy.

One of Clausen's early admissions gave the prosecution a pretty problem. He stated that the ring was part of the Intelligence Section of the Red Army, whereas Miyagi and Ozaki, while admitting their headquarters was in Moscow, claimed to be working for the Comintern.[28] Of course, each told the truth as he saw it. Ozaki knew only what Sorge had chosen to tell him. Miyagi and Voukelitch had been told just what their local Communist parties wanted them to believe. However, Clausen could not be thus gulled, for he belonged to the Red Army and had embarked on the venture directly from Fourth Department headquarters in Moscow. All the members of the ring understood quite well that by whatever name they called it, they worked for the Soviet Union, so from that angle the point is academic.

But to the procurator's office and the Tokko the question had a very practical application. Both diplomatic and legal reasons existed for handling the Sorge case as a Comintern matter. The last thing on earth Tokyo wanted at that time was trouble with Moscow. By maintaining the fiction that the Comintern had no connection with the Soviet government and that the Sorge ring was a Comintern *apparat,* the Japanese forestalled any possible attempt by the Russians on behalf of their devoted servants and gave them no excuse for official protests.

Then, too, the tried-and-true Peace Preservation Law was

in effect an anti-Comintern statute, aimed at the Japanese Communist Party and so-called international groups working against the "national polity." Under this law sentences were comparatively light, but conviction was virtually certain. The new National Defense Security Law, promulgated to protect state secrets, was relatively untested. Loopholes in it might appear under pressure, and moreover, it fell within the purview of the War Ministry. The Justice Ministry would have been superhuman had it viewed with pleasure the prospect of having its case, so painstakingly worked out, taken out of the hands of the procurator's office and the Tokko to the greater glory of the War Ministry and the Kempeitai. All these things considered, it is no wonder that throughout the case Clausen's claim to be working for the Red Army was blandly ignored.[29]

So far Sorge had said nothing about his allegiance or anything else of practical interest. Days went by with nothing from him but one denial after another. Yoshikawa became grimmer with each passing day, for as he had expected, he and his colleagues were under extreme pressure to produce a confession from the ring's chieftain.[30]

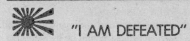

CHAPTER 62

"I AM DEFEATED"

As the Japanese had anticipated, Sorge's arrest produced strong reactions in the German Embassy. The general assumption was that it was "a typical case of Japanese espionage hysteria" or perhaps "an act of revenge as Sorge had always been very critical of the government." Representatives of the German press brought to the embassy "a declaration signed by all of them attesting to Sorge's human and political reliability." Local Nazis as well as Meisinger protested "the obvious blunder of the overzealous Japanese secret police."[1]

No one was more upset than the ambassador and his wife. Ms. Ott was furious, and her husband was convinced that the police had made a terrible mistake.[2] Indeed, he sent to Berlin a sketchy report of the arrests of Sorge and Clausen, indicating that the Japanese had given him little information, the investigation still being in progress. He expressed his belief that this affair was a setup designed to embarrass the ex-prime minister by implying that a Japanese adviser to Konoye had been leaking material about the United States-Japanese talks.[3]

Ott also promptly issued a formal protest to the Japanese Foreign Office. Along with it, through proper government channels, he sent "a strong demand" to see Sorge. The Foreign Office carried this hot potato straight to Tojo himself. Tojo hastily dumped it on Minister of Justice Iwamura, who tossed it down the line to Supreme Prosecutor Hiromasa Matsuzaka. Naturally Matsuzaka bucked it down to Yoshikawa, who had been expecting this development and knew that he had to handle it. The army, firmly in the saddle with Tojo as premier, kept

a wary eye on these events, and Yoshikawa would not have
been surprised to find that Ott's protest had slid along so rapidly
because of army grease on the official rails.[4]

   Yoshikawa had expected that as soon as Sorge was clapped
behind bars, an official German protest would be forthcoming,
and he felt confident that sooner or later he could produce a
case the Germans would have to accept. But with Ott demanding to see Sorge, it was no longer a matter of sooner or
later; it had to be sooner. Ott might raise such an official stink
that Tojo would have to call off the investigation to placate his
Nazi allies. Yoshikawa could not fend off Ott for more than a
week at the outside limit; therefore, he had to secure an admission of guilt from Sorge within the next few days.[5]

   Moreover, Yoshikawa needed the truth from Sorge to
clarify the whole puzzling business. The stories of the other
members of the ring contained certain discrepancies which only
Sorge could resolve. And Yoshikawa still had a nagging fear
at the back of his mind that Sorge was playing a double game.
"If I cannot get the real truth from Sorge, then I cannot get
the real story of the ring, and there will always be this question
in my mind: Is Sorge a double agent?" Thus Yoshikawa brooded.[6]

   Sorge was not yet agreeable to smoothing Yoshikawa's
path for him. Although physically far below par and in a state
of nervous excitement, he summoned up his strong will and
incisive brain for a duel to the death. He was much too clever
to pretend that he had not been collecting information, but he
denied that he had done so on behalf of the Soviet Union. He
was working for Ott, whom he frequently asked to see. "He
apparently hoped that Ott would come to his rescue if he delayed
his confession," stated Tamazawa.[7]

   With shrewd psychology Sorge attempted to put his ad-
versaries on the defense. He complained that the police interpreter's German was so poor that he could not be sure he
understood the questions or that the police understood his answers. But neither Yoshikawa nor Ohashi was a newcomer at
this game. They simply switched to English and kept right after
him, boring in relentlessly. When one questioner tired, another
one, fresh and eager, took up the interrogation.[8]

   Meanwhile, Ohashi cracked down on his assistants to
complete translating and studying the documents found in Sorge's

home. Every evening, when he had finished questioning the prisoner, he hurried back to Tokko headquarters to work with them on the documents. Ohashi noted that some of the items had no apparent connection with Sorge's work for either the *Frankfurter Zeitung* or the German Embassy. In fact, they looked suspiciously like the code material found in Clausen's home; even the paper appeared to be the same. These interesting documents included seven pages of reports and charts in English, which later proved to have originated with Ozaki and Miyagi, and two pages of typewritten drafts in English. Sorge's home also yielded two volumes of the *German Statistical Yearbook*, a copy each for 1932 and 1935, which by now looked to the Tokko like old friends. The 1935 volume was the one currently in use as a code book for the ring. By the third day of questioning these and other items had connected Sorge with Clausen. Even confronted with this evidence, Sorge maintained his innocence and demanded permission to see Ott.[9]

In stepping up their investigation, inevitably the Tokko came across the name of Kawai. On October 22, at about 10:45 A.M., the blow fell. Kawai was in his office, leisurely reading a newspaper and sipping tea, when a messenger boy came in to announce that a Mr. Makino wanted to see him. Inasmuch as Kawai knew no one of that name, he jumped to the conclusion that the visitor was a policeman. For once a jumped-to conclusion was correct.

Resigned to his fate, Kawai opened the office door and stood face-to-face with Kenji Omata, whom he recognized as the Tokko agent who had been trailing him for almost a year. Two other policemen who had been hidden behind the door pounced on Kawai and tied-him up with a rope; then they marched him to the nearby Nishiki Chu Police Station. There Kawai suffered no brutality, but after assuring him that they knew all about him, the police left him alone in a cell for three days before they got around to questioning him. Knowing that Ozaki and Miyagi were already in custody, Kawai saw no point in trying to brazen it out.[10] Actually he had little of importance to tell about the Tokyo ring's activities that the police did not already know or were in the process of finding out.

On October 24 Ohashi set about preparations for his usual questioning of Sorge. This was the sixth day since Sorge's arrest, and Ohashi felt acutely his responsibility to obtain a confession. Yoshikawa could not put Ott off much longer without direct insult. Moreover, the accumulated material evidence plus the confessions of the other major members of the ring made further resistance on Sorge's part less heroic than futile.

So Ohashi was in no mood for more nonsense when he met with Sorge, along with two interpreters and a policeman rather late in the afternoon. Since fuel shortages did not allow extra comforts for prisoners, Ohashi brought along some of his own charcoal to burn in a brazier to take the chill out of the air. The two men sparred verbally for a short time, a routine which in less tension-ridden circumstances both would have rather enjoyed. Then Ohashi put it to Sorge squarely: They had the goods on him, his confederates had already confessed, so why not admit like a man that he had been spying? "You have engaged in spying activities," Ohashi told Sorge. "Your answer must be yes."

And to Ohashi's surprise, Sorge said just that: "Yes."

Feeling like a man who has been tugging at an obstinate doorknob that has suddenly given way, Ohashi continued, "You have been active for the Comintern?"

Once more Sorge replied, "Yes." Delighted with his success, Ohashi told Sorge that he would question him at length the next day and brought the interrogation to an end. The hour was already late, and Ohashi did not want to push his luck too far.[11]

Yoshikawa awoke the next morning unrefreshed. He could look back over a grueling week. His normal stream of work continued unabated; he had spent many hours in Sugamo and elsewhere in Tokyo on the Sorge case; the German ambassador was breathing down his neck. Surely he was entitled to a weekend of rest. Yet an intuition, a nagging sense of something left undone, drove him on. "I did not wish to question Sorge anymore that week," said Yoshikawa, "and yet for some reason I went out to Sugamo. Perhaps this would be the day, I thought." So he asked his boss if he would care to accompany him to the prison. Although it was Saturday, Tamazawa readily agreed.[12]

Ohashi was already with Sorge at Sugamo when the two prosecutors arrived. He and Sorge were chatting casually over their morning tea when Yoshikawa, Tamazawa, Nakamura, Ogata, and Tatsuji Yamaura of the Tokko's Foreign Section walked in. Because the room was small, only Sorge, Yoshikawa, Nakamura, and Tamazawa could be seated. Ohashi yielded his chair, and the others present also stood up. Thus for the first time Tamazawa saw Sorge. His impression was of a man "very polite, very well brought up." Sorge rose to his feet when the group entered, bowed courteously, and resumed his seat. Yoshikawa handled the interrogation and started off by addressing the prisoner almost genially. "Sorge-san, don't you think it is about time that you should confess? How about telling the truth today?"

Sorge returned to his position of unequivocal denial,[13] as though his confession to Ohashi had been a dream. Perhaps it seemed dreamlike to him; prolonged sleeplessness and tension can bring a man to the point at which the line between reality and unreality is ill-defined indeed. Possibly he had repented of his weakness the preceding day and decided to continue the battle. Evidently the Japanese wanted his confession urgently, so why not drag his heels a little longer?

Abandoning his coaxing, Yoshikawa spoke to Sorge firmly and directly in a mixture of broken English and German. "All your colleagues have confessed," he said. "We have your radio, your codes, and we know everything about you. In order to lessen the sentence on your assistants and on yourself, don't you think it is time for you to confess?"

For an instant the duel continued silently, Sorge's blue eyes clashing with Yoshikawa's brown ones. Slowly Sorge seemed to sense a change in atmosphere, for blood surged into his face and his body stiffened. His expression serious and intent, suddenly he said to Yoshikawa, "Give me a piece of paper and pencil."[14]

Surprised, Yoshikawa handed over pencil and paper. Sorge gripped the pencil and slowly, laboriously, like a child carefully spelling out his first sentence, wrote a few words on the sheet of paper. Then he picked it up and tossed it defiantly at the prosecutor. Yoshikawa read a sentence in German: "I have been an international Communist since 1925." Yoshikawa looked across at Sorge. "You have been spying for the Comintern," he stated more than asked.

Abruptly Sorge sprang from his chair, drew himself up
as if to attention, pulled off his coat, slammed it on the floor,
and began pacing back and forth, hands in pockets. He whirled
to face Yoshikawa. "Indeed, I am a Communist and have been
doing espionage. I am defeated!" he shouted despairingly. "I
have never been defeated since I became an international Communist. But now I am beaten by the Japanese police."[15]

Every eye in the room followed Sorge. Then, as abruptly
as he had risen, he dropped into his chair, buried his face in
his hands, and wept bitterly. The Japanese avoided one another's glances, deeply embarrassed and discomfited at the sight
of a man's tears. "It was obvious that he was emotionally very
disturbed," said Yoshikawa. "The atmosphere in the room
was very tense, and we were all surprised and aghast at Sorge's
behavior. He completely broke down before us. He was a
pathetic picture of a caught, defeated, and emotionally defeated
person."[16]

Eager as Yoshikawa was to get to the bottom of Sorge's
espionage activities as rapidly as possible, he could not bring
himself to badger this broken fellow creature anymore that day.
Sorge was exhausted emotionally and physically. Lifting to
Yoshikawa a face drained of all defiance, he told the prosecutor
that he had had not one wink of sleep for a week and was very
tired. "I will confess everything if I can have a rest," he said
dully.

"You may have a long sleep over the weekend, and then
we will begin our work on Monday," Yoshikawa promised.
"I want to know whether you worked for the Comintern or the
Soviet government."

Sorge nodded. "Very well, I understand," he replied.
A flash of his old spirit gleamed for a second in his bloodshot
eyes. "I want to confess to you and not to the police," he told
Yoshikawa. It was a gesture between equals, the refusal of a
fighter to surrender his sword to a lesser being than himself.[17]

This arrangement suited Yoshikawa. He explained to
Sorge that the police would question him on Monday morning
about the general details of his life, but in the afternoon he
himself would come. At that time he and Sorge would talk
over the political aspects of his work and his relationship with
the Soviet Union.

The turn of events relieved Yoshikawa tremendously. No longer need he fear repercussions from either his own government or the Germans. "I was over the first obstacle," said Yoshikawa. "I had Sorge's confession."[18]

Some have read sinister implications into Sorge's breakdown only one week after his arrest. This school of thought cannot believe that he would have yielded so soon unless he were subjected to the most brutal force. Some have patronized General Willoughby for backing up with sworn affidavits from police officers and prosecutors who worked on the case his contention that Sorge was not tortured.[19] Affidavits are better evidence than none at all; however, such questioning was understandable in view of the hideous record of Japanese atrocities during World War II. But the Sorge case was something far out of the ordinary. Sorge's own defense attorney, Sumitsugu Asanuma, a man of the highest probity who held his client in great affection and esteem, stated emphatically that Sorge was handled with extreme care. "Normally Japanese prisoners are treated much more roughly and carelessly," said Asanuma. "The treatment of Sorge is unheard-of and unseen in Japan."[20]

Aside from the political considerations that made torture taboo, maltreatment of Sorge was unnecessary. This was not a case of beating a confession out of a prisoner for want of solid evidence. The Japanese authorities already possessed an abundance of material evidence. No collaborator of any importance requiring Sorge's protection remained at large, and those arrested were telling their own stories. He had brought his espionage mission to a successful close. In Yoshikawa's opinion, such practical considerations were behind Sorge's confession.[21]

Ohashi disclaimed any credit for Sorge's admission of espionage. Sorge had no feeling of guilt; he was very proud of his exploits. So as Ohashi saw it, his role was not to break down a suspect in the usual sense of the term; it was a case of persuading Sorge to talk as at heart he wanted to do and of being on hand to record the flood when the dam broke.[22]

Physically and psychologically Sorge was in no condition to withstand a siege. A reputable life insurance firm would hardly have cared to take out a policy on Sorge in October 1941. A combination of too much alcohol, too much heavy food, and extreme tension in working conditions without any counterbalancing factor—this is the classic pattern preceding sudden collapse as a man nears the half-century mark.

Throughout October, prior to his arrest, Sorge had been so ill that Miyagi thought he should be hospitalized, and on at least one occasion Clausen found a nurse from the German Embassy on duty in Sorge's house.[23] There can be no doubt that he was an exceedingly heavy drinker, and with his arrest, perforce he quit cold turkey. At the very least this circumstance alone must have left him in an unenviable state of nerves.

Emotionally, too, Sorge was ripe for a breakdown. His pattern of crying spells in these last months and years of his life, his morbid preoccupation with death, his maudlin outbursts to Hanako, his near collapse early in October, his unprofessional slipups in care and memory—all point to a man on the verge of losing control of himself.

Furthermore, Sorge's ego had always been outsized. To a man so supremely confident, discovery and arrest must have come as a shattering experience. With this shock more than likely would have come an enormous need for reassurance, to convince himself and his captors that he occupied a very special place in the world. As long as he had been master of his fate, he had been content to gloat over his secret, like a collector who has purchased a stolen masterpiece. Now the Tokko had discovered his hidden treasure, dealing a tremendous blow to his sense of privacy and his self-esteem. All things considered, there is little room for astonishment that by the end of a week Sorge was ready to call it quits.

Before Yoshikawa left that Saturday, the prosecutor had one more obstacle to overcome. He had to arrange for the meeting between Sorge and Ott that Ott was demanding insistently. At first Sorge refused to cooperate. "No," he told Yoshikawa. "I do not want to meet the ambassador. As a foreign correspondent and as a German I am his friend. But politically we are on opposite sides of the fence. I have betrayed the ambassador, and therefore, I do not want to see him."[24] For eight years Sorge had betrayed Ott without a qualm. Now he had been caught and had to face his friend no longer the master of the situation but a defeated prisoner. Sorge's ego, not his conscience, recoiled from looking Ott in the eye.

Yoshikawa took exception to Sorge's stand. "You may

be politically of different minds," he said, "yet you ought to say good-bye to him as a friend." Sorge thought this over for a few minutes, then reluctantly agreed to the meeting. With that, Yoshikawa permitted the prisoner to return to his cell and to long hours of urgently needed sleep.

Yoshikawa reported to Matsuzaka that a meeting between Ott and Sorge was now in order, and arrangements were made for early the following week.[25] Yoshikawa stipulated that all questions Ott intended to put to Sorge be submitted in advance and translated into Japanese, so that his office would have a complete, accurate record of the meeting. He further requested that Ott not discuss the espionage angle with Sorge and that he ask no new questions until Sorge had answered the previous one. Yoshikawa did not inform Ott that Sorge had confessed. The prosecutor did not believe in parting with information unnecessarily.[26]

Ott agreed to Yoshikawa's conditions. On the appointed day he drove to Sugamo, accompanied by a large, impressive retinue of associates. Yoshikawa, Tamazawa, Nakamura, Ohashi, and several others lined up on the Japanese side. The ambassador presented the perfect model of a high-ranking German who has been affronted. "Ott was proud, stern, angry, and very serious as he walked into the big conference room," recalled Yoshikawa. When the Germans had taken their seats and all was in readiness, his captors ushered in Sorge. "When Sorge walked in, he had a very pained expression on his face," said Yoshikawa. "He sat down; he and Ott looked intently at one another, and then the questions began."[27]

The conversation was stiff and stilted as Ott asked the group of prepared questions already agreed upon. The give-and-take went somewhat as follows:

OTT: How are you?
SORGE: I am well.
OTT: How is the food you are receiving?
SORGE: It is satisfactory.
OTT: Are you being well treated?
SORGE: Yes, I am.

The exchange floundered along in this heavy, monotonous fashion for about ten minutes. Then Ott reached the end of his prepared questions. Fixing Sorge with a look of the utmost interest, the ambassador asked his friend if he had anything to say to him.

For a moment of strained silence Sorge returned Ott's regard, a somber, foreboding expression on his face. In a voice low and solemn but clearly audible he replied, "Mr. Ambassador, this is our final farewell."[28]

Ott and his entire entourage sat as if turned to stone. "When Sorge uttered these words," reminisced Yoshikawa, "Ott's face suddenly became pale and weak. It seemed to me as though he had now for the first time caught the true meaning of things and that he understood the significance of Sorge's words *final farewell*. Sorge's words provided an emotional and dramatic climax to their close friendship."[29]

To the best of our knowledge, Ott left no record of his thoughts on that poignant occasion, but one can imagine some degree of his sorrow and sense of loss. With Sorge at his side tendering advice and support, he had risen from assistant military attaché to ambassador to one of the world's great powers. Who knows to what heights this extraordinary team might have climbed in time? Ott and Sorge had matched wits in many a game of chess, had clinked many a convivial glass together after hammering out dispatches and discussing the military and political situation. Now Ott realized that it all had been built on quicksand, that Sorge had been using him for his own purposes. And if Sorge was false, what man was true? To whom could he ever turn again in friendship and trust?

Perhaps it was to rid himself of this unbearable psychological burden that in 1959 Ott defended Sorge in a rare interview. "No, it is impossible, I still don't believe that he was a spy," Ott is quoted as saying. Later in the same interview he added, "Of course, perhaps he played a double game, but that is nothing beside the calumnies that have been written about him!"[30]

Possibly upon reflection Ott convinced himself that Sorge had indeed been a superagent of some sort for Germany, that he played a double game for the benefit of Germany and allowed himself to be convicted as a Soviet spy out of duty and patriotism. But if any secret understanding flashed between the two men in that last long look they exchanged, any unspoken instruction to say nothing, to keep up the game, it escaped the closely watching eyes of the Japanese present on that October day in 1941.

The silence grew until it threatened to burst the walls of the room. Yoshikawa rose to the occasion. "Quickly I realized that I should not keep Sorge there any longer," he said. "So I asked that he be taken back to his cell. He rose quietly from his chair, made a slight bow to the ambassador, and walked slowly out of the room."

As the door closed behind him, the atmosphere returned to normal. Ott's entire attitude had changed. He strode up to Yoshikawa and thanked him for his kindness and cooperation. "For the good of our two countries, investigate this case thoroughly," he said earnestly. "Get to the bottom of it!"[31]

CHAPTER 63

"A HARD WORKER EVEN IN PRISON"

Following his confession and final encounter with Ott, Sorge snapped back into his usual self-confident form. Like Napoleon at Elba, he set about becoming master of his little realm, and he succeeded to an astonishing extent. He turned the full force of his magnetism on Ohashi and Yoshikawa. Both men became his warm admirers. Once over the hurdle of confession, he appears to have enjoyed his many sessions with them. At first the police, particularly Ohashi, questioned him in the morning, and Yoshikawa took over in the afternoon. When the police investigation ended in the spring of 1942, Yoshikawa met with him both morning and afternoon.[1]

Yoshikawa talked with Sorge about fifty times over a period of four months, all lengthy sessions ranging from early afternoon until as late as 10:00 P.M. Some of these conferences took the nature of lectures by Sorge on a variety of subjects: international communism; nazism; geopolitics and Haushofer; China. The Russo-German war particularly concerned him, and he went into considerable detail in his description of just how he would fight the war if he were in charge of the Soviet military establishment. Apparently he had no doubt that he was capable of running the entire Russian war effort.

Hearing expositions of these subjects from the viewpoint of an intelligent European interested and impressed Yoshikawa. "Sorge had the gifts of a great teacher," he explained. "He had a very sharp intellect, and he was a hard worker even in prison. He also had a good sense of humor." Sorge did not hesitate to tell the procurator that he believed Japan would be defeated eventually. He wanted to publish a prison newspaper explaining the modern history of Japan. Also, he had been working on a book when arrested, and the authorities allowed him to have boxes of manuscripts and notes on Japanese history with him in his cell.[2]

Sorge's association with the German Embassy fascinated Yoshikawa. It was a great lesson for him and for the Japanese in general how Sorge, a civilian, could get so close to the ambassador and acquire such a position of influence. "Generally speaking," said Yoshikawa, "the Germans are so stiff, detached, and guarded. How then could Sorge move in the way he did?"

Sorge told Yoshikawa that he never forgot that as a Caucasian his color, features, and height made it very difficult to work as a spy in Japan. But, he added, "Japan is like a crab. Its outside has a hard, durable surface, but once you get on the inside, it is soft. And if you arrive at that point, it is easy to get information."

Yoshikawa made no effort to work on Sorge's political convictions. The prisoner was a Communist through and through, and the procurator preferred to gather whatever facts he could from Sorge without engaging in any ideological arguments. He also liked and admired the prisoner as a person. "Sorge had a wonderful personality," said Yoshikawa. "He was open and warmhearted."[3]

Indeed, one cannot escape the impression that at the time Yoshikawa was more deeply under the influence of Sorge's hypnotic charm than he realized. For instance, Ohashi and Yoshikawa entered into an agreement with him not to discuss the various women in his Tokyo life, who numbered at least thirty. In particular, Sorge gave his word that Hanako had had no part in his espionage activities. The authorities had no interest in probing Sorge's personal life as such, so they let her alone. It speaks volumes for Sorge's personality that these men of intelligence and integrity unquestioningly accepted the word of a confessed spy. Both put this stipulation down to an admirable chivalry on Sorge's part.[4]

Nevertheless, from the practical point of view, as a result of this omission an entire field of Sorge's career in Tokyo remained unplowed.

One comment of Yoshikawa's is revealing both of Sorge and of the procurator's admiration for him. "In all the time he was in prison, he never said a bad word about his colleagues," said Yoshikawa. "They betrayed him, but he never mentioned the fact."[5] Of course, Sorge did quite a bit of talking on his own and betrayed his colleagues no less than they him.

Sorge evolved a special technique for dealing with Miyagi and Voukelitch in his testimony. If the interrogator put a question concerning their evidence in sufficiently generalized terms so as to indicate that the authorities were fishing for information, Sorge either replied, "I do not remember," or answered in terms as nebulous as the question. Yet if the query was direct and specific, obviously based on definite information received from Miyagi or Voukelitch, Sorge remembered the incident very well but denigrated its accuracy or importance.

Needless to say, Yoshikawa was not so hypnotized that he forgot his principal duty, which was to pry a complete confession out of the prisoner. As Sorge's defense attorney acknowledged, in brainpower the spy had met his match, for Asanuma considered Yoshikawa one of the most brilliant men in Japan.[6] Yoshikawa used the judo trick of letting Sorge's own weight throw him.

Sorge stuck his neck out by offering "to prepare and submit a statement on the general outline of his espionage activities."[7] The suggestion was natural enough. He was a professional writer and could express himself more clearly on paper than orally. This gave Yoshikawa exactly the handle he needed. He anticipated that Sorge would not be able to resist the temptation to spell out to an admiring world just how clever he had been. So Yoshikawa arranged for Sorge's own typewriter, confiscated as evidence, to be placed in his cell. Sorge's first efforts were too ambiguous for the procurator to swallow, so he told him to go into greater detail. Sorge fell to with a will, busily weaving his own rope. During the trial the prosecution kept this opus at its elbow, and as Sorge could not help admitting what he had freely written, the trial went remarkably smoothly.[8] Asanuma admitted ruefully that "without this product of Yoshikawa's inspiration, Sorge would have and could have denied some of the charges put up against him."

A short, plump, and youthful-looking man with a jolly

round face, Asanuma became Sorge's counsel obliquely.[9] Because of the importance of the case, the Ministry of Justice was extremely careful that no lost cause specialist or inexperienced young law graduate be involved in it.[10] In January 1942 Asanuma had been selected the custodian of Sorge's property "because his landlord was threatening to attach it as a result of his failure to pay the rent since his arrest in 1941." Sorge and Asanuma hit it off at once. Somehow the Clausens and Voukelitch found that Sorge's affairs were in the hands of a reputable lawyer who spoke excellent German, so they asked that Asanuma act in a similar capacity for them. Somewhat to his own surprise Asanuma found himself property custodian for the major members of the notorious spy ring.

Sorge requested Asanuma as his defense counsel, so the lawyer was in Sorge's employ; he was not an appointee of the Ministry of Justice. He came to be greatly impressed with Sorge and charged him only a token fee.[11] Yoshikawa was happy to confirm the appointment, for Asanuma met all his specifications—namely, a lawyer "well known for his fairness, his fine principles, and, of course, with absolutely no connection with the leftists."[12]

In the early stages Asanuma could see Sorge only about once a week for five-minute periods, a guard watching them, all conversations to be in Japanese. Because Sorge needed time to grope through his Japanese vocabulary, they could not transact much business in five minutes. Asanuma obtained special permission from Yoshikawa to mix some German in their conversations, and from that point the pace stepped up. Sorge seemed to be starving for news of the outside world, especially of the European war, and spent a good deal of their strictly rationed moments together pumping Asanuma about progress of the conflict.[13]

He also obtained war news through the prison underground. Certain trusties and prisoners with light sentences were assigned jobs such as cleaning prison offices. In emptying wastebaskets and straightening out desktops, they had access to newspapers. To their fellow prisoners they whispered bits of information thus obtained. A prison shop sold books and magazines, such as the *Economist*. All these were heavily censored and even had some pages torn out, but a man who had kept pace with events before coming to prison could figure out well enough how the war was going.[14]

Sorge also had his own sharp eyes and long training in deduction. At he beginning of his sessions with Yoshikawa the procurator always offered Sorge some of his cigarettes. Toward the end of their association, however, cigarette rationing had grown so stringent that Yoshikawa no longer could afford this little courtesy. One smokeless day, Sorge cocked a quizzical eye at Yoshikawa and remarked, "Are things that bad in Japan?"[15]

What with weekly visits from Asanuma, smuggled items of news, and censored periodicals, Sorge was probably as well informed as any prisoner in Japan, but the absence of daily newspapers, radio, and letters irked him. Twice he swallowed his pride and asked for a visit with Seiichi Ichijima, the prison governor. Ichijima had refrained deliberately from visiting either Sorge or Ozaki lest he be accused of favoring these famous prisoners, but when Sorge asked for an interview, the governor granted it. On each of these occasions Sorge had only one question: "How is the war progressing?" And each time Ichijima briefed him on the news insofar as he knew it himself.[16]

Meanwhile, Sorge made the best of his situation. He had enough money to smooth his path in prison. Under Japanese law Sorge could spend as he saw fit any funds belonging to him, and he was well-heeled. When the Tokko searched his house, they found 1,000 yen, plus a black leather wallet containing $1,782 in American currency. In addition, the police confiscated a suitcase Sorge had left with Wenneker, which contained about $2,000.[17] Almost $4,000 went a long way in Japan in the early 1940s.

He had nothing on which to spend his money except books and food to supplement the monotonous, painfully frugal prison diet. The prison store offered snacks and lunches for those who could buy. Ohashi observed that Sorge ate 5-yen lunches, which was considerably higher on the hog than Ohashi could live. At one time Sorge's complexion turned almost orange, a circumstance which Yoshikawa attributed to the inordinate number of tangerines he consumed.[18]

Evidently Sorge entertained no malice toward Miyagi for upsetting the apple cart. Miyagi was in hard straits, for he had no money to soften the rigors of prison life, and his tuberculosis was in the advanced stage. The prison officials asked Sorge if he would be willing to allow them to use some of his money to make Miyagi's life more comfortable. Sorge replied cordially that he would be delighted.[19]

Prison was bringing out the more admirable side of Sorge's nature no longer blurred by alcohol and the tensions of a double life. Asanuma admired his client more with every visit. Sorge never complained to him about prison conditions or said a word against the police or his prosecutors. In fact, Asanuma found his duties as defense counsel rapidly becoming those of a book buyer. Sorge always had a list of volumes he wanted Asanuma to find for him. "Sorge almost ate up the books, he read so quickly," remarked Asanuma. Some of these were in German, others in English, and because of wartime restrictions, Asanuma encountered any number of difficulties in finding them. Most were virtually collector's items and, as Asanuma said, "terribly expensive." He recalled paying for one book 1,000 yen—$25 at the current exchange—which seemed to him a fantastic sum.[20]

Kawai kept an eager watch for a glimpse of Sorge. Only once did their glances meet, and Sorge's eyes lit up in recognition. On the way to the bathhouse prisoners had to wear straw baskets over their heads, but Kawai had no difficulty in recognizing Sorge's large white feet and Westerner's cramped toes beneath Sorge's bathrobe. In the bathhouse, out of sight of the guards, Kawai removed his basket and peeped through a small hole in the wall, through which he often saw Sorge talking with the guard. Once he heard a reference to *ohki saiben* and guessed that the "big trial" meant that his case might come before the Supreme Court.[21]

Sorge's cell was quite near Ozaki's and Kawai's, but they had no opportunity to exchange greetings or communicate directly. Such minor miscreants as drunks and petty thieves were herded together in a common cell and exercised en masse, but major prisoners were taken to exercise one by one, so no communal games gave the chance for personal contact. The cells were small, about three-mat size with one mat taken up by an ingenious arrangement. A toilet became a chair when the lid was shut, and facing it was a simple washstand, also with a lid, which closed to become a desk.[22] Thus Sorge had the facilities to write, the bread of life to him.

Early in his interrogation Sorge requested that the Japanese get in touch with the Soviet Embassy with the view to initiating a diplomatic exchange of prisoners.[23] This was amazingly naïve of Sorge. At the time he had confessed to spying only for the Comintern, and the Soviet Union was still maintaining the fiction that it did not control it. By flying his true colors as an agent of the Red Army, Sorge might have forced the Soviet Embassy to espouse his cause, but this is by no means certain. Sorge should have been well aware that in the vast majority of spy cases the country concerned would sacrifice the agent rather than suffer official embarrassment. Had the Russians agreed to exchange Sorge, the Japanese probably would have been more than willing to spring him. Unlike Ozaki's case, no treason was involved, and Japanese national interests would have been served satisfactorily by exposing Sorge and the workings of his ring, then sending him back to the Soviet Union in exchange for one of their own spies. But the Russians did not choose to acknowledge a self-avowed agent of the Comintern; in fact, more than two decades passed before Moscow admitted that Sorge was its man.

If Sorge had identified himself as a Red Army spy, he would have fallen under the jurisdiction of the War Ministry. This did not suit him at all, for this would have meant exchanging his relatively pleasant chats with Ohashi of the Tokko and Yoshikawa of the Justice Ministry for the far from tender mercies of the Kempeitai. Later, after he had admitted his connection with the Red Army, Sorge frankly told his interrogators that he feared being turned over to the military police. He remembered the case of Cox, the British journalist, though not his name.[24] So Sorge was all in favor of taking his chances with the Justice Ministry and the Peace Preservation Law. Possibly he did not understand that much as he preferred to remain in the civil sector, the Tokko and the procurators were just as eager to keep him there.

CHAPTER 64

"THE TRANSITION PERIOD"

Sorge continued to type away at his statement in such free time as he had between questionings by Ohashi and Yoshikawa. Much of it was destroyed in the bombing of Tokyo, which burned much material relating to the Sorge case. What remains are those portions Yoshikawa had in his personal possession when the bombing took place. The surviving portion was completed in translation in April 1942. The Japanese immediately whacked the cover chart with a stamp reading *kimitsu* ("top secret"), with the further qualification "The contents of this document vitally affect domestic administration and foreign relations and should be kept absolutely secret." The reason is not difficult to find.

After beating around the bush for several paragraphs, Sorge admitted, "If we leave the realm of 'belief' and 'conviction,' we must limit consideration exclusively to the facts with which I dealt. Only the following can then be definitely stated: from Nov 1929 on, my espionage groups and I were technically and organizationally a direct part of Red Army Intelligence; i.e., of the so-called 4th Bureau."[1]

Here Sorge admits that he had lied in telling Ohashi and Yoshikawa that he was a Comintern agent. In later conversations with them he dodged the issue by referring to his superiors vaguely as "Moscow authorities," explaining:

When questioned during the early phase of the interrogation with regard to the agency which delegated authority and issued orders to me, I deliberately employed a general and ambiguous term, the "Moscow authorities." For reasons of my own, I did not elaborate on the question of whether that term referred to an organ within the Comintern or to a key agency situated in Moscow. At the time, it was impossible to explain to the police officer through an interpreter all the complexities surrounding the change in my field of operations and the shift in Communist leadership which I have endeavored to describe in the preceding paragraphs. During the minute interrogation conducted by Procurator Yoshikawa, I barely managed to cover the complicated details concerning the changes which occurred in my direct superiors in Moscow. I have related herein in detail that prior to 1929 the Comintern organization was my "Moscow authorities" and that after 1929 my chain of command underwent a basic change corresponding to the change in the general world political situation. Had I attempted to cover all this complicated material in the early interrogation conducted by the police, it would certainly have caused delay and confusion.[2]

To Ohashi, the Comintern expert, this hairsplitting about Red Army versus Comintern was irrelevant. Almost from the beginning he considered Sorge a Russian working for his own country and as such respected him.[3]

Sorge's surviving narrative* is a fascinating memoir, even a lecture, well polished in the florid German manner.

Emphatically it is not the work of a man who feels the chill shadow of the hangman; it is the effort of a man who expects to be free eventually and who is presenting his case to his masters. Ostensibly Sorge addressed a Japanese audience; actually he spoke over their heads to his Kremlin superiors.

* It is possible that somewhere, perhaps in Germany, a complete copy of Sorge's statement may exist. As Sorge completed each section, Yoshikawa had three copies made: one for the Justice Ministry; one for the Foreign Ministry; and one for Ambassador Ott (interview with Yoshikawa, January 16, 1965). If Ott did not destroy his copy, it might turn up eventually.

Above all, this document is the work of an egotist. He knew himself to be a spy, but he wanted to be sure history would record him as the Spy Extraordinary, citing the many times he received high praise from Moscow and the respect in which his superiors held his judgment.[4]

He took great pains to hammer home his prowess as a newsman: "My research was likewise of importance to my position as a journalist, since, without it, I would have found it difficult to rise above the level of the run-of-the-mill German news reporter, which was not particularly high. It enabled me to gain recognition as the best reporter in Japan."[5] As for his fellow journalists: "My scathing remarks were famous, and nobody could refute them."[6]

Sorge presented himself as a man of learning: ". . . had I lived under peaceful social conditions and in a peaceful environment of political development, I should perhaps have been a scholar—certainly not an espionage agent. . . ."[7] Against this it must be noted that his every action proves he genuinely enjoyed espionage and went about it with zest. In emphasizing his scholarly turn of mind, he stressed, "My studies did not interfere with my development as an expert intelligence agent. When necessary, I performed my duties with speed, resolution, courage and resourcefulness."[8]

Sorge did admit to one defeat: his failure to master the Japanese language. In extenuation he remarked, "The best excuse I have to offer for my failure is that I suffered from a lack of time caused by the pressure of my newspaper duties, my work in the German Embassy, my research and my secret activities.[9]

In general, his statement is as interesting for its omissions as for its contents. He polished off in three short sentences the vital meeting at the Nara deer park that resulted in Ozaki's joining the ring: "I never traveled with any members of the intelligence group because I considered it too much of a risk. The single exception was when I met Ozaki in Nara for a certain purpose. Our meeting there was of short duration."[10]

The most notable omission in Sorge's memoirs concerns the important period from 1924, when he went to Moscow from Germany, through 1929, when he left the Comintern for the Fourth Department. These were the years of the duel between

Stalinists and Trotskyites. The German Communist Party inclined toward Trotsky. It would be interesting to know how Sorge managed to tiptoe across the shaky suspension bridge over the gulf that swallowed so many of his comrades. This period was of no direct interest to the Japanese in building up their case, so he got away with the omission.

His recorded political judgments were variable, some accurate, some wholly inaccurate and influenced by his unquestioning belief in the Soviet Union.

Take, for example, the following: Sorge claimed at great length that his research into and study of Japanese history lighted the way for him to understand its present, a reasonable assumption. Yet a few pages later one finds this gem: "Unlike Czarist Russia, the Soviet Union is not an aggressive state either in structure or historical development, nor will she or can she become one in the near future."[11] Shades of Bessarabia, the Baltic states, eastern Poland, Sinkiang, and Karelia! And here was Sorge, with a doctorate in political science and a reputation as a political thinker, presenting the idea that the Soviet Union sprang upon the scene full-panoplied with no roots in its Russian past.

Sorge also wrote, "Unlike Berlin and Washington, Moscow knew China and Japan too well to be fooled easily. The Soviet level of knowledge of Far Eastern affairs was far above that of the American and German Governments. . . ."[12] Yet less than a year before, Sorge had been almost sweating blood because Stalin was so obsessed by the fear of a Japanese attack on Siberia that he withheld moving troops westward until the German advance units were practically in his front yard. This despite the clear evidence of the China Incident, the Japanese economic situation, and Sorge's own repeated assurance that the Japanese were not planning such an attack.

Sorge did not confine his opinions to the written word. On March 24, 1942, almost at the end of his questioning, Yoshikawa asked him for his predictions concerning world events. After protesting that no experienced politician would attempt such a forecast, he proceeded to do so volubly.

He was confident that Britain would collapse whether or not the Axis won the war. Canada had already "economically changed into a U.S. territory." Britain had lost or would soon lose the rest of its empire. But, he cautioned, the British did not know they were licked, and while they might let their possessions go without too much of a fight, they would put up a strong resistance as long as the homeland was in danger.[13]

Sorge nominated Japan, Germany, or the United States as the possible heir to Britain's position. As a Communist he did not think much of any of them. He saw the current war between the Americans and the Japanese as "an endless one economically and militarily. . . . Historically speaking, the United States has not yet finished its role, and it is impossible completely to defeat the United States politically, economically, or militarily." Yet even the United States could not defeat Japan utterly. It would have to compromise with Japan eventually, one reason being that the United States was tottering on the verge of revolt, "and a single mistake might have a social revolution break out."[14] Sorge believed a social revolution in the United States was inevitable. Again, as in the case of the British, he warned the Japanese not to "undervalue the capacity of the American people." He added patronizingly, "I believe that when the American people are thrown out of the present agreeable life, they may possibly stand up and make a good nation." Still, he insisted that the United States could not attack Japan "with all its national energy."[15]

In Sorge's opinion, Germany was riding for a fall. If during 1942 it conquered Russia, occupying the oil fields of the Caucasus, the granaries of the Ukraine, and the military capital of Moscow, it might continue as ruler of Europe for a little while, but ultimate German control of Europe was impossible. "Nazi Germany is extremely poor spiritually. Its policy might work for the people at the level of American negroes, but is almost powerless for the Europeans who have a long tradition."[16]

Next Sorge turned his attention to Japan. "Among the three countries I have mentioned, Japan must be considered the most blessed country," he gushed. "Judging from any point, Japan today can be said to have acquired an unbeatable ground. . . . At the end of this year or next year, the United States offensive against Japan may accelerate its severity, but nevertheless it seems that Japan will still remain as a victor psychologically and materially."

Then he switched to a minor key, "Even if Japan becomes the chief of Asia, the living of the Asian people will
never be improved. Japan cannot help using up all this harvest
for the war, and therefore cannot improve the living standard
of people or truly liberate these people." She might not even
want to do so. Eventually she was sure to fall into the British
pattern of "exploitation and oppression."[17]

It was "entirely unthinkable" that the Soviet Union would
be decisively beaten. Its vast expanses would preclude defeat.
No matter how big the sacrifice, it would remain a Socialist
nation. He was sure the Soviet Union would "make it her
policy foundation to keep a friendly relation with Japan as much
as she can."[18] Sorge was walking a slippery tightrope between
pleasing and flattering the Japanese while hewing to the Marxist
line.

In another cell another compulsive reader and writer was
trying in his own fashion to cope with his environment. Ozaki
was not ill-treated in prison, nor did he suffer material priva-
tions. He was well-off financially and even if his food had not
been sent in by his family, he could have eked out his rations
with purchases from the prison commissary.[19] The prison food
was almost a starvation diet, consisting chiefly of rice, sometimes beans, and a thin soup, with neither meat nor fish. No
labor was required before sentence, but if an internee requested
work, he received extra food. Kawai was one of those who
took advantage of this offer, pasting envelopes in exchange for
additional rations.[20] Ozaki, however, had enough to keep him
busy, for like Sorge, he had plenty to read and write.

In many respects prison life was much more difficult for
Ozaki than for Sorge. Sorge was used to solitary work, had a
chameleonlike gift for blending in with whatever scenery fate
had given him, and fell into a quiet regimen without complaint.
To Ichijima he seemed completely detached and at ease.[21] Sorge
lived in the present and had no personal ties in the outside
world of any genuine importance to him. On the other hand,
Ozaki tended to live in the past, and he was gregarious, so a
solitary cell was a real punishment to him, alone with his
memories.

He asked to see Ichijima frequently, not for information,
as did Sorge, but for the governor's company. Ichijima guessed

that Ozaki was extremely lonely and longed for someone to whom he could pour out his thoughts. He found the prisoner a man of quick intelligence and much charm. His deep love for his family particularly impressed him.[22]

During his incarceration, Ozaki wrote his wife a long series of exquisite and profound letters, a selection of which were published after his death under the title *Aijo Wa Hoshi no Furu Gotoku* (*Love Was Like a Falling Star*). The book became a best seller and helped Ms. Ozaki keep her head above financial water.[23] In view of the acute shortage of paper during the war years, keeping Ozaki supplied with that necessity posed something of a problem. Ichijima managed to wangle a bundle of his daughter's school examination papers, which he brought to the prisoner. Ozaki was so grateful for this and the governor's many other kindnesses that he showed Ichijima the manuscripts of two complete volumes he had written in prison entitled *Haku-en Roku* (*The White Cloud Report*). He told the governor that he wished to leave these documents with him after his death. Following Ozaki's execution Ichijima found the manuscript in Ozaki's cell. After reading it, he presented it to the Ministry of Justice. Unfortunately this book was one of the many documents lost in the massive fire raids.[24]

The Tokko retained primary interest in Ozaki somewhat longer than they did in Sorge. Yosuke Takahashi's interrogation continued until March 11, 1942, when Tamazawa took over.[25] In that period of Japan's history, following such police and prosecution questioning, the prisoner faced a preliminary investigation called a *yoshin*, which could last for months. Ozaki's obvious adherence to the Communist line during his questioning made this second step inevitable. His statement of February 14, 1942, is a perfect outline of what was supposed to happen in the Far East according to Marxist theories and proves that Ozaki dutifully swallowed his ideology whole without troubling to chew, let alone digest it:

> I believed that, just as the First World War created Soviet Russia, the Second World War would create many Socialist countries, first from the side which was defeated in the war or was exhausted, and that thus a world revolution would be achieved soon.

And I estimated that events would appear in the following order:

(a) Russia by all means should stand outside of this struggle among the imperialist nations through a policy of peace, and actually she will do so.

(b) The struggle of Japan, Germany, and Italy against Britain and the United States (a struggle between partially imperialist countries and wholly imperialist countries) may become a long, serious war. As a result, they will either all fall together, or one side will win a temporary victory. In that case there will be a social revolution on the defeated side.

(c) Even the victorious powers will be exhausted, and the possibility will be high that the relative weight of Soviet Russia will increase to the point that even these powerful nations may be compelled to turn Socialist.

. . . even if she [Japan] may achieve a temporary military success during the course of the war, the possibility of social revolution inside Japan would be high due to the internal exhaustion and the deadlock which would soon come, and at the earliest the transition period of Japan, which is the first step to such a social revolution, would appear during 1942. . . .

The idea of the East Asia New Order Society which I advocate conceives that in reality the revolutionary force in Japan during this transition period will be very weak, and such a transformation cannot be achieved by Japan alone, or even if it could be, it would not be stable. Hence a close mutual cooperation and assistance are necessary among the three nations—Russia; Japan, which had rid herself of the capitalist structure; and China, in which the Chinese Communist Party had completely grasped its hegemony—in order for Japan to achieve such a transition in her hostile relations with the British Empire and the United States. . . . [26]

Ozaki did not expect to die and was addressing his superiors in Moscow. In fact, he fretted somewhat in case his efforts should escape the notice of the Kremlin. When Ohashi discovered from Takahashi Ozaki's worry on this score, he asked Sorge if Moscow knew about Ozaki's work. Sorge assured Ohashi that Ozaki was well and favorably known to the Soviet authorities. Ohashi, who frequently carried messages between Sorge and Ozaki, relayed this information, and Ozaki was delighted.[27]

He spent a great deal of time catching up on his reading. He devoured several volumes on philately, an old interest, and meteorology, a new one. He also went through much of Goethe in the original, Machiavelli's *The Prince*, and among other biographies one of Benjamin Franklin—in short, the usual reading most people promise themselves to do when they have the time. He perused volume after volume on China, and certain comments in his letters to Eiko indicate that he was starting to wonder if his whole attitude toward that country needed rethinking. He was no longer complacent about his former interpretations of Chinese sociology and economics, yet he could not swallow in their entirety any of the other theories current in intellectual circles.[28] For all the study and thought that had made him an acknowledged authority on China, something in the subject eluded him. China burst the confines of any straitjacket that he or any other theorist imposed upon it.

This self-questioning was a sign that Ozaki was beginning to think, as opposed to studying, evaluating, analyzing, and writing. Although later Eiko brought him books by the armload, he was separated from his library, and of course, the prison censorship kept out Marxist literature. So when a question vexed Ozaki, he could no longer prowl through his bookshelves to see what someone else had to say about the matter. He was thrown onto his own resources. The imprisonment of Ozaki's body was freeing his mind. Inevitably that mind was the product of what he had fed it for years, but the basic substance was sound. In his last months of life Ozaki revealed the stirrings of a mind starting at last to question.[29] He might have reached the same answers that he had before, but at least they would have been his answers, not hand-me-downs.

CHAPTER 65

"SORGE-SAN IS A SPY"

For about a week after parting with Sorge, Hanako stayed in her home, eager to hear from him but not unduly alarmed when she did not. At the end of the week she was tempted to use her key to his house, but Sorge had asked her to stay away, so she tried to be patient.[1]

On the evening of October 19 she heard the front gate open, and the face of Mr. M. appeared at the lattice. He was alone and seemed nervous. Hanako escorted him to her quarters. To spare her mother the stairs, she had arranged the first floor as an apartment for the older woman, while she herself occupied the second.

As soon as Mr. M. made sure no one could overhear them, he blurted, "Miyake-san, Sorge-san has been arrested." Utterly taken aback, Hanako collapsed onto her cushion.

Mr. M. looked at her compassionately. "I understand that this is a great shock to you." Seeing that Hanako could not utter a word, he continued. "He was in danger, just as I feared. It happened yesterday. . . . He is still under examination and I don't know anything except that he is involved in black marketing in dollars."

The discovery of a large sum in American money in Sorge's house may have been behind this suggestion, which snapped Hanako out of her speechless shock. "There must be a mistake," she declared positively. "He is not the kind of man to do that."

"It may be true," the chief countered, "because they say that he is a Jew." Hanako rallied to a gentle denial. The chief produced another masterstroke: "He worships the sun every morning. He is not a Christian." Presumably Mr. M. founded this belief on Sorge's habit of rising regularly at the stroke of six to do setting-up exercises in front of the window facing the rising sun.

On the subject of Sorge's atheism Hanako stood on firm ground. "No, he never prays to the sun. He doesn't pray to anything," she assured her visitor.

The investigation was still under way, Mr. M. admitted. Then he came to the real reason for his visit. He had burned the affidavit she had signed that summer, and in view of Sorge's arrest he was seriously alarmed for his job, even his liberty.[2]

He urged Hanako to be careful. He felt fairly sure that Sorge would not implicate her, "but still, since he is a foreigner, we can't tell how much he is thinking of his Japanese friends." Mr. M. had liked and sympathized with Sorge and Hanako and had permitted his feelings to lead him into "a big mistake." He switched to the practical side of the matter. "You should have gotten that money sooner," he mourned. No doubt her visitor meant well, but his attitude made Hanako furious. Sorge might be undergoing torture, and the man stood there talking about money.

Asking her to be calm and keep control of herself if called in for questioning, Mr. M. took his departure.[3]

Hanako remained in suspense for another week. Then Mr. M. returned. As soon as they were seated, he told her gently, "Sorge-san is a spy. He turned out to be a Russian spy." This time Hanako made no denial. Immediately she saw that this was the truth. Everything about Sorge that had puzzled her fell into place. It may well have been that she was the one of Sorge's acquaintances in Japan outside his spy ring whom this revelation did not stun. Nothing could reveal more clearly how much of his true self he had let her see.

Mr. M. thought her in no immediate danger, but it would be best not to draw attention to herself by visiting the area of Sorge's house. Again he stressed, "I would be in big trouble if anyone in our police station saw me coming here."

He had seen Sorge, he continued, and brought her a message from him. Sorge was very worried about her and would send her some money as a Christmas present. "Look forward to Christmas," he had said. Evidently sensing her instinctive recoil at the mention of money, he pointed out, "You may be helpless unless you get even as little as a thousand or two yen. Your living is going to be tough from now on."

Hanako brushed aside finances and sped to the crux of the situation. "If it is proved that he is a spy, what will happen?"

"He will be shot," he answered heavily. "There is no hope for him to survive." He added that while final proof had not yet developed, the investigation had turned up substantial evidence. "I understand your feeling, but don't be discouraged. I myself will do my best to get money for you."[4]

"Don't tell Sorge-san that I want money," she pleaded. "I have never asked him for money. He has always given it to me before I asked for it. I didn't come together with him for money. I don't want to be regarded as that sort of woman."

"No, no!" he protested. "He wants to give you a Christmas present. So you shouldn't say no. . . . The world is hard. . . . That is why Sorge-san is worried about you." Then he kindly urged her to cheer up for the sake of her old mother, and promised to call again.[5]

Hanako had no way to get in touch with Sorge. Only wives could visit or write to prisoners. Christmas came and went without the promised gift or any other sign from him. At New Year's Mr. M. visited her briefly to say only that no hope for Sorge remained. Again he urged her to cheer up, but this time he made no promise that he would come again.[6]

Meanwhile, the Tokko continued mopping-up operations. Four days after Sorge's confession to Yoshikawa its men picked up Ugenda Taguchi, one of Miyagi's assistants. In terms of actual service to the Sorge ring, Taguchi was small change, but the court took a serious view, for eventually it hit him with a sentence of thirteen years, one of the stiffest received by anyone outside the higher spy echelon.[7]

Next to attract official attention was Torao Shinotsuka who had provided Miyagi with valuable military information. He was pulled in on November 14, 1941, and by some miracle managed to squirm off the hook.[8]

On November 19 the Tokko finally arrested Anna Clausen. Her information proved a valuable check and confirmation of her husband's and may have helped save his life. Her expressed aversion to communism, as well as her testimony that she had cooperated reluctantly and to keep her husband out of trouble, substantially agreed with what Clausen had told the police. In view of this she received lenient treatment and one of the lightest of the sentences: three years.[9]

Masazano Yamana, the agrarian expert in Miyagi's subring, was arrested on December 15. Although he had severed his connection with the ring in 1938, he drew a stern punishment: twelve years. Like Taguchi, he had served a previous term for Communist-related offenses and again like Taguchi, received his freedom in October 1945 at the hands of the occupation forces.[10]

On January 4, 1942, the Tokko's long arm stretched as far as Peiping to bring in Hisao Funakoshi. When Sorge left Shanghai, he had willed Funakoshi to his successor, and Funakoshi had no further connection with the Sorge ring after that time. Funakoshi was sentenced to ten years in prison. He died there in February 1945.[11]

Late March and early April 1942 saw a spate of arrests as the investigators probed more deeply into the case. No fewer than eleven people were involved, but only three of them received sentences. Of these, by far the most important was Koshiro, the only soldier in the ring. Sorge's written statement implicated him heavily. Koshiro was on active duty in South China when the Tokko pulled him in. In January 1943 the army gave him a dishonorable discharge to permit his trial by civil law. The court took an exceedingly dim view of Koshiro's offense—betrayal of his soldier's oath to nation and Emperor in time of war—and handed down a fifteen-year sentence, the stiffest given anyone but the top four. Technically Koshiro merited hanging, and undoubtedly the fact that Japan was not at war with the Soviet Union is all that saved him. He was another the Americans released in October 1945.[12]

Yoshio Kawamura, arrested on March 31, 1942, remains a shadowy figure. He had worked with Ozaki during the period of Sorge's Shanghai operation. As chief of the Shanghai office of *Manshu Nichi-nichi Shimbun* (*Manchukuo Daily News*), he had been in a position to give Ozaki information about Manchuria. Kawai had introduced Kawamura to Sorge, who claimed that no personal relationship developed between them. He died in prison on December 15, 1942, before sentence could be pronounced.[13]

Tokutaro Yasuda, the doctor Miyagi recruited, was arrested on June 8, 1942. Apparently the court did not consider him too important, for he received only two years' imprisonment with a five-year suspended sentence. In 1964, when the Sorge ring was all the rage in the Soviet press, Yasuda told a Russian journalist a dramatic tale of being taken into custody by no fewer than ten policemen and claimed he was so severely beaten that he developed heart attacks. However, the story appeared in an article so laced with romanticized exaggerations that it is difficult to accept it as factual.[14]

That spring of 1942 Japanese in the know were intrigued by the spectacle of two exceedingly prominent men in the dock—Prince Kinkazu Saionji and Ken Inukai. Inukai's indiscretions appear to have resulted from no illegal intentions; nevertheless, he was guilty of serious violations of security. Had he been less well connected, matters might have gone much harder for him. However, he was the son of a former premier, and Konoye went to bat for him. Konoye likewise pleaded for Saionji, who was much more deeply implicated. Saionji's three-year suspended sentence was more a tribute to his venerated adoptive grandfather than to his own innocence.[15]

The Japanese government released nothing about the Sorge case to the newspapers until May 17, 1942, but naturally two such prominent residents as Ozaki and Sorge could not disappear overnight without giving rise to a torrent of speculation. The coincidence of the fall of the Konoye cabinet on the very day of Sorge's arrest was indeed coincidence, but many in political life, including, apparently, Konoye himself, believed that the case was politically motivated.

Konoye was not a personal friend of Ozaki, as Ott was of Sorge, yet he had reposed great trust in Ozaki, and he, too, felt the shock of betrayal. A close friend of his has stated that in their long friendship he saw Konoye completely down only twice—when Ozaki was arrested and when Japan surrendered.

The militarist faction had been scheming to topple Konoye's government, so Konoye and his followers understandably wondered if the whole business might not be a plot Tojo and his supporters had cooked up. Konoye and his friends were running scared in those early months and became even more alarmed when they discovered that Ozaki was indeed a spy, not the victim of a frame-up. They had good cause to fear, because certain army and navy brass were demanding Konoye's head. But his connections stood him in good stead. He skirted the case with no more personal involvement than being called upon to testify. He played down his connection with Ozaki somewhat, but nothing was to be gained by hair-splitting, so the authorities accepted his testimony without challenge.[16]

Police headquarters felt the reverberations of the public announcement of Ozaki's arrest, which generated widespread shock. Opinion was divided into two main camps. Representatives of the pro-Konoye faction kept bursting in on the police, shouting angrily that Ozaki's arrest was a political plot. The all-has-not-been-told group, which surfaces in the wake of every cause célèbre, likewise badgered the Tokko, complaining that the case as publicized only scratched the surface. The ring must have been much larger; the real masterminds and highly placed operators had not been discovered.[17]

Hanako's brother was in Tokyo on business, and the announcement brought him posthaste to his sister's door, worried in case the neighbors learn of her relationship with Sorge. She reassured him on that score. He tried to persuade her to leave Tokyo if not for her own sake, then for that of their mother, who was very depressed. Japan's victories had turned his head, and he was abandoning his Christian faith in favor of Buddhism and nationalism. All Japanese were children of God, so they could not lose the war. The divine wind (*kamikaze*) would blow, and the United States would be defeated. Somewhat satirically Hanako assured him that she would wait and see. Under no circumstances would she leave the city where she had lived so long with Sorge.

Her brother fired a parting shot: "They say that for those who are executed or commit suicide there is no place for their souls to rest in eternity." In that case, Hanako replied, Sorge's spirit might wander forever beneath Tokyo's sky. All the more reason for her to stay in the capital.[18]

Soviet sources in Tokyo disassociated themselves from the revelation. An unofficial comment ran thus: "The announcement creates the impression that the Moscow Comintern is involved, but the whole thing is a plot engineered by the fifth column of Hitler's Elite Guards and Special Police. Moscow knows nothing about it." A Tass correspondent issued a rambling statement ending, "No member of the Soviet Government or the Soviet Embassy is directly connected with the case.[19]

The German colony registered shock and surprise, sugared with fulsome praise of the Japanese police for breaking the case. Possibly the most outspoken comment came from one of Sorge's colleagues on the *Frankfurter Zeitung*, Elizabeth "Lili" Abegg:

> I have known Sorge since 1936, but I never imagined that he was a Communist. He was a heavy drinker and loafer, but he wrote excellent articles. The paper trusted him. . . .
>   Practically every local German knows that Ambassador Ott was on intimate terms with him, so Ott must be worried. But aren't all the members of the Embassy staff equally to blame? Meisinger is even more embarrassed than Ott because the arrest had to be made by the Japanese authorities. . . .[20]

Meisinger was not the only member of the embassy staff who had cause for embarrassment. According to one postwar account, some of Sorge's closest associates hastily attempted to disassociate themselves from this scandal. "Wenneker was the first to completely distance himself from Ott, and the one who most blackened Ott's name in Berlin."[21] This same report claimed that Wenneker, Gronau, and Kretschmer went to Ott in a body, demanding his resignation on the grounds that he had "kept a journalist continuously abreast of the most secret matters, thereby causing unheard-of damage to Germany." But Ott continued to insist that Sorge was innocent.[22]

None of the three service attachés had protested this arrangement while it existed, and Wenneker, in particular, had been Sorge's friend. It was to him that Sorge always entrusted a suitcase of his valuables whenever he left Tokyo, so that they would be safe from Japanese searchers. After Sorge had been arrested, the embassy surrendered a suitcase Wenneker had been keeping for Sorge to the Japanese authorities. It was claimed that when the Foreign Ministry turned it over to the prosecutors near the end of October, "it was also apparent that it had been opened in the German Embassy."

Among other things, the suitcase yielded a number of letters to Sorge from both Christiane and Katcha.[23] Why a seasoned agent like Sorge kept these letters is something only he could explain. Few circumstances could have been more damaging to his image than the discovery that he had a former wife in the United States and a current wife in the Soviet Union. No doubt he considered his effects safe with his good friend Wenneker, and probably this would have been the case ordinarily.

On the night of the announcement the Otts visited the Mohrs. "On the surface," stated the official report, "there appeared to be nothing unusual about Ott's behavior, but it is said that the Germans employed by the Embassy received secret orders to maintain complete silence about the Sorge case."[24]

The official announcement left Ott and Meisinger, the Gestapo agent, no alternative but to send to Berlin the unhappy news of Sorge's deception of them, which as yet they had not done. Both had good reasons for lying low. Ott had taken one blow after another, beginning with Sorge's oblique confession at the time of their last meeting. He had been astounded to learn from the Foreign Office that Sorge understood Russian, although he spoke it poorly.[25] A report from Berlin outlining Sorge's Communist background "knocked us all for a loop," to use Gronau's expression.[26] Yet as late as Christmas 1941 Ott is reported to have said that Sorge's friends could expect him, "the martyr to Japanese suspicion and spy mania," to be freed.[27] Perhaps Ott still hoped against hope that the whole affair had been a grotesque mistake and that Sorge might emerge with clean hands. Along with his friendship with Sorge he had professional reasons for minimizing the story. Berlin might charge him with criminal stupidity at the least, active complicity with Sorge at the worst.

Nor had Meisinger given Berlin any advance information. He was in an embarrassing position. Schellenberg had charged him with watching and reporting on Sorge, yet with his man practically in his pocket the Japanese police had snatched him away. What is more, Meisinger had cultivated Sorge until the two appeared to be close cronies. His superiors might well choose to wonder whether Sorge had bought him off.

Schellenberg's memoirs make it clear that his office did not know of Sorge's arrest until Tokyo announced the fact, for he wrote, "Sorge was arrested by the Japanese in the summer of 1942. . . . Meisinger reported Sorge's arrest to us as soon as it happened. . . ."[28] Meisinger did nothing of the sort; he waited until he no longer could avoid it, and then obviously did not tell his superiors the actual date of the event.

"In a long and uncomfortable session with Himmler, I had to justify our collaboration with Sorge," Schellenberg recounted economically. The imagination lingers lovingly over that "long and uncomfortable session." No doubt Himmler subjected the discomfited Schellenberg to a battery of triumphant I-told-you-so's, for upon succeeding to power, Himmler had decided to make no further use of the information from Sorge because he "refused to be responsible for it to Hitler." Schellenberg continued, "On the one hand, he wanted to protect me, but on the other he considered it necessary from his own point of view to inform Hitler of the whole business."[29]

It is evident from Schellenberg's account that much heart searching and wire pulling took place behind the scenes when the news of Sorge's arrest hit Berlin:

> As far as Ambassador Ott was concerned, Meisinger did his best to ruin him. After a careful examination of the evidence, however, it became quite clear that, while Ott had been thoroughly exploited by Sorge, he had never been guilty of knowing complicity in espionage activities. From this point of view I defended him energetically in front of Himmler and Ribbentrop. . . .[30]

Himmler made a clean breast of the whole business to Hitler, who fortunately took a lenient view, according to Schellenberg:

> In a confidential discussion between Hitler and Himmler, Hitler agreed that no blame could be placed on the German Secret Service in this affair. However, Himmler was never able to allay Hitler's deep suspicion of Ott. Hitler held to the opinion that a man in Ott's position should never allow trust and friendship to carry him so far as to reveal confidential political information. It was lucky for Ott that Hitler took such an objective view of the matter. He was recalled from his post as Ambassador, and, although Meisinger received secret instructions to look out for additional evidence, nothing was ever found and no further measures were taken against him.[31]

Since Meisinger would have done all possible to implicate Ott, if only to clear himself, presumably no such evidence existed to be found. Meisinger remained in Tokyo until the American occupation dispatched him to Poland for trial.[32]

Ott requested permission to return to Germany for duty at the front, but Berlin refused. He was ordered to stay in the Far East, "in some remote place away from Tokyo." So he settled in Peiping for the duration,[33] and Dr. Heinrich Stahmer of Tripartite Pact fame became ambassador to Japan in January 1943. Indeed, it is surprising that Ott remained in position as long as he did. Had it not been for Sorge's connection with Schellenberg and the RSHA, Ott might have received short shrift.

Sorge fascinated and puzzled Schellenberg. He dug deeply enough into Sorge's background to know something about his family and early life and kept abreast of his later statements. He noted that "neither in his confession nor during his long period of imprisonment did Sorge once admit having also worked for Berlin." Schellenberg concluded that Sorge kept silent because he did not want Moscow to know of his close friendship with Ritgen, head of the German Press Department, a logical conclusion as far as it went.

Other aspects of the case intrigued Schellenberg. Why had the Red Army's Fourth Department, in contrast with its usual policy of iron discipline, "granted him the individual freedom which both he and they despised . . ."? Why had it overlooked his escapades with women, his drinking, his careless talk? Had Sorge had powerful protectors in Moscow as he had in Berlin? Why had Sorge, a dedicated Communist, also served the German Secret Service without attempting to mislead it? For frantic checkups provided one final enigma: The information Sorge had sent to Ritgen was valid. So like many others after him, Schellenberg mulled over the puzzle that was Richard Sorge.[34]

On June 16, 1942, Judge Nakamura commenced the *yoshin* (preliminary hearing) of Ozaki, and on June 24 that of Sorge. Ozaki's case came to an end on November 27, 1942; Sorge's, on December 5 of that year. On December 15 both prisoners were adjudged guilty of violations of the Peace Preservation Law and the National Defense Security Law, and in Ozaki's case, an assortment of military security laws as well. The verdict meant that a full-fledged trial would be held in the Tokyo District Criminal Court, with the prisoners remaining in jail under indictment.[35]

The *yoshin* and prospect of trial made little difference in Sorge's prison life. He was convinced that eventually the Soviet Union would bail him out.[36] In view of his past relations with his superiors, one can understand this optimism. As Schellenberg noted, with shrewd psychology the Russians had given Sorge the long rein that his unconventional spirit required, and had soothed his ego with large pats of the very best butter. Yet Sorge should have known the usual fate of a discovered spy. Of course, he never ranked himself with the majority: He was unique, and the cause could not spare him!

Kawai had a glimpse of Sorge dancing with joy and banging a guard jovially on the back when he heard the news of the German defeat at Stalingrad. Kawai deduced that Sorge hoped Stalingrad presaged victory for the Soviet Union, eventual defeat for Japan, and hence his release. He also believed that Sorge felt exultant satisfaction in having supplied Russia with information that would help toward these highly desirable results.[37]

In later years the whole weight of Soviet officialdom rallied to build up the image of Sorge as a Marxist saint and champion of peace. A street in Baku bore his name; the good ship *Richard Sorge* plied the waters; his wickedly handsome features gazed out from a USSR postage stamp. In death he became a Hero of the Soviet Union. In his hour of need, however, the nation he served abandoned him.

CHAPTER 66

"I TAKE FULL RESPONSIBILITY"

The indefatigable Shin'ichi Matsumoto and his adviser Juso Miwa took counsel together to plan a defense campaign for Ozaki. As an attorney Miwa knew the strength of the prosecution's case, so he recommended that the defense rest upon recantation. Matsumoto agreed and permitted the court to choose defense counsel.[1] In accordance with the policy of appointing only top men in their fields to the Sorge case, the court selected Shunzo Kobayashi, a future Supreme Court justice and one of the most capable lawyers in Japan.[2]

Kobayashi was not happy with his assignment and wanted no part in justifying Ozaki's treason. He agreed to serve on the basis of a defense of ideology, which Ozaki must spell out for the court in a detailed statement. Apparently he observed signs of complacency in his client, for he gave Ozaki a brief list of books to read before he started to write, in case Ozaki's statement should appear brash or superficial.[3]

He had reason to caution his client thus, for Judge Nakamura noted that throughout his preliminary hearings Ozaki seemed to be "in the best of spirits," answering questions in a "clear, frank, and eloquent manner," making "long and diffuse" statements.[4]

After dutifully reading the books his counsel suggested, Ozaki set to work on his statement, or *tenkosho*. This is a document peculiar to Japan. It is not a confession but a written self-examination, explanation, and recantation. To understand it, one must understand another Japanese word, *kokutai*. This term is usually translated "national polity," which does not quite convey the flavor of this vague and controversial concept. And the Japanese Supreme Court's definition of 1929 does not help much: ". . . the condition whereby a line of Emperors unbroken for ages eternal deigns to rule over our Empire and to combine in itself the supreme right to rule. . . ."[5] The word is made up of two ideographs: *nation* and *body*. This nation-body represents a mystical interweaving of Emperor and people, soil and ancestral spirits, government and Shinto.

An offense against the *kokutai* was more than treason; it was an insult to the very soul the criminal shared with his nation. For this reason a Japanese who became a Communist or otherwise sinned against the *kokutai* was considered officially no longer a Japanese—a terrible judgment of national and spiritual excommunication. The offender was cut off from his nation-body in life, and if he died in error, his spirit could not join the honorable souls that hovered in loving protection over the homeland. To be spared this unthinkable fate, the erring one came under pressure to prepare a *tenkosho*. The Japanese authorities would not dream of sentencing him without giving him the opportunity to square himself with gods and men.[6]

Just how much of Ozaki's *tenkosho* was sincere, how much opportunistic, and how much simply the product of a writer absorbed in that most fascinating of topics, himself, is difficult to assess. A picture emerges of a self-satisfied man, sure of his good intentions, attempting to discover why society considers him a criminal, but so conditioned to the Marxist frame of reference that genuinely free thought is impossible. A number of Japanese involved in the interrogations and trials believed that Ozaki was moving away from communism, but he never said so, and a retreat is not visible in his *tenkosho*.

In fact, he was in a nasty dilemma. While he hoped to escape with a lighter sentence if he cried *mea culpa* loudly enough, he had no expectation whatever of a death verdict. A life sentence was the worst possibility he considered. As he would be a model prisoner with influential friends, at most "life" would mean ten years, probably considerably less.[7] Once free, what then? If he had recanted abjectly, he would never be able to pick up the threads of his very satisfactory former life. So Ozaki tried to carry water on both shoulders and could not make up his mind to drop one bucket or the other.

Then, too, an exercise in self-blame ran counter to the Japanese culture pattern in which Ozaki had been reared. While generalizations are often misleading, there is considerable truth in Joseph Newman's words, "Nothing cuts Nipponese pride more than an admission of guilt. . . . [The] Japanese appear to have inherited a conviction that they never can be wrong. . . . When a Japanese convicted of murder recants, he seldom does so from a sense of guilt but rather from one of expediency."[8]

An aura of unreality hovers over Ozaki's defense structure. It never seems to have occurred to any of these men that Ozaki was being tried for criminal activities, not for his political opinions. He had already written a document far more relevant than any *tenkosho*—a long memorandum dated February 25, 1942, listing the date, source, method of collection, and to whom delivered, of each item of information he had procured and which he remembered at the time.[9]

Sorge and Ozaki were tried together before presiding Judge Masahi Takada, a man renowned in Japanese legal circles for his wisdom, fairness, and ability. In accordance with custom, the trial was not open to the public, so only a handful of people with official reason for being there witnessed the drama. "The time and procedure of the trial itself were absolutely the same as all Japanese cases," said Asanuma. "The only difference was that an interpreter translated everything (questions and answers) in German for Sorge to get a correct and clear idea of what was going on."[10]

Between the German translations and Sorge's own Japanese, there can be little question that he understood the proceedings. Even after his capture Sorge studied the language. After he had become acquainted with his questioners, almost playfully he refused to answer certain queries unless they were put to him in Japanese along with the German and English translation.[11] With his native intelligence and unlimited chances to practice, this conversational method must have netted Sorge an adequate vocabulary by the time his trial started. The question of a *tenkosho* did not arise in his case. As a foreigner he stood outside the *kokutai*.

Asanuma fought for his client with every ounce of his considerable ability, not only because it was his duty but also because he was striving to save the life of a friend. He found

Sorge the ideal client—easy to get along with and cooperative: "Sorge was a man of the highest caliber in philosophy, principles, intelligence, and human character."[12]

On September 11, 1943, the prosecution demanded the death penalty for Ozaki. This shook him to his foundations. He had great faith in his own powers of persuasion and built high hopes on his *tenkosho*, which he trusted would outweigh at least some of the prosecution's case.[13] Asanuma thought that Ozaki probably would get away with life imprisonment because of his "high prestige and social status and his many powerful friends." Therefore, he was genuinely surprised when, early in the morning of September 29, Judge Takada handed down the death sentence. It happened that sentence was imposed first on Ozaki. Asanuma believed that this was done to erase from Sorge's mind any doubt that Ozaki might be "receiving special treatment because he was Japanese and also such a big shot."[14]

Asanuma's defense for Sorge was based largely on the premise that Sorge did not bear the full burden of guilt because he could not have obtained so many top secrets of the Japanese government without such a powerful ally as Ozaki. Because this was his line of defense and because such was his belief, Asanuma was startled and somewhat puzzled by Sorge's last words to the court.

The clock stood at approximately ten-thirty that September 29, 1943, when Sorge rose to speak his final words before sentence was imposed. He was erect and calm; his whole being radiated dignity. "I had absolutely no thought or plan to start a Communist revolution in Japan or spread communism in Japan whatsoever," he declared firmly.[15]

Then Sorge added the sentence that lifted him above political tactics: "I take full responsibility, however, so please treat my Japanese colleagues as lightly as possible."

Asanuma believed that Sorge hoped to lessen his sentence by putting across the idea that technically he had done nothing to disturb the peace of Japan in the sense of violating the Peace Preservation Law. He further believed that Sorge wished to convince the court of his sincerity as a human being and also for Asanuma's respect for Sorge did not blind him—to impress the judge.[16]

All this is no doubt true. Asanuma did not understand

that with Sorge's last sentence he spoke for the Occidental concept of responsibility: A subordinate may be accountable, but the chief alone is responsible; the captain is the last to leave the ship. But Asanuma's defense, however earnest, and Sorge's sentiments, however commendable, could not alter facts. The sentence of death was in accordance with the evidence and the law.

Appeal was automatic. In Ozaki's case this triggered a shake-up of his defense structure. Matsumoto was almost as stunned by the verdict as Ozaki himself. He fired Kobayashi and consulted no more with Miwa. Instead, he sought advice from Hideo Shinoda, Michitaro Kazami, and Yoshishige Kozai, stout leftists one and all, and with Kinkazu Saionji, unchastened by his own narrow squeak with justice. This unofficial committee settled on two sympathetic lawyers to take over. Ironically, all the battery of left-wing advisers and lawyers could come up with was another try via the *tenkosho* route.[17]

Ozaki had aged in these past months; his black hair had turned almost completely gray, and he kept it clipped short to try to disguise the change. He seemed resigned to his fate.[18] All things considered, stoical acceptance appeared to him a more dignified and fitting course than composing a hypocritical recantation. He consented to do so only at Ms. Ozaki's earnest appeal.

Once more Ozaki sought inspiration in the words of others, this time volumes on Shinto and nationalism, but his heart was not in it. As he wrote his wife on February 8, 1944, he could not write the confession of a true convert.[19]

Not surprisingly the appeal was denied. It is difficult to see what other decision the court could have handed down. Repentance and recantation are not legal matters; they are matters between a man and his conscience and in no way alter facts and evidence.

Sorge accepted the verdict in his own case equably enough. The summary of his appeal is well worth pondering:

> Japanese laws are subject to interpretation, either broadly or according to the strict letter of the text. Although leakages of information may, strictly speaking, be punishable by law in practice the Jap-

anese social system is not amenable to the keeping of secrets. . . . I consider that in the drawing up of the indictment insufficient consideration was given to our activity and to the nature of the information which we obtained. Data which Voukelitch supplied was neither secret nor important; he brought in only news which was well known to every press correspondent. The same may be said of Miyagi who was in no position to obtain state secrets. What may be termed political information was procured by Ozaki and by me.

I obtained my information from the German Embassy, but here again I consider that little if any of it could be termed "state secret." It was given to me voluntarily. To obtain it I resorted to no strategy for which I should be punished. I never used deceit or force. Ambassador Ott and Commander [sic] Schol asked me to help them write reports, especially Schol, who put much confidence in me and asked me to read all of his own reports before he sent them to Germany. As for me, I placed much trust in this information because it was compiled and evaluated by competent military and naval attachés for the use of the German General Staff. I believed that the Japanese government, in giving data to the German Embassy expected some of it to leak out.

Ozaki obtained much of his news from the Breakfast Group. But the Breakfast Group was not an official organization. Such information as was exchanged within the group must have been discussed by other similar cliques, of which there were many in Tokyo in those days. Even such data as Ozaki considered important and secret was actually no longer so, because he had procured it directly after it had left its secret source.[20]

This specious reasoning struck no sympathetic chord in the breasts of the Supreme Court, which denied the appeal. Only once did a representative of the German Embassy visit Sorge, and that was on the initiative of the Japanese to "receive Sorge's last will and testament." The embassy sent an interpreter named Hamel. He was surprised to see Sorge looking so well. The harsh lines on his face had smoothed out; he was neatly shaved and clothed, showing no evidence whatever of torture or any kind of coercion. On the contrary, he freely, almost triumphantly acknowledged his actions, giving the impression of "a man who is proud to have accomplished a great work and is now ready to leave the scene of his accomplishments."

He asked that his mother, eighty years old and living in Hamburg, be spared from persecution as she knew nothing of his life over the past twenty years. Typically he wanted more history books to read.[21]

Even after the rejection of Ozaki's appeal Matsumoto and his advisers did not abandon hope. A story drifted out of a cabinet meeting that the government was considering sending two former members of the Japanese Communist Party to Chinese Communist headquarters with the view to arranging peace with that element. Matsumoto, Saionji, and Teizo Taira seized this opportunity to try to persuade the government that Ozaki, with his long interest in and knowledge of China and his connections with the Chinese leftists, would be the ideal emissary. Needless to say, the Justice Ministry did not share this belief.[22]

Of the Sorge ring, only its leader and Ozaki were sentenced to death. Mizuno, Ozaki's crown prince, received a sentence of thirteen years. He did not survive to be freed when the Americans released the Japanese political prisoners early in October 1945. He died on March 22 of that year.[23]

Not even a long term in a Japanese jail could kill off Kawai. The tough little adventurer was transferred from Sugamo to Toyotama Prison in Nakano in July 1944. Sugamo was heavily bombed throughout 1945, and as bit by bit it became uninhabitable, prisoners were transferred to other institutions. So it was that in March 1945, when some of these evacuees reached Toyotama, Kawai heard with profound grief the news that his beloved patron, Ozaki, and his much respected chieftain, Sorge, had been executed. Later Kawai became high priest of the Ozaki shrine, although he left the Communist Party. First and always he was Ozaki's man.[24]

In view of the importance of Miyagi's position in the spy ring, it is likely that he would have drawn the death penalty. But on August 2, 1943, his tired lungs gave up the struggle, and death released him from his sufferings while his trial was still under way. Despite his confession to the police, he remained a convinced Communist to the last.[25]

Kawai learned of Miyagi's death after his own release from prison in October 1945. He understood him to have been buried in the prison graveyard at Zoshigaya but made no effort to verify this information. Almost twenty years later he heard from Hotsuki Ozaki, his patron's half brother, that according to information from the United States, Miyagi's remains were in Mexico.[26]

And what of Voukelitch? Until April 1944 his adored Yoshiko visited him frequently, bringing him clothes, books, and money for food and other small comforts obtainable in the prison commissary. From that time on, however, she was allowed to see him only once a month. Then, in July of that year, Voukelitch was transferred to Abasiri Prison in Hokkaido. Before he left, the authorities permitted his wife to spend thirty minutes with him instead of the customary five, and she brought little Yo with her. Her husband had become so thin that Ms. Voukelitch could not hold back her tears. The emaciated prisoner comforted his wife, summoning up his old optimistic smile. He vetoed her wish to come to Hokkaido as soon as possible, saying that their son was too young.[27]

Hokkaido is savagely cold in winter, and the prison was even more than normally arctic because of the wartime fuel shortage. No kindly Suzuki was there to intercede for Voukelitch as he had in Sugamo, so the prisoner had no special privileges. Weakened by malnutrition, he caught pneumonia. With a life sentence imposed on him, seemingly with nothing to live for, Voukelitch lacked the stubborn will to survive that might have carried him through. He died on January 13, 1945.[28]

On the night of January 15 Yoshiko received a telegram from Abasiri summoning her to come for the corpse of her husband. She found his pitifully wasted body clad in white, the Japanese color of mourning, already in his coffin. Sadly she took her burden to the crematory.[29]

Of the ring elite, only Clausen returned to life victoriously. Despite his heart trouble, which for a time sent him to the prison infirmary, he had the solid strength of the earth. On January 29, 1943, he and Anna saw each other for the last time for more than two and a half years. At first Sugamo was not too bad as prisons go. It was run along modern lines, and if not exactly the Imperial Hotel, at least it was clean. Clausen received better treatment than he expected, a fact which he attributed—no doubt correctly—to his German nationality. He had an unpleasant time during the Tokyo bombings, with choking smoke filling his cell and flaming debris raining down on his bed.

Soon thereafter he was transferred to another prison. There he found himself subjected to another form of attack and whiled away the time killing fleas. Through the prison underground he heard of Sorge's and Ozaki's deaths, then of the surrender of Germany. As the war drew to a close, he was transferred again, this time to a secret prison in Akita. His weight dropped to 99 pounds and he was almost too weak to walk. One day the doctor from Sugamo, who had given Clausen special care, called on him and whispered, "Hold on! Pluck up your courage!" This hint gave Clausen a real handle on hope.

On October 8, 1945, U.S. Army troops occupied the prison, rushed Clausen to a military hospital, and after his recuperation sent him to Tokyo aboard a military train.[30] There he hunted up Asanuma, who put him in touch with Anna. The two were so worn that they almost did not recognize each other, then fell sobbing into each other's arms. The kindhearted lawyer put them up in his home for several months before the unsinkable pair could return to Europe. The Soviets flew them by military aircraft to Vladivostok, then put Clausen in a naval hospital, where he recovered from an infection. After his release he and Anna traveled by train to Moscow, to a hearty reception by old friends. "We were and are communists, we did it for our sacred cause," they chirped.[31]

Soon they settled in East Germany under the name of Christiansen. (This may, in fact, have been Clausen's real name; Tamazawa believed it was.) There Clausen and Anna lived as dyed-in-the-wool Communists.[32]

CHAPTER 67

"FIGHT THE COLD BRAVELY"

The luminous dawn of November 7, 1944, haloed each bare branch and twig outside the home of Tamon Yuda in Suginami-ku, Tokyo. Because this was no usual morning, he rose early and groomed himself with painstaking care. If Ms. Yuda wondered why her husband had donned his best formal morning clothes instead of the depressing national uniform, a khaki-colored fiber suit that Japanese civilians wore during the war years, she gave no sign. A high Tokko official never discussed his work with anyone, not even his wife—perhaps least of all with his wife.[1]

His devotions completed, Yuda ate a meager breakfast. At about eight, he stubbed out his precious rationed cigarette and stepped outside. The morning sun beamed down with the soft glow of autumn, and the air was as tartly sweet as the taste of apples.[2]

From Yuda's broad, businesslike face peered the eyes of a surgeon—searching, diagnostic. He looked more serious than usual as he strode through his garden to the street. No late bloom lifted its head, for the Yudas had long since sacrificed the cherished flower beds to the family's need for vegetables. But on this day Yuda had no regret to spare for his lost plants. The task before him filled his mind, a task he hated. Yuda was on his way to watch two men die.[3]

By a spin of fortune's wheel, today was his turn to act as the Tokko's official witness to an execution. The Tokko always selected for this duty an officer not directly connected with the case in question. It so happened that at the top of the list of those eligible to witness the double execution of Sorge and Ozaki stood the name of Tamon Yuda.

The coming New Year's Day would see Yuda's forty-sixth birthday, and he was no stranger to unnatural death. In the course of his police duties and through the circumstances of war he had seen death in its most gruesome forms. But something about the deliberate taking of a man's life by the process of law set such a death apart from the common fate of humankind. Yuda had witnessed four executions before this date. He opposed the death penalty both on principle and because the sight revolted him.[4]

Yuda hurriedly joined the commuters' crush on the electric train. He had to remember to watch the crowd at Shinjuka Station and not miss his assistant, Kikuyasa Akiyama, who would join him there and ride with him the rest of the way to Sugamo Prison. Akiyama was in charge of the paper work on the day's two executions. Yes, there he was, twisting his way through a mass of humanity. Once aboard the train the two men settled down for the long ride to Sugamo.[5]

The prison governor, Ichijima, looked forward to the grim events of the day even less than Yuda, if that was possible. Yuda witnessed only an occasional execution; Ichijima had to see them all. He was not a career warden but a Ministry of Justice official temporarily assigned to Sugamo, a post he heartily disliked. He endured the ordeal of an execution by doing all possible to convince himself that the victim was an enemy of humankind who had forfeited his right to live. Ichijima's task being to supervise the prison, he had no connection with the investigation of any case and knew nothing about the prisoners committed to Sugamo until the reports came to his office. Inasmuch as these numbered in the hundreds, he could give each record only a quick reading, unless for some reason it called for special attention.[6]

Before every execution Ichijima took the official record home with him and pored over it in detail for several days to give himself "a sense of justice." On that lovely November morning he spent an hour or so refreshing his memory about the activities of the two condemned men. He also attempted to compose himself by withdrawing in solitude to meditate and empty his mind of troubling thoughts. In this case the task was more difficult than usual. Most of the prisoners were strangers to him, but he had come to know Ozaki quite well and Sorge slightly. And he liked them both.[7]

During breakfast and for the time left to them that morning he and Ms. Ichijima kept up the pretense that she did not know an execution was scheduled. Ichijima strictly isolated his home life from the distasteful details of his position. He even kept his full-dress uniform in his office so that his wife would never know when some official occasion was at hand.

Since his home lay just outside the prison walls, Ichijima walked to his office.[8] Ordinarily the execution of Sorge and Ozaki would have taken place on the morrow. The approval of execution signed by the minister of justice bore the date November 4, 1944. Once signed, the order had to be carried out within five days, so technically Ichijima had until midnight of the eighth to comply. In ordinary times he would have held off until the last minute, but these were not ordinary times. Because of the astounding Japanese success at Pearl Harbor on December 8, 1941 (Japanese time), the eighth of every month carried a special significance, never more than now when Japan had so few occasions for celebration. All over the nation dreary little ceremonies harking back to Japan's hour of greatest glory would be taking place. An execution on that day would have insulted the spirit of the moment.

Still another reason entered into the selection of the seventh as a suitable day to send Sorge and Ozaki to their ancestors. For November 7 was the Soviet Union's national holiday, the anniversary of the Bolshevik takeover of Russia in 1917.[9] The selection of that particular date has led to some peculiar speculations. One Karl Kindermann, a wartime interpreter in Japan, used this as a factor to bolster his thesis that the Japanese did not execute Sorge.

Hotsuki Ozaki, while accepting that both his half brother and Sorge were executed on November 7, produced an equally strange explanation: "The Japanese government at that time was negotiating for peace through the Soviet Union and offered Sorge as a condition. But the offer was turned down. I heard that he was executed on the anniversary of the Soviet Revolution as a retaliation for failure of the peace negotiations."[10]

The actual reason was far less outré but, being typically

Japanese, might be difficult for a Westerner to understand and appreciate. Quite simply the authorities chose November 7 because, inasmuch as Sorge and Ozaki served the Soviet Union, it seemed fitting and proper to execute these two men on that auspicious occasion. Perhaps no other people on earth would have taken such a consideration into account. The Japanese kept anniversaries reverently and in that spirit chose November 7 to honor the doomed men for their dedication to Russia.[11]

In his office Ichijima changed to full dress—a plain dark uniform with epaulets and brass buttons—buckled on his police sword, and laid ready his white gloves and ceremonial hat. He wore this costume with a somewhat deprecating air, as if he were more at home in civilian clothes. One by one the official party gathered, all in full morning dress except for the prison chaplain, Kato Sensho, in Buddhist robes. The Japanese considered no criminal so depraved that his spirit should not be dispatched with all due courtesy. So Ichijima and the others dressed as carefully for Sorge and Ozaki as they would have for an imperial reception.[12]

Yuda and Akiyama joined the group shortly after nine. The men greeted one another with slight bows and delicate hissing. In addition to Ichijima, Yuda, Akiyama, and Chaplain Sensho, the group included Shoichiro Omata, the prison doctor; Otsubo, Ichijima's assistant; and his secretary. A group of guards and executioners stood slightly apart. Beyond polite salutations and a few murmured generalities there was no conversation, for these men had not met for a social occasion.[13]

The clang of the morning bell woke Ozaki in his cell at six. He rose as usual, washed, and breakfasted on the Spartan prison fare of rice, bean soup, and pickles. Then he seated himself at the little desk-washstand to pen his daily postcard to his wife. "It is gradually getting colder," he wrote. "I am going to fight the cold bravely." The note, full of concern for Eiko's aged father, conveyed no hint of any suspicion that this morning would be different from any other since Ozaki's conviction.[14]

At exactly nine, just as he finished his postcard, a key rattled in the lock of his cell. The door swung open to frame two minor prison officials. Ozaki received the notification of his imminent execution with calm dignity. He asked only for fifteen minutes to change into proper attire. With his wish granted, he stripped off his clothes and put on clean undergarments. He removed from his small storage box the black ceremonial kimono that Eiko had sent him for this day, shook the wrinkles from its folds, and shrugged himself into it. Then he pulled over his feet a pair of black tabi instead of the customary white ones to symbolize the dark ordeal ahead. Anything ropelike was strictly prohibited to a prisoner, but from somewhere, perhaps a sympathetic guard, Ozaki had procured a sash and tied it about his waist. Then he said that he was ready.[15]

The cell door swung open, and he walked through it for the last time. Flanked by his two guards, he moved slowly down the bleak corridor. As the three men crossed the prison courtyard, for a fleeting moment the sun caught Ozaki in its golden rays. Presently they reached the death house, which high walls concealed from the rest of the prison. Ozaki stepped through the door into a small anteroom. Near a corner a Buddhist altar blazed with gold and lighted candles. In the center of the room stood a small table and a chair, to which his guards escorted him. Ozaki sat down and surveyed the scene with tired, resigned eyes. He showed no emotion, revealed no fear, nothing but a slight tension. The witnesses who had foregathered in Ichijima's office were in place, seated about the room so that, along with the prisoner in his chair, they formed roughly a hollow square. Opposite Ozaki glowed the altar.[16]

"Are you Shujitsu Ozaki?" Ichijima asked the condemned man.

"No, I am Hotzumi Ozaki," the prisoner answered quietly but distinctly.*

Ichijima followed the ritual for an execution to the letter. Not only did he thus uphold Japanese decorum, but also the prisoner gained strength and courage by having a program to follow, by the sight of officialdom clad in its best to honor their common humanity, and by the comfort of his faith.

Ichijima read aloud the formal order of execution. Then he stepped back in favor of the chaplain. Sensho asked Ozaki

---

* The ideographs for Ozaki's given name are frequently rendered as "Shujitsu," but Ozaki preferred "Hotzumi."

whether he had a will, what disposition he wanted made of his effects, what he desired done with his body, and if he had any final statement to make. Ozaki answered all these questions politely, specifying that he wanted his lawyer to receive his remains. These details completed, Sensho offered Ozaki ceremonial tea and cakes. Ozaki extended his hand as if to accept, then hesitated and refused the refreshment.[17]

Ozaki knelt with the priest before the serene, taper-lit visage of Buddha, burning incense with closed eyes, while Sensho intoned the *Dai Muryoju Kyo* ("The Three Promises of the Great Sutra of Constant Life"). The ceremony over, the two worshipers bowed and rose to their feet. Ozaki turned to Ichijima and thanked him for all his kindness.

The two guards moved into place to guide Ozaki into the execution chamber. The officials silently rose and filed out. Witnesses and prisoner entered the death room by different doors. The witnesses seated themselves in a single row facing the death trap, the prison personnel on the extreme left, then Ichijima, Yuda, Akiyama, and the doctor.[18]

Slowly, serenely Ozaki stepped forward. The last room he entered was not, as morbid imagination might picture, small and dark but fairly large, with plain wooden walls. A broad shaft of morning light slanted in through the single window. Ozaki took his place approximately in the center of the room directly under the rope that would strangle his last breath. One of the attendants bound his ankles, legs, and arms. This was part of the usual procedure, to ensure that no unseemly struggle marred the occasion, to create the image of disorder or sordidness.[19]

The attendants adjusted the hood over his head. From his place in the row before the gallows, Yuda watched Ozaki's hands—small, articulate hands, hands that had written brilliantly about China, hands now motionless in final resignation. At last the noose slipped around the dark curve of Ozaki's neck. With all adjustments completed, the attendants stole away. Four or five executioners stood ready to spring the trap simultaneously, so that no one person should have the death of a fellowman on his conscience.[20]

A moment of taut stillness. Then the trap flew open. Ozaki's body dropped, and his neck snapped like a broken stick. Yuda could not take his eyes from Ozaki's hands, which shook as the breath of life struggled out of him. A deep, compelling silence engulfed the room. Dr. Omata looked at his watch. Ten minutes had elapsed. Normally a hanged person required about twelve minutes to die, but Ozaki looked as though life had left him. Dr. Omata checked Ozaki's pulse. The steady beat had stilled.* The unruffled composure with which Ozaki went to his death sincerely moved Ichijima and the others in attendance.[21]

As soon as his body had been removed from the execution chamber, the witnesses returned to the anteroom and took their seats as before. Within minutes Sorge entered in the company of two guards. Yuda watched with interest this man of whom he had heard so much but never seen. He wore dark trousers, a shirt with no necktie, and a loose jacket. His rugged features "looked very calm" and showed no fear or apprehension as he took the seat Ozaki had vacated so recently. "Are you Richard Sorge?" Ichijima asked.

"Yes, I am Richard Sorge." The reply came clearly and distinctly.

Then Ichijima advised him that in accordance with the orders of the minister of justice, he would be executed on this day. Sorge's expressive brows lifted, and his eyes sprang open like an animal's, but his voice held no tension. "It is today?" he inquired.

"Yes, today," Ichijima replied. To make sure that Sorge comprehended his Japanese, the governor asked, "Do you understand?"

"Yes, I understand," answered Sorge.

Then the chaplain took over. Once more Sensho asked the questions concerning the prisoner's final requests. Listening intently, Yuda understood the condemned man to say he wished to leave his property to "Anna."[22] Sorge hastily scribbled his

---

* The G-2 study "The Sorge Spy Ring . . ." (Washington, D.C., 1949, pp. A722-723) indicated that Ozaki murmured, "*Namu Amida Butsu*" twice before the trap was sprung (see also Charles A. Willoughby, *Shanghai Conspiracy* [New York, 1952, p. 126]). Neither Ichijima nor Yuda, both of whom paid acute attention to all the details of this execution, heard Ozaki say a word after his final thanks to Ichijima in the anteroom.

wishes in a will, which he entrusted to the Procurator's office.
Yuda had heard correctly. Sorge left his remaining funds to
Anna Clausen.[23] He also requested that a letter be sent to his
mother and sister through the German Embassy. He presented
those concerned in his execution with his dictionaries and his
Leica camera as tokens of thanks for their consideration.[24]

Sorge being a European and an atheist, the chaplain had
closed the door of the golden shrine before Sorge entered the
antechamber, but now Sensho offered him tea and cakes and
the opportunity to pray if he wished. Sorge refused both politely. He appeared completely at ease, very much master of
himself. Yet just as the guards moved forward to escort him
from the anteroom, Sorge turned to Ichijima and made one
final request. "May I have a cigarette?" he asked.

Ichijima was a compassionate man who had come to like
and respect Sorge. But he was also a prison governor of integrity. He could not break regulations out of favoritism. "No,"
he replied regretfully but firmly, "it is against the rules."

Yuda broke in impulsively. "Oh, let him have a cigarette!" he urged. "I know it is against the rules, but it is his
last wish. You can say you let him have some medicine at the
last minute."

But Sorge's request struck a wrong note with Ichijima.
It was too flippant; it smacked of bravado; it jarred in this
awesome hour. "No," he repeated with quiet finality, "it is
against the rules."

Sorge seemed neither disappointed nor resentful.[25] Like
Ozaki, he remained calm, dignified, a gentleman to the last.
With sincerity he thanked Ichijima and the other prison officials
for all they had done for him. Then with composure he walked
into that bare, sunlit room that had already claimed Ozaki.
From death he feared nothing and expected nothing. Once again
the functionaries left the anteroom and took their places in the
death chamber.[26]

The attendants bound his arms and legs, then melted into
the background. In that precise moment Sorge spoke clearly
and distinctly. His words tolled in the taut silence like funeral
bells:

"*Sakigun* [The Red Army]!"

"*Kokusai Kyosanto* [The International Communist Party]!"

"*Soviet Kyosanto* [The Soviet Communist Party]!"[27]

Man must worship as he must eat and drink and breathe. Let him deny there is a God, and he will invest with divinity some force within his understanding. So Sorge had set up his own trinity and called upon it in his last hour. Yet he spoke neither in German, the language of his boyhood, nor in the broken Russian of his adopted tongue; he spoke in Japanese, which always came haltingly to his lips. Thus Sorge's last words did not well up spontaneously; he had carefully selected them. He had to be sure that his audience understood, that they would report his words correctly, so that all would know he had died in the faith.

A second time Sorge intoned his litany. The words, the dedication with which Sorge uttered them, his whole attitude impressed Yuda to his very soul. "There was no show-off in his manner," said Yuda in retrospect. "Sorge was loyal and faithful to his cause to the end. He repeated his words like a person saying a prayer."

For the third time Sorge spoke his farewell salute to the world.* Then he snapped to attention. Instinctively recognizing the sure moment, the executioners sprang the trap. It was exactly 10:20 A.M.

Yuda's eyes moved irresistibly to Sorge's hands—much bigger than Ozaki's, hands that quivered in the death struggle. Watching them, Yuda asked himself, "What are we accomplishing by executing these two men? Will this be a plus for us or a minus?"

Ozaki's body, submissive to fate, had released his spirit willingly. Sorge's body had always kept his spirit earthbound; now it clung fiercely to life. Sorge took nineteen minutes to die.[28]

---

* Sorge's last words have been variously reported. According to the G-2 study, he said, "I thank you for all your kindnesses" ("Sorge Spy Ring," p. A723, see also *Shanghai Conspiracy*, p.127). Hans-Otto Meissner pictured him as crying out, "To hell with mankind!" (*The Man with Three Faces* [New York, 1955], p. 235). To Yuda, the Tokko's official witness to Sorge's execution, the scene remained one of the most unforgettable incidents of his life: he remembered Sorge's words exactly as recorded here.

"FOREVER A STRANGER"

Ichijima, Yuda, and the others filed silently out of the execution chamber and into the sun-washed air of the courtyard. The scenes they had just witnessed had moved them profoundly. Death was no stranger to Ichijima, but he never became hardened to an execution. In all his experience he had "never seen anyone act as nobly as Ozaki and Sorge at their deaths."[1]

In the governor's office the little group gratefully drank steaming tea. Printed certificates of execution were duly completed, names, date, and times filled in with sumi (Japanese calligraphy ink). Ichijima, Yuda, and Akiyama affixed their ideograph signatures attesting the certificates were accurate. Then Yuda and Akiyama returned to their offices to report that they had fulfilled the morning's mission. Soon the bustling routine of a busy day pushed the executions into the past.[2]

In accordance with prison custom the bodies of Ozaki and Sorge rested for twenty-four hours in the prison morgue to permit relatives or friends to claim the corpses. In general the outside world knew nothing about the executions, not because Ozaki and Sorge were hanged in unusual secrecy but because the Japanese press never played up executions. Normally a small notice would appear on an inner page, but with the paper shortage cutting all Japanese newspapers to the bone, items of limited interest fell by the wayside. In the vast majority of cases, after notifying the lawyers of the victims, the prison authorities had nothing further to do with the bodies.[3]

As soon as Kintaro Takeuchi, Ozaki's lawyer, received

the routine telegram, he informed Ms. Ozaki of her husband's death. Grief and shock stunned that faithful lady. "There is nothing before me, not even colors," she wrote drearily. "All that exists is a weary, endless amount of empty hours and empty space."[4]

Eiko had never dreamed that the execution would take place so quickly. Japanese justice was ponderous. Usually at least five years, often ten, frequently even more years elapsed between sentence and execution. The deaths of Sorge and Ozaki, long delayed by Western standards, seemed to Ms. Ozaki, her counselors, and to Asanuma as having been carried out with almost indecent haste.[5]

Eiko had trusted implicitly in Shin'ichi Matsumoto's assurances that the executions would be delayed for some time, and indeed, they had much cause for this belief. Not only was delay customary, but also the trials of some of the minor members of the ring were still in progress, and Saionji and other friends of Ozaki's were working frantically behind the scenes to have him freed.[6]

It is well that the grief-stricken Eiko could not have foreseen that a wait of less than a year almost certainly would have brought her husband the key to freedom; by October 1945 the American occupation would be emptying Japan's jails of political prisoners. The chances are about 99 percent that both Ozaki and Sorge would have been turned loose, as were a number of their associates.

But fortunately for her peace of mind Ms. Ozaki lacked the gift of prophecy. Having no sense of urgency, she had been out of Tokyo briefly. Back in the capital on November 6 she had intended to visit her husband the next day but mercifully postponed it, promising herself to go to Sugamo on November 8. Now on that date she went to the prison with Takeuchi and Yuho Morikawa to claim her husband's body. She brought a sheaf of chrysanthemums to place in his coffin and poured French perfume on his body "because he was so fond of it."[7]

Then she escorted the coffin to the crematorium in Ochiai in what is now Shinjiku-ku, Tokyo. There cremation took place at 3:00 P.M. "I walked through the dark road in the rain holding the still warm ashes of my husband in my arms," Ms. Ozaki described her sad trip home. "I said to the ashes of my husband,

'This is the home to which you wanted to come so much. Now you have your study.' I put the ashes on the table in his study with tears in my eyes. Outside, it was pouring rain.''[8]

On the second anniversary of Ozaki's execution his ashes were interred at Tama Cemetery.[9] There Ozaki's remains rest today.

Sorge's body presented a problem. No one knew who was responsible for it. The German Embassy was notified but wanted nothing to do with Sorge's remains. If the Soviet Embassy knew he had been executed, it gave no sign. The Japanese had no alternative but to bury Sorge in the prison graveyard with a wooden marker on the spot.[10]

On the date of the execution Asanuma was in Kobe, buying books for his client. He returned to find a message that Sugamo Prison had telephoned him. Promptly he returned the call and thus learned that Sorge had died on the gallows. The lawyer did not go to Sugamo, nor did he contact anyone concerning disposition of the body, for he had no idea what Sorge wanted done with his remains. He had never mentioned his living relatives to Asanuma.

Asanuma busied himself liquidating the estate in accordance with Sorge's directions. He realized about 15,000 yen* and deposited this in Sorge's bank account, after deducting a very modest sum for his own expenses. Anna Clausen's inheritance was awaiting her when she and Clausen were released from prison and sought Asanuma's aid.

Asanuma could not bring himself to break up Sorge's magnificent book collection and donated it to the Procurator's Office, where it burned to the last page in the fire bombings of 1945. He never ceased to mourn the loss of Sorge's library.[11]

Time passed. Sun and rain warmed and washed the shallow grave in Sugamo's dismal little graveyard. One by one the wooden markers disappeared into the fires of nearby households, sacrificed to the acute shortage of fuel.[12] Tokyo burned like a vast torch in the bombings. Among the thousands of homes feeding the flames was Sorge's ramshackle house. Asanuma saw the Procurator's Office bombed to rubble. With it burned not only Sorge's beloved books but also irreplaceable

---

* At that time the dollar exchange rate was 4 yen to the dollar.

evidence on his case.[13] Sugamo, too, was bombed. Fate seemed determined to erase from Japan every tangible reminder of Richard Sorge.

But one had not forgotten him and would not while she could breathe. For many months after her world so unexpectedly and shockingly had shattered in October 1941, grief for Sorge and terror for herself tore at Hanako. In spite of Mr. M.'s assurance it seemed too much to hope that she would not be accused of complicity in Sorge's spying.[14]

Human existence cannot continue at this shrill pitch. Gradually the recurring cycle of daily routine quiets the wounded spirit in spite of itself. Slowly Hanako came to accept the fact that she stood in no danger of arrest. She did not know that this was because of the gentlemen's agreement among Sorge, Ohashi, and Yoshikawa.

She wished neither to return to her old life at the Rheingold nor to marry; her duty was to make a home for her mother and niece. With characteristic practicality she counted her assets: a house, a piano, and her own vigorous, sensible self. She secured a government loan to build an extension to the house and, by renting two rooms and her piano to students, brought in a modest income sufficient for three frugal women.[15]

She thought of Sorge constantly but had few clues to his fate. In July 1943 the Yodobashi Police Station had her under investigation. She deduced shrewdly that if she still interested the police, Sorge must be alive. On November 7, 1944, she was at the home of her brother-in-law. She remembered Sorge on that day but later claimed no intuition of disaster. Her thoughts of Sorge, as he breathed his last, were no more and no less gloomy than usual.[16]

Hanako learned of Sorge's death for the first time when, in October 1945, the occupation authorities released the story to the press. The news came almost as a relief, bringing the freedom of finality. Death itself she could accept with resignation. Carefully she scanned the published list of those connected with the Sorge ring but recognized none of the Japanese names. These newspaper stories did not mention Sorge's burial place, so Hanako assumed that his body had been returned to his mother and sister in Germany.[17]

The Sorge case had generated much interest in Japan

because the main action had taken place on Japanese soil and many Japanese were involved. The two leading spirits of a society to study the matter were Kawai and Ozaki's half brother, Hotsuki Ozaki. Naturally this movement took a strong pro-Ozaki tilt.[18] By 1948 this cult was gathering momentum, and a group of the admirers of Sorge and Ozaki commissioned Hanako to write her memoirs of Sorge for publication in their magazine, *Junken News*. Economic necessity swallowed any qualms Hanako might have felt at opening her life with Sorge to public view.

It so happened that while engaged on this manuscript, she stopped in a bookstore to browse. Riffling through a magazine she spotted a story about Sorge, from which she learned that his body still rested in the Zoshigaya graveyard near Sugamo Prison. Reverent disposition of remains so that loved ones can pay their frequent respects to the departed spirit is a matter of real importance to a Japanese, so this information upset Hanako exceedingly.

She was not the woman to wring her hands in ineffectual grief. With her to think was to act. On November 23, 1948, she called on Asanuma. The visit much surprised him, for he had not the slightest inkling that such a person as Hanako existed. Sorge had never mentioned her name, not even that he had a Japanese sweetheart. Hanako wanted to learn the exact location of the Zoshigaya Cemetery, but this he did not know. Not easily balked, she soon located the graveyard. On December 17 she presented herself at the office of the custodian to ask the site of Sorge's grave. Although sympathetic, he was unable to help at the time. He explained that the markers had long since disappeared for firewood; however, he promised to do what he could to locate the grave and would notify her.[19]

In the meantime, she kept up the search. Three days later she spoke with a Mr. Uno, chief of the Administrative Section at Tokyo Prison in Kosuge. He checked what few records were available, the Sugamo files having perished in the bombing of that prison. All Uno could find was the date and time of the execution, with Sorge's name and nationality—evidently a copy of the certificate of execution.

On January 6 she returned and received a severe setback.

Uno would only say coldly, "All administrative affairs of the Japanese Ministry of Justice are now under the jurisdiction of the American occupation, and as the international situation is extremely delicate at the moment, they could not touch upon Sorge's incident in any manner." Back to Asanuma she sped to beg his assistance. The lawyer promised he would make the necessary arrangements. He counseled Hanako to wait before trying anything else.[20]

To this she agreed, for the magazine was pressing her to have her manuscript ready for publication by February 9. Working intensively, she completed the last touches by the deadline. Then frustration raised its head on this front, too. On February 10, 1949, MacArthur's headquarters released its report concerning the Sorge case. This brought to a halt the projects of the Ozaki-Sorge group.[21]

This perforce delayed Hanako's project to rebury Sorge. She had counted on royalties for the considerable sum necessary to pay for the exhumation and for a plot in Tama Cemetery. Finally, in July 1949, her book came off the press. Now she had the means to purchase the cemetery lot. The custodian of Tama Cemetery took care of the preliminaries: hired the gravediggers for the exhumation, set up the cremation, and submitted to Hanako a bill of roughly 5,500 yen—a very tidy sum for a woman in Hanako's circumstances.[22]

Not until November 16, 1949, slightly more than a year since she first started her project, did the spades bite into the earth of the Zoshigaya graveyard at the spot pinpointed after much research as the exact site of Sorge's burial. The little group surrounding the spot consisted of Hanako, a representative of the custodian's office, a young man from the Tama Cemetery Masonry as witness, and three gravediggers. The sky was cloudy, so no warming sun took the edge off the sharp November air.[23]

More than physical chill shook Hanako as she peered into the slowly deepening excavation. But time, circumstances, and nature had been kind. Sorge's corpse had been consigned to the earth close to the surface, protected only by a flimsy coffin and the clothes he wore when the trap was sprung. By the time Hanako came for her last tribute, decomposition was complete, leaving only the skeleton, as clean and impersonal as a scientific exhibit.[24]

This was Sorge's skeleton, no doubt about that. Those big bones were not those of a Japanese. There on his right leg was the place where his World War I wound had lamed him; the bone had not knit properly, one end of the fracture slightly overlapping the other. There, too, were his well-remembered spectacles and a belt buckle. Gently, reverently she lifted the skull and picked up the gold bridgework that had so pained and annoyed him in life.[25]

The hour was just short of noon when the laborers filled in the excavation and Hanako was free to escort the bones to the Shimo-Ochiai Cremation Center, where the cleansing fire had reduced Ozaki's body to ashes so long ago. That evening she brought Sorge's ashes back to her home in Mitikaya City, near Tokyo. She also kept his spectacles, belt buckle, and teeth.

Shortly thereafter Hanako took the bridgework to a jeweler, to be fashioned into a ring.[26]

Almost a year elapsed before Hanako placed Sorge's ashes in his final resting place.[27]

So Richard Sorge lies with Japan's honored dead in the somber beauty of Tama Cemetery. Above him stands a stone inscribed in graceful Japanese ideographs, "Here lies a hero who sacrificed his life fighting against war and for world peace." Hanako and her friends of the Society to Aid the Victims of the Ozaki-Sorge Incident erected this final tribute.[28] It is grimly just that Sorge, shaped and rent by the blood of Russia and Germany, should rest in the end in neither, "forever a stranger" in the alien soil of Japan.

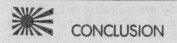 CONCLUSION

Many, probably most, soldiers on both sides of World War I who survived that conflict emerged with a bone-deep hatred of war as a personal experience and as an instrument of national policy. Of these, many left the battlefield disillusioned with the government and society that had brought this horror upon them. To a portion of these men, communism, which professed to reach across national boundaries, seemed to offer a fresh start for humanity. Of these, a few were not content to talk and dream; they became members of the Communist Party and worked actively for the revolution. Sorge typified every ring in this ever-narrowing spiral.

Experience of war did not trigger the other major members of his ring on their trajectory toward communism. Clausen had served briefly in the German Army's Signal Corps, but Ozaki, Miyagi, and Voukelitch had no direct combat experience. If they had a common starting point, it was the fact that none of them had a homeland that meant to him what his native soil means to the average human being.

Clausen's path was simple, grass-roots economics. German industry was on the rocks, unemployment was rife, and when he caught a glimpse of Russian heavy industry, he decided that this society had the answer. Police repression in Yugoslavia had alienated Voukelitch, but it is doubtful if his involvement with communism would have gone beyond intellectual dabbling had not two former comrades talked him into becoming an *apparatchik*. Miyagi was an almost predestined victim of any movement that offered him an alternative to Japanese imperialism, on the one hand, and American racial discrimination, on the other.

Ozaki was possibly the most complex of the lot. He could sympathize with underdogs but had no desire to be one. He loved luxury, made a good salary, and lived up to every yen of it. His early remark to the effect that if he could not be the best in one field, he would choose another, provides the key to his actions. He was not cut out to be a humble worker; he liked the air on top of the heap.

Sorge and his ring were not working for democracy and political freedom. One can readily understand why the Japanese members held the current military state in abhorrence, but the totalitarian pattern was so deeply embedded in them that they could see no remedy except in another equally statist regime. Nor were they consciously forwarding the Allied cause in World War II, as some have sentimentally suggested. They were spying for the Soviet Union, the interests of which during the war years happened to coincide with those of the Allies. These men worked, and some of them died, for a cause in which they believed, and it does their memory no honor to drape them figuratively in any flag but their revered hammer and sickle.

Nor were they crusaders for world peace—another sentimental suggestion. Their devotion to peace in the abstract is questionable. There is no evidence that any one of them expressed a qualm about the Soviet Union's aggression in Finland, its swallowing the Baltic states, its attack upon Poland in concert with Hitler. They were trying to preserve the Soviet Union from attack, quite a different aim. They seem to have accepted—certainly they used—the curious rationale that passing German and Japanese state secrets to Moscow would keep the Soviet Union out of war. In fact, such knowledge could help the Russians cope with war only if it came, either on their own initiative or another nation's.

The Sorge case offers a sobering example of the height and breadth a Soviet *apparat* could reach, even in a closed society like Japan of the 1930s and 1940s. Was a spy ring ever so highly placed? Possibly, for the only ones of which the outside world hears are those that have been found out. But to the best of our knowledge, Sorge's ring must take its place at or very near the top.

What was Sorge's position in history? On the German side this is difficult, if not impossible, to assess. Ott respected Sorge's evaluations and depended on him for reliable information, so to that extent Sorge influenced the thinking and attitude of the German Embassy. However, Ott was not in high favor with Hitler, and it is highly doubtful that Ott's opinions carried much weight in Berlin.

On the Russian side two factors vitiated what could have been an outstanding contribution to history prior to the German invasion of the Soviet Union in June 1941. At the Tokyo end Clausen's destruction or cutting of messages intended for the Fourth Department, plus Sorge's haphazard management, which enabled such sabotage to take place under his nose, watered down the nature and importance of his many warnings of imminent attack. Had the Kremlin possessed all of Sorge's detailed material, the Fourth Department might have taken his reports much more seriously and insisted that they receive due consideration at the highest levels of Soviet command. Yet such was Stalin's obstinate stupidity and willful blindness that he and his hierarchy ignored not only Sorge's warnings but also those from other sources much nearer the scene of action.

The coup most frequently credited to Sorge is that he personally saved the Soviet Union by his assurance that Japan was going south on its program of conquest, instead of north against Siberia and that as a result of this intelligence, the Red Army released the troops from the eastern stations that enabled them to stop the Nazi advance in the West. While Sorge did provide such information, the corollary is pure speculation. There is no evidence that Sorge's messages provided the only reason the Soviets moved troops to European Russia. Stalin really had no other choice; Japan might strike, but Germany had already struck. He had to deal with the current reality, and take a chance on the problematical future. This would have been the case had no such person as Sorge ever existed. His messages provided valuable confirmation of Japanese intentions, but he cannot be credited with having been the sole savior of the Soviet Union.

Sorge did enough for his adopted homeland without our enhancing his image. If we cannot credit him with a few spectacular coups of surpassing importance, we can credit him with what in the long run was a more valuable service. His contribution consisted of a steady stream of dependable information straight from some of the most authoritative sources in Japan: his own foothold in the German Embassy and through Ozaki the South Manchurian Railroad, the Konoye cabinets, and a whole network of Japanese political and intellectual circles, as well as Miyagi with his subring of agents and his contacts with the Japanese Army.

For more than two decades, long after much of Sorge's story had been known in the West, Moscow maintained a cryptic silence about him. The Soviet Union only began to honor him after the Stalin cult of personality had gone out of style. This is ironic because Sorge was an ardent admirer of Stalin. On November 6, 1964, the Kremlin proclaimed Sorge posthumously a Hero of the Soviet Union. Sorge fully merited the official and journalistic honors, however belated, for he had well served the cause in which he believed and the nation for which he lived and died.

APPENDIX

NOTES

CHAPTER 1
"Mr. R. Sorge"

1. *Japan Advertiser* and *Japan Times and Mail*, both September 7, 1933.
2. Ibid., September 1, 1933.
3. *Japan Advertiser*, September 2, 1933.
4. *Japan Times and Mail*, September 3, 1933.
5. *Japan Advertiser*, September 3, 1933.
6. Ibid., September 7, 1933. *Japan Times and Mail*, September 8, 1933.

CHAPTER 2
"Slightly Different from the Average"

1. F. W. Deakin and G. R. Storry, *The Case of Richard Sorge* (New York, 1966), pp. 23–24; hereafter *Case of Richard Sorge*. This work contains by far the best account of Sorge's early life available in English. The facts about Sorge's family are already blurred. Nine seems the most authentic figure available of the number of children.
2. Partial Memoirs of Richard Sorge, Part 2, p. 30. Sorge typed this autobiographical material while in Sugamo Prison. Unfortunately it is incomplete, the rest lost when the Ministry of Justice burned in the bombing of Tokyo during World War II. The English translation quoted herein appears in "A Partial Documentation of the Sorge Espionage Case," prepared in the Intelligence Section (G-2), Far East Command, 1950; pages cited herein are those of this "Partial Documentation"; hereafter Sorge Memoir. This same memoir, in slightly different format, appears in Charles A. Willoughby, *Shanghai Conspiracy* (New York, 1952), pp. 133–230; hereafter *Shanghai Conspiracy*.

3. Obi Toshito, ed., *Gendai-shi Shiryo, Zoruge Jiken (Materials on Modern History, The Sorge Incident)* (Tokyo, 1962), Vol. I, p. 320; hereafter *Gendai-shi Shiryo*.

4. See, for example, Viktor Mayevsky, "Comrade Richard Sorge," *Pravda*, September 4, 1964, p. 4; hereafter "Comrade Richard Sorge."

5. *Case of Richard Sorge*, pp. 35–36.

6. Sorge Memoir, Part 2, p. 30.

7. Ibid., pp. 30–31.

8. Ibid., p. 31.

9. Ibid.

10. Ibid. *Gendai-shi Shiryo*, Vol. I, p. 321.

11. Sorge Memoir, Part 2, p. 32. *Gendai-shi Shiryo*, Vol. I, p. 321.

12. Ibid.

13. *Gendai-shi Shiryo*, Vol. I, p. 319.

14. Sorge Memoir, Part 2, p. 33.

15. Ibid., pp. 33–34.

16. Ibid., p. 34.

17. Ibid. *Case of Richard Sorge*, p. 26.

18. Julius Mader, Gerhard Stucklik, and Horst Pehnert, *Dr. Sorge funkt aus Tokyo: Ein Dokumentarbericht über Kundschafter des Friedens mit auggewählten Artikeln von Richard Sorge* (Berlin, 1968), p. 45; hereafter *Dr. Sorge funkt aus Tokyo*.

19. Sorge Memoir, Part 2, p. 34.

20. Ibid.

21. *Case of Richard Sorge*, pp. 29–30.

22. *Dr. Sorge funkt aus Tokyo*, p. 56.

23. Christiane Sorge, *"Mein Mann, Richard Sorge." Die Weltwoche* (Zurich), December 1, 1964; hereafter "My Husband."

24. Sorge Memoir, Part 2, pp. 34–35.

25. Message, Berlin to Tokyo, February 9, 1942, signed Braunstumm, German Foreign Office Archives, State Security File, Japan (1941–1944), files on Sorge case; hereafter German Archives.

26. *Case of Richard Sorge*, pp. 32–33.

27. Sorge Memoir, Part 2, p. 35.

28. Hede Massing, *This Deception* (New York, 1951), p. 71; hereafter *This Deception*.

29. Sorge Memoir, Part 2, p. 35.

30. *Gendai-shi Shiryo*, Vol. I, p. 324.

31. Sorge Memoir, Part 2, p. 35.

32. I. Dementieva and N. Agayantz, "Richard Sorge, Soviet Intelligence Agent," *Sovietskaya Rossiya*, September 6, 1964, p. 4; hereafter "Richard Sorge."

33. Sorge Memoir, Part 1, p. 4; Part 2, p. 35. These books were published in Germany under the pseudonym of R. Sonter and were translated into Russian.

34. *This Deception*, p. 74.

35. "My Husband." *Case of Richard Sorge*, p. 43.

36. *Der Spiegel*, June 27, 1951, p. 25. From June 13 to October 3, 1951, this West German magazine ran a series of articles entitled *"Herr Sorge sass mit zu Tische: Porträt*

eines Spions"; hereafter *Der Spiegel*.

37. Alain Guerin and Nicole Chatel, *Camarade Sorge* (Paris, 1965), pp. 16, 274; hereafter *Camarade Sorge*.

38. Ibid., p. 330.

39. Sorge Memoir, Part 1, p. 4.

40. Ibid.

41. Ibid., pp. 4–5; *Case of Richard Sorge*, p. 45. Message, February 9, 1942, German Archives.

42. *This Deception*, pp. 75–77.

43. Sorge Memoir, Part 1, pp. 5, 13.

44. Ibid., pp. 13–14; Part 2, p. 39. *Gendai-shi Shiryo*, Vol. I, p. 335.

CHAPTER 3
"We Could Work Well Together"

1. *Gendai-shi Shiryo*, Vol. I, pp. 336–38. Sorge Memoir, Part 1, pp. 16–17. By autumn "Alex" had returned to Russia, leaving Sorge in sole charge.

2. Sorge Memoir, Part 1, pp. 19–23.

3. *Gendai-shi Shiryo*, Vol. III, pp. 437, 172; Vol. I, p. 338. Sorge Memoir, Part 1, p. 23. This name is often spelled "Klausen." But the name Clausen appears on his driver's license as well as his signature; see photo in *Shanghai Conspiracy*, p. 75.

4. *Camarade Sorge*, p. 72.

5. *Gendai-shi Shiryo*, Vol. III, pp. 84–85, 141. His birth date was February 27, 1899.

6. Ibid., pp. 85–86, 91, 142, 146–47.

7. Ibid., p. 425. Dieter Wolf, *"Der Funker des Senders 'Ramsai'; Wie Max und Anna Christiansen-Klausen an der Seite Kundshafters Dr. Sorge kämpften,"* *Neues Deutschland*, November 2, 1965: hereafter *"Der Funker."*

8. Ibid.

9. *Gendai-shi Shiryo*, pp. 451–53, 443. Anna was born on April 2, 1899. Her mother died in that childbirth, and a Russian adopted Anna when she was three years old. She received no schooling beyond the fourth grade.

10. Ibid., pp. 425, 453.

11. Ibid., p. 437. *"Der Funker."* Sorge Memoir, Part 1, p. 8.

12. "Extracts from an Authenticated Translation of Foreign Affairs Yearbook, 1942, Criminal Affairs Bureau, Ministry of Justice, Tokyo, Japan" (hereafter "Extracts"), Clausen Testimony, original p. 566, Record Group 319 Army Staff, Numerical Section of Intelligence Documents (ID Files) ID 923289, Collection and Dissemination Division, Office of the Assistant Chief of Staff, G-2 (Intelligence), Box 5F8-18, located in Military Records Division, National Archives Records Center, Suitland, Maryland.

13. *Gendai-shi Shiryo*, Vol. III, pp. 426–27, 454–55. Mishin was a radio technician who worked for Sorge in Shang-

hai and Canton. The term *White Russian* usually is understood to mean one who opposed the Reds, but both Anna and Sorge (Sorge Memoir, Part 1, p. 17) referred to him as such. Possibly they meant a Russian immigrant, or he may have been a native of Byelorussia.

14. *Gendai-shi Shiryo*, Vol. III, pp. 436–37.

15. Ibid., p. 437. Years later, interviewed by a Soviet reporter in East Germany, Anna gushed that she was already a Communist sympathizer, that Sorge "patiently and cautiously" indoctrinated her, going into detail "only later when he was sure of my firm resolve to devote my life to the struggle. . . ." (B. Orlov, "Centre Listens in to Ramsay," *Izvestia*, October 28, 1964; hereafter "Centre Listens"). This is in direct contradiction of Anna's testimony under oath.

16. *"Der Funker."*

17. *Gendai-shi Shiryo*, Vol. III, p. 227.

18. U.S. House of Representatives, 82d Congress, First Session, Un-American Activities Committee, *Hearings on Un-American Aspects of the Richard Sorge Spy Case*, Washington, 1951, p. 1156; hereafter *Hearings*. "Extracts," Clausen testimony, original p. 595, op. cit.

19. Message, Shanghai to Berlin, December 5, 1941, signed Zinsser, German Archives. Sorge Memoir, Part 1, p. 16. An entire book could be written about Sorge's Shanghai ring.

20. Sorge Memoir, Part 1, pp. 19–22. *Hearings*, pp. 1178, 1221.

21. Sorge Memoir, Part 1, pp. 14, 17. In view of the teapot tempest Smedley stirred up in the late 1940s when Major General Charles A. Willoughby, G-2 of General Douglas MacArthur's Far East Command, accused her of being a Soviet agent, Sorge's words are noteworthy. If Smedley was not an agent of the Soviet Union in the narrow sense of being paid expressly for that purpose, she was the willing and knowing accomplice of a major Soviet agent and "a direct member" of his Shanghai ring.

22. *Gendai-shi Shiryo*, Vol. I, p. 520.

23. "Extracts," Part XV, Sorge's Notes, p. 195, Record Group 319, File ID 923289, Part 37, Box 7482.

24. Ibid., Part XVI, Clausen Notes, p. 233, Record Group 319, File ID 923289, Part 37, Box 7482.

25. Sorge Memoir, Part 1, p. 15. *Gendai-shi Shiryo*, Vol. I, p. 338.

26. *Gendai-shi Shiryo*, Vol. II, p. 207. The given name is variously Hotsumi and Jotzumi. Shigeharu Matsumoto, who knew Ozaki well, told

Dr. Prange that "Hotzumi" is correct.

27. Shin Aochi, *Chisei* (August 1956), p. 219.

28. Sorge Memoir, Part 1, p. 18. *Gendai-shi Shiryo*, Vol. II, p. 207. Hotzumi Ozaki, *Aijo-wa furu hoshi no gotoku* (*Love Was Like a Falling Star*) (Tokyo, 1946), p. 193; hereafter *Falling Star*. Chalmers Johnson, *An Instance of Treason: Ozaki Hotsumi and the Sorge Spy Ring* (Stanford, Calif., 1964), p. 36; hereafter *Instance of Treason*.

29. *Gendai-shi Shiryo*, Vol. II, pp. 5, 117. Hotsuki Ozaki, *Zoruge Jiken* (*Sorge Incident*) (Tokyo, 1953), pp. 11–15; hereafter *Sorge Incident*.

30. *Gendai-shi Shiryo*, Vol. II, pp. 109, 99, 107. An interesting account of Ozaki's early life appears in *Instance of Treason*, pp. 23–39.

31. *Gendai-shi Shiryo*, Vol. II, p. 198. Charles A. Buss, *Asia in the Modern World* (New York, 1964), p. 310, hereafter *Asia in the Modern World*.

32. Michitaro Kazama, *Aru Hangyaku, Ozaki Hotzumi no Shogai* (*A Case of Treason: The Life of Ozaki Hotzumi*) (Tokyo, 1959), pp. 29–39.

33. Ibid., p. 25. *Gendai-shi Shiryo*, Vol. II, pp. 198, 7.

34. Takeo Mitamura, *Senso to Kyosanshugi* (*War and Communism*) (Tokyo, 1950), pp. 339–40.

35. *Gendai-shi Shiryo*, Vol. II,

p. 7. *Instance of Treason*, p. 34.

36. *Sorge Incident*, pp. 30–32. Eiko Ozaki, "Omeide," in Yuichi Horie and Yoshishige Kozai, eds., *Edai-naru Aijo* (*The Great Love*) (Tokyo, 1949), pp. 4–5. Yoko, born in China in 1929, was the Ozakis' only child.

37. *Gendai-shi Shiryo*, Vol. II, pp. 7, 100.

38. This brief sketch is based upon *Asia in the Modern World*, pp. 304–11; Edwin O. Reischauer, *The Japanese* (London, 1977), pp. 88–97.

39. *Gendai-shi Shiryo*, Vol. II, pp. 7, 197.

40. Ibid., p. 7. *Sorge Incident*, p. 72.

41. Sorge Memoir, Part 1, pp. 18, 22.

42. Sorge Memoir, Part 1, p. 18. *Gendai-shi Shiryo*, Vol. II, p. 111.

43. *Gendai-shi Shiryo*, Vol. II, pp. 100, 205. *Instance of Treason*, p. 89. U.S. Army, Far East Command, Military Intelligence Section, "The Sorge Spy Ring—A Case Study in International Espionage in the Far East," reproduced in *Congressional Record*, Vol. 95, Part 12 Appendix, 81st Congress, First Session, February 9, 1949, p. A715; hereafter "Sorge Spy Ring."

44. *Gendai-shi Shiryo*, Vol. II, p. 208. *Instance of Treason*, p. 69.

45. Interview with Teikichi Ka-

wai, January 13, 1965; hereafter titled Kawai. Replies
submitted by Kawai to a
questionnaire from Dr.
Prange; this document is undated but was completed early
in 1965; hereafter Kawai
questionnaire. *Gendai-shi
Shiryo*, Vol. II, p. 208. *Instance of Treason*, p. 80.

46. Sorge Memoir, Part 1, p. 18.

47. Dr. Prange formed the
impression of Kawai as described herein at their initial
interview, January 13, 1965.
Kawai broke with the Com-
munist Party when he finally
recognized that the Comintern had been a tool of the
Soviet Union's interest. But
he remained hopefully de-
voted to communism as an
ideology. He might have
made a clean break had he
not been engaged in polish-
ing Ozaki's postmortem halo.
Interviews with Kawai, January 13 and 19, 1965.

48. *Gendai-shi Shiryo*, Vol. III,
p. 683. "Sorge Spy Ring,"
pp. A708, A715. *Instance of
Treason*, pp. 58, 79.

49. *Gendai-shi Shiryo*, Vol. II,
p. 105.

50. Ibid., pp. 208–209. Sorge
Memoir, Part 1, p. 118. For
a summation of Funakoshi's
background, see "Sorge Spy
Ring," p. A715; *Shanghai
Conspiracy*, pp. 79–80; and
Instance of Treason, pp. 58,
60, 81–82.

51. Sorge Memoir, Part 1, p. 23.
Gendai-shi Shiryo, Vol. I, p.

346. It is incredible that a man
of Sorge's mentality could
confer with his principal assistant in China on an average of once a week for more
than six months and recall
nothing that passed between
them.

CHAPTER 4
"You Might Try Tokyo"

1. *Gendai-shi Shiryo*, Vol. I, p.
347.

2. Ibid., p. 348. Sorge Memoir,
Part 2, p. 27.

3. *Der Spiegel*, June 27, 1951,
p. 25. *Dr. Sorge funkt aus
Tokyo*, p. 108, states that
Sorge and Christiane "had
mutually agreed to dissolve
their marriage in 1932."
Deakin and Storry indicate
that Sorge may have met
Christiane in Berlin during
the summer of 1933 and there
secured "an amicable di-
vorce" (*Case of Richard
Sorge*, p. 101). After his arrest in 1941 Sorge told his
questioners that he had no wife
(*Gendai-shi Shiryo*, Vol. I,
p. 329).

4. *Camarade Sorge*, pp. 302–
03. *Dr. Sorge funkt aus Tokyo*, p. 108.

5. Sorge Memoir, Part 2, p. 27.

6. *Gendai-shi Shiryo*, Vol. I, p.
348. Sorge Memoir, Part 2,
p. 27. "Extracts," Part XV,
Sorge's Notes, p. 190, Record Group 329, File ID
923289, Box 7482. Borov-

itch, an associate of Sorge's of long standing, was destined to die, like Berzin, in the Stalin purges; Radek, too, would fall from grace during that specific period ("Richard Sorge").

7. This thumbnail sketch of Japanese-Russian relations is largely based upon *Asia in the Modern World*, pp. 279–322, 378–382.

8. *Gendai-shi Shiryo*, Vol. I, p. 348.

9. Ibid., p. 449; Vol. III, p. 163. "Extracts," Part XV, Sorge's Notes, p. 192, op. cit. Because only the head of the spy ring was permitted to know the code, Sorge guarded the secret in his early years in Japan, never sharing it with his first radioman, Bruno Wendt, alias Bernhardt.

10. *Gendai-shi Shiryo*, Vol. I, pp. 348, 449.

11. "Extracts," Interrogation of Richard Sorge, December 20, 1941, p. 25, Record Group 319, File ID 923289, Part 47, Box 7484.

12. Hede Massing, "The Almost Perfect Russian Spy," *True* (December 1951), p. 96; hereafter "The Almost Perfect Russian Spy." Ms. Massing claimed that at the party's direction, she wrote to an influential German "both introducing and recommending Sorge to him as a foreign correspondent." This article is riddled with errors, accepts secondhand accounts, and is heavily embroidered. But she knew Sorge, and her tales of direct experience should not be discounted in the absence of proof to the contrary.

13. *Der Spiegel*, August 8, 1951, p. 28. Benno Reifenberg, who in 1933 and 1934 headed the *Frankfurter Zeitung's* Far East section, claimed that Heinrich Simon, grandson of the newspaper's founder, engaged Sorge before 1934, prior to his departure for Japan, upon the recommendation of Eugen Ott. Paul Sethe, a former editor of the newspaper, stated that he remembered Ott's recommendation but claimed that he himself compiled and wrote the reports for Japan through 1935. If these accounts are true, it would mean that Ott knew Sorge, or at least knew of him, before he reached Japan, contradicting more direct evidence. In 1933 Ott was an obscure lieutenant colonel, no great favorite with the Nazis, and it is unlikely that his recommendation would have meant much to the prestigious newspaper in that year. By 1935, however, he wielded considerably more clout, and might well have recommended Sorge in that year or early in 1936.

14. *Case of Richard Sorge*, p. 204.

15. "Extracts," Interrogation of Richard Sorge, op. cit. *Ca-*

marade Sorge, pp. 344–45. Unfortunately Goriev gave no specific examples of how he and Sorge worked together, confining himself to generalities.

16. *Gendai-shi Shiryo*, Vol. I, p. 228.

17. Curt Reiss, *Total Espionage* (New York, 1941), pp. 88–89, 219; hereafter *Total Espionage*. *Democratic Idea: The Myth and Reality* is perhaps Haushofer's best-known work.

18. *Total Espionage*, pp. 88–89.

19. *Gendai-shi Shiryo*, Vol. I, p. 228.

20. Ibid., pp. 229, 348. Sorge also obtained credentials from the financial sheet *Berliner Börsen Zeitung* and the Dutch *Amsterdam Algemeen Handelsblad*.

21. *Gendai-shi Shiryo*, Vol. I, p. 229.

22. Sorge Memoir, Part 2, pp. 9–10.

23. *The Deception*, p. 69.

24. "Extracts," Interrogation of Richard Sorge, op. cit. *Gendai-shi Shiryo*, Vol. I, p. 348.

25. "Sorge Spy Ring," p. A710.

26. "The Almost Perfect Russian Spy," p. 96.

27. *Gendai-shi Shiryo*, Vol. I, p. 349. *Hearings*, p. 1206. Who gave Sorge these instructions remains unknown.

28. *Gendai-shi Shiryo*, Vol. I, p. 228. *Hearings*, p. 1206.

29. *Gendai-shi Shiryo*, Vol. I, p. 349. *Hearings*, pp. 1156, 1206–07. The Japanese authorities, the Far East Command G-2, and the House Un-American Affairs Committee all tried to discover the identity of the *Washington Post* man but were unsuccessful.

30. "Extracts," Testimony of Richard Sorge, op. cit. Ralph de Toledano, *Spies, Dupes, and Diplomats* (New York, 1951), pp. 70–71; hereafter *Spies, Dupes, and Diplomats*.

CHAPTER 5
"No Equivalent in History"

1. Herbert von Dirksen, *Moscow, Tokyo, London* (London, 1951), pp. 135, 142; hereafter *Moscow, Tokyo, London*.

2. *Gendai-shi Shiryo*, Vol. I, pp. 228, 359.

3. Ibid., pp. 228–29. Many years later Etzdorff was German ambassador to Great Britain.

4. Ibid., p. 227.

5. Ibid., p. 230.

6. Ibid., p. 245.

7. *Moscow, Tokyo, London*, p. 128.

8. Ibid., p. 142.

9. Interview with Ms. Mitsutaro Araki, January 6, 1965; hereafter Araki.

10. *Der Spiegel*, June 20, 1951, p. 29.

11. Interview with Araki, January 11, 1965.

12. *Der Spiegel*, June 20, 1951, p. 28. *Total Espionage*, p. 9. *Moscow, Tokyo, London*, p. 143. For an absorbing ac-

count of Schleicher's career, see John W. Wheeler-Bennett, *The Nemesis of Power: The German Army in Politics, 1918–1945* (London, 1954); hereafter *Nemesis of Power.*

13. *Total Espionage*, p. 218.

14. Ellis M. Zacharias, *Secret Missions* (New York, 1946), p. 159; hereafter *Secret Missions.*

15. *Der Spiegel*, June 20, 1951, p. 29.

16. *Moscow, Tokyo, London*, pp. 142–43.

17. *Gendai-shi Shiryo*, Vol. I, p. 230.

18. Interview with Araki, January 6, 1965.

19. Sorge Memoir, Part 2, p. 21.

20. *Der Spiegel*, June 20, 1951, p. 29.

21. *Gendai-shi Shiryo*, Vol. I, p. 230.

22. Interviews with Araki, January 6 and 11, 1965.

23. *Der Spiegel*, June 27, 1951, p. 23.

24. Interviews with Araki, January 6 and 11, 1965.

25. *Der Spiegel*, June 27, 1951, pp. 23–24.

26. *Camarade Sorge*, p. 86.

27. Hanako Ishii, *Ningen Zoruge, Aijin Miyake Hanako no Shuki (The Man Sorge, Memoirs of His Mistress Miyake Hanako)* (Tokyo, 1949), pp. 52–53; hereafter *Ningen Zoruge.* Interview with Hanako Ishii, February 7, 1965; hereafter Ishii.

28. *Moscow, Tokyo, London*, p. 143.

29. Interview with Araki, January 11, 1965.

30. *Gendai-shi Shiryo*, Vol. I, p. 230.

31. Interview with Araki, January 6, 1965.

32. Interview with Ishii, January 7, 1965.

33. Interview with Shigeharu Matsumoto, January 8, 1965; hereafter Matsumoto.

34. *Gendai-shi Shiryo*, Vol. I, pp. 234–35.

35. Sorge Memoir, Part 2, p. 19.

36. *Der Spiegel*, August 8, 1951, p. 28.

37. Sorge Memoir, Part 2, p. 19.

38. *Gendai-shi Shiryo*, Vol. I, p. 227.

39. Sorge Memoir, Part 2, pp. 19–20.

40. Ibid., p. 20.

41. Ibid., p. 21. *Gendai-shi Shiryo*, Vol. I, pp. 246–47.

42. Walter Schellenberg, *The Labyrinth* (New York, 1951), pp. 158–59; hereafter *The Labyrinth.*

43. Sorge Memoir, Part 2, p. 20.

44. Ibid., p. 17.

45. Ibid., p. 18.

46. *Gendai-shi Shiryo*, Vol. I, p. 235. Message, Ott to Berlin, February 23, 1942, German Archives.

47. Sorge Memoir, Part 2, p. 18.

CHAPTER 6
"You Are Going to Japan"

1. *Gendai-shi Shiryo*, Vol. III, p. 623. It is possible that Olga was Lydia Chekalova Stahl,

photographer for the Communist Party's Paris cell. In 1935 Ms. Stahl was tracked down by means of a postcard addressed to her from Finland. No firm evidence exists that Olga was Ms. Stahl, but the coincidence is striking. Whittaker Chambers, *Witness* (New York, 1952), p. 87; hereafter *Witness*. See also David J. Dallin, *Soviet Espionage* (New Haven, 1955), pp. 60–66.

2. *Gendai-shi Shiryo*, introduction to Vol. III, p. xiii.

3. Dusan Cvetič, "Who Was Branko Vukelič?" *Review—Yugoslavia Monthly Magazine* (October 1964), p. 38; hereafter "Who Was Branko Vukelič?" *Gendai-shi Shiryo*, Vol. III, p. 635. There are various ways of spelling Voukelitch's name. This study uses the one nearest the English pronunciation. He may have added the "de" in his Paris days, and it appears as part of his name in the telephone book of foreigners in Tokyo during his stay in that city. His birth date was August 15, 1904.

4. *Gendai-shi Shiryo*, Vol. III, p. 635.

5. Ibid., pp. 66–67.

6. Ibid., p. 635.

7. Ibid., p. 621.

8. Ibid., pp. 621–22.

9. Ibid., p. 622.

10. Ibid.

11. Ibid., p. 623.

12. Ibid.

13. Ibid., p. 624.

14. Voukelitch may have joined the Communist Party at this time. Sorge believed him to be a member of the French party (Sorge Memoir, Part 1, p. 7).

15. *Gendai-shi Shiryo*, Vol. III, p. 624; introduction to Vol. III, p. xiii. Interview with Ken Fuse, January 22, 1965; hereafter Fuse. Fuse was one of Voukelitch's interrogators following his arrest.

16. *Gendai-shi Shiryo*, Vol. III, p. 624.

17. Ibid., pp. 624–25. Voukelitch was not sure of the date of this rendezvous but placed it near the end of April or the beginning of May.

18. Ibid., pp. 625, 629.

19. Ibid., pp. 625, 628.

20. Ibid., pp. 625, 629. Since this man was the culminating contact and the one who gave specific instructions, obviously he was a comrade of some importance, perhaps the "neurotic Rumanian" who Chambers stated was head of the Paris cell (*Witness*, p. 387).

21. *Gendai-shi Shiryo*, Vol. III, pp. 625, 635.

22. Ibid., p. 626. *Case of Richard Sorge*, pp. 124–25.

23. *Gendai-shi Shiryo*, Vol. III, p. 308.

24. Ibid., pp. 313–14.

25. Ibid., pp. 307, 313–14.

26. Ibid., pp. 307, 314–16. *Case of Richard Sorge*, pp. 129–30; *Shanghai Conspiracy*, p.

53. "Sorge Spy Ring," p. A711.

27. *Gendai-shi Shiryo,* Vol. III, p. 315.

28. Ibid., pp. 308, 315–16.

29. Ibid. *Shanghai Conspiracy,* p. 54.

30. "Sorge Spy Ring," p. A711.

31. *Gendai-shi Shiryo,* Vol. III, pp. 308, 311. Roy remains a mysterious figure. Willoughby suggested he was a certain "East Indian member of the Comintern" who also used the name Roy (*Shanghai Conspiracy,* p. 54). Chalmers Johnson gave this man's name, Manebendra Nath Roy, but pointed out that he was in prison at the time (*Instance of Treason,* p. 94 n.). Deakin and Storry suggested that Roy might have been Miyagi's cousin, who lived in Los Angeles and used that name in his business; if this man was a Nisei with U.S. citizenship, Miyagi was technically correct in calling Roy an American (*Case of Richard Sorge,* pp. 131–32).

32. *Gendai-shi Shiryo,* Vol. III, p. 311.

33. Ibid., pp. 311–12; Vol. I, p. 27.

34. Ibid., Vol. III, p. 312. "Sorge Spy Ring," p. A716.

CHAPTER 7
"He Will Be Your Boss"

1. *Gendai-shi Shiryo,* Vol. III, p. 626. Interview with Tomiki Suzuki, January 18, 1965; in 1941, Suzuki was an inspector in the Foreign Section and chief of the American-European Division, Tokyo Metropolitan Police; he had primary responsibility for interrogating Voukelitch.

2. *Gendai-shi Shiryo,* Vol. III, p. 626. Voukelitch did not tell source of this allowance.

3. Ibid., p. 636.

4. Ibid., Vol. I, p. 350. "Extracts," Interrogation of Richard Sorge, December 20, 1941, p. 25, Record Group 319, File ID 923289, Part 47, Box 7484.

5. *Gendai-shi Shiryo,* Vol. I, p. 350.

6. Kinjiro Nakamura, *Zoruge, Ozaki Hotzumi Supai Jiken No Zenbo: Soren Wa Subete o Shitte Ita* (*The Entire Picture of the Sorge-Ozaki Hotzumi Spy Incident*) (Tokyo, 1949); hereafter *The Entire Picture.* Article IV, "How the Spy Ring Was Born," p. 17.

7. *Gendai-shi Shiryo,* Vol. I, p. 350; Vol. III, pp. 628–29. "Extracts," Interrogation of Richard Sorge, December 22, 1941, p. 27, Record Group 319, File ID 923289, Part 47, Box 7484.

8. *Gendai-shi Shiryo,* Vol. III, p. 637. Sorge Memoir, Part 2, p. 7.

9. *Gendai-shi Shiryo,* Vol. III, p. 162. Voukelitch did not use his home as a sending site until May 1938.

10. Police Bureau Report of Sorge Case, p. 34. This document was furnished Dr. Prange by courtesy of Harutsugu Saito; hereafter Police Report.

11. *Gendai-shi Shiryo,* Vol. III, pp. 308–09, 636. *Japan Advertiser,* December 6 through 9, 1933.

12. *Gendai-shi Shiryo,* Vol. III, pp. 308–09, 636. According to the case summary in Vol. I, p. 29, Wendt made the initial contact with both Miyagi and Voukelitch. But both Miyagi's and Sorge's testimony (Vol. I, p. 349) indicate that the go-between with Miyagi was Voukelitch.

13. Ibid., Vol. I, pp. 27, 351.

14. Ibid., Vol. II, p. 307. Interview with Kawai, January 13, 1965. Sorge Memoir, Part 2, p. 21.

15. *Gendai-shi Shiryo,* Vol. III, p. 308.

16. Ibid., pp. 308–09, 27.

17. Ibid., p. 317.

18. Ibid.

19. *Instance of Treason,* pp. 88–89. *Case of Treason,* p. 110.

20. *Gendai-shi Shiryo,* Vol. II, p. 9. *Instance of Treason,* pp. 37, 86–87.

21. Hugh Byas, *Government by Assassination* (New York, 1942), pp. 28–29; hereafter *Government by Assassination.*

22. Ibid., p. 29.

23. *Gendai-shi Shiryo,* Vol. II, p. 120; *Instance of Treason,* pp. 88–89.

24. *Instance of Treason,* p. 89.

CHAPTER 8
"Spy Activity with Sorge"

1. *Gendai-shi Shiryo,* Vol. I, p. 28. Sorge did not remember the exact date, which could have been late April.

2. Ibid., Vol. II, p. 211; Vol. III, p. 308. Miyagi recalled his initial meeting with Ozaki as being in late spring, probably May.

3. Ibid., Vol. II, pp. 107–08.

4. Ibid., p. 211.

5. For a brief discussion of this reaction, see *Instance of Treason,* p. 98. The thesis of Ozaki's apologists is that he agreed to work with Sorge because of his commitment to world revolution, but only after a bitter inner conflict. Nothing in Ozaki's background or testimony supports this thesis.

6. *Gendai-shi Shiryo,* Vol. II, pp. 131–32.

7. "Extracts," Part XV, Sorge's Notes, p. 192, Record Group 319, File ID 923289, Part 37, Box 7482.

8. *Gendai-shi Shiryo,* Vol. II, p. 152.

9. Ibid., pp. 274–75.

10. Interview with Mitsusada Yoshikawa, January 16, 1965; hereafter Yoshikawa.

11. *Gendai-shi Shiryo,* Vol. II, pp. 106–08. *Instance of Treason,* pp. 99–100.

12. *Gendai-shi Shiryo,* Vol. II, p. 117; Vol. I, p. 478. "Extracts," Interrogation of Richard Sorge, December 20,

1941, p. 25, Record Group 319, File ID 923289, Part 47, Box 7484.

13. *Gendai-shi Shiryo*, Vol. II, p. 126. *Instance of Treason*, pp. 99–100. Ozaki's translation was entitled *A Woman Walks the Earth Alone*. He used the nom de plume Jiro Shirakawa. In 1951 and 1958, uncensored editions were published with Ozaki's true by-line.

14. *Gendai-shi Shiryo*, Vol. II, pp. 197, 219. *Instance of Treason*, pp. 99–100.

15. *Gendai-shi Shiryo*, Vol. II, pp. 219–20; Vol. I, p. 236.

16. *Moscow, Tokyo, London*, p. 150.

17. *Gendai-shi Shiryo*, Vol. I, p. 237.

18. *Moscow, Tokyo, London*, pp. 144–45.

19. *Asia in the Modern World*, pp. 382–83.

20. *Moscow, Tokyo, London*, pp. 145–46.

21. Ibid., Vol. I, pp. 237, 232. In the summer of 1938 Thomas was involved in a plot with several other disaffected German generals to capture Hitler and proclaim Germany under a military dictatorship, in an attempt to save the country from the Nazis. Later Thomas was associated with the abortive, disastrous attempt on Hitler's life (*Nemesis of Power*, pp. 414–27, 560).

22. *Gendai-shi Shiryo*, Vol. II, p. 158.

23. *Moscow, Tokyo, London*, p. 147.

24. *Gendai-shi Shiryo*, Vol. II, p. 212. "Extracts," Kawai Statement, p. 11, Record Group 319, File ID 923289, Part 46, Box 7384.

25. *Gendai-shi Shiryo*, Vol. II, p. 300. "Sorge Spy Ring," p. A716.

26. Sorge Memoir, Part 2, p. 15.

27. *Gendai-shi Shiryo*, Vol. III, p. 300. "Sorge Spy Ring," p. A716. Interview with Kawai, January 19, 1965. Exactly when Akiyama commenced working for the Sorge ring is questionable. Miyagi's testimony gives the impression that this was in the summer of 1934: however, the Introduction to *Gendai-shi Shiryo*, Vol. I, p. 29, asserts that Miyagi had Akiyama submit his reply to the *Japan Advertiser* ad of December 1933 that put Miyagi in touch with Sorge.

28. *Gendai-shi Shiryo*, Vol. III, p. 298; Vol. II, p. 212.

29. Interview with Kawai, January 13, 1965. "Extracts," Kawai Statement, op. cit.

30. Masau Maruyama, *Thought and Behaviour in Modern Japanese Politics*, ed. Ivan Morris (London, 1969), p. 360; hereafter *Thought and Behaviour*.

31. Interview with Kawai, January 13, 1965.

32. Ibid. *Gendai-shi Shiryo*, Vol. III, p. 298.

33. *Gendai-shi Shiryo*, Vol. III,

p. 315, lists eleven addresses between October 1933 and the end of 1937, when he settled into his final lodgings.

34. *Witness*, pp. 364, 367, 388.

CHAPTER 9
"Collecting Information and Intelligence"

1. Sorge Memoir, Part 2, p. 3.
2. Ibid.
3. Ibid., pp. 3–4, 22.
4. Ibid., p. 22.
5. Ibid., p. 6.
6. "Extracts," Part XV, Sorge's Notes, p. 199, Record Group 319, File ID 923289, Part 37, Box 7482.
7. *Camarade Sorge*, p. 262. Most of Voukelitch's testimony from the trial of the Sorge ring has been lost.
8. Relman Morin, *East Wind Rising* (New York, 1960), p. 312; hereafter *East Wind Rising*.
9. *Camarade Sorge*, pp. 262–64.
10. Ibid.
11. Ibid., p. 263. One of Voukelitch's interrogators indicated that Branko had married Edith by order of the party as a cover (interview with Suzuki, January 18, 1965). If true, this would suggest that in Paris both were involved in communism considerably more deeply than Voukelitch ever admitted. In view of the circumstances of the marriage as related by Clausen, the story is questionable.

12. *Camarade Sorge*, p. 268.
13. Interview with Suzuki, January 18, 1965.
14. *Gendai-shi Shiryo*, p. 635.
15. Sorge Memoir, Part 2, pp. 7–8.
16. *Camarade Sorge*, p. 90.
17. *Gendai-shi Shiryo*, Vol. II, p. 62.
18. Sorge Memoir, Part 2, pp. 4, 5, 7.
19. Ibid., p. 5.
20. *Gendai-shi Shiryo*, Vol. I, p. 247.
21. Sorge Memoir, Part 2, p. 15.
22. Ibid., p. 4.
23. Interview with Ishii, January 11, 1965. Sorge's house succumbed to the fire bombings late in World War II.
24. "Extracts," Sorge's Notes, op. cit.
25. Interview with Ishii, January 7, 1965. Hans-Otto Meissner, *The Man with Three Faces* (New York, 1955), pp. 50–51; hereafter *Man with Three Faces*.
26. *Der Spiegel*, August 3, 1951, p. 28.
27. Interview with Kawai, February 13, 1965.
28. Interviews with Ishii, January 7 and 9, 1965.
29. Ibid., January 7, 9 and 11, 1965.
30. *Der Spiegel*, August 1, 1951, p. 29.
31. Interviews with Ishii, January 9 and 11, 1965. "Extracts," Sorge's Notes, p. 198, op. cit. One account avers that Mrs. Fukuda gave information about Sorge to the police, rather amusing him

(*Der Spiegel*, August 8, 1951, p. 27), but no reliable confirmation has turned up.

CHAPTER 10
"The Bright Prospects I Foresaw"

1. *Gendai-shi Shiryo*, Vol. I, p. 349; Vol. II, pp. 137, 276. We have used Johnson's dating, which was based on *Asahi* records (*Instance of Treason*, pp. 100, 238), although Ozaki recalled the trip as taking place from late in 1935 to January 1936.
2. "Extracts," Part XV, Sorge's Notes, pp. 201–03, Record Group 319, File ID 923289, Part 37, Box 7482.
3. Ibid., p. 202.
4. Sorge Memoir, Part 2, p. 5.
5. Yu Geller, "On the 70th Anniversary of the Birth of S. P. Uritskii," *KrasnayaZveda*, March 2, 1965. Uritskii was killed in the Stalinist purges.
6. Sorge Memoir, Part 2, p. 27. *Gendai-shi Shiryo*, Vol. I, p. 360.
7. Sorge Memoir, Part 2, p. 9.
8. Ibid., p. 10.
9. *Gendai-shi Shiryo*, Vol. I, p. 360.
10. Sorge Memoir, Part 2, p. 27. *Gendai-shi Shiryo*, Vol. I, p. 356. "Extracts," Interrogation of Richard Sorge, December 22, 1941, p. 28, Record Group 319, File ID 923289, Part 47, Box 7484.
11. Sorge Memoir, Part 2, p. 27.
12. Sorge Memoir, Part 2, p. 27. "Extracts," Interrogation of Richard Sorge, op. cit.
13. *Gendai-shi Shiryo*, Vol. III, p. 61.
14. Ibid., pp. 60–62.
15. "Extracts," Part XVI, Clausen Notes, p. 246, Record Group 319, File ID 923289, Part 37, Box 7482. "Extracts," Interrogation of Richard Sorge, December 20, 1941, Record Group 319, File ID 923289, Part 47, Box 7484. *Case of Richard Sorge*, p. 156.
16. "Sorge Spy Ring," p. A709.
17. *Gendai-shi Shiryo*, Vol. III, pp. 455–56, 437, 55–56.
18. Ibid., pp. 36, 458.
19. Ibid., pp. 456, 56–57. *Camarade Sorge*, p. 78. "Sorge Spy Ring," p. A709.
20. *Gendai-shi Shiryo*, Vol. III, pp. 57–58. Until two years before, Engels had been Pekrovsk.
21. *Gendai-shi Shiryo*, Vol. III, p. 58.
22. Ibid., pp. 58, 456.
23. Ibid., p. 58.
24. Ibid., p. 59.
25. Ibid.
26. Ibid., pp. 60–61.
27. Sorge Memoir, Part 2, p. 28.
28. *Gendai-shi Shiryo*, Vol. I, pp. 352–53. Sorge kept this to himself until sure his case would not be turned over to the Kempeitai.
29. *Gendai-shi Shiryo*, Vol. III, p. 151; Vol. I, p. 359. *Ogonek* (April 1965), p. 25; this

issue of this magazine contains a number of what it claims to be letters between Sorge and Katcha.

30. "Extracts," Part XV, Sorge's Notes, p. 201, Record Group 319, File ID 923289, Part 37, Box 7482. The documentation of the Sorge case is silent concerning this interim, but common sense suggests that Sorge took these steps.

31. *This Deception*, pp. 67–68.

32. *Camarade Sorge*, p. 241. In this account the date is mistakenly given as 1937.

33. "Extracts," Part XV, Sorge's Notes, p. 202, op. cit.

CHAPTER 11
"I Am Sorge"

1. *Ningen Zoruge*, pp. 1–10. Interviews with Ishii, January 7 and 9, 1965. The Rheingold was located at 5 Chome in the West Ginza.

2. This description is taken from a picture which Ms. Ishii showed Prange.

3. Interviews with Ishii, January 9 and 11, 1965, which Ms. Chi Harada conducted with Ms. Ishii on Prange's behalf, March 18, 1965; hereafter Ishii/Harada interview. Interview which Ms. Harada conducted with Karl Ketel, son of Helmut ("Papa") Ketel, on Prange's behalf, March 23, 1965. Ott and Wenneker were among the embassy personnel who patronized the Rheingold at

the time of this chapter's events.

4. *Ningen Zoruge*, p. 12.

5. Ibid. Interviews with Ishii, January 7 and 11, 1965.

6. *Ningen Zoruge*, p. 13.

7. Ibid., p. 14.

8. Interviews with Ishii, January 7 and 11, 1965.

9. *Ningen Zoruge*, p. 13. Actually she was twenty-five years old. Papa Ketel liked his waitresses to subtract a few years when anyone asked their ages (*Ningen Zoruge*, p. 91).

10. This description is based on the impression she made upon Prange in their initial interview of January 7, 1965. More than twenty-eight years after her first meeting with Sorge, Ms. Ishii remained remarkably young-looking and attractive.

11. *Ningen Zoruge*, p. 13.

12. Ibid., p. 14.

13. Interview with Ishii, January 7, 1965. *This Deception*, p. 69.

14. *Ningen Zoruge*, p. 13.

15. Interview with Ishii, January 9, 1965.

16. *Ningen Zoruge*, p. 14.

17. Ibid., p. 15.

18. Ibid., p. 48.

19. Ishii/Harada interview, March 18, 1965.

CHAPTER 12
"A Useful Man"

1. *Gendai-shi Shiryo*, Vol. III, pp. 61–62.

2. Ibid., pp. 3, 159, 84.

3. Ibid., p. 432. "Extracts," Part XVI, Clausen Testimony, original p. 566, Record Group 319, File ID 923289, Box 5F8-18.

4. *Gendai-shi Shiryo*, Vol. III, pp. 63–64.

5. Ibid., pp. 234, 64.

6. Ibid., p. 152.

7. Ibid. *Camarade Sorge*, p. 80.

8. *Gendai-shi Shiryo*, Vol. III, p. 153. *Camarade Sorge*, pp. 80–81.

9. *Gendai-shi Shiryo*, Vol. III, p. 153.

10. Ibid. *Camarade Sorge*, p. 82.

11. *Camarade Sorge*, p. 82. *Gendai-shi Shiryo*, Vol. I, p. 351.

12. *Der Spiegel*, August 8, 1951, p. 25.

13. *Gendai-shi Shiryo*, Vol. I, p. 231. V. Kudriatsev, "I Meet Richard Sorge," *Izvestia*, November 1–7, 1964; hereafter "I Meet Richard Sorge." *Case of Richard Sorge*, p. 141.

14. *Der Spiegel*, August 8, 1951, pp. 25–26.

15. Sorge Memoir, Part 2, p. 7.

16. *Gendai-shi Shiryo*, Vol. III, pp. 3, 103.

17. "Extracts," Part XI, Summary of Radio Communications Facilities, p. 156, Record Group 319, File ID 923289, Box 5F8-18.

18. Ibid. Clausen believed, no doubt correctly, that "Wiesbaden" was Vladivostok, but he also suggested Khabarovsk or Komsomolsk.

19. Interview with Yoshikawa, January 16, 1965.

20. "Extracts," Part XI, Summary of Radio Communications Facilities, op. cit.

21. Ibid. *Gendai-shi Shiryo*, Vol. III, p. 162. *Der Spiegel* claimed that Clausen's specifying "a wooden house . . . exonerates Günther Stein, who at that time lived in a stone house. . . ." (August 15, 1951, p. 33). Actually Clausen's testimony made it clear that the house's frame must be wooden rather than steel.

22. *Gendai-shi Shiryo*, Vol. III, pp. 155, 159, 187.

23. Sorge Memoir, Part 2, p. 8.

24. *Gendai-shi Shiryo*, Vol. III, p. 162. "Extracts," Clausen Testimony, p. 9, Record Group 319, File ID 923289, Part 48, Box 7484. *Camarade Sorge*, pp. 84–85.

25. "Extracts," Interrogation of Richard Sorge, December 22, 1941, p. 28, Record Group 319, File ID 923289, Part 47, Box 7484: Police Report, p. 22. *Instance of Treason*, p. 107.

26. "Extracts," Interrogation of Richard Sorge, pp. 28–29, op. cit.

27. *Gendai-shi Shiryo*, Vol. III, p. 69.

28. *Der Spiegel*, July 18, 1951, pp. 24–25.

29. Sorge Memoir, Part 1, p. 9. "Extracts," Interrogation of Richard Sorge, December 22, 1941, p. 29, op. cit.

30. "Extracts," Interrogation of Richard Sorge, December 22, 1941, p. 29, op. cit.

31. Sorge Memoir, Part 2, p. 16.

Sir George was a renowned expert on Japan, author of a three-volume history of that country.

32. Ibid., p. 5. *Gendai-shi Shiryo*, Vol. III, p. 439.

33. For Sorge's testimony indicating that Stein was a ring member, see Sorge Memoir, Part 1, p. 9, and *Gendai-shi Shiryo*, p. 361. For his testimony that Stein was a "sympathizer" or "more than a sympathizer," see *Gendai-shi Shiryo*, Vol. I, pp. 351, 354; Sorge Memoir, Part 2, p. 16; and "Extracts," Interrogation of Richard Sorge, December 22, 1941, p. 29, op. cit.

34. *Gendai-shi Shiryo*, Vol. III, pp. 438, 156, 105. Clausen's least ambiguous statement was "There is no doubt that he was a member of our group" ("Extracts," Clausen Testimony, p. 9, op. cit.). Anna Clausen also understood that Stein and his girl friend, Margot Gantenbein, "belonged to this ring" (*Gendai-shi Shiryo*, Vol. III, pp. 431, 438, 458).

35. *Gendai-shi Shiryo*, Vol. I, p. 449; Vol. III, p. 105.

36. *Hearings*, p. 1194.

37. Sorge Memoir, Part 2, p. 7.

38. Ibid., pp. 6–7. *Camarade Sorge*, p. 82.

39. *Gendai-shi Shiryo*, Vol. III, pp. 159, 309, 105.

40. Ibid., Vol. II, p. 111; Vol. III, pp. 65, 104, 308–09. Interview with Taiji Hasebe, January 19, 1965; hereafter Hasebe. He participated in the questioning of Clausen. Clausen believed he met Ozaki rather more frequently.

41. *Gendai-shi Shiryo*, Vol. III, p. 154.

CHAPTER 13
"He Himself Respected Ozaki Very Much"

1. *Gendai-shi Shiryo*, Vol. III, p. 398.

2. Ibid., p. 250. This situation exists in any literate society, the United States very much included. Much information of interest and use to spies is readily obtainable in bookstores and on newsstands.

3. Ibid., p. 298.

4. Ibid., p. 272; Vol. II, pp. 213–14.

5. Sorge Memoir, Part 2, p. 14. Johnson wrote that Shinotsuka "was dropped before he learned too much" (*Instance of Treason*, p. 110). Yet Shinotsuka testified that he met Ozaki and Miyagi from about autumn 1935 to about February 1941 (*Gendai-shi Shiryo*, Vol. II, p. 265). Sorge referred to his arrival from Moscow in 1935.

6. *Gendai-shi Shiryo*, Vol. II, p. 265.

7. Ibid., Vol. III, pp. 303, 272–73.

8. Ibid., Vol. II, pp. 152, 214.

9. Ibid., Vol. III, p. 398.

10. Ibid., Vol. II, pp. 210, 9. "Extracts," Interrogation of

Kawai, Record Group 319, File ID 923289, Part 46, Box 7484. *Sorge Incident*, p. 104. *Instance of Treason*, p. 110. Johnson rendered this name as Fukujima Ryuki. Kawai stated that the correct form is Tatsuoka Soejima (Kawai questionnaire).

11. Kawai questionnaire.
12. Ibid.
13. Ibid.
14. Ibid.
15. *Gendai-shi Shiryo*, Vol. II, pp. 208, 321.
16. Kawai questionnaire.
17. Ibid.
18. *Total Espionage*, pp. 221–22.
19. Kawai questionnaire.

CHAPTER 14
"Risen in Revolt"

1. *Ningen Zoruge*, p. 16.
2. *Government by Assassination*, pp. 120–21.
3. Ibid., pp. 121–22.
4. Ibid., pp. 123–24.
5. Ibid., p. 36.
6. *Gendai-shi Shiryo*, Vol. I, p. 241.
7. Sorge Memoir, Part 2, pp. 10, 3.
8. *Gendai-shi Shiryo*, Vol. I, p. 253.
9. *Moscow, Tokyo, London*, pp. 150–52.
10. *Gendai-shi Shiryo*, Vol. I, p. 253.
11. Ibid. *Total Espionage*, pp. 220–21. *Der Spiegel*, June 20, 1951, p. 29.
12. For an excellent exposition of this situation, see *Government by Assassination*, pp. 74–83.
13. See, for example, Tracy Dahlby, "For Japan, '36 Revolt Has Modern Refrain," *Washington Post*, February 2, 1982.
14. *Japan Times*, February 28, 1936.
15. Joseph C. Grew, *Ten Years in Japan* (New York, 1944), pp. 188–89; hereafter *Ten Years in Japan*.
16. *Gendai-shi Shiryo*, Vol. I, pp. 369–70.
17. *Government by Assassination*, p. 122.
18. *Gendai-shi Shiryo*, Vol. I, p. 253.
19. Ibid., Vol. II, p. 137; see also pp. 158–59. Kita's book, *A Reconstruction Program for Japan*, had Marxist overtones and had long been banned. Possibly the Kita connection plus Ozaki's hints that the uprising had an agrarian background may account for Sorge's telling Urach that the Japanese Communists might have been connected with the incident (*Case of Richard Sorge*, p. 174). Here Kita's first name is given as Ikki.
20. *Ningen Zoruge*, p. 17.
21. Ibid., p. 18.
22. *Gendai-shi Shiryo*, Vol. III, p. 253.
23. *Der Spiegel*, July 11, 1951.
24. *Government by Assassination*, pp. 227–29.
25. *Gendai-shi Shiryo*, Vol. III, p. 253.
26. Ibid., Vol. I, pp. 369, 372.

Government by Assassination, pp. 124–25.

27. *Gendai-shi Shiryo*, Vol. III, p. 255.

28. *Government by Assassination*, pp. 125–26.

29. Dr. B. V. A. Röling and Dr. C. F. Rüter, *The Tokyo Judgments: The International Military Tribunal of the Far East (I.M.T.F.E.), 29 April 1946–12 November 1948*, Amsterdam, Netherlands, 1977, Vol. I, pp. 65, 253–54; hereafter *Tokyo Judgments*. *Government by Assassination*, pp. 134–35. Maj. Gen. Sir Francis S. G. Piggott, *Broken Thread* (Aldershot, England, 1950), pp. 266–67; hereafter *Broken Thread*.

30. *Gendai-shi Shiryo*, Vol. III, pp. 253, 251.

31. Ibid., pp. 253–54.

32. Ibid., Vol. I, p. 241.

33. Ibid., p. 371.

34. *Case of Richard Sorge*, pp. 204–05.

35. *Gendai-shi Shiryo*, Vol. I, pp. 241–42. *Pravda* printed a condensed version of this article, and it turned up in the embassy, much to Sorge's displeasure. He hurriedly had Clausen inform Moscow that essays in the *Zeitschrift für Geopolitik* were his and urgently requested they never be reprinted in *Pravda*. Sorge did not so state, but it is incredible that Ott should not have recognized "R. S." of the *Pravda* article. There was no real reason why the Soviet newspaper should not have picked up an interesting article from Haushofer's magazine, but Sorge could not be too careful.

36. *Gendai-shi Shiryo*, Vol. I, p. 371.

CHAPTER 15
"Hot After Some Sort of Queer Enterprise"

1. *Gendai-shi Shiryo*, Vol. II, pp. 112–13.

2. Interview with Yoshikawa, January 16, 1965.

3. "Sorge Spy Ring," p. A716.

4. Interview with Kawai, January 19, 1965.

5. *Gendai-shi Shiryo*, Vol. III, p. 253. "Sorge Spy Ring," p. A716. Interview with Kawai, January 19, 1965.

6. "Sorge Spy Ring," p. A716. B. Chekhonin, "Heroes Do Not Die," *Izvestia*, September 8, 1964; hereafter "Heroes Do Not Die."

7. "Sorge Spy Ring," p. A717.

8. *Gendai-shi Shiryo*, Vol. III, p. 301.

9. Ibid., p. 301. "Sorge Spy Ring," p. A717.

10. "Sorge Spy Ring," p. A717.

11. Sorge Memoir, Part 2, p. 15.

12. *Gendai-shi Shiryo*, Vol. III, pp. 295, 305. Little is known of this man except his name, for he was not among the many arrested in connection with the Sorge case.

13. *Gendai-shi Shiryo*, Vol. III, p. 259.

14. Sorge Memoir, Part 2, pp.

14–15. Yabe's name does not appear among those arrested, so concrete examples of his participation are lacking.

15. Ibid., p. 15.

16. *Gendai-shi Shiryo*, Vol. III, p. 302; Vol. I, p. 356.

17. Sorge Memoir, Part 2, p. 15.

18. Prange's translator, Kyoshi Kawahito, commented on these characteristics of Miyagi, which were evident from Miyagi's Japanese testimony.

19. *Gendai-shi Shiryo*, Vol. III, p. 310.

20. Ibid., p. 68.

21. Letter, Masataka Chihaya to Prange, May 15, 1965. Interview with Harutsugu Saito, January 23, 1965; hereafter Saito. *Instance of Treason*, p. 8.

22. *Man with Three Faces*, p. 48.

CHAPTER 16
"Busy with the Secret Work"

1. *Gendai-shi Shiryo*, Vol. II, p. 456.

2. Ibid., p. 431.

3. Ibid., p. 456. Apparently the Fourth Department wanted to be sure Anna boarded the train.

4. Ibid.

5. Ibid., p. 457.

6. Ibid., p. 108.

7. *Shanghai Conspiracy*, pp. 98–99.

8. Material which Harutsugu Saito submitted to Prange early in 1965; hereafter Saito material. In 1941 Saito was in the Foreign Section of the Tokko and handled all cases pertaining to Germans. He had been assigned to trail Sorge in October 1939 and participated in the arrest of Sorge.

9. *Gendai-shi Shiryo*, Vol. I, p. 449; Vol. III, p. 103.

10. Ibid., Vol. III, pp. 104–05.

11. Ibid., Vol. I, pp. 378, 453, 461.

12. Ibid., Vol. III, p. 7.

13. Ibid., p. 155. *"Der Funker,"* p. 18.

14. *"Der Funker,"* p. 18. *Camarade Sorge*, p. 83.

15. *Gendai-shi Shiryo*, Vol. III, pp. 4, 232.

16. Ibid., pp. 4, 232.

17. Ibid., p. 4.

18. Ibid.

19. Ibid., pp. 3, 193.

20. Ibid., p. 3.

21. Ibid., p. 457.

22. Ibid., pp. 193, 457.

23. Ibid., pp. 425–26. *Camarade Sorge*, p. 84.

24. Ibid.

CHAPTER 17
"Love and Tenderness"

1. *Ogonek* (April 1965), p. 25.

2. Ibid.

3. Ibid. This letter was probably one of the items Sorge carried when he made a courier run to Peking in August 1936 (*Gendai-shi Shiryo*, Vol. I, pp. 305–06; Sorge Memoir, Part 2, p. 5).

4. *Ningen Zoruge*, pp. 18–19.

5. Ibid., pp. 19–20.

6. Ibid., pp. 20–21.

7. Ibid., pp. 22–23.
8. Ibid., p. 23.
9. Ibid., pp. 23–24.
10. Ibid., p. 24.
11. Ibid., p. 25.
12. Interviews with Ishii, January 9 and 14, 1965.
13. *Ningen Zoruge*, p. 26.
14. Ibid.
15. Ibid., p. 27.
16. Ibid., p. 28.
17. Ibid., p. 29. Interview with Ishii, January 7, 1965.
18. *Gendai-shi Shiryo*, Vol. III, p. 226. "Extracts," Clausen Testimony, p. 40, Record Group 319, File ID 923289, Part 37, Box 7482.
19. *Ningen Zoruge*, pp. 29–31.

CHAPTER 18
"On the Edge of a Precipice"

1. *Gendai-shi Shiryo*, Vol. II, p. 279. *Instance of Treason*, pp. 111, 113. *Spies, Dupes, and Diplomats*, p. 87.
2. *Government by Assassination*, pp. 321–22.
3. *Gendai-shi Shiryo*, Vol. II, pp. 222, 224. *Instance of Treason*, p. 204. The full extent of Saionji's commitment to communism in 1936 is difficult to assess.
4. *Gendai-shi Shiryo*, Vol. II, p. 222.
5. Ibid., p. 224.
6. Ibid., p. 222.
7. *Instance of Treason*, p. 111.
8. *Spies, Dupes, and Diplomats*, pp. 182–83.
9. *Gendai-shi Shiryo*, Vol. II, p. 279.
10. Ibid.
11. Ibid.
12. Japanese Council Paper No. 14, Hotzumi Ozaki, "Recent Developments in Sino-Japanese Relations," June 28, 1936, prepared for the Sixth Conference of the Institute of Pacific Relations to be held at Yosemite, California, August 15 to 20, 1936, Japanese Council, Institute of Pacific Relations, p. 3.
13. Ibid., p. 4.
14. Ibid., pp. 8–9.
15. Ibid., pp. 9–11.
16. Ibid., pp. 19, 22.
17. *Gendai-shi Shiryo*, Vol. II, p. 224.
18. *Instance of Treason*, p. 113. The wholesale arrests in the Sorge case caught up Saionji, but he escaped with a three-year suspended sentence ("Sorge Spy Ring," p. A722).
19. *Gendai-shi Shiryo*, Vol. II, pp. 107–08.

CHAPTER 19
"Work Only with Sorge"

1. *Man with Three Faces*, p. vi.
2. *Gendai-shi Shiryo*, Vol. I, p. 231.
3. Ibid., p. 233.
4. *Der Spiegel*, August 8, 1951, p. 28.
5. Interview with Araki, January 11, 1965. In 1936 Dr. Alois Tichy became head of the embassy's Economic Section. Sorge became acquainted with him but spoke

little about him (*Gendai-shi Shiryo*, Vol. I, p. 233). Tichy was a leading light in the *Auslands-Organization* in Japan (*Dr. Sorge funkt aus Tokyò*, p. 451).

6. *Man with Three Faces*, pp. 77, 150. Meissner seems to have swallowed any lurid yarn fed him about the Sorge ring. However, his reminiscences of events he witnessed personally deserve the same attention as any firsthand account, no more and no less. If Ott did indeed believe Sorge was some sort of agent for Berlin, as Meissner thought, this would go far toward explaining why he accepted Sorge so readily. The exact degree of Sorge's involvement with Germany remains unresolved.

7. *Gendai-shi Shiryo*, Vol. I, p. 254.

8. Ibid., p. 255.

9. Ibid., p. 256.

10. Ibid., p. 281.

11. Ibid. Sorge Memoir, Part 2, p. 25.

12. *Gendai-shi Shiryo*, Vol. I, p. 281.

13. *Moscow, Tokyo, London*, p. 153.

14. Ibid., p. 171.

15. *Gendai-shi Shiryo*, Vol. I, pp. 248, 255.

16. "Extracts," Part XV, Sorge's Notes, p. 199, Record Group 319, File ID 923289, Part 37, Box 7482.

17. *Gendai-shi Shiryo*, Vol. I, p. 256.

18. *Moscow, Tokyo, London*, pp. 173–74. At about the same time as this conference, Sorge visited Inner Mongolia. The next year he sent an essay on the subject to Thomas, then published a revised version as an article in *Zeitschrift für Geopolitik* (*Gendai-shi Shiryo*, Vol. I, p. 238).

19. *Moscow, Tokyo, London*, p. 175.

20. *Ogonek* (April 1965), p. 18.

21. The full text of the Anti-Comintern Pact, the accessory protocol, and the secret agreement which accompanied it appear, among other sources, in *Tokyo Judgments*, Vol. II, pp. 832–33.

22. Ibid.

23. *Ten Years in Japan*, p. 191.

24. *Gendai-shi Shiryo*, Vol. I, p. 256.

25. Ibid., Vol. I, p. 281.

26. Sorge Memoir, Part 2, p. 21.

27. *Total Espionage*, p. 219. *Der Spiegel*, June 20, 1951, p. 29.

CHAPTER 20
"Dangerous Political
Experiments"

1. *Gendai-shi Shiryo*, Vol. II, p. 15; Vol. III, p. 297.

2. Ibid., Vol. II, p. 109.

3. Ibid., pp. 112–13.

4. Ibid., pp. 137–38, 160.

5. Ibid., p. 160.

6. Ibid., pp. 137, 138, 160.

7. "Extracts," Kawai statement, p. 12, Record Group 319, File ID 923290, Part 46, Box 7484. "Sorge Spy Ring," pp. A715, A717. *In-*

stance of Treason, pp. 82, 56. A member of the China Problems Research Institute was Ko Nakanishi of the Investigations Department of the South Manchurian Railway at Dairen, a long-time Communist worker. His name crops up regularly in relation to organizations with which various members of Sorge's group were connected. Arrested in June 1942, he was sentenced to life imprisonment in September 1945, but he was released some two weeks later in the Allied amnesty of political prisoners.

8. *Gendai-shi Shiryo*, Vol. II, p. 124.
9. "Extracts," Kawai statement, p. 12, op. cit.
10. "Sorge Spy Ring," p. A715. *Instance of Treason*, p. 110.
11. *Chuo Koron* (January 1937), pp. 406–14.
12. *The Entire Picture*, Article VII, p. 11.
13. *Gendai-shi Shiryo*, Vol. II, p. 220.
14. Sir Robert Craigie, *Behind the Japanese Mask* (London, 1945), p. 69; hereafter *Behind the Japanese Mask*.
15. *Gendai-shi Shiryo*, Vol. II, p. 220.
16. Ibid., p. 226.
17. Ibid., p. 225.
18. *Instance of Treason*, p. 122 n.
19. *Gendai-shi Shiryo*, Vol. II, p. 109.
20. *Government by Assassination*, pp. 138–40.
21. *Gendai-shi Shiryo*, Vol. II, p. 161.
22. Ibid., Vol. I, p. 373.
23. Ibid., Vol. II, p. 161.

CHAPTER 21
"Very Strenuous Work"

1. "I Meet Richard Sorge." Koudriatsev recalled this incident took place in late 1936 or early 1937.
2. Ibid.
3. Ibid.
4. *Gendai-shi Shiryo*, Vol. I, p. 235.
5. Sorge Memoir, Part 2, p. 22.
6. *Gendai-shi Shiryo*, Vol. I, p. 238.
7. Ibid., Vol. II, p. 297.
8. Ibid., Vol. I, pp. 238, 232. So far as is known, Thomas and Sorge never met in the flesh, but at least on the German side, the friendship by mail was cordial and trusting. Many official visitors from Berlin to Tokyo brought letters of introduction and oral greetings from Thomas to Sorge.
9. For a summation of Sorge's published works, see *Case of Richard Sorge*, pp. 357–58.
10. *Ningen Zoruge*, p. 47.
11. Sorge Memoir, Part 2, p. 19.
12. *East Wind Rising*, pp. 304–12.
13. *Ningen Zoruge*, pp. 38–40.
14. *Ogonek* (April 1965), p. 19.
15. "I Meet Richard Sorge."
16. *Gendai-shi Shiryo*, Vol. III, p. 157. *Camarade Sorge*, p. 91.

17. "Extracts," Clausen Testimony, p. 11, Record Group 319, File ID 923289, Part 48, Box 7484.
18. "Extracts," Interrogation of Richard Sorge, December 22, 1941, pp. 29–30, Record Group 319, File ID 923289, Part 47, Box 7484.
19. *Ningen Zoruge*, p. 45.
20. *Camarade Sorge*, p. 336.
21. *Ningen Zoruge*, p. 51.
22. *Der Spiegel*, August 1, 1951, p. 30.
23. Interview with Araki, January 6, 1965.
24. Sorge Memoir, Part 2, pp. 17–18.
25. *Der Spiegel*, July 27, 1951, p. 24; August 8, 1951, p. 25.

CHAPTER 22
"An Incident in Northern China"

1. *Gendai-shi Shiryo*, Vol. II, pp. 221, 138.
2. Ibid.
3. *Tokyo Judgments*, Vol. I, p. 261.
4. Ibid., p. 87.
5. Ibid., Vol. I, p. 235. Sorge Memoir, Part 2, p. 3.
6. *Gendai-shi Shiryo*, Vol. III, p. 258.
7. Ibid., pp. 301, 259.
8. Ibid., p. 318.
9. Ibid., Vol. II, pp. 138, 161–62.
10. Ibid., p. 162.
11. Ibid.
12. Ibid.
13. Ibid.
14. *Instance of Treason*, pp. 122, 242.
15. *Gendai-shi Shiryo*, Vol. II, p. 162.
16. Ibid., Vol. I, p. 235.
17. *Man with Three Faces*, p. 108.
18. *Moscow, Tokyo, London*, pp. 188–89, 192.
19. *Gendai-shi Shiryo*, Vol. I, p. 374.
20. Ibid., p. 259.
21. Ibid., pp. 259–60.

CHAPTER 23
"The China Incident Will Spread"

1. *Gendai-shi Shiryo*, Vol. III, p. 258. About this time Miyagi settled down at 28 Tatsudo Cho, Azabu-ku, in a room he was to occupy until his arrest (ibid., p. 315).
2. *Gendai-shi Shiryo*, Vol. III, p. 260.
3. Ibid., Vol. II, p. 220. Despite his meetings, newspaper job, and work with Sorge, Ozaki published two books in 1937: *China Facing the Storm: The Foreign Relations, Politics, and Economics of China at a Turning Point* in September; *China Seen from the Point of View of International Relations* in November. He also wrote fourteen articles that also survive and in October 1937 found time to translate Agnes Smedley's *Macao—Pearl of the East*, once more using his

pen name, Jiro Shirakawa. For a list of Ozaki's published work, see *Instance of Treason*, pp. 259–62.

4. *Gendai-shi Shiryo*, Vol. I, p. 256.
5. Ibid., p. 257.
6. Ibid.
7. Ibid.
8. Ibid.
9. Ibid., p. 375. Vol. II, p. 276. In his testimony, Ozaki did not mention having met Sorge in Hong Kong.
10. *Gendai-shi Shiryo*, Vol. I, pp. 238–39. *Case of Richard Sorge*, p. 358.
11. *Gendai-shi Shiryo*, Vol. II, p. 223.
12. Interview with Matsumoto, January 8, 1965.
13. *Gendai-shi Shiryo*, Vol. II, pp. 223–24.

CHAPTER 24
"Secret and Important"

1. *Gendai-shi Shiryo*, Vol. III, p. 432.
2. Ibid., pp. 432, 108.
3. Ibid., pp. 432–33.
4. Ibid., pp. 434, 458. In later accounts Clausen painted the picture of a beautiful three-way friendship between Sorge and the Clausens. See, for example, *Camarade Sorge*, pp. 85–86. But this is greatly at variance with the sworn testimony of all concerned.
5. *Man with Three Faces*, p. 78.

6. *Gendai-shi Shiryo*, Vol. III, pp. 86, 159.
7. *Camarade Sorge*, p. 85.
8. Ibid., p. 4.
9. Interview with Ishii, January 7, 1965.
10. *Gendai-shi Shiryo*, Vol. III, p. 69.
11. Ibid., p. 321. Whether or not Edith knew Miyagi is not certain but it is quite likely, for he had numerous personal contacts with Voukelitch.
12. Ibid., pp. 439, 462.
13. Ibid., pp. 434, 439.
14. Ibid., pp. 434, 462.
15. Ibid., pp. 433, 439.
16. Ibid., pp. 434, 462.
17. Ibid., pp. 433, 435, 439, 462. The extent of Anna's participation in the ring and her motivation are difficult to assess. Clausen later claimed that he, Sorge, and Anna agreed to pretend, if caught, that she was reluctant (*Camarade Sorge*, p. 96). This is in conflict with the sworn testimony of all concerned.
18. *Gendai-shi Shiryo*, Vol. III, p. 462.
19. Ibid., p. 4.

CHAPTER 25
"Free Run of the Embassy"

1. *Moscow, Tokyo, London*, pp. 180–81.
2. Ibid., p. 180.
3. *Man with Three Faces*, pp. vi, vii.
4. Ibid., p. 144.
5. *Japan Advertiser*, February

7, 1938. Dirksen's next post was ambassador to the Court of St. James's.

6. *Camarade Sorge*, pp. 336–37.

7. *Gendai-shi Shiryo*, Vol. I, p. 236.

8. Ibid., pp. 362, 396.

9. Ibid., pp. 247, 251.

10. *Moscow, Tokyo, London*, p. 143. Apparently the Reich did not care to entrust Ott with a military command, in view of his long association with Schleicher (*Nemesis of Power*, p. 299 n.).

11. *Der Spiegel*, July 18, 1951, p. 25.

12. Ibid., July 25, 1951, p. 23.

13. *Japan Advertiser*, February 9, April 28–29, 1938.

14. *Gendai-shi Shiryo*, Vol. I, pp. 232, 239.

15. *Der Spiegel*, August 15, 1951, p. 32.

16. *Man with Three Faces*, pp. 175–76.

17. *Gendai-shi Shiryo*, Vol. I, p. 231.

18. Ibid., pp. 232, 247–48.

19. Ibid., pp. 236–37, 305.

20. Sorge Memoir, Part 2, p. 4. *Gendai-shi Shiryo*, Vol. III, p. 439.

21. Interview with Araki, January 11, 1965.

22. *Gendai-shi Shiryo*, Vol. I, p. 233.

23. Ibid., p. 231.

24. Ibid., p. 233.

25. Wolfgang von Gronau, *Weltflieger: Erinnerungen 1926–1944* (Stuttgart, 1955), p. 267; hereafter *Weltflieger*.

26. Ibid.

27. Ibid., p. 268..

CHAPTER 26
"The Accident Could Have Killed Me"

1. *Case of Richard Sorge*, pp. 197–98. *Der Spiegel*, August 1, 1951, p. 31.

2. Interviews with Ishii, January 7 and 9, 1965.

3. *Der Spiegel*, August 1, 1941, p. 31. *Case of Richard Sorge*, p. 198. It is impossible to give a definitive account of Sorge's accident. He did not elaborate on the subject in his testimony, and secondhand accounts are somewhat conflicting.

4. Ibid. Interview with Ishii, January 7, 1965.

5. *Case of Richard Sorge*, p. 198.

6. Interviews with Ishii, January 7, 9, and 11, 1965. *Der Spiegel*, August 1, 1951, p. 31.

7. *Gendai-shi Shiryo*, Vol. III, pp. 5, 181. *"Der Funker,"* p. 23.

8. *Gendai-shi Shiryo*, Vol. I, p. 251.

9. Interview with Ishii, January 9, 1965. *Ningen Zoruge*, p. 55. Finding "Richard" unmusical, Hanako always called him "Sorge."

10. Interviews with Ishii, January 9, 1965. *Ningen Zoruge*, pp. 56–58, 124.

11. *Case of Richard Sorge*, pp. 198–99.
12. Interview with Ishii, January 9, 1965.
13. *Japan Times and Advertiser*, May 13, 1938. *Gendai-shi Shiryo*, Vol. I, p. 378.
14. *Gendai-shi Shiryo*, Vol. II, pp. 138–40; Vol. I, p. 376.
15. Ibid., Vol. I, pp. 376–77.
16. Ibid., pp. 377–78.
17. Interview with Ishii, January 9, 1965.
18. *Man with Three Faces*, p. 159.
19. Interview with Araki, January 6, 1965.
20. Interview with Ishii, January 9, 1965.
21. Letter, April 23, 1965, Thompson to J. Mader, quoted in *Dr. Sorge funkt aus Tokyo*, p. 119.
22. *Der Spiegel*, August 1, 1951, p. 31. *Japan Times and Advertiser*, May 13 and 29, June 2, 1938.
23. Interview with Ishii, January 9, 1965. *Ningen Zoruge*, p. 57.
24. Message, Ott to Berlin, February 23, 1942, German Archives.

CHAPTER 27
"If It Is Shanghai, I Will Go"

1. *Gendai-shi Shiryo*, Vol. II, pp. 7, 226.
2. Ibid., pp. 66–67.
3. Ibid., pp. 67, 162. Sorge Memoir, Part 1, p. 8.
4. *Gendai-shi Shiryo*, Vol. III, p. 235.

5. Ibid., p. 5.
6. Ibid., p. 155.
7. Ibid., pp. 103, 156.
8. Ibid., p. 222.
9. Ibid., p. 224.
10. Ibid., p. 232.
11. Ibid., pp. 172, 440. This message was dated September 5, 1938.
12. Ibid., p. 434.
13. Ibid., pp. 440, 172. This reply came on October 7, 1938.
14. Ibid., p. 462.
15. Ibid., p. 173.
16. Ibid., pp. 433–34.
17. Ibid., pp. 462–63.
18. Ibid., pp. 434–35, 440.
19. Ibid., pp. 463, 434.
20. Ibid., pp. 440, 435, 462.
21. Ibid., p. 439.

CHAPTER 28
"A Big Trouble"

1. *Tokyo Judgments*, Vol. I, pp. 115–16, 321; Vol. II, p. 1074.
2. *Gendai-shi Shiryo*, Vol. II, pp. 140, 164–65.
3. Ibid., Vol. I, pp. 64, 379.
4. *Ten Years in Japan*, p. 251.
5. *Gendai-shi Shiryo*, Vol. I, p. 379.
6. Ibid., Vol. II, p. 165.
7. Ibid., Vol. III, p. 191; Vol. I, p. 379.
8. For a good account of this incident, see *Instance of Treason*, pp. 146–48.
9. *Gendai-shi Shiryo*, Vol. II, p. 318.
10. Ibid., Vol. I, p. 379.
11. Ibid., p. 265.
12. Ibid., p. 379.

13. Ibid., p. 265.
14. Ibid., p. 379; Vol. III, p. 263.
15. Ibid., Vol. III, p. 262.
16. Ibid., pp. 191–92, 180.
17. Ibid., Vol. I, p. 265.
18. Ibid., p. 282.
19. Ibid., p. 266.
20. Ibid., pp. 265–66.
21. *The Entire Picture*, Article II, "Why the Spy Ring Was Created," p. 24. This message was dated September 5, 1938.
22. *Gendai-shi Shiryo*, Vol. III, p. 175.
23. Ibid., Vol. I, p. 250.
24. Ibid., pp. 248, 365.
25. Ibid., pp. 45, 266.
26. Ibid., p. 280.
27. *Instance of Treason*, p. 149.
28. *Gendai-shi Shiryo*, Vol. I, p. 258.

CHAPTER 29
"The Time Is Not Ripe Enough"

1. *Gendai-shi Shiryo*, Vol. II, pp. 222, 164. In later days Kazami wrote an essay on Ozaki subtitled "Elegy for a Martyr."
2. Unpublished student paper by Hideo Kaneko, "Ozaki Hotsumi (1901–1944)," submitted to Prange in June 1966, p. 25.
3. *Gendai-shi Shiryo*, Vol. II, p. 222.
4. Ibid.
5. Ibid., p. 133.
6. *Tokyo Judgments*, Vol. I, pp. 284–85.

7. *Gendai-shi Shiryo*, Vol. I, p. 401.
8. Ibid., Vol. II, pp. 140, 165.
9. Ibid., Vol. I, p. 380; Vol. II, pp. 140–41.
10. *Instance of Treason*, p. 120.
11. *Gendai-shi Shiryo*, Vol. II, pp. 225–26.
12. Ibid., pp. 140, 226.
13. Ibid., pp. 168–69.
14. "Richard Sorge."
15. *Camarade Sorge*, pp. 337–38.
16. *Gendai-shi Shiryo*, Vol. II, p. 213. *Instance of Treason*, pp. 133–34.

CHAPTER 30
"Much Valuable Information on Japanese Politics"

1. Reiko Chiba, *The Japanese Fortune Calendar* (Rutland, Vt., 1965), p. 12; hereafter *Fortune Calendar*.
2. *Gendai-shi Shiryo*, Vol. III, pp. 266–68.
3. Ibid., p. 262; Vol. II, p. 153.
4. Ibid., Vol. II, p. 141.
5. Ibid., Vol. II, p. 223.
6. Ibid. *Instance of Treason*, pp. 118, 128.
7. *Gendai-shi Shiryo*, Vol. II, pp. 128–29. At least some of the officials involved in Ozaki's interrogation and trial had no doubt that his ambition was "that in coöperation with Soviet Russia he himself would preside over the revolutionary government of Japan. This had been expected by Ozaki with confidence." (*The Entire Picture*,

Article XII, "Secrets of the Codes," p. 16. See also Ibid., Article VII, "Ozaki's Activities in Japan," p. 11.)

8. *Instance of Treason*, p. 119.

9. Ibid., pp. 119, 129.

10. Ibid., pp. 134–36.

11. *Gendai-shi Shiryo*, Vol. I, p. 267; Vol. II, p. 118.

12. Ibid., Vol. II, p. 227. *Tokyo Judgments*, Vol. I, p. 37. *Instance of Treason*, p. 136.

13. *Tokyo Judgments*, Vol. I, pp. 54, 79.

14. *Gendai-shi Shiryo*, Vol. II, p. 227.

15. Ibid., pp. 227, 115.

16. "Sorge Spy Ring," p. A717.

17. Kodama Daizo, "A Secret Record: The Mantetsu Chosabu," *Chuo Koron* (December 1960), pp. 192–96.

18. *Gendai-shi Shiryo*, Vol. III, p. 175.

19. "Sorge Spy Ring," pp. A715–16. Koshiro's name is sometimes rendered as Kodai.

20. Ibid., p. A716.

21. Ibid.

22. Ibid.

23. Sorge Memoir, Part 1, p. 8. *Gendai-shi Shiryo*, Vol. I, pp. 441, 452. "Sorge Spy Ring," p. A716. Some question exists whether Sorge asked for Koshiro or Shinotsuka as a formal member (*Gendai-shi Shiryo*, Vol. III, pp. 107, 156, 220). He may well have requested both of them.

24. *Gendai-shi Shiryo*, Vol. III, p. 176.

25. Ibid., Vol. I, p. 361.

26. Sorge Memoir, Part 2, p. 15.

CHAPTER 31
"A Very Crucial Meaning"

1. Leonard Mosley, *Hirohito, Emperor of Japan* (Englewood Cliffs, 1966), pp. 189–91; hereafter *Hirohito*.

2. Robert J. C. Butow, *Tojo and the Coming of the War* (Princeton, 1961), pp. 33, 74, 115; hereafter *Tojo*.

3. Sorge Memoir, Part 2, p. 17.

4. *Gendai-shi Shiryo*, Vol. III, pp. 156, 221–22. At this time, Sorge paid himself between 600 to 800 yen a month and gave 300 to 400 yen a month to Miyagi. Ozaki had no regular wages, although Sorge helped defray transportation and social expenses. According to Sorge, Moscow allowed him $10,000 a year, with a maximum expenditure of $1,000 each month (*Gendai-shi Shiryo*, Vol. I, pp. 478–79; Vol. II, pp. 116–17).

5. For an interesting discussion of the early moves toward the Tripartite Pact, see *Tojo*, pp. 136–38.

6. *Gendai-shi Shiryo*, Vol. II, pp. 150–51.

7. Ibid., Vol. I, p. 266.

8. Ibid., p. 282.

9. Winston S. Churchill, *The Gathering Storm* (Boston, 1948), pp. 343–46; hereafter *Gathering Storm*.

10. *Gendai-shi Shiryo*, Vol. I, p. 282.

11. Ibid., p. 267.

12. Ibid., Vol. II, pp. 170, 223, 226.

13. *Ningen Zoruge*, pp. 70–71.

Interview with Ishii, January 20, 1965.

14. *Ningen Zoruge,* p. 71.

15. *Tokyo Judgments,* Vol. I, pp. 147–49.

16. *Gathering Storm,* p. 377. Alan Bullock, *Hitler: A Study in Tyranny* (New York, 1962), pp. 507–08.

17. *Gendai-shi Shiryo,* Vol. III, p. 268.

18. *Gathering Storm,* pp. 365–68.

19. Ibid., pp. 362–64.

20. *Gendai-shi Shiryo,* Vol. I, p. 267.

21. *Gathering Storm,* p. 379.

22. *Gendai-shi Shiryo,* Vol. I, p. 383.

23. *Gathering Storm,* p. 393.

24. *In Stalin's Secret Service,* p. 3. For a brief but interesting discussion, see Victor Kravchenko, *I Chose Freedom,* New York, 1946, pp. 332–35.

25. *Nemesis of Power,* pp. 446–48.

26. Office of U.S. Chief of Council for Prosecution of Axis Criminals, *Nazi Conspiracy and Aggression, VII,* pp. 753–54; quoted in David J. Dallin, *Soviet Russia and the Far East* (New Haven, 1948), p. 150.

27. *Gendai-shi Shiryo,* Vol. II, p. 142.

28. Ibid., Vol. I, p. 384.

CHAPTER 32
"A Russian Victory"

1. For an account of Nomonhan (Khalkhin Gol) from the Russian standpoint, see G. K. Zhukov, *The Memoirs of Marshal Zhukov* (New York, 1971), pp. 147–71; this book was originally published in Moscow in 1969 under the title *Reminiscences and Reflections;* hereafter *Zhukov Memoirs.*

2. *Tokyo Judgments,* Vol. I, pp. 152, 321. *Zhukov Memoirs,* p. 147.

3. Interview with Ishii, January 11, 1965.

4. *Gendai-shi Shiryo,* Vol. I, p. 381. Sorge Memoir, Part 2, p. 3.

5. *Gendai-shi Shiryo,* Vol. II, p. 169.

6. Ibid., p. 154; Vol. I, pp. 440–41. This distinction was later abolished.

7. Ibid., Vol. I, pp. 388, 381.

8. Ibid., p. 381.

9. *Zhukov Memoirs,* p. 149.

10. *Gendai-shi Shiryo,* Vol. I, p. 282.

11. *Zhukov Memoirs,* pp. 148–49, 169.

12. *Gendai-shi Shiryo,* Vol. I, p. 381.

13. Interview with Ishii, January 20, 1965.

14. *Gendai-shi Shiryo,* Vol. III, pp. 276–77, 270.

15. *Zhukov Memoirs,* pp. 150–51, 169.

16. *Gendai-shi Shiryo,* Vol. I, pp. 381–82.

17. Ibid., p. 388.

18. Ibid., pp. 382, 388.

19. *Zhukov Memoirs,* pp. 151–54.

20. *Gendai-shi Shiryo,* Vol. I, p. 382.

21. Ibid., p. 388.
22. Ibid., Vol. III, p. 629.
23. Ibid., Vol. I, pp. 397, 382, 282.
24. Ibid., Vol. III, p. 299.
25. Ibid., p. 269; Vol. I, p. 382.
26. Ibid., Vol. III, p. 270. *Zhukov Memoirs*, pp. 159–60.
27. *Zhukov Memoirs*, p. 157.
28. Ibid., p. 162. *Gendai-shi Shiryo*, Vol. III, p. 270.
29. *Hearings*, p. 1147. *Tokyo Judgments*, Vol. I, p. 323.
30. *Gendai-shi Shiryo*, Vol. III, p. 270.
31. *Zhukov Memoirs*, pp. 168–69.
32. *Gendi-shi Shiryo*, Vol. III, p. 270.
33. Ibid., p. 323.
34. Ibid., Vol. I, p. 437.
35. Ibid., pp. 282–83.
36. Ibid., Vol. II, p. 169; Vol. I, p. 387.
37. Interview with Ishii, January 20, 1965.

CHAPTER 33
"Something Fishy Was Going On"

1. *Man with Three Faces*, p. 47.
2. February 3, 1938.
3. *Total Espionage*, p. 225.
4. *Instance of Treason*, p. 110.
5. "Sorge Spy Ring," p. A716.
6. Ibid.
7. *Gendai-shi Shiryo*, Vol. III, p. viii. Saito material, pp. 45, 47.
8. Interview with Shigeru Aoyama conducted on behalf of Prange by Ms. Chi Harada; the record of this interview is undated, but was held early in 1965; hereafter Aoyama/Harada interview.
9. *Ningen Zoruge*, pp. 60–61.
10. *Gendai-shi Shiryo*, Vol. III, p. 5.
11. Interview with Saito, January 23, 1965.
12. Joseph Newman, *Goodbye Japan* (New York, 1942), pp. 161, 163: hereafter *Goodbye Japan*.
13. Interview with Saito, January 23, 1965.
14. This description of Saito is based upon the impression he made upon Prange during interview of January 23, 1965.
15. Interview with Saito, January 23, 1965.
16. Ibid.

CHAPTER 34
"A Considerably High Position"

1. Interview with Araki, January 6, 1965.
2. *Der Spiegel*, September 5, 1951.
3. Interview with Araki, January 6, 1965.
4. Ibid., January 11, 1965.
5. *Der Spiegel*, September 5, 1951.
6. In addition to interviewing Ms. Araki for this study, Prange knew her from occupation days and had a high opinion of her mental sharpness.
7. *Ningen Zoruge*, p. 89.
8. Interview with Araki, January 6, 1965.

9. *Gendai-shi Shiryo*, Vol. III, p. 176.
10. Ibid., Vol. II, pp. 170–71.
11. Ibid., Vol. I, pp. 267–68.
12. Ibid., pp. 268–69.
13. Ibid.
14. Ibid., Vol. III, pp. 278–81.
15. Ibid., pp. 112, 173–74; Vol. I, p. 451.
16. Ibid., Vol. I, p. 243. *Hearings*, p. 1147.
17. *Gendai-shi Shiryo*, Vol. I, p. 243.
18. Ibid.
19. *Der Spiegel*, August 15, 1951, p. 31.
20. Interview with Araki, January 11, 1965. "Sorge Spy Ring," p. A712.
21. *Gendai-shi Shiryo*, Vol. I, p. 243. *Der Spiegel*, August 15, 1951, p. 31.
22. Sorge Memoir, Part 2, p. 23.
23. *Dr. Sorge funkt aus Tokyo*, p. 317.
24. *Case of Richard Sorge*, pp. 204–06.
25. Sorge Memoir, Part 2, p. 23.
26. *Dr. Sorge funkt aus Tokyo*, p. 317.
27. Margret Boveri, *Der Verrat im XX Jahrhundert* (Reinbech bei Hamburg, 1957), p. 72; hereafter *Der Verrat*.
28. Richard Sorge, *"Die japanische Expansion," Zeitschrift für Geopolitik* (August/September 1939), pp. 617–22.
29. Interview with Araki, January 6, 1965.
30. *East Wind Rising*, p. 309.
31. *Gendai-shi Shiryo*, Vol. I, pp. 243–44.
32. Ibid., p. 251.
33. Ibid., pp. 260, 434.
34. Ibid., pp. 260, 435.
35. Ibid.

CHAPTER 35
"Clausen Has Had a Heart Attack"

1. *Japanese Fortune Calendar*, p. 14.
2. Saito material, p. 33.
3. "Sorge Spy Ring," p. A712.
4. *Gendai-shi Shiryo*, Vol. III, p. 222.
5. Ibid., pp. 162, 69.
6. "Extracts," Clausen testimony, p. 10, Record Group 318, File ID 923289, Part 48, Box 7484.
7. *Gendai-shi Shiryo*, Vol. III, p. 69.
8. *Camarade Sorge*, p. 268.
9. Interviews with Suzuki, January 18, 1965, and Fuse, January 22, 1965.
10. *Camarade Sorge*, p. 268.
11. Sorge Memoir, Part 2, p. 7.
12. Ibid., p. 6.
13. Interview with Ishii, January 7, 1965.
14. *Gendai-shi Shiryo*, Vol. III, pp. 222–23.
15. Ibid., Vol. I, pp. 478–79.
16. Ibid., Vol. III, pp. 173, 221. "Sorge Spy Ring," p. A718.
17. *Gendai-shi Shiryo*, Vol. III, pp. 221, 173, 109, 108. "Sorge Spy Ring," p. A718.
18. *Gendai-shi Shiryo*, Vol. III, pp. 159, 227.
19. Ibid., Vol. III, p. 435.
20. Ibid., p. 173.
21. "Extracts," Clausen Testimony, p. 41, Record Group

319, File ID 923289, Part 37, Box 7482.

22. *Gendai-shi Shiryo*, Vol. III, pp. 173–74.

23. Ibid., p. 194.

24. Ibid., pp. 461, 228.

25. Ibid., p. 227.

26. Ibid., p. 108.

27. Ibid., pp. 31, 162.

28. Ibid., pp. 194–95. "Extracts," Clausen testimony, p. 41, Record Group 319, File ID 923289, Part 37, Box 7482.

29. *Gendai-shi Shiryo*, Vol. III, pp. 226–28, 65.

30. *Camarade Sorge*, pp. 87, 89.

31. *Gendai-shi Shiryo*, Vol. III, p. 6.

32. "Richard Sorge."

33. *Gendai-shi Shiryo*, Vol. III, p. 8.

34. Ibid., pp. 8, 234.

35. Ibid., p. 227.

CHAPTER 36
"The Flow of Information"

1. "Richard Sorge." If these letters are genuine, one wonders why the Soviet Union published them as part of its glorification of the spy. They reveal him as pompous, whining, conceited, and mendacious.

2. *Gendai-shi Shiryo*, Vol. II, pp. 141, 165–66.

3. Ibid., Vol. I, p. 390.

4. *Instance of Treason*, p. 153.

5. *Gendai-shi Shiryo*, Vol. II, p. 166. According to Saionji, Ozaki visited him at his, Saionji's, home in January 1940, at which time Saionji mentioned the treaty and showed him his copy at Ozaki's request. By this account Saionji, like Inukai, committed an impromptu violation of security because Ozaki dropped in, and the prince often consulted him on Chinese affairs (*Gendai-shi Shiryo*, Vol. III, pp. 491–92).

6. *Instance of Treason*, pp. 197, 204 n. Throughout Ozaki's imprisonment and trial Saionji worked desperately to have him released and put to work for the Japanese government in negotiating with China. He inscribed the calligraphy carved on Ozaki's tombstone and still later abandoned Japan in favor of Red China.

7. *Gendai-shi Shiryo*, Vol. II, p. 167; Vol. I, p. 285.

8. Ibid., Vol. II, p. 155.

9. Ibid., p. 168.

10. Ibid., Vol. I, pp. 390, 403.

11. Ibid., Vol. II, pp. 217–18.

12. Ibid., p. 118.

13. Ibid., p. 225.

14. Ibid., pp. 142–43; Saito material, p. 80.

15. Herbert Feis, *The Road to Pearl Harbor* (Princeton, 1950), pp. 45, 52; hereafter *Road to Pearl Harbor*.

16. *Gendai-shi Shiryo*, Vol. I, p. 268.

17. *Government by Assassination*, p. 136.

18. *Gendai-shi Shiryo*, Vol. II, p. 170.

19. Ibid., p. 225.

20. Ibid., pp. 221, 226.

21. Ibid., p. 276. The date is not certain.
22. Sorge Memoir, Part 2, p. 14.
23. *Gendai-shi Shiryo*, Vol. I, p. 437. This comment runs through Sorge's testimony.
24. Sorge Memoir, Part 2, p. 14. *Gendai-shi Shiryo*, Vol. I, p. 437.
25. *Gendai-shi Shiryo*, Vol. II, p. 277.
26. Ibid., p. 143.
27. Ibid., pp. 120–21.
28. Ibid., pp. 171–72.
29. *Instance of Treason*, pp. 169, 173–74.

CHAPTER 37
"An Overcoat for a Very Cold Country"

1. Interview with Araki, January 11, 1965.
2. *Der Spiegel*, August 15, 1951.
3. *Gendai-shi Shiryo*, Vol. III, p. 176. *The Entire Picture*, Article II, "Why the Spy Ring Was Created," p. 24.
4. *Gendai-shi Shiryo*, Vol. III, p. 182; Vol. I, p. 452.
5. Ibid., Vol. III, p. 179; Vol. I, p. 453.
6. Ibid., Vol. III, p. 177; Vol. I, p. 453.
7. *Camarade Sorge*, p. 356.
8. *Gendai-shi Shiryo*, Vol. I, p. 453. Saito material, p. 98.
9. *Gendai-shi Shiryo*, Vol. I, p. 553. Saito material, p. 99.
10. *Ningen Zoruge*, pp. 96–97.
11. Ibid., p. 104.
12. *Gendai-shi Shiryo*, Vol. I, p. 553; Vol. III, p. 179.

13. Ibid., Vol. III, p. 176. *The Entire Picture*, Article II, op. cit., p. 24.
14. *Gendai-shi Shiryo*, Vol. III, p. 177.
15. "Richard Sorge."
16. *Gendai-shi Shiryo*, Vol. III, p. 284. Around this time Sorge kept the engagement Clausen had made for him to meet "the Moscow man"; the two men exchanged passwords and packages (Sorge Memoir, Part 2, pp. 4–6).
17. *Road to Pearl Harbor*, pp. 58–59. *Tokyo Judgments*, Vol. I, p. 169.
18. Winston S. Churchill, *Their Finest Hour* (Boston, 1949), p. 134; hereafter *Their Finest Hour*.
19. *The Entire Picture*, Article II, op. cit., p. 24.
20. *Camarade Sorge*, p. 92.
21. *Road to Pearl Harbor*, p. 66.
22. Saito material, p. 83. This message went out on June 15, 1940.
23. *Road to Pearl Harbor*, pp. 67–68.
24. *Gendai-shi Shiryo*, Vol. III, p. 284.
25. Ibid., Vol. II, p. 143.
26. Sorge Memoir, Part 2, p. 18.

CHAPTER 38
"Konoye Came Up Again"

1. *Tokyo Judgments*, Vol. I, p. 177. *Road to Pearl Harbor*, p. 78.
2. *Government by Assassination*, p. 137.

3. *Gendai-shi Shiryo*, Vol. II, p. 172. In June 1940 Ozaki had published *On Chinese Society and Economy*, the last of his books to reach the press during his lifetime. In Ozaki's opinion, this was his masterpiece. This same month he also contributed to a book of essays by six authors, *The Theory and Method of Constituting a New Order in Asia*, issued by Showa Kenkyu Kai (*Instance of Treason*, pp. 131, 260).

4. *Tojo*, pp. 140–41.

5. *Gendai-shi Shiryo*, Vol. II, p. 172.

6. Ibid., Vol. III, p. 285.

7. *Road to Pearl Harbor*, pp. 80–81. *Behind the Japanese Mask*, p. 107.

8. *Gendai-shi Shiryo*, Vol. II, p. 176.

9. Ibid., Vol. III, p. 285.

10. For an interesting in-depth study, see *Tojo*.

11. *Gendai-shi Shiryo*, Vol. II, p. 172.

12. Ibid., p. 161.

13. *Gendai-shi Shiryo*, Vol. II, p. 173.

14. Ibid., Vol. I, pp. 389–90.

15. Ibid., Vol. II, pp. 150–51.

16. Ibid., pp. 133–34.

17. Sorge Memoir, Part 2, p. 13.

18. *Gendai-shi Shiryo*, Vol. II, p. 224.

19. Ibid., p. 135.

20. Ibid., p. 280.

21. "Extracts," Kawai Statement, p. 12, Record Group 319, File ID 923289, Part 46, Box 7484; *Gendai-shi Shiryo*, Vol. II, p. 213; Vol. III, p. 399.

22. *Gendai-shi Shiryo*, Vol. II, p. 117.

23. Interview with Kawai, January 13, 1965.

24. Ibid., January 19, 1965.

25. Ibid., January 13, 1965.

CHAPTER 39
"I Spy You"

1. *Ningen Zoruge*, p. 96.

2. *Instance of Treason*, p. 175.

3. Ibid., p. 174. *Case of Richard Sorge*, p. 248.

4. Interview with Kawai, January 19, 1965. *Case of Richard Sorge*, p. 249.

5. Interview with Yoshikawa, January 21, 1965.

6. Ibid. "Extracts," Part I, Outline of the Case, p. 3., Record Group 319, File ID 923289, Box 5F8-18. *Instance of Treason*, p. 177.

7. *Case of Richard Sorge*, p. 249.

8. "Sorge Spy Ring," p. A721.

9. Interview with Hotsuki Ozaki, June 23, 1965; hereafter Ozaki.

10. Interview with Yoshikawa, January 14, 1965.

11. *The Entire Picture*, Article I, "Clue to Discovery and Developments Up to the Arrest," p. 21.

12. Ibid.

13. "Sorge Spy Ring," p. A716.

14. *The Entire Picture*, Article I, op. cit.

15. *Instance of Treason*, p. 175.

Case of Richard Sorge, p. 249. Interview with Kawai, January 14, 1965.

16. Interview with Yoshikawa, January 16, 1965.

17. *Instance of Treason*, p. 175. This book devotes an appendix to the involvement of Ito in the breakup of the Sorge ring (pp. 217–26).

18. "Extracts," Interrogation of Kawai, November 10, 1941, p. 16, Record Group 319, File ID 923289, Part 46, Box 7484.

19. Interview with Kawai, January 14, 1965. *Sorge Incident*, pp. 123, 125.

20. *East Wind Rising*, pp. 335–36.

21. *Behind the Japanese Mask*, p. 112.

22. Sorge Memoir, Part 2, p. 19.

23. *East Wind Rising*, pp. 335–41.

24. *Ningen Zoruge*, p. 101.

25. *Gendai-shi Shiryo*, Vol. III, p. 64.

26. *Ningen Zoruge*, p. 102.

CHAPTER 40
"Russia Was Excluded"

1. *Gendai-shi Shiryo*, Vol. I, p. 269.

2. Ibid., Vol. II, p. 171.

3. Ibid., Vol. I, p. 269.

4. *Tokyo Judgments*, Vol. I, p. 189. *Road to Pearl Harbor*, p. 113.

5. *Gendai-shi Shiryo*, Vol. III, p. 173.

6. *Tojo*, p. 142 n. *Tokyo Judgments*, Vol. I, p. 189.

7. *Road to Pearl Harbor*, p. 113 n.

8. Ibid., pp. 114–15.

9. Ibid., pp. 115–16.

10. *Gendai-shi Shiryo*, Vol. III, p. 286.

11. Ibid., Vol. I, p. 269.

12. Ibid.

13. Ibid., Vol. III, p. 210.

14. Ibid., Vol. I, p. 475.

15. *Road to Pearl Harbor*, pp. 103–05.

16. *Gendai-shi Shiryo*, Vol. I, p. 269. *Road to Pearl Harbor*, pp. 103–04.

17. *Behind the Japanese Mask*, p. 108. *Ten Years in Japan*, p. 339.

18. *Gendai-shi Shiryo*, Vol. III, p. 287.

19. *Goodbye Japan*, p. 46.

20. *Tojo*, p. 180.

21. "Sorge Spy Ring," p. A712. *Spies, Dupes, and Diplomats*, p. 99.

22. *Gendai-shi Shiryo*, Vol. I, p. 269.

23. Quoted in *Tokyo Judgments*, Vol. II, p. 837.

CHAPTER 41
"Japan Is Demanding Too Much"

1. *The Entire Picture*, Article II, "Why the Spy Ring Was Created," p. 25; *Gendai-shi Shiryo*, Vol. III, p. 178.

2. *Gendai-shi Shiryo*, Vol. I, pp. 453–54; Vol. III, p. 178.

3. Ibid., Vol. III, p. 190.

4. *Behind the Japanese Mask*, p. 88.
5. *Gendai-shi Shiryo*, Vol. III, p. 190.
6. *Road to Pearl Harbor*, p. 96, 96 n.
7. *Gendai-shi Shiryo*, Vol. III, p. 107.
8. Ibid., p. 192.
9. *Road to Pearl Harbor*, p. 105.
10. *Gendai-shi Shiryo*, Vol. III, pp. 397–98.
11. Ibid., p. 400.
12. Ibid., Vol. II, p. 144.
13. Ibid., p. 277.
14. *Ten Years in Japan*, p. 327.
15. *Thought and Behaviour*, pp. 351, 361.
16. *Tojo*, pp. 158–59. *Instance of Treason*, p. 121.
17. *Gendai-shi Shiryo*, Vol. II, pp. 277–78, 153; Vol. I, p. 437.
18. Ibid., Vol. II, p. 167.
19. Ibid., Vol. III, p. 300.
20. Ibid., Vol. I, pp. 285–86. Sorge Memoir, Part 2, p. 7. Ozaki testified that he had Miyagi report to Sorge (Vol. II, p. 168). However, Sorge's recollection was that Ozaki reported to him personally (Vol. I, pp. 285–86, 403).
21. *Gendai-shi Shiryo*, Vol. I, p. 286.
22. Ibid.
23. Ibid.
24. Interview with Kawai, January 15, 1965.
25. Ibid.
26. *Gendai-shi Shiryo*, Vol. III, p. 398.
27. Ibid. "Extracts," Interrogation of Kawai, November 10, 1941, p. 14, Record Group 319, File ID 923289, Part 46, Box 7484.
28. *Gendai-shi Shiryo*, Vol. III, p. 399.
29. Ibid., Vol. II, pp. 222–23.

CHAPTER 42
"Sick and Tired of Spy Work"

1. "Richard Sorge." This letter is undated, but Sorge's reference to having just turned forty-five places it fairly early in October 1940.
2. *Gendai-shi Shiryo*, Vol. III, p. 65.
3. "Extracts," Clausen Testimony, pp. 41–42, Record Group 319, File ID 923289, Part 37, Box 7482.
4. *Gendai-shi Shiryo*, Vol. III, pp. 433, 440.
5. Ibid., p. 461.
6. In one portion of his testimony Clausen dated the meeting as around December, elsewhere as October 20, in accordance with Moscow's arrangement (*Gendai-shi Shiryo*, Vol. III, p. 195; "Extracts," Clausen Testimony, p. 42, Record Group 319, File ID 923289, Part 37, Box 7482).
7. "Extracts," Clausen Testimony, op. cit. *Gendai-shi Shiryo*, Vol. III, p. 195.
8. *Gendai-shi Shiryo*, Vol. III, p. 224.
9. Ibid., p. 160.
10. Ibid., pp. 8, 109, 234–35.
11. Ibid., p. 157.
12. Ibid., pp. 8–9, 234.

13. Ibid., p. 234.
14. Ibid., p. 8.
15. Ibid., p. vii.
16. Ibid., pp. 64–65. Later, living in East Germany, Clausen protested that he, Anna and "Richard" were the best of friends (*Camarade Sorge*, pp 85–86; "*Der Funker*").
17. Interview with Ishii, January 7, 1965.
18. *Gendai-shi Shiryo*, Vol. III, pp. 164, 234.
19. Ibid., pp. 224–25.
20. Ibid., pp. 108–09.

CHAPTER 43
"Many Anxious Moments"

1. *Der Spiegel*, August 8, 1951, p. 26.
2. Interview with Ishii, January 7, 1965.
3. *Der Spiegel*, August 8, 1951, p. 27.
4. Ibid., p. 28.
5. H. W. Henzel, "*Der Zeitungssorger Sorge*," unpublished student paper prepared for Dr. Prange's 1966 course, History 372, at the University of Maryland; hereafter "*Der Zeitungssorger Sorge*."
6. *Gendai-shi Shiryo*, Vol. I, pp. 240–41.
7. Ibid., p. 232.
8. *Road to Pearl Harbor*, pp. 134–35.
9. *Gendai-shi Shiryo*, Vol. III, p. 145.
10. Ibid., Vol. I, p. 271.
11. Ibid.
12. Ibid., p. 272.
13. Ibid., pp. 271–72.

14. Ibid., Vol. II, p. 252.
15. Ibid., Vol. I, p. 391.
16. Ibid.
17. Ibid., p. 277.
18. Ibid.
19. Ibid.
20. *Ningen Zoruge*, pp. 103–06.
21. Ibid., p. 99.
22. *East Wind Rising*, p. 313.
23. *Ningen Zoruge*, p. 100. *Der Spiegel*, August 8, 1951, p. 28.
24. *Ningen Zoruge*, pp. 100–01. Interview with Ishii, January 7, 1965.
25. Interview with Ishii, January 6, 1965.
26. *Camarade Sorge*, p. 356.
27. *Their Finest Hour*, p. 589.
28. *Gendai-shi Shiryo*, Vol. III, p. 118.

CHAPTER 44
"Continue to Be on the Lookout"

1. *Gendai-shi Shiryo*, Vol. I, pp. 270–72.
2. Ibid., p. 271.
3. Ibid.
4. Ibid.
5. *Their Finest Hour*, pp. 577–87.
6. *Road to Pearl Harbor*, p. 146.
7. *Their Finest Hour*, pp. 582–87.
8. *Road to Pearl Harbor*, pp. 146–47.
9. *Tojo*, pp. 205–06. A liaison conference consisted of the premier and the foreign, war, and navy ministers, plus the chiefs of the army and navy general staffs. The secre-

taries of the conference were the chief cabinet secretary and the heads of the powerful military and naval affairs bureaus of the respective ministries. Other cabinet members participated from time to time, but the predominantly military cadre remained. They and their subordinates planned and pushed through national policy. This group eclipsed the cabinet, and the imperial conference could do little but ratify its decisions. For an interesting discussion of this unique feature of Japan's governmental system, see ibid., pp. 149–51.

10. *Gendai-shi Shiryo*, Vol. II, p. 230.
11. Ibid., pp. 145, 230; Vol. I, p. 272.
12. *Road to Pearl Harbor*, p. 182.
13. Ibid.
14. *Gendai-shi Shiryo*, Vol. III, p. 289.
15. Ibid., p. 290.
16. Ibid., Vol. I, pp. 273, 287.
17. Ernst L. Presseisen, *Germany and Japan: A Study in Totalitarian Diplomacy 1933–1941* (The Hague, 1958), p. 289; hereafter *Germany and Japan*. Ms. Ott seems to have preceded her husband by way of the United States. Early in the year she dropped in on Christiane in New York with greetings from Sorge. The message evidently encouraged Christiane to try to visit him, for later she procured a visa to Japan. But her cable

to Sorge went unanswered, and when she arrived in Tokyo, he was already incommunicado in Sugamo Prison (*Case of Richard Sorge*, p. 259 n.).
18. *Road to Pearl Harbor*, pp. 183–84.
19. Ibid., pp. 184–85. Winston S. Churchill, *The Grand Alliance* (Boston, 1950), pp. 190–91; hereafter *Grand Alliance*.
20. *Grand Alliance*, pp. 162–63, 361.
21. Ibid., p. 191.
22. *Road to Pearl Harbor*, pp. 186–87.
23. *Gendai-shi Shiryo*, Vol. II, p. 176.
24. Ibid., p. 231.
25. Ibid., p. 176.
26. Ibid., p. 231.
27. Ibid., p. 176.
28. Ibid., pp. 176–77.
29. Ibid., Vol. I, p. 392.
30. Ibid., Vol. III, p. 345.
31. Ibid., p. 97.
32. Ibid., Vol. I, p. 272.
33. Ibid., p. 273.
34. *Case of Richard Sorge*, p. 226 n.

CHAPTER 45
"Difficulties for Sorge"

1. *Gendai-shi Shiryo*, Vol. III, p. 5.
2. Interviews with Kawai, January 13 and 14, 1965. *Gendai-shi Shiryo*, Vol. III, pp. 398, 400. "Extracts," Interrogation of Kawai, November 10, 1941, p. 15, Record

Group 319, File ID 923289, Part 46, Box 7484.

3. Interview with Kawai, January 14, 1965.

4. Interviews with Yoshikawa, January 16, 1965, and Mitsusaburo Tamazawa, January 21, 1965; hereafter Tamazawa. In 1941 Tamazawa was an official of the Tokko and closely connected with the Sorge case.

5. Ibid. Deakin and Storry state that the arrest of Ms. Aoyagi took place sometime in September 1941 (*Case of Richard Sorge*, p. 250); however, the interviews with Yoshikawa and Tamazawa strongly indicate that this happened early in 1941.

6. Ibid. *Case of Richard Sorge*, p. 250.

7. Interview with Tamotsu Sakai, January 31, 1965; hereafter Sakai. In 1941 Sakai was a detective in the First Section of the Tokko. Interviews with Yoshikawa, January 16, 1965; Tamazawa, January 21, 1965; and Sakai, January 31, 1965.

8. *Instance of Treason*, p. 170.

9. Interviews with Kawai, January 11 and 14, 1965.

10. Ibid.

11. *Gendai-shi Shiryo*, Vol. III, p. 345. Interview with Kawai, January 14, 1965. Elsewhere Kawai testified that this meeting took place "around the end of March or early April" ("Extracts," Interrogation of Kawai, November 10, 1941, p. 15, Record Group 319, File 923289, Part

46, Box 7484). But the reference to the passage of the National Defense Security Law establishes it in May.

12. *Instance of Treason*, p. 170.

13. *Gendai-shi Shiryo*, Vol. III, p. 345.

14. Interviews with Kawai, January 13 and 14, 1965. "Extracts," Interrogation of Kawai, op. cit.

15. Interviews with Kawai, January 13 and 14, 1965.

16. Ibid., January 14, 1965.

17. *The Labyrinth*, p. 158.

18. Ibid., pp. 158–59.

19. Ibid., pp. 160–61.

20. Ibid., p. 160.

21. Erich Kordt, *Nicht aus den Akten* (Berlin, 1950), p. 428; hereafter *Nicht aus den Akten*.

22. *Case of Richard Sorge*, p. 336.

23. *The Labyrinth*, p. 160.

24. Ibid., pp. 160–61.

25. *Instance of Treason*, pp. 172–73. *Hearings*, p. 1144.

26. *Total Espionage*, pp. 275–76.

27. *Gendai-shi Shiryo*, Vol. I, p. 251.

CHAPTER 46
"The Soviet Union Ignored Our Report"

1. "Richard Sorge." According to Soviet releases, on March 5 Sorge sent to Moscow microfilm of cables from Ribbentrop to Ott warning that Hitler planned to attack the Soviet Union during the latter half of June (V. Cher-

nyavsky, "Richard Sorge's Exploit," *Pravda*, November 6, 1964). There is reason to question this statement. Clausen's diary indicated only one contact with the middleman in March. This took place late in the month, and no material changed hands (*Gendai-shi Shiryo*, Vol. III, p. 195). In early March Hitler's timetable still called for zero hour on May 15.

2. Papers of Franklin D. Roosevelt, Presidential Secretary's File No. 22, Franklin D. Roosevelt Library, Hyde Park, New York; hereafter FDR Papers.

3. *Gendai-shi Shiryo*, Vol II, p. 175.

4. Ibid., Vol. I, pp. 247–49. Niedermayer was an authority on the Soviet Union, having lived there for about ten years following World War I, when the Russians permitted the Germans to conduct secret military training on Soviet territory. He was a staunch advocate of a German liaison with the USSR (*Nemesis of Power*, pp. 127–29, 611–12 n.).

5. *Gendai-shi Shiryo*, Vol. I, p. 274.

6. Ibid., p. 273.

7. Ibid., p. 274.

8. Ibid., Vol. III, p. 109. Clausen's total for May 6 was 802 word groups.

9. "Richard Sorge."

10. *Gendai-shi Shiryo*, Vol. III, pp. 164, 197.

11. Ibid., pp. 109, 164, 178.

12. Ibid., Vol. I, pp. 249, 274.

13. Ibid., p. 274.

14. Ibid.

15. Ibid., Vol. III, p. 190.

16. "Richard Sorge."

17. *Gendai-shi Shiryo*, Vol. III, pp. 109, 164.

18. *Camarade Sorge*, pp. 87–88.

19. *Gendai-shi Shiryo*, Vol. III, p. 292.

20. *Ningen Zoruge*, p. 109.

21. Interview with Ishii, January 7, 1965.

22. A number of translations of this phrase exist. Dr. Prange preferred this one.

23. Interview with Ishii, January 7, 1965.

CHAPTER 47
"Attack Soviet Russia"

1. *Der Spiegel*, September 5, 1951.

2. *Gendai-shi Shiryo*, Vol. I, p. 249.

3. *Der Spiegel*, September 5, 1951.

4. Ibid.

5. *Gendai-shi Shiryo*, Vol. III, pp. 346–47.

6. Ibid., p. 346.

7. Ibid., pp. 292, 290.

8. Interview with Kawai, January 14, 1965.

9. Ibid.

10. *Gendai-shi Shiryo*, Vol. II, p. 192.

11. "Richard Sorge."

12. *Gendai-shi Shiryo*, Vol. III, pp. 110, 191. Clausen sent 728 word groups on that day.

13. Ibid., p. 191.
14. *Ningen Zoruge*, p. 112.
15. Ibid., pp. 112–13.
16. *Der Spiegel*, September 5, 1951. *Ningen Zoruge*, p. 125.
17. "Richard Sorge."
18. *Gendai-shi Shiryo*, Vol. III, p. 110.
19. Ibid., p. 197.
20. *Izvestia*, June 14, 1941, quoted in Vladimir Petrov, comp., "June 22, 1941": Soviet Historians and the German Invasion (Columbia, S. C., 1968), p. 201; hereafter *June 22, 1941*.
21. *Gendai-shi Shiryo*, Vol. II, pp. 177, 232–33.
22. Ibid., p. 177.
23. *"Der Zeitungssorger Sorge."*
24. *Gendai-shi Shiryo*, Vol. I, p. 223.
25. *Nicht aus den Akten*, p. 426.
26. Ibid., pp. 426–27.
27. Ibid., p. 427.
28. Ibid., pp. 427–28.

CHAPTER 48
"Some Influence on Japanese Policy"

1. *Der Spiegel*, September 5, 1951, p. 24.
2. *Nicht aus den Akten*, p. 429.
3. *"Der Funker,"* p. 22.
4. *June 22, 1941*, pp. 169 n., 184, 188.
5. "Richard Sorge."
6. For an interesting study of this complicated and controversial subject, see *June 22, 1941*.

7. J. C. Masterman, *The Double-Cross System in the War of 1939–1945* (New Haven, 1972), p. 32.
8. *Gendai-shi Shiryo*, Vol. II, p. 229.
9. Ibid., Vol. I, p. 276.
10. Ibid., Vol. III, p. 292.
11. Ibid., Vol. I, pp. 280–81, 406.
12. Ibid., Vol. II, p. 234.
13. Ibid., p. 257.
14. Ibid., pp. 258, 187.
15. Ibid., Vol. I, p. 279.
16. Ibid., p. 280.
17. Ibid., Vol. III, p. 292; Vol. II, p. 178.
18. Ibid.
19. Ibid., pp. 346–47.
20. Ibid., p. 347.
21. Ibid., Vol. I, pp. 288, 411. Certain accounts indicate that Ott had sent an agent to Shanghai that spring to solicit support for what he claimed was Hitler's plan to restore the Romanov dynasty in the person of Grand Duke Vladimir, grandnephew of Nicholas II. *Total Espionage*, p. 276.
22. *Gendai-shi Shiryo*, Vol. I, p. 288.
23. Ibid., p. 280. Sorge Memoir, Part 2, p. 24.
24. *Gendai-shi Shiryo*, Vol. I, p. 284.
25. Ibid.
26. Ibid., Vol. II, p. 187.
27. Interview with Matsumoto, January 8, 1965.
28. Ibid.
29. *Gendai-shi Shiryo*, Vol. II, p. 187.
30. Sorge Memoir, Part 2, p. 24.

31. *Gendai-shi Shiryo*, Vol. II, p. 258.
32. Ibid., p. 187.
33. Ibid., p. 258.

CHAPTER 49
"A Fateful Day"

1. *Gendai-shi Shiryo*, Vol. I, p. 454; Vol. III, p. 178.
2. Ibid., Vol. III, p. 178.
3. Ibid., p. 163.
4. Ibid., pp. 110, 197–98.
5. Ibid., pp. 110, 6. This day's total was 8 messages, 544 word groups in the first session, 340 the second.
6. Interview with Matsumoto, January 8, 1965.
7. From a number of available translations, Prange selected the version reproduced in the record of the *Hearings before the Joint Committee on the Investigation of the Pearl Harbor Attack, Congress of the United States, Seventy-ninth Congress*, Part 20, pp. 4018–19. Hereafter PHA.
8. Interview with Matsumoto, January 8, 1965.
9. Ibid.
10. *Gendai-shi Shiryo*, Vol. II, pp. 236–37.
11. Ibid., Vol. III, p. 350.
12. Ibid., p. 351.
13. Ibid., Vol. II, p. 112.
14. Ibid., Vol. I, p. 275.
15. Ibid., p. 409.
16. Ibid., p. 275.
17. Ibid., Vol. II, p. 236.
18. *Instance of Treason*, p. 170.
19. *Gendai-shi Shiryo*, Vol. I, p. 405.
20. Ibid., p. 409.
21. Ibid., p. 275.
22. Ibid., Vol. III, p. 110. This day's total was 637 word groups.
23. Ibid., Vol. II, p. 237.
24. Ibid., Vol. I, p. 275.
25. Ibid., Vol. III, p. 226.
26. Ibid., Vol. I, p. 271. *Road to Pearl Harbor*, pp. 213–14.
27. *Gendai-shi Shiryo*, Vol. I, p. 275.
28. Ibid., pp. 275–76.
29. Ibid., p. 283.
30. Ibid., Vol. III, p. 198.
31. Ibid., p. 351.
32. Ibid., p. 361.
33. Ibid., pp. 200, 110.
34. Ibid., p. 174; Vol. I, p. 274.

CHAPTER 50
"Too Early To Make a Final Judgment"

1. *Gendai-shi Shiryo*, Vol. II, pp. 154, 192.
2. Ibid., Vol. III, p. 296.
3. Ibid., p. 303.
4. Ibid., pp. 297, 322.
5. Ibid., Vol. I, p. 291.
6. Ibid., Vol. II, p. 192.
7. Ibid., Vol. I, p. 292.
8. Ibid., p. 292; Vol. II, p. 192.
9. Ibid., Vol. I, p. 292.
10. Ibid., pp. 292, 438.
11. Zaitsev gave Clausen $1,000 in American currency and 4,500 yen. Later Clausen gave $800 and 2,000 yen of this money to Sorge, holding the rest in the ring's fund. *Gendai-shi Shiryo*, Vol. III, pp. 195, 211, 223. "Extracts,"

Clausen Testimony, pp. 42–43, Record Group 319, File ID 923289, Part 37, Box 7482.

12. *Gendai-shi Shiryo*, Vol. I, p. 288.
13. Ibid., pp. 288–89.
14. Ibid., p. 293.
15. Ibid., pp. 293–94.
16. Ibid., p. 294.
17. Ibid., p. 412.
18. Ibid., pp. 276, 412.
19. Ibid., Vol. III, pp. 292–93. This was very good strategic intelligence.
20. Ibid., Vol. I, p. 427.
21. Ibid., Vol. III, p. 293.
22. Ibid., pp. 110, 115.
23. Ibid., p. 185.
24. Ibid., Vol. I, p. 294; Vol. II, p. 254.
25. Ibid., Vol. III, p. 198.
26. Ibid., Vol. I, p. 276.
27. Ibid., Vol. II, p. 182.
28. Ibid., p. 238. Ozaki did not recall the exact figures, but testified that this proportion was roughly correct.
29. Ibid., Vol. III, pp. 216–17.
30. Ibid., Vol. II, p. 239. Sato soon became a general.
31. Ibid.
32. Ibid., p. 237.
33. Ibid., p. 238.
34. Ibid.

CHAPTER 51
"Japan–United States Negotiations"

1. For an authentic, readable account of these discussions, see *Road to Pearl Harbor* and Cordell Hull, *The Memoirs of Cordell Hull* (New York, 1948), Vol. II.
2. *Road to Pearl Harbor*, p. 193.
3. *Gendai-shi Shiryo*, Vol. II, p. 243.
4. Ibid., Vol. I, p. 277.
5. Ibid., p. 418. Matsuoka informed Grew that if the United States convoyed ships to Britain and lost ships to Germany as a result, and war with Germany ensued, Japan would consider the United States an aggressor under Article III of the Tripartite Pact (*Ten Years in Japan*, pp. 388–89). This was bellicose enough, but much less so than his words as reported by Sorge.
6. Ibid., p. 277.
7. Ibid., p. 417.
8. Ibid., Vol. II, p. 188.
9. Ibid., Vol. I, p. 279.
10. Ibid., p. 278.
11. Ibid., pp. 278, 419.
12. Ibid., Vol. II, p. 189.
13. Ibid., Vol. I, p. 457.
14. Ibid., Vol. II, p. 149.
15. Ibid., Vol. I, p. 419.
16. Ibid., p. 278.
17. Ibid., Vol. II, p. 245; Vol. I, pp. 290, 420.
18. Ibid., Vol. I, p. 420.
19. Ibid., Vol. II, p. 246.
20. Ibid., p. 264.
21. Ibid., p. 246.
22. Ibid., pp. 246, 193.
23. Ibid., p. 246.
24. Ibid., p. 253.
25. *Ten Years in Japan*, pp. 413–14.
26. *Gendai-shi Shiryo*, Vol. II, p. 248.
27. Interview with Kawai, Jan-

uary 13, 1965. There is some indication that Ozaki hoped to arrange an even more outré encounter—one between Konoye and Stalin (*Instance of Treason*, p. 6 n.).

28. *Gendai-shi Shiryo*, Vol. I, p. 461; Vol. III, pp. 200–01.

29. Ibid., Vol. II, pp. 189–90; 247–48. Ozaki claimed that these exchanges did not take place "on the same occasion but fractionally from time to time" (p. 248).

CHAPTER 52
"Worried About Miyake-san"

1. *Gendai-shi Shiryo*, Vol. III, p. 6.
2. Aoyama/Harada interview.
3. Ibid.
4. Ibid.
5. Ibid.
6. Interview with Saito, January 23, 1965.
7. Interview with Tamazawa, January 21, 1965.
8. *Ningen Zoruge*, p. 128.
9. *Ningen Zoruge*, p. 113. Interview with Ishii, January 14, 1965. In this interview, Hanako dated this incident as late July 1941, but in *Ningen Zoruge*, she placed it in August.
10. Ibid., pp. 113–14. Interview with Ishii, January 14, 1965.
11. *Ningen Zoruge*, p. 114.
12. Interviews with Ishii, January 11 and 14, 1965.
13. Ibid., January 14, 1965.
14. Ibid.

15. Ibid. *Ningen Zoruge*, p. 115–16.
16. Interview with Ishii, January 14, 1965. *Ningen Zoruge*, p. 128.
17. Interview with Ishii, January 14, 1965.
18. *Ningen Zoruge*, p. 120.
19. *This Deception*, p. 75.

CHAPTER 53
"Sorge Will Become a God"

1. Interview with Ishii, January 14, 1965.
2. *Ningen Zoruge*, pp. 116–17.
3. Interview with Ishii, January 14, 1965. *Ningen Zoruge*, pp. 118–19.
4. Interview with Ishii, January 14, 1965.
5. Ibid. *Ningen Zoruge*, p. 119.
6. Ibid. *Ningen Zoruge*, p. 120.
7. Ibid. *Ningen Zoruge*, pp. 120–21.
8. *Ningen Zoruge*, pp. 121–22.
9. Interview with Ishii, January 14, 1965.
10. *Ningen Zoruge*, pp. 123–28.
11. Interview with Ishii, January 14, 1965. *Ningen Zoruge*, p. 130.
12. *Ningen Zoruge*, p. 131.
13. Interview with Ishii, January 11, 1965. In this interview she mentioned the location and purpose of this dinner but gave no further details.
14. *Ningen Zoruge*, p. 132.
15. Ibid., p. 133.
16. Ibid., p. 134.
17. *Ningen Zoruge*, p. 137. Interview with Ishii, January 7, 1965.

18. *Ningen Zoruge*, pp. 138–39.
19. Ibid., p. 140.
20. Ibid., p. 141.
21. Ibid., p. 142.
22. Ibid., p. 143.
23. Ibid., p. 144.
24. Ibid., p. 145.

CHAPTER 54
"Getting into Dangerous Ground"

1. Interview with Tamazawa, January 21, 1965.
2. Interview with Yoshikawa, January 14, 1965. *The Entire Picture*, Part I, pp. 21–22.
3. *The Entire Picture*, Part I, p. 21.
4. Interview with Yoshikawa, January 14, 1965.
5. *The Entire Picture*, Part I, p. 21.
6. *Gendai-shi Shiryo*, Vol. III, p. 400.
7. Interview with Kawai, January 14, 1965.
8. Ibid.
9. *Gendai-shi Shiryo*, Vol. III, pp. 637–38.
10. *Dr. Sorge funkt aus Tokyo*, p. 168. It is not clear whether Thompson paid Voukelitch out of his own pocket or on behalf of the United Press.
11. *Camarade Sorge*, p. 268.
12. *Gendai-shi Shiryo*, Vol. III, pp. 66–67. Voukelitch said much the same thing to the men who recruited him in Paris.
13. Ibid., p. 67.
14. Ibid., p. 157.
15. Ibid., Vol. I, p. 431.
16. Ibid., Vol. III, p. 186. *Case of Richard Sorge*, p. 256.
17. *Gendai-shi Shiryo*, Vol. III, pp. 185, 230. Edith joined her sister and brother-in-law, Mr. and Ms. G. Pederson, in a suburb of Perth. Letter, D. R. Anderson to Dr. Prange, September 26, 1967.
18. *Gendai-shi Shiryo*, Vol. III, pp. 160, 225.
19. Ibid., p. 195. "Extracts," Clausen Testimony, p. 42, Record Group 319, File ID 923289, Part 37, Box 7482.
20. *Gendai-shi Shiryo*, Vol. III, pp. 195–96. "Extracts," Clausen Testimony, p. 43, op. cit.
21. Sorge Memoir, Part 2, p. 6.
22. *Gendai-shi Shiryo*, Vol. III, p. 185. "Extracts," Clausen Testimony, op. cit.
23. *Gendai-shi Shiryo*, Vol. III, p. 164.
24. Ibid., p. 163.
25. Ibid., p. 6.

CHAPTER 55
"Released from a Heavy Burden"

1. *Gendai-shi Shiryo*, Vol. I, p. 443.
2. Ibid., Vol. III, p. 198.
3. Ibid., pp. 110, 196. Clausen's output for the day was 12 messages, totaling 812 word groups.
4. Ibid., p. 183.
5. Ibid., p. 199.
6. Ibid., Vol. I, p. 458; Vol. III, p. 203.
7. Ibid., Vol. I, p. 276.

8. Ibid., Vol. II, pp. 182, 238.
9. Ibid., pp. 182–83.
10. Ibid., Vol. III, pp. 304, 353.
11. Ibid., Vol. II, p. 183.
12. Ibid., p. 239.
13. Ibid., Vol. I, p. 413.
14. Ibid., Vol. II, p. 240.
15. Ibid., Vol. I, p. 289; Vol. II, p. 240.
16. Ibid., Vol. II, pp. 147, 184, 240.
17. Ibid., pp. 147, 186, 240.
18. Ibid., p. 240.
19. Ibid., pp. 184, 240.
20. Ibid., pp. 181–85, 241.
21. Ibid., p. 185.
22. "Richard Sorge."
23. Gendai-shi Shiryo, Vol. III, p. 183.
24. Ibid., p. 110. The total was 903 word groups.
25. Ibid., Vol. II, pp. 184–85.
26. Ibid., Vol. III, p. 356.
27. Ibid., Vol. II, p. 262.
28. Ibid., Vol. III, p. 110.
29. The Entire Picture, Part II, p. 25. Gendai-shi Shiryo, Vol. I, p. 473. Sorge always maintained that he spied to keep the peace and that the Soviet Union would never attack Japan. He barely admitted that Russia might defend itself if Japan attacked. (Gendai-shi Shiryo, Vol. I, p. 480). This message, with its emphasis upon potential bombing targets, makes Sorge's pose somewhat shaky.
30. Gendai-shi Shiryo, Vol. I, p. 276. Unfortunately this message, if it ever existed, has not survived.
31. Ibid., Vol. II, pp. 185–86.
32. Ibid., p. 184.
33. Ibid., p. 186.
34. Ibid., pp. 250, 190.
35. Ibid., p. 282.
36. Ibid., pp. 148, 190, 248, 250.
37. Ibid., pp. 249–50.
38. Ibid., p. 149.
39. Ibid., p. 251.
40. PHA, Part 20, pp. 4022–23.
41. Gendai-shi Shiryo, Vol. II, p. 250.
42. Ibid., p. 262.
43. Ibid., p. 263.

CHAPTER 56
"Guaranteed Against Japanese Attack"

1. Gendai-shi Shiryo, Vol. III, pp. 110, 186. The word groups totaled 551.
2. "Richard Sorge."
3. Gendai-shi Shiryo, Vol. III, pp. 116, 200; Vol. I, p. 461.
4. "Comrade Richard Sorge." The Soviet Union remained silent about Sorge for twenty years.
5. Case of Richard Sorge, p. 233.
6. FDR papers, PSF Box 85.
7. Japanese Special Studies on Manchuria, Vol. XIII, Study of Strategical and Tactical Peculiarities of Far Eastern Russia and Soviet Far East Forces (Tokyo, 1955), pp. 64–66.
8. Gendai-shi Shiryo, Vol. III, pp. 199–200.
9. Ibid., p. 202.
10. New York Daily News, May 17, 1954.
11. Washington Evening Star, August 23 and 24, 1951.

12. *Spies, Dupes, and Diplomats*, p. 4.
13. Ralph de Toledano, "Moscow Plotted Pearl Harbor," *The Freeman* (June 1952), p. 569.
14. *Washington Post*, October 8, 1952.
15. Robert A. Theobald, *The Final Secret of Pearl Harbor* (New York, 1954), p. 80.
16. *Man with Three Faces*, p. 218.
17. Sorge Memoir, Part 2, p. 9.
18. *Gendai-shi Shiryo*, Vol. III, p. 201.
19. Ibid.
20. Interview with Ishii, January 11, 1965. *Ningen Zoruge*, pp. 146–47.
21. Interview with Ishii, January 11, 1965. *Ningen Zoruge*, p. 148.
22. Interview with Ishii, January 11, 1965. *Ningen Zoruge*, p. 149.
23. *Der Spiegel*, September 5, 1951, p. 24.
24. *Gendai-shi Shiryo*, Vol. II, pp. 251–52.
25. Ibid., p. 251.
26. Ibid., p. 388.
27. Interview with Araki, January 6, 1965. Possibly related to professor of music Eta Harich-Schneider, a harpsichord specialist, who lived in Tokyo during 1941 and remembered Sorge well (*Der Spiegel*, June 27, 1951, p. 23).
28. *Gendai-shi Shiryo*, Vol. I, p. 428; Vol. III, pp. 186, 226. "Extracts," Clausen Testimony, p. 40, Record Group 319, File ID 923289, Part 37, Box 7482.
29. *Gendai-shi Shiryo*, Vol. III, pp. 213–14, 226, 297, 300.
30. Ibid., Vol. I, p. 445.
31. Ibid., pp. 429–30.
32. *Ten Years in Japan*, pp. 452–53.
33. Sorge Memoir, Part 2, p. 116.
34. *Gendai-shi Shiryo*, Vol. I, p. 429.
35. Ibid., pp. 463, 278–79.
36. Ibid., Vol. III, pp. 196, 213. "Extracts," Clausen Testimony, p. 43, op. cit.

CHAPTER 57
"He Had Crossed the Barrier of Death"

1. Interviews with Yoshikawa, January 14, 1965; Tamazawa, June 21, 1965; Kawai, January 14, 1965.
2. *The Entire Picture*, Part 1, p. 22.
3. Ibid. Interview with Tamazawa, January 21, 1965. *Hearings*, p. 1135. At the trials, Yoshisaburo was found innocent. Tomo received a five-year sentence and was released with time off for good behavior ("Sorge Spy Ring," p. A716).
4. Interview with Yoshikawa, January 14, 1965.
5. Interview with Sakai, January 31, 1965.
6. Ibid.
7. Ibid.
8. Interview with Tamazawa, January 21, 1965; *Hearings*, p. 1136; *The Entire Picture*, Part 1, p. 22.

9. Interview with Sakai, January 31, 1965.
10. Ibid.
11. Ibid.
12. Ibid.
13. See, for example, *Instance of Treason*, p. 178.
14. Interview with Yoshikawa, January 16, 1965.
15. Interview with Sakai, January 31, 1965.
16. Ibid.
17. Ibid.
18. Ibid. Interview with Yoshikawa, January 14, 1965. *The Entire Picture*, Part 1, p. 23.
19. Interview with Sakai, January 31, 1965. Taiji Hasebe, who worked on Clausen's case, told Prange in an interview of January 19, 1965, that Miyagi fractured a leg in his fall; hereafter Hasebe. Deakin and Storry have written likewise (*Case of Richard Sorge*, p. 251). But according to Yoshikawa, Miyagi injured his thigh (interview of January 14, 1965). Sakai confirmed that the hospital found nothing wrong with Miyagi (interview of January 31, 1965).
20. *The Entire Picture*, Part 1, p. 23. Interviews with Tamazawa, January 21, 1965; Yoshikawa, January 14, 1965; and Sakai, January 31, 1965.
21. Interviews with Sakai, January 31, 1965; and Tamazawa, January 21, 1965. *The Entire Picture*, Part 1, p. 23.
22. Interview with Sakai, January 31, 1965.
23. Interview with Yoshikawa, January 14, 1965.
24. Ibid.
25. *Hearings*, p. 1134.
26. Miyake Masataro, *An Outline of the Japanese Judiciary* (Tokyo, 1935), quoted in *Hearings*, p. 1134.
27. Such was the impression Yoshikawa made upon Prange at their first interview of January 14, 1965.
28. *Hearings*, p. 1135.
29. Interview with Yoshikawa, January 14, 1965.
30. Statement of Mitsusaburo Tamazawa, April 2, 1949, Record Group 319, ID 923289, Part 41, Box 7483. Collection and Dissemination Division, Office of the ACS/G2, located in Washington National Records Center, Suitland, Maryland; hereafter Tamazawa statement.
31. Interview with Yoshikawa, January 14, 1965; Tamazawa statement.
32. Interviews with Yoshikawa, January 14 and 16, 1965; *Hearings*, p. 1136.
33. Interviews with Yoshikawa, January 14 and 16, 1965.
34. Ibid., January 14, 1965.

CHAPTER 58
"A Very Quiet Arrest"

1. Interview with Kawai, January 19, 1965.
2. *Gendai-shi Shiryo*, Vol. II, p. 388.

3. Ibid., Vol. III, p. 229; Vol. I, p. 479.
4. Ibid., Vol. II, p. 388.
5. Tamazawa statement. *The Entire Picture*, Part 1, pp. 23–24.
6. *The Entire Picture*, Part 1, p. 24.
7. *Sorge Incident*, p. 130.
8. *Gendai-shi Shiryo*, Vol. II, p. 99.
9. *The Entire Picture*, Part 1, p. 24.
10. Hiroshi Miyashita, *Tokko no Kaiso (Reminiscences of the Tokko)* (Tokyo, 1978), p. 212; hereafter *Tokko no Kaiso. The Entire Picture*, Part 1, p. 24.
11. *Tokko no Kaiso*, p. 212.
12. *The Entire Picture*, Part 1, p. 25.
13. Ibid., p. 24.
14. Ibid., p. 25.
15. *Instance of Treason*, p. 189.
16. Interview with Matsumoto, January 8, 1965.
17. *Gendai-shi Shiryo*, Vol. I, pp. 465, 480; Vol. III, p. 229.
18. Ibid., Vol. III, p. 229.
19. Ibid., Vol. I, p. 479.
20. Ibid., Vol. III, p. 229.
21. Interview with Saito, January 23, 1965.
22. Ibid.
23. Interview with Yoshikawa, January 14, 1965.
24. Tamazawa statement. Konoye was officially listed as his own minister of justice, but apparently Iwamura functioned as such.
25. Interview with Yoshikawa, January 14, 1965.
26. Ibid.
27. *Gendai-shi Shiryo*, Vol. III, p. 360.
28. Interview with Suzuki, January 18, 1965.

CHAPTER 59
"An Uneasy Feeling"

1. Interviews with Yoshikawa, January 14 and 16, 1965.
2. *The Entire Picture*, Part 1, p. 25.
3. Ibid.
4. *Instance of Treason*, p. 189.
5. *Gendai-shi Shiryo*, Vol. I, pp. 479–80.
6. Ibid., Vol. III, p. 229. *Camarade Sorge*, p. 93.
7. *Gendai-shi Shiryo*, Vol. III, p. 230.
8. Ibid., pp. 227, 230.
9. Interview with Suzuki, January 18, 1965.
10. Ibid.
11. Ibid.
12. In his interview of January 23, 1965, Saito made no mention of any comings and goings at Sorge's house on October 17 until that night. In a follow-up interview which Ms. Chi Harada conducted on Prange's behalf in May 1965, Saito stated definitely that he did not see Clausen, Voukelitch, or anyone else visit Sorge until around 10:00 P.M.; hereafter Saito/Harada interview.
13. *Gendai-shi Shiryo*, Vol. I, p.

480. *Modern Japan* was an annual published by *Asahi Shimbun*.

14. Ibid., Vol. III, pp. 7, 230.
15. Interview with Suzuki, January 18, 1965.
16. *Gendai-shi Shiryo*, Vol. III, p. 230.
17. Ibid., pp. 7, 104.
18. Ibid., pp. 7, 230.
19. Ibid.
20. Ibid., p. 7.
21. Ibid., pp. 7, 230.
22. Tamazawa statement. Interviews with Yoshikawa, January 14 and 16, 1965, and Tamazawa, January 21, 1965.
23. Interviews with Tamazawa, January 21, 1965, and Yoshikawa, January 14, 1965. Also interview which Ms. Harada conducted with Yoshikawa on Prange's behalf in May 1965; hereafter Yoshikawa/Harada interview.
24. Interview with Tamazawa, January 21, 1965; Yoshikawa/Harada interview.
25. Interview with Suzuki, January 18, 1965.
26. Interview with Saito, January 23, 1965; Saito/Harada interview.
27. Ibid.
28. During Prange's interview with Taiji Hasebe on January 19, 1965, Suzuki was present. Toward the end of the session, while Hasebe and Prange were talking together, Suzuki told this story about Ms. Ott to Ms. Harada, who was translating.

CHAPTER 60
"This Is the End"

1. Interview with Saito, January 23, 1965.
2. Japan *Times and Advertiser*, October 18, 1941.
3. Interview with Suzuki, January 18, 1965.
4. *Camarade Sorge*, p. 268.
5. Interview with Suzuki, January 18, 1965.
6. Ibid.
7. Ibid. Interview with Yoshikawa, January 14, 1965.
8. Interview with Suzuki, January 18, 1965.
9. *Gendai-shi Shiryo*, Vol. III, pp. 7–8, 230.
10. Ibid., pp. 8, 230. Aoyama/Harada interview. Aoyama gave Ms. Harada an account of what he remembered as the arrest of Sorge. While this contained numerous discrepancies with the recollections of other participants in Sorge's arrest, it dovetailed in all essentials with Clausen's testimony on his own arrest. Evidently Aoyama mixed up memories of his participation in Sorge's arrest with the earlier taking of Clausen.
11. *Gendai-shi Shiryo*, Vol. III, p. 230. Interviews with Hasebe, January 19, 1965, and Shinichi Ogata, January 20, 1965; hereafter Ogata.
12. Interview with Tamazawa, January 21, 1965.
13. Ibid.
14. Interview with Ogata, January 20, 1965.

15. Interview with Saito, January 23, 1965. Saito/Harada interview.

16. Testimony on this individual's identity is conflicting. Suzuki claimed that it was Ms. Ott and that the police held off because they anticipated enough trouble with the German Embassy without involving the ambassador's wife (See Note 28, Chapter 59). Saito emphatically denied this (Saito/Harada interview, May 1965). On the basis of an article by Ohashi, Deakin and Storry identified the caller as Wilhelm Schulz of DND (*Case of Richard Sorge*, p. 254 n.). Yet Ohashi told Prange that the visitor was the embassy's second secretary (interview with Ohashi, January 21, 1965). Yoshikawa only stated that someone was there; he did not know who (interview with Yoshikawa, January 14, 1965; also *Hearings*, p. 1137).

17. Aoyama/Harada interview.

18. Interview with Hideo Ohashi, January 21, 1965. Hereafter Ohashi.

19. Ibid. Interview with Yoshikawa, January 14, 1965. Saito/Harada interview. *Hearings*, p. 1137.

20. Saito/Harada interview.

21. Interview with Saito, January 23, 1965.

22. Ibid. Saito/Harada interview.

23. Ibid. Interview with Ohashi, January 21, 1965.

24. Aoyama/Harada interview. Interview with Saito, January 23, 1965. Saito/Harada interview. Interview with Ohashi, January 21, 1965.

25. Aoyama/Harada interview.

26. Interview with Ohashi, January 21, 1965.

27. Interviews with Ogata, January 20, 1965, Yoshikawa, January 14, 1965, and Saito, January 23, 1965.

28. Interview with Yoshikawa, January 14, 1965.

29. Ibid. Interview with Ohashi, January 21, 1965. *Hearings*, p. 1137.

30. Interview with Yoshikawa, January 14, 1965.

31. Aoyama/Harada interview.

32. Ibid.

33. Interview with Ogata, January 20, 1965.

34. Interview with Kawai, January 14, 1965.

35. *Instance of Treason*, p. 189.

36. Interview with Saito, January 23, 1965.

CHAPTER 61
"Clausen's Fatal Error"

1. Interview with Yoshikawa, January 14, 1965.

2. *The Entire Picture*, Part 1, p. 26. Interview with Suzuki, January 18, 1965.

3. Interview with Fuse, January 22, 1965.

4. Interview with Suzuki, January 18, 1965.

5. "Sorge Spy Ring," p. A712.

6. Interviews with Yoshikawa, January 14, 1965, and Su-

zuki, January 18, 1965. Tamazawa statement.

7. Interview with Suzuki, January 18, 1965.
8. Interview with Fuse, January 22, 1965.
9. Ibid. Interview with Suzuki, January 18, 1965.
10. Interview with Suzuki, January 18, 1965.
11. Interview with Fuse, January 22, 1965.
12. Ibid. Interview with Suzuki, January 18, 1965.
13. "Extracts," Clausen Testimony, orig. p. 482, Record Group 319, File ID 923289, Box 5F8-18.
14. Interview with Hasebe, January 19, 1965.
15. Ibid. Interview with Ogata, January 20, 1965.
16. Interview with Hasebe, January 19, 1965.
17. Ibid. "Sorge Spy Ring," p. A721.
18. Interview with Hasebe, January 19, 1965.
19. "Extracts," Clausen Testimony, original pp. 481–82, op. cit.
20. Ibid. Interview with Ogata, January 20, 1965.
21. Interviews with Hasebe, January 19, 1965, and Ogata, January 20, 1965.
22. Interviews with Ogata, January 20, 1965, and Yoshikawa, January 14, 1965. "Extracts," Clausen Testimony, original pp. 481–82, op. cit.
23. Interviews with Ogata, January 20, 1965, Hasebe,

January 19, 1965, and Yoshikawa, January 16, 1965.
24. Interview with Yoshikawa, January 16, 1965.
25. Interview with Hasebe, January 19, 1965.
26. *Der Spiegel,* January 18, 1951, p. 22.
27. "Sorge Spy Ring," pp. A722–23.
28. Interview with Yoshikawa, January 16, 1965.
29. For an interesting discussion of this point, see *Instance of Treason,* pp. 183–86.
30. Interview with Yoshikawa, January 16, 1965.

CHAPTER 62
"I Am Defeated"

1. *Nicht aus den Akten,* p. 429.
2. Interviews with Yoshikawa, January 16, 1965, and Araki, January 6, 1965.
3. Message, Ott to Berlin, October 23, 1941, German Archives.
4. Interview with Yoshikawa, January 16, 1965.
5. Ibid.
6. Ibid.
7. Tamazawa statement.
8. Interviews with Hasebe, January 19, 1965, and Yoshikawa, January 16, 1965.
9. Interview with Ohashi, January 21, 1965; "Extracts," Clausen Testimony, original p. 481, Record Group 319, File ID 923289, Box 5F8-18.
10. Interview with Kawai, January 19, 1965. This station was later renamed Kanda.

11. Interview with Ohashi, January 21, 1965.
12. Interview with Yoshikawa, January 16, 1965.
13. Interviews with Ohashi, January 21, 1965, Yoshikawa, January 16, 1965, and Tamazawa, January 21, 1965.
14. Interviews with Yoshikawa, January 16, 1965, and Tamazawa, January 21, 1965.
15. Interviews with Yoshikawa, January 16, 1965, Ohashi, January 21, 1965, and Tamazawa, January 21, 1965. *Hearings*, p. 1144. *The Entire Picture*, Part 1, p. 26.
16. Interviews with Yoshikawa, January 16, 1965, and Tamazawa, January 21, 1965.
17. Interview with Yoshikawa, January 16, 1965.
18. Ibid.
19. See for example, *Instance of Treason*, p. 181.
20. Interview which Ms. Harada held on Dr. Prange's behalf on May 25, 1965 with Sumitsugu Asanuma. Hereafter Asanuma/Harada interview.
21. *Hearings*, pp. 1139, 1158.
22. Interview with Ohashi, January 21, 1965.
23. "Extracts," Clausen Testimony, p. 40, Record Group 319, File ID 923289, Part 37, Box 7482.
24. Interview with Yoshikawa, January 16, 1965. *Hearings*, p. 1142.
25. Ibid.
26. Interview with Yoshikawa, January 16, 1965.
27. Ibid. *Hearings*, p. 1142.
28. Interviews with Yoshikawa, January 16, 1965, and Ohashi, January 21, 1965. Kordt, who claimed to have been present, wrote that this interview lasted only three minutes (*Nicht aus den Akten*, p. 430), but Yoshikawa's estimate of at least ten minutes seems more likely.
29. Interview with Yoshikawa, January 16, 1965.
30. *Camarade Sorge*, p. 248.
31. Interview with Yoshikawa, January 16, 1965.

CHAPTER 63
"A Hard Worker Even in Prison"

1. *Hearings*, p. 1151.
2. Interview with Yoshikawa, January 16, 1965.
3. Ibid.
4. Ibid. Interview with Ohashi, January 21, 1965. "Sorge Spy Ring," p. A706.
5. Interview with Yoshikawa, January 16, 1965.
6. Asanuma/Harada interview.
7. Yoshikawa statement, April 1, 1949, Record Group 319, File ID 923289, Part 41, Box 7483; Tamazawa statement.
8. Ibid. Interview with Yoshikawa, January 16, 1965.
9. Yoshikawa/Harada interview.
10. Asanuma/Harada interview.
11. Ibid. Statement of Asanuma, April 4, 1949, Record Group

319, File ID 923289, Part 41, Box 7483.

12. Yoshikawa/Harada interview.

13. Asanuma/Harada interview.

14. Kawai questionnaire.

15. Interview with Yoshikawa, January 16, 1965.

16. Interview which Ms. Harada conducted on behalf of Prange with Seiichi Ichijima, February 1965; hereafter Ichijima/Harada interview No. 1.

17. Interview with Ohashi, January 21, 1965; "Extracts," Clausen Testimony, original p. 481, Record Group 319, File ID 923290, Box 5F8-18.

18. Interviews with Ohashi, January 21, 1965, and Yoshikawa, January 16, 1965.

19. Interview with Ohashi, January 21, 1965.

20. Asanuma/Harada interview.

21. Kawai questionnaire.

22. Ibid., interview which Ms. Harada conducted on behalf of Prange with Ichijima, May 1965. Hereafter Ichijima/Harada interview No. 2.

23. *Case of Richard Sorge*, p. 329.

24. *Gendai-shi Shiryo*, Vol. I, pp. 329, 355.

CHAPTER 64
"The Transition Period"

1. Sorge Memoir, Part 1, p. 9.
2. Ibid., p. 13.

3. Interview with Ohashi, January 21, 1965.

4. Sorge Memoir, Part 2, p. 31.

5. Ibid., p. 23.

6. Ibid., p. 25.

7. Ibid., p. 22.

8. Ibid., p. 23.

9. Ibid., p. 20.

10. Ibid., p. 22.

11. Ibid., pp. 20–21, 25.

12. Ibid., p. 23.

13. *Gendai-shi Shiryo*, Vol. I, pp. 295–96.

14. Ibid., p. 296.

15. Ibid., p. 297.

16. Ibid., pp. 297–98.

17. Ibid., p. 298.

18. Ibid., p. 299.

19. Interview with Ohashi, January 21, 1965. Ichijima/Harada Interview No. 2.

20. Kawai questionnaire.

21. Ichijima/Harada interview No. 1.

22. Ibid.

23. *Instance of Treason*, pp. 2, 36.

24. Ichijima/Harada interview No. 1.

25. Interview with Ohashi, January 21, 1965.

26. *Gendai-shi Shiryo*, Vol. II, pp. 128–29.

27. Interview with Ohashi, January 21, 1965.

28. *Instance of Treason*, pp. 197–98.

29. Interview with Yoshikawa, January 16, 1965. Others who believed that Ozaki had begun to waver were Procurators Toneo Nakamura (Statement of April 4, 1949)

and Isamu Hiramatsu (Statement of April 11, 1949), Record Group 319, ID 923289.

CHAPTER 65
"Sorge-san Is a Spy"

1. Interview with Ishii, January 11, 1965.
2. Ibid. *Ningen Zoruge*, pp. 149–50.
3. Interview with Ishii, January 11, 1965. *Ningen Zoruge*, p. 151.
4. Interview with Ishii, January 11, 1965. *Ningen Zoruge*, p. 152.
5. Interview with Ishii, January 11, 1965. *Ningen Zoruge*, p. 153.
6. *Ningen Zoruge*, p. 154. Interview with Ishii, January 11, 1965.
7. "Sorge Spy Ring," pp. A717, 721. He was one of those whom the U.S. Army released in October 1945.
8. Ibid., p. A721.
9. Ibid., pp. A709, 721–22.
10. Ibid., pp. A717, 721.
11. Ibid., pp. A715, 721.
12. Ibid., pp. A716, 721.
13. Ibid., pp. A716, 721. Sorge Memoir, Part 1, p. 8.
14. "Sorge Spy Ring," pp. A717, 721; "Heroes Do Not Die."
15. "Sorge Spy Ring," pp. A721–22. *Instance of Treason*, p. 180.
16. *Instance of Treason*, pp. 179–

80. *The Entire Picture*, Part 12, p. 14.
17. *The Entire Picture*, Part 1, p. 27; Part 12, p. 14.
18. *Ningen Zoruge*, pp. 155–56.
19. "Extracts," Part XIV, Effect of Public Announcement of Case, Record Group 319, File ID 923289, Part 37, Box 7482.
20. Ibid.
21. *Der Spiegel*, August 15, 1951, p. 31.
22. Ibid., September 19, 1951, p. 24.
23. Sorge Incident, p. 135; Sorge Notes.
24. "Extracts," Part XIV, Effects of Public Announcement of Case, op. cit.
25. "Sorge Spy Ring," p. A721. *Der Spiegel*, September 19, 1951, p. 24.
26. *Weltflieger*, p. 268. *Nicht aus den Akten*, p. 430. "Sorge Spy Ring," p. A721.
27. *Der Spiegel*, September 19, 1951, p. 24.
28. *The Labyrinth*, p. 162.
29. Ibid., p. 163.
30. Ibid., p. 164.
31. Ibid., pp. 164–65.
32. "Sorge Spy Ring," p. A721.
33. *Der Spiegel*, September 26, 1951.
34. *The Labyrinth*, pp. 163–64.
35. *Instance of Treason*, pp. 187, 190. Sorge was arrested under the Peace Preservation Law, but when months after he had been arrested he finally admitted he had been spying for the Red Army, the

Justice Ministry charged him with violation of both laws. Ozaki came under the National Defense Security Law from the first. Anyone interested in the legal ramifications of the Sorge case trials is referred to *Instance of Treason*, which gives a rather detailed account.

36. "Sorge Spy Ring," p. A706.
37. Kawai questionnaire.

CHAPTER 66
"I Take Full Responsibility"

1. *Instance of Treason*, p. 192.
2. Joint statement of Associate Judges Masaru Higuchi and Fumihiko Mitsuda, April 4, 1949, Record Group 319, File ID 923289, Part 41, Box 7483.
3. *Instance of Treason*, pp. 192–93.
4. Statement of Judge Mitsuzo Nakamura, April 4, 1949, Record Group 319, File ID 923289, Box 7483.
5. *Thought and Behaviour*, p. 376.
6. *Instance of Treason*, p. 189.
7. Ibid., p. 194.
8. *Goodbye Japan*, p. 151.
9. *Gendai-shi Shiryo*, Vol. II, pp. 135–56.
10. Asanuma/Harada interview.
11. Interview with Suzuki, January 18, 1965.
12. Asanuma/Harada interview.
13. *Instance of Treason*, p. 194.
14. Asanuma/Harada interview.
15. Ibid.
16. Ibid.
17. *Instance of Treason*, p. 194.
18. Interview with Yoshikawa, January 16, 1965.
19. *Instance of Treason*, p. 195.
20. "Sorge Spy Ring," p. A722.
21. *Der Spiegel*, October 3, 1951.
22. *Instance of Treason*, p. 197.
23. "Sorge Spy Ring," pp. A715, 722.
24. Kawai questionnaire.
25. "Sorge Spy Ring," p. A722. *Gendai-shi Shiryo*, Vol. III, p. 307.
26. Kawai questionnaire. Since Miyagi's testimony revealed no connection with Mexico, rumor might have confused Miyagi with Hideo Noda of the abortive Don *apparat*, Noda's having been a pupil of Diego Rivera. See Chapter 7.
27. Letter from Ms. Voukelitch to her mother-in-law, Ms. Vilma Voukelitch, December 15, 1946, quoted in "Who Was Branko Vukelič?," p. 39.
28. Interviews with Suzuki, January 18, 1965, and Fuse, January 22, 1965. "Sorge Spy Ring," p. A722.
29. Voukelitch letter, op. cit.
30. *"Der Funker."* "Centre Listens in to Ramsay." *Gendai-shi Shiryo*, Vol. III, p. 8.
31. Asanuma/Harada interview. *"Der Funker."*
32. Interview with Tamazawa, January 21, 1965. *"Der Funker."* "Centre Listens in to Ramsay."

CHAPTER 67
"Fight the Cold Bravely"

1. Interview which Ms. Harada conducted on behalf of Prange with Tamon Yuda, May 1965; hereafter Yuda/Harada interview No. 2.
2. Ibid. Interview with Yuda, January 18, 1965.
3. Yuda/Harada interview No. 2.
4. Ibid.
5. Ibid. Interview which Ms. Harada conducted on behalf of Prange with Yuda, February 1965; hereafter Yuda/Harada interview No. 1.
6. Ichijima/Harada interview No. 2.
7. Ichijima/Harada interviews Nos. 1 and 2.
8. Ichijima/Harada interview No. 2.
9. Interview with Yuda, January 18, 1965.
10. *Washington Post,* January 17, 1977.
11. Interview with Yuda, January 18, 1965.
12. Ichijima/Harada interview No. 2.
13. Ichijima/Harada interviews Nos. 1 and 2. Yuda/Harada interview No. 2.
14. *Sorge Incident,* p. 6. "Sorge Spy Ring," p. A722. Ichijima/Harada interview No. 2.
15. Interview with Yuda, January 18, 1965. Ichijima/Harada interview No. 2.
16. Ibid. "Sorge Spy Ring," p. A722.
17. Ibid. Yuda/Harada interview No. 2.
18. Interview with Yuda, January 18, 1965. "Sorge Spy Ring," p. A722.
19. Interview with Yuda, January 18, 1965. Yuda/Harada interview No. 2.
20. Interview with Yuda, January 18, 1965.
21. Ibid. Ichijima/Harada interview No. 2. "Sorge Spy Ring," p. A723.
22. Interview with Yuda, January 18, 1965.
23. Asanuma/Harada interview.
24. Ibid. Yuda/Harada interviews Nos. 1 and 2. Yuda took these items to his office; they were destroyed in the Tokyo bombings. So far as is known, Sorge did not mention his wife, Katcha. Whether he knew it or not, she had died on August 4, 1943. She had been working in a chemical factory near Krasnoyarsk in southern Siberia, and perished of mercury poisoning and general weakness due to famine. (*Camarade Sorge,* p. 306).
25. Interview with Yuda, January 18, 1965.
26. Ibid. "Sorge Spy Ring," p. A723.
27. Interview with Yuda, January 18, 1965.
28. Ibid. "Sorge Spy Ring," p. A723.

EPILOGUE
"Forever a Stranger"

1. Ichijima/Harada interview No. 1.

2. Yuda/Harada interview No. 2.

3. Ichijima/Harada interview No. 2.

4. Answers to undated questionnaire submitted to Hotsuki Ozaki by Ms. Harada on behalf of Prange; hereafter Ozaki questionnaire. *Sorge Incident*, p. 6.

5. Ibid. Asanuma/Harada interview.

6. Ozaki questionnaire.

7. Ibid. *Sorge Incident*, p. 6.

8. Ibid.

9. Ozaki questionnaire.

10. Interview with Yuda, January 18, 1965.

11. Asanuma/Harada interview.

12. Interviews with Yuda, January 18, 1965, and Ishii, January 7, 1965.

13. Asanuma/Harada interview. Interview with Ishii, January 7, 1965.

14. Interview with Ishii, January 11, 1965. *Ningen Zoruge*, pp. 155–56.

15. Answers to undated questionnaire submitted to Hanako Ishii by Ms. Harada on behalf of Prange; hereafter Ishii questionnaire. Interview with Ishii, January 9, 1965.

16. Ishii questionnaire.

17. Ibid. Interview with Ishii, January 11, 1965.

18. Hotsuki Ozaki never met his half-brother but understandably worked hard to prove that Hotzumi had been a hero and patriot. The reader interested in a masterly account of the Sorge case's aftermath, the Japanese Communists' elevation of Ozaki to virtual sainthood, and the shock waves in those circles through the revelations about Ritsu Ito, can do no better than read Chalmers Johnson's book *An Instance of Treason*.

19. Ishii questionnaire. Asanuma/Harada interview.

20. Ishii questionnaire.

21. Ibid. Anyone wishing to delve into the MacArthur report and the American aspects of the Sorge aftermath should read the hearings before the House Un-American Activities Committee which took place on August 9, 22, and 23, 1951, and General Willoughby's book *Shanghai Conspiracy*, which is based largely upon his testimony at those hearings, the G-2 study of the case, and the statements of Sorge and Clausen.

22. Ishii questionnaire.

23. Ibid.

24. Ibid.

25. Ibid. Interview with Ishii, January 7, 1965. Rumors that Sorge was not really executed have been rife for years. Meissner seems to have been one of the prime originators of this tale (*Man with Three Faces*, pp. 238–43). According to one story, the Japanese Communist Party rushed the gates at Sugamo and saved Sorge at the last minute (interview with Yuda, January 18, 1965). The latest legend arose when Karl Kindermann, a wartime interpreter

in Japan, wrote that the Japanese traded Sorge to the Soviet Union in exchange for Soviet neutrality in the war and that later he was executed in one of the Stalinist purges (*Washington Post,* January 17, 1977).

26. Ishii questionnaire. Interview with Ishii, January 9, 1965. She wore this ring during her interviews with Dr. Prange.

27. Ishii questionnaire.

28. *Instance of Treason,* p. 254. *Case of Richard Sorge,* p. 345. Interview with Ishii, January 9, 1965.

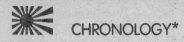

CHRONOLOGY*

Pre-1920

October 4, 1895	Richard Sorge born.
February 27, 1899	Max Clausen born.
May 1, 1901	Hotzumi Ozaki born. Some six months later his family moves to Taiwan.
February 10, 1903	Yotoku Miyagi born.
August 15, 1904	Branko de Voukelitch born.
1905	Sorge family returns to Berlin from Russia.
1915	Sorge wounded at Ypres; returns to battle; sent to Russian front.
1916	Sorge wounded twice; hospitalized.
January 1918	Sorge discharged from German Army.
June 1919	Miyagi moves to California.
August 1919	Sorge receives Ph.D. in political science at University of Hamburg.

1920 through 1932

1920–1921	Sorge engaging in Communist activity in Germany.
May 1921	Sorge marries Christiane Gerlach.
1922–1923	Sorge and Christiane in Frankfurt.
Late 1924	Sorge and Christiane to Moscow.
1925	Sorge becomes citizen of Soviet Union.
March 1925	Ozaki graduates from Tokyo Imperial University.

*With the exception of certain specific dates, timing cannot be determined exactly because much of it depends upon testimony taken some years after the events in question.

1926	Voukelitch to Paris to study.
May 1926	Ozaki joins Tokyo *Asahi Shimbun*.
October 1926	Christiane leaves Sorge.
October 1927	Ozaki moves to Osaka.
November 1927	Ozaki marries Eiko Ozaki, née Hirose, his former sister-in-law.
November 1928	Ozaki and Eiko move to Shanghai.
1929	Sorge becomes part of Red Army's Fourth Department (Intelligence).
1929	Voukelitch graduates from University of Paris.
Late 1929 or early 1930	Voukelitch marries Edith Olsen after their son, Paul, is born.
January 1930	Sorge arrives in Shanghai.
1930	Sorge meets Clausen.
October or November 1930	Sorge meets Ozaki through Smedley.
1931	Miyagi joins American Communist Party.
September 18, 1931	Manchuria Incident begins.
October 1931	Ozaki introduces Kawai to Sorge.
Early 1932	Ozaki and family return to Osaka.
January 1932	Voukelitch returns to Paris; out of work; returns to Communist activity.
March 1932	Olga recruits Voukelitch for Tokyo ring.
April 1932	Miyagi rents room from Yoshisaburo and Tomo Kitabayashi.
Late 1932	Miyagi recruited for Tokyo ring.
Late 1932	Sorge leaves Shanghai for Moscow.

1933

February 11	Voukelitch and family arrive in Japan.
Early spring	Sorge marries Katcha Maximova.
Late April or early May	Sorge ordered to Tokyo.
May	Sorge arrives in Berlin to establish cover.
August	Sorge en route to Japan. Spends fifteen days in the United States.
August	Clausen ordered from China to Moscow.
September 6	Sorge arrives in Japan.
September	Sorge contacts German Embassy.
October	Miyagi arrives in Japan.
November	Wendt contacts Voukelitch; Voukelitch meets Sorge.

December   Miyagi meets Voukelitch; meets Sorge.
December   Dirksen arrives as German ambassador.

1934

Early spring   Clausen and Anna to Volga Republic.
March   Ott becomes German military attaché in To-
                        kyo.
May   Sorge recruits Ozaki at Nara.
Mid-May   Wendt finishes radio set at Voukelitch's
                        house.
August   Miyagi recruits Akiyama as translator.
August   Sorge meets Prince Albrecht von Urach.
Mid-September   Ozaki moves to Tokyo with East Asia Prob-
                        lems Investigation Association.
Early autumn   Voukelitch meets Yoshiko Yamasaki.
Early autumn or   Sorge to Manchukuo with Ott. On return
    late summer   writes essay that Ott sends to General
                        Thomas in Berlin.

1935

January   Miyagi contacts Yasuda.
April   Voukelitch accredited to Havas.
Spring   Sorge meets Stein.
May   Ozaki introduces Kawai to Miyagi.
Summer   Sorge to Moscow. Uritskii assigns him mis-
                        sion to report re Japanese intentions toward
                        USSR; confirms Ozaki as member of ring,
                        gives Sorge carte blanche to work through
                        German Embassy; okays Clausen for
                        Sorge's Tokyo ring.
September 26   Sorge reaches Japan by plane.
October 4   Sorge meets Hanako Ishii.
Early December   Clausen arrives in Tokyo; shortly thereafter
                        Sorge introduces him to Voukelitch.

1936

February 10 or 11   Kawai tortured in Manchuria.
February   Stein agrees to let Clausen use his home to
                        broadcast.
February 26   Start of February 26 Incident. Sorge's analysis
                        and reporting to Moscow the ring's first
                        real triumph.

March	Miyagi recruits Ms. Kuzumi.
March	Ms. Kuzumi introduces Miyagi to Yamana.
March	Yamana introduces Miyagi to Taguchi.
March	Miyagi recruits Hashimoto.
March	Ott brings Sorge into Oshima-Ribbentrop discussions on Japanese-German military alliance. Sorge actively argues against the pact.
Spring and summer	As result of Sorge's messages to Moscow, Oshima, Ribbentrop, and Canaris shadowed.
May	Clausen and Voukelitch destroy old radio.
June 25	Kawai released from jail in Manchuria.
July 4	Tokko reorganizes and expands.
August	Clausen and Anna married in Shanghai.
August 15–29	Ozaki to IPR conference at Yosemite. Meets Saionji; renews friendship with Ushiba.
September	Ott reports on Japanese military capacity; too early to conclude a Japanese-German military alliance.
November 25	Anti-Comintern Pact announced.
November	Ms. Kitabayashi returns to Japan.
November	Ozaki joins China Problems Research Institute.
Late autumn	Sorge introduces Ozaki to Stein.
December	Mizuno arrested; released after a few days.
Late 1936	Ozaki meets Prince Konoye.

1937

January	Ozaki publishes famous article on kidnapping of Chiang Kai-shek (December 1936). Prophesies Kuomintang-Chinese Communist rapprochement against threat of Japanese aggression.
February	Ozaki joins Showa Research Association, founded in 1936 to bring experts together as advisers for Konoye.
May	Kawai sets up branch of China Research Institute in Tokyo.
Summer	Clausen's firm, M. Clausen Shokai, opens.
June	Konoye forms first cabinet.
July 7	Marco Polo Bridge Incident. Start of China war.

July	Ott, Schol, and Sorge form a study group to investigate Japanese Army in relation to China Incident.
July	Ozaki becomes director of China Department of Showa Research Association; holds post until 1940.
August	Ozaki publishes article predicting a long war with determined Chinese resistance.
November	Ozaki becomes charter member of Breakfast Group.
December	Ozaki to China for three months for *Asahi Shimbun*.
December	Sorge and his embassy associates working on German effort to mediate Sino-Japanese war.

1938

February 6	Dirksen leaves Japan on permanent change of station.
February	Mizuno arrested again, receives suspended sentence.
April	Miyagi recruits Ms. Kitabayashi.
April 28	Ott becomes German ambassador to Japan.
May 14	Sorge has severe motorcycle accident.
May 26	Ugaki becomes foreign minister. Miyagi thus has direct line into Foreign Ministry through Yabe. (Ugaki leaves office on October 29.)
June 13	Gen. Lyushkov defects from USSR. Sorge sends important information to Moscow.
Summer	Voukelitch and Edith separate pending divorce.
Summer	Ozaki enters government as a cabinet consultant.
July 12–August 11	Chang-kufeng Incident.
August	Stein leaves Japan.
Autumn and winter	Ozaki works on National Reorganization Plan.
December 18	Wang Ching-wei flees Chungking. Japan's attempts to establish Wang as head of a Chinese government a long-term project for Sorge.
December	Ozaki an original member of China Research Bureau; he brings in Mizuno.

December	Wenneker returns to Germany to command *Deutschland*.

1939

Early	Schol leaves embassy on permanent change of station.
Early	Sorge gives Clausen certain financial responsibilities.
Early	Showa Research Association and Ozaki backing the Greater East Asia Co-Prosperity Sphere.
February 10	Japanese take Hainan Island.
Early	Oshima, Shiratori, and Ott working hard for full Japan-Germany-Italy alliance. Sorge tries to discourage Ott.
March	Sorge hears of possible USSR-German rapprochement.
March	Clausen begins to use Edith Voukelitch's house for transmissions.
Late April or early May	Miyagi recruits Koshiro.
May 11	Start of Nomonhan Incident.
May	Ozaki publishes his best-known book, *On Modern China*.
June 1	Ozaki joins South Manchurian Railroad's Investigation Department.
June	Railroad sends Ozaki to Shanghai, Hong Kong, and Hankow.
July 3–15	Voukelitch to Nomonhan as observer for Havas.
July	Sorge reports to Moscow on failure of Japan-Great Britain discussions.
August 20	Zhukov counterattacks at Nomonhan.
August 24	Hitler-Stalin pact signed.
August 28	Hiranuma cabinet falls; Abe transition cabinet in.
September 1	European war begins. No longer possible to send couriers to China, for Germany now a belligerent.
September 15	Japanese agree to cease-fire at Nomonhan.
Early autumn	Sorge takes unofficial position in embassy Press Section at Ott's insistence; security tightens in embassy.
October	Tokko assigns Saito to check up on Sorge.

Late autumn	Sorge reports on Japanese-German naval discussions. This project continues into 1940.
November	Tokko arrests Ritsu Ito, an assistant of Ozaki's at the South Manchurian Railroad.
November 25	Moscow arranges first Tokyo courier contact.
December 18	Voukelitch divorce becomes final.
December	Draft of Wang Ching-wei treaty completed; Saionji secures a copy.

1940

January 26	Voukelitch marries Yoshiko Yamasaki.
January	Moscow extends Sorge's tour of duty another year.
January	Saionji shows Ozaki draft of highly classified Wang treaty.
Late January	Admiral Yonai, opponent of full alliance with Germany, becomes premier.
January 27	Max and Anna Clausen make first Tokyo courier rendezvous. Their contact is a representative of the Soviet Embassy.
February	Wenneker returns to Tokyo as naval attaché.
March 7	Sorge warns USSR Germany intends to strike in Western Europe.
Mid-March	Ozaki becomes member of Foreign Policy Department of Showa Research Association.
Late March	Ozaki secures firsthand information on Wang regime, established March 30. Tokko and Kempeitai screen his writings in connection with security leak in South Manchurian Railroad.
April-May	Clausen ill with heart trouble and bedridden until August but still encodes and sends from his bed.
May	Ito gives Tokko the name of Tomo Kitabayashi.
June 15	Miyagi predicts Japan will move into Hanoi and Saigon. Sorge disagrees.
June	Ozaki publishes book, *On Chinese Society and Economy*.
July	Tokko locates Ms. Kitabayashi and sets watch on her.
July 22	Second Konoye cabinet takes office. Again Ozaki is in close touch with the premier's office.

August	Tokko releases Ito, who returns to South Manchurian Railroad as a police informer.
August	Kawai returns to Japan; Miyagi takes him in charge.
September 9	Matsuoka-Stahmer talks begin for Tripartite Pact. Sorge keeps current on discussions and advises Moscow.
September	Clausen up and back on the job, but his beliefs begin to waver.
September 27	Tripartite Pact signed.
Late September– mid-October	Ozaki in Tsinking for Concordia Society meeting. Reports to Sorge on location of Japanese Army units.
Late summer	Inukai shows Ozaki the new Wang treaty. Ozaki copies it and gives it to Sorge.
October	Clausen meets Zaitsev (Serge), his new courier contact from the Soviet Embassy.
October	Police close down Showa Research Association.
October	Voukelitch's son Yo born.
Autumn	Clausen begins to destroy some draft messages.
Autumn	Moscow orders Clausen's money used for ring. He refuses.
Fall and winter	Sorge carefully following relations between Matsuoka and Ott.
December	Ozaki to Shanghai re Chinese resistance, also visits Peking and Dairen.
December	Colonel Kretschmer replaces Matzky as military attaché.

1941*

Early	Tokko arrests Ms. Aoyagi. Reactivates watch on Ms. Kitabayashi.
Early	Ott urging Japanese to attack Singapore. Sorge sees all the related material.
Early	Ozaki, Miyagi, and Voukelitch report about Japan's demands on southern areas.
Early	M. Clausen Shokai incorporates and opens branch in Mukden.
February	Matsuoka and Ott plan trip to Berlin.
March 10	Peace Preservation Law stiffened.

*Courier contacts took place at least monthly during 1941. Only the most significant listed herein.

March	Saito taken off Sorge's case for several months.
March 27	Hitler postpones Operation Barbarossa from May 15 to June 15. Later postpones another week.
March	Ozaki gives Sorge report on Japanese Army divisions.
April 13	Japan-USSR Neutrality Pact signed.
Late April	Ott returns and briefs Sorge on his trip.
Late April or early May	Sorge to Shanghai for Ott on Japanese–U.S. talks.
Early May	Niedermayer tells Sorge Germany has decided to attack USSR; Kretschmer tells Sorge Germans have completed large-scale preparations. Ott trying to bring Japan into war.
May 6	Clausen wires Moscow. This is probably the date on which he sends a message that Germany would begin war with USSR that month.
May 10	National Security Defense Law passed.
May	Miyagi returns Kawai to Ozaki's control.
May	Meisinger arrives at German Embassy with orders from Schellenberg to watch Sorge.
May	Schol gives Sorge very important information about German plan to attack USSR.
May 21	Clausen on air to Moscow. Now destroying or drastically cutting Sorge's drafts. Moscow ignores ring's warnings of impending attack.
May	Kawai finds Ozaki being watched.
May	Miyagi predicts Germans will attack USSR within a month.
May 31	Clausen on air to USSR. Warns Germany will attack on "left wing war front."
June 22	German attack on USSR. Stalin has ignored all warnings, including Sorge's.
Late June	Sorge discourages Ott and Kretschmer from expecting Japan to join war as "cat's-paw of Germany."
Late June	Ozaki agitates in Breakfast Group to turn Japan's war effort south.
June 26	Miyagi reports on conference of June 19 and 23, with decision of "north-to-south integration."

June 27	Moscow wires Sorge for information on Japanese government's decision in regard to entering the war.
June 28	Berlin advises Ott to urge Japanese participation in Russo-German war.
June 29	Clausen wires USSR concerning Big Mobilization going on in Japan.
July 2	Imperial conference. Decision is to go south but may still strike USSR if events so indicate. Ozaki secures result of this secret session and gives it to Sorge, probably on July 7. Ozaki still very worried about the USSR.
Summer	Throughout late spring, summer, and early autumn, Sorge follows and reports on progress of Japanese-U.S. talks.
July 16	Second Konoye cabinet falls; Matsuoka out.
July 18	Third Konoye cabinet formed.
Late July	Miyagi reports Japan is sure to go south; Sorge disagrees, for troops are building up in north.
July	Saito back on Sorge's track. Aoyama checking up on Clausen.
July, August, and September	Big Mobilization under way. Koshiro back on active duty and reporting. Sorge fears mobilization may lead to Japan's attacking USSR.
Early August	Police question Hanako about association with Sorge.
August 7	Clausen on air concerning Big Mobilization. Sends only a portion of available material.
Mid-August	Police question Hanako again.
Mid-August	Long message to USSR based on information from Ozaki concerning Japanese preparations in Manchuria.
August 20–23	Kwantung Army officials and senior Japanese Army officials decide not to fight the USSR.
August 25 or 26	Ozaki hears the above decision from Saionji.
September 2–19	Ozaki, in Manchuria for South Manchurian Railroad, secures very important information on Japanese military activities.
September 14	Clausen sends eleven messages, including the information Japan will not attack USSR unless certain conditions are met.

September 22	Ozaki reports to Sorge on his Manchurian findings, which indicate no Japanese attack on USSR planned for the rest of the year.
September 24	Saionji shows Ozaki draft of Japanese proposals to United States.
September 25	Edith Voukelitch and her son, Paul, leave for Australia.
September 28	Tokko arrests Mr. and Ms. Kitabayashi.
September 29	Ozaki briefs Sorge on U.S.-Japanese draft and southern operations.
October 4	Sorge's forty-sixth birthday; last meeting with Hanako.
October 4	Clausen's last transmission. Includes message telling USSR it is guaranteed safe for remainder of 1941; also on Japanese-U.S. discussions and southern operations.
October 6	Sorge's last meeting with Ozaki.
October 6	Sorge's last article appears in *Frankfurter Zeitung*.
October 7	Sorge ill in bed. Miyagi and Clausen meet at his bedside.
October 9	Ms. Kitabayashi gives Tokko Miyagi's name.
October 10	Last courier contact at Clausen's home; Miyagi arrested.
October 11	Miyagi confesses. Voukelitch under observation.
October 11–12	Nakamura and Yoshikawa appointed procurators in the case.
October 13	Akiyama and Ms. Kuzumi arrested.
October 15	Ozaki arrested.
October 16	Yoshikawa prepares brief for minister of justice.
October 16	Third Konoye cabinet falls.
October 17	Mizuno arrested.
October 17	Yoshikawa receives permission to arrest Sorge, Clausen, and Voukelitch.
October 18	Arrest of Sorge, Clausen, and Voukelitch.
October 22	Kawai arrested.
October 25	Sorge confesses.
November 19	Anna Clausen arrested.
Late 1941–early 1942	Sorge composes his memoir.

Post-1941

May 17, 1942	Case announced in Japanese newspapers.
August 2, 1943	Miyagi dies in prison before sentencing.
September 29, 1943	Death sentences pronounced on Sorge and Ozaki.
November 7, 1944	Sorge and Ozaki executed.
January 13, 1945	Voukelitch, serving life sentence, dies in prison.
March 27, 1945	Mizuno dies in prison.
October 1945	Clausen released from prison.
November 16, 1949	Sorge reburied in Tama Cemetery in Tokyo, in accordance with Hanako's arrangements.
November 6, 1964	Sorge made Hero of the Soviet Union.

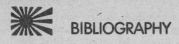 BIBLIOGRAPHY

Primary Sources

German Foreign Office Archives. State Security File, Japan (1941–1944), file on Sorge Case.

Japanese police reports and other related materials, courtesy of Harutsugu Saito.

Obi, Toshito, ed. *Gendai-shi Shiryo, Zoruge Jiken* (*Materials on Modern History, the Sorge Incident*). Misuzu Shobo, 3 vol. Tokyo, 1962.

Papers of Harry Hopkins, Franklin D. Roosevelt Library, Hyde Park, N.Y.

Papers of Franklin D. Roosevelt, Franklin D. Roosevelt Library, Hyde Park, N.Y.

U.S. Congress, 79th Congress, Joint Committee on the Investigation of the Pearl Harbor Attack. *Hearings before the Joint Committee on the Investigation of the Pearl Harbor Attack*. U.S. Government Printing Office. Washington, D.C.: 1945–1946.

U.S. House of Representatives, 82nd Congress, First Session: Un-American Activities Committee. *Hearings on Un-American Aspects of the Richard Sorge Spy Case*. U.S. Government Printing Office. Washington, D.C.: 1951.

Books

Boveri, Margret. *Der Verrat im XX Jahrhundert*. Reinbeck bei Hamburg: Rowalt, 1957.

Bullock, Alan. *Hitler: A Study in Tyranny*. New York: Harper & Row, 1962.

Buss, Claude A. *Asia in the Modern World*. New York: Macmillan, 1964.

Butow, Robert J. C. *Tojo and the Coming of the War*. Princeton, N.J.: Princeton University Press, 1961.

Byas, Hugh. *Government by Assassination*. New York: Alfred A. Knopf, 1942.

Chambers, Whittaker. *Witness*. New York: Random House, 1952.

Chiba, Reiko. *The Japanese Fortune Calendar*. Rutland, Vt.: Charles E. Tuttle Co., 1965.

Churchill, Winston S. *The Gathering Storm*. Boston: Houghton Mifflin, 1948.

———. *The Grand Alliance*. Boston: Houghton Mifflin, 1950.

———. *Their Finest Hour*. Boston: Houghton Mifflin, 1949.

Craigie, Sir Robert. *Behind the Japanese Mask*. London: Hutchinson & Co., 1945.

Dallin, David J. *Soviet Espionage*. New Haven: Yale University Press, 1955.

———. *Soviet Russia and the Far East*. New Haven: Yale University Press, 1948.

Deakin, F. W. and Storry, G. R. *The Case of Richard Sorge*. New York: Harper & Row, 1966.

Dement'yeva, I., Agayants, N., and Yakolev, Y. *Tovaritch Sorge (Comrade Sorge)*. Moscow: Sovietskaya Rossiya, 1965.

De Toledano, Ralph. *Spies, Dupes, and Diplomats*. New York: Duell, Sloan & Pearce, 1952.

Dirksen, Herbert von. *Moscow, Tokyo, London*. London: Hutchinson & Co., 1951.

Erickson, John. *The Soviet High Command: A Military-Political History, 1918–1941*. London: St. Martin's Press, 1962.

Feis, Herbert. *The Road to Pearl Harbor*. Princeton: Princeton University Press, 1950.

Grew, Joseph C. *Ten Years in Japan*. New York: Simon & Schuster, 1944.

Gronau, Wolfgang. *Weltflieger: Erinnerungen 1926-1944*. Stuttgart: Deutsche Verlaganstalt, 1955.

Guérin, Alain, and Chatel, Nicole. *Camarade Sorge*. Paris: Julliard, 1965.

Hori, Yuichi, and Kozai, Yoshishige, eds. *Idai Naru Aijo (The Great Love)*. Tokyo: Ikuseisha, 1949.

Hull, Cordell. *The Memoirs of Cordell Hull*. New York: Macmillan, 1950.

Ind, Allison. *Short History of Espionage*. New York: McKay, 1963.

Ishii, Hanako. *Ningen Zoruge, Aijen Miyake Hanako no Shuki (The Man Sorge, Memoirs of His Mistress, Miyake Hanako)*. Tokyo: Masu Shobo, 1956.

Johnson, Chalmers. *An Instance of Treason: Ozaki Hotsumi and the Sorge Spy Ring*. Stanford: Stanford University Press, 1965.

Kawai, Teikichi. *Aru Kakumeika No Kaiso (Memoirs of a Revolutionary)*. Tokyo: Nihon Shuppan Kyokai, 1953.

Kazama, Michitaro. *Aru Hangyaku, Ozaki Hotsumi no Shogai (A Case of Treason, the Life of Ozaki Hotsumi)*. Tokyo: Shinseido, 1959.

Kordt, Erich. *Nicht aus den Akten*. Stuttgart: Deutsch Verlagsanstalt, 1950.

Kravchenko, Victor. *I Chose Freedom*. New York: Charles Scribner's Sons, 1946.

Krivitsky, Walter G. *In Stalin's Secret Service*. New York: Harper & Bros., 1939.

Mader, Julius; Stucklik, Gerhard; and Pehnert, Horst. *Dr. Sorge funkt aus Tokyo: Ein Dokumentarbericht über Kundschafter des Friedens mit ausgewählten Artikeln von Richard Sorge*. Berlin: Deutscher Militarverlag, 1968.

Makai, Gyorgy. *Ki Volt dr. Sorge?* Budapest: Kossuth Konyokiado, 1965.

Maruyama, Masau. *Thought and Behaviour in Modern Japanese Politics*, Ivan Morris. London: Oxford University Press, 1963.

Massing, Hede. *This Deception*. New York: Duell, Sloan & Pearce, 1951.

Masterman, J. C. *The Double-Cross System in the War of 1939-1945*. New Haven: Yale University Press, 1972.

Meissner, Hans-Otto. *The Man with Three Faces*. New York: Reinhart & Co., 1955.

Mitamura, Takeo. *Senso to Kyosanshugi, Showa Seiji Hiroku (War and Communism, Secret Records of Showa Politics)*. Tokyo: Minshu Seida Fukyu Kai, 1950.

Miyashita, Hiroshi. *Tokko no Kaiso (Reminiscences of the Tokko)*. Tokyo: Tabata Shoten, 1978.

Moore, Harriet L. *Soviet Far Eastern Policy, 1931–1945*. Princeton: Princeton University Press, 1945.

Morin, Relman. *East Wind Rising*. New York: Alfred A. Knopf, 1960.

Mosley, Leonard. *Hirohito, Emperor of Japan*. Englewood Cliffs: Prentice-Hall, 1966.

Nakamura, Kinjiro (pen name Hachiro Yamamura). *Zoruge, Ozaki Hotzumi Supai Jiken No Zenbo: Soren Wa Subete o Shitte Ita (The Entire Picture of the Sorge-Ozaki Hotzumi Spy Incident)*. Osaka: Korinsha, 1949.

Newman, Joseph. *Goodbye Japan*. New York: L. B. Fischer, 1942.

Ozaki, Hotsuki. *Zoruge Jiken: Ozaki Hotzumi no Riso to Zasetsu (The Sorge Incident: The Ideals and Frustrations of Ozaki Hotzumi)*. Tokyo: Chuo Koron Cha, 1963.

Ozaki, Hotsumi. *Aijo Wa Furu Hoshi no Gotoku (Love Was Like a Falling Star)*. Tokyo: Sekai Hyoron Sha, 1946.

Petrov, Vladimir, comp. *"June 22, 1941": Soviet Historians and the German Invasion*. Columbia: University of South Carolina Press, 1968.

Piggott, Major General Sir Francis S. C. *Broken Thread*. Aldershot, England: Gale and Polden, 1950.

Presseisen, Ernst L. *Germany and Japan: A Study in Totalitarian Diplomacy, 1933–1941*. The Hague: Nijhoff, 1958.

Reischauer, Edwin O. *The Japanese*. London: Belknap, 1977.

Reiss, Curt. *Total Espionage*. New York: G. P. Putnam's Sons, 1941.

Röling, Dr. B. V. A., and Rüter, Dr. C. F. *The Tokyo Judgments: The International Military Tribunal of the Far East, (I.M.T.F.E.), 29 April 1946–12 November 1948*. Amsterdam, Netherlands: APA University Press, 1977.

Schellenberg, Walter. *The Labyrinth: Memoirs of Walter Schellenberg*. New York: Harper and Bros., 1956.

Theobald, Robert A. *The Final Secret of Pearl Harbor*. New York: Devin-Adair, 1954.

U.S. Army, Far East Command, Military Intelligence Section. *A Partial Documentation of the Sorge Espionage Case*. Tokyo: Toppan Printing Co., 1950.

————. *Extracts from an Authenticated Translation of Foreign Affairs Yearbook, 1942, Criminal Affairs Bureau, Ministry of Justice, Tokyo, Japan*. Tokyo: Toppan Printing Co., 1950.

————. "The Sorge Spy Ring—A Case Study in International Espionage in the Far East," reproduced in U.S. 81st Congress, First Session, *Congressional Record*, Vol. 95, Part 12, Appendix, February 9, 1949.

Wheeler-Bennett, John W. *The Nemesis of Power*. London: Macmillan, 1954.

Wighton, Charles. *World's Greatest Spies*. London: Odhams Press, 1962.

Willoughby, Charles A. *Shanghai Conspiracy: The Sorge Spy Ring*. New York: E. P. Dutton, 1966.

Young, John. *The Research Activities of the South Manchurian Railway Company, 1907–1945: A History and Bibliography*. New York: East Asia Institute, Columbia University, 1966.

Zacharias, Ellis M. *Secret Missions*. New York: G. P. Putnam's Sons, 1946.

Zhukov, G. K. *The Memoirs of Marshal Zhukov*. New York: Delacorte Press, 1971.

Articles

Chekhonin, B. "Heroes Do Not Die." *Izvestia*, September 8, 1964.

Chernyavsky, V. "Richard Sorge's Exploit." *Pravda*, November 6, 1964.

Cvetič, Dusan. "Who Was Branko Voukelič?" *Review—Yugoslav Monthly Magazine* (October 1964).

Daizo, Kodama. "A Secret Record: The Mantetsu Chosa-bu." *Chuo Koron* (December 1960).

Dementieva I. and Agayants, N. "Richard Sorge, Soviet Intelligence Agent." *Sovietskaya Rossiya*, September 5–6, 1964.

De Toledano, Ralph. "Moscow Plotted Pearl Harbor." *The Freeman* (June 1952).

Eisler, Gerhart. *"Erinnerungen an Richard Sorge."* *Neues Deutschland*, November 2, 1964.

Geller, Yu. "On the 70th Anniversary of the Birth of S. P. Uritskii." *Krasnaya Zvezda*, March 2, 1965.

Kalinin, A. "The Feat of an Intelligence Officer." *Krasnaya Zvezda*, November 7, 1964.

Kudriatsev, V. "I Meet Richard Sorge." *Izvestia*, November 1–7, 1964.

Marich, N., and Dzhuvarevich, M. "Sorge's Assistant." *Krasnaya Zvezda*, October 17, 1964.

Massing, Hede. "The Almost Perfect Russian Spy." *True* (December 1951).

Mayevsky, Viktor. "Comrade Richard Sorge." *Pravda*, September 4, 1964.

Orlov, B. "Centre Listens in to Ramsay." *Izvestia*, October 28, 1964.

Ozaki, Hotzumi. "Recent Developments in Sino-Japanese Relations." June 28, 1936, Japanese Council Paper No. 14, Japanese Council, Institute of Pacific Relations. Tokyo: Nihon Kokusai Kyoki, 1936.

————. *"Taiheyo Kaigi No Shina Mondai"* ("The China Problem at the Pacific Conference"). *Chuo Koron* (November 1936).

Pekelnik, N. "The Exploits of Richard Sorge: The Story of a Soviet Spy's Heroism." *Izvestia*, September 4, 1964.

Prange, Gordon W. "Master Spy." *Reader's Digest* (January 1967).

Semichastny, Vladimir. "Soviet Chekists in the Great Patriotic War." *Pravda*, May 7, 1945.

Series of articles, *"Herr Sorge Sass mit zu Tische: Porträt eines Spions,"* *Der Spiegel* June 13–October 3, 1951.

Series of letters between Sorge and his second wife Katcha, *Ogonek* (April 1965).

Smedley, Agnes. "The Tokyo Martyrs." *Far East Spotlight* (March 1949).

Sorge, Christiane. *"Mein Mann, Richard Sorge."* *Die Weltwoche* (Zurich), December 1, 1964.

Sorge, Richard. *"Die Japanische Expansion."* *Zeitschrift für Geopolitik* (August/September 1939).

Wolf, Dieter. *"Der Funker des Senders 'Ramsai': Wie Max und Anna Christiansen-Klausen an der Seite Kundshafters Dr. Sorge kampfen."* *Neues Deutschland*, November 2, 1965.

Newspapers

In addition to those cited under "Articles," the following newspapers proved useful:

Japan Advertiser
Japan Times and Advertiser
Japan Times and Mail

New York Daily News
Washington Evening Star
Washington Post

Interviews Conducted by Prange

Araki, Ms. Mitsutaro
Fukuoka, Seiichi
Fuse, Ken
Hasebe, Taiji
Ishii, Hanako
Kawai, Teikichi
Matsumoto, Shigeharu
Ogata, Shinichi

Ohashi, Hideo
Ozaki, Hotsuki
Saito, Harutsugu
Sakai, Tamotsu
Suzuki, Tomiki
Tamazawa, Mitsusaburo
Ushiba, Tomohiko
Yoshikawa, Mitsusada
Yuda, Tamon

Interviews Conducted on Prange's Behalf by Ms. Chi Harada

Aoyama, Shigeru
Asanuma, Sumitsugu
Ichijima, Seiichi
Ishii, Hanako

Ketel, Karl
Saito, Harutsugu
Yoshikawa, Mitsusada
Yuda, Tamon

Miscellaneous

Letter, D. R. Anderson to Prange, September 26, 1967.

Questionnaire completed by Teikichi Kawai.

Questionnaire completed by Hanako Ishii.

Unpublished student paper, Arisumi, Mark, "The Tokko."

Unpublished student paper, Carter, James H., "The Soviet View of Sorge—Myth and Reality."

Unpublished student paper, Henzel, H. W., *"Der Zeitungssorger Sorge."*

Unpublished student paper, Volz, Thomas E., "Richard Sorge as a Journalist."

Military History Section, Military History Division, Headquarters, U.S. Army Forces Far East, Japanese Special Studies on Manchuria, Vol. XIII, Study of the Strategical and Tactical Peculiarities of Far Eastern Russia and Soviet Far East Forces, Tokyo, 1955. This study was prepared in the main by Saburo Hayashi, former Colonel, IJA.

ARTICLES BY RICHARD SORGE
FOR THE *FRANKFURTER
ZEITUNG*—1940

ARTICLES BY RICHARD SORGE
FOR THE *FRANKFURTER*
ZEITUNG—1941

	24	1	Matsuoka wieder in Tokio
	29	1	Matsuoka berichtet über seine Reise
May	9	1	Reis, Gummi und Zinn
	10	1	Der Frieden am Mekong
	19	2	Keine Verhandlung mit Tschiang Kai-shek
	22	1	Vermittlung unter ungünstigem Stern
	24	2	Ablehnung auf allen Seiten
	27	1	Grosse Beachtung in Japan
	28	1	Die Kämpfe in China
	29	1	Japan ist bereit
June	1	2	Auf der Basis des Dreimächtepakts
	16	2	Wang Tsching-wei reist nach Tokio
July	1	1	Eine japanische Anleihe an Nanking
	2	2	Eine Überschwemmungskatastrophe in Japan
	8	1	Vier Jahre Krieg in China
	9	1	Yamashita über seine Eindrucke in Deutschland
	11	1	Die Besetzung Islands
	18	1	Umbildung des japanischen Kabinetts
	20	2	Das dritte Kabinett Konoe
	21	1	Unveränderte Grundlinie
	26	1	Die Grundlagen des Kabinetts Konoe
	28	1	Das Abkommen über Indochina
	29	2	Die Verteidigung Indochinas
	30	2	Japan lässt sich nicht einschüchtern
August	2	6	Japan beobachtet
	16	1	Japan's Interessen im Südwest Pazifik
	17	6	Heerse, Schiffahrt, Preise
	20	1	Japanische Wachsamkeit
	21	1	Japanische Wachsamkeit
	23	1	Der Ring der Einkreisung
	28	2	Japanische Blätter antworten Churchill
	29	1	Japan protestiert in Washington und Moskau
September	3	4	Wichtige Personalveränderungen in der japanischen Marine
	4	1	Japan's Blockadeabwehr
			Das japanische Heer gegen passives Abwarten
	4	2	Japan bleibt wachsam
	10	1	Japan's Interesse für den Fall "Greer"
	13	2	Rückzug aus Ostasien
	14	1	Yoshizawa in Indochina
	16	1	Japan und die "Freiheit der Meere"
	19	1	Japan erinnert sich an 1931
	22	2	Neue Personalveränderungen in der japanischen Marine

ARTICLES BY RICHARD SORGE (R.S.) FOR THE *ZEITSCHRIFT FÜR GEOPOLITIK*

 INDEX

ABOUT THE AUTHORS

The late Gordon Prange was a Professor of History at the University of Maryland and the former Chief of the Historical Section at Japan under General MacArthur. The author of two distinguished best-sellers, *At Dawn We Slept* and *A Miracle at Midway*, he personally interviewed many of the principals involved in the Sorge affair.

Donald M. Goldstein is Associate Professor of Public and International Affairs at the University of Pittsburgh.

Katherine V. Dillon is a Chief Warrant Officer, USAF (Ret.)